May 18–21, 2014
Denver, Colorado, USA

I0054871

**Association for
Computing Machinery**

Advancing Computing as a Science & Profession

SIGSIM-PADS'14

Proceedings of the 2014 ACM Conference on
SIGSIM Principles of Advanced Discrete Simulation

Sponsored by:
ACM SIGSIM

Association for Computing Machinery

Advancing Computing as a Science & Profession

The Association for Computing Machinery
2 Penn Plaza, Suite 701
New York, New York 10121-0701

Notice to Past Authors of ACM-Published Articles

ISBN: 978-1-4503-2794-7 (Digital)

ISBN: 978-1-4503-3078-7 (Print)

Additional copies may be ordered prepaid from:

ACM Order Department
PO Box 30777
New York, NY 10087-0777, USA

Phone: 1-800-342-6626 (USA and Canada)
+1-212-626-0500 (Global)
Fax: +1-212-944-1318
E-mail: acmhelp@acm.org
Hours of Operation: 8:30 am – 4:30 pm ET

Printed in the USA

Message from the Program Co-Chairs

Welcome to the 2nd AC M SIG SIM/PADS c onference on principles of a dvanced di screte simulation. T he use of si mulation-based t ools has bec ome ubi quitous i n nearl y al l sci ence an d engineering di sciplines, a nd conferences such as PADS a re key t o re porting a dvances in critical simulation m ethods a nd i mportant ap plication domains. A s a pa per aut hor or at tendee in AC M SIGSIM/PADS, you are helping to advance the state of the art in simulation methodologies.

We have an e xcellent p rogram t o of fer o ur at tendees t his y ear. All papers s ubmitted t o t he conference were rigorously reviewed with most papers receiving 4 to 5 referee reports. We thank the program committee and additional referees for th eir diligent efforts to provide timely, critical reviews and feedback to the authors. This process resulted in a total of 19 submissions accepted as full pa pers. T wo a dditional papers were a ccepted for the work-i n-progress session. We e xpect everyone will appreciate the high-quality papers and presentations in the conference this year.

The best paper candidates for this year are:

GPU-Assisted Hybrid Network Traffic Model by Jason Liu, Yuan Liu, Zhihui Du and Ting Li

Multi-fidelity Modeling & Simulation Methodology for Simulation Speed Up by Seon Han Choi, Sun Ju Lee and Tag Gon Kim

A Stream-based Architecture for the Management and On-Line Analysis of Unbounded Amounts of Simulation Data by Johannes Schutzel, Holger Meyer, and Adelinde M. Urhmacher.

The winner will be announced at the conference and will be mentioned in the Chair's message for the 2015 conference.

As is traditional with SIGSIM/PADS, we are pleased to confirm that the 2013 SIGSIM/PADS best paper award went to:

Modeling Communication Software for Accurate Simulation of Distributed Systems
by Stein Kristiansen, Thomas Plagemann and Vera Goebel

Congratulations to Stein, Thomas, and Vera on this well-deserved award!

Enjoy Denver, enjoy th e camaraderie and friendships, a nd above all com e away with m any ne w ideas for further advances in simulation tools and methods for the years to come.

George F. Riley
SIGSIM-PADS'14 Program Co-Chairs
Georgia Institute of Technology

Richard M. Fujimoto
SIGSIM-PADS'14 Program Co-Chairs
Georgia Institute of Technology

Table of Contents

SIGSIM-PADS 2014 Conference Organization

General Chair: John A. (Drew) Hamilton, Jr. *(Mississippi State University, USA)*

Program Co-Chair: George F. Riley *(Georgia Institute of Technology, USA)*
Richard M. Fujimoto *(Georgia Institute of Technology, USA)*

Publicity Chair: Navonil Mustafee *(University of Exeter, UK)*

Steering Committee Chair: George Riley *(Georgia Institute of Technology, USA)*

Steering Committee: Osman Balci *(Virginia Tech, USA)*
Paul Fishwick *(The University of Texas at Dallas, USA)*
Richard M. Fujimoto *(Georgia Institute of Technology, USA)*
John A. (Drew) Hamilton, Jr. *(Mississippi State University, USA)*
Jason Liu *(Florida International University, USA)*
David M. Nicol *(University of Illinois at Urbana-Champaign, Urbana, USA)*
George F. Riley *(Georgia Institute of Technology, USA)*

Program Committee: Khaldoon Al-Zoubi, Blackberry, Canada
Michele Amoretti, Università degli Studi di Parma, Italy
Osman Balci, Virginia Tech, USA
Fernando J. Barros, University of Coimbra, Portugal
Wengtong Cai, Nanyang Technological University, Singapore
Christopher D. Carothers, Rensselaer Polytechnic Institute, USA
Rodrigo Castro, University of Buenos Aires, Argentina
Olivier Dalle, INRIA/University of Nice Sophia-Antipolis, France
Andrea D'Ambrogio, University of Rome "Tor Vergata", Italy
Umut Durak, Roketsan Inc. System Simulations, Turkey
Roland Ewald, University of Rostock, Germany
Tony Field, Imperial College, UK
Paul Fishwick, The University of Texas at Dallas, USA
Richard M. Fujimoto, Georgia Tech, USA
Drew Hamilton, Mississippi State University, USA
David Hill, Blaise Pascal University, France
Jan Himmelspach, University of Rostock, Germany
Xiaolin Hu, Georgia State University, USA
Shafagh Jafer, University of Milwaukee, USA
David R. Jefferson, Lawrence Livermore National Lab, USA
Cameron Kiddle, University of Calgary, Canada
Franziska Klügl, Orebro University, Sweden
Sunil Kothari, Hewlett Packard Development Company, L.P., USA
Hillel Kugler, Microsoft Research, UK

Sponsors:

Applying Modeling and Simulation for Development of Embedded Systems

Gabriel A. Wainer
Department of Systems and Computer Engineering
Carleton University
Ottawa, Ontario Canada
gwainer@sce.carleton.ca

Abstract

Embedded real-time software construction has usually posed interesting challenges due to the complexity of the tasks executed. Most methods are either hard to scale up for large systems, or require a difficult testing effort with no guarantee for bug-free software products. Formal methods have showed promising results; nevertheless, they are difficult to apply when the complexity of the system under development scales up. Instead, systems engineers have often relied on the use of modeling and simulation (M&S) techniques in order to make system development tasks manageable. Construction of system models and their analysis through simulation reduces both end costs and risks, while enhancing system capabilities and improving the quality of the final products. M&S let users experiment with "virtual" systems, allowing them to explore changes, and test dynamic conditions in a risk-free environment. This is a useful approach, moreover considering that testing under actual operating conditions may be impractical and in some cases impossible.

In this talk, we will present a Modeling and Simulation-based framework to develop embedded systems based on the DEVS (Discrete Event systems Specification) formalism. DEVS provides a formal foundation to M&S that proved to be successful in different complex systems. This approach combines the advantages of a simulation-based approach with the rigor of a formal methodology. Another advantage of using DEVS is that different existing techniques (Bond Graphs, Cellular Automata, Partial Differential Equations, Queuing models, etc.) have been successfully transformed into DEVS models. We will discuss how to use this framework to incrementally develop embedded applications, and to seamlessly integrate simulation models with hardware components. Our approach does not impose any order in the deployment of the actual hardware components, providing flexibility to the overall process. The use of DEVS improves reliability (in terms of logical correctness and timing), enables model reuse, and permits reducing development and testing times for the overall process. Consequently, the development cycle is shortened, its cost reduced, and quality and reliability of the final product is improved.

SIGSIM-PADS'14, May 18–21, 2014, Denver, Colorado, USA.
ACM 978-1-4503-2794-7/14/05.
http://dx.doi.org/10.1145/2601381.2601400

Categories and Subject Descriptors

simulation and modeling; discrete event simulation; algorithms.

Keywords

embedded simulation; real-time systems

Short Bio

GABRIEL A. WAINER, SMSCS, SMIEEE, received the M.Sc. (1993) at the University of Buenos Aires, Argentina, and the Ph.D. (1998, with highest honors) at the Université d'Aix-Marseille III, France. In July 2000 he joined the Department of Systems and Computer Engineering at Carleton University (Ottawa, ON, Canada), where he is now Full Professor. He has held visiting positions at the University of Arizona; LSIS (CNRS), Université Paul Cézanne, University of Nice, INRIA Sophia-Antipolis (France); UCM, UPC (Spain) and others. He is the author of three books and over 280 research articles; he edited four other books, and helped organizing numerous conferences, including being one of the founders of SIMUTools and SimAUD. Prof. Wainer is the Vice-President Conferences, and was a Vice-President Publications and a member of the Board of Directors of the SCS. Prof. Wainer is the Special Issues Editor of SIMULATION, member of the Editorial Board of IEEE Computing in Science and Engineering, Wireless Networks (Elsevier), Journal of Defense Modeling and Simulation (SCS), and International Journal of Simulation and Process Modelling (Inderscience). He is the head of the Advanced Real-Time Simulation lab, located at Carleton University's Centre for advanced Simulation and Visualization (V-Sim). He has been the recipient of various awards, including the IBM Eclipse Innovation Award, SCS Leadership Award, and various Best Paper awards. He has been awarded Carleton University's Research Achievement Award (2005), the First Bernard P. Zeigler DEVS Modeling and Simulation Award, the SCS Outstanding Professional Award (2011) and Carleton University's Mentorship Award (2013), the SCS Distinguished Professional Award (2013) and Carleton University's Research Achievement Award (2014).

LORAIN: A Step Closer to the PDES "Holy Grail"

Justin M. LaPre, Elsa J. Gonsiorowski, and Christopher D. Carothers
Department of Computer Science, Rensselaer Polytechnic Institute
Troy, NY U.S.A.
laprej@cs.rpi.edu, gonsie@cs.rpi.edu, chrisc@cs.rpi.edu

ABSTRACT

Automatic parallelization of models has been the "Holy Grail" of the PDES community for the last 20 years. In this paper we present *LORAIN – Low Overhead Runtime Assisted Instruction Negation* – a tool capable of automatic emission of a reverse event handler by the compiler. Upon detection of certain instructions, LORAIN is able to account for, and in many cases reverse, the computation without resorting to state-saving techniques. For our PDES framework, we use Rensselaer's Optimistic Simulation System (ROSS) coupled with the LLVM [18] compiler to generate the reverse event handler.

One of the primary contributions of this work is that LO-RAIN operates on the LLVM-generated Intermediate Representation (IR) as opposed to the model, high-level source code. Through information gleaned from the IR, LORAIN is able to analyze, instrument, and invert various operations and emit efficient reverse event handlers at the binary code level.

This preliminary work demonstrates the potential of this tool. We are able to reverse both the PHOLD model (a synthetic benchmark) as well as Fujimoto's airport model. Our results demonstrate that LORAIN-generated models are able to execute at a rate that is over 97% of hand-written, parallel model code performance.

Keywords

discrete event simulation; compiler analysis; reverse computation; slicing

1. INTRODUCTION

Since the early 1990's, the "Holy Grail" for parallel discrete-event simulation has been the automatic parallelization of event- and process-driven models which yield performance improvements on par with hand-written models. The belief in this goal is rooted in the Time Warp protocol's ability to be "blind" with respect to a model's event scheduling behavior both in terms of space (e.g., which logical processes

(LPs) communicate) and time (i.e., model lookahead) [12, 17]. The promise of Time Warp has been its ability to automatically uncover parallelism within a discrete-event model. On the surface this appears to be a very easy problem to solve compared with the more general problem of automatically parallelization of a serial piece of software. That has clearly turned out to not be the case.

At the 1994 PADS conference, Fujimoto correctly asserted that the PDES "Holy Grail" would not be reached in that century [22]. This view was driven from experience in the automatic parallelization of the Simscript II.5 models which were built for and executed by a Time Warp kernel [29]. The principal challenge was LP state-saving, more specifically the issue of sharing state among LPs. This was addressed via *Space-Time Memory*, however, its functionality came with potentially large overheads that diminished overall parallel performance. There were also related issues in that Simscript allowed an event to examine the event list.

To address part of the Time Warp state-saving challenge, Carothers, Perumalla, and Fujimoto [9] devised a new approach called *reverse computation*. As the name implies, only the control state (e.g., which `if`-block was taken) is stored during the forward processing of any event, as opposed to incrementally or fully saving an LP's state changes. To support the rollback operation, a reverse event handler is created that uses the control state information to select which control path to take during event rollback processing. It then reverses or undoes each state change. Due to the fact that many operations performed on state are *constructive*, such as an increment or decrement on integer statistics, the model's execution time is dramatically reduced by using this approach. Performance increases with reverse computation have been attributed to significant improvements in cache and TLB hit rates within the overall memory hierarchy [9].

Reverse computation has been applied to a number simulation areas including Hodgkin-Huxley neuron models [20], Internet models [32], HPC network models [19, 21], particle simulations [26], and gate-level circuit models [15]. Most recently, Barnes et al. [5] executed the PHOLD benchmark with reverse computation on nearly two million cores and was able to achieve an event-rate exceeding half a trillion events per second.

Besides improving overall Time Warp simulator performance, reverse computation also opened the door to revisit the question of automatic model parallelization. In 1999, Perumalla created the first reverse C compiler called *RCC* [25]. This was a source-to-source compiler that took a model built to a specific PDES engine (in this case Georgia Tech Time

Warp) and produced both the instrumented forward event handlers as well as the reverse event handler. RCC was based on a direct statement by statement reversal of the forward event handler's C code statements. The key to this approach is that the model developer had to insert pragma statements to provide hints to RCC in order to produce correct forward and reverse event handlers. This work demonstrated for the first time that an automatic parallelization tool could produce event processing code that was as good as the hand written code (i.e., having negligible performance loss).

The most recent effort to automatically parallelize event-driven models with reverse computation has been the *Backstroke* framework [16, 30]. Here, the ROSE source-to-source compiler framework is used to develop a set of algorithms that operate on an Abstract Syntax Tree (AST) to produce both a modified forward event processing code as well as the reverse event handler code. What is unique about Backstroke is that it takes on the challenge of working with models developed in C++ at the source-level.

In this paper, we introduce a new automatic parallelization approach called *LORAIN – Low Overhead Runtime Assisted Instruction Negation*. LORAIN is a collection of compiler passes that leverage the LLVM [18] compiler framework to create both a modified forward event handler, which records the control state, as well as the corresponding reverse event handler for a specific Time Warp simulator's API. For this research, ROSS (Rensselaer's Optimistic Simulation System) [5] is used.

The key contribution of this work is that it operates not on the source code of the model but on LLVM's Intermediate Representation (IR). This can be viewed as a very high level abstract machine instruction set. LLVM IR instructions use Static Single Assignment (SSA) [10] which aids in the analysis of the model code and forward/reverse code generation process. LORAIN's overall approach is twofold: first, it analyzes the forward handler per the specifics of the ROSS API; second, it synthesizes the proper state-restoring reverse handler. The analysis stage includes evaluating the IR to find locations at which *destructive* assignments take place. Transformations are also made that make certain code patterns more amenable to reversal. In the synthesis stage, LORAIN passes the instrumented forward IR into secondary transformation pass which traverses the Control Flow Graph (CFG) and finds and reverses "store" instructions. Once the model's IR is complete, LLVM can directly produce an executable, as opposed to modified source code. Thus, the developer need not be concerned with additional compilation steps of model source code nor do they need to insert pragmas.

The principal advantage of operating at the LLVM IR level is LORAIN gains independence from the syntax complexities that occur at the source code level, such as multi-expression if-statements that contain potentially destructive assignment statements. The LLVM compiler design-view endorses this separation between language syntax and representation by enabling nearly all compiler passes to operate exclusively at the IR level and not on the front-end's AST (which is contained in a separate tool called *clang*).

The remainder of this paper is organized as follows: Section 2 describes the ROSS Time Warp engine and LLVM compiler. Section 3 describes our LORAIN framework. The specific details on how LORAIN performs the IR modifica-

tion and generation is presented in Section 4 for two models along with parallel performance results. Finally, additional related work and conclusions are presented in Sections 5 and 6 respectively.

2. BACKGROUND

2.1 ROSS

In this study, we will be using ROSS [8], an open-source, discrete event simulation engine that supports both conservative and optimistic (Time Warp) simulation (http://ross.cs.rpi.edu). ROSS is written in C and assembly language atop MPI, with targeted support for supercomputing platforms such as the IBM Blue Gene/Q. ROSS takes a different approach from other Time Warp simulation systems which use bulk state-saving. Instead, ROSS utilizes reverse computation to undo state changes programmatically. To help achieve this programmatic reversal, ROSS employs a reversible random number generator. Through reverse computation, ROSS enables quick state restoration, often many times faster than classical state-saving.

Within ROSS, MPI Tasks are represented as *Processing Elements* (PEs). PEs contain multiple *Logical Processes* (LPs) capable of independently executing *events* in time-stamp order. Events are created by sending messages between LPs and inter-PE messages are permitted. During optimistic simulation, out of order execution is permitted until a temporal anomaly is detected. For example, an LP receives an event in its past. At this point ROSS uses reverse computation to incrementally undo all operations that potentially modified the LP's state. Through multiple anti-messages, the LP's state is reversed until the system can process the erroneous event in proper time-stamp order. At this point, normal forward execution of events will resume.

A central assumption of all ROSS models is that LPs only share state by exchanging time-stamped event messages. This is a typical restriction of many PDES systems and allows ROSS to scale to hundreds of thousands of processors or more. Currently, Space-Time Memory (STM) [29] is not supported in ROSS but could be in the future. Design and implementation of STM on a million core supercomputer is still an open PDES problem. Additionally, static or global variables are not supported unless they are read-only once the model initialization step is complete. This assumption greatly simplifies LORAIN's analysis and instrumentation steps.

The functions within the ROSS API that need to be reversed are relatively straightforward. All of the RNG functions in ROSS rely on the `tw_rand_unif()` macro, which itself calls the `rng_gen_val()` function. Other functions exist, such as `tw_rand_integer()` and `tw_rand_exponential()`, which must be caught and handled appropriately. All other function calls are either re-emitted or ignored as they are immaterial to the various LORAIN passes.

Finally, the function prototypes for the forward and reverse event handlers must be identical and are critically important for this work; all parameters play a role: `void name(state *lp_state, bitfield *bf, message *msg, LP *lp);`, where `lp_state` is the pointer to the LP state, `bf` is a pointer to the control state bit field, `msg` is the pointer to the current event's message data and `lp` is the pointer to the current LP. LORAIN's use of the ROSS API will be discussed further in Section 3.

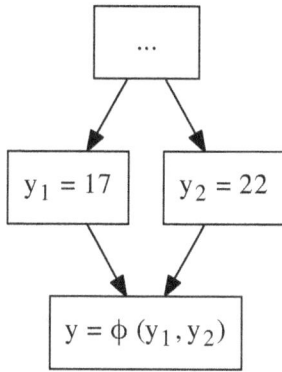

Figure 1: SSA ϕ construction. y is assigned the appropriate value based on the path taken through the control flow graph.

```
%1 = load i32* @test_add_x , align 4
%2 = add nsw i32 %1, 1
store i32 %2, i32* @test_add_x , align 4
```

Figure 2: A use-def chain example. The `store` instruction uses %2, which in turn uses %1. Using this information, we can generate a topological ordering of an instruction's dependencies.

2.2 LLVM

LLVM is a compiler framework developed at University of Illinois at Urbana-Champaign by Lattner and Adve [18]. The virtual instruction set is very similar to RISC, where most instructions are represented as three-address code. Instructions for accessing memory are an exception. Memory is only accessed via `load` and `store` instructions. LLVM utilizes SSA [10] assigning a value to each identifier exactly once. Strict typing is used to ensure consistency within virtual instructions. LLVM has a modern C++ code base and enjoys heavy interest from academia and industry alike.

The LLVM virtual instructions are collated into *basic blocks*. Basic blocks are sequences of instructions that *will* execute once they have been entered (i.e. there are no exits other than completing the block). Each basic block concludes with exactly one *terminator* instruction such as a jump or `return` instruction.

A key feature of LLVM is its application of SSA virtual registers. Here, new SSA virtual registers are assigned the result of any operation that generates a value e.g., `%22 = add %x, %y` adds x and y and assigns that value to the temporary `%22`. `%22` may be used in future computations requiring that value, for example common sub-expression elimination. Having the same value in multiple paths through the CFG can be problematic. SSA solves this at merge points with ϕ functions. See figure 1. For example, y is assigned the output of a ϕ function on y_1 and y_2. The ϕ function "knows" which path was taken to get here and is therefore able to choose the correct value.

Finally, LLVM is object oriented and many classes derive from the *Value* class such as *Argument*, *BasicBlock*, and *Instruction* to name a few. To be precise, the *Instruction* class is a subclass of the *User* class, which itself is a subclass of the *Value* class. The *User* class keeps track of *Value*s it

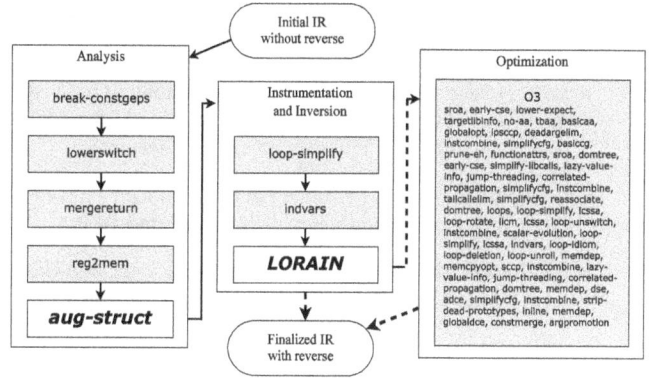

Figure 3: The various LLVM passes that are run by LORAIN. LLVM-authored passes are shown in gray, our passes are shown in white.

uses and is helpful in the construction of *use-def* chains [2]. LORAIN uses use-def chains to ensure that all instruction dependencies are satisfied (see figure 2).

3. LORAIN

LORAIN makes the key assumption that only instructions that affect memory have the capacity to alter state. Therefore, restoring the contents of memory to its previous values is sufficient to effectively negate an erroneous event. By inverting the CFG and reversing the stores along the basic block path taken through the function, the contents of memory following a reverse function call should be restored to its original values (assuming there is no bit loss in the instruction reversal step). Currently, LORAIN only reverses the LLVM store instruction, although other instructions do exist which may alter memory. In practice, these are rarely seen.

Most operations are capable of being programmatically inverted (i.e., they are constructive). However, for those that are not we must resort to state-saving. Values which are destructively assigned must store their data elsewhere to ensure proper reversal. This is explained further in Section 3.1

LORAIN's reversal process begins with a standard C language file which adheres to the ROSS API and includes the forward event handler as well as a declaration for its reverse event handler. ROSS builds a table of function pointers which is used by the simulation runtime to determine which function to call. Therefore, ROSS requires all model-specific function handlers to be declared ahead of time thereby necessitating the declaration of the reverse event handler. Note that at this stage the function body of of the reverse event handler has yet to be defined. This file is then compiled down to its corresponding IR bitcode. The resulting bitcode file can then be passed into the LLVM `opt` tool. `opt` is used to run code transformation and analysis passes. The following list of compiler passes are utilized by LORAIN's overall work-flow. Figure 3 shows how these pass are organized and ordered. The passes developed in this paper are highlighted in bold italics.

- break-constgeps: de-optimizes the instruction sequence for analysis purposes (e.g., struct member references).

This pass is from the latest version of the open-source SAFECode compiler [1, 11].

- lowerswitch: convert `switch` instructions into a sequence of `if` conditions. This allows the developer to *not* have to implement `switch` instructions.

- mergereturn: create a single `return` point and have all other earlier termination instructions jump to it.

- reg2mem: de-optimize the SSA code into non-SSA form. This allows for easier modification of the IR.

- *aug-struct*: append members to the `message` struct which enables state-saving for destructively-assigned LP state members (see Section 3.1).

- loop-simplify: apply transformations to natural loops to more easily allow future analysis and transformations.[1]

- indvars: simplify loop induction variables.[1]

- *LORAIN*: This step is implemented as several passes for automatic reversal of parallel discrete-event simulation models. These passes are described in the Sections 3.2 and 3.3.

3.1 Analysis & Message Augmentation

A first pass is executed by LORAIN to find all state values which are destructively overwritten. Upon detection of such a value, the value's type must be retained as well as other identifying aspects of that value. The pass iterates over all `store` instructions, marks them with metadata, and saves them in a set. At this point, the `message` struct provided by the ROSS model is augmented with types matching the overwritten values. This provides a location to store values that may be overwritten by the current event. This approach has been used extensively by hand written models, such as the Yaun et al. TCP model [32].

Given a forward event handler, we need to evaluate all store instructions to the LP state. First, we find all "destructive" stores. Destructive stores are stores in which the original value cannot be recovered given the final value and sequence of steps taken. For example, i = i * 3; is reversible: simply divide the new value of i by 3. i = 27; is non-reversible: given 27, there is no way of knowing the previous value for i. If any destructive stores exist, we must make space to save these values prior to overwriting them. We do this by augmenting the `message` struct. This requires modifying the forward and reverse event handler function prototypes. These destructive store instructions are marked with LLVM metadata indicating they have already been taken care of and will not be reversed.

3.2 Instrumentation

Instrumentation is a pass done primarily to facilitate proper reversal. For readability and debugging purposes, all basic blocks are renamed. Basic blocks with two or more predecessors are found and the edge from the predecessor to the current basic block is *split* and an empty basic block is inserted (see figure 4). An instruction to turn on a particular bit in the bit field is inserted in these blocks. The purpose

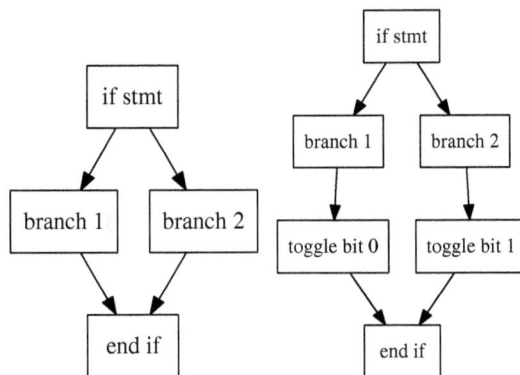

Figure 4: The CFG of the original function *F* (left subfigure) and the modified CFG (right subfigure). The branch 1 and branch 2 blocks are split and instructions to toggle the appropriate bit fields are inserted into the newly created basic blocks.

of this construction is to ensure bits are toggled so it is possible to retrace the path through the function's CFG. This leverages the existing bit field `bf` of the ROSS model event handler that developers use in their hand-written models.

The next part of the instrumentation pass deals with the `store` instructions. For each `store` instruction LORAIN analyzes it uses and determine if it affects the memory of the LP state. If the `store` instruction has no bearing on the LP state, it is marked with metadata to be ignored in future LORAIN passes. If the `store` instruction affects the LP state but is destructive, we save the value for future rollback. The value is saved in the augmented `message` struct which is created during the `aug_struct` pass as previously noted in Section 3.1. These instructions are also marked with metadata since the reversal is handled in the opposite order with a restorative assignment operation from the `message` struct back to the LP state.

3.3 Inversion

We begin our reverse event handler function with its prototype. Since the forward and reverse event handlers have identical types, we simply request a function type matching the forward event handler. We must do this for ROSS compliance.

For each basic block in our forward event handler we create an empty analog block in our reverse event handler. The entry block always has certain special properties, namely stack allocations for local variables and stack-allocated temporary variables for arguments. A bidirectional, one-to-one mapping is established between the individual forward and reverse basic blocks.

Next, LORAIN analyzes each forward basic block separately. Instructions which are important enough to be reversed are placed on a stack. LORAIN then goes through the stack to build the corresponding reverse basic block. For each forward instruction, LORAIN takes advantage of the LLVM's InstVisitor class which provides a Visitor pattern [14] implementation for all available instruction types. We have the potential to visit any of the following instructions:

---

[1]This pass is not exemplified by the examples in this paper, though is typically required.

- `visitSExtInst`: sign extend the given value. LLVM requires all operands in a comparison are the same length.

- `visitBitCast`: cast between compatible types.

- `visitGetElementPtrInst`: all array and struct accesses must use this instruction to perform proper pointer arithmetic.

- `visitTerminatorInst`: all basic blocks finish with a terminator instruction (e.g., a `return` instruction).

- `visitAllocaInst`: a stack space allocation instruction.

- `visitStoreInst`: a store instruction (can access memory).

- `visitLoadInst`: a load instruction (can access memory).

- `visitCallInst`: for the sake of this work, this should be viewed as a standard function call.

- `visitBinaryOperator`: standard three-address code binary operator. For example, arithmetic operations, shifting operations, etc.

The Terminator instruction requires special consideration. In LLVM, all basic blocks end with a single terminator instruction with no exceptions. Typical terminators are branches to other basic blocks, function calls, or return instructions. A critical observation is that, based on the terminator instructions alone, we are able to reconstruct the control flow graph or in this case, its inverse.

For example, if a given basic block B from the forward event handler F has no predecessors, we can conclude that this block is in fact the entry block. In the reverse event handler F', we must make its counterpart, B', the exit block. Similarly, if B has one predecessor P, then clearly there is an unconditional jump from P to B. This requires the reverse edge from B' to P'. Two or more predecessors means there are multiple paths through the CFG to B. Reversing this will require an instruction that supports two or more possible exits, namely a `switch` statement terminating block B'. Determining which route to take involves evaluating the bit field corresponding to this particular branch point, see figure 5.

Another key instruction is `store`. If it is unmarked with metadata it is reversed. Upon detecting a store instruction in B, we first check to see if it exists in our forward-to-reverse value mapping, i.e. if we have previously seen it from another path. If so, this store has already been successfully reversed and inserted into F'. This could have happen during dependency lookups. If we have not encountered this value before, all of the instruction's dependencies must be found and also reversed. All reversals are again carried out by the InstVisitor class. Here, for each *use* of the value being stored, we must recursively visit each member of the instruction's use-def chain. When all dependencies are satisfied, we can construct the final store and insert it into F'. Any store instruction we have visited is saved in the forward-to-reverse value mapping.

Some function call instructions must also be reversed. For example, RNG calls must be "uncalled" to preserve deterministic behavior. In particular, LORAIN supports the

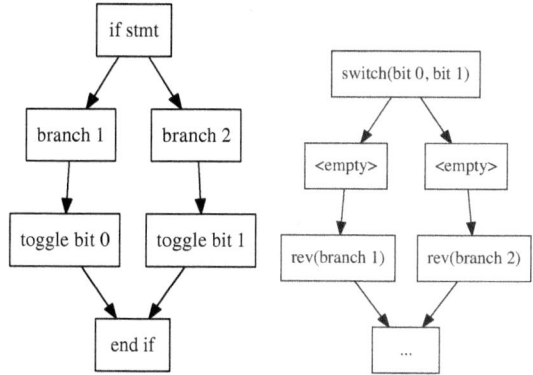

Figure 5: The forward event handler (left subfigure) and reverse event handler (right subfigure), which are inverses of one another. Based on which bit is set, we can find our way back through the CFG.

RNG calls that are provided with the ROSS framework. Some ROSS macros may also ultimately call RNG functions. This is not a problem as the macros have already been expanded by the time we examine the IR. LORAIN's passes catch all RNG calls and emit the corresponding reverse RNG calls. These are supplied by the ROSS framework. All other unrecognized function calls, e.g. `printf()`, are not reversed.

Finally, all function exits must be coalesced; this can be accomplished by using LLVM's `mergereturn` pass. This is required due to the C language invariant that any function must have exactly one entry point. If F had multiple exits, F' would have multiple entry points: a nonsensical proposition for the C language. Having a single exit blocks also gives us an ideal location to restore the values that were previously state-saved in the augmented message struct. This corresponds to destructive store instructions which were marked with metadata.

4. MODELS & PERFORMANCE STUDY

To investigate LORAIN's performance, two complete ROSS models were selected. First, we present the PHOLD model [12] and the entirety of its reversal. This demonstrates a full LORAIN reversal and consists of several complex calls to the RNG. Second, we present Fujimoto's airport model [13]. This is a larger model which demonstrates additional features of LORAIN such as recovering from both constructive and destructive state changes.

4.1 PHOLD

PHOLD is simple benchmark for discrete-event simulations [12]. Upon startup, the system is primed with n starting events. These events are then processed in time-stamp order on their respective starting LP. Only during event processing can another event be dispatched.

The PHOLD pseudo-code is shown in figure 6. Observe that there are potentially two or three RNG calls depending on whether or not the `if` block is entered. Figure 7 is the corresponding basic block representation of figure 6. Figures 8 through 15 are the actual IR from the basic blocks contained within this function. As a whole, we denote the IR of forward event handler with the name F.

```
initialization;
if tw_rand_unif() <= percent_remote then
 |  dest = tw_rand_integer(0, ttl_LPs - 1);
else
 |  dest = local_PE;
end
if dest < 0 || dest >= (g_tw_nlp * tw_nnodes()) then
 |  tw_error(TW_LOC, "bad dest");
 |  return;
end
tw_event *e = tw_event(dest,
tw_rand_exponential(mean));
tw_event_send(e);
```

Figure 6: PHOLD forward event handler.

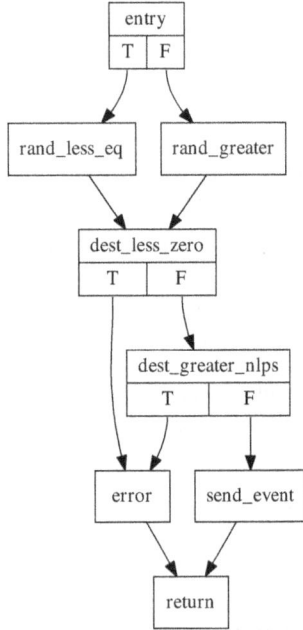

CFG for 'phold_event_handler' function

Figure 7: The CFG of the PHOLD forward event handler. The basic block titles have been renamed for clarity.

The `entry` (figure 8) block begins by creating four stack allocations to hold the program parameters and one additional allocation for the `dest` variable. All four parameters are stored into their allocations. Next, a zero value is written over the bit field parameter. The `tw_rng_stream` is extracted from the LP parameter and `rng_gen_val()` is called on it to determine whether PHOLD is generating a remote event or not. If it does, then PHOLD jumps to `rand_less_eq`, otherwise it jumps to `rand_greater`. Note, that in LLVM IR, `getelementptr` is used for calculating memory addresses when dealing with `struct` or array indexing, `bitcast` is used to transform the integer bit field to the appropriate type, and `fcmp` is a floating-point comparison instruction.

The `rand_less_eq` block (figure 9) again extracts `tw_rng_stream` from the LP and calls `rng_gen_val()`. `ttl_lps` is

```
%1 = alloca %struct.PHOLD_state*, align 8
%2 = alloca %struct.tw_bf*, align 8
%3 = alloca %struct.PHOLD_message*, align 8
%4 = alloca %struct.tw_lp*, align 8
%dest = alloca i64, align 8
store %struct.PHOLD_state* %s, %struct.
    PHOLD_state** %1, align 8
store %struct.tw_bf* %bf, %struct.tw_bf** %2,
    align 8
store %struct.PHOLD_message* %m, %struct.
    PHOLD_message** %3, align 8
store %struct.tw_lp* %lp, %struct.tw_lp** %4,
    align 8
%5 = load %struct.tw_bf** %2, align 8
%6 = bitcast %struct.tw_bf* %5 to i32*
store i32 0, i32* %6, align 4
%7 = load %struct.tw_lp** %4, align 8
%8 = getelementptr inbounds %struct.tw_lp* %7,
    i32 0, i32 7
%9 = load %struct.tw_rng_stream** %8, align 8
%10 = call double @rng_gen_val(%struct.
    tw_rng_stream* %9)
%11 = load double* @percent_remote, align 8
%12 = fcmp ole double %10, %11
br i1 %12, label %13, label %21
```

Figure 8: PHOLD entry block.

```
; <label>:13                         ; preds = %0
%14 = load %struct.tw_lp** %4, align 8
%15 = getelementptr inbounds %struct.tw_lp* %14,
    i32 0, i32 7
%16 = load %struct.tw_rng_stream** %15, align 8
%17 = load i32* @ttl_lps, align 4
%18 = sub i32 %17, 1
%19 = zext i32 %18 to i64
%20 = call i64 @tw_rand_integer(%struct.
    tw_rng_stream* %16, i64 0, i64 %19)
store i64 %20, i64* %dest, align 8
br label %25
```

Figure 9: PHOLD `rand_less_eq` block.

loaded and 1 is subtracted from it and is then passed into `tw_rand_integer()`. The returned value is assigned to the `dest` variable.

```
; <label>:21                         ; preds = %0
%22 = load %struct.tw_lp** %4, align 8
%23 = getelementptr inbounds %struct.tw_lp* %22,
    i32 0, i32 1
%24 = load i64* %23, align 8
store i64 %24, i64* %dest, align 8
br label %25
```

Figure 10: PHOLD `rand_greater` block.

```
; <label>:25                  ; preds = %21, %13
%26 = load i64* %dest, align 8
%27 = icmp ult i64 %26, 0
br i1 %27, label %35, label %28
```

Figure 11: PHOLD is `dest_less_zero` block.

```
; <label>:28                    ; preds = %25
%29 = load i64* %dest, align 8
%30 = load i64* @g_tw_nlp, align 8
%31 = call i32 @tw_nnodes()
%32 = zext i32 %31 to i64
%33 = mul i64 %30, %32
%34 = icmp uge i64 %29, %33
br i1 %34, label %35, label %36
```

Figure 12: PHOLD `dest_greater_nlps` block.

```
; <label>:35                    ; preds = %28, %25
call void (i8*, i32, i8*, ...)* @tw_error(i8*
    getelementptr inbounds ([58 x i8]* @.str1,
    i32 0, i32 0), i32 90, i8* getelementptr
    inbounds ([9 x i8]* @.str2, i32 0, i32 0))
br label %47
```

Figure 13: PHOLD `error` block.

```
; <label>:36                    ; preds = %28
%37 = load i64* %dest, align 8
%38 = load %struct.tw_lp** %4, align 8
%39 = getelementptr inbounds %struct.tw_lp* %38,
    i32 0, i32 7
%40 = load %struct.tw_rng_stream** %39, align 8
%41 = load double* @mean, align 8
%42 = call double @tw_rand_exponential(%struct.
    tw_rng_stream* %40, double %41)
%43 = load double* @lookahead, align 8
%44 = fadd double %42, %43
%45 = load %struct.tw_lp** %4, align 8
%46 = call %struct.tw_event* @tw_event_new(i64
    %37, double %44, %struct.tw_lp* %45)
call void @tw_event_send(%struct.tw_event* %46)
br label %47
```

Figure 14: PHOLD `send_event` block.

```
; <label>:47                    ; preds = %36, %35
ret void
```

Figure 15: PHOLD `return` block.

The `rand_greater` block, as shown in figure 10, loads the LP identifier into `dest`. The `dest_less_zero` block shown in figure 11 compares `dest` with zero. If it's less, PHOLD jumps to the error block. Otherwise, it jumps to the `dest_greater_nlps` block. The `dest_greater_nlps` block (figure 12) calls `tw_nnodes()` and multiply the result with `g_tw_nlp`. If `dest` is greater than the product, jump to the `error` block. Otherwise jump to the `send_event` block. The `error` block (figure 13) is the error state. Despite the appearance, this state will terminate the program. The `send_event` block (figure 14) creates a random number using `tw_rand_exponential()` to which we add `lookahead`. PHOLD then calls `tw_event_new()` with `dest` as the destination LP, a new future time-stamp, and the current LP as the third argument. Finally, PHOLD calls `tw_event_send()` and jumps to the `return` block. Last, PHOLD's `return` block, shown in figure 15) exits from the event handler function.

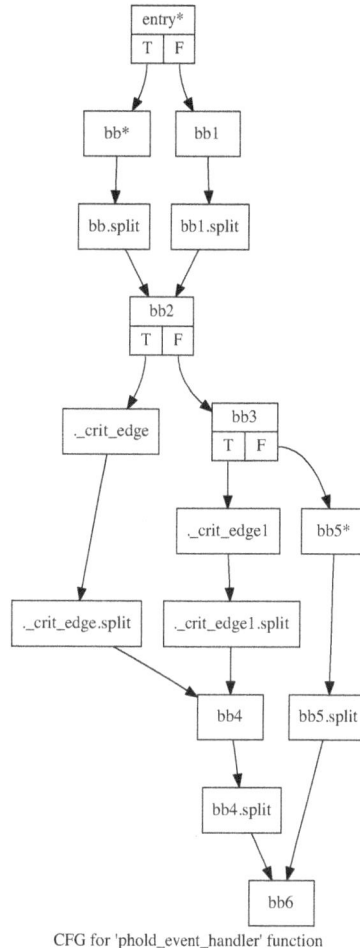

Figure 16: The CFG of the instrumented PHOLD forward event handler function. RNGs calls are marked with *.

With the forward event handler IR of F in hand, LORAIN must both instrument it (figure 16) and then invert the resulting function in order to generate F'. Please note that there are no stores to the simulation (LP) state in the PHOLD model. There are therefore no stores that need to be reversed to generate F'. There are, however, varying numbers of RNG calls that must be un-called. By retracing our steps in reverse through the CFG of F', all RNGs will be successfully rolled back as shown in figure 17.

4.2 Airport

While PHOLD is fairly simple and requires no state changes to be reversed, Fujimoto's airport model [13] does require handling of state modifications while simultaneously maintaining a degree of simplicity. As ROSS has an implementation of this, the airport model was deemed an ideal target for demonstrating further reversing capabilities. Additionally, this model contains examples of all three operations which must be reversed: constructive operations, destructive operations, and random number generation.

Each airport in the airport model maintains three variables: `In_The_Air`, `On_The_Ground`, and `Runway_Free`. The first two are integers: the number of planes in the airport's

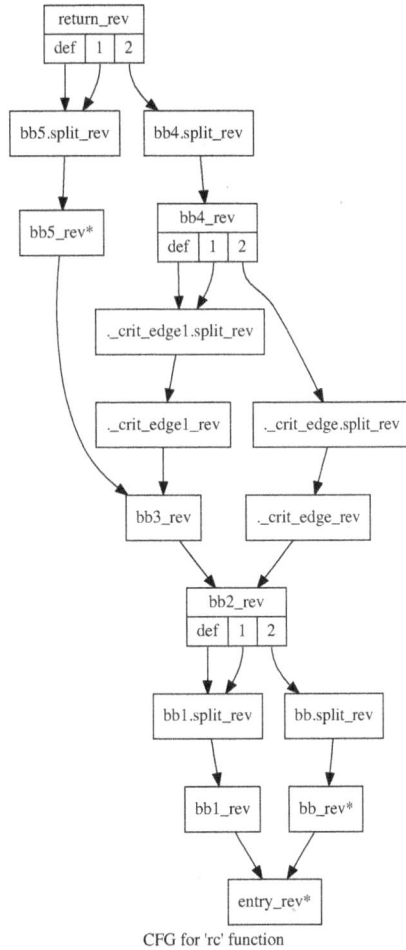

CFG for 'rc' function

Figure 17: The CFG of the reverse PHOLD event handler. Reverse RNG calls are marked with *.

```
bb4:                      ; preds = %LeafBlock1
%91 = load %struct.airport_state** %0, align 8
%92 = getelementptr inbounds %struct.
   airport_state* %91, i32 0, i32 2
%93 = load i32* %92, align 4
%94 = add nsw i32 %93, -1
store i32 %94, i32* %92, align 4
%95 = load %struct.tw_lp** %3, align 8
%96 = getelementptr inbounds %struct.tw_lp* %95,
   i32 0, i32 7
%97 = load %struct.tw_rng_stream** %96, align 8
%98 = load double* @mean_flight_time, align 8
%99 = call double @tw_rand_exponential(%struct.
   tw_rng_stream* %97, double %98)
store double %99, double* %ts, align 8, !jml !10
%100 = load %struct.tw_lp** %3, align 8
%101 = getelementptr inbounds %struct.tw_lp*
   %100, i32 0, i32 7
%102 = load %struct.tw_rng_stream** %101, align 8
%103 = call i64 @tw_rand_integer(%struct.
   tw_rng_stream* %102, i64 0, i64 3)
%104 = trunc i64 %103 to i32
store i32 %104, i32* %rand_result, align 4, !jml
   !10
store i64 0, i64* %dst_lp, align 8, !jml !10
%105 = load i32* %rand_result, align 4
store i32 %105, i32* %.reg2mem, !jml !10
br label %NodeBlock20
```

Figure 18: Demonstration of constructive operations. For example, the blue region consists of subtracting 1 from the On_The_Ground state variable. The green and red regions perform RNG calls.

```
bb4_rev:                  ; preds = %NodeBlock20_rev
%31 = load %struct.tw_lp** %0
%32 = getelementptr %struct.tw_lp* %31, i32 0,
   i32 7
%33 = load %struct.tw_rng_stream** %32
%34 = call double @rng_gen_reverse_val(%struct.
   tw_rng_stream* %33)
%35 = load double* @mean_flight_time
%36 = load %struct.tw_lp** %0
%37 = getelementptr %struct.tw_lp* %36, i32 0,
   i32 7
%38 = load %struct.tw_rng_stream** %37
%39 = call double @rng_gen_reverse_val(%struct.
   tw_rng_stream* %38)
%40 = load %struct.airport_state** %3
%41 = getelementptr %struct.airport_state* %40,
   i32 0, i32 2
%42 = load i32* %41
%43 = sub i32 %42, -1
store i32 %43, i32* %41
br label %LeafBlock1_rev
```

Figure 19: Demonstration of "reverse" constructive operations. The blue region consists of adding 1 to the On_The_Ground state variable. The green and red regions are reverse RNG calls.

air-space and the number of planes on the ground at this particular airport. Runway_Free is a boolean indicating whether or not the runway is available. In this model, each LP represents an airport and an event represents the action of an airplane (arrive, land, depart). As different events are scheduled, the airplane "moves" between airports.

As aircraft flow from airport to airport, these variables are adjusted appropriately. When a plane x moves from airport A to airport B, the In_The_Air variable at A is decremented by one while B's is incremented by one. If x is destined for airport B, Runway_Free must be checked to determine whether or not the runway is available for a landing. If so, a landing event must be scheduled. In_The_Air will again be decremented and On_The_Ground will be incremented. After some amount of time, this aircraft may again be scheduled to depart this airport.

Figure 18 demonstrates a basic block from the forward event handler while figure 19 demonstrates its corresponding basic block from the reverse event handler. These basic blocks represent the forward and reverse cases of the departure event. The blue region in the forward decrements (in the reverse it increments) the state variable On_The_Ground. The green and red regions handle random number generation in both forward and reverse directions.

Likewise, as destructive operations are performed on the various values in the forward event handler, they must be collated and their values saved for possible future restoration. These values are determined at an earlier stage by an analysis pass and passed to the current stage via metadata. The forward event handler is configured to save these values at the beginning of the function (before their values are overwritten). The emitted reverse event handler will restore the values in its (single) exit block.

The time deltas for each event will be generated by ROSS' reversible RNG. For example, when a landing event is scheduled, it must be at some (bounded) random time in the future from the current event time. RNG calls must be un-called so as to not disturb the random sequence. In other words, if RNG R produces r_1 and is un-called, the very next call on R must produce an identical value to r_1.

4.3 Experimental Setup

For our experimental study, we consider the following three code versions for both PHOLD and airport models:

- *O0: unoptimized.* Both models were passed through LORAIN and the modified forward and synthesized reverse event handlers were compiled without applying any further optimization (-O0)

- *O3: optimized.* Both models were passed through LO-RAIN but the modified and forward and synthesized reverse event handlers were further optimized (-O3)

- *HW: hand-written.* Both models had modified forward and reverse event handlers written by hand and used optimization level -O3. We emphasize here that the LORAIN passes are not used.

The ROSS framework itself is always compiled with -O3 turned on regardless of which approach we were using. The results were gathered using a 2.1 GHz 64 core AMD machine with 512 GB of RAM running GNU/Linux and clang 3.2. Only 32 cores were ever used in experimentation.

The PHOLD model is configured with 16 LPs and 1 event per LP when run on 2 cores (small workload case) and 1,048,576 LPs with 16 events per LP when run on 32 cores (large workload case). The airport model is configured 1024 airport LPs with 1 plane event per airport LP using 2 cores (small workload case) and 1,048,576 airport LPs with 16 plane events per airport LP using 32 cores (large workload case). All box-plot graphs were generated by running each simulation 100 times.

A first pass ROSS model verification relies on a simulation's net event count. This count indicates the number of committed events that occurred for a specific experiment. It is necessary (but not sufficient) that the net event count is identical for all parallel (any number of processors) and serial runs of the same model configuration. This approach was used as a sanity check when model development was done by hand.

Table 1: Median performance of PHOLD and airport models measured in net events per second.

Experiment	O0	O3	HW
2 core PHOLD	946,164.80	971,834.45	974,658.30
32 core PHOLD	6,070,813.30	6,155,326.35	6,178,446.40
2 core Airport	1,921,355.20	2,039,775.40	2,062,018.85
32 core Airport	6,713,835.70	6,854,997.75	7,044,712.05

4.4 Performance Results

The performance graphs for the PHOLD and airport models configured with 2 processors and small workload are

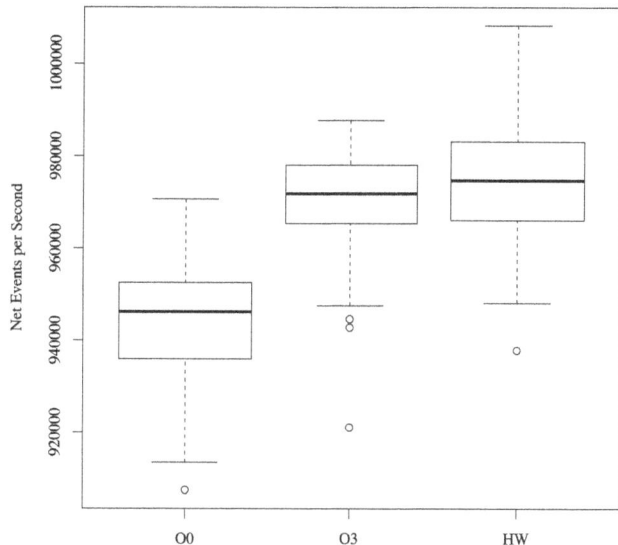

Figure 20: The performance of the PHOLD model using 2 cores. The three plots are O0, the unoptimized generated IR, O3, the optimized generated IR, and HW, the model including a hand-written reverse event handler.

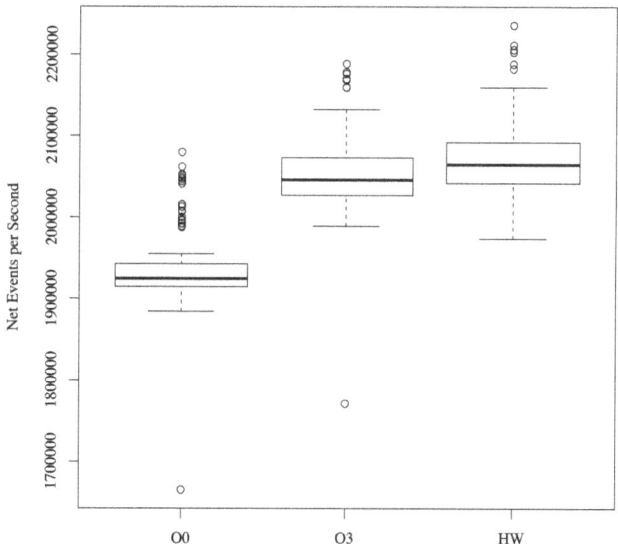

Figure 21: The performance of the airport model using 2 cores. The three plots are O0, the unoptimized generated IR, O3, the optimized generated IR, and HW, the model including a hand-written reverse event handler.

shown in figures 20 and 21. The 32 core, large workload performance graphs are shown in figure 22 for PHOLD and figure 23 for the airport model. For both models, the unoptimized version generated by LORAIN is always worse than the other two executions. However, the gap narrows between optimized LORAIN model code and the hand-written approach. Using the median from the hand-written approach as the baseline, the LORAIN-generated airport model was only 1% less efficient while running with 2 cores and 2.7% less efficient when running with 32 cores. The PHOLD

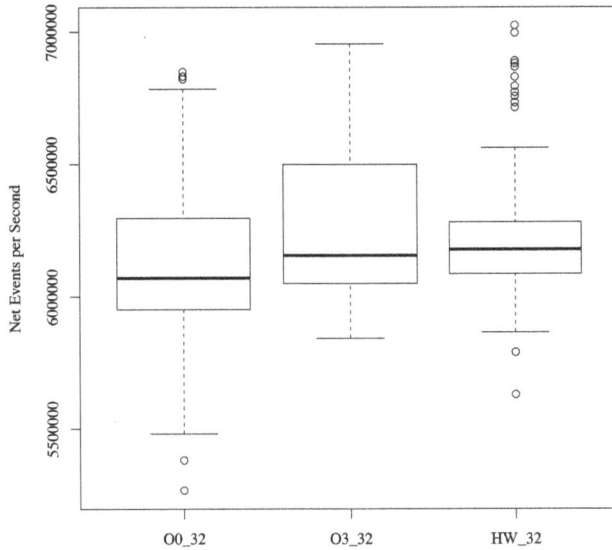

Figure 22: The performance of the PHOLD model using 32 cores. The three plots are O0, the unoptimized generated IR, O3, the optimized generated IR, and HW, the model including a hand-written reverse event handler.

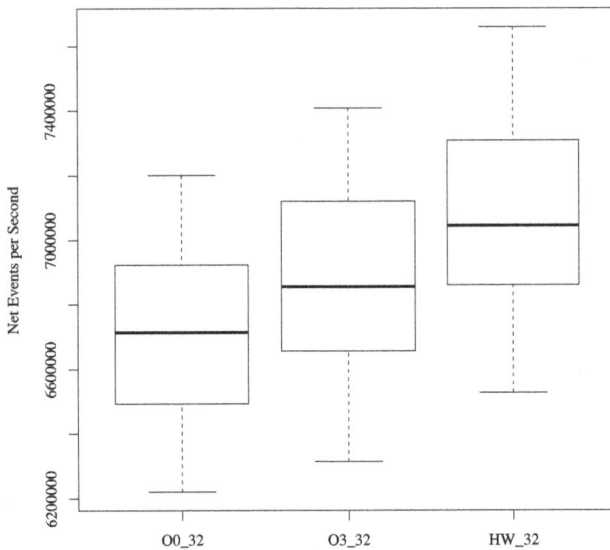

Figure 23: The performance of the airport model using 32 cores. The three plots are O0, the unoptimized generated IR, O3, the optimized generated IR, and HW, the model including a hand-written reverse event handler.

model was 0.3% less efficient than the corresponding hand-written model when run with 2 cores and only 0.4% less efficient when run on 32 cores.

As expected, hand-written instrumentation and reverse event handlers always outperform their synthesized counterparts. Despite the hand-written approach always having the best performance, the optimized LORAIN approach is able to come very close to the hand-written performance in all cases. Although the hand-written model appears to be more efficient in figure 23, table 1 indicates a median performance

difference of 189,714.30 events-per-second (for models that are executing at a rate of 6 to 7 million events-per-second) between hand-written and optimized LORAIN code.

Notably, the range of the performance results was larger than one might expect. This is attributed to OS jitter [6]. The Linux machine on which we performed these measurements had quite a few extraneous processes, network traffic, and other external factors that would contribute to a variance in the runtimes. Additionally, no attempt at locking the MPI processes to specific PEs, which may have tightened the results slightly, was made.

5. RELATED WORK

Beyond Parallel Simscript II.5 [29], RCC [25] and Backstroke [30], there are number of previous related works within the PDES community that have a similar goal. For example, Nicol and Heidelberger [22] create the Utilitarian Parallel Simulator (UPS) which creates a set of modeling language extensions that enable model components developed for serial execution to execute in parallel using a conservative event scheduling approach. A similar idea is that of the High-Level Architecture (HLA) [13] except that the end goal is one of simulator interoperability and not improved parallel performance. The idea here is that a heterogeneous, federation of serial simulators is combined and made to interoperate with much less effort than a fully, integrated rewrite of all models executing within the federation. In the context of network simulation, Riley et al. [27] create a specialized approach called *Backplane* that enables the federations of different network simulators. They demonstrate the capability of *Backplane* using a parallel version of *ns* (pdns), GTNetS and GloMoSim.

Outside of the PDES community, there has been growing interest automatic reverse execution of programs, especially in the context of program debugging. Akgul et al. [3] provide an assembly language level reverse execution approach for the purposes of application debugging. Biswas and Mall [7] provide an reverse execution approach for purposes of debugging. The earliest work (e.g., 1988) in reverse execution for debugging appears to have been done by Pan and Linton [23]. This early work is especially interesting because there target was not serial programs but parallel programs that are much harder to debug. Like other approaches, it involved some varying degree of program state-saving to support the reverse program execution.

LORAIN's overall approach is similar to Weiser's slicing methodology [31]. Slicing is a method of reducing the program down to specific *slicing criterion*, or points of interest (in this case, LLVM Values), as well as the remainder of the program that may possibly affect it. This subset of the program is referred to as a *slice*. Slicing is useful in many areas [28]; applications include debugging purposes, parallelization, and more directly related to this work, reverse engineering.

Bahi and Eisenbeis [4] present a lower bound on the spatial complexity of a DAG with reversible operations and an approach for finding the minimum number of registers required for a forward and backward execution of a DAG. They also define an energy-based garbage collection metric as the additional number of registers needed for the reversible execution of the original computation. Experimental results report that garbage size is never more than 50% of the DAG size.

Finally, Perumalla [24] provides an excellent survey of the field of reverse/reversible computing.

6. CONCLUSIONS & FUTURE WORK

In this work we have presented LORAIN, a tool capable of automatic analysis and instrumentation of a specific forward event handler and the emission of a reverse event handler capable of inverting all model state changes. Early results show the automatically generated code is on par with hand-written reverse event handlers. LORAIN currently only supports models adhering to the ROSS simulator API.

LORAIN can deliver over 99% the performance of hand-written models and our results have shown no less than 97% of the performance on a more complex model. While at an early stage, having such a tool will undoubtedly ease the burden on model developers and allow them to more quickly develop optimistic models that better exploit current and future HPC systems.

Currently, LORAIN does not support inter-procedural analysis or transformations, though such support may be added in the future. Preliminary loop support exists although loop handling improvements are certainly a high-priority addition. All primary simulation languages such as C, C++, and Fortran are supported in LLVM, paving the way for future support in LORAIN.

Additionally, we are interested in leveraging other LLVM advances that may help to improve the overall quality of LORAIN's modified forward and synthesized reverse event handler functions. For example, Zhao et al. [33] develop a proof technique for proving SSA-based program invariants and compiler optimizations. Here, they apply this technique and formally verify a variant of LLVM's mem2reg transformation and show the verified code generation performs on par with LLVM's unverified implementation.

The overall issue of verification is very much an open question in the context of reverse computation especially at the IR level. It is clear from the *Backstroke* compiler that source-to-source tools can maintain program semantics that may enable improved reverse code transformations. However, it is unclear if verification of the generated code at the LLVM IR level is equally good as source-to-source reverse code.

7. ACKNOWLEDGMENTS

This research was partially supported by the Office of Science of the U.S. Department of Energy under Contracts DE-SC0004875 and DE-AC02-06CH11357.

8. REFERENCES

[1] SAFECode (latest version). http://sva.cs.illinois.edu/index.html, 2014.

[2] A. V. Aho, M. S. Lam, R. Sethi, and J. D. Ullman. *Compilers: Principles, Techniques, and Tools (2Nd Edition)*. Addison-Wesley Longman Publishing Co., Inc., Boston, MA, USA, 2006.

[3] T. Akgul and V. J. Mooney III. Assembly instruction level reverse execution for debugging. *ACM Trans. Softw. Eng. Methodol.*, 13(2):149–198, Apr. 2004.

[4] M. Bahi and C. Eisenbeis. Spatial complexity of reversibly computable dag. In *Proceedings of the 2009 International Conference on Compilers, Architecture, and Synthesis for Embedded Systems*, CASES '09, pages 47–56, New York, NY, USA, 2009. ACM.

[5] P. D. Barnes, Jr., C. D. Carothers, D. R. Jefferson, and J. M. LaPre. Warp speed: Executing time warp on 1,966,080 cores. In *Proceedings of the 2013 ACM SIGSIM Conference on Principles of Advanced Discrete Simulation*, SIGSIM-PADS '13, pages 327–336, New York, NY, USA, 2013. ACM.

[6] P. Beckman, K. Iskra, K. Yoshii, S. Coghlan, and A. Nataraj. Benchmarking the effects of operating system interference on extreme-scale parallel machines. *Cluster Computing*, 11(1):3–16, 2008.

[7] B. Biswas and R. Mall. Reverse execution of programs. *SIGPLAN Not.*, 34(4):61–69, 1999.

[8] C. Carothers, D. B. Jr, and S. Pearce. ROSS: A high-performance, low-memory, modular time warp system. *Journal of Parallel and Distributed Computing*, 62(11):1648 – 1669, 2002.

[9] C. D. Carothers, K. S. Perumalla, and R. M. Fujimoto. Efficient optimistic parallel simulations using reverse computation. *ACM Trans. Model. Comput. Simul.*, 9(3):224–253, July 1999.

[10] R. Cytron, J. Ferrante, B. K. Rosen, M. N. Wegman, and F. K. Zadeck. Efficiently computing static single assignment form and the control dependence graph. *ACM Trans. Program. Lang. Syst.*, 13(4):451–490, Oct. 1991.

[11] D. Dhurjati, S. Kowshik, and V. Adve. SAFECode: enforcing alias analysis for weakly typed languages. In *PLDI '06: Proceedings of the 2006 ACM SIGPLAN conference on Programming language design and implementation*, pages 144–157, New York, NY, USA, 2006. ACM.

[12] R. M. Fujimoto. Parallel discrete event simulation. *Commun. ACM*, 33(10):30–53, Oct. 1990.

[13] R. M. Fujimoto. *Parallel and Distribution Simulation Systems*. John Wiley & Sons, Inc., New York, NY, USA, 1st edition, 1999.

[14] E. Gamma, R. Helm, R. Johnson, and J. Vlissides. *Design Patterns: Elements of Reusable Object-oriented Software*. Addison-Wesley Longman Publishing Co., Inc., Boston, MA, USA, 1995.

[15] E. Gonsiorowski, C. Carothers, and C. Tropper. Modeling large scale circuits using massively parallel discrete-event simulation. In *Modeling, Analysis Simulation of Computer and Telecommunication Systems (MASCOTS), 2012 IEEE 20th International Symposium on*, pages 127–133, Aug 2012.

[16] C. Hou, G. Vulov, D. Quinlan, D. Jefferson, R. Fujimoto, and R. Vuduc. A new method for program inversion. In *Compiler Construction*, pages 81–100. Springer, 2012.

[17] D. R. Jefferson. Virtual time. *ACM Trans. Program. Lang. Syst.*, 7(3):404–425, 1985.

[18] C. Lattner and V. Adve. LLVM: A compilation framework for lifelong program analysis & transformation. In *Proceedings of the International Symposium on Code Generation and Optimization: Feedback-directed and Runtime Optimization*, CGO '04, pages 75–, Washington, DC, USA, 2004. IEEE Computer Society.

[19] N. Liu and C. D. Carothers. Modeling billion-node torus networks using massively parallel discrete-event simulation. In *Proceedings of the 2011 IEEE*

Workshop on Principles of Advanced and Distributed Simulation, PADS '11, pages 1–8, Washington, DC, USA, 2011. IEEE Computer Society.

[20] C. J. Lobb, Z. Chao, R. M. Fujimoto, and S. M. Potter. Parallel event-driven neural network simulations using the hodgkin-huxley neuron model. In *PADS '05: Proceedings of the 19th Workshop on Principles of Advanced and Distributed Simulation*, pages 16–25, Washington, DC, USA, 2005. IEEE Computer Society.

[21] M. Mubarak, C. D. Carothers, R. Ross, and P. Carns. Modeling a million-node dragonfly network using massively parallel discrete event simulation. In *3rd International Workshop on Performance Modeling, Benchmarking and Simulation of High Performance Computer Systems (PMBS12) held as part of SC12*, 2012.

[22] D. Nicol and P. Heidelberger. Parallel execution for serial simulators. *ACM Trans. Model. Comput. Simul.*, 6(3):210–242, July 1996.

[23] D. Z. Pan and M. A. Linton. Supporting reverse execution for parallel programs. In *Proceedings of the 1988 ACM SIGPLAN and SIGOPS Workshop on Parallel and Distributed Debugging*, PADD '88, pages 124–129, New York, NY, USA, 1988. ACM.

[24] K. Perumalla. *Introduction to Reversible Computing.* CRC Press, 2013.

[25] K. S. Perumalla and R. M. Fujimoto. Source-code transformations for efficient reversibility. 1999.

[26] K. S. Perumalla and V. A. Protopopescu. Reversible simulations of elastic collisions. *ACM Trans. Model. Comput. Simul.*, 23(2):12:1–12:25, May 2013.

[27] G. F. Riley, M. H. Ammar, R. M. Fujimoto, A. Park, K. Perumalla, and D. Xu. A federated approach to distributed network simulation. *ACM Trans. Model. Comput. Simul.*, 14(2):116–148, Apr. 2004.

[28] F. Tip. A survey of program slicing techniques. Technical report, Amsterdam, The Netherlands, The Netherlands, 1994.

[29] J.-J. Tsai and R. M. Fujimoto. Automatic parallelization of discrete event simulation programs. In *Proceedings of the 25th Conference on Winter Simulation*, WSC '93, pages 697–705, New York, NY, USA, 1993. ACM.

[30] G. Vulov, C. Hou, R. Vuduc, R. Fujimoto, D. Quinlan, and D. Jefferson. The backstroke framework for source level reverse computation applied to parallel discrete event simulation. In *Proceedings of the Winter Simulation Conference*, WSC '11, pages 2965–2979. Winter Simulation Conference, 2011.

[31] M. Weiser. Program slicing. In *Proceedings of the 5th International Conference on Software Engineering*, ICSE '81, pages 439–449, Piscataway, NJ, USA, 1981. IEEE Press.

[32] G. Yaun, C. D. Carothers, and S. Kalyanaraman. Large-scale TCP models using optimistic parallel simulation. In *Proceedings of the seventeenth workshop on Parallel and distributed simulation*, PADS '03, pages 153–, Washington, DC, USA, 2003. IEEE Computer Society.

[33] J. Zhao, S. Nagarakatte, M. M. Martin, and S. Zdancewic. Formal verification of SSA-based optimizations for LLVM. *SIGPLAN Not.*, 48(6):175–186, June 2013.

Lock-Free Pending Event Set Management in Time Warp

Sounak Gupta
Dept of of Electrical Engineering and Computing Systems
Cincinnati, OH 45221-0030
sounak.besu@gmail.com

Philip A. Wilsey
Dept of of Electrical Engineering and Computing Systems
Cincinnati, OH 45221-0030
wilseypa@gmail.com

ABSTRACT

The rapid growth in the parallelism of multi-core processors has opened up new opportunities and challenges for parallel simulation discrete event simulation (PDES). PDES simulators attempt to find parallelism within the pending event set to achieve speedup. Typically the pending event set is sorted to preserve the causal orders of the contained events. Sorting is a key aspect that amplifies contention for exclusive access to the shared event scheduler and events are generally scheduled to follow the time-based order of the pending events. In this work we leverage a Ladder Queue data structure to partition the pending events into groups (called buckets) arranged by adjacent and short regions of time. We assume that the pending events within any one bucket are causally independent and schedule them for execution without sorting and without consideration of their total time-based order. We use the Time Warp mechanism to recover whenever actual dependencies arise. Due to the lack of need for sorting, we further extend our pending event data structure so that it can be organized for lock-free access. Experimental results show consistent speedup for all studied configurations and simulation models. The speedups range from 1.1 to 1.49 with higher speedups occurring with higher thread counts where contention for the shared event set becomes more problematic with a conventional mutex locking mechanism.

Categories and Subject Descriptors

D.1.3 [**Programming Techniques**]: Concurrent Programming—*parallel programming, distributed programming*
; I.6.8 [**Simulation and Modeling**]: Types of Simulation—*parallel, distributed, discrete event*

General Terms

Algorithms, Performance

Keywords

Time Warp, pending event lists, multi-core, threads, lock-free

1. INTRODUCTION

The adoption of parallelism through core replication to produce multi-core and many-core processors is widespread and growing. Inexpensive processors with core counts of 4–8 are common. At a slightly higher (but still affordable) price point, core counts of 12–16 are readily available. Furthermore, there is every expectation that these numbers will continue to increase. The introduction of these multi-core and many-core processors into mainstream Beowulf Clusters means that distributed algorithms must be developed that support parallelism both within and between the nodes of the cluster [6]. Shared data must be represented and organized to support high speed, access with a minimum of contended accesses by the parallel threads that need to read and update the shared data. This is especially true for fine-grained applications such as parallel discrete event simulation.

The central data structure on a discrete event simulator is the pending event set. This set records and organizes the events yet to be processed by the simulation kernel. For a parallel simulation kernel with multiple threads accessing a shared pending event set, the organization and management of the pending event set must be carefully planned. The pending event set is frequently accessed as the event processing threads dequeue events for processing and enqueue any generated events (for purposes of this manuscript, we will ignore the details of remote event transmission to other nodes of a Beowulf Cluster). Furthermore, since the processing of discrete events is often a fine-grained computation, significant contention for the protected pending event set can rapidly grow to negatively impact performance. As few as 5-6 threads can easily result in performance loss triggered by contention [18].

This manuscript examines the management of a shared pending-event set for a Time Warp [9, 5] synchronized parallel simulation kernel executing on a single node many-core processing platform. The work builds on the two-level approach for managing the pending event set that was originally developed by Karthik [18] and extended by Dickman *et al* [4]. The extension by Dickman *et al* used the ladder queue data structure [29] to manage the scheduling event queue. The ladder queue is a variant of the calendar queue [3] that arranges events into *months* (or *buckets*) so that their timestamp falls within a bounded time window assigned to that bucket. Thus, the events in each bucket are guaranteed to fall within a small window of time. In the ladder queue, these buckets are not sorted (to save time) until the actual dequeue operations occur on a particular bucket.

At the end of their experimental analysis section, Dickman *et al* suggest that the small time window for the pending events in a particular bucket may be such that the contained events are mostly causally independent. Should this be true, in a Time Warp synchronized parallel simulation, one could manage all of the buckets in the ladder queue as unsorted queues and potentially use atomic operations to build a lock-free data structure for managing the pending event set. Given the relatively high costs of locks or other mechanisms to provide a critical region of access, a lock-free pending event set could substantially reduce access time and contention to this critical shared resource. Time Warp is a critical contributor to this possibility since it can recover, by rollback, should a causal dependency actually be experienced when processing the unsorted events from the ladder queue bucket. In this manuscript, we examine this idea more fully and show experimental results for a parallel Time Warp simulator with a lock-free unsorted ladder queue data structure for managing the pending event set.

The remainder of this manuscript is organized as follows. Section 2 provides a brief review of studies related to pending event set and non-blocking, lock-free lists/queues. Section 3 provides details about the software architecture of WARPED, the Time Warp simulation kernel which has been used in this work. Section 4 describes our proposed non-blocking ladder queue design in details. Section 5 presents the results of our experimental analysis. Section 6 is a discussion about the possibilities of further change in the pending event set design. Finally, Section 7 presents the conclusions we can draw from this experiment.

2. RELATED WORK

2.1 Pending Event Sets

WARPED is a parallel simulation kernel that implements the Time Warp synchronization protocol [12, 23]. Management of the pending event set in WARPED follows the model outlined in [26] and decomposes it into Unprocessed and Processed event pools. The Unprocessed pool stores the events that are yet to be executed. The Processed pool refers to those events that have been processed but not yet committed (they must be preserved in case of rollback). As per the Time Warp protocol, WARPED has been designed to greedily process events without strict adherence to causal order. Whenever causal violations are detected, WARPED rolls back to a consistent state (usually the last commit point) and re-executes the events in their proper order. To support this rollback, the Processed queue serves as the holding list for events that might need re-execution in case of a rollback [4, 18]. Similar models have been adopted for other time warp synchronized simulators. For example, a simple implementation of a doubly-linked list to store all processed and unprocessed events along with their execution status was proposed by Ronngren *et al* [26]. Although this design allows quick and efficient rollbacks and fossil collection, it cannot effectively insert and delete events when the Unprocessed event pool is large. An improved skew heap was suggested by Ronngren as a possible data structure that can be effective for large Unprocessed event pools.

A medium to coarse-grained simulator was built by Prasad *et al* [22] using a parallelized Calender Queue. They provided each processor with a different calender queue. Their study showed that load balancing of a local queue-based simulator was comparable to that of a global queue-based simulator. However, the global queue-based simulator was faster with fewer rollbacks. Using an array and hierarchical bitmap, Santoro *et al* [27] created a Least-Timestamp-First (LTSF) scheduler. Although similar to a Calendar Queue, this low-overhead scheduler provides a constant access-time.

Dickman *et al* [4] proposed the use of multiple LTSF queues in scheduler to reduce contention on a many-core processing platform. A comparative analysis also showed that Ladder Queue [29] performed better as a LTSF queue in WARPED scheduler compared to STL multiset (a sorted doubly-linked list) and Splay tree [28].

2.2 Lock Free Lists

Valois [31] proposed the first lock-free list that required only atomic compare-and-swap (CAS) operations. He used the technique of encoding in-progress operations in auxiliary nodes. This technique was improved by Michael *et al* [15]. A lock-free ordered list was implemented by Harris [7] using pointer marking technique. The least significant bit of the next pointer of a deleted node is marked to denote logical deletion. Physical removal of that node takes place in a separate phase. Memory reclamation in Harris' algorithm was improved by Michael [13] using hazard pointers [14]. A lock-based linked list was designed by Heller *et al* [8] that used wait-free look up operations. Harris and Michael used this wait-free approach to improve the performance of their algorithm. A wait-free queue was proposed by Kogan and Petrank [10]. Their fast-path-slow-path method is composed of a slower wait-free algorithm coupled with a comparatively faster lock-free algorithm. This approach shows better performance than Harris-Michael algorithm. Timnat *et al* used ideas from [30] to design a wait-free ordered linked list. They used Harris-Michael algorithm as the fast path.

Liu *et al* [11] proposed a lock-free scheduler for conservative parallel simulation. Their implementation uses fetch-and-add atomic operations to improve performance on a shared-memory multiprocessor platform. They observed that with increases in the number of logical processes, the performance improvement was marginal.

3. BACKGROUND: EVENT MANAGEMENT AND PROCESSING IN WARPED

WARPED is a parallel discrete event simulation kernel that implements the Time Warp synchronization protocol [12, 23]. Initially designed and optimized for parallel simulations on single core processor-based Beowulf Clusters, it incorporates extensive configurable features and sub-algorithms of the Time Warp Mechanism (*e.g.,* adaptive periodic checkpointing [19] and lazy, aggressive, and dynamic cancellation [25]). On each processing node, the Logical Processes (LPs) of a simulation are grouped together and scheduled according to a Least-Timestamp-First (LTSF) event scheduling policy. The Time Warp housekeeping functions such as GVT estimation, termination detection, and fossil collection are organized into a set of common services for the entire LP population on that node. This node-based architecture is similar to that reported in [1] and [24].

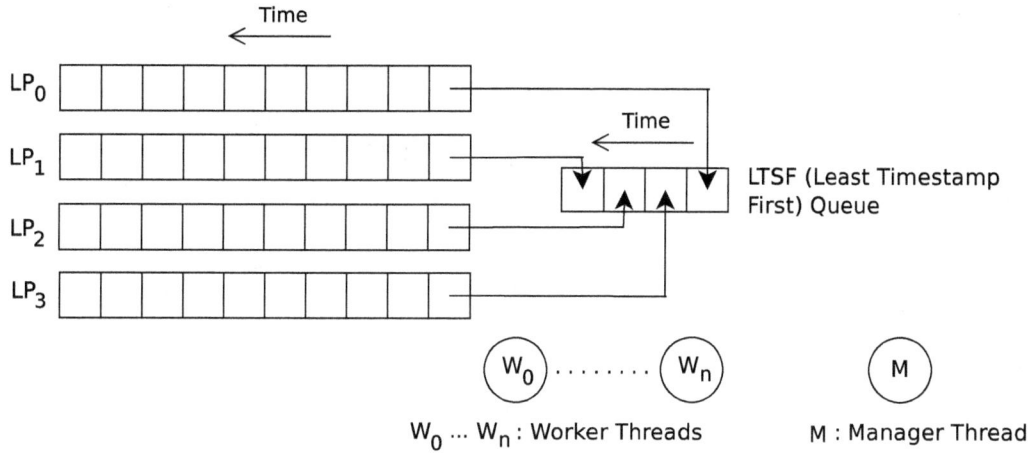

Figure 1: Threaded structure of warped.

Recently, WARPED was extended to incorporate threaded execution for multi-core and many-core processors and Beowulf Clusters composed of such [17, 18]. Figure 1 shows the overall design structure consisting of the main pending event pool and the executing threads. The initial design worked reasonably well for smaller multi-core processor systems. A high level overview of the thread operation and pending event set organization is provided below.

A manager thread and one or more worker threads constitute a threaded instance of WARPED. The Time Warp housekeeping functions are processed by the *manager thread* (labeled M in Figure 1). The receipt and transmission of event messages exchanged with remote nodes in the cluster is also handled by the *manager thread*. However, the local event insertion is performed by the worker threads. Additional details on the operation of the manager thread design are provided in [18]. The dequeueing and execution of pending events and the subsequent generation of new events is handled by the *worker threads* (depicted as $W_0 \cdots W_n$ in Figure 1).

The pending event sets are organized into a two level structure. At the first level, each LP managed a separate sorted linked list of its pending events. These lists are locked and accessed by the manager and worker threads. At the second level is (one or more) common LTSF pending event queue where the lowest timestamped event from each LP event list is enqueued. The *worker threads* use the (locked) LTSF queue to schedule the next event for execution. After dequeueing and processing an event from the LTSF queue, a worker thread will replenish the LTSF queue by removing the new lowest timestamped event from the pending event list of the LP corresponding to the event just processed and insert it into the LTSF queue. The algorithm shown in Figure 2 provides a pseudo code representation of the general event processing performed by the worker threads.

When configured with only a few worker threads, this system works well. However, once the number of worker threads exceeds 5–6, there is a negative impact on the performance due to contention for the LTSF queue. Contention is not a problem for the LP event pools as these structures are independently locked and only one worker thread and the manager thread can simultaneously access the same LP event pool. The LTSF queue is the focal point of contention for

```
worker_thread()
    lock the LTSF queue
    dequeue the smallest event from the LTSF
    unlock the LTSF queue

    while !done loop
        process event
            (assume this event belongs to LP[i])
        lock LP[i] queue
        dequeue smallest event from LP[i]
            (assume this event to be k)
        lock the LTSF queue
        insert event k into the LTSF
        dequeue the smallest event from the LTSF
        unlock the LTSF queue
        unlock LP[i] queue
    end loop
```

Figure 2: Generalized event execution loop for any worker thread.

pending events in this architecture. The organization of the pending event list needs modification, especially the LTSF queue.

The principle solution to the contention issue in threaded WARPED kernel is to support multiple LTSF queues (Figure 3). The worker threads are uniformly (or near uniformly) divided into a number of independent groups. The number of such groups equals the number of LTSF queues desired. Each worker thread group is statically assigned to a LTSF queue. Figure 3 illustrates the binding of worker thread groups to LTSF queues (the worker threads are denoted by the bubbles labeled $W_0 \cdots W_n$). Correspondingly, the LPs are divided into a number of independent groups bound to specific LTSF queues. The LTSF queues are then populated with events from their assigned LPs in a manner similar to the single LTSF implementation. The assignment of worker thread groups is designed to be fixed throughout the simulation. LP groups, however, can be reassigned among the LTSF queues dynamically during simulation to facilitate

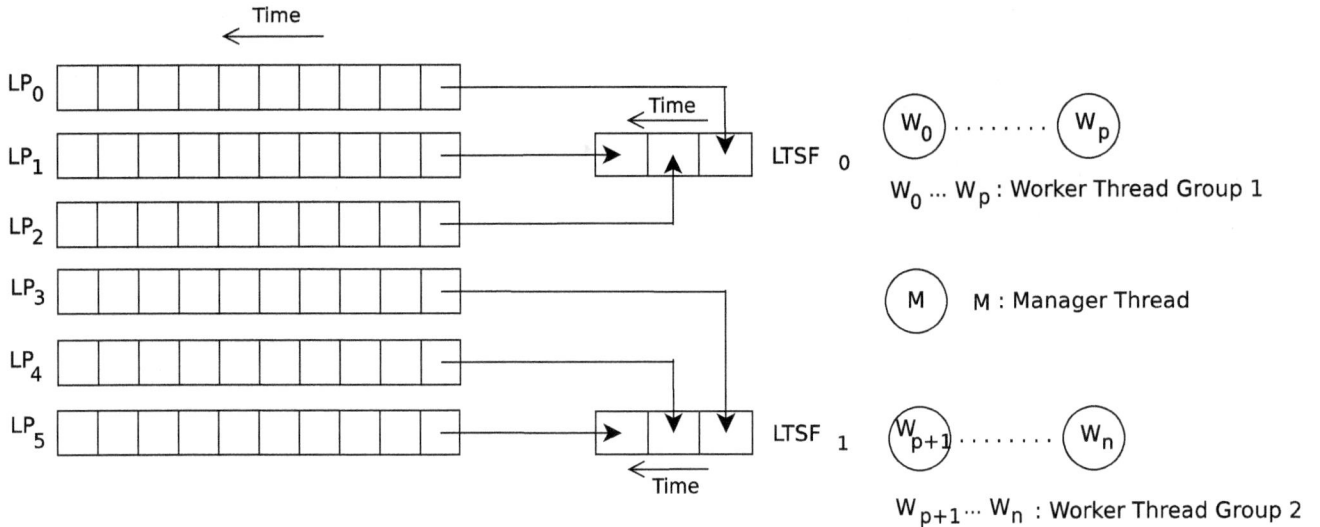

Figure 3: Threaded structure of warped with multiple LTSF queues.

load balancing (or more precisely to distribute the critical path of events for processing) [4].

Partitioning the LPs into groups, each serving as event pool to a specific LTSF queue, does improve the performance due to reduction in contention for individual LTSF queues. However, this re-organization can prove to be a "double-edged sword". The basic problem with this organization is the challenge of statically partitioning the LP groups. The unique aspect of the Time Warp scheduling is that events are aggressively processed and the system is rolled back to a consistent state when any inconsistency is detected. This makes it difficult to determine which processes are working effectively and which are not. One approach is to "kick-start" the simulation with arbitrary initial partitions of the LPs followed by intermittent monitoring and rectification of the imbalance through load balancing [4].

The underlying data structures for Implementing the LTSF queue were also explored [4]. In these studies, the `Ladder Queue` [29] delivered superior performance over both the `STL multiset` and `Splay tree` [28] implementations. The significant characteristic of the `Ladder Queue` (also its principal difference with `Calendar Queue` [3]) is the dynamic splitting of buckets (months) that store events. When the number of stored events exceeds some threshold, `Calendar queue` requires a dynamic resizing of the entire data structure. In contrast, the `Ladder queue` dynamically splits a bucket (when it exceeds some specified threshold) into a collection of buckets and therefore requires no resizing operations. The principal components of a `Ladder Queue` are shown in Figure 4. An overview of the operation of a `Ladder Queue` is outlined below.

Initially the ladder queue is empty. Incoming events are inserted into the `Top` component in order of their arrival (not sorted based on event timestamp). While receiving events into `Top`, the minimum and maximum timestamps of the events placed therein are recorded. On receiving the first dequeue request, the events in `Top` are transferred to a collection of buckets in the first rung of the ladder (`Rung[1]`). Each bucket in `Rung[1]` holds events for the timestamp range that equally divides the time range be-

tween the minimum and maximum timestamp of events that were originally stored in `Top`. Each event is placed, without sorting, into the bucket encompassing its timestamp value. There is an upper threshold on the number of events in each bucket. If the first non-empty bucket of the rung exceeds this threshold, a new lower `Rung` is defined and events from the overflowing bucket are transferred to the collection of buckets in the next lower rung (`Rung[2]`). This redistribution is illustrated in Figure 4.

To complete the dequeue operation, the events from the first non-empty bucket (containing the elements with timestamp ranges smaller than all of the remaining buckets) of the lowest rung are *sorted* and placed in `Bottom`. The first event (having the lowest timestamp) is then dequeued from `Bottom`. The events are pulled from `Bottom` for successive dequeue operations until it becomes empty. This condition triggers another pull of events from the first non-empty bucket of the lowest rung in the ladder. The dequeue activity continues in this way until there are no more events left in the `Rungs` and `Bottom`. New events from `Top` are then allowed to re-populate the `Rungs` and `Bottom` in the manner discussed above.

In the ladder queue, timestamp values govern the incoming event distribution once the initial ladder structure is populated. The ladder queue then partitions the event timeline into epochs. Events with timestamp value between t and $t + \Delta t$ are held by the `Bottom` and `Rung` structures while the `Top` acts as temporary storage for events with timestamp above $t + \Delta t$. When the dequeue operation empties the `Bottom` and `Rung` contents, another ladder queue epoch occurs. Events in `Top` are transferred to the `Rungs` and `Bottom`. The additional special cases are discussed in [29]. For use in threaded WARPED, the `Ladder Queue` algorithms were modified slightly (see to Section 5.2 of [4]).

4. A LOCK-FREE AND UNSORTED LTSF QUEUE

In our past work [4], a comparative analysis of the original `Ladder Queue`'s performance was presented. In this paper, we discuss two significant modifications to the Ladder Queue

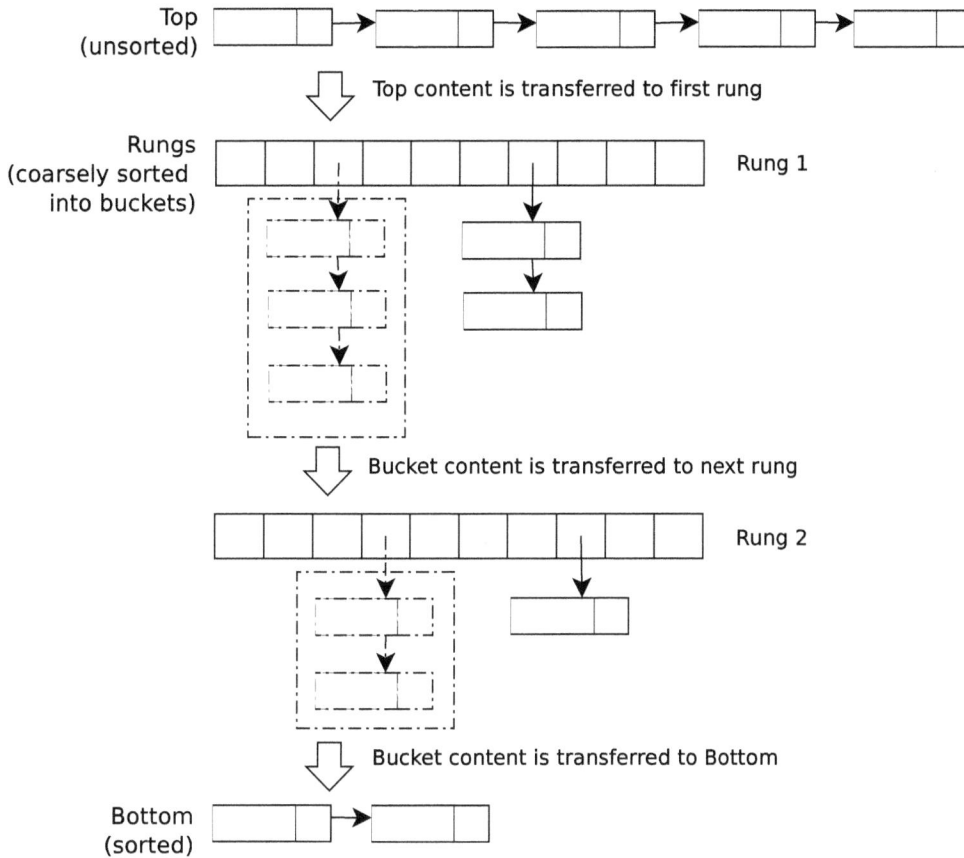

Figure 4: Illustration of the Ladder Queue Structure

structure to further optimize its use in the WARPED simulation kernel. In particular, we consider:

1. replacing the sorted list in the `Bottom` ladder queue structure with an unsorted list, and

2. replacing the mutex locks used in the management of the structures of the ladder queues with lock-free accesses.

The first modification is motivated by an observation that the limited size of the time window in `Bottom` is such that most events contained there are likely to be causally independent. Since the Time Warp mechanism is non-strict in its adherence to causal order and since it can also recover from causal violations, an accidental out-of-order processing of events is not a catastrophic happening. The simulator can merely rollback and reprocess events in their proper order. Thus, the partitioning of events into buckets (as normally required by the ladder queue) also partitions the events into coarse time windows that can be greedily scheduled by the event scheduler. Ideally, the generation of new events will fall outside the time window of the current bucket and the system will operate without significant rollback and without a full sort of input events. While this style of processing may not work efficiently for all simulation models, those models are also not likely to be suitable for Time Warp in general. Thus, this approach should not be a significant drawback for a Time Warp synchronized parallel simulator. The concept of event partitioning (into ladder queue buckets) and the

unsorted processing of events in a bucket, will be referred to as "relaxed order of event causality" (or relaxed causality) in the remainder of this paper. Events scheduled using the original `Ladder Queue` are said to have a "strict order of event causality" (or strict causality).

The opportunity to use a lock-free modification arises because once the need to sort the queues are removed, it becomes possible to use a simpler data structure that can be implemented with high performance lock-free access. The details of the implementation and use of a suitable lock-free data structure in WARPED is described in the next section. There is, however one additional small change that we made to our Ladder Queue implementation. Namely we removed the check to split the `Bottom` queue when additional insertions would normally trigger such a split. This is done to further optimize performance. The revised algorithm that illustrates this change to the implementation is shown in Figure 5.

4.1 The Lock-Free Ladder Queue

The WARPED LTSF queue supports the following operations for an event `e`:

`void enqueue(e)`: insert the event `e` into the LTSF queue,

`event* dequeue()`: return the event from the LTSF queue that has the smallest timestamp, and

`void remove(e)`: remove the event `e` from the LTSF queue.

```
void enqueue() {
    /* Try inserting into Top */
    if( timestamp of new event >= minimum timestamp of event in Top ) {
        insert into Top
        return;
    }

    /* Try to locate a suitable rung */
    while( timestamp of new event < min. timestamp of event in rung[i] &&
                                  i <= available number of rungs       ) {
        i++;
    }

    /* Check if rung found */
    if( i <= available number of rungs ) {
        determine the bucket number (j) suitable for the new event
        insert the event in the bucket j of the rung[i].
    } else {

#ifdef SORTED_BOTTOM
        /* Check if number of events in bottom exceeds threshold */
        if( number of events in bottom > threshold ) {
            create a lower rung (if possible)
            transfer Bottom to this lowest available rung
            insert the new event in an appropriate bucket of this rung
        } else {
            insert into Bottom
        }
#endif

#ifndef SORTED_BOTTOM
        insert into Bottom
#endif

    }
}
```

Figure 5: Ladder Queue enqueue() for unsorted Bottom written in C style. Some details have been omitted.

The remove(e) operation is needed so that when an LP receives an event e with a timestamp that is smaller than the timestamp for the event at the head of its unprocessed events, the system can replace the entry in the LTSF queue. Migrating to the Ladder queue with an unsorted bottom, these operations are maintained, however, the dequeue() event is redefined to simply return the event at the head of Bottom; the sorting of events in Bottom is no longer maintained.

Since the implementation of a functionally correct lock-free algorithms can be quite difficult, using a existing algorithm is most desirable. Examining the literature, we found two promising candidate solutions, namely: the queue algorithm developed by Michael and Scott [16], and the LFList algorithm developed by Zhang *et al* [33]. To support our needs, the queue algorithm would have to be extended to include the remove(e) operation and the LFList algorithm would have to be extended to include an operation to remove the head element. After studying the problem and developing several strategies to extend each algorithm, it became apparent that the simpler (yet still highly efficient) solution would be to adapt and extend the LFList algorithm for our needs. This adaption and extension is described below.

4.2 LFList

The LFList algorithm supports an unsorted doubly-linked list of elements using lock-free compare-and-swap (CAS) instructions. For uncontended cases, the insert operation requires 2 CAS instructions and a remove operation requires 1 CAS instruction. To facilitate lock-free access, the LFList algorithm defines four states for elements in the list, namely: INS (insert), REM (remove), DAT (valid data), and INV (invalid). INS and REM are intermediate states that correspond to nodes that are, respectively being "inserted" and "removed". The DAT state is assigned to a node that has been successfully linked into the list and the INV state is assigned to a node that has been marked for removal. The actual removal of INV states occurs during some later insert or remove operation.

Pseudo code representations of the INSERT (enqueue) and REMOVE (dequeue) operations are shown in Figures 6 and 8. Graphical representations of a representative list being operated on by the INSERT and REMOVE function are shown in Figures 7 and 9. In Figure 7 we can see how the inserted node is initially placed in the list in state INS. Upon completion of the insert operation, the state is changed to

```
Node:
  key  : stores the Event pointer
  next : points to successor
  state: current status of any node
         (insert, remove, data, invalidate)
List:
  head : starting node (initially NULL)

function INSERT( Event *k in, bool out ) :

  1. create a new node with 'k' as key and
     'insert' as status

  2. add the new node at the front of list
     and mark it as head using CAS.

  3. check whether key 'k' is already
     present in the list; this determines
     the return value. Remove existing
     'invalid' nodes during this search.

  4. using CAS try to change the state of
     the node from 'insert' to 'data' if
     key is unique in the list;
     else, try to 'invalidate' it.

  5. if CAS not successful, clean up the
     invalidated nodes in the list.

end INSERT
```

Figure 6: **Non-blocking unsorted list details and insert function. Some details have been omitted.**

DAT. Note also that the list has a (previously deleted) node marked as state INV. Due to the nature of this lock-free algorithm, the remove operation actually marks nodes with state INV (Figure 9) which is then removed on a later operation (by either INSERT or REMOVE) on the list. More complete details on the operations of LFList are available in [33].

In our implementation of LFList, we removed the backward link (**prev**) and the thread id (**tid**) that was part of the algorithm presented by Zhang *et al* [33]. We did not require a doubly linked list and the thread id was needed for a wait-free derivation of their list that we also did not require. Finally, we also had to define a **dequeue()** operation for the LFList. This is easily achieved by finding an event e from the LTSF queue and simply using the **remove(e)** operation of LFList. Pseudo code for the **dequeue()** operation is shown in Figure 10.

5. EXPERIMENTAL ANALYSIS

The purpose of this study is to analyze the effectiveness of causality relaxation in threaded WARPED. The use of an unsorted list as Bottom in Ladder Queue [29] allows us to study the overall effect of out-of-order event processing on the simulation. The effect of lock-free operations in the above mentioned Ladder structure is another aspect that has been studied in this paper.

All simulations were run multiple times on the same machine and the results averaged. The machine used for our

Step 1 and 2 :

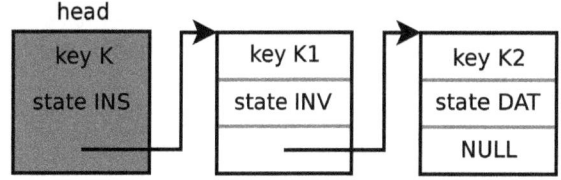

Step 3 and 4 :

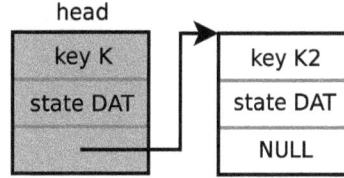

Figure 7: **Illustrative example of LFList Insert**

```
function REMOVE( Event *k in, bool out ) :

  1. create a new node with 'k' as key and
     'remove' as status

  2. add the new node at the front of list
     and mark it as head using CAS.

  3. search for the node with key 'k' in the
     rest of the list and 'invalidate' it if
     it is in 'data' mode; this determines
     the return value. Remove existing
     'invalid' nodes during this search.

  4. move the state of the created node to
     'invalidate'.

end REMOVE
```

Figure 8: **Non-blocking unsorted list remove function. Some details have been omitted.**

Step 1 and 2 :

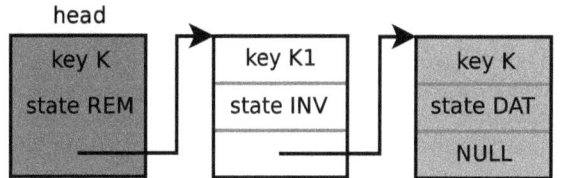

Step 3 and 4 :

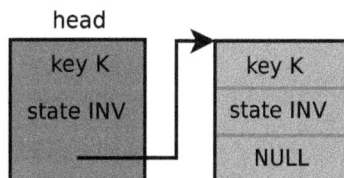

Figure 9: **Illustrative example of LFList Remove**

```
function DEQUEUE() :

  while the list has nodes with state DAT {
    find the first available node k with state DAT
    if (REMOVE(k) == true) {return k;}
  }
  return NULL;

end DEQUEUE
```

Figure 10: A Dequeue operation for LFList.

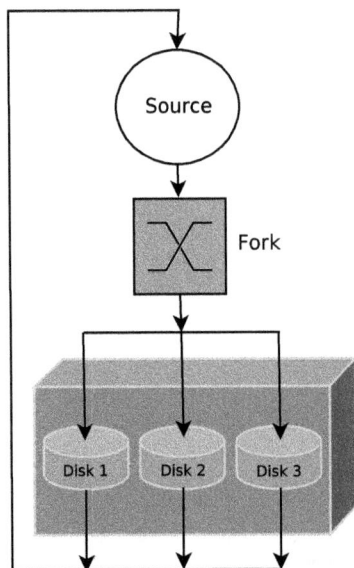

Figure 11: RAID-5 Simulation Model

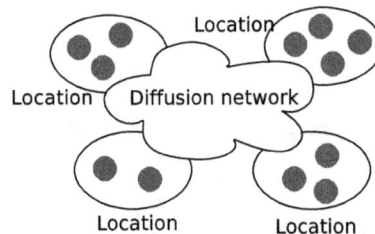

Figure 12: Epidemic Simulation Model

simulations has 48 cores — four 12-core AMD Opteron 6168 processors, each core running at a clock rate of 1.9GHz. It is configured with 64 GB of RAM.

The following two simulation models were used for the experimental analysis:

RAID-5: This model represents a Level 5 RAID (Redundant Array of Inexpensive Disks) setup. Figure 11 shows the schematics of this model. It consists of 136 logical processes (LPs) that simulate 32 disks, 8 forks and 96 sources. Requests for data from the array are generated by the sources. These requests pass through their respective forks. The forks forward each request to the necessary disks. After a predetermined amount of time, each disk responds to any data request received from the fork. This model simulates the access time to any sector of the disk. The simulation is allowed to continue till the global execution time reaches one hundred thousand seconds.

Epidemic Disease Propagation: This model simulates the spread of disease during an epidemic outbreak. It consists of 56 logical processes each of which simulates a different location. Each location has a group of people, each with different stages of the disease (infected, latent, incubating, infectious, asymptotic or recovered). The progress of disease in a person is controlled by a finite state machine proposed

by Barrett *et al* [2]. People can travel between locations at any point during the simulation. There is a pre-defined travel time between any two locations. A reaction-diffusion model based on [20] has been employed to simulate the intra-location and inter-location spread of the disease. The reaction function determines the intra-location spread of disease. The diffusion network models the inter-location movement pattern of persons. Two types of diffusion network have been used, namely:

1. **Fully Connected** : A person can travel to any location in a single hop.

2. **Watts-Strogatz** [32]: This models the small-world behavior of human networks where a person has the option of traveling to any location in a short number of hops.

Similar to RAID-5, the simulation is allowed to continue until the global execution time reaches one hundred thousand seconds. Figure 12 shows the schematics of this model.

Different configurations with varying numbers of worker threads were used for the simulations. The number of worker threads used were 4, 8, 16 and 32. These worker thread configurations were also permuted with varying number of LTSF queues (1, 2 and 4). The number of LTSF queues is always kept less than the number of worker threads and increased by a power of two. This allows even distribution of worker threads for each LTSF queue and helps to keep the simulations balanced. All results were obtained by taking the mean of ten simulation runs. The results from these LTSF queue experiments are described below.

Figures 15, 18 and 21 compare the performance of WARPED scheduler by replacing its sorted `Ladder Queue`-based LTSF with a lock-free `Ladder Queue` having an unsorted `Bottom`. When using a single LTSF queue, we observe significant speedup as the number of threads increase. This is most likely due to role thread contention plays in slowing access to the shared pending event set.

A sorted `Ladder Queue` uses traditional locks to make its operations thread-safe. Contention for locks increase as the number of threads is increased. Figures 13, 16 and 19 show the effect of contention on simulation time when the number of threads is increased. In case of Raid-5 model (Figure 13), we notice the simulation time increases as the number of threads is increased. There is some anomaly in case of 8 threads for Epidemic: Watts-Strogatz (Figure 19) and 16 threads for Epidemic: Fully Connected (Figure 16). This is most likely due to load imbalance on the WARPED scheduler. The simulation times for sorted 2 and 4 LTSF queues steadily increase except for some anomalies in case of (2

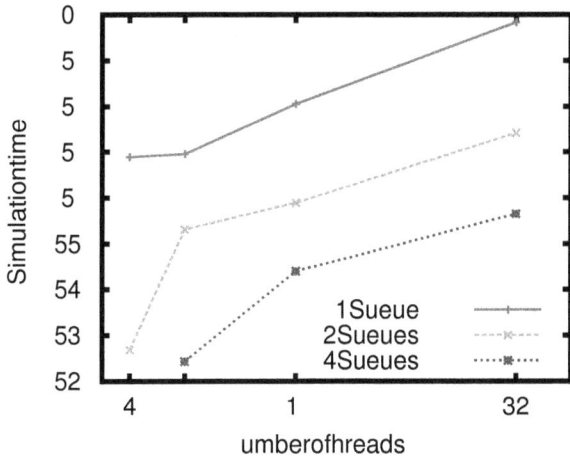

Figure 13: Raid-5 model: Sorted Ladder Queue simulation time

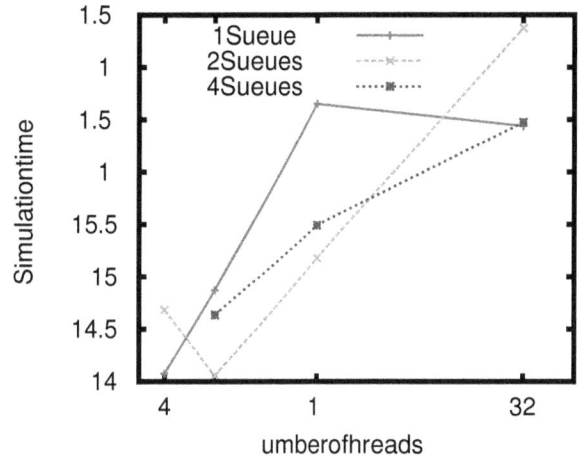

Figure 16: Epidemic model (Fully Connected): Sorted Ladder Queue simulation time

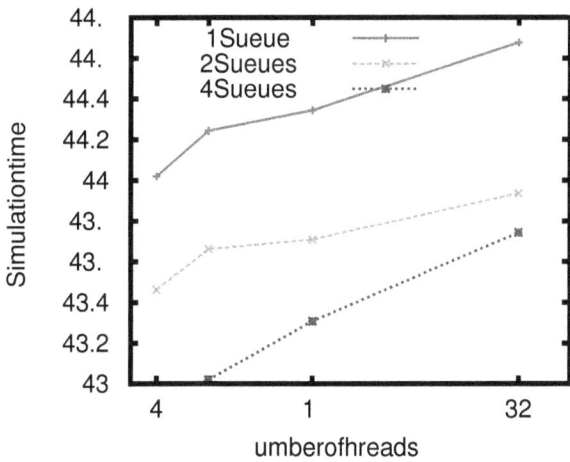

Figure 14: Raid-5 model: Lock-free unsorted Ladder Queue simulation time

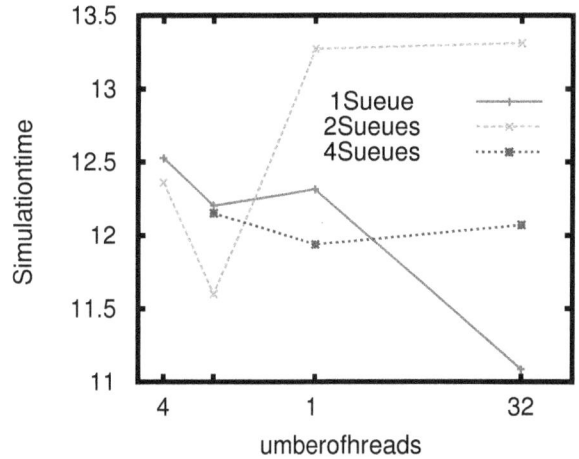

Figure 17: Epidemic model (Fully Connected): Lock-free unsorted Ladder Queue simulation time

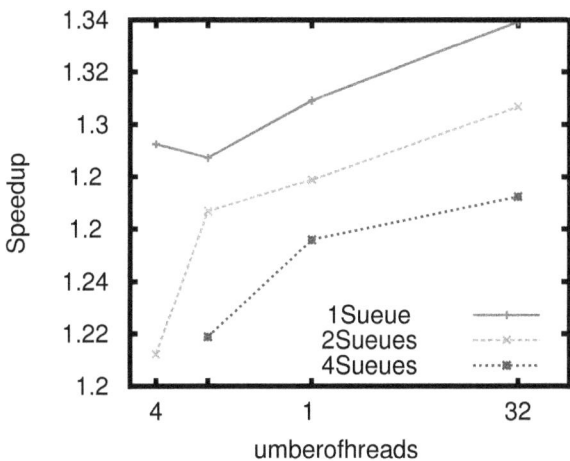

Figure 15: Raid-5 model: Lock-free unsorted Ladder Queue vs. Sorted Ladder Queue.

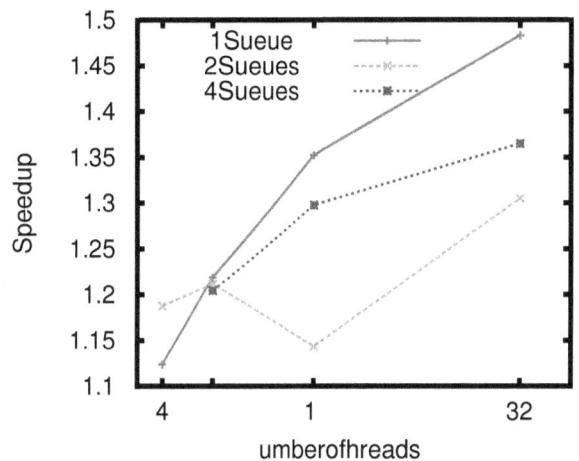

Figure 18: Epidemic model (Fully Connected): Lock-free unsorted Ladder Queue vs. Sorted Ladder Queue.

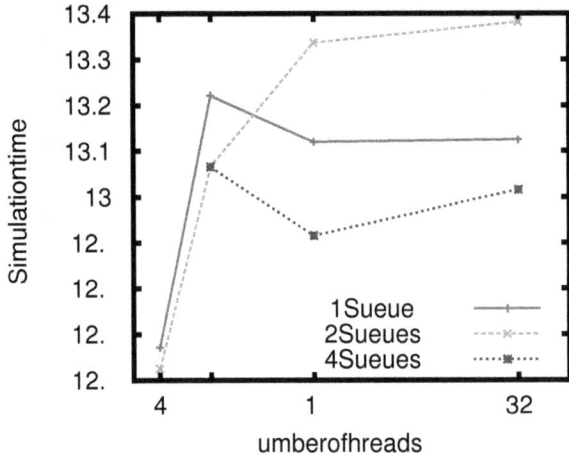

Figure 19: Epidemic model (Watts-Strogatz): Sorted Ladder Queue simulation time

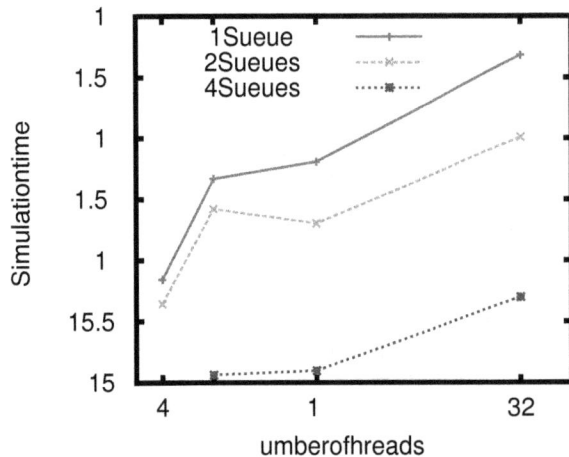

Figure 20: Epidemic model (Watts-Strogatz): Lock-free unsorted Ladder Queue simulation time

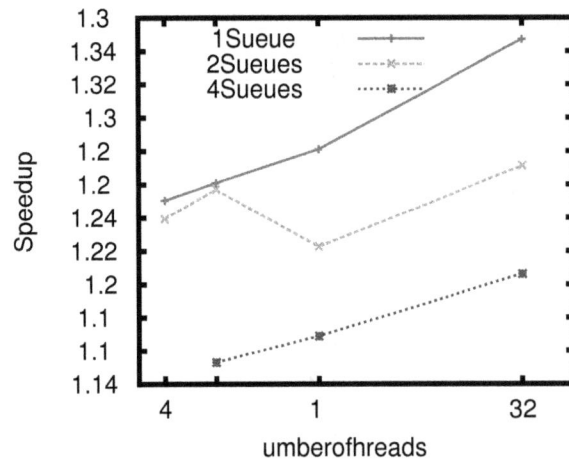

Figure 21: Epidemic model (Watts-Strogatz): Lock-free unsorted Ladder Queue vs. Sorted Ladder Queue.

LTSF, 4 threads) for Epidemic: Fully Connected (Figure 16) and (4 LTSF, 8 threads) for Epidemic: Watts-Strogatz (Figure 19).

On the other hand, a lock-free queue shows relatively steady performance even when the number of threads is increased. Figures 14, 17 and 20 show a relatively steady behavior as the number of threads is increased. However, Epidemic: Fully Connected (Figure 17 shows some anomaly in case of 2 LTSF queues. The Fully Connected model essentially relies on a random network and hence such anomalies are possible. If there are very few causality violations when events are scheduled using Unsorted Ladder Queue, the number of rollbacks will remain relatively low — effectively improving the simulation runtime.

In general, the speedup ratio should increase as the number of threads per LTSF queue increases and vice versa. In case of 4 threads, we notice significant speedup in spite of limited contention overhead for a sorted `Ladder Queue`. This is due to effectiveness of `relaxed causality` in the unsorted `Ladder Queue`. The Raid-5 model (Figure 15) shows up to 29% speedup while the Epidemic: Fully Connected (Figure 18) and Epidemic: Watts-Strogatz (Figure 21) shows up to 20% and 25% speedup respectively for 4 threads. The unsorted `Bottom` in lock-free `Ladder Queue` encourages relaxed causality (refer Section 4). Speedup figures for 8, 16 and 32 threads too are boosted by relaxed causality and show an upward trend except in case of (2 LTSF, 16 threads) for the two epidemic models.

6. DISCUSSION

Based on the results presented in Section 5, it can be said that the `Lock-Free Ladder Queue` with unsorted `Bottom` performs very well. The `Ladder Queue`'s ability to coarsely sort events into groups which are causally independent is a key feature that we have attempted to highlight in this paper. However, this property is dependent on the nature of event pool. If a model generates a considerable amount of causally dependent events within any given epoch, then the benefits of using unsorted `Bottom` would be considerably diminished. A `Sorted Ladder Queue` might yield better results under such circumstances. That said, our models did not show this behavior.

Pienta et al [21] analyzed the effect of scale-free model topology on conservative parallel simulation. They found that with increase in degree of any hub node, the hub node needs to process more events during each epoch leading to loss of parallel speedup. The scheduler design we have proposed in this paper should ameliorate the speedup problem for such hub nodes.

The other aspect of this paper is the `lock-free` nature of the WARPED scheduler. While we have migrated to atomic moves for the `Ladder Queue` with unsorted `Bottom`, we have retained the locks for sorted `Ladder Queue`. The `Bottom` structure in sorted `Ladder Queue` uses STL `multiset` to hold events in sorted order. Heller et al [8] proposed a lock-based optimistic list implementation with wait-free lookup options. Based on the results presented in [33], this lock-based implementation shows performance superior to the lock-free list implementation used for the `Ladder Queue` with unsorted `Bottom`. Whether or not this lock-based list implementation will boost performance of WARPED can only be answered through experimental analysis in future.

7. CONCLUSIONS

In this paper, we explore the concept of `relaxed causality` using an unsorted `Bottom` in a `Ladder Queue` that is used to manage the pending event sets for a Time Warp parallel simulation engine. We propose the replacement of unsorted lists in `Top`, `Rungs` and `Bottom` with unsorted lock-free queues. Experimental analysis shows a speedup of 1.1 to 1.49 for two different simulation models in various configurations of threads and schedule queues. The results further show that the speedup results are in the higher region of these speedups with larger thread counts. These results help to support our hypothesis that multiple LTSF queues, each made of lock-free coarsely partitioned events in a `ladder queue`, is an efficient candidate for scheduling events in a Time Warp simulator.

The organization and management of the pending event set is critical to the performance of a multi-threaded Time Warp synchronized parallel simulation engine. The two-level pending event set implemented with an unsorted lock-free Ladder Queue provides the best performance among the variety of configurations that we have examined. In a separate and as yet unreported study, we have initiated studies with hardware-based transactional memory to manage the updates to the pending event set. These studies are showing a slight improvement in performance (on the order of 10%) over the conventional mutex locked ladder queue implementation of the LTSF queues. The reason these speedup numbers are not higher is due to the collisions that still occur among the threads to this shared structure. Interestingly enough, the studies with transactional memory have also caused us to identify an approach that should further improve performance for several of our existing solutions. Specifically we now believe that it is best to decouple the worker threads from the LTSF queues and then to rotate each access by a worker thread to the next LTSF queue (in a circular manner).[1] This will spread out the concurrent access into different data segments (each of the different LTSF queues), reducing collisions to transactional data accesses and/or mutex locks/shared data. Almost even more importantly, this will also have the side benefit of distributing the critical path of LPs among the LTSF queues. Thus, load balancing will occur naturally as a result of the event management process rather than as a separate disruptive process (such as the technique outlined in [4]).

8. ACKNOWLEDGMENTS

Support for this work was provided in part by the National Science Foundation under grant CNS–0915337.

9. REFERENCES

[1] H. Avril and C. Tropper. Clustered time warp and logic simulation. In *Proceedings of the Ninth Workshop on Parallel and Distributed Simulation (PADS'95)*, pages 112–119, June 1995.

[2] C. L. Barrett, K. R. Bisset, S. G. Eubank, X. Feng, and M. V. Marathe. Episimdemics: An efficient algorithm for simulating the spread of infectious disease over large realistic social networks. In *Proceedings of the 2008 ACM/IEEE Conference on Supercomputing*, pages 37:1–37:12, 2008.

[3] R. Brown. Calendar queues: A fast O(1) priority queue implementation for the simulation event set problem. *Communications of the ACM*, 31(10):1220–1227, Oct. 1988.

[4] T. Dickman, S. Gupta, and P. A. Wilsey. Event pool structures for pdes on many-core beowulf clusters. In *Proceedings of the 2013 ACM SIGSIM conference on Principles of advanced discrete simulation*, pages 103–114, May 2013.

[5] R. Fujimoto. Parallel discrete event simulation. *Communications of the ACM*, 33(10):30–53, Oct. 1990.

[6] A. Ghuloum. Face the inevitable, embrace parallelism. *Communications of the ACM*, 52(9):36–38, Sept. 2009.

[7] T. L. Harris. A pragmatic implementation of non-blocking linked-lists. In *Proceedings of the 15th International Conference on Distributed Computing*, pages 300–314. Springer-Verlag, 2001.

[8] S. Heller, M. Herlihy, V. Luchangco, M. Moir, W. N. Scherer, and N. Shavit. A lazy concurrent list-based set algorithm. In *Proceedings of the 9th International Conference on Principles of Distributed Systems*, OPODIS'05, pages 3–16, 2006.

[9] D. Jefferson. Virtual time. *ACM Transactions on Programming Languages and Systems*, 7(3):405–425, July 1985.

[10] A. Kogan and E. Petrank. Wait-free queues with multiple enqueuers and dequeuers. In *Proceedings of the 16th ACM Symposium on Principles and Practice of Parallel Programming*, PPoPP '11, pages 223–234, 2011.

[11] J. Liu, D. M. Nicol, and K. Tan. Lock-free scheduling of logical processes in parallel simulation. In *Proceedings of the Fifteenth Workshop on Parallel and Distributed Simulation*, PADS '01, pages 22–31. IEEE Computer Society, 2001.

[12] D. E. Martin, T. J. McBrayer, and P. A. Wilsey. WARPED: A Time Warp simulation kernel for analysis and application development. In H. El-Rewini and B. D. Shriver, editors, *29th Hawaii International Conference on System Sciences (HICSS-29)*, volume Volume I, pages 383–386, Jan. 1996.

[13] M. M. Michael. High performance dynamic lock-free hash tables and list-based sets. In *Proceedings of the Fourteenth Annual ACM Symposium on Parallel Algorithms and Architectures*, SPAA '02, pages 73–82, 2002.

[14] M. M. Michael. Hazard pointers: Safe memory reclamation for lock-free objects. *IEEE Trans. Parallel Distrib. Syst.*, 15(6):491–504, June 2004.

[15] M. M. Michael and M. L. Scott. Correction of a memory management method for lock-free data structures. Technical report, University of Rochester, Rochester, NY, USA, 1995.

[16] M. M. Michael and M. L. Scott. Nonblocking algorithms and preemption-safe locking on multiprogrammed shared memory multiprocessors. *Journal of Parallel and Distributed Computing*, 51(1):1–26, May 1998.

---

[1]This will introduce yet another location of contention for the worker threads. However it should be nothing more than a fetch-and-add type operation by each worker thread to retrieve the next index into the pool of LTSF queues.

[17] R. Miller. Optimistic parallel discrete event simulation on a beowulf cluster of multi-core machines. Master's thesis, University of Cincinnati, 2010.

[18] K. Muthalagu. Threaded warped: An optimistic parallel discrete event simulator for clusters fo multi-core machines. Master's thesis, School of Electronic and Computing Systems, University of Cincinnati, Cincinnati, OH, Nov. 2012.

[19] A. Palaniswamy and P. A. Wilsey. Parameterized Time Warp: An integrated adaptive solution to optimistic pdes. *Journal of Parallel and Distributed Computing*, 37(2):134–145, Sept. 1996.

[20] K. S. Perumalla and S. K. Seal. Discrete event modeling and massively parallel execution of epidemic outbreak phenomena. *Simulation*, 88(7):768–783, July 2012.

[21] R. S. Pienta and R. M. Fujimoto. On the parallel simulation of scale-free networks. In *Proceedings of the 2013 ACM SIGSIM Conference on Principles of Advanced Discrete Simulation*, SIGSIM-PADS '13, pages 179–188, 2013.

[22] S. K. Prasad, S. I. Sawant, and B. Naqib. Using parallel data structures in optimistic discrete event simulation of varying granularity on shared-memory computers. In *IEEE First International Conference on Algorithms and Architectures for Parallel Processing*, pages 365–374, Apr. 1995.

[23] R. Radhakrishnan, D. E. Martin, M. Chetlur, D. M. Rao, and P. A. Wilsey. An Object-Oriented Time Warp Simulation Kernel. In D. Caromel, R. R. Oldehoeft, and M. Tholburn, editors, *Proceedings of the International Symposium on Computing in Object-Oriented Parallel Environments (ISCOPE'98)*, volume LNCS 1505, pages 13–23. Springer-Verlag, Dec. 1998.

[24] R. Radhakrishnan, L. Moore, and P. A. Wilsey. External adjustment of runtime parameters in Time Warp synchronized parallel simulators. In *11th International Parallel Processing Symposium, (IPPS'97)*. IEEE Computer Society Press, Apr. 1997.

[25] R. Rajan and P. A. Wilsey. Dynamically switching between lazy and aggressive cancellation in a Time Warp parallel simulator. In *Proc. of the 28th Annual Simulation Symposium*, pages 22–30. IEEE Computer Society Press, Apr. 1995.

[26] R. Rönngren, R. Ayani, R. M. Fujimoto, and S. R. Das. Efficient implementation of event sets in time warp. In *Proceedings of the 1993 workshop on Parallel and distributed simulation*, pages 101–108, May 1993.

[27] T. Santoro and F. Quaglia. A low-overhead constant-time ltf scheduler for optimistic simulation systems. In *Proceedings of the The IEEE symposium on Computers and Communications*, pages 948–953, June 2010.

[28] D. Sleator and R. Tarjan. Self adjusting binary search trees. *Journal of the ACM*, 32(3):652–686, July 1985.

[29] W. T. Tang, R. S. M. Goh, and I. L.-J. Thng. Ladder queue: An o(1) priority queue structure for large-scale discrete event simulation. *ACM Transactions on Modeling and Computer Simulation*, 15(3):175–204, July 2005.

[30] S. Timnat, A. Braginsky, A. Kogan, and E. Petrank. Wait-free linked-lists. In *Proceedings of the 17th ACM SIGPLAN Symposium on Principles and Practice of Parallel Programming*, PPoPP '12, pages 309–310, 2012.

[31] J. D. Valois. Lock-free linked lists using compare-and-swap. In *Proceedings of the Fourteenth Annual ACM Symposium on Principles of Distributed Computing*, PODC '95, pages 214–222, 1995.

[32] D. J. Watts and S. H. Strogatz. Collective dynamics of 'small-world' networks. *Nature*, 393:440–442, June 1998.

[33] K. Zhang, Y. Zhao, Y. Yang, Y. Liu, and M. Spear. Practical non-blocking unordered lists. In *Distributed Computing*, volume 8205 of *Lecture Notes in Computer Science*, pages 239–253. Springer Berlin Heidelberg, 2013.

A Case Study in Using Massively Parallel Simulation for Extreme-Scale Torus Network Codesign

Misbah Mubarak
Christopher D. Carothers
Department of Computer Science
Rensselaer Polytechnic Institute
Troy, NY 12180
{mubarm,chrisc}@cs.rpi.edu

Robert B. Ross
Philip Carns
Mathematics and Computer Science Division
Argonne National Laboratory
Chicago, IL 60439
{rross,carns}@mcs.anl.gov

ABSTRACT

A high-bandwidth, low-latency interconnect will be a critical component of future exascale systems. The torus network topology, which uses multidimensional network links to improve path diversity and exploit locality between nodes, is a potential candidate for exascale interconnects.

The communication behavior of large-scale scientific applications running on future exascale networks is particularly important and analytical/algorithmic models alone cannot deduce it. Therefore, before building systems, it is important to explore the design space and performance of candidate exascale interconnects by using simulation. We improve upon previous work in this area and present a methodology for modeling and simulating a high-fidelity, *validated*, and scalable torus network topology at a packet-chunk level detail using the Rensselaer Optimistic Simulation System (ROSS). We execute various configurations of a 1.3 million node torus network model in order to examine the effect of torus dimensionality on network performance with relevant HPC traffic patterns. To the best of our knowledge, these are the largest torus network simulations that are carried out at such a detailed fidelity. In terms of simulation performance, a 1.3 million node, 9-D torus network model is shown to process a simulated exascale-class workload of nearest-neighbor traffic with 100 million message injections per second per node using 65,536 Blue Gene/Q cores in a simulation run-time of only 25 seconds. We also demonstrate that massive-scale simulations are a critical tool in exascale system design since small-scale torus simulations are not always indicative of the network behavior at an exascale size. The take-away message from this case study is that massively parallel simulation is a key enabler for effective extreme-scale network codesign.

General Terms

Design, Experimentation, Performance, Measurement.

Keywords

High-performance computing, Parallel discrete-event simulation, Massively parallel architectures, Torus networks, Exascale systems.

Categories and Subject Descriptors

I.6.4 [**Computing methodologies**]: Modeling and simulation

1. INTRODUCTION

A key factor that largely determines the effectiveness of massively parallel systems is its interconnect network. With future exascale systems having up to one million compute nodes [1, 2], considerable research is in progress to determine a suitable network topology that maximizes the bandwidth of a network under different traffic patterns. One viable option is to continue using k-ary, n-dimensional torus networks that have been extensively used in modern supercomputers such as the IBM Blue Gene (BG) series [3, 4], Cray XT, and Cray XE series networks [5]. Another option is to use low-latency, low-diameter interconnect topologies (such as the dragonfly used by Cray XC30 system [6, 7], flattened butterfly [8], or PERCS [9]) that will enable fast communication at large node counts while keeping power usage and physical construction parameters in check.

While a number of network topologies have been proposed for exascale systems, the search for a topology that yields high performance for most scientific applications is still under way. The torus networks are attractive for local communication patterns because they exploit physical locality between compute nodes. Torus networks also have good path diversity, since they offer multiple minimal paths for transporting packets between the source and destination [10]. One disadvantage of torus networks is that they have a high hop count when communication involves far ends of the network.

Simulation and modeling are important tools to answer "what if" questions and guide network topology design decisions. While analytical modeling helps to make initial design decisions about the networks, an accurate and high-fidelity simulation is required to predict the network performance [10]. Such a simulation will not only help explore the design space of the interconnect topologies but also help find a high-performance network configuration by enabling parameter tuning of these topologies. Additionally, modeling exascale systems requires a simulation that can efficiently model an interconnect having millions of compute nodes in a reasonable amount of time. The Rensselaer Optimistic Simulation System (ROSS) is a high-performance, low-memory massively parallel discrete-event simulator [11] that can process billions of events in a second.

The potential system architecture for exascale systems is predicted to have $O(100,000)$ or $O(1M)$ compute nodes and a node interconnect bandwidth in the range of 200-400 GB/sec [12, 2]. In this paper, we use ROSS to develop a high-fidelity torus model to simulate 1.3 million compute nodes/endpoints torus network. Our torus model routes packets similar to the Blue Gene architecture, where variable-sized packets are routed in 'packet-chunks' of $n * 32$ bytes each, where $n = 1$ to 16.

The main contributions of this paper are as follows: (1) we developed the methodology for simulating exascale size torus network topology at a packet-chunk level granularity using the optimistic event scheduling and reverse computation capabilities of ROSS [13], in a time frame allowing for parameter exploration of these networks on HPC systems, (2) by using simulation to investigate the network performance at a detailed fidelity, we identify the pros and cons of certain torus configurations with relevant HPC traffic patterns including local and far-end network communication, prior to building them, (3) we demonstrate the need for executing models at scale and show how small node configurations mis-predict network performance trends compared with large-scale node configurations, (4) we have built on our previous work on torus modeling to make our torus network simulation capable of modeling the BG/P and BG/Q class of networks and (5) by using large-scale torus network simulations, we can also instrument our ROSS torus network model to gain an insight into exactly why are we seeing these performance results. Taken together, these contributions underscore the need for a massively parallel simulation capability to enable effective extreme-scale network codesign.

Our work extends previous work in extreme-scale torus network models by Liu et. al [14]. Specifically, we emphasize the following key improvements:

- [14] used packet-based deterministic routing for a uniform random traffic pattern. According to Dally and Towles [10], reporting simulation results using uniform random traffic only is a common simulation measurement pitfall since uniform random is a benign traffic pattern which naturally balances load across the network. To accurately measure network performance, one has to consider both benign and adversarial traffic patterns.

   Our model operates at the packet-chunk level detail with performance dynamics shown for both benign (nearest neighbor) and adversarial (diagonal pairing) traffic patterns. The diagonal paring traffic stresses the torus network topology as reported in [15].

- [14] uses infinite buffering for packets without any flow-control methodology. Moreover, the packets are buffered and transported as full-sized packets whereas the BG architecture divides the packets further into chunks of 32 bytes for transportation and buffering. Our new model uses finite buffering with token-based flow control at packet-chunk level which closely approximates the BG architecture's implementation.

- [14] focuses on the implementation of the torus network model and the simulation performance of the ROSS torus model. In this paper, our focus is to use ROSS torus network simulation as a tool to predict and closely approximate the behavior of different synthetic communication patterns on real torus networks.

- [14] performed a preliminary validation of a 1x32x32, 3-D torus on the BG/L using MPI ping-pong test that involved two MPI processes only. In our work here, we validate our updated torus model against the 3-D torus of the BG/P and 5-D torus of BG/Q machines by testing against both near and far-end network communication patterns. In particular, we validate MPI messaging for 1 hop to 11 hops on BG/Q and up to 12 hops on BG/P with variable message lengths (4 bytes - 131K bytes). The *mpptest* performance benchmark is used to record the latency of MPI point-to-point messages on the BG/P and BG/Q networks and we force the BG eager message protocol for all MPI communication. All MPI processes participate in the point-to-point messaging.

The road-map for this research begins with an overview of torus networks, ROSS optimistic event scheduling, and the experimental platform for our massively parallel simulations (Section 2). We then discuss the design, validation, and a 1.3 million node scalability study of the torus network simulation (Section 3). We also identify the configurations in which the torus network model yields high or limited performance under different traffic patterns. We then present the simulation performance results of our massively parallel torus network model (Section 4). We then present a literature review on torus network simulations (Section 5), followed by conclusions and future work (Section 6).

2. BACKGROUND

In this section, we first introduce the layout and properties of the torus network topology and then explain the optimistic event scheduling that enables ROSS to schedule billions of events per second on HPC systems. We also discuss the massively parallel experimental platform on which we have executed our million node torus simulation.

2.1 Torus Network

A torus is a k-ary n-cube network with $N = k^n$ nodes arranged in an N-dimensional grid with k nodes in each dimension [10]. Each node of a torus network is connected to $2 * n$ other nodes typically via short electrical cables. Each torus node can be identified with a unique *n-digit*, *radix k* address. Torus networks have been extensively used for the Blue Gene [3, 4], Cray XT and Cray XE [5, 16] series of supercomputers. Since each torus node is connected to its neighbor via a dedicated link, torus networks can yield high throughput for nearest-neighbor communication patterns. Therefore, they are well suited for applications such as anisotropic mesh adaptation in CFD solvers [17]. Torus networks also offer good path diversity because several distinct paths exist between any given source and destination node. This property can be leveraged to balance load across network channels. Unlike other hierarchical networks like the butterfly and dragonfly [7, 8], torus networks have a higher average number of hop counts traversed.

Network designers determine the properties of a torus network primarily by torus dimensionality and link bandwidth. Physical channel bandwidth is an important factor in the design of torus networks and is a costly resource of an interconnection network [18]. Another key factor is its dimensionality: at the low extreme of dimension, latency is dominated by the high hop count; at the high extreme of dimension, serialization latency dominates due to narrow channel width, according to Dally and Towles [10]. Therefore, while designing a torus network, one has to balance the number of dimensions and channel bandwidth to get high performance.

2.2 Optimistic Event Scheduling with ROSS

Massively parallel ROSS models are made up of thousands to millions of logical processes (LPs), where each LP models a distinct state of the system. The LPs interact with each other via events in the form of time-stamped messages. MPI tasks in ROSS are abstracted as a processor element (PE), where a PE can have multiple LPs. Events destined for an LP on another PE are called remote messages. Using ROSS, we have developed a detailed simulation that models the behavior of the torus network topology for massively parallel architectures with millions of nodes.

ROSS uses a Time Warp synchronization protocol [19] to process events. If the synchronization mechanism detects an out-of-order event, the events are rolled back and re-executed in the correct order. Optimistic scheduling in ROSS has been shown to dramatically improve the parallel performance and reduce the amount of state-saving overhead [11, 20]. The reverse computation improves the scalability of our parallel simulations especially in instances where the model exhibits a low level of look-ahead [21].

In terms of performance, ROSS can process billions of events per second as indicated in a number of recent performance studies [21, 22, 23]. In [22], ROSS has been shown to scale on 7.86 million MPI tasks with an event rate of over 500 million events per second for the PHOLD benchmark model.

2.3 Experimental Platform

The largest network simulations presented in this work were executed on 65,536 MPI tasks (1 rack) of the Mira Blue Gene/Q system operated by the Argonne Leadership Computing Facility. Mira consists of 48 racks with each rack containing 1024 nodes. Each node has 16, 1.6 GHz compute cores. Each core in turn supports four hardware threads, bringing the maximum number of compute threads per node to 64. The Blue Gene/Q also has a five-dimensional torus network that provides both point-to-point and collective communication facilities [24]. By utilizing the threading capability of Blue Gene/Q, we scheduled 64 MPI tasks per node, which provides the best performance for ROSS given its memory pointer-intensive structure. A parallel performance evaluation of our ROSS torus network simulation on a 1.3 million node test-case is presented in Section 4.

3. TORUS NETWORK SIMULATION

To design the ROSS torus model, we closely followed the design features and configuration parameters of the existing torus network of the BG series supercomputers so that (1) we can validate our simulation results of torus network model against the existing BG architecture and (2) our model uses realistic design parameters of a torus network. The

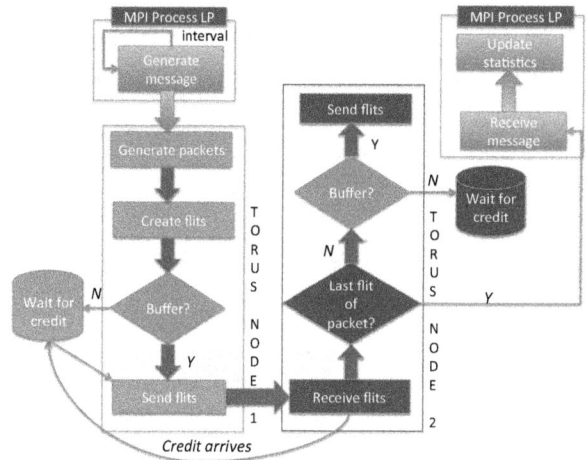

Figure 1: Basic discrete-event flow of the ROSS torus model.

BG/Q torus network uses a 5-D torus network with packets having a maximum size of 512 bytes, where each packet is broken into chunks of 32 bytes each for transportation over the network [4]. The torus network uses multiple virtual channels (VCs) to avoid head-of-line blocking for packets [3]. A bubble-escape virtual channel is used for deterministic routing and to avoid deadlocks [25]. Each VC has buffers for storing packets to be processed. A token-flow control mechanism is used to prevent a VC buffer from over flowing.

To align the ROSS torus network model with the BG configuration, we model two LP types in the ROSS torus model: The MPI process LP and the torus node LP. The MPI process LP generates MPI messages that are forwarded to the torus node LP in the form of network packets. Each torus node LP is connected to its neighbors via channels having a fixed buffer capacity. The ROSS events in the torus model are of three types:

1. MPI messages: these messages are sent to/from MPI process LP.

2. Torus network packets: MPI messages are passed on to the torus node LPs by dividing them into network packets where the torus node LPs send and receive network packets. A full-sized network packet can be up to 512 bytes in our torus model.

3. Network packet chunks: similar to the BG network, when communicating between torus node LPs, the network packets are further divided into packet chunks of 32 bytes each.

Figure 1 shows the event flow of the ROSS torus network model. Each torus node LP has an incoming and outgoing virtual channel with VC buffers. The VC buffers are also allocated in the form of 32-bytes packet-chunks, thereby incorporating virtual channel flow control. The MPI process LP generates MPI messages that are divided into packets and sent to the torus node LP. The torus node LP divides the packets into chunks and injects them into the network if the VC buffer space is available. Before sending the packet-chunks over a VC, the torus node checks for the available

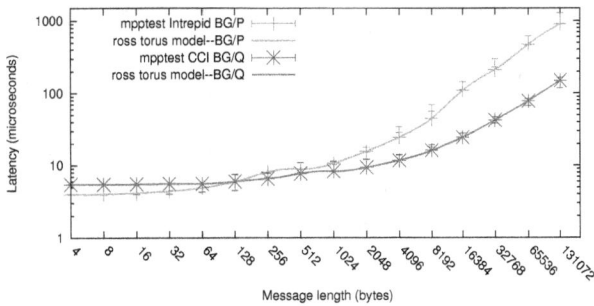

Figure 2: Latency comparison of mpptest on Intrepid BG/P and CCI BG/Q with ROSS 3-D and 5-D tori models. Each packet traverses 8 hops between the source and destination (512 nodes on Intrepid and 1,024 nodes on CCI BG/Q with 1 MPI rank per node).

buffer space. If the buffer space is not available for the next torus node, the packet-chunk keeps waiting for the next buffer slot in its current buffer location. Whenever a packet-chunk arrives at a torus node LP, it sends a credit event back to the sender torus node LP indicating that the buffer can be reused for the next packet-chunk in the queue. We model a simple input-queued router in which whenever a packet-chunk arrives at the router, a hop delay based on the router speed and port bandwidth, is added to simulate the processing time of the packet-chunk. The router can forward multiple packet-chunks at a time as long as the path from the input to output VC is available. If the path from the input VC to output VC is not available, the packet-chunk is queued and proceeds only when the earlier packet-chunks have processed.

The ROSS torus network model uses dimension order routing to route packets. With such routing, the radix-k digits of the destination are used to direct network packets, with one dimension at a time [26]. Although the BG architecture supports both dynamic and dimension-order routing, the dynamic routing for BG is strictly vendor specific, and details of this routing algorithm are not available [3, 4]. Therefore, in this paper, the results are presented with dimension order routing only.

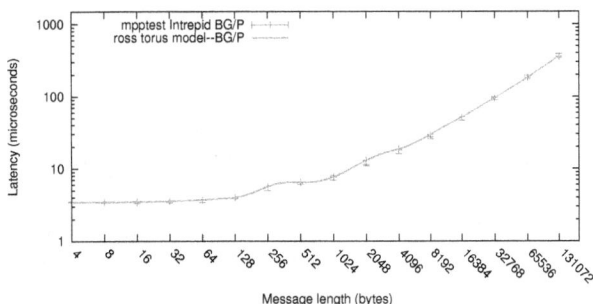

Figure 3: Latency comparison of mpptest on Intrepid BG/P with ROSS 3-D torus model using nearest-neighbor communication (512 nodes of intrepid BG/P with 1 MPI rank per node).

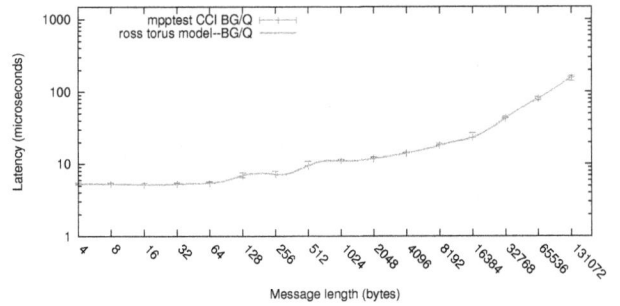

Figure 4: Latency comparison of mpptest on CCI BG/Q with ROSS 5-D torus model using farthest node communication (hop count set to 11 hops, 1,024 nodes of CCI BG/Q with 1 MPI process per node).

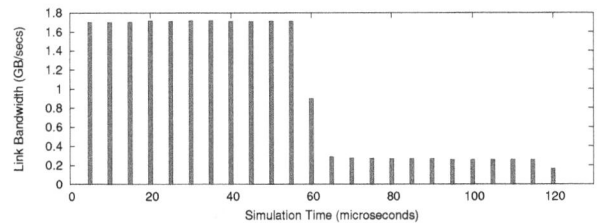

Figure 5: Bandwidth (GB/sec) of a 9-D 1.3 million node torus link over 500 nanoseconds interval with nearest-neighbor traffic, packet injection is stopped after 2 microseconds with an injection rate of $2*10^8$ injections/sec (1.8 GB/s of the 2.0 GB/s bandwidth is the maximum available for user data).

3.1 Validation of Torus Model with Blue Gene Architectures

To verify the accuracy of our torus network model, we validated the latency results of our ROSS torus model against the mpptest benchmark for measuring MPI performance [27]. Mpptest measures the performance of MPI message passing routines with many participating MPI processes, it can isolate sudden changes in system performance by choosing various message sizes. In the mpptest bisection test, each MPI process communicates with exactly one other process such that half of the processes in the communicator are communicating with the other half. One can configure the distance between the MPI processes such that two processes communicating with each other can exchange MPI messages that traverse a fixed number of hops. This strategy also helps measure the bisection bandwidth of a network where packets traversing through a fixed number of hops cross the mid-point of a network.

We measured the MPI performance on Argonne's BG/P system 'Intrepid' and RPI CCI's BG/Q 'Amos' system using mpptest. We ran the mpptest performance benchmark on 512 compute nodes on Argonne Intrepid BG/P and 1,024 compute nodes on CCI BG/Q using bisection traffic pattern with 1 MPI rank per compute node. We used only 1 MPI rank per compute node as we were interested in observing the network behavior, not how the nodes internally manage the contention for the network. The MPI eager protocol, which uses deterministic routing, was used to measure MPI performance on the BG systems since the BG allows one to force the eager or rendezvous protocol on messages [24]. The torus configuration on the BG/P is 8 x 8 x 8 (1 mid-plane) and on the BG/Q is 8 x 4 x 4 x 4 x 2 (1 rack). We ran our torus network simulator in the following four configurations simulating an MPI job with one MPI rank per node:

1. BG/P configuration with 8 x 8 x 8 (1 mid-plane) nodes with messages traversing 8 hops between the source and destination.

2. BG/Q configuration with messages traversing exactly 8 hops between source and destination

3. BG/P mid-plane nearest-neighbor configuration with messages traversing exactly 1 hop between source and destination nodes.

4. BG/Q farthest-node communication with messages traversing 11 hops.

The channel bandwidth of the ROSS torus model was configured according to the BG systems: 2 GB/sec (1.8 GB/s available to user) per torus link on BG/Q and 425 MB/sec (374 MB/sec available to user) per torus link on BG/P.

Figure 2 presents a latency comparison of the `mpptest` benchmark on a BG/P mid-plane and a BG/Q rack vs. the ROSS 3-D and 5-D tori models with 512 and 1,024 nodes respectively. The distance between the communicating MPI processes is 8 hops for both `mpptest` and the ROSS torus models (configurations 1 and 2). One can see close latency agreement between the MPI performance prediction of the ROSS torus model and the `mpptest` benchmark for message size ranging from 4 bytes to 130 Kilobytes.

Figure 3 provides a latency comparison of the ROSS 3-D torus model and `mpptest` performance benchmark on the Argonne Intrepid BG/P for 512 compute nodes with nearest-neighbor traffic (configuration 3). The distance between the communicating MPI processes is 1 hop for both `mpptest` and ROSS torus models.

Figure 4 presents the latency comparison of the ROSS 5-D torus model with the `mpptest` performance benchmark on BG/Q using farthest-node communications (configuration 4). The distance between communicating MPI processes is 11 intermediate hops on BG/Q which is the maximum number of hops that a MPI message can traverse on a 1,024 nodes torus configuration.

From these latency comparison statistics, one can see close latency agreement between the MPI performance prediction of the ROSS torus model and the `mpptest` performance benchmark for message sizes ranging between 4 bytes and 130 Kilobytes.

3.2 A Million-Node Torus Network Model

After validating our ROSS torus model for the BG/P and BG/Q architectures, we set out to scale our torus model to anticipated exascale configurations. Exascale systems are expected to have up to 1 million compute nodes [1]. In this section, we evaluate the network performance trends for a 1.3 million node torus network model for a 5-D (32 x 32 x 32 x 20 x 2 configuration), 7-D (16 x 16 x 16 x 10 x 4 x 4 x 2 configuration), and 9-D (10 x 8 x 8 x 8 x 4 x 4 x 4 x 2 x 2 configuration) tori.

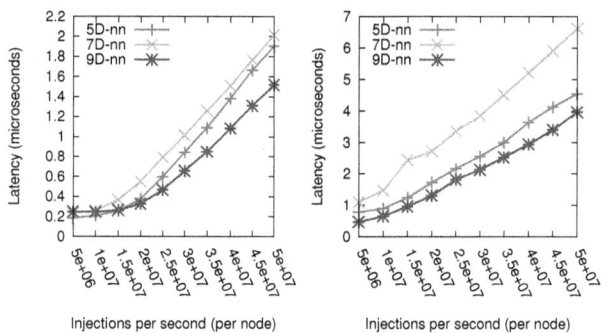

Figure 6: Average (left) and maximum (right) latency of a 1,024 node 5-D, 7-D, and 9-D torus model with 9-D nearest-neighbor traffic (the 9-D nearest-neighbor traffic is executed on 5-D and 7-D tori).

While designing a torus network, one has to balance the number of dimensions and channel bandwidth to get high performance for expected applications. In this section, we take a large-scale torus network with a fixed peak bandwidth (i.e. sum of the link bandwidths for all network links is the same) and experiment with the key properties of the torus networks (i.e. torus dimensions and link bandwidths) in order to identify the configuration that yields better network performance. We assume that the overall cost of the network stays relatively the same. To evaluate the network performance, we choose well-known synthetic communication patterns, including nearest-neighbor traffic, to determine performance of local communication patterns [10], and diagonal traffic, to determine the bisection bandwidth of the torus network [15]. We keep the channel bandwidth to a maximum of 2 GB/sec out of which 1.8 GB/s of the bandwidth is available for user data in ROSS, which is the default bandwidth configuration of the BG/Q. We keep the buffer capacity of a channel to 128 full sized packets per channel. Through out the simulation results presented in this section, we inject packets at a specific injection rate during an injection interval of 2 microseconds, followed by which we stop injecting more packets and observe how long the network takes to completely process the injected data. We also collect various network performance statistics such as link utilization, aggregate buffer queue utilization and the average number of hops traversed by packets to monitor the progress of injected data over the network.

3.2.1 Nearest Neighbor Traffic Pattern

The torus networks yield high throughput for applications that frequently communicate within a set of nearest-neighbors. In our synthetic nearest-neighbor traffic pattern, each torus node sends 512-byte MPI messages to all its torus neighbors. Torus networks tend to achieve a large fraction of the peak network bandwidth when communication involves neighboring torus nodes only [24].

A. Link utilization of a 9-D million-node torus: First we observe the performance and link utilization of the 9-D torus model using the 9-D nearest-neighbor traffic pattern. In this case, each torus node sends messages to its immediate neighboring node, which makes a message traverse only 1 hop. The simulation sends messages at a link bandwidth of 1.8 GB/sec which is the maximum bandwidth available

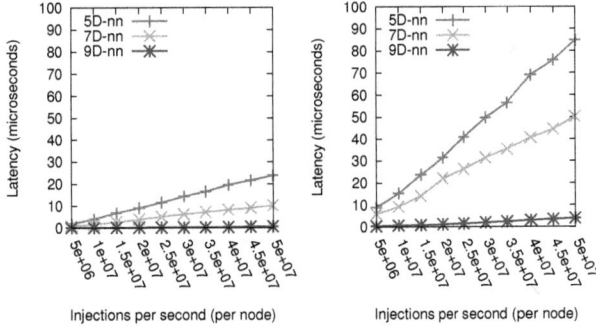

Figure 7: Average (left) and maximum (right) latency of a 1.3 million node 5-D, 7-D, and 9-D torus model with 9-D nearest-neighbor traffic (the 9-D nearest-neighbor traffic is executed on 5-D and 7-D tori).

for user data in the BG/Q (1.8 GB/s of 2.0 GB/s is available to user data). The ROSS torus model simulation injects packets to the neighboring torus nodes to the maximum capacity of channel buffers. During this interval, the torus buffer queues grow quickly, and the maximum fraction of the link bandwidth is utilized (roughly 1.73 GB/sec out of 1.8 GB/sec of available link bandwidth). As shown in Figure 5, given a very high peak injection rate of $2 * 10^8$ injections per second, the 9-D torus network has maximum link utilization with nearest-neighbor traffic and it takes 120 microseconds of simulation time for all packets in the torus buffer queues to reach their destinations (the channels hold a large number of torus packets in their buffer queues). As the channel queue size starts shrinking, the link bandwidth starts decreasing until all packets have arrived at their destinations. This experiment is an example of how we can instrument our ROSS torus network model to gain insight into the network behavior by collecting simulation performance statistics such as link utilization over simulation time.

B. Behavior of torus network with 9-D nearest neighbor traffic: To compare the effectiveness of various torus configurations on a traffic pattern that communicates with a wide set of neighboring torus nodes, we take a fixed nearest-neighbor traffic pattern for a 9-D torus network and execute the 9-D nearest-neighbor traffic pattern on a 9-D, 7-D, and 5-D tori. In turn, we also test the three tori configurations by executing a 5-D nearest-neighbor traffic on a 9-D, 7-D, and 5-D tori, in order to evaluate the effectiveness of the torus configurations on a traffic pattern that communicates with relatively modest number of neighboring torus nodes. Choosing a fixed traffic configuration and mapping it on different torus dimensions reflects the fact that the communication patterns of applications are based on their own physics and they are not dependent on the system architecture. Therefore, in the next set of experiments, we keep a constant sum of link bandwidths per node and change the dimensions of the torus network. The bandwidth per link for a 5-D, 7-D, and 9-D tori is fixed at 2.0 GB/sec, 1.428 GB/sec, and 1.111 GB/sec respectively; 90% of the bandwidth in each case is available for the user data.

First, to see the impact of scale, we execute a small 1,024 node torus model configured as 5-D (4 x 4 x 4 x 4 x 4), 7-D (4 x 4 x 4 x 2 x 2 x 2 x 2) and 9-D (4 x 4 x 2 x 2 x 2 x 2 x

2 x 2 x 2) topologies. The average and maximum nearest-neighbor traffic latency is shown in Figure 6 with a constant on-node bandwidth using the 9-D nearest-neighbor traffic pattern. Next, we take a 5-D, 7-D, and 9-D configuration of a 1.3 million node with a constant on-node bandwidth and execute the 9-D nearest-neighbor traffic pattern on these configurations. Figure 7 shows the performance results of a 1.3 million nodes 5-D, 7-D, and 9-D tori networks. In both 1,024 node and 1.3 million node cases, packets on a 5-D and 7-D tori traverse more than one hop, since we have configured a 9-D torus traffic pattern on a 5-D and 7-D tori networks and the 9-D torus traffic nearest neighbors may not be immediate neighbors on a 5-D and 7-D tori networks.

Looking at the performance results of the above 1,024 node configuration, we observe a dramatically different performance picture from which is shown for the notional exascale network configuration of 1.3 million nodes. In particular, we see that for the 1,024 node case in Figure 6, the 5-D network out-performs the 7-D network by yielding lower average and maximum latencies. Moreover, for lower injection rates, the 5-D network also outperforms the 9-D torus in terms of average latencies at a small-scale of 1,024 nodes (Figure 6 average latency on the left). We attribute this phenomena to the 5-D torus being symmetric for 1,024 nodes while the 7-D has become asymmetric which lowers overall bisection bandwidth of the network in comparison to the 5-D network. In this case, the 9-D network provides a lower latency at high injection rates because it's neighbors align exactly with the 9-D nearest-neighbor traffic, thus avoiding the degree of congestion encountered in the 5-D network. On the other hand, for the 1.3 million node case in Figure 7, one can see that when communication involves a large number of MPI processes including nearest-neighbors, despite of their wider channel bandwidth, 5-D and 7-D tori yield 3 to 5 times higher latency than does a 9-D torus network with relatively narrower channel bandwidth. Overall, this experiment demonstrates the importance of modeling this class of network at scale since one could not make reliable predictions about network latency performance at larger scales based on smaller scale configurations for the same number of torus dimensions.

C. Behavior of torus network with 5-D nearest neighbor traffic: As our third test case, we tested the three tori configurations by using the nearest-neighbor traffic pattern of a 5-D torus for 1.3 million node configuration. Figure 8 shows the performance results of this test case, in terms of average and maximum latency, for the 5-D, 7-D, and 9-D torus configurations. With 5-D nearest-neighbor traffic, packets on a 5-D torus network traverse one hop only as they are being sent to direct neighbors. However, packets on a 7-D and 9-D tori may traverse more than one hop, since the first five dimensions of a 5-D nearest neighbor traffic are different on a 7-D and 9-D tori than a 5-D torus. We note that the 9-D nearest-neighbor traffic pattern gives a lower latency when executed on a 5-D torus as opposed to the 5-D nearest neighbor traffic when executed on a 9-D torus (Figures 7 and 8 respectively). In case of a 5-D nearest neighbor traffic pattern executed on a 9-D torus, some of the 9-D torus links are left un-utilized, whereas the remaining links become congested because of the lower link bandwidth (1.11 GB/sec) with an average of 5 to 6 torus hops traversed by the packets. When the 9-D nearest-neighbor pattern is executed on a 5-D torus, all the 5-D torus links are utilized

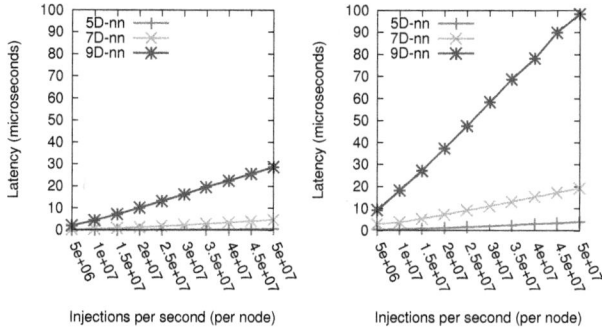

Figure 8: Average (left) and maximum (right) latency of a 1.3 million node 5-D, 7-D, and 9-D torus model with 5-D nearest-neighbor traffic (torus 5-D nearest-neighbor traffic executed on 7-D and 9-D tori).

at a higher link bandwidth (2.0 GB/sec) with packets following a diverse set of torus paths (on average 10 to 12 torus hops are being traversed in this case). Therefore, one can see that when communication involves a limited set of MPI processes, because of the narrower channel bandwidth, the serialization latency of the 9-D torus dominates its high dimensionality, and the 5-D torus network yields better performance because of its wider channel bandwidth.

D. Findings for nearest neighbor traffic: In the case of nearest-neighbor traffic, we have observed that the network performance depends on the nature of the traffic pattern. Overall, given a choice between moderate number of torus dimensions with wide channel bandwidth and a high number of torus dimensions with narrower channel bandwidth, one should carefully align the number of torus dimensions and bandwidth with the neighborhood communication requirements of the applications. Having more torus dimensions than the application's communication requirements can lead to load imbalance, because the dimension order routing uses selected neighboring links on a node for communication, leaving the remaining neighboring links under utilized. We also observe that the performance impact of the nearest neighbor traffic pattern is significantly different on a small-scale torus network than the 1.3 million node torus. At a small-scale, we see the 5-D torus network giving improved performance in terms of average latencies than a 9-D torus at lower injection rates. We also see a 5-D torus performing better than a 7-D torus network at 1,024 nodes. However, these performance trends are entirely different at the 1.3 million node case where the 9-D torus always outperforms the 5-D and 7-D tori. We attribute this performance difference to the symmetric nature of the small-scale 5-D torus and emphasize that reliable predictions about performance of exascale interconnects cannot be done through small-scale simulations.

3.2.2 Diagonal Pairing Traffic

Diagonal pairing in torus networks is an effective communication pattern for measuring the bisection bandwidth of a network. The bisection bandwidth of a torus network is calculated using the following equation (Bi_w is the bisection bandwidth of the network, N is the number of nodes in the

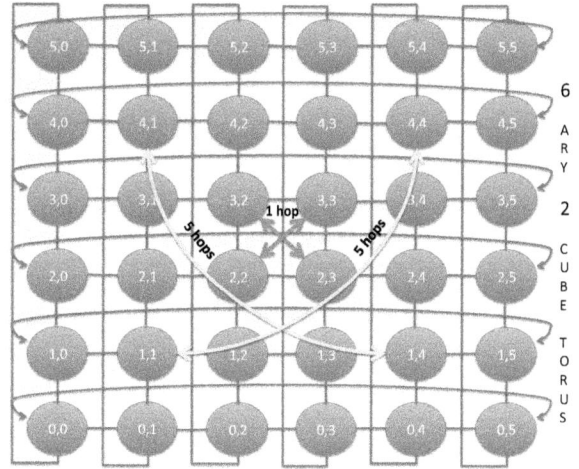

Figure 9: Example of diagonal traffic pattern in a 6-ary 2-cube torus network.

network, M is the maximum length of a torus dimension, B is the link bandwidth):

$$Bi_w = N * \frac{4}{M} * B \qquad (1)$$

In the diagonal pairing method, each torus node communicates with exactly one other torus node which is a reflection across the mid-point of each dimension, according to [15]. As shown in Figure 9, each torus node is assigned an index k for each dimension. Each node with index k in the nth dimension communicates with another torus node having index $L - k - 1$, where L is length of the nth torus dimension. The packets sent from nodes in the mid-point of the network traverse fewer hops than do the packets that are sent from the far end of the torus dimension.

A. Network performance statistics of a million node 9-D torus: Figure 10 shows the bandwidth of a 1.3 million 9-D ROSS torus network model recorded over 1 microsecond intervals with a 9-D diagonal traffic pattern. Unlike the nearest-neighbor traffic pattern, diagonal pairing can quickly fill up the buffer space of the network as packets traverse multiple network hops between the source and destination. Additionally, since the packets cross the notional mid-point of the network and may wait in the buffer queues at intermediate hops, it takes more time for the packets to arrive at their destinations. We model the diagonal pairing traffic scenario in ROSS by injecting the network packets at a very high injection rate. In our ROSS torus model, we stop injecting packets in the simulation right before the network buffers start overflowing. In Figure 10, the torus network configuration is 10 x 8 x 8 x 8 x 4 x 4 x 4 x 2 x 2, which produces a maximum hop count of 25. Due to the nature of this traffic pattern, most of the packets traverse $h/2$ hops (h is the number of hops traversed by a packet), while a few packets traverse more or less than $h/2$ hops. Figure 10 also shows the average number of hops traversed by the packets and the aggregate buffer utilization at corresponding points in the simulation. The majority of the packets issued have an average hop count of 13, and the network reaches its peak bisection bandwidth during simulation intervals of 30 to 58 microseconds, while packets traversing an average of 13 hops are arriving at their destination nodes.

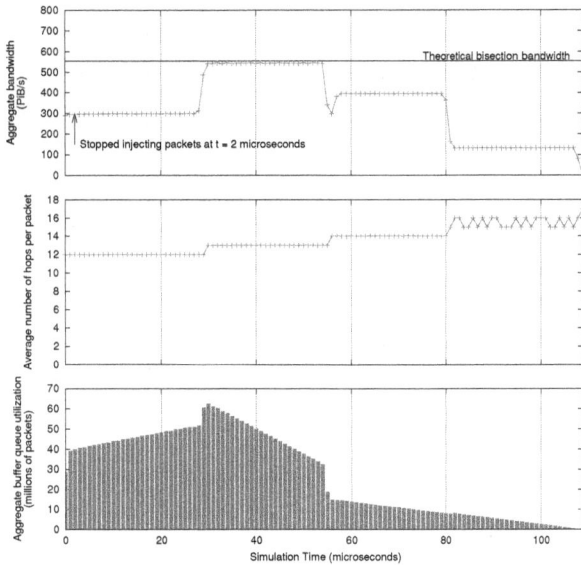

Figure 10: Aggregate bandwidth (GB/sec), average hop count and buffer queue utilization of a 9-D 1.3 million node torus model over 1-microsecond intervals with diagonal pairing traffic at injection rate $3 * 10^7$ Packets were stopped injecting after 2 microseconds of simulation time.

Figure 10 also shows that the aggregate buffer utilization starts declining after 58 microseconds of simulation time, since majority of the total packets injected reach their destinations by this time. Towards the end of the simulation, only packets with a hop count of 14 and more are left in the queue. This experiment is another example of how we can instrument our ROSS torus network model to understand why we are seeing the performance results by collecting a number of additional simulation statistics like aggregate buffer queue utilization with simulation time, number of average hops traversed with simulation time etc.

B. Behavior of torus network with 9-D diagonal traffic pattern: Next, we set out to measure the performance of 5-D, 7-D, and 9-D tori network models for diagonal traffic pattern to see the performance benefits of changing torus dimensionality on traffic that communicates with the far-end of the network. We execute a 9-D diagonal pairing traffic pattern on a 5-D, 7-D, and 9-D tori. The injection rates are kept high so that the network reaches a state of congestion. The maximum injection rate is the point after which the network channel buffers start overflowing.

To see the impact of scale, we execute the diagonal traffic pattern on a small 1,024 node torus and then on a large 1.3 million node torus. Figure 11 shows the latency comparison of a 5-D, 7-D, and 9-D tori networks with diagonal traffic pattern on 1,024 nodes. Figure 12 shows the latency comparison of the three tori configurations on a 1.3 million node torus. Here, we also observe a dramatically different performance for 1,024 nodes. For a 1,024 node case, the latency trends of a 5-D torus are the lowest whereas for the 1.3 million node case, the 9-D torus yields lowest latencies despite of its lower channel bandwidth (1.11 GB/s vs. 1.428 GB/s and 2 GB/s). Since the bisection bandwidth is de-

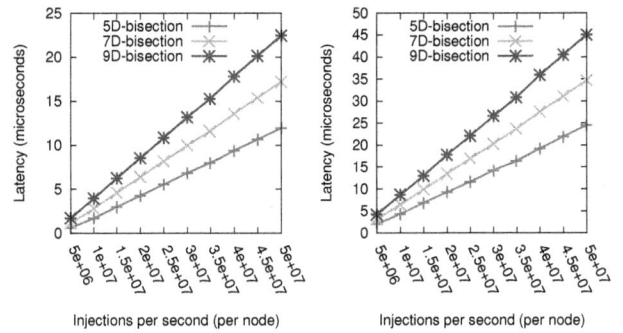

Figure 11: Average (left) and maximum (right) latency of a 1,024 node 5-D, 7-D, and 9-D torus model with 9-D diagonal traffic (the 9-D diagonal traffic is executed on 5-D and 7-D tori).

pendent on the maximum length of the torus dimension and the link bandwidth (See Eq. 1 for bisection bandwidth), the 5-D torus has the highest bisection bandwidth at the 1,024 node configuration whereas at the 1.3 million node case, the 9-D torus configuration has a significantly higher bisection bandwidth than a 1.3 million node 5-D and 7-D tori.

C. Findings for diagonal pairing traffic: Overall, our simulation results show that the benefits of having higher dimensions for far-end network traffic are not evident at a small-scale of 1,024 nodes since increasing torus dimensions at a small-scale may cause little or no improvement over the bisection bandwidth of the network. However, increasing torus dimensions significantly improves performance for a large network of 1.3 million nodes since we can get a higher bisection bandwidth by carefully configuring the maximum lengths of the torus dimensions even if the bandwidth available per link is narrower.

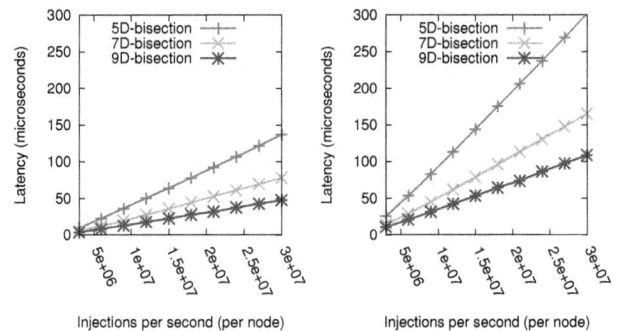

Figure 12: Average (right) and maximum (left) latency of a 1.3 million node 5-D, 7-D, and 9-D torus model with diagonal traffic with torus 9-D bisection traffic pattern mapped on 5-D and 7-D.

4. MASSIVELY PARALLEL SIMULATION PERFORMANCE

In this section, we explore the simulation performance of the 1.3 million node torus model. The objective of this study is to demonstrate that with ROSS we are able to simulate

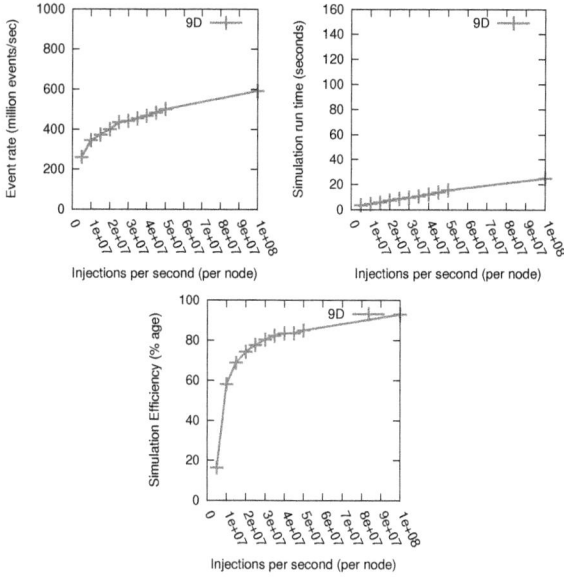

Figure 13: Event rate, run time and efficiency for a 1.3 million node 9-D torus model with nearest-neighbor traffic using 64 MPI tasks per node on 1 Mira rack (65K MPI tasks).

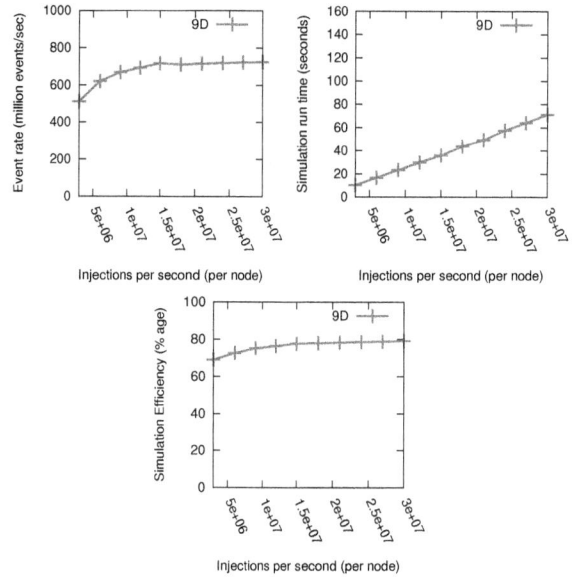

Figure 14: Event rate, run time and efficiency for a 1.3 million 9-D torus model with bisection traffic pattern using 64 MPI tasks per node on 1 Mira rack (65K MPI tasks).

million node network models under very high traffic work loads in a reasonable amount of time. Similar to the previous experiments presented in Section 3.2, we inject packets at a specific injection rate during an injection interval of 2 microseconds, followed by which we allow these packets to propagate through the network and stop injecting more packets.

4.1 Reverse Computation

Our torus network model uses reverse computation to support the *undo* operation as part of optimistic event scheduling within the ROSS model execution framework. The torus model node and MPI process LPs have reverse event handlers such that if any of the MPI message/packet/chunk generation, packet-chunk sending, and MPI message/packet/chunk arrival events are out of order, the incorrect events are rolled back, and the corresponding LP state variables are correctly undone (see Figure 1). To write the reverse event handlers, one has to develop a "state rollback mindset" since every possible update to the state of a LP has to be reversible. However, the size of the reverse event handler code for the torus models is only 1/5 than that of its corresponding forward event handlers. Therefore, with a small amount of effort for writing reverse handlers, the optimistic event scheduling and reverse computation capability in our models enables us to avoid the look-ahead limitations of the simulators that use conservative event processing [28, 29], while at the same time eliminating the traditional time warp overheads associated with LP state saving. As a result, this network model executes efficiently on 65,536 MPI tasks on Mira. To the best of our knowledge, this capability has not been previously demonstrated for this class of network models.

4.2 Parallel Simulation Performance of Torus Network Models

The simulation performance in ROSS is measured by using three parameters: ROSS simulation efficiency, committed event rate, and the time to complete the simulation. These metrics provide a picture of how ROSS performs with various network models and configurations. ROSS event efficiency determines the amount of useful work performed by the simulation. It is defined in Equation 2 [23] :

$$event\_efficiency = 1 - \frac{rolled\_back\_events}{total\_committed\_events} \quad (2)$$

To reduce state-saving overheads, ROSS employs an event rollback mechanism by developing event computations such that they can be reverse processed [30]. The simulator efficiency is inversely proportional to the number of rollbacks. With no rollbacks, the simulator yields 100% efficiency.

Figures 13 and 14 show the ROSS committed event rate, simulation run time, and ROSS event efficiency of a 1.3 million node 9-D torus network model under different traffic work loads. The tests were executed on 1 rack of Mira utilizing all 4 threads per core, with each compute node have 64 MPI processes. As seen in the figures, as the injection rates of the torus model simulation keeps on increasing, the ROSS committed event rate also increases. With maximum injection rates of 100 million packets per second in Figure 13, the ROSS event rate increases to 600 million events per seconds, whereas the simulation run time does not exceed 25 seconds. Also, the ROSS event efficiency of the torus model simulation increases with increasing traffic work loads. As the injection rates increase, ROSS simulation has more events to process than it can roll-back. With more events to process, the ratio of rolled-back events to the total committed events becomes less, which in turn increases ROSS event efficiency (Equation 2). Since the injection rates of the torus network with bisection traffic are at a smaller scale than that of nearest-neighbor traffic (Figure 14), the variance in ROSS event rate and efficiency is less for bisection traffic. The simulation run time of the torus bisection traffic (Figure 14) is more than the run time of the nearest-neighbor traffic (Figure 13) because the bisection traffic traverses multiple hops (up to 25 hops) whereas the nearest-neighbor traffic traverses only a single network hop.

The ROSS simulation performance measurements show that the run times and event rate of the torus network model are scalable with high packet injection rates. The efficiency of the models increases when we increase the work loads, since more events are processed than the events being rolled back. Therefore the model can efficiently process high injection rates as the simulation is being assigned more work.

5. RELATED WORK

A number of efforts have been done to analytically model and/or simulate torus network and related network topologies.

We first start with the analytic models. Agarwal [31] improves upon the latency analytic results of Dally [32] by considering the node or switch delays in addition to wire delays in the model. These results countered Dally's at the time by showing that a 3-D network has a lower latency as opposed to a 2-D network when switch delays are four times the wire delay. The results here are concerned with symmetric torus networks where K is the same for all dimensions.

For asymmetric torus networks, Ciciani [33], presents an average latency delay model for an asymmetric 3-D torus network that considers both uni-directional and bi-directional links. Here, configurations are considered up to 1000 nodes (e.g., 10 x 10 x 10) with uniform random traffic flows with Poisson arrival times.

Additionally, Min et al. [34] developed an analytic model for computing communication delays in torus networks with circuit switching under multiple time-scale bursty and correlated traffic. The probability of message blocking in practical torus topologies was calculated using the model. Probabilistic methods were also used to determine traffic characteristics on network channels. The accuracy of the analytical model was validated by comparing analytical results with simulation experiments of the real system.

For serial simulation, Dally et al. developed *Booksim* which is a cycle-accurate network simulation framework, to study the performance of the torus network and others topologies in comparison to a dragonfly network topology [7, 35]. While *Booksim* provides the support for a number of network topologies, the maximum size of the network is limited to only 1024 nodes.

Further, Wang et al. presented Orion [36], a power and performance interconnection simulator aimed at providing network designers with a framework for exploring interconnected microprocessor systems. It also provides fast design-level power estimation to enable research in power-efficient hardware. Orion uses a component-based approach by letting the users plug-in routers and links in order to investigate their impact on network performance. As a case study, Orion uses a 16-node 4x4 torus network and explores different router configurations such as wormhole and virtual channel routers under collective and uniform workloads.

Related parallel simulation results include Adiga et al. [3]. Here, the BG/L torus network was simulated by using a cycle-accurate simulator in which the simulation time was defined as the time it takes to transfer one byte This simulator, driven by application pseudo-codes, runs on a 16-way shared memory machines. Each processor thread simulates a BG 512-node mid-plane and is synchronized using the YAWNS (yet another windowing network simulator) protocol [37].

Additionally, Abhinav et al. [38] use a parallel simulation framework called *BigSim*, to study the performance of the PERCS network. This is a two-level direct network which connects the compute nodes into groups using high-bandwidth links at the lowest level and at the next level connects the groups using another type of link . They explore various intelligent topology-aware mappings and routing techniques to avoid hot spots due to multiple levels in the PERCS topology. The BigSim simulator predicts the application performance for a future machine by obtaining traces through emulation on existing architectures. The simulation for future machines is then carried out using these traces. The PERCS network topology is simulated for up to 307,200 cores at the packet-level detail.

Finally, the Structural Simulation Toolkit (SST) [29] uses a component-based parallel discrete-event model built on top of MPI. The SST uses a conservative distance-based optimization without support for rollbacks. SST models a variety of hardware components including processors, memory, and networks under different accuracy and details. When the simulation starts, a system topology graph is loaded, which is then load-balanced across multiple processes. SST supports generic router models that uses wormhole routing for messages, though there is no flow-control in place and the router links have infinite buffer capacity. The network topologies currently supported are two- and three-dimensional meshes, binary tree, binary fat tree, hypercubes, flattened 2-D butterfly and a fully connected graph.

In summary, while a number of simulations accurately model the torus network topology, none of these simulations have been shown to scale to exascale network levels for a torus topology. We do note that the *BigSim* model of the IBM PERCS network has been shown to scale to modeling 300K cores, but the PERCS topology layout is much different from the torus network.

6. CONCLUSION AND FUTURE WORK

As we get closer to the exascale era, the search is under way for an interconnect topology that yields high bandwidth with relevant HPC traffic patterns. Simulation is an increasingly important tool for exploring the design space of massively parallel architectures yet most of the current simulation infrastructures have been shown to scale on a modest network size only. In this paper, we have applied massively parallel discrete-event simulation to efficiently model high-fidelity torus interconnects at a size of future exascale systems. We have used relevant HPC traffic patterns to explore the behavior of these network topologies under different configurations. We have shown that with the help of these network simulations, we can not only see realistic performance results, but we can instrument our ROSS network models to provide useful network performance statistics that help us gain an insight into exactly why are we seeing these performance results. We show that large-scale simulations are critical in the design of exascale systems, because trends at a modest scale are do not necessarily reflect network behavior at exascale size. We have also demonstrated that we have the ability to simulate these large-scale network topologies in a reasonable amount of time which strongly suggests that massively parallel discrete-event simulation can be a key enabler for effective, efficient extreme-scale network codesign.

As part of future work, we plan to use the torus network model as the underlying interconnect in exascale storage architectures as part of the CODES simulation toolkit [39]. In terms of exploring other candidate interconnect topologies for exascale systems, we are also working to simulate a million node high-fidelity dragonfly network topology using ROSS [40]. We also plan to explore the behavior of the torus and dragonfly interconnects using real application network workloads in addition to the currently used, synthetic traffic patterns.

7. ACKNOWLEDGEMENT

The manuscript has been created by UChicago Argonne, LLC, Operator of Argonne National Laboratory ("Argonne"). Argonne, a U.S. Department of Energy Office of Science laboratory, is operated under Contract No. DE-AC02-06CH11357. The U.S. Government retains for itself, and others acting on its behalf, a paid-up nonexclusive, irrevocable worldwide license in said article to reproduce, prepare derivative works, distribute copies to the public, and perform publicly and display publicly, by or on behalf of the Government. This research used resources of Argonne Leadership Computing Facility at Argonne National Laboratory, which is supported by the Office of Science of the U.S. Department of Energy under contract DE-AC02-06CH11357.

We gratefully acknowledge Ning Liu, Ph.D. student at the Illinois Institute of Technology, for his help with the torus network model development.

8. REFERENCES

[1] Jack Dongarra. Impact of architecture and technology for extreme scale on software and algorithm design. Presented at the Department of Energy Workshop on Cross-cutting Technologies for Computing at the Exascale, February 2010.

[2] Jack Dongarra. *On the future of high-performance computing: how to think for peta and exascale computing.* Hong Kong University of Science and Technology, 2012.

[3] Narasimha R Adiga, Matthias A Blumrich, Dong Chen, Paul Coteus, Alan Gara, Mark E Giampapa, Philip Heidelberger, Sarabjeet Singh, Burkhard D Steinmacher-Burow, Todd Takken, et al. Blue Gene/L torus interconnection network. *IBM Journal of Research and Development*, 49(2.3):265–276, 2005.

[4] Dong Chen, Noel A Eisley, Philip Heidelberger, Robert M Senger, Yutaka Sugawara, Sameer Kumar, Valentina Salapura, David L Satterfield, Burkhard Steinmacher-Burow, and Jeffrey J Parker. The IBM Blue Gene/Q interconnection network and message unit. In *2011 International Conference for High Performance Computing, Networking, Storage and Analysis (SC), 2011.*, pages 1–10. IEEE, 2011.

[5] Sadaf R Alam, Jeffery A Kuehn, Richard F Barrett, Jeff M Larkin, Mark R Fahey, Ramanan Sankaran, and Patrick H Worley. Cray XT4: an early evaluation for petascale scientific simulation. In *Proceedings of the 2007 ACM/IEEE Conference on Supercomputing, 2007. SC'07.*, pages 1–12. IEEE, 2007.

[6] Bob Alverson, Edwin Froese, Larry Kaplan, and Duncan Roweth. Cray XC® series network. 2012.

[7] John Kim, William Dally, Steve Scott, and Dennis Abts. Cost-efficient dragonfly topology for large-scale systems. *Micro, IEEE*, 29(1):33–40, 2009.

[8] John Kim, James Balfour, and William Dally. Flattened butterfly topology for on-chip networks. In *Proceedings of the 40th Annual IEEE/ACM International Symposium on Microarchitecture*, pages 172–182. IEEE Computer Society, 2007.

[9] Baba Arimilli, Ravi Arimilli, Vicente Chung, Scott Clark, Wolfgang Denzel, Ben Drerup, Torsten Hoefler, Jody Joyner, Jerry Lewis, Jian Li, et al. The PERCS high-performance interconnect. In *IEEE 18th Annual Symposium on High Performance Interconnects (HOTI), 2010.*, pages 75–82. IEEE, 2010.

[10] William J Dally and Brian P Towles. *Principles and Practices of Interconnection Networks*. Morgan Kaufmann, 2004.

[11] Christopher D Carothers, David Bauer, and Shawn Pearce. Ross: A high-performance, low-memory, modular Time Warp system. *Journal of Parallel and Distributed Computing*, 62(11):1648–1669, 2002.

[12] Exascale initiative: Design forward program, 2013.

[13] Christopher D Carothers, Kalyan S Perumalla, and Richard M Fujimoto. Efficient optimistic parallel simulations using reverse computation. *ACM Transactions on Modeling and Computer Simulation (TOMACS)*, 9(3):224–253, 1999.

[14] Ning Liu, Christopher Carothers, Jason Cope, Philip Carns, and Robert Ross. Model and simulation of exascale communication networks. *Journal of Simulation*, 6(4):227–236, 2012.

[15] Dong Chen, Noel Eisley, Philip Heidelberger, Sameer Kumar, Amith Mamidala, Fabrizio Petrini, Robert Senger, Yutaka Sugawara, Robert Walkup, Burkhard Steinmacher-Burow, et al. Looking under the hood of the IBM Blue Gene/Q network. In *Proceedings of the International Conference on High Performance Computing, Networking, Storage and Analysis*, page 69. IEEE Computer Society Press, 2012.

[16] Courtenay Vaughan, Mahesh Rajan, Richard Barrett, Douglas Doerfler, and Kevin Pedretti. Investigating the impact of the Cielo Cray XE6 architecture on scientific application codes. In *Parallel and Distributed Processing Workshops and Phd Forum (IPDPSW), 2011 IEEE International Symposium on*, pages 1831–1837. IEEE, 2011.

[17] Aleksandr Ovcharenko, Kedar Chitale, Onkar Sahni, Kenneth E Jansen, and Mark S Shephard. Parallel adaptive boundary layer meshing for CFD analysis. In *Proceedings of the 21st International Meshing Roundtable*, pages 437–455. Springer, 2013.

[18] William J Dally. Virtual-channel flow control. *IEEE Transactions on Parallel and Distributed Systems.*, 3(2):194–205, 1992.

[19] David R Jefferson. Virtual time. *ACM Transactions on Programming Languages and Systems (TOPLAS)*, 7(3):404–425, 1985.

[20] Akintayo O Holder and Christopher D Carothers. Analysis of time warp on a 32,768 processor IBM Blue gene/L supercomputer. In *proceedings of European Modeling and Simulation Symposium (EMSS), 2009.*, 2008.

[21] C. D. Carothers and K. S. Perumalla. On deciding between conservative and optimistic approaches on massively parallel platforms. In *Winter Simulation Conference'10*, pages 678–687, 2010.

[22] Peter D Barnes Jr, Christopher D Carothers, David R Jefferson, and Justin M LaPre. Warp speed: executing time warp on 1,966,080 cores. In *Proceedings of the 2013 ACM SIGSIM conference on Principles of advanced discrete simulation*, pages 327–336. ACM, 2013.

[23] David W Bauer Jr, Christopher D Carothers, and Akintayo Holder. Scalable time warp on Blue Gene supercomputers. In *Proceedings of the 2009 ACM/IEEE/SCS 23rd Workshop on Principles of Advanced and Distributed Simulation*, pages 35–44. IEEE Computer Society, 2009.

[24] Megan Gilge. IBM system Blue Gene Solution: Blue Gene/Q Application Development. *IBM Redbook Draft SG24-7948-00*, 2012.

[25] Valentin Puente, Cruz Izu, Ramón Beivide, José A Gregorio, Fernando Vallejo, and JM Prellezo. The adaptive bubble router. *Journal of Parallel and Distributed Computing*, 61(9):1180–1208, 2001.

[26] William J Dally and Charles L Seitz. The torus routing chip. *Distributed computing*, 1(4):187–196, 1986.

[27] William Gropp and Ewing Lusk. Reproducible measurements of MPI performance characteristics. In *Recent Advances in Parallel Virtual Machine and Message Passing Interface*, pages 11–18. Springer, 1999.

[28] Philip Heidelberger and David M. Nicol. Conservative parallel simulation of continuous time Markov chains using uniformization. *IEEE Transactions on Parallel and Distributed Systems.*, 4(8):906–921, 1993.

[29] Arun F Rodrigues, K Scott Hemmert, Brian W Barrett, Chad Kersey, Ron Oldfield, Marlo Weston, R Risen, Jeanine Cook, Paul Rosenfeld, E CooperBalls, et al. The structural simulation toolkit. *ACM SIGMETRICS Performance Evaluation Review*, 38(4):37–42, 2011.

[30] Garrett Yaun, Christopher D Carothers, and Shivkumar Kalyanaraman. Large-scale TCP models using optimistic parallel simulation. In *Proceedings of the seventeenth workshop on Parallel and Distributed Simulation*, page 153. IEEE Computer Society, 2003.

[31] A. Agarwal. Limits on interconnection network performance. *IEEE Transactions on Parallel and Distributed Systems*, 2(4):398–412, 1991.

[32] W.J. Dally. Performance analysis of k-ary n-cube interconnection networks. *Computers, IEEE Transactions on*, 39(6):775–785, 1990.

[33] B. Ciciani, M. Colajanni, and C. Paolucci. An accurate model for the performance analysis of deterministic wormhole routing. In *Parallel Processing Symposium, 1997. Proceedings., 11th International*, pages 353–359, 1997.

[34] Geyong Min and Mohamed Ould-Khaoua. Prediction of communication delay in torus networks under multiple time-scale correlated traffic. *Performance Evaluation*, 60(1):255–273, 2005.

[35] John Kim, Wiliam J Dally, Steve Scott, and Dennis Abts. Technology-driven, highly-scalable dragonfly topology. *ACM SIGARCH Computer Architecture News*, 36(3):77–88, 2008.

[36] Hang-Sheng Wang, Xinping Zhu, Li-Shiuan Peh, and Sharad Malik. Orion: a power-performance simulator for interconnection networks. In *35th Annual IEEE/ACM International Symposium on Microarchitecture, 2002.(MICRO-35).*, pages 294–305. IEEE, 2002.

[37] Phillip M. Dickens, David M. Nicol, Paul F. Reynolds, Jr., and J. M. Duva. Analysis of Bounded Time Warp and Comparison with YAWNS. *ACM Trans. Model. Comput. Simul.*, 6(4):297–320, October 1996.

[38] Abhinav Bhatele, Nikhil Jain, William D Gropp, and Laxmikant V Kale. Avoiding hot-spots on two-level direct networks. In *International Conference for High Performance Computing, Networking, Storage and Analysis (SC), 2011.*, pages 1–11. IEEE, 2011.

[39] Jason Cope, Ning Liu, Sam Lang, Phil Carns, Chris Carothers, and Robert Ross. Codes: Enabling co-design of multilayer Exascale storage architectures. In *Proceedings of the Workshop on Emerging Supercomputing Technologies*, 2011.

[40] Misbah Mubarak, Christopher D Carothers, Robert Ross, and Philip Carns. Modeling a million-node dragonfly network using massively parallel discrete-event simulation. In *High Performance Computing, Networking, Storage and Analysis (SCC), 2012 SC Companion*, pages 366–376. IEEE, 2012.

Mesoscopic Traffic Simulation on CPU/GPU*

Yan Xu and Gary Tan
School of Computing
National University of Singapore
Singapore 117417
xuyan.nus@gmail.com

Xiaosong Li
School of Computing Engineering
Nanyang Technological University
Singapore 639798
xli15@e.ntu.edu.sg

Xiao Song
School of Automation
Beihang Univ.
Beijing, China
songxiao@buaa.edu.cn

ABSTRACT

Mesoscopic traffic simulation is an important branch of technology to support offline large-scale simulation-based traffic planning and online simulation-based traffic management. One of the major concerns using mesoscopic traffic simulations is the performance, which means the required time to simulate a traffic scenario. At the same time, the GPU has recently been a success, because of its massive performance compared to the CPU. Thus, a critical question is "whether the GPU can be a potential high-performance platform for mesoscopic traffic simulations?" To the best of our knowledge, there is no clear answer in the research area. In this paper, we firstly propose a comprehensive framework to run a traditional time-stepped mesoscopic traffic simulation on CPU/GPU. Then, we design a boundary processing method to guarantee the correctness of running mesoscopic supply traffic simulations on the GPU. Thirdly, the proposed mesoscopic traffic simulation framework is demonstrated to simulate 100,000 vehicles moving on a large-scale grid road network. In this case study, running a mesoscopic supply traffic simulation on a GPU (GeForce GT 650M) gives 11.2 times speedup, compared with running the same supply simulation on a CPU core (Intel E5-2620). In the end, this paper explains the theoretical limitation of running mesoscopic supply traffic simulations on the GPU. In conclusion, regardless of high system complexity, the proposed mesoscopic traffic simulation framework on CPU/GPU provides an innovative and promising solution for high-performance mesoscopic traffic simulations.

Categories and Subject Descriptors

I.6.8 [Types of Simulation: Parallel]; D.1.3 [Concurrent Programming: Parallel Programming]

Keywords

Mesoscopic Traffic Simulation, GPU, Correctness, Scalability

1. INTRODUCTION

Traffic simulation is an appealing solution for traffic planners and engineers to solve Dynamic Traffic Assignment (DTA) problems for offline system planning and online operation management. Technically, any traffic simulation consists of two components: 'demand' and 'supply' [1]. Modeling from the travelers' point of view, the former is to understand how travel decisions are made, such as mode choice, departure time choice and route choice.

Modeling from the traffic flow's point of view, the latter is to understand how traffic demand is assigned to available road resources. This paper focuses mainly on the supply part which is often more computational costly because the supply models the traffic flow dynamics with vehicles moving on road networks [2].

To simulate the supply part of an entire city such as Singapore [1] or Beijing [4] in peak hours, when a few hundred thousand to a few million vehicles are on the road, the amount of time it would require a single von Neumann-style serial processor to track and compute the states of such large numbers of vehicles makes traffic simulations nearly infeasible on these architectures. To tackle this performance problem, researchers have made efforts on two main approaches, structurally improve supply framework and enhance performance with parallel computing.

To improve efficiency of the supply framework, mesoscopic traffic simulators, such as DynaMIT [3, 4] and DynaSMART [5], were created to reduce the computational requirement of microscopic traffic simulators. Compared with microscopic traffic simulators, individual vehicle dynamics in mesoscopic traffic simulators are approximated by a speed-density model in the moving part of a link and a queuing model in the queue part of a link [1]. At the same time, in contrast to aggregated macroscopic models [6], vehicles are modeled as agents in mesoscopic traffic simulations to gain the advantage that they are consistent with the detailed demand models of traveler behaviors, such as route choice. For their well designed tradeoff between performance and accuracy, mesoscopic traffic simulators have been widely used to support large-scale simulation-based DTA systems [3-5]. A recent work is ETSF [16], which reduces the theoretical time complexity of the mesoscopic supply simulation, with an assumption that vehicles on the same lane of a segment are moving at the same speed at a time step. ETSF is introduced in Section 2.2. However, mesoscopic traffic simulations are still not efficient enough to satisfy the intensive computational requirement of real-world large-scale DTA applications [1]. Moreover, in most cases, tens or hundreds of runs are required for statistical analysis before any decision making, which make the problem more challenging.

Thus many researchers addressed the problem from a parallel computing perspective. They have used multi-core CPUs or CPU clusters to handle the large computational load [7-9]. Traffic network is typically decomposed into segments that are handled by different processors. Load balancing, inter-processor communication, and synchronization then become important considerations. For optimal use of computing resources, segments must be distributed evenly among processors based on the estimated computation cost of each segment. At the same time, the communication cost between processors should be minimized. For this purpose multi-core parallel algorithms and data structures

* This research was supported by the National Research Foundation Singapore through the Singapore MIT Alliance for Research and Technology's FM IRG research programme (sub contract R-252-001-459-592).

have been developed in [8, 9] and Message Passing Interface (MPI)-based communication among CPU clusters is used in [2]. In summary, traditional parallel computing using either CPU clusters or multi-core processors is the main-stream technology to support large-scale mesoscopic traffic simulations. However, it is still a challenge to run a large-scale mesoscopic traffic simulation on a CPU cluster efficiently. Besides, the cost and complexity of maintenance of such computing resources makes these approaches expensive and sometimes undesirable.

Graphics processing unit (GPU) has recently been a success, because of its massive performance compared to the CPU. While GPUs were primarily meant to do three-dimensional rendering in graphics applications, rapid developments in their architectures have enabled their use in scientific computing [11, 22], computational finance [12], computational biology [12], simulations [17, 19-21] and high performance computing [13]. Moreover, the development of direct computing application protocol interfaces (APIs) such as CUDA (compute unified device architecture) [10] and OpenCL have significantly reduced the programming efforts. However, fundamental differences in GPU and CPU architectures mean that traditional technique of converting serial implementations to parallel using standards such as OpenMP and MPI is inapplicable. Thus, a critical question is "whether the GPU can be a potential high-performance platform for mesoscopic traffic simulations?"

There have been some research work to enhance the solution to traffic simulation on GPUs. Perumalla et al. [14] introduced a method to simulate the vehicle movement on GPU by using a field based model. This model maps the real world road data onto a 2D lattice, with each element in lattice representing the possibility of turning either left/right or up/down. By using this possibility data, the vehicles will be directed from one position in the 2D array to another position. The proposed field based model is similar to the classic Cellular Automata Model. However, the contribution of this work within the global traffic simulation research framework is not clarified. The MATSIM team recently released a research work to implement an event-driven mesoscopic traffic simulation framework on the GPU [15]. The paper introduced two kernel functions (*moveLink* and *moveNode*) to implement the core queue simulation. They also talked about three different implementations of the vehicle array in the GPU memory. Their work is pioneering and obtained a speedup over serial applications between 5.5 and 60 times depending on different data structures and NVIDIA GPU series. However, the paper did not confirm the correctness of running MATSIM on the GPU and also did not explain how to migrate a real-world mesoscopic traffic simulation from the CPU to the GPU. Besides, compared to time-stepped mesoscopic traffic simulation (e.g. DynaMIT [1]), event-driven mesoscopic traffic simulation has limitations for online simulation-based operation management [2].

In this paper, we use both the CPU and the GPU to enhance performance of a traditional time-stepped mesoscopic traffic simulation enabled by Entry Time based Supply Framework (ETSF) described by [16]. This paper has four contributions:

1. This paper proposes a comprehensive framework to run a time-stepped mesoscopic traffic simulation on CPU/GPU, including time management, network and vehicle modeling on the GPU, kernel functions on the GPU and incident modeling on the GPU.

2. This paper introduces an innovative boundary processing method to guarantee the correctness of running mesoscopic supply traffic simulations on the GPU.

3. The proposed mesoscopic traffic simulation framework is demonstrated to simulate 100,000 vehicles moving on a grid road network and the supply traffic simulation on a GPU (GeForce GT 650M) gets 11.2 times speedup, compared with running the same supply simulation on a CPU core (Intel E5-2620).

4. Based on profiling results, we found that the theoretical limitation (or the bottleneck) of running mesoscopic supply simulation on the GPU is the memory access latency. It is also a challenge that should be solved in future.

The paper is organized as follows. In Section 2 the GPU is introduced and a brief overview of ETSF method is provided. Section 3 introduces the mesoscopic traffic simulation framework on CPU/GPU. Section 4 discusses the correctness of running mesoscopic supply traffic simulation on the GPU and proposes a boundary processing method. Section 5 further talks about optimization of data transfer between the CPU and the GPU. In Section 6 we provide comparison results of our benchmarks with the serial implementation and analyze the theoretical limitation. Finally, we list conclusions and future works in Section 7.

2. BACKGROUND
2.1 Combination of CPU and GPU
NVIDIA GPUs can be found in roughly 70 million PCs and notebooks around the world [15]. The key to the success of GPU computing has partly been its massive performance compared to the CPU [18]. Nowadays, there is a performance gap between the GPU and the CPU, when comparing theoretical peak bandwidth and gigaflops performance. The performance gap has its root in the physical restraints and the architecture differences between the two processors. GPUs are designed to gain massive performance to address problems that can be expressed as data parallel computations (i.e., the same program is executed on many data elements in parallel) with high arithmetic intensity (i.e., the ratio of arithmetic operations to memory operations). On the contrary, CPUs are designed to address general-purpose problems, which usually have complex execution logic.

One of the major performance factors of CPUs has traditionally been its steadily increasing frequency [18]. However, in the 2000s, this increase came to an abrupt stop. At the same time, GPUs were growing exponentially in performance due to massive parallelism. Parallelism appears to be a sustainable way of increasing performance and there are many applications that are perfectly suited for GPUs. However, increased parallelism can only increase the performance of the parallel code section, meaning that the serial part will soon become the bottleneck. Thus, the combination of traditional CPU cores and a massively parallel GPU can benefit a large number of applications. It is true for mesoscopic traffic simulations.

However, it is a challenge to migrate traditional mesoscopic traffic simulation from the CPU to CPU/GPU, because the GPU programming is quite different from the CPU programming in many ways. First, the GPU can support thousands of light-weight threads, which requires the target problem to be divided into thousands of parallel sub-problems. Second, the GPU has three memory spaces, listed in decreasing order by speed: registers, the shared memory, and the global memory. GPU programming requests users to decide which memory space to use for each dataset in the GPU memory. Besides, in most cases, the amount of total registers and total shared memory is limited. Third, the GPU and the CPU are currently using different memory spaces. The data communication between the CPU and the GPU is time costly. Fourth, the performance of GPU programming is sensitive to coalesced global memory access and bank conflicts in shared memory access, which do not exist in CPU programming. Finally, the available APIs on GPUs are still not sufficient.

2.2 Entry Time-based Supply Framework

The time complexity of simulating a lane at a time step in current mesoscopic supply framework [1, 2, 4, 5] is linear to *the number of vehicles on the lane*. To simulate an entire city the computation cost is often practically unacceptable, especially in congested traffic scenarios. To tackle this problem, an approach named 'Entry Time based Supply Framework (ETSF)' is proposed to improve the performance of mesoscopic applications. The main idea is that ETSF updates the '*entry_time_to_pass*' and '*entry_time_to_queue*' parameters of each lane to compute the moving/queuing parts of link/lane vehicles. The key feature of ETSF is to reduce the theoretical time complexity of simulating a lane at a time step to *the number of vehicles passing the lane*. ETSF significantly reduces the time to simulate a congested traffic scenario [16]. In the following paragraphs of this section, we try to explain ETSF approach before presenting GPU based ETSF in the next section.

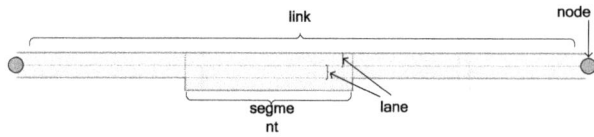

Figure 1. Network-related terminologies used in this paper

As shown in Figure 1, in ETSF, a road network is modeled as *nodes*, *links*, *segments* and *lanes*. The nodes correspond to intersections of the actual road network, while links represent unidirectional path ways between nodes. Each link is divided into a number of segments, according to geometry features. Each segment contains lanes. Each lane contains a number of vehicles which are located on the lane. Each lane has capacity constraints at the upstream end and the downstream end, referred to as the input capacity and the output capacity. A queue occurs in a lane if vehicles cannot pass the lane. A spill-back occurs if a lane is blocked, which means the length of the queue on the lane is equal to the length of the lane.

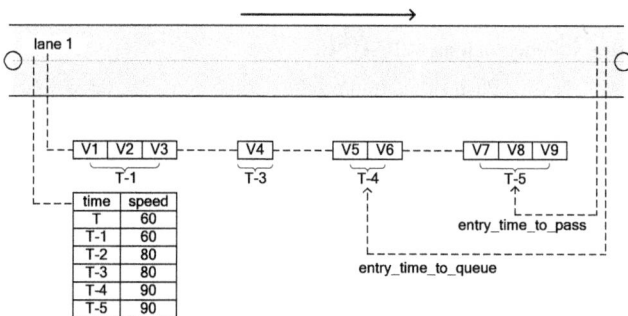

Figure 2. An example of vehicles in a lane of a link in ETSF

Figure 2 shows an example of vehicles in a lane of a link in the ETSF. First, each lane of the link has a list of vehicles which are ordered by their *entry time*, referring to the time a vehicle enters the lane. Second, in ETSF, each lane of the link is devised to have a speed table (see in Figure 2), which contains the lane speeds of recent time steps, with the assumption that vehicles in the same lane are moving using the same speed at a time. Given

the speed table and the *entry time* of a vehicle, the accumulated travel distance of the vehicle can be calculated. Third, each lane of the link has a key attribute: *entry_time_to_pass* (t_p), which means that at a time t, if the lane entry time of a vehicle is earlier (or smaller) than (or equal to) t_p, its accumulated movement distance equals to or bigger than the length of the lane and has the potential to pass current lane. For example, in Figure 2 the current time is T and t_p is T-5. Fourth, each lane of the link has another key attribute: *entry_time_to_queue* (t_q), which denotes that at a time T, if the lane has a queue and the entry time of a vehicle is earlier than (or equal to) t_q, the vehicle either enters the queue or passes the lane. For example, in Figure 2, t_q is T-4. It means vehicles whose entry time is earlier than T-4 are either in the queue or have passed the lane. Note that the queue length of a lane is calculated by adding up the occupancy space of vehicles in the queue and t_q also takes into account the vehicles whose accumulated movement distances are smaller than the length of the lane but catch the end of the queue.

3. Mesoscopic Traffic Simulation Framework on CPU/GPU

3.1 The Framework

The major motivation to design a new simulation framework is to make full use of two types of computational resources: central processing unit (CPU) and graphics processing unit (GPU). In this framework, the GPU is responsible for the supply part of mesoscopic traffic simulation, which includes speed calculation, vehicle movement on a road and between roads and queue calculation. A key feature of supply simulation is that the simulation of a road is only related with its surrounding roads, which fits GPU's data parallel requirement. The CPU is responsible for the demand part and the I/O part of mesoscopic traffic simulation, which includes vehicle generation, departure time choice, pre-trip route choice, en-trip route choice and pushing simulation results to files. A key feature of demand simulation is that vehicles are making decisions based on the information on the global road network. Figure 3 shows the mesoscopic traffic simulation framework on CPU/GPU, which explains the logic procedure and the simulation time management. This framework is suitable for general time-stepped mesoscopic traffic simulation [3-5].

The traditional simulation time, which controls the turnover of the system status, is divided into three components: a demand time step (t_d), a supply time step (t_s) and an I/O time step (t_{io}). A traffic simulation is completed only if t_d, t_s and t_{io} are all reaching the simulation end. In this framework, multiple time steps enable to identity the exact progress of different components in a traffic simulation. Note that at an instantaneous time, the three time steps can be different. The time management in this framework is controlled by three rules:

❖   Rule 1: $t_d >= t_s$

❖   Rule 2: $t_s >= t_{io}$

❖   Rule 3: $t_d <= t_s + DPP$

First, t_d is always not smaller than t_s, because only if vehicles entering the simulation at time t are generated, the supply simulation at t can start. Second, t_s is always not smaller than t_{io}, because only if the supply simulation at t is completed, the simulation results at t can be outputted to files. The third rule

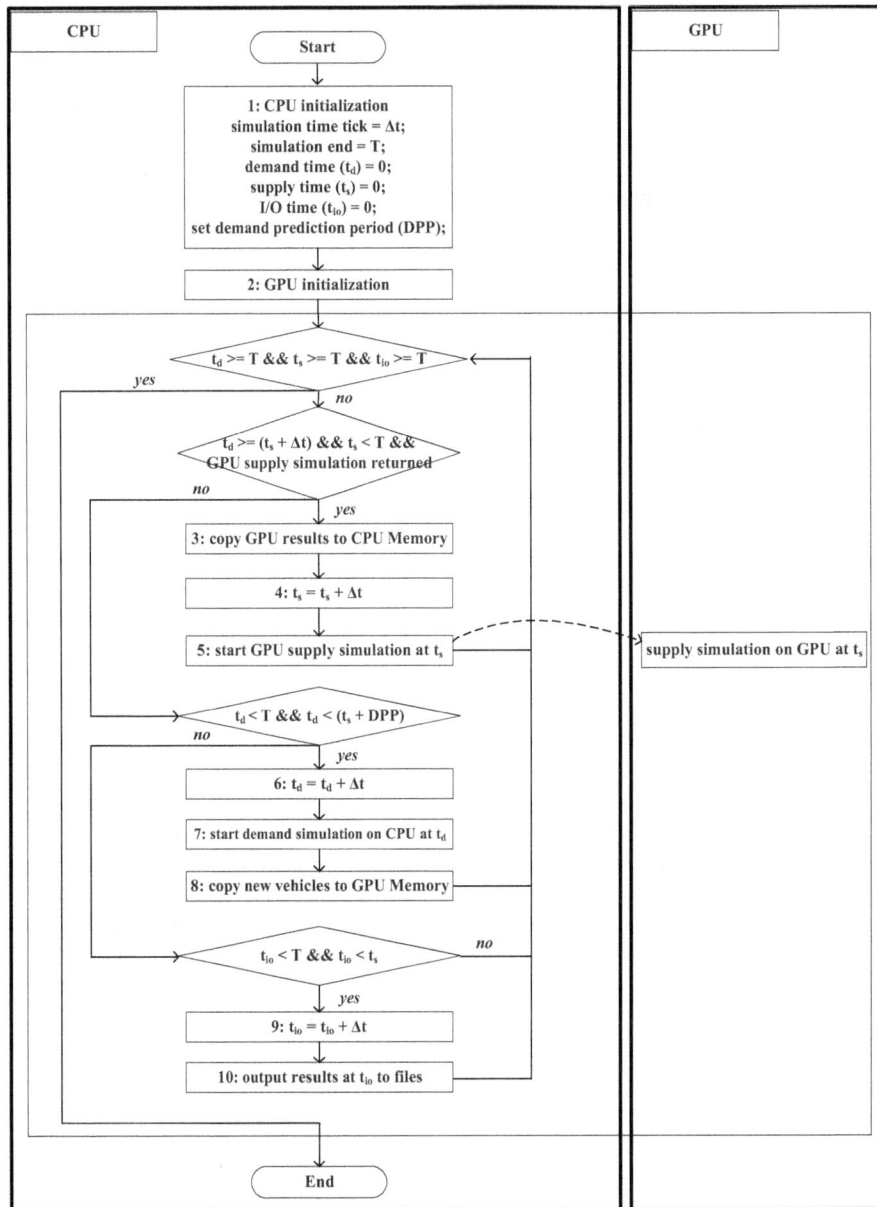

Figure 3. Mesoscopic Traffic Simulation Framework on CPU-GPU

involves a concept in traffic simulation: demand prediction period (DPP). Vehicles generated at time t requires the simulated results at $t - DPP$, for departure time choices and route choices. The minimum value of DPP is 1, which means vehicles have real-time instantaneous information about the global traffic status in last time step (e.g. 1 second). However, DPP tends to be larger in real-world traffic systems (e.g. 15 minutes).

In the logic procedure in Figure 3, step 1 and 2 initialize the required data structures on the CPU and the GPU, including the road network, traffic scenario configurations and other parameters. After initialization, the CPU controls the simulation logic, in order to manage the simulation time and also to make full use of computational resources. Without breaking the three rules in time management, the following tasks can be executed in parallel:

❖ Task 1: The supply simulation at time t_s on GPU (step 3-5).

❖ Task 2: The demand simulation at time t_d on CPU (step 6-8).

❖ Task 3: Push simulation results at time t_{io} to files (step 9-10).

Within a loop of the logic procedure, the CPU firstly checks whether the GPU has finished the supply simulation at time t_s. If yes, the simulation results on the GPU (e.g. road-based speed and density) are copied to the CPU and the supply time t_s is advanced. Then, the supply simulation at next time step is started on the GPU. Note that the CPU will not wait for the GPU supply simulation to finish. If the supply simulation on the GPU is ongoing, the CPU checks whether the demand simulation can be started. If the simulation results required for demand simulation are available, the demand simulation will be started on the CPU. Otherwise, the CPU checks whether there are available simulation results that need to be written into files. The CPU will continue the loop until the three time t_s, t_d and t_{io} are all reaching the simulation end. The logic of the supply simulation and the demand simulation are explained in [1, 16].

Road Network

vector<Link*>
vector<Node*>

Link

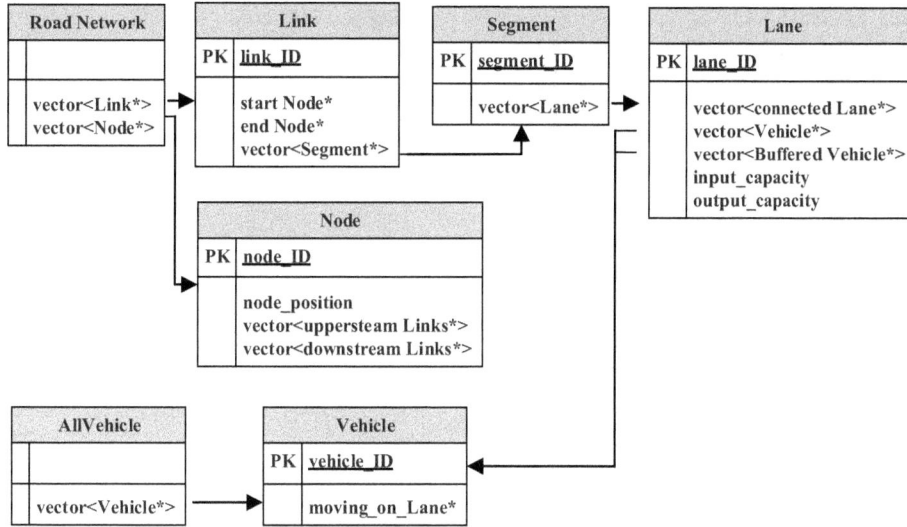

PK	link_ID
	start Node*
	end Node*
	vector<Segment*>

Segment

PK	segment_ID
	vector<Lane*>

Lane

PK	lane_ID
	vector<connected Lane*>
	vector<Vehicle*>
	vector<Buffered Vehicle*>
	input_capacity
	output_capacity

Node

PK	node_ID
	node_position
	vector<uppersteam Links*>
	vector<downstream Links*>

AllVehicle

vector<Vehicle*>

Vehicle

PK	vehicle_ID
	moving_on_Lane*

(A) Road network and vehicle modeling on the CPU

Link on GPU

PK	link_Index
	start_node_index
	end_node_index
	segment_index[]
	link_ID

Segment on GPU

PK	segment_Index
	lane_index[]
	segment_ID

Road Network on GPU

Link[LINK_SIZE]
Node[NODE_SZIE]
Segment[SEGMENT_SIZE]
Lane[LANE_SIZE]

Node on GPU

PK	node_Index
	node_position
	uppersteam_link_Index[]
	downstream_link_Index[]
	node_ID

Lane on GPU

PK	lane_Index
	connected_lane_Index[]
	vehicles_index[]
	buffered_vehicles_index[]
	lane_ID
	input_capacity
	output_capacity

Vehicles on GPU

Vehicle[]

Vehicle on GPU

PK	vehicle_Index
	move_on_lane_index
	vehicle_ID

(B) Road network and vehicle modeling on the GPU

Figure 4. Key differences in road network and vehicle modeling on the CPU and the GPU

3.2 Road Network and Vehicle Modeling on the GPU

Figure 4 (A) shows the road network and vehicle modeling on the CPU memory. A road network is composed of a list of links and a list of nodes. Each link consists of a number of segments and each node consists of a list of upstream links and downstream links. Each segment consists of multiple lanes and each lane contains a number of lane connections. Vehicles are moving on lanes or segments. Figure 4 (B) shows a similar road network and vehicle modeling on the GPU memory. Note that the purpose is to show the difference of network modeling between CPU memory and GPU memory. Figure 4 contains only a portion of network-related parameters.

There are two key differences between the road network modeling in the CPU memory and the GPU memory. **First**, on the CPU memory, the large number of road elements and vehicles are stored in random separated memory spaces and the objects are connecting with each other using *pointers* (or memory addresses). While on the GPU memory, these elements are kept in *arrays* in a continuous memory space and different elements are connecting each other using the *index* inside the *array*. The reasons of doing this on the GPU memory include making it easy to copy the entire road network from the CPU memory to the GPU memory and more importantly to allow efficient *coalesced memory access*, which means GPU threads in a warp tend to access continuous memory space. **Second**, on the CPU memory, dynamic memory allocation (e.g. std::vector) is widely used in the data structure of a road network and vehicles, because of its flexibility and efficiency. However, on the GPU memory, dynamic memory allocation (e.g. std::vector) has to be replaced by fixed memory allocation (e.g. array). It is a limitation of GPU programming, because it is not efficient to dynamically malloc and release GPU memory in kernel/device functions. It generates some memory issues. For example, as shown in Figure 4 (B), each lane has an array named

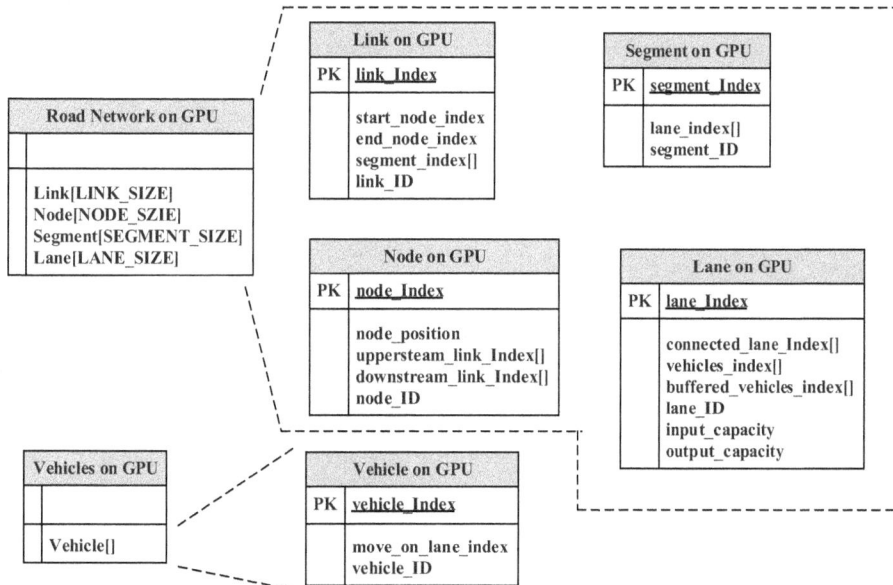

"vehicle_index", which contains the index of all vehicles located on the lane. The size of the array is the maximum number of vehicles the lane has space for. The memory space for the array is mandatory, even if there is no vehicle moving on the lane during the traffic scenario.

3.3 Kernel Functions on the GPU

There are four kernel functions in supply simulation on the GPU:

❖ Kernel function 1: *check_entrip_route_choice*
❖ Kernel function 2: *pre_vehicle_passing*
❖ Kernel function 3: *vehicle_passing*
❖ Kernel function 4: *copy_simulation_results_to_cpu*

The first kernel function identifies vehicles that require en-trip route choices, because of immerging traffic conditions (e.g. traffic congestions). The update unit of this kernel function is a vehicle, which means each individual vehicle is updated using a GPU thread. If a vehicle decides to change its route, it sets an attribute "entrip_route_choice" to be true. En-trip route changing behavior is simulated on the CPU and then the new routes are copied back to the GPU. As explained in Section 3.2, the attribute of all vehicles are kept in a continuous memory space, in order to minimize the communication cost between the CPU and the GPU. The first kernel function involves the CPU program to update the routes, thus, it is costly. There are three methods to reduce the cost. Firstly, if the en-trip route choice behavior is not required in the traffic scenario, this kernel function can be disabled. Second, in most traffic scenarios, there is no need to check en-trip route choice at each time step. Third, if a vehicle's route changing decision does not immediately change his status in the next time, the GPU does not need to wait for the end of this kernel function.

The second kernel function updates the status of each road (e.g. density, speed and t_p), before passing vehicles to the downstream roads. The update unit of this kernel function is a road (e.g. a lane), which means each individual road is simulated on a GPU thread. This kernel function firstly inserts vehicles, which passed to this road at the previous time, into the road. After that, it loads new generated vehicles into the road. Then, the kernel function calculates speed of the road based on a speed density relationship. After that, it calculates the *entry_time_to_pass*. The calculation algorithms are explained in [16].

The third kernel function scans vehicles on the road and passes some vehicles to the downstream roads. If a vehicle is moved from the current road to a downstream road, the corresponding output capacity, input capacity and empty space should be updated. The index of the vehicle should be removed from the current road and inserted to the target road since vehicles from links, which have the same end node, might conflict each other, if they are moving to the same downstream link. Each node, including its upper stream links, is considered as a basic process unit and is updated in a separate GPU thread. One example is shown in Figure 5. In this small road network, node 1 has two upstream links: link 1 and link 4. Thus, vehicles on link 1 and link 4 are processed on the same GPU thread, to remove the potential conflicts. On the other hand, since each link has only one upstream node, from where vehicles might pass through, there is also no conflicts when updating nodes in massive parallel. After passing vehicles to downstream roads, this kernel function updates the queue length, t_q and empty

space of each road. The calculation of queue length is also explained in [16].

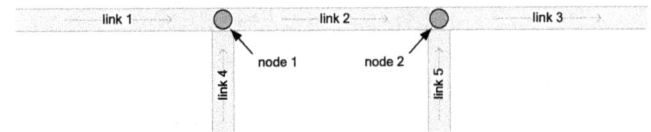

Figure 5. Each node and its upstream links are updated on the same GPU thread

The last kernel function copies the simulated results, which include speed, density, flow, queue length and empty space of each road, from the GPU memory to the CPU memory. As shown in Figure 4(B), these data are stored in a contiguous GPU memory space, in order to reduce the time cost of data transfer from the GPU memory to the CPU memory.

3.4 Incident Simulation

Incident simulation captures the impact of traffic incidents on the road capacity and traveler's response during a period, and predicts future traffic conditions, by simulating the interaction between the changed traffic demand and the reduced traffic supply. Incident simulation is critical for simulation-based traffic planning and simulation-based traffic management. In this framework, an incident is characterized by the ID of the affected road, incident start time and end time and a capacity reduction factor (e.g. 40%) on the road [4].

When simulating a traffic incident on CPU/GPU, the CPU reads the incident information from offline files (for offline traffic planning) or real-time data channel (for online traffic prediction). When the supply simulation time t_s reaches the incident start time, the CPU reduces the capacity reduction factor of the corresponding roads and then updates the road capacity in the GPU memory before starting the traffic simulation on the GPU at the next time step. When the supply simulation time t_s reaches the incident end time, the CPU recovers the road capacity and then updates the original capacity in the GPU memory.

During an incident period, vehicles moving on the road network might change their routes, based on their perceived traffic information. The drivers' intention to change routes is simulated in the first kernel function. If a vehicle decides to change its route, the new route is calculated on the CPU. Note that the current design involves additional data copy between the CPU and the GPU, which is time costly in current NVIDIA architectures [10]. However, the cost will be reduced in future architectures when the CPU and the GPU share the same memory space. Compared to en-trip route choice, pre-trip user behaviors are more efficient. The CPU is responsible to choose the updated departure time and the updated routes for drivers, taking into consideration the incident simulation results from the GPU. There is no additional data copy between the CPU and the GPU.

4. CORRECTNESS

The purpose of running mesoscopic supply simulation on the GPU is to boost its massive computational power. However, it is critical to guarantee that the supply simulation on GPU gives the same results as the supply simulation on CPU, or at least the difference is acceptable.

4.1 Problem Definition

A challenging problem is that mesoscopic traffic simulations in a road network cannot be naturally spatially divided into multiple independent traffic simulations in a large number of sub-networks, because of *upstream downstream dependence* when vehicles cross the boundaries of sub-networks. An example is shown in Figure 6. When a vehicle crosses from link 1 to link 2, there are three conditions to check:

1.   Whether there is available output capacity at link 1.
2.   Whether there is available input capacity at link 2.
3.   Whether there is enough empty space at link 2.

As explained in the third kernel function in Section 3.3, each individual node and its upstream links are simulated on a GPU thread. Before starting a supply traffic simulation on the GPU, the pre-configured input capacity and output capacity of links are available. Besides, the input capacity of each link is updated by only 1 node (or 1 GPU thread). It means the capacity of links does not cause problems when running mesoscopic traffic simulations on the GPU. However, the empty spaces at downstream links depend on the traffic movement of downstream links. The requirement to know the empty space of the downstream links when simulating traffic movement in the upstream links is defined as *upstream downstream dependence*. When running mesoscopic traffic simulations in a sequential way, *upstream downstream dependence* is complied by ordering the links from downstream to upstream. For this example in Figure 6, it means that in the mesoscopic supply simulation, traffic movement on link 2 is simulated before traffic movement on link 1. If there is a road circle in the road network, the road circle can be break at a random node. However, when a mesoscopic supply simulation is spatially divided into multiple traffic simulations in a number of sub-networks, it is a challenge to comply with all *upstream downstream dependencies*.

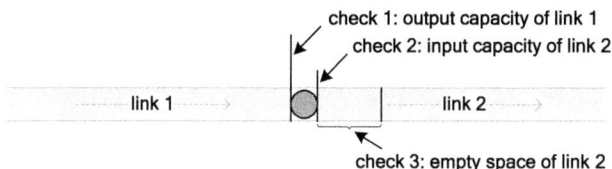

Figure 6. An example upstream downstream dependence in mesoscopic traffic simulations

When perfect knowledge of the empty space in a downstream road is not available, the upstream link has to move vehicles based on its best estimate. This could lead to two types of unrealistic vehicle movements [2]:

Pessimistic biased movement: If vehicles' movement in an upstream links is based on overly conservative estimate of the downstream empty space, when empty space of downstream link at time t is estimated to be the empty space of that link at the end of t-1, vehicles might move slower than the sequential simulation. For example, if a downstream link is blocked at time t-1, an upstream link may assume that the downstream link will be still blocked at time t, which might be wrong. It will force upstream vehicles to stay on the upstream link.

Optimistic biased movement: An upstream link could over-estimate the empty space available at a downstream link. For instance, it may optimistically assume a downstream link always has enough empty space for vehicles. In this case, the simulator may fail to capture exactly the same queuing and spill-backs from the sequential traffic simulation.

Moving vehicles on upstream links based on estimated empty spaces on downstream links in parallel might generate simulation errors (compared to a sequential traffic simulation), when simulating congested traffic scenarios. In free-flow traffic scenarios, the empty spaces of most links are large and the speeds on roads are high. Thus, empty spaces are less likely to be a limitation for vehicles on upstream links to cross. In this case, optimistic vehicle movement can get almost the same results with the sequential simulation. However, in congested traffic scenarios, the empty spaces of links can be small (or even zero). It becomes critical to have an accurate estimation of empty spaces in downstream links, in order to decide whether or not to pass a vehicle.

4.2 Boundary Processing Method for Massive Parallelism on the GPU

The concept of boundary processing has been previously used in spatial parallel traffic simulations [2]. The boundary area means a portion of a road network which connects the traffic flow from different road partitions. In most cases, traffic movement in a boundary area requires a different procedure compared with traffic movement on a normal road. In this paper, when running traffic supply simulation on the GPU and each node of a road network is simulated on a separate GPU thread, the boundary area is in fact the global road network.

The purpose of the boundary processing method is to support an accurate estimation of empty spaces in downstream links, before moving vehicles to cross links. Thus, the simulation results from a massive parallel traffic simulation on the GPU are similar to the sequential simulation. As shown in formula 1, the update of an empty space on a road at a time step t (ES(t)) depends on three variables: the empty space of the road at the previous time step t-1, the speed of the road at time t ($v(t)$) and the queue length of the road at t ($q(t)$).

$$ES(t) = \min\{ES(t\text{-}1) + v(t) \,,\, RL - q(t)\} \qquad (1)$$

Where, RL is the length of the road, $ES(t\text{-}1) + v(t)$ reflects the traffic movement on the road and $RL - q(t)$ reflects the feedback of the queue on the road.

The proposed boundary processing method consists of two steps. First, an additional synchronization (or a barrier) is inserted between speed calculation and vehicle movement. It does not affect the simulation results. Since empty spaces are calculated in the phase of vehicle movement, the speed of all roads turns to be available before empty space calculation. As explained in Section 3.3, the speed calculation happens in the second kernel function and the empty space calculation happens in the third kernel function. These two operations are naturally separated. Thus, the synchronization does not bring additional cost to the framework. Besides, when this paper is written, the time cost to switch between different kernel functions on the GPU is trivial. Second, the queue length of each road in the current time t is predicted before empty space calculation using formula 2.

$$q(t) = \max\{q(t\text{-}1) + a * (q(t\text{-}1) - q(t\text{-}2)), RL\} \qquad (2)$$

Where RL is the length of the road, $(q(t\text{-}1) - q(t\text{-}2))$ reflects the short-term trend of the queue length and a is a parameter, which indicates how much the predicted queue length depends on the short-term trend.

4.3 Evaluation

This section evaluates the efficiency of the boundary processing method. As shown in Figure 7(A), a grid road network is used in this section. There are 121 nodes and 220 unidirectional links in the road network. The length of each link is 1000 meters. Each node has an ID, from 0 to 120. For example, the nodes in the first (top) row have IDs from 0 to 10. Vehicles are loaded into the road network from nodes in the top and the left, which are moving to the bottom and the right. When a vehicle is loaded into the road network, the vehicle randomly chooses a route from pre-calculated candidate routes. Vehicles on the same road are moving using the same speed, which is calculated using a linear speed-density relationship [16]. 50,000 vehicles are loaded into the road network within an hour. As the traffic simulation is on-going, the road densities in the bottom right corner turns to be higher than the road densities in the top left corner. The basic simulation time step is 1 second, which means the system status is updated every 1 second and there are 3600 simulation ticks in this traffic scenario. Speed, density, flow, queue length and empty space of each link at each time are outputted to files as the simulation results.

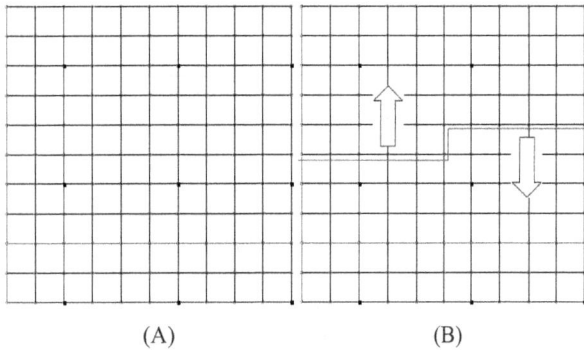

(A)   (B)

Figure 7. (A) a grid road network with 121 nodes and 220 unidirectional links; (B) the grid road network is divided into two partitions, running on 2 threads.

In a sequential traffic simulation, nodes (and the upstream links) are updated in order (from downstream to upper stream). For example, nodes in the bottom-right corner are updated before nodes in the top-left corner. All *upstream downstream dependencies* are followed in a sequential traffic simulation. Comparatively, the grid network will be divided into a number of sub-networks in a parallel traffic simulation. As shown in Figure 7 (B), the grid road network is divided into two partitions. Nodes in each individual partition are updated in order, to follow the *upstream downstream dependencies* within the partition. But there is no guarantee of the *upstream downstream dependencies* between these two partitions. For the vehicle movement in upstream links nearby the boundary, this section evaluates two methods: the pessimistic biased movement and the proposed boundary processing method. Since the traffic scenario is congested, the optimistic biased movement is not suitable. The simulation results (road-based speeds and densities) are compared with the sequential traffic simulation to measure the correctness at each simulation time tick. The performance indicator is the Normalized Root Mean Square error (RMSN), which measures the proportional difference between two vectors [4].

$$RMSN = \frac{\sqrt{N * \sum_{i=1}^{N}(s_i - p_i)^2}}{\sum_{i=1}^{N} s_i} \qquad (3)$$

Where, N is the length of vectors, S_i is a simulation result of the sequential traffic simulation and p_i is a simulation result of the parallel traffic simulation.

The results (simulation correctness) are shown in Figure 8. Figure 8(A) shows the speed and density simulation error using pessimistic biased movement when the simulation is divided into 2 partitions. As shown in Figure 7(B), the boundary area is in the middle of the road network. It is a surprise to see the simulation results of the parallel traffic simulation using pessimistic biased movement are exactly the same with the sequential traffic simulation before the 2800 tick, even though it is using inaccurate empty spaces. We found that in this traffic scenario, congestion starts in the bottom area and gradually spills back to the middle area of the road network. It indicates the pessimistic biased movement might give an acceptable correctness when parallel traffic simulations are run on a small number of partitions and there are no traffic congestions around the boundary area. When traffic congestion spills back to the boundary area, a maximum 2.9% speed error and a maximum 0.4% flow error are observed in this case study. Figure 8(B) shows the speed and density simulation error using pessimistic biased movement when the simulation is divided into 121 partitions, which is the case to run the mesoscopic supply simulation on the GPU. The simulation error using pessimistic biased movement happens when congestion starts in the bottom area and grows fast when the congestion spills back to the middle of the road network. Finally, a maximum 36.0% speed error and a maximum 8.6% flow error are observed in this case study. It means that the pessimistic biased movement gives an unacceptable correctness when running congested traffic scenarios on the GPU in a massive parallel way. On the other side, for these two cases, the proposed boundary processing method gets exactly the same simulation results with the sequential traffic simulation, or the speed error and the flow error during the whole simulation period are 0%.

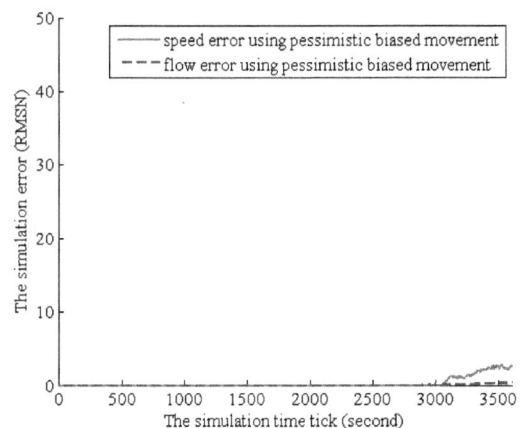

(A)

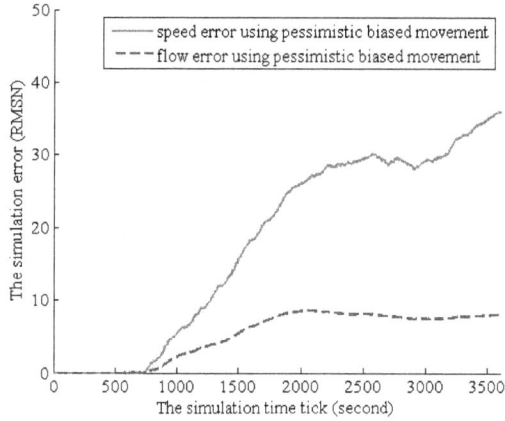

(B)

Figure 8. (A) The speed and density simulation error when divided into 2 partitions using pessimistic biased movement. (B) The speed and density simulation error when divided into 121 partitions using pessimistic biased movement. (Note: there is no speed and density simulation error in A and B when using the proposed boundary processing method)

Even though the experiment results prove the efficiency of the proposed boundary processing method, there are two limitations. First, the quantitative results from this experiment (e.g. 2.9% and 36%) are not significant and it is difficult to directly generalize the quantitative results to other mesoscopic traffic simulations on other road networks. The road network topology and the behavior models (e.g. the speed-density relationship) in mesoscopic traffic simulations might change experiment results. Second, there is no theoretical guarantee for the proposed boundary processing method to always get the same results with the sequential traffic simulation, because the predicted queue length might be wrong in the boundary processing method.

5. Double-Buffer Data Channel on the GPU

The process of copying simulation results from the GPU memory to the CPU memory at each time step (step 3 in Figure 2) is time costly in CPU/GPU. As shown in Figure 9, a double-buffer data channel is designed on the GPU to minimize the data communication cost. There are two optimizations in the double-buffer data channel. Firstly, the frequency to copy simulation results from the GPU memory to the CPU memory is reduced. For example, in this case, each buffer can keep simulation results of up to 8 time steps (known as "*buffer size*"). When the buffer is full, the supply simulation on the GPU starts to write simulation results to the other buffer space. At the same time, the simulation results in the buffer are copied to the CPU memory in one time step. Secondly, the data transfer from the GPU to the CPU is done asynchronously. It means the supply simulation on the GPU does not wait for the data transfer to finish. However, the double-buffer data channel brings two additional rules in time management.

❖ Time management rule 4: *buffer size* <= DPP
❖ Time management rule 5: $t_s < t_{io} + 2 *$ *buffer size*

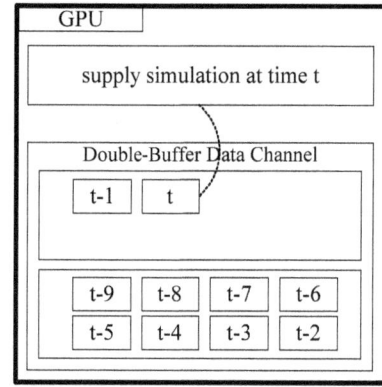

Figure 9. An example double-buffer data channel on GPU (the buffer size is 8)

If the buffer size is larger than the demand prediction period (DPP), there will be a deadlock in time management. The buffer is waiting for additional supply simulation results before transfer its data to the CPU. At the same time, the demand simulation on the CPU is waiting for the simulation results from the GPU to generate future vehicles and the supply simulation on the GPU is blocked because of the lack of new vehicles. The mutual waiting between the three components is a deadlock. The suggested *buffer size* should be much smaller than DPP. In this paper, DPP is 15 minutes and *buffer size* is 1 minute (or 60). Besides, rule 5 says the supply simulation on the GPU cannot write simulation results to a buffer, if the data in the buffer has not been transferred to the CPU. It means a slow data transfer or I/O will finally force the supply simulation on the GPU to stop and wait.

6. Experiments

In this section, the proposed mesoscopic traffic simulation framework on CPU/GPU is implemented and evaluated to simulate a large-scale traffic scenario. This section focuses on the performance comparison of the supply simulation on the CPU and the GPU.

6.1 Testbed

An artificial large grid road network, which is similar to the road network in Figure 7(A), is used as the testbed, with 10201 nodes and 20200 unidirectional links. Each node has an index from 0 to 10200, indicating the store location on the GPU memory. Each link also has an index from 0 to 20199. 100,000 vehicles are loaded into the road network during 1000 simulation ticks (each tick is 1 second). Same with the experiment configuration in Section 4.3, vehicles are loaded into the road network from nodes in the top and the left, which are moving to the bottom and the right. Each vehicle randomly picks a route from the pre-calculated candidate routes before starting a trip. En-trip route choice is not included in this traffic scenario.

The traffic scenario is simulated on two types of platforms: the CPU and CPU/GPU. Only the total time cost of the supply simulation during the 1000 simulation ticks is measured in this experiment. The CPU platform includes an Intel E5-2620, 32 GB main memory and a 500GB SATA 7.2K RPM. The GPU platform is a GeForce GT 650M, which has 384 CUDA cores and 2 GB global memory. The supply simulations on the CPU and the GPU follow the same logic. The source codes are both implemented using C++ on Ubuntu 12.04 and compiled using g++_4.6.3 and CUDA 5.5. The release version executable file is used to measure the time cost.

6.2 Results and Analysis

The experiment results are shown in Table I. The time cost column shows the average time cost of 5 different measurements of each configuration. The speedup is measured by comparing the time cost of supply simulation on a GPU to the time cost of supply simulation on a CPU core. In the first configuration, executing the supply simulation on a CPU core takes 4720.88 ms to finish the traffic scenario. In the second configuration, directly executing the proposed supply simulation on a GPU takes 704.72 ms to finish the same traffic scenario, which means the speedup is 6.7. The performance is sensitive to the configuration of the kernel functions. When the number of threads in a block is 192, the maximum performance is achieved. In the third configuration, the double-buffer data channel on the GPU is enabled to allow asynchronous data transfer between the CPU and the GPU. We found that the double-buffer data channel is efficient and the data transfer cost is almost hidden by the supply simulation on the GPU. The total time cost is reduced by 35% and the speedup is significantly improved from 6.7 to 10.3. Besides, we found that the registers are not efficiently used in the third configuration. In the fourth configuration, internal variables, which will not be used by other kernel functions and not transferred to the CPU, are moved from the global memory to the registers. The speedup is slightly improved from 10.3 to 10.7. Finally, there are parameters which are never changed during the traffic simulation, such as the simulation end time and settings in the speed-density relationship. In the fifth configuration, constant parameters are moved from the global memory to the constant memory for efficient memory access. The speedup is slightly improved from 10.7 to 11.2.

Table I: the time cost of running a traffic supply simulation on the CPU and the GPU

Case ID	Configuration Description	Time Cost (ms)	Speedup
1	Supply simulation on a CPU core	4720.88	1.0
2	Supply simulation on a GPU	704.72	6.7
3	Case 2 + Double-buffer data channel optimization on the GPU	457.29	10.3
4	Case 3 + Push internal variables from the global memory to the registers	439.29	10.7
5	Case 4 + Push constant parameters from the global memory to the constant memory	423.37	11.2

Table II shows major profiling measurements of two major kernel functions in the framework: *pre_vehicle_passing* and *vehicle_passing*. First, the processing unit in the first and the second kernel function are a road and a node. In this experiment, the two kernel functions launched 20200 GPU threads and 10201 GPU threads. The occupancies of these two kernel functions are high, which indicates the GPU cores are fully utilized. Though internal variables are moved from the global memory to the registers, registers are still not a bottleneck. Second, as explained in Section 3.2, the network data and vehicle data are stored into a contiguous memory space. Thus, threads in a warp tend to access a contiguous memory space, which is also known as *coalesced memory access*. As shown in the table, the number of memory transaction per request (both load and store) for these two kernel functions are small, which

indicates the memory load and store is efficient. Third, the branch taken ratio (within threads in the same warp) for the first kernel function is 72%. Threads in the first kernel function do not take exactly the same branch, because different roads have different number of new vehicles and different number of passed vehicles. The branch taken ratio for the second kernel function is much lower (41.7%). It is expected, because in the second kernel function there are many for-loops in the logic of finding and passing vehicles to downstream roads. The number of upstream links and the number of vehicles on nodes are different. However, there is no much branch divergence in these two kernel functions. The instruction serialization ratio of these two kernel functions are 15.5% and 18.6%. It means that the low branch taken ratio is not a big problem in this framework. Fourth, the numbers of instruction per clock (IPC) for the two kernel functions are 0.9 and 1.0, which are far below the hardware's peak value (4.0). As shown below, the major reason for low issue efficiency is the execution dependency. Based on our knowledge of the framework, the major problem is that most data (e.g. the road network and vehicles) is stored in the global memory, which causes high memory latency. The high memory latency cannot be completely hidden by the large number of threads. Finally, the achieved GLOPS for the two kernel functions are also lower than the hardware's peak, which is also related with high global memory latency.

Table II: The profiling of major kernel functions in mesoscopic traffic simulations

	Parameters	pre_vehicle_passing	vehicle_passing
1	Launched GPU threads	20200	10201
2	GPU occupancy	81%	90%
3	Registers (used / available)	3072 / 65536	1920 / 65536
4	Transaction per request (load/store)	1.73/1.49	1.67/1.83
5	Branch taken ratio (%)	72.1%	41.7%
6	Instruction serialization	15.5%	18.6%
7	Instruction per clock (IPC) (measurement/ maximum)	0.9 / 4.0	1.0 / 4.0
8	Warp issue efficiency (no eligible %)	49.7%	36.1%
9	Issue Stall Reasons (execution dependency)	92.3%	88.4%
10	CUDA achieved GFLOPS	14.8	6.0

This paragraph discusses additional thoughts about running mesoscopic traffic simulations on CPU/GPU. First, it is beneficial to run the demand simulation on the CPU, the supply simulation on the GPU and the data communication between the CPU and the GPU in an asynchronous way. In this experiment, the supply simulation on GPU is the bottleneck and the time costs of the other two tasks are almost hidden. Second, this paper demonstrates a supply simulation framework (ETSF) on the GPU. Running the ETSF framework on the GPU gets a speedup of 11.2, compared with running the same logic on the CPU. However, when generalizing the conclusion to other supply simulation frameworks, it should be noted that ETSF naturally guarantees a good load balance on each road. In ETSF, the workload of a road is not sensitive to the number of vehicles on the road and the length of the road. This feature might do not exist in other supply simulation frameworks, in which case, load balance should be considered. Third, the memory access latency is a bottleneck in the proposed mesoscopic traffic simulation framework. In current mesoscopic supply simulation frameworks [1, 4, 5, 16], the update logic of a road majorly depends on its own road status (e.g. road density and queue status) and requires a small number of parameters from its downstream roads. There is few shared data access among nearby roads and nodes, which limits the usage of the efficient shared memory in the GPU. It is the major reason of high memory latency.

7. CONCLUSIONS AND FUTURE WORK

Mesoscopic traffic simulation is hungry for computational resources to support aggressive large-scale simulation-based traffic planning and simulation-based traffic management. The GPU has recently been a success, because of its massive performance compared to the CPU. Thus, a critical question is "whether the GPU can be a potential high-performance platform for future mesoscopic traffic simulations?" In this paper, we proposed a comprehensive mesoscopic traffic simulation framework on CPU/GPU. Then, we designed an innovative boundary processing method to guarantee the correctness of running massive parallel mesoscopic traffic simulations on the GPU. The proposed mesoscopic traffic simulation framework is evaluated to simulate a large-scale traffic scenario and gets a speedup of 11.2, compared with running the same logic on the CPU. Based on our view, the proposed mesoscopic traffic simulation framework on CPU/GPU provides an innovative and promising solution for high-performance mesoscopic traffic simulations.

Further research on the topic of mesoscopic traffic simulation on CPU/GPU includes two directions. First, the proposed mesoscopic traffic simulation framework needs to be evaluated to simulate a real-world large-scale traffic scenario. Second, the proposed mesoscopic traffic simulation framework needs to be improved to make better use of the shared memory in the GPU.

8. ACKNOWLEDGMENTS

The authors would like to thank Kakali Basak, Stephen Robinson, Lu Yang, Francisco Pereira and Harish Loganathan for their comments to this paper.

9. REFERENCES

[1] Barcelo J. (editor), "Fundamentals of Traffic Simulation", International Series in Operations Research & Management Science, 2010, Springer, New York.

[2] Yang W., "Scalability of Dynamic Traffic Assignment", Ph.D. thesis, Massachusetts Institute of Technology, 2009.

[3] Ben-Akiva, M., Gao, S., Wei, Z. and Yang, W., "A dynamic traffic assignment model for highly congested urban networks", Transportation Research Part C, 2012, 24: 62–82.

[4] Ben-Akiva, M., Bierlaire, M., Burton, D., Koutsopoulos, H. N., and Mishalani, R., "Network state estimation and prediction for real-time traffic management", Networks and Spatial Economics, 2001, 1(3/4):293-318.

[5] Mahmassani H.S., Hu T., and Jaykrishnan R., "Dynamic traffic assignment and simulation for advanced network informatics (DYNASMART)", Proceedings of the 2nd International Capri Seminar on Urban Traffic Networks, Capri, Italy, 1992.

[6] Ziliaskopoulos A. K., Waller S. T., Li Y., and Byram, M., "Large-scale dynamic traffic assignment: Implementation issues and computational analysis", Journal of Transportation Engineering, 2004, 130(5): 585-593.

[7] Gordon D. B. C. and Gordon I. D. D., "Paramics - Parallel Microscopic Simulation of Road Traffic". The Journal of Supercomputing, 1996, pp. 25-53.

[8] Çetin, N., "Large-scale parallel graph-based simulations", Ph.D. thesis, ETH Zurich, Switzerland, 2005.

[9] Aydt H., Yadong X., Michael L., and Alois K., "A Multi-threaded Execution Model for the Agent-Based SEMSim Traffic Simulation", Proceedings of AsiaSim 2013.

[10] Nvidia, "CUDA C Programming Guide", 2013, available at http://www.nvidia.com/CUDA.

[11] Michalakes J. and Vachharajani M., "GPU acceleration of numerical weather prediction", IPDPS 2008: IEEE Int'l Symp. Parallel and Distributed Processing, 2008.

[12] Buck I., "GPU computing with NVIDIA CUDA". In SIGGRAPH '07, New York, NY, USA, 2007.

[13] Fan, Z., Qiu, F., Kaufman, A., and Yoakum-Stover, S., "GPU cluster for high performance computing". In Proceedings of SC'04, 2004.

[14] Perumalla, K. S., Brandon G. A., Srikanth B. Y., and Sudip K. S., "GPU-based real-time execution of vehicular mobility models in large-scale road network scenarios", International Workshop on Principles of Advanced and Distributed Simulation, 2009.

[15] Strippgen, D. and Nagel, K., "Multi-agent traffic simulation with CUDA", Proceedings of International Conference on High Performance Computing & Simulation, Leipzig, 2009.

[16] Yan X., Xiao S., Zhiyong W. and Gary T., "An Entry Time based Supply Framework (ETSF) for Mesoscopic Traffic Simulations", submitted to Simulation Modelling Practice and Theory, 2014.

[17] Denis G., Jose-Juan T., Samuel A. and Roshan M. D. S., "Graphics processing unit based direct simulation Monte Carlo", Simulation: Transactions of the Society for Modeling and Simulation International, 2012, 88(6): 680-693.

[18] Brodtkorb A. R., Trond R. H. and Martin L. S., "Graphics processing unit (GPU) programming strategies and trends in GPU computing", Journal of Parallel and Distributed Computing, 2013, 73: 4-13.

[19] Perumalla, K. S., "Discrete Event Execution Alternatives on Gen-eral Purpose Graphical Processing Units (GPGPUs)", International Workshop on Principles of Advanced and Distributed Simulation, 2006.

[20] Passerat-Palmbach, J.; Mazel, C.; Hill, D. R C, "Pseudo-Random Number Generation on GP-GPU," International Workshop on Principles of Advanced and Distributed Simulation, 2011.

[21] Xiaosong L., Wentong C. and Stephen J. T., "GPU Accelerated Three-stage Execution Model for Event-parallel Simulation", International Workshop on Principles of Advanced and Distributed Simulation, 2013.

[22] Park H. and Fishwick P. A., "An analysis of queuing network simulation using GPU-based hardware acceleration", ACM Transactions on Modeling and Computer Simulation. 2011, 21(3).

Sim-Tree: Indexing Moving Objects in Large-Scale Parallel Microscopic Traffic Simulation*

Yan Xu and Gary Tan
Dept of Computer Science, School of Computing
National University of Singapore
Singapore 117417
xuyan.nus@gmail.com, gtan@comp.nus.edu.sg

ABSTRACT

Performance is one of the major concerns in large-scale parallel microscopic traffic simulations. This paper focuses on one of the most time-costly data structures: the two-dimensional spatial index. A drawback of using popular two-dimensional tree-based spatial indexes (e.g. the R*-Tree) in large-scale microscopic traffic simulation is the heavy cost to rebalance the tree structure when a large number of vehicles frequently update their locations. This heavy location update cost also reduces the scalability of parallel microscopic traffic simulations. We observe that in real-world traffic systems the road density during a short period is stable, which is not sensitive to an individual vehicle's location. Thus, why not build a balanced tree structure based on the average road density in a road network? Motivated by this observation, this paper proposes Sim-Tree. The key feature of the Sim-Tree is that there is no need to check or rebalance its tree structure when individual vehicles frequently update their locations. In addition, a rebalance function and a bottom-up region query function are designed to optimize Sim-Tree's region query operations. The results of experiments simulating a city-scale traffic scenario on a 6-core machine show that the Sim-Tree is scalable and performs significantly better than the R*-tree family of spatial indexes.

Keywords

Large-scale Microscopic Traffic Simulation; Two-dimensional Spatial Index; Frequent Location Updates; Scalability

1. INTRODUCTION

A typical microscopic traffic simulator [1, 2, 3] models the behavior of individual vehicles and the interaction between vehicles and road infrastructure, in order to allow users to interact with the complex traffic system (e.g. to simulate a "what-if" traffic scenario), without changing the real-world traffic system. Various national and local transportation agencies, academic institutions and consulting firms use traffic simulation to enhance their management of transportation networks. However, as the number of simulated vehicles increases and the size of the simulated road network grows in a traffic scenario, simulation of the scenario takes disproportionately longer to complete. Thus, the performance, which means the time to simulate a traffic scenario, has been one of the major concerns in the design and deployment of large-scale microscopic traffic simulations.

This paper focuses on one of the most time-costly data structures in large-scale parallel microscopic traffic simulation: the two-dimensional spatial index. A spatial index is a data structure that manages locations of objects (e.g. a vehicle, a pedestrian, etc.) in a simulated road network. The spatial index supports two functions: a region query function and a location update function. The region query function is used to get objects located in a region. The interface is "Objects *getObjectsInsideARegion* (a region)". For example, a vehicle can use the function to retrieve nearby objects (e.g. the front vehicle). The region query function is a fundamental function to support various traffic behavior models [4] to determine a vehicle's speed, acceleration and location. The location update function is used by a vehicle to update its new location in the spatial index, so that other vehicles can query this vehicle based on its new location. The interface is "void *updateLocation* (object_id, new_location)".

Based on the number of dimensions in objects' locations, the spatial index is classified into one-dimensional spatial indexes (e.g. linear referencing [8]) and two-dimensional spatial indexes. In one-dimensional spatial indexes, the location of an object is formulated as <segment_ID, lane_ID, offset>. Each object's location is associated with a segment. In two-dimensional spatial indexes, the location of an object is formulated as <latitude, longitude>, which does not depend on its underlying geometries. A one-dimensional spatial index is sufficient for traditional vehicles' car following models, lane changing models and gap acceptance models [4]. However, it has limited capability in more complex conditions, such as vehicles' cooperative driving [9], pedestrians' behaviors [10] and the interactions between objects on different roads. This paper focuses on two-dimensional spatial indexes to support various behavior models of different types of objects on different types of geometries (e.g. segments and intersections) in general-purpose microscopic traffic simulations. An example two-dimensional region query is shown in Figure 1.

An efficient two-dimensional spatial index is important for the performance of large-scale microscopic traffic simulation. First, the region query function is used by each vehicle at each simulation time step. For example, if the simulation time step (or the frequency of updating drivers' status) is 0.1 seconds, to simulate a traffic scenario with 100,000 vehicles for 60 minutes in a city, the region query function will be used 3.6 billion times in this scenario. A poorly-implemented region query function will check the 100,000 vehicles one by one to determine which vehicles are in the target region. Second, the location update function is also used by each vehicle at each simulation time step.

*This research was supported by the National Research Foundation Singapore through the Singapore MIT Alliance for Research and Technology's FM IRG research programme (sub contract R-252-001-459-592).

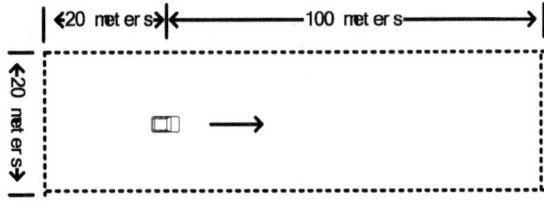

Figure 1: An example of a driver's region query using a two-dimensional spatial index (a plan view)

The tree-based spatial index [11, 12, 13] is a popular candidate solution to index moving objects in two-dimensional road networks. Figure 2(A) shows an example R*-tree based spatial index (the *fanout* is 3). Each node in the tree can have child nodes. Each leaf node is mapped to a two-dimensional area in the simulated road network and contains a list of objects located in this area. Each father node has a mapping area which contains all child nodes' mapping areas and has a pointer to the list of child nodes. With such a tree structure, to do a region query, we do not need to check all objects in the simulated road network. Instead, we only need to scan the tree structure to get leaf nodes whose mapping areas overlap the target region and then check only objects in these leaf nodes. In order to make region queries efficient, the tree structure should be balanced [11], which means that objects in the simulated road network are evenly distributed under leaf nodes of the tree structure.

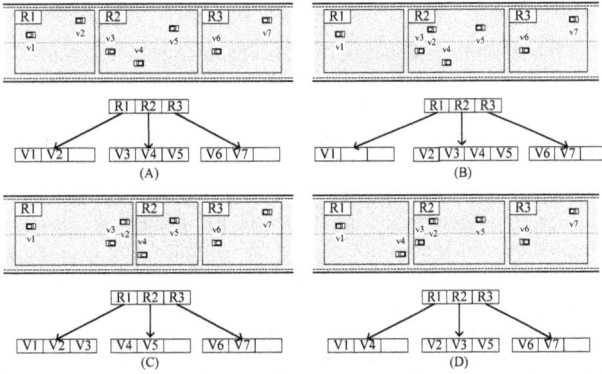

Figure 2: An example two-dimensional R*-tree based spatial index (the *fanout* is 3). (A) The tree structure is balanced; (B) The tree structure is unbalanced when v2 goes from R1 to R2; (C) The tree structure is rebalanced; (D) The tree structure is re-balanced again when v4 goes from R2 to R1.

A drawback of tree-based spatial index is that it may adjust (or rebalance) its tree structure when vehicles update locations. As shown in Figure 2, the example R*-tree is balanced in (A). But when a vehicle v2 moves from R1 to R2, the tree is not balanced any more in (B). A split operation is executed and half of the drivers are re-inserted. Besides, the mapping areas of R1 and R2 also change. The rebalanced tree structure is shown in (C). When a vehicle v4 moves from R2 to R1, another rebalance operation is executed. The rebalanced tree structure is shown in (D). Rebalancing the tree structure aims to guarantee that future region queries are efficient. However, in large-scale microscopic traffic simulation, thousands (or even millions) of vehicles are updating their locations at each simulation time step, making the time cost to update vehicles' locations and to adjust the tree structure expensive. So, the question is "is there a way to build an efficient two-dimensional tree-based spatial index without incurring

expensive location update cost (including the rebalance cost) in a large-scale microscopic traffic simulation?"

There is another reason that makes this question important. Parallel microscopic traffic simulation is becoming popular to support simulating large-scale traffic scenarios. The main idea of parallel microscopic traffic simulation [5, 6] is to assign vehicles to cores (or CPUs), and then vehicles can be simulated in parallel. However, it is not trivial to parallelize the location update function, because parallel location updates may conflict with each other when adjusting the tree structure. Thus, the expensive time cost of the location update function in two-dimensional tree-based spatial index also affects the scalability of parallel microscopic traffic simulation.

This paper proposes Sim-Tree, a novel two-dimensional tree-based spatial index which greatly reduces the time cost of location update operations and improves the scalability of large-scale parallel microscopic traffic simulations. The contributions of this paper are listed below:

1. This paper introduces four observations in real-world traffic systems and traffic simulations (Section 2), which imply special requirements of a two-dimensional spatial index in large-scale parallel microscopic traffic simulation.

2. Motivated by the observations, this paper proposes Sim-Tree (Section 4). The key feature of Sim-Tree is that its tree structure is build based on the average road density in the traffic scenario, thus there is no need to check or rebalance its tree structure when individual vehicles frequently update their locations. The results of experiments simulating a city-scale traffic scenario on a 6-core machine (Section 8) show that Sim-Tree is scalable and performs significantly better than the popular R*-Tree [12] and the LUR-tree [14].

3. A rebalance function (Section 5) and a bottom-up region query function (Section 6) are designed in Sim-Tree, to reduce the time cost of the region query function.

2. OBSERVATIONS AND MOTIVATIONS

This section introduces four observations in real-world traffic systems and traffic simulations. These observations imply special requirements of a two-dimensional spatial index in large-scale parallel microscopic traffic simulation. They are also the motivation to design a new tree-based spatial index.

Observation 1: During a short period (e.g. 5 minutes) and a reasonably large area (e.g. a 100 meter road), the number of vehicles in the area is stable.

For example, Figure 3(A) shows the distribution of the number of vehicles (per second) in 5 minutes on a 100 meter section of a real-world 4-lane road on the Ayer Rajah Expressway in Singapore. The average number of vehicle in the 5 minutes is 15.8 and the standard deviation is 2.85. 94% of the numbers of vehicles in the 5 minutes are in [10, 20]. Figure 3(B) shows the trend of the number of vehicles in the 5 minutes on the section. You can see that whenever the number of vehicles departs from the average number of vehicles during the period, the number of vehicles will inadvertently return to the average number of vehicles.

The traffic flow theory gives another explanation. The number of drivers in an area is determined by the drivers' demand on the area and the supply capacity of the area. During peak hours, the drivers' demand on the area is high, so the expected number of vehicles in the area is high. If an incident happens in the area, the supply capacity of the area is reduced, so traffic congestion might happen and the expected number of vehicles in the area is also high. If both the drivers' demand on the area and the supply capacity of the area are not changed, during a short period and a reasonable large area, the expected number of vehicles in the area is stable.

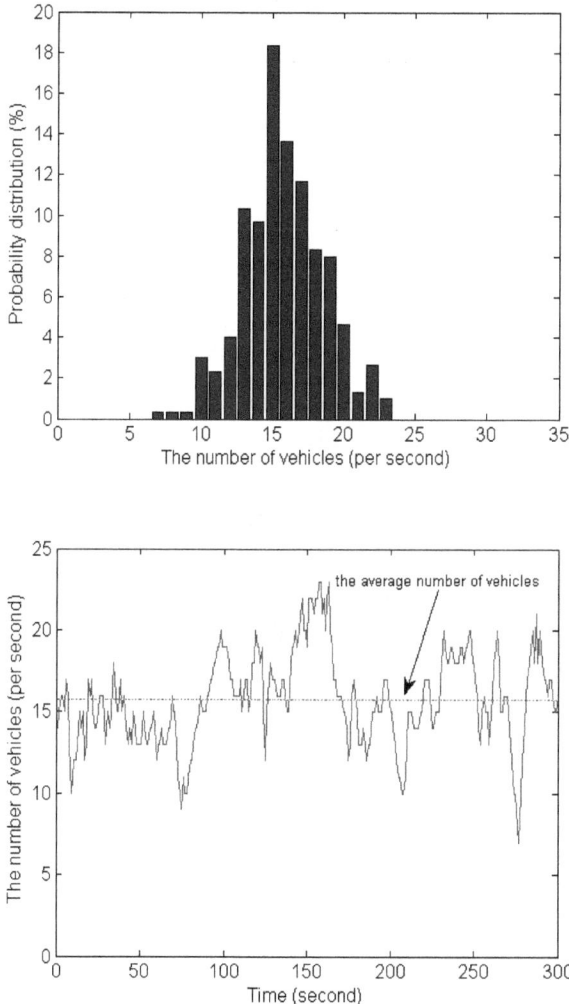

Figure 3: (Top) the distribution of the number of vehicles (per second) in 5 minutes on a 100 meter section of a real-world 4-lane road on the Ayer Rajah Expressway in Singapore. (Bottom) the trend of the number of vehicles (per second) in the 5 minutes on the section.

This observation means that if a balanced tree structure of a spatial index is built based on the average road density in a road network during a period, the tree structure tends to be balanced at each simulation time step within the period. More importantly, since the road density in a road network is not sensitive to an individual vehicle's location, there is no need to check or rebalance the tree when individual vehicles update their locations. "Building a balanced (and stable) two-dimensional spatial index based on the average road density in a road network during a period" is the main idea of this paper.

Observation 2: The region query function and the location update function are used separately in a simulation time step in microscopic traffic simulations.

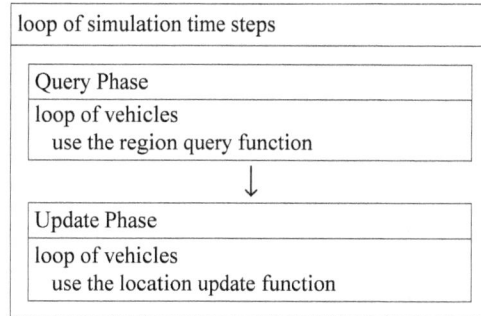

Figure 4: The region query function and the location update function in microscopic traffic simulations.

As shown in Figure 4, there are two phases in a simulation time step in microscopic traffic simulations. In the query phase, vehicles use the region query function to get nearby objects and determine speeds, accelerations and locations. When all vehicles complete the region query function, the traffic simulation goes to the update phase. In the update phase, vehicles use the location update function to update their new locations in the spatial index. When all vehicles complete the location update function, the traffic simulation goes to the next simulation time step.

This observation implies two things. First, there are no location updates in the query phase. Thus, if a tree structure is balanced in the beginning of the query phase, all region queries in the query phase are efficient. Second, there are no region queries in the update phase. Thus, an unbalanced tree structure is acceptable in the update phase. In summary, we only need to check and rebalance (if required) the tree structure once at the beginning of each simulation time step.

Observation 3: Drivers are configured to use the same-sized rectangles in the region query function.

As shown in Figure 1, a driver queries its nearby objects in a two-dimensional region (in this paper, it is a rectangle). The shape of the region depends on the requirement of traffic behavior models [4]. In microscopic traffic simulations, the shape reflects the view of drivers' surrounding traffic. In this particular example, the configuration means that a vehicle can see 100 meters in front, 20 meters behind, 10 meters to the left and 10 meters to the right. The size of the region is small compared to the road network. Besides, the shape of the region does not change after starting a traffic simulation. This observation suggests optimizing this particular type of region queries. Note that this paper focuses on vehicles. However, pedestrians are another critical component in microscopic traffic simulations. If the cost of region query by pedestrians is significant, the size of rectangle used by pedestrians should also be considered in the design of Sim-Tree, which is explained in Section 4.1.

Observation 4: The region query function can be efficiently parallelized in a parallel traffic simulation. However, it is not trivial to parallelize the location update function.

In microscopic traffic simulation, the region query function fetches vehicle's local traffic environment in the last time step. It reads the tree structure and does not write (or change) the tree structure, so different region queries can be done naturally in parallel. In contrast, the location update function writes (or changes) the tree structure, so there are potential conflicts when performing location updates in parallel. This observation suggests reducing the cost of the location update function as much as possible, even at the expense of some additional costs in the region query function, because the cost of the region query function can be reduced by increasing the number of cores (or CPUs) in parallel traffic simulation.

3. RELATED WORK

One-dimensional spatial indexes (e.g. linear referencing [8]) are still popular in current microscopic traffic simulations [1, 2, 3]. In a linear reference system, an object is located by a segment ID, a lane ID and an offset. Each object is mapped to a segment and each segment has a list of objects that are located on the segment. Objects' movement is considered as a one-dimensional movement on the segment. If an object crosses from the current segment to a downstream segment, the offset of the object is initialized to zero. One-dimensional spatial indexes are used together with the network topology, if the query region covers multiple roads. One-dimensional spatial indexes are sufficient for traditional car following models, lane changing models and gap acceptance models [4] and has the advantage that an object can efficiently fetch nearby objects on the same segment. However, it has limited capability in more complex conditions, such as vehicles' cooperative driving [9], pedestrians' behaviors [10] and the interactions between objects on different roads. Besides, one-dimensional spatial indexes are not accurate in curved segments and complicated intersections.

Indexing moving objects in a two-dimensional space is a hot research topic in spatial simulations [28, 29], computer games and spatial databases. R-Tree [11], R*-Tree [12] and extended B+-Tree [26, 27] are three of the most popular two-dimensional tree-based spatial indexes and remain a focus of attention in the research community. The key idea of tree-based two-dimensional spatial index is to map spaces into nodes on a tree, and objects within a space are linked to the corresponding node. A region query in a large-scale road network is then transferred into an efficient region query on a tree, which scans only a smaller portion of the road network. Considerable work has been done to reduce the I/O cost of tree-based spatial indexes [13, 26]. In current large-scale microscopic traffic simulations, in most cases, data can fit into main memory, so, this paper focus on two-dimensional spatial indexes in main memory. The major drawback of using tree-based spatial indexes in main memory (e.g. R-Tree and R*-Tree) is the heavy time cost of update operations. In case of frequent location update operations in large-scale microscopic traffic simulations, there will be lots of node splitting and node merging, making the time cost of update operations heavy. To support frequent updates in the R-family trees, [14] proposes the LUR-tree. The main idea of the LUR-tree is to update the structure of the index only when an object moves out of the corresponding node. If a new position of an object is in the same leaf node, it changes only the position of the object in the same leaf node. Besides, a secondary index (a hash table) is introduced in the LUR-tree to allow starting an update operation from the bottom. This method can update positions of an object quickly and reduce the update cost. The work in [17] proposes a similar bottom-up update function to reduce the cost of frequent updates. Another branch of work [27] maps two-dimensional data to a one-dimensional space by using a recursive space-filling curve and then inserts the data to a B+-Tree. As these works are based on

B+-Tree, it can be easily integrated to existing DBMSs. The most relevant recent work to this paper is MOVIES [15]. This approach does not require a sophisticated index structure to be adjusted for each incoming update. Instead, it constructs conceptually simple short-lived throwaway indexes which are only kept for a very short period of time (sub-seconds). This work has similarities with the Sim-Tree approach, where both of them do not modify the tree structure for large-number of location updates. The key difference is that Sim-Tree is designed especially for traffic simulations, where the road density in traffic scenarios is valid for a longer period (e.g. 5 minutes). Sim-Tree is re-built only if the traffic condition has been significantly changed (e.g. an incident happens). A recent summary of tree-based spatial index can be found in [16].

Another type of two-dimensional spatial index is the grid [20, 21, 22]. The grid is a simple space-partitioning index where a predefined monitored area is divided into rectangular cells. Objects with coordinates within the boundaries of a grid cell belong to that particular cell. Each cell has a list of objects that located in the cell. Similar to the tree-based spatial indexes, location update operations in the grid are categorized as local or non-local. When an object's new position belongs to the same cell as its currently stored position, the update is local; otherwise, the update is non-local and involves deletion of the object from its current cell and insertion into a new cell. The bottom-up update function [14] can also be used in the grid. Recent researches [23, 24, 25] are targeting to remove conflicts between concurrent queries and updates. Grid-based spatial index has the advantage that the structure of the grid is not changed when objects update locations. When directly using the grid in large-scale traffic simulations, most of the cells in the grid tend to be empty and the distribution of objects in cells is skewed. It will make the region query inefficient. However, recent work [22] shows that with a careful choice of the cell size, the grid can compete with the R-tree in terms of the query performance and it is robust to varying workloads. This paper focus on tree-based spatial indexes and the key idea of Sim-Tree can also be implemented in the grid.

4. SIM-TREE

Motivated by the four observations listed in Section 2, this paper proposes Sim-Tree, a novel two-dimensional tree-based spatial index for large-scale parallel microscopic traffic simulations.

4.1 Data Structure

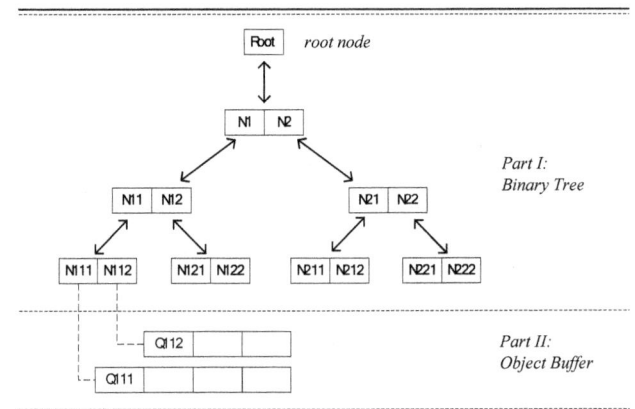

Figure 5: Sim-Tree Data Structure

The data structure of Sim-Tree is shown in Figure 5. Each node in the tree structure has pointers to its child nodes and a pointer to its parent node. Each node has a two-dimensional mapping area (e.g. a rectangle) in a road network. The root node is mapped to the whole road network. The inner nodes are mapped to smaller areas. Each leaf node has an object buffer, which contains a list of objects which are located inside the leaf node's mapping area. Locations of objects (e.g. drivers and pedestrians) are modeled as points. Leaf nodes' mapping areas have no overlap, thus, each object is located inside only one leaf node.

The innovation of Sim-Tree is not on its shape, but on its fit to the requirements of large-scale parallel microscopic traffic simulation. First, the binary tree structure in Sim-Tree is constructed based on the average road density in a road network during a period (observation 1). Second, the tree structure is checked only once in the beginning of each simulation time step (observation 2). Third, the major driver's region query operations are optimized (observation 3), which is discussed in Section 6. Fourth, Sim-Tree is designed to minimize the time cost of the location update function to improve the scalability of parallel microscopic traffic simulation (observation 4).

This paragraph explains why a binary tree is used in Sim-Tree. Assuming that objects are evenly distributed in leaf nodes and a query region is inside the mapping area of a leaf node, let w be the average number of objects in a leaf node, k be the number of child nodes in each node and N be the total number of leaf nodes, the average cost of a region query operation can be estimated using a formula:

$$Average\,Query\,Cost = k * log_k^N + w, \ (k \geq 2, w \geq 0) \quad (1)$$

where, log_k^N is the depth of the tree structure, $k * log_k^N$ is the cost of finding the target leaf node, and w is the cost of check objects in the target leaf node. The cost unit is a rectangle operation, e.g. to check whether a rectangle overlaps with another rectangle. To minimize the region query cost, the best value of k is e (the calculation is in Appendix I). In this paper, k equals to 2.

There are two types of road densities used in Sim-Tree: pre-simulation road density and in-simulation road density. Pre-simulation road density indicates that the density on each road at each time step for a similar traffic scenario is available before simulating a traffic scenario. Pre-simulation road density is firstly divided into multiple periods, in order that the density pattern within each period is not significantly different. For example, the road density in a normal day can be divided into six periods: morning {pre-peak, peak, post-peak} and afternoon {pre-peak, peak and post-peak}. Then, the average road density during each period is used to build the initial balanced binary tree for that period. In-simulation road density indicates that the average road density during a recent period (e.g. 5 minutes) is available when simulating a traffic scenario. It is true for most microscopic traffic simulations [1, 2, 3, 18], because the density of each road is an important output of traffic simulations.

This paragraph explains how to build a balanced binary tree in Sim-Tree, given the average density on each road during a period. Firstly, the road network is evenly divided into a large number of cells (e.g. 1 m^2). Then, each road is related with multiple overlapping cells. Assuming vehicles are evenly distributed on a road, the average densities on roads are transformed into the average density in cells, according to the portion of road length in each cell. The relationship between roads and cells is pre-calculated before simulating a traffic scenario and

is not changed during the simulation. Given the average density in cells at a time step (e.g. the simulation time is 0) during the simulation, Sim-Tree starts with only a root node, which is mapped to the whole road network (all cells) and contains all objects in the road network. Then, the node is divided into two child nodes vertically or horizontally. Each child node is mapped to a smaller area and contains half of the objects in the road network. These two child nodes' mapping areas do not overlap with each other. After that, each child node is divided into two nodes using the same method. The node division process is repeated until:

1. The average number of objects in one node is smaller than 5.
2. The size of one node's mapping area is smaller than a pre-defined threshold.

Rule 1 means that if there are no more than 4 objects in a node, there is no benefit to divide the node into 2 child nodes. If dividing the node into 2 child nodes, the depth of the branch is increased by 1 and the cost of finding the correct leaf node is increased by two rectangle operations. At the same time, the benefit comes from checking less number of objects. In the best case, if objects are evenly distributed in the two child nodes, the benefit is also two rectangle operations. Thus, if the number of objects in a node is not more than 4, there is no benefit to divide the node. As in observation 3, drivers are configured to use the same-sized rectangles in the region query function. Rule 2 means that if the mapping area of a node is smaller than a pre-defined threshold (e.g. ¼ of the rectangle's size), a driver's region query tends to contain the mapping area of the node. In this case, all objects contained in the node can be returned immediately without additional checking. Thus, there is no benefit to divide the node. If the time cost of range queries from pedestrians is significant, the rectangle size of pedestrians' query region should be used instead.

4.2 Functional Design

As shown in Table 1, Sim-Tree has five public functions and two private functions. The first function is *InitializeTreeStructure*. It is used before a simulation run. This function builds a balanced tree structure based on the historical road density in a road network. The second public function is *Insert*. It is used to insert a new object in Sim-Tree. After inserting an object in Sim-Tree, other objects can query (or can see) this object using the region query function. Besides, an object is automatically removed from Sim-Tree when the object is removed from the simulation. The third public function is *RegionQuery*. Given a target rectangle, this function scans the tree structure from the root node and finds all leaf nodes whose mapping areas overlap the target rectangle. Then, this function checks objects in these leaf nodes to determine which objects are in the target rectangle. The next is *BottomUpRegionQuery*. This function has the same purpose with the function *RegionQuery*, but it is implemented using a different way. The bottom-up region query function is explained in Section 6. The last public function is *UpdateAll*. This function is used once in each simulation time step to update objects' new locations in the Sim-Tree. If a vehicle's new location is still inside its current leaf node, there is no need to update anything. Otherwise, the vehicle will be moved to the appropriate leaf node. The two private functions are used by Sim-Tree to check and rebalance its tree structure. The rebalance function is explained in Section 5. Note that the function *InitializeTreeStructure* is not a strictly mandatory function, because Sim-Tree can rebalance its tree structure. However, starting from a reasonable tree structure is always better than starting from an empty tree structure. Besides, the work in [7] gives algorithms to estimate road density in the road network before starting a traffic simulation. The estimated road density can also be used to build an initially balanced tree structure.

Table 1: The interface of Sim-Tree

public functions:
1. InitializeTreeStructure ()
2. Insert (OneObject)
3. RegionQuery (A Rectangle)
4. BottomUpRegionQuery (OneObject, A Rectangle)
5. UpdateAll ()
private functions:
1. MeasureBalance ()
2. Rebalance ()

5. THE REBALANCE FUNCTION

Although the target of Sim-Tree is to avoid rebalancing the tree structure, there are two conditions where Sim-Tree has to adjust its tree structure. First, if there is no prior information about the average road density in a road network before simulating a traffic scenario, the Sim-Tree has to learn the road density while the simulation is ongoing and adjust its tree structure. Second, if road density in the road network changes significantly during a traffic scenario (e.g. an incident happens), Sim-Tree has to learn new road densities and adjust its tree structure. To be exact, a rebalance operation happens if any of the follow rules is true.

1. The average number of objects in all leaf nodes is smaller than 2.
2. The average number of agents in all leaf nodes is larger than 32 and the average rectangle size of all leaf nodes is larger than a pre-defined threshold.
3. The unbalance ratio of the tree structure is larger than 0.3.

Rule 1 means that if the depth of a Sim-Tree is too high and many leaf nodes have only 1 object or even have no object, the Sim-Tree needs to be rebalanced. Rule 2 means that if the depth of a Sim-Tree is too low (there are a large number of agents in most of the leaf nodes) and the average rectangle size of leaf nodes is larger than a pre-defined threshold (e.g. half of the size of a driver's query rectangle), the Sim-Tree needs to be rebalanced. If the average number of agents in all leaf nodes is larger than 32, but the average rectangle size of the leaf nodes is smaller than the threshold, it means there is congestion in the road network. Since a typical driver's region query tends to contain leaf nodes' mapping area and objects in leaf nodes can be directly returned without checking individually, the region query function is still efficient and there is no need to rebalance the tree structure. Rule 3 means that if the depth of Sim-Tree is acceptable, but objects are not evenly distributed in leaf nodes, the Sim-Tree needs to be rebalanced. Note that parameters in the 3 rules are configurable. The unbalance ratio of a tree structure is measured by a formula:

$$The\ unbalance\ \text{ratio} = \frac{\sum_{n \in N} |Objects(n) - E(N)|}{\sum_{n \in N} Objects(n)} \quad (2)$$

where, N is the list of leaf nodes, *Objects (n)* means the number of objects in node(n)'s mapping area, $E(N)$ is the average number of objects in all leaf nodes. An unbalance ratio is a variable in [0, 1]. A smaller unbalance ratio means that the tree structure is more balanced. For example, if the unbalance ratio of a tree structure is 0, the tree structure is perfectly balanced.

There are three variables affecting a rebalance operation. The first variable is the checking frequency (f), which controls the frequency to check the three rules. The second variable is the unbalance ratio threshold (u). If the unbalance ratio of a tree structure is larger than u, the tree structure is judged as unbalanced (the default value is 0.3). The last variable is the confirmation threshold (c). Only if a tree structure is continuously judged as unbalanced more than c times, a rebalance operation is started. A rebalance operation is to throw away the previous unbalanced Sim-Tree and to re-build a new Sim-Tree using the average density on road during a recent period and the pre-calculated relationship between roads and cells, which is explained in Section 4.1. The sensitivity of these three variables to the performance of a rebalance operation is studied in Section 8.3.

6. The Bottom-Up Region Query Function

A key step in a region query operation is to find a node whose mapping area is just large enough to contain the target region. This node is named as the root proxy node of the region query operation. Starting a region query operation from the root proxy node will achieve the same result as starting the region query operation from the root node. As shown in Figure 6, a vehicle v2 queries nearby objects in a rectangle and N1 is the lowest node containing the rectangle. Thus, N1 is the root proxy node of this region query. In case of a region query in large-scale traffic simulation, the depth of the Sim-Tree is high and the distance from leaf nodes to the root proxy node is much smaller than the distance from the root node to the root proxy node. Motivated by this, we design a bottom-up region query function. The idea of a bottom-up region query is to find the root proxy node of a vehicle's region query operation from the leaf node of the vehicle in a bottom-up direction, instead of from the root node of the tree structure in a top-down direction.

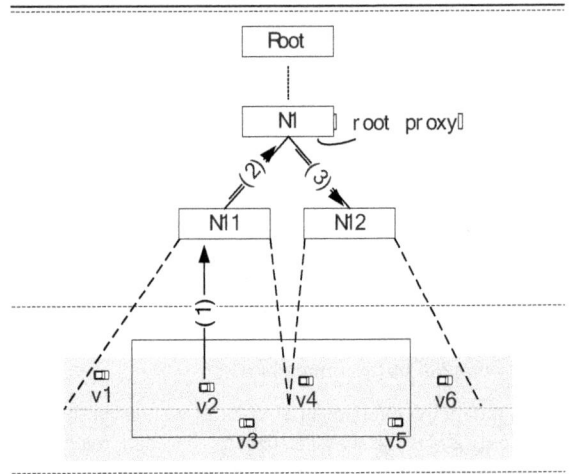

Figure 6: An example bottom-up region query by a vehicle v2

The bottom-up region query function consists of three steps. The first step is to check whether the vehicle's leaf node's rectangle overlaps the vehicle's query region. If not, a normal region query function starting from the root node is executed. If yes, the next step is to find the root proxy node of the region query in a bottom-up direction. The last step is to initiate a normal region query starting from the root proxy node. As shown in Figure 6, a vehicle v2 queries nearby objects in a rectangle. Firstly, the query rectangle overlaps with the vehicle's leaf node (N11), so a bottom-up region query is suitable. Second, an upward step is required to find the root proxy node N1 from the leaf node N11. Finally, a normal region query is initiated from N1.

The bottom-up region query function is more efficient than a normal region query in large-scale traffic simulation. There are two reasons. First, the query region of a vehicle is a rectangle surrounding the location of the vehicle. So, starting from the leaf node of the vehicle is a reasonable choice. Second, as explained in Section 4.1, the mapping area of leaf nodes cannot be much smaller than a vehicle' query region, thus, in most cases, only a small number of upward steps are required to find the root proxy node in a bottom-up direction. In our experiments to simulate 69,567 vehicles in the whole Singapore network, the average number of upward steps is smaller than 3.

7. TESTBED
This section introduces three major components of the testbed: a microscopic traffic simulator, the Singapore road network and a city-scale traffic scenario.

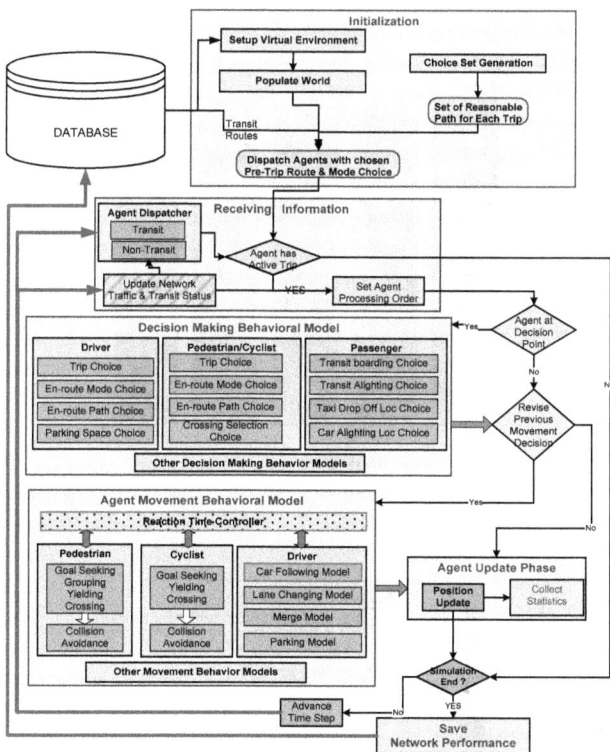

Figure 7: The logic flow of SimMobilityST

7.1 SimMobilityST
The SimMobility short-term simulator (SimMobilityST) is an open-source microscopic traffic simulator, developed by the Future Urban Mobility in Singapore-MIT Alliance for Research and Technology (SMART). SimMobilityST is based on the concept of agent-based or micro-simulation. Representation of

individuals as agents in the model is necessary to simulate how people will react in the future to new infrastructures, new technologies and innovations in system management and policy changes. Figure 7 shows the logic flow of the microscopic traffic simulator. The virtual world is populated during the initialization phase, after which the simulation receives the information/action plan at every time step. It simulates two kinds of behaviors: (1) Decision-making behavior (like route choice) is taken when agents are at some decision point e.g., a bus stop (2) Agent movement behavior occurs during the movement (lateral or longitudinal) e.g., "Car Following" and "Lane Changing". SimMobilityST is also a parallel microscopic traffic simulator to support simulating large-scale traffic scenarios. Vehicles in a road network are evenly distributed on cores (or CPUs), so that vehicles are simulated in parallel. The default simulation time step is 0.1 seconds. More information about the project SimMobilityST is available in [18].

7.2 Road Network
Singapore is a country that is well-known for its advanced transportation system. Figure 8 shows the Singapore road network. The Singapore road network consists of expressways, major arterial roads, collector roads and local roads. In this testbed, the Singapore road network is modeled as a map with 10,702 nodes and 20,918 segments.

Figure 8: the Singapore road network

7.3 Traffic Scenario
A city-scale traffic scenario is created. The time is from 8:00AM to 8:30AM on a weekday. 69,567 trips are generated during this period, based on Singapore's Household Interview Travel Survey (HITS) [19]. The Singapore government conducts the HITS Survey every four to five years to give transport planners and policy makers insights into residents' travelling patterns. Note that the purpose of this paper is not to generate the exact trips on the Singapore road network, but to generate a reasonable large-scale traffic scenario. The first 10 minutes are the warm up period. The number of moving vehicles in this scenario is around 30,000.

8. EXPERIMENTS
This section introduces three experiments to evaluate the efficiency of Sim-Tree, the scalability of Sim-Tree and the rebalance function. The testbed in Section 7 is used. Besides, these experiments are executed on a machine with six 2.67GHz Intel Xeon processors, 48GB main memory and Ubuntu Linux 10.10.

8.1 Experiment 1: Efficiency

This experiment evaluates the time cost of the region query function and the location update function in Sim-Tree. The traffic scenario is to simulate 69,567 trips during a typical morning period in the Singapore road network. The microscopic traffic simulator SimMobilityST is used to simulate the traffic scenario using 1 worker thread. It means that the 69,567 trips are simulated using only 1 thread on 1 core. The only variable in this experiment is the tree-based spatial indexes. Four tree-based spatial indexes are evaluated in this experiment: the R*-tree [12], the LUR-tree [14], Sim-Tree and Sim-Tree-No-BU. The R*-tree and the LUR-tree are introduced in Section 3. Besides, the only difference between Sim-Tree and Sim-Tree-No-BU is that there is no bottom-up region query function (in Section 6) in Sim-Tree-No-BU.

Table 2: Performance comparison of tree-based spatial indexes

	The location update (sec)	The region query (sec)	The total cost (sec)
The R*-Tree	9,643	2,660	32,047
The LUR-tree	1,266	2,633	23,741
Sim-Tree-No-BU	34	2,139	22,172
Sim-Tree	34	1,920	21,970

The results are shown in Table 2. Four tree-based spatial indexes are evaluated and the measurements are the cost of the location update function, the cost of the region query function and the total cost of simulating the traffic scenario. First, and most importantly, the location update cost of the Sim-Tree is significantly lower than both the R*-Tree and the LUR-tree. This is expected, because the major target of Sim-Tree is to reduce the cost of the location update function (based on observations 1 and 2). Compared with Sim-Tree, both the R*-Tree and the LUR-tree spend time on operations (e.g. re-insert, split, merge, shrink and expand) in order to rebalance the tree structure. In addition, when using Sim-Tree in this case study, for more than 90% of location updates, vehicles' new locations are still in the same leaf node, which generates very little additional overhead. Second, the region query cost of Sim-Tree is also better than the R*-Tree and the LUR-tree. This is an interesting finding. In the R*-Tree, one of the key parameters is the fanout of a node (the number of child nodes). If the fanout is large, a node is mapped to a large area in a road network, so the cost of the location update function is reduced (because vehicles' new locations tend to be in the same node). However, the cost of the region query function is also increased (as explained in Formula 1). Thus, the fanout of a node is a compromise between the cost of the location update function and the cost of the region query function. Based on experiments, the fanout of a node in the R*-Tree in this case study is set to 50 to minimize the total simulation cost. However, in Sim-Tree, there is no need to worry about the fanout of a node, which is set to be 2, in order to optimize the region query function. Third, compared with Sim-Tree-No-BU, the bottom-up region query function (in Sim-Tree) reduces the cost of the region query function by 10.6%. It is expected, because the bottom-up region query function scans less number of nodes in the tree in large-scale traffic simulations. Finally, Sim-Tree does not significantly reduce the total simulation cost. It is expected. Sim-Tree is designed to reduce the time cost of the non-parallel location update function and improves scalability.

8.2 Experiment 2: Scalability

This experiment evaluates the scalability of Sim-Tree. Sim-Tree greatly reduces the cost of the location update function, so the next key question is "whether the cost of the region query function can be reduced by increasing the number of cores in parallel traffic simulation?" The traffic scenario is the same as the traffic scenario in the first experiment. But the traffic scenario is simulated using more threads (1-5 worker threads). Each worker thread is executed exclusively on a core and the master thread is executed on the sixth core.

The results of simulating the traffic scenario in parallel are shown in Figure 9. Figure 9 (A) is the time cost of the location update function. The time cost of the location update function is not strongly related to the number of cores (or threads). This is expected, because the location update function is not parallelized. Figure 9 (B) is the time cost of the region query function. The left bar is the measured cost of the region query function when simulating the traffic scenario in parallel. The right bar is the estimated cost of the region query function with linear scalability, which directly divides the measured cost of the region query function using 1 thread over the number of threads. You can see that the measured costs of the region query function are close to the estimated cost with linear scalability. Thus, the time cost of the region query function is scalable to the number of threads (or cores). Besides, part of the difference between the

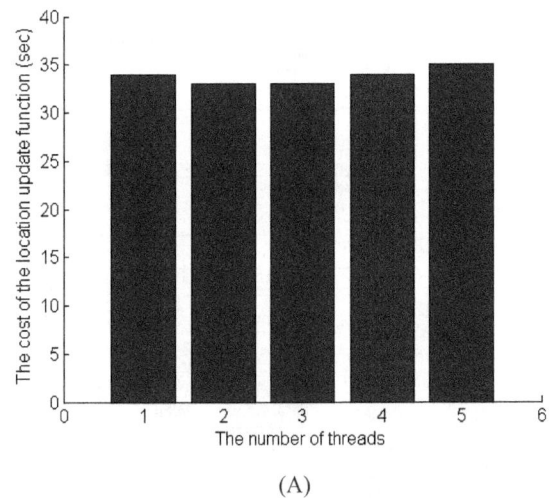

(A)

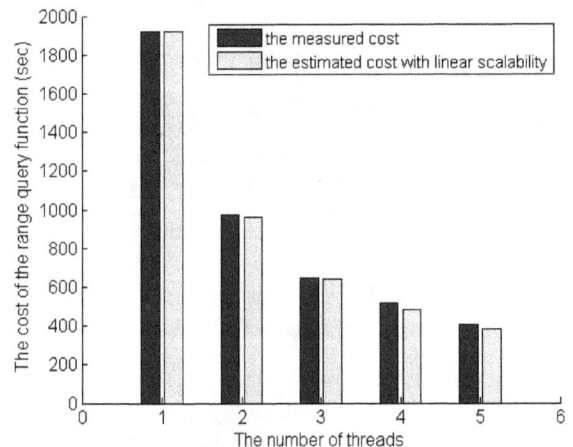

(B)

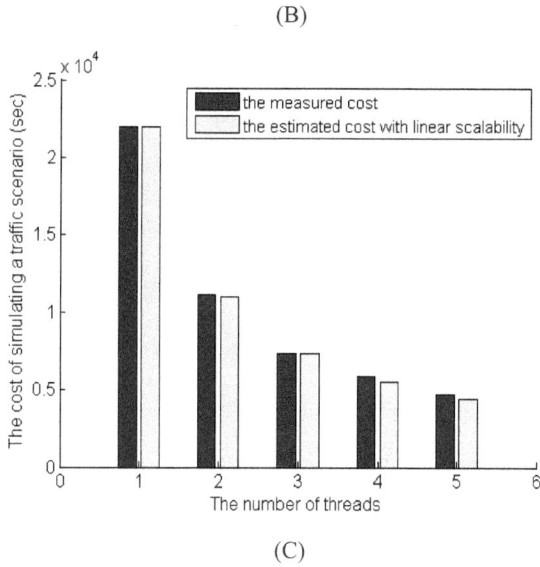

(C)

Figure 9: simulating the traffic scenario in parallel. (A) The time cost of the location update function, (B) the time cost of the region query function and (C) the time cost of simulating the traffic scenario.

left bar and the right bar is caused by other factors, e.g. an imperfect load balance and additional costs in parallel memory operations. Figure 9 (C) is the total time cost of simulating the traffic scenario. First, the time cost of the location update function is not significant compared to the total cost of simulating the traffic scenario. Second, the time cost of simulating the traffic scenario is scalable to the number of threads (or cores). This means that the target of Sim-Tree (to reduce the time cost of the location updates and to make the time cost of the region queries scalable to the number of cores in parallel traffic simulation) is valid.

8.3 Experiment 3: The Rebalance Function

This experiment evaluates the rebalance function. The traffic scenario is the same as the traffic scenario in the first experiment. However, there is no prior information about the average road density in the road network. Thus, Sim-Tree needs to adjust its tree structure when the simulation is ongoing. This traffic scenario is simulated using 5 worker threads. As explained in Section 5, there are three variables controlling the rebalance function: the checking frequency (f), the unbalance ratio threshold (u) and the confirmation threshold (c). Based on our knowledge, the unbalance ratio threshold (u) is the most critical parameter. In this case study, the checking frequency (f) is 10, which means Sim-Tree checks its tree structure every 10 simulation time steps (or 1 second). The confirmation threshold (c) is 1, which means a rebalance operation is triggered only if Sim-Tree is unbalanced in two continuous checking. In this case study, different unbalance ratio thresholds (u) are evaluated. The cost of the rebalance function consists of three parts. The first part (Part 1) comes from checking whether a rebalance operation is required. The second part (Part 2) comes from aggregating the road density in the road network during a previous period. The third part (Part 3) comes from rebalancing a tree structure based on the aggregated road density in the road network in the previous period.

Table 3 shows the performance of the rebalance function using different unbalance ratio thresholds (u). The measurements

are the number of the rebalance operations, the cost of the rebalance function and the cost of the region query function. First, the cost of rebalancing the tree structure (Part 3) dominates the cost of the rebalance function. Both the cost of checking whether a rebalance operation is required (Part 1) and the cost of aggregating the road density in the road network (Part 2) are small. Second, the cost of the rebalance operation (Part 3) is sensitive to the unbalance ratio threshold (u). As u increases from 0.15 to 0.35, the number of the rebalance operation is reduced from 632 to 2 and the cost of the rebalance operation is reduced from 849 seconds to 2 seconds. The cost of a rebalance operation depends on the number of vehicles in the road network. In this case study, the cost of a rebalance operation is around 1.0-1.5 seconds. Besides, the cost of the region query function is not sensitive to u when u is smaller than 0.3. Third, the rebalance operation is used twice (when u is 0.35), which is the same with the case when u is 0.3. However, the time cost of the region query function when u is 0.35 is higher. The reason is that the rebalance operations when u is 0.35 are triggered later, which makes region queries before the rebalance operations inefficient. In summary, in this experiment, when there is no prior information about the road density in the road network, the rebalance function (when u is 0.3) enables the Sim-Tree to do region queries efficiently with small additional time cost.

Table 3: the performance of the rebalance function

unbalance ratio threshold (u)	No. of rebalance	The rebalance function (sec)			The region query function (sec)
		Part 1	Part 2	Part 3	
0.15	632	143e-6	449e-6	849	399
0.20	373	209e-6	499e-6	498	401
0.25	45	138e-6	469e-6	61	404
0.30	2	129e-6	436e-6	2	408
0.35	2	121e-6	434e-6	2	446

9. CONCLUSIONS AND FUTURE WORK

Motivated by our observations in real-world traffic systems and microscopic traffic simulations, this paper proposed a new two-dimensional spatial index: Sim-Tree. The main idea of Sim-Tree is to build a tree structure based on the average road density in a road network. The key feature of Sim-Tree is that there is no need to check or rebalance its tree structure when individual vehicles frequently update their locations. In experiments to simulate a city-scale traffic scenario, Sim-Tree performed significantly better than the state-of-the-art R*-tree family of spatial indexes. To be exact, Sim-Tree reduced the time cost in location update operations by 97% (compared to the LUR-tree based two-dimensional spatial index) and contributes to achieving a near linear speed-up.

There are three ways to enhance Sim-Tree in future. First, the current rebalance function is reactive, which means that a rebalance operation is triggered only if the tree structure is already unbalanced. The rebalance function can be changed to be proactive. If the traffic condition is predictable or if the traffic scenario was simulated before, the distributed of objects on a network in future can be used to make Sim-Tree rebalance its tree structure before the tree structure turns unbalanced. Second, in some traffic conditions, there is no need to update a vehicle's surrounding traffic every simulation time step (e.g. 0.1 second). Reducing the frequency of updating a vehicle's surrounding traffic tends to reduce the total time cost of region query operations. Third, Sim-Tree, as a two-dimensional spatial index, can also be used as a supplement to a one-dimensional spatial index (e.g. a linear reference). Besides, the performance of Sim-Tree in traffic scenarios with incidents will be studied in future.

10. ACKNOWLEDGMENTS

The authors would like to thank Li-Shiuan Peh, Kakali Basak and Seth Hetu, from the Future Urban Mobility group in Singapore-MIT Alliance for Research and Technology, for their support in this work.

11. REFERENCES

[1] Qi Yang and Haris N. Koutsopoulos. (1996). "A Microscopic Traffic Simulator for evaluation of dynamic traffic management systems", Transportation Research Part C: Emerging Technologies, Volume 4, Issue 3, Pages 113-129.

[2] Qi Yang. (2007). "A Simulation Laboratory for Evaluation of Dynamic Traffic Management Systems". Ph.D. Thesis, Center for Transportation Studies, Massachusetts Institute of Technology

[3] Gordon D.B. Cameron and Gordon I.D. Duncan. (1995). "PARAMICS wide area micro-simulation of ATT and traffic management". Proceedings of 28th International symposium on Automative Technology and automation (ISATA), Stuggartt, Germany, Pages 475-484.

[4] Jaume Barcelo. (2010). "Fundamentals of traffic simulation". (ISBN: 978-1-4419-6141-9), Springer.

[5] Gordon D.B. Cameron, Gordon I.D. Duncan. (1996). "Paramics - Parallel Microscopic Simulation of Road Traffic". The Journal of Supercomputing, Pages 25-53.

[6] Klefstad, R., Zhang, Y., Lai, M., Jayakrishnan, R., and Lavanya, R. (2005). "A distributed, scalable, and synchronized framework for large-scale microscopic traffic simulation". In Proceedings of the 8th International IEEE Conference on Intelligent Transportation Systems, Pages 813–818.

[7] Dali Wei; Feng Chen and Xinxin Sun. (2010). "An improved road network partition algorithm for parallel microscopic traffic simulation," Mechanic Automation and Control Engineering (MACE), Pages 2777-2782.

[8] Val Noronha and Richard L. Church. (2002). "Linear Referencing and Alternate Expressions of Location for Transportation", Santa Barbara, California: Vehicle Intelligence and Transportation Analysis Laboratory, National Center for Geographic Information and Analysis.

[9] Mourad Ahmane, Abdeljalil Abbas-Turki, Florent Perronnet, Jia Wu, Abdellah El Moudni, Jocelyn Buisson and Renan Zeo. (2013). "Modeling and controlling an isolated urban intersection based on cooperative vehicles", Transportation Research Part C: Emerging Technologies, Volume 28, Pages 44-62.

[10] Helbing Dirk and Molnar Peter. (2005). "Social force model for pedestrian dynamics". Physical Review, Volume 51, Issue 5, Pages 4282-4286.

[11] Guttman, A. (1984). "R-Trees: A Dynamic Index Structure for Spatial Searching". Proceedings of the 1984 ACM SIGMOD international conference on Management of data. pp. 47-57.

[12] Beckmann, N., Kriegel, H. P., Schneider, R., and Seeger, B. (1990). "The R*-tree: an efficient and robust access method for points and rectangles". Proceedings of the 1990 ACM SIGMOD international conference on Management of data. pp 322-331.

[13] Navathe, Ramez Elmasri, Shamkant B. (2010). "Fundamentals of database systems" (6th ed.). Upper Saddle River, N.J.: Pearson Education. pp. 652–660.

[14] Mong Li Lee, Wynne Hsu, Christian S. Jensen, Bin Cui, and Keng Lik Teo. (2003). "Supporting frequent updates in R-trees: a bottom-up approach". In Proceedings of the 29th international conference on very large data bases (VLDB)

[15] Jens Dittrich, Lukas Blunschi, Marcos Antonio Vaz Salles. (2009). "Indexing Moving Objects Using Short-Lived Throwaway Indexes". In Proceedings of the 11th International Symposium on Advances in Spatial and Temporal Databases.

[16] Sergio Ilarri, Eduardo Mena, and Arantza Illarramendi. (2010). "Location-dependent query processing: Where we are and where we are heading". ACM Computing Surveys (CSUR).

[17] Dongseop Kwon, Sangjun Lee and Sukho Lee, (2002). "Indexing the current positions of moving objects using the lazy update R-tree," Mobile Data Management.

[18] Singapore-MIT Alliance for Research and Technology. (Last accessed: Feb, 2014) http://smart.mit.edu/research/futureurban-mobility/future-urban-mobility.html.

[19] Choi Chik Cheong and Raymond Toh. "Household Interview Surveys from 1997 to 2008 – A Decade of Changing Travel Behaviours".

[20] J. L. Bentley and J. H. Friedman. (1979). "Data structures for range searching". ACM Computer Survey, 11(4), Pages 397–409.

[21] V. Akman, W. R. Franklin, M. Kankanhalli, and C. Narayanaswami. (1989). "Geometric computing and the uniform grid data technique". Computer Aided Design, 21(7), Pages 410–420.

[22] D. Šidlauskas, S. Šaltenis, C. W. Christiansen, J. M. Johansen, and D. Šaulys. (2009). "Trees or grids? Indexing moving objects in main memory". In GIS, Pages 236–245.

[23] Darius Šidlauskas, Kenneth A. Ross, Christian S. Jensen, and Simonas Šaltenis. (2011). "Thread-level parallel indexing of update intensive moving-object workloads". In Proceedings of the 12th international conference on Advances in spatial and temporal databases (SSTD'11), Pages 186–204.

[24] Darius Šidlauskas, Simonas Šaltenis, and Christian S. Jensen. (2012). "Parallel main-memory indexing for moving-object query and update workloads". In Proceedings of the 2012 ACM SIGMOD International Conference on Management of Data.

[25] K. Chakrabarti and S. Mehrotra. (1999). "Efficient concurrency control in multidimensional access methods". In

Proceedings of the 1999 ACM SIGMOD International Conference on Management of Data.

[26] Khaled M. Elbassioni, Amr Elmasry, Ibrahim Kamel. (2005). "An Indexing Method for Answering Queries on Moving Objects". Distributed and Parallel Databases 17(3), Pages 215-249.

[27] C. S. Jensen, D. Lin, and B. C. Ooi. (2004). "Query and update efficient B+-tree based indexing of moving objects". In Proc. VLDB, pages 768–779.

[28] W. Koh and S. Zhou. "Modeling and simulation of pedestrian behaviors in crowded places". ACM Transactions on Modeling and Computer Simulation, 21(3):20:1–20:23, 2011.

[29] N. B. Othman, L. Luo, W. Cai, and M. Lees. 2013. "Spatial indexing in agent-based crowd simulation". In Proceedings of the 6th International ICST Conference on Simulation Tools and Techniques (SimuTools '13).

Appendix I: Calculation of k in Sim-Tree

The average cost of a region query operation in Sim-Tree can be estimated using the formula:

$$Average\, Query\, Cost = k * log_k^N + w, \ (k \geq 2, w \geq 0)$$

where,

k is the number of children in a node in Sim-Tree,

w is the average number of objects in a leaf node,

N is the total number of leaf nodes,

log_k^N is the depth of the tree structure,

$k * log_k^N$ is the cost of finding the target leaf node

To find the turning point (which is also the optimal solution of k),

$$\frac{d(k * log_k^N + w)}{d(k)} = 0$$

$$-> \ln N * \frac{d(\frac{k}{\ln k})}{d(k)} = 0$$

$$-> \ln N * \frac{\ln k - 1}{(\ln k)^2} = 0$$

$$-> \ln k - 1 = 0$$

$$-> k = e$$

GPU-Assisted Hybrid Network Traffic Model

Jason Liu
Florida International University
Miami, Florida, USA
liux@cis.fiu.edu

Yuan Liu
Tsinghua University
Beijing, China
liuy139@gmail.com

Zhihui Du
Tsinghua University
Beijing, China
duzh@tsinghua.edu.cn

Ting Li
Florida International University
Miami, Florida, USA
tli001@cis.fiu.edu

ABSTRACT

Large-scale network simulation imposes extremely high computing demand. While parallel processing techniques allows network simulation to scale up and benefit from contemporary high-end computing platforms, multi-resolutional modeling techniques, which differentiate network traffic representations in network models, can substantially reduce the computational requirement. In this paper, we present a novel method for offloading computationally intensive bulk traffic calculations to the background onto GPU, while leaving CPU to simulate detailed network transactions in the foreground. We present a hybrid traffic model that combines the foreground packet-oriented discrete-event simulation on CPU with the background fluid-based numerical calculations on GPU. In particular, we present several optimizations to efficiently integrate packet and fluid flows in simulation with overlapping computations on CPU and GPU. These optimizations exploit the lookahead inherent to the fluid equations, and take advantage of batch runs with fix-up computation and on-demand prefetching to reduce the frequency of interactions between CPU and GPU. Experiments show that our GPU-assisted hybrid traffic model can achieve substantial performance improvement over the CPU-only approach, while still maintaining good accuracy.

Categories and Subject Descriptors

C.4 [**Performance of Systems**]: Modeling Techniques; I.6.3 [**Simulation and Modeling**]: Applications

Keywords

GPU, network simulation, fluid model

1. INTRODUCTION

Simulation is an effective method for studying network protocols and applications, capable of capturing detailed op-

erations of a complex network, especially the cross-layer interoperation of various network protocols and components that are difficult to reproduce in real network testbeds. Simulation, once validated, can be especially cost effective for studying new network designs and services by offering controlled, diverse, and yet reasonably realistic network scenarios before the actual deployment.

The computational requirement of simulating large-scale network can be extremely high. Consider an example of simulating the core network of a major US Internet service provider, in this case, AS 7018 from the RocketFuel dataset, which consists of about 12,000 routers and 15,000 links [12]. Assuming all links are gigabit connections and assuming the average packet size is 500 bytes, in order to simulate this network with a mere 10% utilization, we can have a back-of-an-envelop calculation which shows that the simulator would need to process on average about 375 million packet events per second. (A packet event is defined as a simulation event representing a packet either arriving at or departing from a host or a router, and can be considered as the unit of simulation workload.) To meet with such computational demand, there are two general approaches.

In one approach we can use parallel simulation to harness the collective computing power of parallel machines [4]. In this case a large network is partitioned among the available processors and cores; each submodel is a logical process that maintains its own event list and simulation clock, and can run on a separate processor. Each logical process must process local simulation events independently in timestamp order, and synchronize and communicate with other logical processes via timestamped messages. Several parallel network simulators (e.g., [3,32,40]) have demonstrated the potential of running large network models on massively parallel computers.

In another approach we can increase the level of abstraction in order to reduce the computational demand of a large-scale network simulation. Fluid traffic models provide a first-order approximation of the aggregate network behavior by capturing the flow rates rather than individual packets. A discrete-event formulation of a fluid flow can describe the changes in the flow rate as the flow traverses the network links and competes for network resources with other traffic [19]. Alternatively, one can use differential equations to represent the behavior of persistent TCP flows and their effect on the network queue length [16]. These differential equations can be numerically solved with efficiency. In both cases the fluid models can demonstratively achieve a speedup over packet-oriented simulation by as much as three orders of magnitude while maintaining good accuracy.

This gives rise to an important distinction between the foreground and background traffic. The foreground traffic consists of detailed transactions of the network protocols and applications that we intend to study and therefore need to be modeled with high fidelity. The background traffic is the stochastic processes that govern the behavior of the bulk of the network traffic that occupies the network links. The background traffic causes the characteristic fluctuations of the network queues and therefore affects the packet delays and losses of the foreground traffic. Since the background traffic does not require significant accuracy, we can model the background traffic as fluid flows. Previously we developed a hybrid network traffic model that integrates the packet-oriented foreground traffic, which is simulated using discrete-event simulation, and the fluid-based background traffic, which is described by a set of differential equations and solved numerically using a time-stepped approach [13].

Once a specialized processing unit dedicated only for graphics rendering, the Graphic Processing Unit (GPU) has now become an important massively parallel computing platform, suitable for high-performance high-throughput data parallel computations. Currently the performance gap between GPU and CPU is roughly 10x, both in the processing rate and the main memory bandwidth. Such a gap is expected to widen in the next decade. Nowadays, GPU is commonly available among workstations; because of its low cost performance ratio and energy efficiency, GPU is already making regular appearances in high-profile enterprise systems and supercomputers. For example, according to the November 2013 list of the top 500 supercomputers [36], although less than 10% of the current supercomputer systems come with GPU, statistics show that nearly one third of the overall performance of these supercomputers has been brought by GPU acceleration.

In this paper, we present an extension to the hybrid network traffic model, which offloads the numerically intensive background traffic calculations to GPU. We propose an integration scheme that can overlap the CPU-based discrete-event simulation of the foreground network packets and the GPU-based differential equation solver for the background fluid dynamics. We describe a novel mechanism that can minimize the effect of inherent communication latencies between CPU and GPU. Our work takes advantage of the GPU capabilities by moving the computationally intensive background traffic calculations to GPU, so that CPU can concentrate on simulating the detailed transactions of network protocols and applications.

The contributions of this paper can be summarized in two folds: (1) We present a hybrid traffic model that cleanly separates packet-oriented foreground traffic simulation that executes on CPU and the fluid-based background traffic calculation that executes on GPU; (2) We propose a set of optimization algorithms for overlapping asynchronous CPU and GPU computations, exploiting the lookahead information in the fluid calculations, and using batch runs and associated fix-up computations to reduce frequent interactions between CPU and GPU. Extensive experiments for validating the GPU-assisted hybrid traffic model using controlled network scenarios, and demonstrate significant performance improvements (as much as 25x) using large network scenar-

ios. In this aspect, our work sets the stage for massive-scale network simulation with realistic traffic behavior on hybrid supercomputing platforms with GPU acceleration.

The rest of the paper is organized as follows. Section 2 reviews the existing work in network traffic modeling and GPU-based simulation and modeling techniques. Section 3 describes the hybrid traffic model and presents the basic method for integrating the packet-oriented simulation on CPU and the fluid-based traffic calculation on GPU. Section 4 describes the optimization techniques that can efficiently overlap CPU and GPU computations and reduce communication overhead between CPU and GPU. Section 5 presents our validation and performance studies. Section 6 concludes the paper and outlines future work.

2. BACKGROUND

In this section we present an overview of fluid network traffic models. We focus on the integration schemes from which we develop our GPU-based solution. We also describe existing work on GPU-based simulation and modeling.

2.1 Fluid Network Traffic Models

Traditional infrastructure network simulations represent network transactions at the packet level. It is computationally expensive since we use at least one simulation event for each packet entering or leaving a network host or router. Modeling network traffic as fluid flows can be traced back to the idea of using packet trains by Ahn and Danzig [2]. Fluid models need to accurately and efficiently capture flow-level characteristics, such as the flow rate, as an approximation of the network effect. For example, Nicol [18] used piecewise linear functions to represent TCP traffic flows and uses simulation events to represent the flow rate changes as the flows are propagated downstream. Guo et al. [7] proposed a time-stepped approach where consecutive packets arriving at a router within a time-step are lumped together and represented by a single flow rate. Recently Li et al. [10] proposed a fast rate-based TCP (RTCP) traffic model that approximates traffic flows as a series of *rate windows*, each consisting of a number of packets considered to possess the same arrival rate.

Misra et al. [17] used a set of ordinary differential equations (ODE) to represent the flow rate changes by capturing the long-term average behavior of persistent TCP flows. Liu et al. [16] later provided several improvements to the Misra's algorithm by explicitly expressing the network topological information using a set of nonlinear time-varying ordinary differential equations, which keep track of the time-varying congestion window size of the fluid flows and the length of the network queues.

These differential equations can be solved numerically using a fixed time-stepped Runge-Kutta method. This can be achieved by having the simulator to schedule an event periodically with a small time interval. At each step, the differential equations are evaluated, and subsequently the congestion window sizes and the queue lengths are updated. To achieve better efficiency, multiple fluid flows with the same source and destination can be consolidated into one flow following the same congestion window trajectory.

2.2 Integration of Packet and Fluid Models

Hybrid network traffic models aim at combining the packet-oriented foreground flows and the fluid-based background flows within the same simulator, and as such they need to focus on the interaction between the two types of network flows. Discrete-event fluid models (e.g., [18]) use simulation events to capture the moments of flow rate changes and thus can be naturally integrated with the packet-level simulation (e.g., [9, 20, 33]).

Special arrangement, however, must be made to integrate the packet-oriented discrete-event simulation and the fluid model based on differential equations. Gu et al. [6] presented a method of integrating two separate networks: a fluid network at the core with states represented by differential equations, and a packet network at the peripheral with network transactions represented by discrete events. Interactions are allowed to happen only at the network boundary: packets entering the core network must be converted into fluid flows, and when they leave, they must be converted back to packet events. Zhou et al. [41] suggested an improvement. In order to achieve a better response time from the ODE solver (implemented in MATLAB), two instances of the same fluid model are included in their system with interleaving simulation clocks. Such redundant computation can effectively double the speed of the ODE solver.

In our previous work we proposed an integration scheme that allows mixing of fluid and packet flows at each network queue [13]. To correctly integrate the fluid and packet models, the scheme takes into consideration the impact of fluid flows on packet flows and vice versa. In particular, one must calculate the aggregate arrival rate of both fluid and packet flows at each network queue for correct queue length and queuing delay for all fluid flows traversing a node. In doing so, one can properly schedule the packet departure events according to the calculated queuing occupancy.

We also proposed several techniques to improve the performance of the hybrid model, such as using efficient data structures, caching, and dynamically varying the Runge-Kutta time step size [15]. We also demonstrated that the hybrid model is highly parallelizable [14]. We observed that the time it takes to propagate fluid characteristics (such as the accumulative delay and loss rate) along the flow paths has a lower bound equal to the minimum link delay, according to the governing ordinary differential equations. As such, parallel simulation can maintain good lookahead and is thus capable of achieving good parallel performance.

2.3 GPU-based Simulation

Modern GPUs have recently evolved beyond simply being the graphics processing units for rasterization of 3D primitives. It is common that contemporary high-end computing systems include GPUs to accelerate computation. Over the years, we have seen many algorithms and applications taking advantage of GPU's unique processing capabilities [5, 23, 29]. The GPU programming tools have also evolved from specific graphics languages, such as OpenGL and Cg, to more generic parallel programming paradigms, such as CUDA [21] and OpenCL [34].

GPU-based simulation has also become more common. Verdesca et al. [37] used GPU to conduct line-of-sight and route planning calculations for battlefield simulations. It is not surprising that simulation can benefit significantly from offloading data parallel tasks onto GPU, including for example, N-body simulation [8, 22], Monte Carlo simulation [30, 38], group mobility models [28], and agent-based models [1, 27].

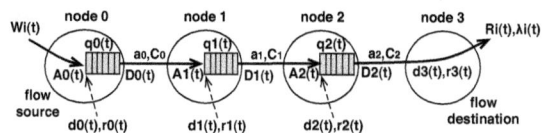

Figure 1: A flow traversing two intermediate nodes.

Perumalla [26] first investigated possible alternatives for conducting discrete event simulation (DES) on GPU. Park and Fishwick [24] developed an application framework based on CUDA to support fast DES. In a consequent paper [25], they conducted an analysis of queuing network simulation using their GPU-based application framework. More recently, Li et al [11] introduced the a three-stage strategy to realize DES on the GPU platform as a cost-efficient alternative to the traditional parallel DES. Tang and Yao [35] developed a new simulation kernel based on GPU to support DES. All the above efforts aimed at accelerating generic discrete-event simulation on GPU. Our method described in this paper is specific for cooperating CPU and GPU for high-performance network traffic modeling.

In this aspect, Xu and Bagrodia [39] presented a hybrid network simulation framework that uses GPU to carry out certain tasks, including a GPU implementation of a fluid TCP model [17]. Our hybrid traffic model is derived from an improved fluid model with detailed network topological information. To achieve better accuracy, our model also requires fine-tuned integration between the fluid and the packet flows, which presents unique challenges for coordinating the computation carried out both on CPU and GPU.

3. HYBRID TRAFFIC MODELING

Our hybrid traffic model consists of a fluid-based background traffic model on GPU, and a discrete-event packet-oriented foreground traffic model on CPU. We describe the fluid model and its GPU-based implementation, and then introduce the integration scheme that combines the GPU-based fluid model and the CPU-based packet simulation.

3.1 Fluid Model

The input to the background fluid traffic model is a graph that represents the network with link delays and bandwidths, and a traffic matrix consisting of fluid flows on the network with distinct sources and destinations as the background traffic. In the following we first describe the set of differential equations that need to be solved on GPU. Compared with the original fluid model [16], here we also present a simplified model for drop-tail queues in addition to the Random Early Detection (RED) queuing policy. Fig. 1 illustrates an example with a fluid flow traversing two intermediate nodes; it shows most of the flow variables maintained by the model.

For TCP flow i, the additive-increase and multiplicative-decrease behavior of the TCP window size $W_i(t)$ (during the TCP congestion avoidance stage) can be described as:

$$dW_i(t)/dt = 1/R_i(t) - W_i(t)\lambda_i(t)/2 \qquad (1)$$

where $R_i(t)$ is the round-trip delay and $\lambda_i(t)$ is the packet loss rate at time t.[1]

---

[1]The boundary conditions of the window size and the queue length (shown later) are not included here in the equations for simple exposition.

Suppose flow i visits a total of n_i nodes from source to destination, where node 0 is the source and node $(n_i - 1)$ is the destination of the flow. At each node k except the destination node, we can calculate its queue length $q_k(t)$ using the following differential equation:

$$dq_k(t)/dt = \Lambda_k(t)(1 - \rho_k(t)) - C_k \qquad (2)$$

where $\Lambda_k(t)$ is the total arrival rate of all fluid flows entering the network queue, $\rho_k(t)$ is the packet drop probability, and C_k is the link bandwidth. The packet drop probability $\rho_k(t)$ is used specifically to model the selective packet dropping mechanism in RED. For drop-tail queues, we set $\rho_k(t)$ to zero. For RED, it is a piece-wise linear function of the average queue length, which can be calculated as a moving average from the instant queue length.

The round trip time, $R_i(t)$, and the packet loss rate, $\lambda_i(t)$, are determined by accumulating queuing delays and packet losses along the flow path. We use $d_k(t)$ to denote the cumulative delay, and $r_k(t)$ to denote the cumulative packet loss rate of flow i arriving at the kth node, where $0 \le k < n_i$. At the source, both $d_0(t)$ and $r_0(t)$ are zero.

The cumulative delay at the downstream node $(k+1)$ can be calculated from the value at node k:

$$d_{k+1}(t_f) = d_k(t) + a_k + q_k(t)/C_k \qquad (3)$$

where $t_f = t + a_k + q_k(t)/C_k$, and a_k is the link propagation delay between node k and node $k + 1$. Here, the cumulative delay at the downstream node is calculated from the cumulative delay at the previous node plus the queuing delay at the previous node and the link's propagation delay. Note that the cumulative delay must consider a time lag equal to the sum of the queuing delay and the propagation delay.

The cumulative packet loss rate for the fluid flow arriving at the downstream node $(k + 1)$ can be calculated from the cumulative packet loss rate at node k plus all the losses occurred at node k (also with the proper time lag). For RED queues, this can be expressed as:

$$r_{k+1}(t_f) = r_k(t) + A_k(t)\rho_k(t) \qquad (4)$$

where $A_k(t)$ is the arrival rate and $\rho_k(t)$ is the RED packet drop probability at node k. For drop-tail queues, we have:

$$r_{k+1}(t_f) = r_k(t) + A_k(t) - D_k(t + q_k(t)/C_k) \qquad (5)$$

Here, $A_k(t)$ is the arrival rate of the fluid flow and $D_k(t + q_k(t)/C_k)$ is departure rate of the same flow. The difference accounts for the loss.

At the flow source, the arrival rate is the flow send rate, which can be calculated from the TCP congestion window size and the round-trip delay:

$$A_0(t) = W_i(t)/R_i(t) \qquad (6)$$

Similar to [16], we allow a fluid flow to include multiple TCP sessions having the same source and destination and therefore following the same congestion window trajectory. For that, we simply multiply the send rate by the number of TCP sessions. Note that if flow i is an UDP flow, we simply set a constant send rate.

For subsequent nodes, the arrival rate is the departure rate of the previous queue after a time lag equal to the link's propagation delay:

$$A_{k+1}(t + a_k) = D_k(t) \qquad (7)$$

The departure rate at node k is determined by the arrival rate after a time lag equal to the queuing delay, which amounts to $q_k(t)/C_k$. If the total arrival rate is less than the bandwidth, the departure rate remains the same as the arrival rate. Otherwise, the departure rate is proportional to the arrival rate as the bandwidth is shared among the competing flows:

$$D_k(t_f') = \begin{cases} A_k(t)(1 - \rho_k(t)) & \text{if } \Lambda_k(t)(1 - \rho_k(t)) \le C_k \\ A_k(t)C_k/\Lambda_k(t) & \text{otherwise.} \end{cases} \qquad (8)$$

where $t_f' = t + q_k(t)/C_k$.

For simplicity, we assume the routing path is symmetrical, and the queuing delays and packet losses are negligible for the ACK flow from the destination traveling back to the source. Let π_i be path delay for flow i, which is the sum of the propagation delay of all links on the path from source to destination. The round-trip delay can be calculated from the cumulative delay at the flow destination:

$$R_i(t) = d_{n_i-1}(t - \pi_i) + \pi_i \qquad (9)$$

Similarly, the packet loss rate can also be calculated from the cumulative packet loss rate at the flow destination:

$$\lambda_i(t) = r_{n_i-1}(t - \pi_i) \qquad (10)$$

In case a flow consists of multiple TCP sessions, we need to divide the total loss rate by the number of TCP sessions to derive the *per-session* loss rate, which we use in Eqn. (1).

The above equations can be solved numerically using the Runge-Kutta method. In general, to solve $y(t)$ given $dy(t)/dt$, and the initial value $y(0) = y_0$, one can iteratively compute the approximate values $y_1, y_2, \cdots, y_n$ of the actual values $y(t_1), y(t_2), \cdots, y(t_n)$, where $t_0 = 0$ and $t_{i+1} = t_i + \delta$ for $i = 0, 1, \cdots, n - 1$. δ is the Runge-Kutta step size, which is set to be at least 10x smaller than the link delay in the implementation in order to maintain numerical accuracy.

In parallel simulation, a fluid flow may traverse multiple sub-networks each assigned to a different processor. We use ghost nodes to represent the next fluid nodes assigned to remote processors. The ghost nodes communicate with the remote processors by the underlying parallel simulation kernel. The fluid nodes along the path of a fluid flow are thus broken into multiple segments assigned to different processors and handled in a parallel fashion. There is a full discussion in [14].

3.2 GPU Implementation

We implement the Runge-Kutta method on GPU using CUDA [21]. In CUDA, a program is composed of a large number concurrently schedulable threads. These threads are organized into thread blocks and dispatched onto GPU's parallel execution units, called Streaming Multiprocessors (SMs), via invocation of the CUDA "kernel" functions. While threads within the same block can synchronize using CUDA's `__syncthreads()` function, synchronization between threads belonging to different blocks is unsupported. In this case, one would have to split calculations into serval kernels so that data modification by threads in one kernel are visible to threads in subsequent kernels.

There exist data dependencies during the evaluation of the differential equations within a Runge-Kutta step. For example, the departure rate at the source of the fluid flow depends on the flow send rate (as well as the queue length), which in turn depends on the congestion window size and the round-trip time. We split the fluid calculations into three kernels. We make sure there is no data dependency within each kernel; therefore, we can employ more threads and assign them to multiple thread blocks for better parallelism.

The first kernel function, `update_flow`, designates a CUDA thread for evaluating the congestion window size $W_i(\cdot)$, the round-trip time $R_i(\cdot)$, and the packet loss rate $\lambda_i(\cdot)$, for each flow i. The second kernel function, `update_queue`, designates a CUDA thread for calculating the queue length $q_l(\cdot)$ for each network queue l that contains fluid flows. Here, each thread performs a gather operation to compute the total arrival rate of all fluid flows entering the queue. The third kernel function, `update_hop`, designates a CUDA thread for each fluid flow at a network queue that the fluid flow traverses. Each thread needs to evaluate the flow arrival rate $A_k(\cdot)$, the flow departure rate $D_k(\cdot)$, the cumulative delay $d_k(\cdot)$, and the cumulative packet loss rate $r_k(\cdot)$. At each Runge-Kutta step, these three kernels will be invoked in sequence. Data transfer between CPU and GPU will happen before and after the kernel invocations. It is obviously inefficient to invoke the kernels and transfer data at such frequency; we discuss further optimizations in Section 4.

CUDA provides users access to different types of memory. Each thread may use *registers* or *shared memory* for fastest access. The latter can be used to communicate with threads within the same block. However, both types of memory are not persistent across kernel invocations. There are also *constant memory* and *texture memory*, but they are used for special purposes: constant memory is used only for storing immutable data, and texture memory requires 2D spatial locality.

Since fluid variables, like the congestion window size $W_i(\cdot)$ and the cumulative packet loss rate $r_k(\cdot)$, need to be kept at GPU across kernel invocations, and they also need to be accessed by threads potentially belonging to different blocks, we use *global memory*, which is a large chunk of memory and can be accessed by all threads belonging to different blocks and across kernel invocations. Although accessing the global memory is about 100x slower than the registers and shared memory, it is still considered to have a higher bandwidth than the CPU memory.

Certain fluid variables need to keep values in the simulated future. For example, the cumulative delay $d_k(\cdot)$ in Eqn. (3) must be able to set values at a future time after the current queuing delay and the link propagation delay. In this case, we allocate memory for an array to keep track of the time series. The size of the array is bounded by the maximum queuing delay and the link propagation delay.

3.3 Packet and Fluid Integration

The fluid background traffic calculation on GPU is invoked as CUDA kernel functions by CPU at each Runge-Kutta step. However, the GPU-based fluid model only considers fluid flows; these fluid flows need to be integrated with the foreground traffic, which is represented by individual packets and simulated as discrete events on CPU.

In particular, when a packet arrives at a node, the simulator needs to determine whether this packet will cause the network queue to overflow with the given queue length calculated from the background fluid model. If so, the packet needs to be dropped. Otherwise, it is inserted into the network queue and the network queue length is adjusted ac-

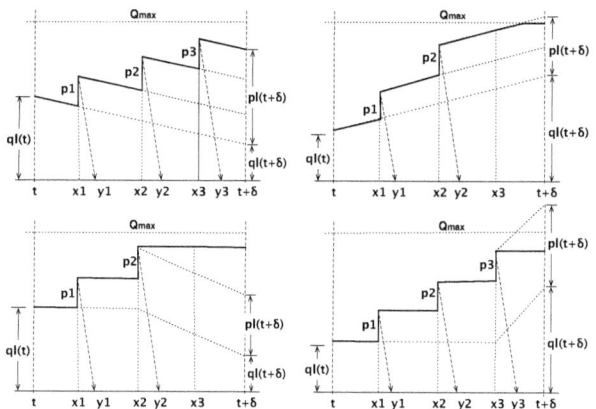

Figure 2: Mixing of fluids and packets.

cordingly. The simulator also needs to schedule a packet departure event after the queuing delay. The fluid model needs to consider the changes to the network queue length due to packet arrivals. The fluid model only calculates the differences in queue length at each Runge-Kutta step (using Eqn. 2).

Fig. 2 shows an example on how fluids and packets are integrated. Suppose at time t and $t+\delta$ (δ is the Runge-Kutta step size), the GPU-based fluid model calculates the network queue length $q_l(t)$ and $q_l(t+\delta)$. The top left plot shows the situation where the aggregate fluid arrival rate is less than the bandwidth and therefore the queue length is decreasing. The top right plot shows the fluid arrival is greater than the bandwidth, and the queue length is increasing. During the time interval, three packets of size p_1, p_2, and p_3 arrive at the network queue at time x_1, x_2, and x_3, respectively. The top left plot shows that all packets are admitted into the network queue; however, the top right plot shows that the third packet is dropped due to queue overflow.

When a packet is inserted into the queue, we need to adjust the queue length. We use variable $p_l(x)$ to keep track of the total size of packets arrived at the queue during the interval before and including time x. We set $p_l(t) = 0$ at the start of the interval. If a packet is allowed to be inserted into the queue upon its arrival at time x, the packet size will be added to $p_l(x)$ and then the simulator will schedule a packet departure event so that it can later simulate the delivery of the packet to the next queue. The departure time y can be calculated from the arrival time x and the current queuing delay, which depends on the length of the queue (including for both fluids and packets) and the link bandwidth C_l:

$$y = x + (q_l(x) + p_l(x))/C_l \qquad (11)$$

The problem is that when packets arrive during the Runge-Kutta time interval between time t and $t+\delta$, the fluid queue length at time $t+\delta$ is not yet available (it's in the simulated future). As a matter of fact, $q_l(t+\delta)$ actually should depend on both fluid and packet arrivals during the interval. In our implementation, we approximate the queuing occupancy by assuming the fluid queue length $q_l(\cdot)$ stays constant during the interval.

This approximation may introduce errors, which are illustrated in the bottom two plots in Fig. 2. The bottom left plot shows the situation where the third packet, which is supposed to be admitted, is dropped due to queue overflow. And the bottom right plot shows the third packet is admitted,

Algorithm 1 Lock-step hybrid simulation on CPU

```
1:  q_l, p_l ⇐ 0 for all network queues
2:  schedule a Runge-Kutta event at time 0
3:  ··· // initialize other simulation variables
4:  While (simulation is not finished) Do
5:     e ⇐ eventlist.getEarliestEvent()
6:     t_c ⇐ e.time // current simulation time
7:     If (e is a Runge-Kutta event) Then
8:        q_l ⇐ q_l + p_l; p_l ⇐ 0 for all network queues
9:        copy q_l for all network queues CPU⇒GPU
10:       invoke update_flow, update_queue, update_hop
11:       wait for the three kernels to complete
12:       copy q_l and ρ_l for all network queues GPU⇒CPU
13:       schedule a Runge-Kutta event at time t_c + δ
14:    Else If (e is a packet arrival event) Then
15:       u ⇐ uniform(0,1)
16:       If (u < ρ_l OR q_l + p_l + packet.size > Q_l^{max}) Then
17:          drop the packet
18:       Else
19:          insert packet into the queue
20:          p_l ⇐ p_l + packet.size
21:          schedule packet departure event at time t_c + (q_l +
             p_l)/C_l
22:       End If
23:    Else
24:       ··· // process other simulation events
25:    End If
26: End While
```

but in reality it should be dropped. Similarly, we assume the packet drop probability for the REQ queue $\rho_l(\cdot)$ also stays constant during the interval. The packet drop probability is calculated from the average queue length, which could change during the interval when the instant queue length changes. In both cases, however, we expect the error to be insignificant. The Runge-Kutta step size must be kept small to maintain numerical accuracy. The differences only occur when the network queue is about to be full. When we keep the Runge-Kutta step size small, the chance of having multiple packets to arrive during the interval and causing such error cannot be significant.

The algorithm for integrating fluid flows and packet flows is described in detail in Alg. 1. At each Runge-Kutta step, CPU needs to copy the updated queue length of all network queues to GPU global memory (at lines 8 and 9). The CUDA kernel functions are then invoked, which calculate the flow values of the current time, which include the congestion window size, the queue length, and the cumulative delay and packet loss rate (at lines 10 and 11). CPU then transfers the queue length and packet drop probability from GPU's global memory back to CPU's main memory (at line 12), so that it is ready for the next Runge-Kutta interval.

Upon each packet arrival, the simulator first draws a random number from the uniform distribution between 0 and 1 (at line 15). If it's less than ρ_l, which means the packet is randomly picked to be dropped according to the RED queuing policy, or if the packet would cause to queue to overflow (at line 16), the simulator drops the packet. Otherwise, the simulator inserts the packet into the queue (at line 19), updates the queue size (at line 20), and then schedules the packet departure with the proper delay (at line 21).

Note that, in this algorithm, the invocation of the GPU kernel functions is synchronous. CPU needs to wait for the GPU kernel functions to complete (at line 11) before it can continue with simulation for the next Runge-Kutta interval. This algorithm therefore is *lock-stepped*: there is no overlap

between CPU and GPU computations. In the next section, we describe several optimizations for CPU and GPU to perform their tasks asynchronously and more efficiently.

4. OPTIMIZATIONS

In the previous section, we introduce a hybrid traffic model which performs the background fluid-based traffic calculation on GPU and the foreground packet-oriented simulation on CPU. The algorithm is inefficient, however, due to the strong coupling between CPU and GPU computations—at each Runge-Kutta step, CPU has to transfer data to GPU, wait for the kernel invocations to complete, and then transfer data back from GPU, before it can continue with the discrete-event simulation for the next interval. In this section, we present optimizations to allow overlapping CPU and GPU calculations with reduced synchronization frequency.

4.1 Exploiting Lookahead

A close inspection on the set of differential equations of the fluid model reveals that the GPU threads evaluating the equations can be made independent of one another for a time interval larger than the Runge-Kutta step size. We observe that the flow values at one queue does not influence the calculation of the flow values of another queue for a period of time no less than the propagation delay of the link in-between.

Specifically, we see that , according to Eqn. (7), the arrival rate at the downstream queue $A_{k+1}(\cdot)$ is only dependent on the departure rate of the previous queue $D_k(\cdot)$ after a time lag equal to the link's propagation delay a_k. Also, in Eqns. (3), (4), and (5), we see that the the cumulative delay $d_{k+1}(\cdot)$ and the cumulative packet loss rate $r_{k+1}(\cdot)$ at the downstream queue are all dependent on corresponding values at the predecessor queue after a time lag equal to the sum of the link's propagation delay and the queuing delay, $a_k + q_k(t)/C_k$. Similarly, in Eqns. (9) and (10), the round-trip delay $R_i(\cdot)$ and the packet loss rate $\lambda_i(\cdot)$ are calculated from the cumulative delay and the cumulative packet loss rate, respectively, with a time lag as large as the path delay π_i.

This means that the thread responsible for evaluating the flow variables associated with a queue can run independently from the other threads within the same time window of size equal to the minimum propagation delay. Note that this concept is similar to the lookahead we use for parallel simulation. Lookahead is defined to be the minimum simulation time it takes for one simulation process to affect the state of another. With good lookahead, a process can safely process simulation events and advance its simulation clock in parallel with the other processes.

In this context, a simulation process is analogous to a GPU thread. To exploit this lookahead, we still keep the three GPU kernel functions, update_flow, update_queue, and update_hop; however, we make the threads to evaluate for as many as τ number of Runge-Kutta steps at each kernel invocation, where $\tau = \min\{a_k\}/\delta$, and δ is the Runge-Kutta step size. Consequently, data transfer between CPU and GPU happens only at each kernel invocation every $\tau\delta$ units of time. Given that the minimum link propagation delay is at least 10 times larger than the Runge-Kutta step size (for numerical stability), this optimization can significantly reduce the overhead associated with the kernel invocations and data transfers between CPU and GPU.

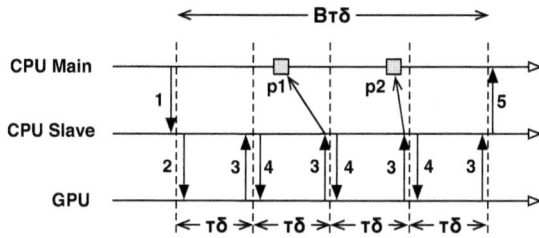

Figure 3: Overlapping CPU/GPU computation.

4.2 Overlapping CPU and GPU Computations

GPU is a separate computing device and can be treated as a co-processing unit to CPU. To improve performance, we need to overlap CPU and GPU computations and have CPU and GPU to perform tasks in parallel. For our hybrid traffic model, this means we want CPU to process simulation events associated with the foreground traffic and GPU to calculate the background traffic, *concurrently*.

We solve this problem by creating a separate thread on CPU to handle GPU kernel invocations for GPU to coast forward for a batch of Runge-Kutta steps without further update from CPU. As illustrated in Fig. 3, the method maintains two threads on CPU: the main thread for processing simulation events, and the slave thread for invoking the GPU kernel functions. The following steps corresponds to the numbers shown in the figure:

1. The CPU main thread schedules a Runge-Kutta batch event periodically every $B\tau\delta$ units of simulation, where B is the batch size, τ is determined by the lookahead described in the previous section, and δ is the Rung-Kutta step size. When processing this event, the main thread first check that the slave thread has completed the previous batch run and if so, signals the slave thread to set off a new batch run. CPU will continue processing events until the next Runge-Kutta batch event.

2. The CPU slave thread waits for the signal from the main thread to start a batch run. Upon receiving this signal, the slave thread transfers the updated queue lengths for all network queues from CPU to GPU. It then invokes the three GPU kernel functions in order: `update_flow`, `update_queue`, and `update_hop`. Each thread will run for τ number of Runge-Kutta steps.

3. The CPU slave thread waits for all three GPU kernels to complete and then copies the resulting fluid queue values from GPU. The CPU main thread processes packet arrival events (p_1 and p_2 in the figure) using the fluid queue values of the corresponding Runge-Kutta step, like in Alg. 1. This means that GPU may need to run ahead of CPU by as much as $\tau\delta$ time. In other words, the CPU main thread may need to wait for the slave thread (and the GPU) to get ahead. Synchronization between the CPU main thread and slave thread can be easily implemented using thread conditional variables.

4. The CPU slave thread sets off for the next τ number of Runge-Kutta steps by invoking the three GPU kernel functions. This step is similar to step 2, except here it does not include data transfers from CPU to GPU. Steps 3 and 4 alternates until GPU completes the whole batch.

5. The CPU slave thread signals the main thread that the batch run has completed, so that the main thread can start with the next batch run.

The above method allows GPU to run the fluid model for a batch of $B\tau$ steps using the updated queue lengths received from CPU at the beginning each batch (in step 2). The resulting fluid values (fluid queue length and drop probability) are copied back to CPU every τ steps. In the next section, we introduce a fix-up computation to avoid the accumulation of errors. In another section to follow, we also introduce an on-demand prefetching technique to further reduce data transfers during a batch run.

4.3 Fix-up Computation

In Section 3.3, we introduce an approximation method for mixing fluid and packet flows within a Runge-Kutta interval. We observe that the approximation may introduce errors due to possible queue overflow. Here we call it an *overflow problem*. We expect the overflow problem should not be significant because of the small step size.

When we consider multiple Runge-Kutta steps for batch runs (as detailed in the previous section), we face two other problems. One problem is how to set the batch size B. The fluid model on GPU only receives an update of the queue length from CPU at the beginning of each batch run. It then carries out the calculations for the next $B\tau$ number of Runge-Kutta steps independent of the changes happen at CPU. This is the same as to assume that the fluid traffic may not be significantly influenced by the packet arrivals during this time period. In general, the background traffic is the dominant traffic on the network, in which case the influence of packet flows on fluid flows is not as important as the other way around. Setting a bigger batch size can make fluid traffic to be less responsive to the changes in the packet flows. One must determine whether this situation is desirable for the simulation problem at hand, and set the batch size cognizant of the performance and accuracy tradeoff.

The other problem we face when dealing with batch runs is what we call an *underflow problem*, an example of which is illustrated by the top plot of Fig. 4. The figure shows the network queue size fluctuates as a function of fluid and packet arrivals over time. For a batch run that starts at time t_B, GPU calculates the background traffic flows and their effect on the fluid queue length, $q_l(\cdot)$, at time $t_B + \delta, t_B + 2\delta, \cdots, t_B + B\tau\delta$. For packet arrivals, the simulator accumulates the packet queue length $p_l(\cdot)$, as shown in Alg. 1 (at line 20). The sum of fluid and packet queue lengths determines the departure time of the arrived packet (see Eqn. 11). The underflow problem is that this method can gravely over-estimate the actual queue length when dealing batch runs having multiple Runge-Kutta steps.

The error occurs at the time when the fluid queue length gets close to zero. The fluid model calculates the queue length, $q_l(\cdot)$, according to the aggregate arrival rate and the bandwidth (Eqn. 2). When the queue becomes empty, for example, during the interval between $t_B + 2\delta$ and $t_B + 3\delta$ in Fig. 4, the queue length simply stays at zero. However, this does not affect the packet accumulations at CPU, $p_l(\cdot)$, which in fact should also be decreased at a rate according to the aggregate arrival rate and the bandwidth.

We solve this problem by asking GPU to calculate the quantity of *projected reduction* in queue length as if the fluid queue were not empty during this Runge-Kutta in-

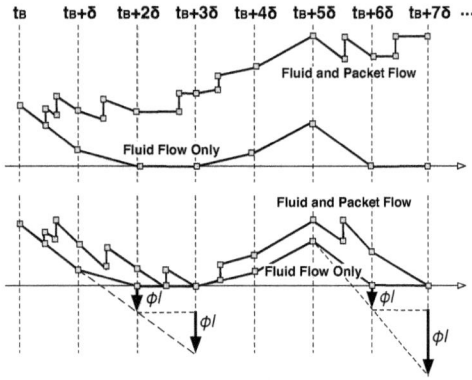

Figure 4: Underflow and fix-up computation.

terval. Suppose the fluid queue l becomes empty or stays empty during the interval between t and $t+\delta$; that is, when $q_l(t+\delta) = 0$. We can calculate the projected reduction in queue length for this interval as:

$$\phi_l(t+\delta) = \max\{(C_l - \Lambda_l(t))\delta - q_l(t), 0\} \quad (12)$$

We can then obtain the cumulative projected reduction in queue length from the beginning of the batch for each Runge-Kutta step of the batch:

$$\Phi_l(t_B + i\delta) = \sum_{k=1}^{i} \phi_l(t_B + k\delta) \quad (13)$$

where $i = 1, 2, \cdots, B\tau$.

On CPU, at the beginning of each batch run, we set $p_l(t_B)$ to zero and set t_l^p to t_B. t_l^p is a variable which we use to record the time at which p_l is last updated. Suppose a packet arrives at the network queue l at time x. We can adjust the current packet queue length p_l:

$$p_l(x) = \max\{p_l(t_l^p) - \Phi_l(x) + \Phi_l(t_l^p), 0\} \quad (14)$$

where $\Phi_l(t)$ (for an arbitrary time t) can be obtained using a linear interpolation of the values at the Runge-Kutta step boundaries, $t_B + i\delta$, where $i = 1, 2, \cdots, B\tau$. After that, we update t_l^p to be x, and we can now correctly schedule the corresponding packet departure event using Eqn. (11).

4.4 On-Demand Prefetching

Fig. 3 shows that the CPU slave thread needs to wait for the invocation of the three GPU kernel functions to complete and then copy the fluid queue values (including the fluid queue size $q_l(\cdot)$, the packet drop probability $\rho_l(\cdot)$, and the cumulative projected reduction in queue size $\Phi_l(\cdot)$) from GPU to CPU (shown as step 3). Such interaction happens once every τ number of Runge-Kutta time steps. In low packet traffic situations when the packets arrive sparingly, maintaining this level of interaction between CPU and GPU, however, may not be necessary. For better efficiency, CPU needs to be able to determine *on demand* whether to synchronize with GPU, and if so, what data needs to be transferred from GPU to CPU.

Let T_{CPU} be the time of the fluid values required by the CPU main thread to process a packet arrival at time t. We set T_{CPU} to be the end time of its current Runge-Kutta interval:

$$T_{CPU} = t_B + \lceil (t - t_B)/\delta \rceil \delta \quad (15)$$

Similarly, we use T_{GPU} to indicate the time up to which GPU has progressed. If the CPU main thread is processing a packet arrival, it needs to determine whether GPU has the needed fluid values ready to be used. If T_{GPU} is less than T_{CPU}, it means the main thread must wait for GPU to catch up. We accomplish this by using a conditional variable to synchronize between the CPU main thread and slave thread, which is overseeing the progress of GPU. We let the CPU main thread block on the conditional variable if GPU is lagging behind.

The CPU slave thread can determine whether or not to synchronize with GPU between the kernel invocations by choosing whether or not to wait for the completion of all previous invoked kernels. In our implementation the CPU slave thread can invoke the three GPU kernels consecutively at most B times (that's the entire batch) before it is forced to wait for all of them to complete. When GPU is ahead of CPU, the CPU main thread can copy the fluid values from T_{CPU} to T_{GPU} in one swoop. Prefetching data from GPU can reduce the frequency of such data transfers and thus improves efficiency. To facilitate that, we use a variable t_{up} to indicate the time of the fluid variables that have already been copied to the CPU main memory.

The complete algorithm, including all optimization techniques mentioned in this and previous sections, is summarized in Alg. 2 and Alg. 3. Alg. 2 describes logic of the CPU main thread and Alg. 3 describes the logic of the CPU slave thread that manages GPU computation.

5. EXPERIMENTS

We implemented the GPU-assisted hybrid network traffic model in our network simulator PRIME [31]. The simulator is designed for parallel and distributed simulation of large-scale networks. For now, the implementation of the hybrid model allows for only sequential execution. We conducted several experiments to validate the hybrid model and assess its performance.

The machine we used for the experiments is a Linux workstation equipped with an Intel i5-750 2.66 GHz CPU, 5 GB memory, and an NVIDIA GeForce GTX 260+ graphics card. We use GCC and CUDA compilers to compile the program with optimization level 2.

5.1 Validation Results

To demonstrate the correctness of the GPU-assisted hybrid model, we use a small network model, which was designed originally by Gu et al. to evaluate their hybrid model [6]. The network topology, as shown in Fig. 5, consists of only 12 nodes and 11 links. The delay and bandwidth of all links are set to be 10 ms and 100 Mbps, respectively. There are 22 RED queues in this example. We place four flows on the network: flow 0 and flow 1 each has 10 long-lasting TCP sessions, all starting at time 0; flow 2 has 20 long-lasting TCP sessions, also starting at time 0; flow 3 has 40 short-lived TCP sessions, starting at 30 seconds and lasting for only 30 seconds. We set the maximum queue length to be 5 MB for all network queues. All TCP sessions in the experiments are assumed to be TCP Reno with a maximum window size of 128 KB.

In the first validation test, we set all flows except flow 2 to be the background fluid traffic calculated on GPU. For flow 2, we select 0, 10, or 20 out of the 20 TCP sessions as the foreground packet-oriented traffic and simulate them on

Algorithm 2 Async hybrid simulation: CPU main thread
1: $q_l, p_l, t_l^p, \Phi_l \Leftarrow 0$ for all network queues
2: REQ $\Leftarrow$ false // whether CPU is requesting data from GPU
3: create and run CPU slave thread
4: schedule a Runge-Kutta batch event at time 0
5: $\cdots$ // initialize other simulation variables
6: **While** (simulation is not finished) **Do**
7:    e $\Leftarrow$ eventlist.getEarliestEvent()
8:    $t_c \Leftarrow$ e.time // current simulation time
9:    **If** (e is a Runge-Kutta batch event) **Then**
10:      **If** ($t_c > 0$) **Then**
11:        wait for signal from slave thread previous batch has completed
12:        copy q_l, ρ_l, and Φ_l for all network queues GPU$\Rightarrow$CPU
13:      **End If**
14:      $T_{GPU}, t_{up}, t_l^p, t_B \Leftarrow t_c$; // start time of the batch
15:      $T_{CPU} \Leftarrow T_{GPU} + \delta$
16:      update p_l for all network queues using Eqn. (14)
17:      $q_l \Leftarrow q_l + p_l$; $p_l \Leftarrow 0$ for all network queues
18:      signal slave thread to start a new batch
19:      schedule a Runge-Kutta batch event at time $t_c + B\tau\delta$
20:    **Else If** (e is a packet arrival event) **Then**
21:      $T_{CPU} \Leftarrow t_B + \lceil (t_c - t_B)/\delta \rceil \delta$ // round up
22:      **If** ($t_{up} < T_{CPU}$) **Then**
23:        **If** ($T_{CPU} > T_{GPU}$) **Then**
24:          REQ $\Leftarrow$ true // main thread is requesting GPU progress
25:          wait for signal from slave thread when $T_{GPU} \geq T_{CPU}$
26:        **End If**
27:        copy q_l, ρ_l, and Φ_l for $T_{CPU} \leq t \leq T_{GPU}$ GPU$\Rightarrow$CPU
28:        $t_{up} \Leftarrow T_{GPU}$ // time of prefetching
29:      **End If**
30:      update p_l using Eqn. (14), $t_l^p \Leftarrow t_B$
31:      u $\Leftarrow$ uniform(0,1)
32:      **If** ($u < \rho_l$ OR $q_l + p_l +$ packet.size $> Q_l^{max}$) **Then**
33:        drop the packet
34:      **Else**
35:        insert packet into the queue
36:        $p_l \Leftarrow p_l +$ packet.size
37:        schedule packet departure event at time $t_c + (q_l + p_l)/C_l$
38:      **End If**
39:    **Else**
40:      $\cdots$ // process other simulation events
41:    **End If**
42: **End While**

Algorithm 3 Async hybrid simulation: CPU slave thread
1: **While** (**True**) **Do**
2:    wait for signal from main thread to start a new batch
3:    copy q_l for all network queuesCPU$\Rightarrow$GPU
4:    $i \Leftarrow 0$
5:    **While** ($i < B$) **Do**
6:      invoke **update_flow**, **update_queue** and **update_hop**
7:      $i \Leftarrow i + 1$
8:      **If** (REQ = true AND $t_B + i\tau\delta \geq T_{CPU}$) **Then**
9:        wait for all previously invoked kernels to complete
10:        $T_{GPU} \Leftarrow t_B + i\tau\delta$
11:        REQ $\Leftarrow$ false
12:        signal CPU main thread $T_{GPU} \geq T_{CPU}$
13:      **End If**
14:    **End While**
15:    wait for all previously invoked kernels to complete
16:    signal CPU main thread the batch has completed
17: **End While**

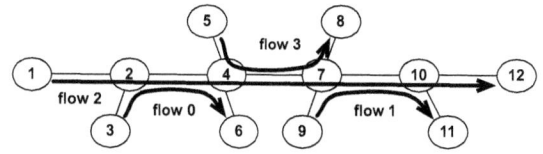

Figure 5: A small network topology with 4 flows.

flows, the queue length exhibits larger variations since the pure fluid model can only capture average traffic behavior. We observed the same result from the CPU-only model.

In the next validation test, we study the effect of different batch sizes on accuracy. As we mentioned earlier, having a large batch can introduce errors, because CPU can only push the information about the effect of the packet flows (as updated queue length) to GPU at the start of a batch. That is, the influence of packet flows on fluid flows can be delayed if the batch size is large; the result is that the background fluid flows can become less responsive to the changes in the foreground packet flows.

To study this effect, we use the same network model as in the previous experiment. We designate 10 TCP sessions in flow 2 to be packet flows. All other flows are modeled as fluid flows. We compare the results with various batch sizes. Fig. 7 shows the TCP congestion window size of the four flows changes over time for three cases: $B = 1, \tau = 1$; $B = 1, \tau = 20$; and $B = 20, \tau = 20$. Note that the lookahead τ can be set as large as 20; however, we include the case for $B = 1, \tau = 1$ as the baseline for comparison.

We observe similar results for the three test cases. Flow 0 and flow 1 have very similar congestion window trajectories. In comparison, flow 2 has a smaller congestion window because it has a longer round-trip time. At 30 seconds, flow 3 (with 40 TCP sessions) arrives and immediately causes congestion at the link between node 4 and node 7, as shown in Fig. 6. Because of the congestion, flow 2 reduces its congestion window size during this period. Consequently, both flow 0 and flow 1 increase their window size to reclaim the bandwidth handed out by flow 2. The $B = 20$ case shows slightly larger variations than the other two cases. If we keep increasing B more than 20, the delay effect becomes evident and the results become unrecognizable (therefore, it's not shown). This experiment tells us that we cannot arbitrarily increase the batch size; however, we do not yet know exactly

CPU using the detailed TCP implementation in the simulator. The rest of flow 2 are fluid flows and set as part of the background traffic calculated on GPU. In the case of 0 TCP sessions, we have a pure fluid model, which we use as the baseline for comparison.

We fix the Runge-Kutta step size to be 0.5 ms. Therefore, the lookahead τ is 20 (because the minimum link delay is 10 ms and the Runge Kutta step size δ is 0.5 ms). We start with the batch size $B = 1$. Fig. 6 shows the length of the network queue in node 4 (in the network interface connecting to node 7). We see that the queue length increases rapidly at 30 seconds when flow 3 (with 40 TCP sessions) enters the network causing congestion at the link between node 4 and node 7. The TCP sessions in flow 3 end at 60 seconds, at which time the congestion is relieved and the fluid queue length comes back zero. The results are similar with different mixture of packet and fluid flows. As expected, with more packet

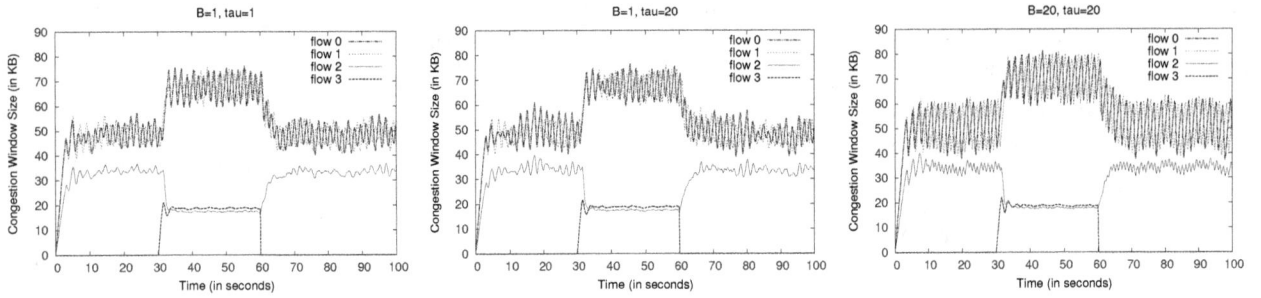

Figure 7: TCP window trajectory under different batch sizes.

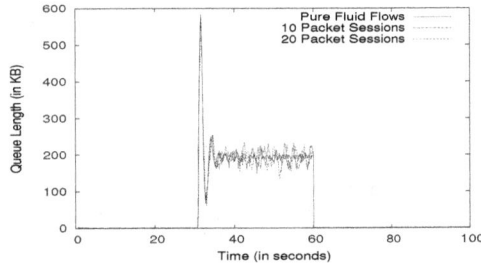

Figure 6: Result from different traffic mixtures.

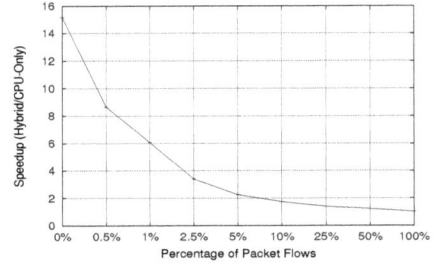

Figure 9: Speedup decreases with more packet flows.

what would be the largest batch size one can choose to get reasonable results.

5.2 Performance Experiments

Next we focus on evaluating the performance of our GPU-assisted hybrid network traffic model. For this experiment, we use the standard campus network model, which has been used for benchmarking the performance of various network simulators. The network consists of a variable number of stub networks, call "campuses". At the top level, the campuses are connected as a ring with additional shortcuts between the campuses that are far apart. Each campus has 504 end hosts, organized into 12 local area networks (LANs) connected by 18 routers. Each campus also has a server cluster with 4 end hosts that can be used as the traffic source. Each LAN consists of a gateway router connecting to 42 end hosts with 10 Mb/s bandwidth and 1 ms delay. A campus is divided into 4 OSPF areas. The links between the routers in the OSPF backbone area and those in the server cluster are configured with 1 Gb/s bandwidth and 10 ms delay. All other router links have 100 Mb/s bandwidth and 10 ms delay.

For the experiment, we choose to simulate 4, 8, and 16 campuses. We cannot run 32 campuses because of the memory limitation on the machine. Traffic on the campus network is generated randomly by the end hosts requesting data from a server in the server cluster either at the same campus or on another campus. Each end host generates 10 TCP flows. Therefore, each campus gets 5,040 traffic flows; for 16 campuses, that's more than 80,000 flows. On average, 50% of the flows are set between campuses. In separate tests, we designate 0%, 0.5%, and 1% of these flows as foreground packet flows simulated using detailed TCP implementation; the rest of the flows are treated as background fluid flows. In this experiment, we set the Runge-Kutta step size to be 0.5 ms and the batch size to be 3.

We compared the performance of our GPU-assisted hybrid model against the original CPU-only implementation. The results are shown in Fig. 8. The normalized execution time is the run time of the model divided by the simulation time. That is, if the normalized execution time is bigger than 1, we have a slow-down: the simulation runs slower than real time. Otherwise, if it's smaller than 1, the simulation is running faster than real time. The CPU-only implementation (left plot) has a slow-down factor ranging from 1.3 for 4 campuses with 0% packet flows to 9.3 for 16 campuses with 1% packet flows. In comparison, our GPU-assisted hybrid model (middle plot) is running faster than real time, except for the case of 16 campuses with 1% packet flows. The right plot in Fig. 8 shows the speedup of the GPU-accelerated model over the CPU-only implementation. With more campuses, more speedup is achieved as the model is benefiting from the more data parallelism available on GPU. As expected, the highest speedup (25x) is achieved by the pure fluid model (i.e., with 0% packet flows).

With increasing packet flows, the speedup decreases. Fig. 9 shows the speedup of our GPU-accelerated model over the CPU-only implementation as we vary the portion of packet flows (for 8 campuses). With more packet flows, the CPU computation is taking over; also, the communication is becoming more expensive as more data needs to be transfered between CPU and GPU. Eventually, the speedup becomes 1 when all flows are packet flows.

Our final experiment looks at the effect of batch size on performance. Fig. 10 shows that the normalized execution time of our GPU-assisted hybrid model decreases as we increase the batch size from 1 to 7. We observe that increasing batch size has a diminishing return in terms of performance improvement. The results show that the performance levels off after the batch size reaches 3 or 4. Beyond that, having a larger batch size does not produce much better perfor-

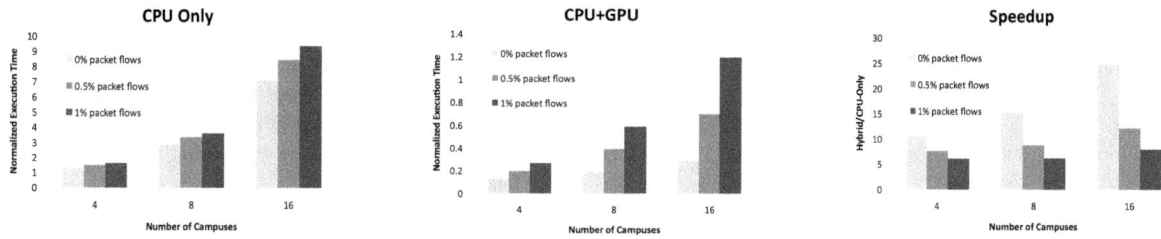

Figure 8: Performance comparison between CPU-only and GPU-accelerated implementations.

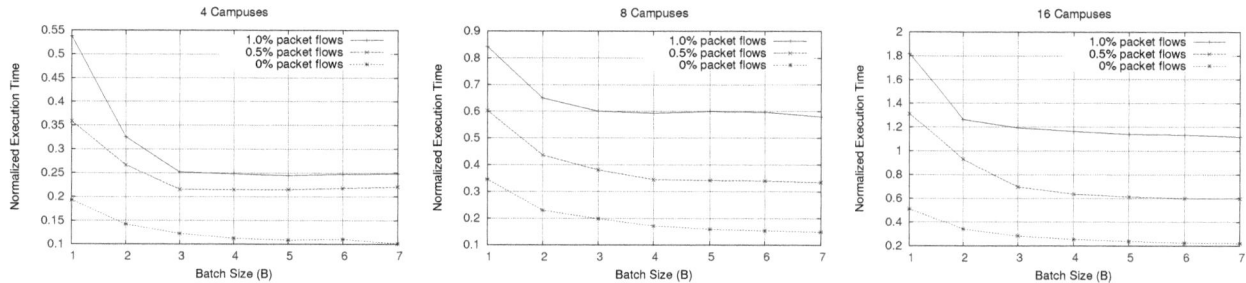

Figure 10: GPU performance decreases with increasing batch size.

mance; in doing so, however, may cause larger errors that can jeopardize the validity of the simulation results.

6. CONCLUSION

In this paper, we propose a GPU-assisted hybrid network traffic model which offloads the numerically intensive background traffic calculations to GPU, and keeps the discrete-event simulation of the foreground packet-oriented transactions on CPU. A novel mechanism that integrates fluid-based and packet-oriented network traffic is introduced, with several optimization techniques that can effectively overlaps CPU and GPU computations and minimize the effect of the inherent communication latencies between CPU and GPU. Experiments show that our method can achieve significant speedup over the CPU-only approach, while still maintaining desirable accuracy.

Our immediate future work includes comparison of the performance impact among the various optimization techniques and further investigation of the loss of accuracy introduced by batch runs. We would like to develop a method for determining the batch size given simulation scenarios. Our current implementation of the hybrid model is sequential. To parallelize the GPU model, we recognize the same lookahead inherent to the fluid equations. However, in order to achieve better parallelism, necessary mechanisms need to be in place to support batch runs. Together with the parallel packet-oriented network simulation, the GPU model shall be able to support massive-scale network simulations with realistic traffic characterization on today's hybrid supercomputing platforms with GPUs.

Acknowledgment

We thank Dr. Kalyan Perumalla at Oak Ridge National Laboratory for the initial discussion of the GPU design. We also thank the anonymous reviewers for their constructive comments. This research is supported in part by the United States National Science Foundation grants (CNS-0836408, CCF-0937964, HRD-0833093), a subcontract from the GENI Project Office at Raytheon BBN Technologies (CNS-0714770, CNS-1346688), and by the National Natural Science Foundation of China (No. 61272087, No. 61363019, No. 61073008 and No. 60773148), Beijing Natural Science Foundation (No. 4082016 and No. 4122039).

7. REFERENCES

[1] B. G. Aaby, K. S. Perumalla, and S. K. Seal. Efficient simulation of agent-based models on multi-GPU and multi-core clusters. In *Proceedings of the 3rd International ICST Conference on Simulation Tools and Techniques (SIMUTools'10)*, 2010.

[2] J. S. Ahn and P. B. Danzig. Packet network simulation: Speedup and accuracy versus timing granularity. *IEEE/ACM Transactions on Networking (TON)*, 4(5):743–757, October 1996.

[3] J. Cowie, D. Nicol, and A. Ogielski. Modeling the global Internet. *Computing in Science and Engineering*, 1(1):42–50, 1999.

[4] R. M. Fujimoto. Parallel discrete event simulation. *Communications of the ACM*, 33(10):30–53, 1990.

[5] GPGPU. General-purpose computation using graphics hardware. http://www.gpgpu.org/.

[6] Y. Gu, Y. Liu, and D. Towsley. On integrating fluid models with packet simulation. *INFOCOM*, 2004.

[7] Y. Guo, W. Gong, and D. Towsley. Time-stepped hybrid simulation (TSHS) for large scale networks. *INFOCOM*, pages 441–450, 2000.

[8] P. Jetley, L. Wesolowski, F. Gioachin, L. V. Kalé, and T. R. Quinn. Scaling hierarchical N-body simulations on GPU clusters. In *Proceedings of the 2010 ACM/IEEE International Conference for High Performance Computing, Networking, Storage and Analysis (SC'10)*, pages 1–11, 2010.

[9] C. Kiddle, R. Simmonds, C. Williamson, and B. Unger. Hybrid packet/fluid flow network simulation. In *Proceedings of PADS'03*, pages 143–152, 2003.

[10] T. Li, N. V. Vorst, and J. Liu. A rate-based TCP traffic model to accelerate network simulation. *Transactions of the Society for Modeling and Simulation International*, 89, 2013.

[11] X. Li, W. Cai, and S. J. Turner. Gpu accelerated three-stage execution model for event-parallel simulation. In *Proceedings of PADS '13*, pages 57–66, 2013.

[12] M. Liljenstam, J. Liu, and D. M. Nicol. Development of an internet backbone topology for large-scale network simulations. In *Proceedings of WSC'03*, 2003.

[13] J. Liu. Packet-level integration of fluid TCP models in real-time network simulation. In *Proceedings of WSC'06*, pages 2162–2169, December 2006.

[14] J. Liu. Parallel simulation of hybrid network traffic models. In *Proceedings of PADS'07*, pages 141–151, June 2007.

[15] J. Liu and Y. Li. On the performance of a hybrid network traffic model. *Simulation Modelling Practice and Theory*, 16(6):656–669, 2008.

[16] Y. Liu, F. L. Presti, V. Misra, D. F. Towsley, and Y. Gu. Scalable fluid models and simulations for large-scale IP networks. *TOMACS*, 14(3):305–324, 2004.

[17] V. Misra, W.-B. Gong, and D. Towsley. Fluid-based analysis of a network of AQM routers supporting TCP flows with an application to RED. *SIGCOMM*, pages 151–160, 2000.

[18] D. M. Nicol. Discrete event fluid modeling of TCP. In *Proceedings of WSC'01*, 2001.

[19] D. M. Nicol, M. Goldsby, and M. Johnson. Fluid-based simulation of communication networks using SSF. In *Proceedings of the 1999 European Simulation Symposium*, 1999.

[20] D. M. Nicol and G. Yan. Discrete event fluid modeling of background TCP traffic. *TOMACS*, 14(3):211–250, July 2004.

[21] NVIDIA. Common Unified Device Architecture (CUDA). http://developer.nvidia.com/cuda.

[22] L. Nyland, M. Harris, and J. Prinsn. Fast N-Body Simulation with CUDA. In H. Nguyen, editor, *GPU Gems 3*, chapter 31. Addison Wesley Professional, August 2007.

[23] J. D. Owens, D. Luebke, N. Govindaraju, M. Harris, J. Krüger, A. E. Lefohn, and T. J. Purcell. A survey of general-purpose computation on graphics hardware. In *Eurographics*, pages 21–51, 2005.

[24] H. Park and P. A. Fishwick. A GPU-based application framework supporting fast discrete-event simulation. *Transactions of the Society for Modeling and Simulation International*, 86(10):613–628, 2010.

[25] H. Park and P. A. Fishwick. An analysis of queuing network simulation using GPU-based hardware acceleration. *ACM Transactions on Modeling and Computer Simulation (TOMACS)*, 21(3), 2011.

[26] K. S. Perumalla. Discrete-event execution alternatives on general purpose graphical processing units (GPGPUs). In *Proceedings of PADS'06*, pages 74–81, 2006.

[27] K. S. Perumalla and B. G. Aaby. Data parallel execution challenges and runtime performance of agent simulations on GPUs. In *Proceedings of the 2008 Spring simulation multiconference (SpringSim'08)*, pages 116–123, 2008.

[28] K. S. Perumalla, B. G. Aaby, S. B. Yoginath, and S. K. Seal. GPU-based real-time execution of vehicular mobility models in large-scale road network scenarios. In *Proceedings of PADS'09*, pages 95–103, 2009.

[29] M. Pharr and R. Fernando. *GPU Gems 2: Programming Techniques For High-Performance Graphics And General-Purpose Computation.* Addison-Wesley, 2005.

[30] T. Preis, P. Virnau, W. Paul, and J. J. Schneider. GPU accelerated Monte Carlo simulation of the 2D and 3D Ising model. *Journal of Computational Physics*, 228:4468–4477, 2009.

[31] PRIME Research Group. Parallel Real-time Immersive network Modeling Environment. http://www.primessf.net/.

[32] G. F. Riley. The Georgia Tech network simulator. *MoMeTools*, pages 5–12, 2003.

[33] G. F. Riley, T. M. Jaafar, and R. Fujimoto. Integrated fluid and packet network simulations. In *Proceedings of MASCOTS'02*, pages 511–518, 2002.

[34] J. E. Stone, D. Gohara, and G. Shi. OpenCL: A parallel programming standard for heterogeneous computing systems. *Computing in Science & Engineering*, 12(3):66, 2010.

[35] W. Tang and Y. Yao. A GPU-based discrete event simulation kernel. *Transactions of the Society for Modeling and Simulation International*, 89, 2013.

[36] TOP500 Supercomputers Sites. http://top500.org/.

[37] M. Verdesca, J. Munro, M. Hoffman, M. Bauer, and D. Manocha. Using graphics processor units to accelerate OneSAF: A case study in technology transition. *JDMS*, 3(3):177–187, 2006.

[38] L. Xu, M. Taufer, S. Collins, and D. G. Vlachos. Parallelization of tau-leap coarse-grained Monte Carlo simulations on GPUs. In *24th IEEE International Symposium on Parallel and Distributed Processing (IPDPS'10)*, pages 1–9, 2010.

[39] Z. Xu and R. Bagrodia. GPU-accelerated evaluation platform for high fidelity network modeling. In *Proceedings of the PADS'07*, pages 131–140, 2007.

[40] G. Yaun, D. Bauer, H. Bhutada, C. Carothers, M. Yuksel, and S. Kalyanaraman. Large-scale network simulation techniques: Examples of TCP and OSPF models. *ACM SIGCOMM Computer Communication Review*, 33(3):27–41, 2003.

[41] J. Zhou, Z. Ji, M. Takai, and R. Bagrodia. MAYA: Integrating hybrid network modeling to the physical world. *ACM Transactions on Modeling and Computer Simulation (TOMACS)*, 14(2):149–169, 2004.

Modeling and Simulation of Data Center Networks

Reem Alshahrani
Department of Computer Science
Kent State University
Kent, Ohio 44236–0001
ralshahr@kent.edu

Hassan Peyravi
Department of Computer Science
Kent State University
Kent, Ohio 44236–0001
peyravi@cs.kent.edu

ABSTRACT

Data centers are integral part of cloud computing that support Web services, online social networking, data analysis, computation intensive applications and scientific computing. They require high performance components for their interprocess communication, storage and sub-communication systems. The performance bottleneck that used to be the processing power has now been shifted to communication speed within data centers. The performance of a data center, in terms of throughput and delay, is directly related to the performance of the underlying internal communication network.

In this paper, we introduce an analytical model that can be used to evaluate the underlying network architecture in data centers. The model can further be used to develop simulation tools that extend the scope of performance evaluation beyond what it can be achieved by the theoretical model in terms of various network topologies, different traffic distributions, scalability, and load balancing. While the model is generic, we focus on its implementation for fat-tree networks that are widely used in data centers. The theoretical results are compared and validated with the simulation results for several network configurations. The results of this analysis provide a basis for data center network design and optimization.

Categories and Subject Descriptors: C.2.1 [Computer Communication Networks]: Data Center Networks.

General Terms: Theory.

Keywords: Data centers; Tandem Queuing; Topology Analysis.

1. INTRODUCTION

A significant portion of Internet applications and communications are taking place in data centers in which thousands of servers and storage systems are interconnected. Scalability becomes a limiting factor in majority of commercial and home-grown simulation models, mainly due to the interac-

tion of protocol stacks that makes it hard to pin-point the performance bottlenecks.

Large-scale data centers are the foundations to support many data-intensive communications such as scientific computations, cloud computing Internet applications, and data analysis. A data center is a large cluster of interconnected servers and routers designed with the goal of optimizing both cost and performance. Figure 1 illustrates an example of a simple data center network (DCN) architecture [1] in which rack-mounted servers are connected to a Top of Rack (ToR) switch. The ToR switch is connected to a primary and back up aggregation switches. Each aggregation switch receives traffic from ToR switches and then forward it to the access routers. The access routers aggregate traffic from several thousand servers and route it to core routers. The core routers connect the data center network to the Internet.

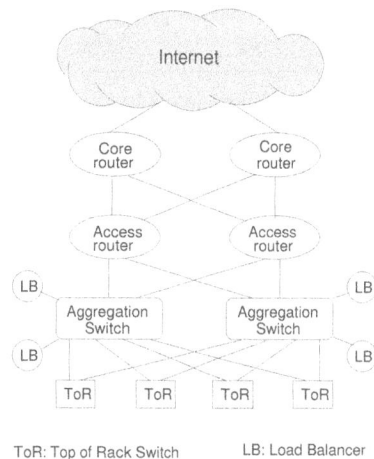

ToR: Top of Rack Switch   LB: Load Balancer

Figure 1: A DCN architecture.

Data centers are anticipated to be the bottleneck in hosting network-based services. It has been observed that data centers contribute to a significant portion of overall delay, and this delay is likely to grow with the increasing use of dynamic Web contents [7]. The gap between communication and computation speeds is widening and communication speed within a data center is becoming a bottleneck. Since computational and communication needs are constrained by the underlying network performance at data centers, the interconnection network plays a significant role for the traffic coming in and going out from a data center and has become a critical element in the overall design. Therefore, researchers and data center designers need to study various design alternatives for data center networks (DCNs).

One of the widely used network topologies is fat-tree [4] which is basically a hierarchical structure where the capacity of the network increases for traffic aggregates upward. Figure 2 illustrates a fat-tree network. A fat-tree network

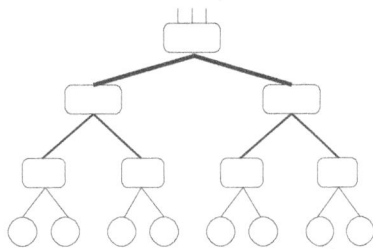

Figure 2: Fat-tree network.

can be viewed as a folded non-blocking rearrangeable Clos network [6]. The topology is used and implemented in the largest data centers worldwide, mainly due to (i) its ability to provide full bisection bandwidth and (ii) aggregate traffic naturally for a tree with low latency and self-routing. However, hierarchical structures in general have the saturation problem as traffic moves upward toward the root, and that limits the overall performance of the network.

In this paper, we develop a theoretical model that reduces the simulation scalability problem significantly. It can be used to evaluate the performance of various interconnection networks for data center design. Second, the model can be used to study various alternative designs theoretically and use it for validation and verification of the the simulation model. Finally, numerical results for a few cases have been presented.

The rest of the paper is organized as follows. Section 1.1 briefly covers major related contributions. Section 2 presents a model that describes and formulates the widely used fat-tree network topology in data centers. Section 3 devise a model for a switching module and network that can be used to compute the throughput of an $n \times m$ switching element as well as the end-to-end throughput for the entire network in close forms. Section 4 develop an open queuing network that can be used to compute the end-to-end delay close forms. Section 5 presents simulation results for the purpose of comparative analysis with the theoretical results. Section 6 describes how the model can be used to design an appropriate network to cluster the servers and interconnect them with aggregation switches and core routers. Finally, conclusions and remarks are given in Section 7.

1.1 Related Work

In data centers, servers are packaged into racks and connected with an aggregation Top of Rack (ToR) switches. The bandwidth at the top-level of a data center is a fraction of the incoming capacity and that raises a blocking (bottleneck) problem. Performance of data centers, in terms of throughput and response time, relies heavily on the performance of underlying networking infrastructure inside the centers.

The main challenge is how to build a scalable DCN that can deliver significant aggregate bandwidth with low latency and meet the requirements of serving applications. One of the proposals is fat-tree [4] network that adopts a folded

Clos network topology [6] to provide higher bisection bandwidth with low latency. However, such a topology with a hierarchical structure suffers from performance bottleneck due to oversubscription at the higher layers of the hierarchy. As a result, new layer-2 networks such as PortLand [15] and VL2 [9] were designed to be implemented on top of any Clos topology [6]. The goal of this kind of network is to solve the issue of oversubscription in Clos-based data centers. While it can be scaled to support massive data centers with high bisection bandwidth, its deployment requires expensive equipment and does not support incremental deployment. With the same goal of solving the issue of oversubscription in Clos-based topologies, other proposals such as Helois in [8], and c-Through in [17] suggest taking an advantage of wireless or optical networks and implement them in conjunction with the hierarchical topologies. Employing these techniques increases material cost and interconnection network complexity.

Other proposals such BCube in [10] and DCell in [11] have utilized hypercube structures to reduce average path lengths and improve the overall bandwidth through inter-cell network connections. This involves using complex network patterns which limits DCN expansion to a certain degree and requires complex cabling. In [12], a dynamic variation of active network elements has been investigated to achieve energy efficiency and fault-tolerance. In [5], an imperial study of network traffic patterns in various data centers has been investigated.

To assess the effectiveness of these solutions, whether they can meet the requirements of data centers or not, large-scale deployment or simulation of the infrastructure network, that supports thousands of nodes would become necessary. Most of the proposed approaches were tested and evaluated on a limited number of hosts ranging from 16 up to 27 hosts. While hardware level of simulation can yield more detailed information, it does not provide a clear estimation of a data center performance. In reality, the size of the data center significantly affects its performance. Limiting the simulation scope to a small number of hosts will underestimate the DCN performance assessments.

2. DCN MODELING

Given the hierarchical and regular structure of a data center interconnection, in this section, we introduce a modeling scheme that can be used to develop a robust simulation model and also be used to verify the simulation model with basic theoretical results. An $N \times M$ multi-rooted multi-stage fat-tree can be constructed by stacking L rows of $n \times m$ switches, where $N = n^L$ and $M = m^L$. An example of 4-rooted 2-stage $4^2 \times 2^2$ network is shown in Figure 3. Clearly, various decompositions of N and M will give different multi-rooted unique path fat-tree networks. There are two ways to increase the end-to-end bandwidth in a fat-tree network; (i) by increasing the bandwidth of upstream links, and (ii) by adding extra stages that provides alternate paths for an end-to-end connection. While the latter increases the network throughput by reducing the internal blocking probability and increases the hardware cost, the former demands for much faster links between stages which is not unlimited. Adding extra stages will also increase the delay and larger lookup tables.

Consider two non-prime integers N and M ($N \geq M > 2$). Let $I = \langle n_1, n_2, \cdots, n_L \rangle$ and $O = \langle m_1, m_2, \cdots, m_L \rangle$ be

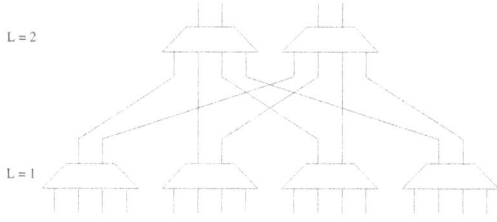

Figure 3: A 2-stage 16×4 fat-tree network.

two decomposition permutation vectors of N and M, respectively, where $N = \prod_{i=1}^{L} n_i$ and $M = \prod_{i=1}^{L} m_i$. An L-stage unique-path fat-tree network can be constructed from vectors I and O, where the i-th stage of the network is made of switches of size $n_i \times m_i$. From graph theory perspective, I and O represent the in-degree and out-degree of nodes (switches) at different stages of the network. Clearly, the number of switches at stage 1 is N/n_1, the number of switches at stage 2 is Nm_1/n_1n_2, and the number of switches at stage i is $Nm_1m_2\cdots m_{i-1}/n_1n_2\cdots n_i$. The last stage of the network consists of $Nm_1m_2\cdots m_{L-1}/n_1n_2\cdots n_L$ switches. Various decomposition of $N = 12, 16$ and $M = 4$ for building a fat-tree network are given in Table 1.

Table 1: Possible fat-tree configurations, $N = 12, 16$, $M = 4$.

	$N = 12,$	$M = 4$	$N = 16,$	$M = 4$
L	I	O	I	O
1	$< 12 >$	$< 4 >$	$< 16 >$	$< 4 >$
2	$< 3, 4 >$	$< 2, 2 >$	$< 4, 4 >$	$< 2, 2 >$
2	$< 4, 3 >$	$< 2, 2 >$	$< 2, 8 >$	$< 2, 2 >$
2	$< 2, 6 >$	$< 2, 2 >$	$< 8, 2 >$	$< 2, 2 >$
2	$< 6, 2 >$	$< 2, 2 >$		

The interconnections between successive stages form an nm-shuffle permutation (σ_{nm}). In effect, σ_{nm} divides nm indices into n sets, each having m indices, such that the first m indices belong to the first set, the second m indices belong to the second set, and so on. It then picks, in order, the first index from each set, the second index from each set, and so on, until all indices are all picked. This is illustrated by the link permutation between stage 1 and stage 2 in Figure 4 in which $\{\{0,1\}, \{2,3\}, \{4,5\}, \{6,7\}\}$ is mapped onto $\{\{0,2,4,6\}, \{1,3,5,7\}\}$. The permutation links between the

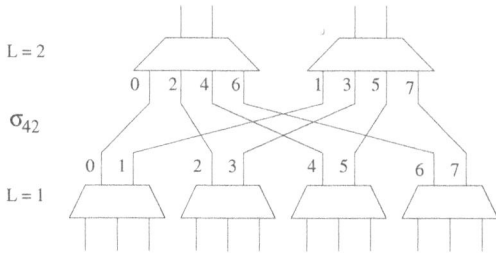

Figure 4: A 12×4 fat-tree network with non-uniform switches.

first stage and the second stage in Figure 4 form a 4-shuffle

of 8 indices. Similarly, the permutation links between the first stage and the second stage in Figure 3 form a 4-shuffle of 8 indices, where an n-shuffle of nm indices, denoted by σ_{nm}, is defined by [16],

$$\sigma_{nm}(i) = \left(n \times i + \left\lfloor \frac{i}{m} \right\rfloor \right) \mod nm, \quad 0 \leq i \leq nm - 1 \tag{1}$$

Alternatively, σ_{nm} can be expressed as,

$$\sigma_{nm}(i) = \begin{cases} n \times i \mod (nm - 1) & 0 \leq i < nm - 1 \\ i & i = nm - 1 \end{cases} \tag{2}$$

It is easy to see that n-shuffle is an inverse permutation of m-shuffle of nm indices for the reverse traffic. Hence,

$$\sigma_{nm} = \sigma_{mn}^{-1}, \text{and} \quad \sigma_{nm}\left(\sigma_{mn}(i)\right) = i, \quad 0 \leq i \leq nm - 1. \tag{3}$$

While the upstream permutation links between successive stages follow σ_{nm}, the down-stream permutation links between successive stages follow σ_{mn}^{-1}.

3. THROUGHPUT MODELING

3.1 Switch Module

Consider an $n \times m$ switch, as shown in Figure 5, where $m \leq n$. Collision occurs when two packets contend for the same output port during the same time slot. Let ρ be the

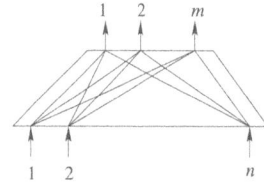

Figure 5: An $n \times m$ switch.

probability that an input buffer is not empty during a time slot, then q_i, the probability of i input buffers are non-empty is

$$q_i = \binom{n}{i} \rho^i (1 - \rho)^{n-i}, \tag{4}$$

where $\binom{n}{i}$ is the binomial coefficient.

Let $E(i)$ be the expected number of packets served by the $n \times m$ switch during a time slot. The number of ways in which i arriving packets can be routed to m distinct output ports, during the time slot, is m^i. Now, assume a particular output port is idle during the time slot. Then, the number of ways the i arriving packets can be routed to $m - 1$ distinct output ports, during the time slot, is $(m - 1)^i$. Thus, $m^i - (m - 1)^i$ is the number of ways in which a particular output port always receives a packet. Therefore, the expected number of packets routed through the switch, given i arriving packets, is

$$E(i) = \frac{m^i - (m - 1)^i}{m^i} \cdot m = m \left[1 - \left(1 - \frac{1}{m} \right)^i \right] \tag{5}$$

Thus, the expected bandwidth of an $n \times m$ switch is.

$$B_{n \times m} = \sum_{i=0}^{n} E(i) \cdot q_i$$

$$= m \sum_{i=0}^{n} \binom{n}{i} \rho^i (1-\rho)^{n-i} \left[1 - \left(1 - \frac{1}{m}\right)^i \right]$$

$$= m \sum_{i=0}^{n} \binom{n}{i} \rho^i (1-\rho)^{n-i} - m \sum_{i=0}^{n} \binom{n}{i} \left(\rho(1-\frac{1}{m})\right)^i (1-\rho)^{n-i}$$

$$= m \left[1 - \left(1 - \frac{\rho}{m}\right)^n \right] \quad (6)$$

Dividing the r.h.s of Equation (6) by m, the number of output lines, gives the traffic rate on any one of m output ports.

$$B_{n \times 1} = 1 - \left(1 - \frac{\rho}{m}\right)^n \quad (7)$$

3.2 Network Module

For any stage of a fat-tree network, the output rate, ρ_{out}, is a function of its input rate, ρ_{in}, and is given by,

$$\rho_{out} = 1 - \left(1 - \frac{\rho_{in}}{m}\right)^n \quad (8)$$

Therefore, the performance of each stage will be affected by the departure rate of the previous stage.

Let P be the probability that an arbitrary arriving packet to an input port successfully depart from an output port during a slot time. P can be defined as the ratio of expected bandwidth to the expected number of packets arriving during a time slot. Hence,

$$P = \frac{B_{n \times m}}{n\rho} = \frac{m}{n\rho} \left[1 - \left(1 - \frac{\rho}{m}\right)^n \right] \quad (9)$$

Let ρ_i be the rate of the packet departure rate on an output port of stage i, then from Equation (8), the following recursive equation gives the bandwidth of the network.

$$B_{N \times M} = M\rho_L, \quad \rho_i = 1 - \left(1 - \frac{\rho_{i-1}}{m}\right)^n, \quad \rho_0 = \rho,$$

$$1 \le i \le L, \quad N = n^L, \quad M = m^L \quad (10)$$

where, $\rho_0 = \rho$ is the input rate for the switches at stage 1. Therefore, the probability that a packet will be routed through the network without any blocking is,

$$P_{N \times M} = \frac{m^L \rho_L}{n^L \rho} \quad (11)$$

Similarly, for non-uniform switches,

$$P_{N \times M} = \frac{m_1 m_2 \cdots m_L \rho_L}{n_1 n_2 \cdots n_L \rho} \quad (12)$$

Now, consider a fat-tree network with $n_i \times m_i$ switching elements at stage i, $1 \le i \le L$. Then, Equation (10) can be generalized to include non-uniform switches.

$$B_{N \times M} = M\rho_L, \quad \rho_i = 1 - \left(1 - \frac{\rho_{i-1}}{m_i}\right)^{n_i}$$

$$\rho_0 = \rho, \quad 1 \le i \le L \quad (13)$$

4. DELAY MODELING

To model the delay performance, we consider the network as a stack of interconnected tandem queuing system, where each node has a FIFO buffer. Exogenous (external) packets arriving to the core nodes are forwarded through the distribution network towards the servers. Similarly, servers forward packets towards the core node via the aggregation network. Given the structure of fat-tree networks, the upstream traffic suffers significantly more delay and throughput degradation than the downstream traffic. Hence, in this paper we analyze the performance of upstream traffic due to the dominant role of the aggregation network.

Consider a partial structure of the network that is illustrated in Figure 6, where γ_j is the cumulative rate of exogenous (external) traffic flows entering node j, λ_j is the aggregate traffic, both exogenous and endogenous (relay) flows, arriving to node j. r_{ij} is the probability of a packet routed from node i to node j. A packet departing from node i may arrive to node j deterministically $r_{ij} = 1$, as in multiplexing sink-tree networks with fixed routing, or it may arrive to the next node probabilistically when alternate routing is provided. In tandem queuing systems, the arrival time

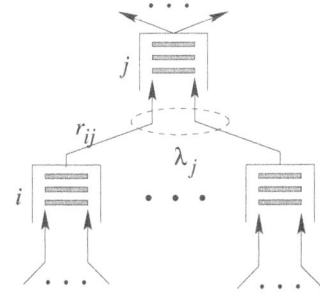

Figure 6: Tandem queues representing a switch.

of a packet to a receiving node is strongly correlated with its departure time from the preceding nodes. There exists no analytical results for such networks in which interarrival and service times are dependent. However, Kleinrock independence approximation [14] states that merging several packet streams on a transmission line has an effect akin to restoring the independence of interarrival times and packet lengths, thus an M/M/1 model can be used to analyze the behavior of each communication link.

Let $\mathbf{R}$ be the $n \times n$ probability matrix describing the routing of packets within an open queuing system [13], $\lambda = (\lambda_1, \lambda_2, \cdots, \lambda_n)$ be the mean arrival rates of the relayed packets, and $\gamma = (\gamma_1, \gamma_2, \cdots, \gamma_n)$ be the mean arrival rates of the exogenous packets. Unlike the state transition used for Markov chains, the rows of $\mathbf{R}$ matrix need not necessarily sum up to one, i.e., $\sum_j r_{ij} \le 1$.

A Jackson queuing network [13] is a network of an n M/M/n state-independent queuing system with the following features. (i) There is only one class of packets arriving to the system. (ii) Exogenous packets arrive at node j according to a Poisson process with rate $\gamma_j \ge 0$. (iii) The service times of the packets at jth queue are exponentially distributed with mean $1/\mu_j$. Upon receiving its service at node i, the packet will proceed to node j with a probability r_{ij} or leave the network at node i with probability $(1 - \sum_{j=1}^{n} r_{ij})$. Finally, the queue capacity at each node is assumed to be infinite, so there is no packet dropping.

Assuming the network reaches equilibrium, then we can write the following traffic equation using the flow conservation principle, in which the total sum of arrival rates entering the system is equal to the total departure rate under steady-state condition.

$$\lambda_j = \gamma_j + \sum_{i}^{n} \lambda_i r_{ij}, \quad j = 1, 2, \cdots, n. \qquad (14)$$

In the steady state, assuming the network is stable, the aggregate input rate λ_j into node j is equal to the aggregate output rate from node i, $i = 1, \cdots, n$. Therefore, we have a system of n equations and n unknowns. These equations can be written in matrix form as,

$$\vec{\lambda} = \vec{\gamma} + \vec{\lambda} \mathbf{R}, \qquad (15)$$

and the aggregate arrival rate vector can be solved by,

$$\vec{\lambda} = \vec{\gamma} (\mathbf{I} - \mathbf{R})^{-1}, \qquad (16)$$

where, $\gamma = (\gamma_1, \gamma_2, \cdots, \gamma_n)$ and the components of the vector $\mathbf{I}$ give the arrival rates into the various stations. It is shown in [13] that $(\mathbf{I} - \mathbf{R})$ is invertible. Assuming the exogenous arriving traffic are independent and identically distributed (*iid*) Poisson process with rate γ_j, and the service time at node j is assumed to be exponentially distributed with rate μ_j, $j = 1, 2, \cdots n$. The service times are assumed to be mutually independent and also independent of the arrival process at that queue, regardless of the previous service times of the same packet in other nodes.

After the net rate into each node is known, the network can be decomposed and each node can be treated as an independent queuing system with Poisson input. This also follows that the average number of packets and the average delay in each queue is the same as the corresponding $M/M/1$ queue. To ensure the steady state distribution of the network model, it is necessary that the aggregate packet arrival rate λ_j, computed in Equation (14), be less than the service rate μ_i, that is $\lambda_j < \mu_j$, $j = 1, 2, \cdots, n$, i.e.,

$$\vec{\gamma} (\mathbf{I} - \mathbf{R})^{-1} < \vec{\mu}. \qquad (17)$$

This is all needed to check the stability of the network. Assuming $\lambda_j < \mu_j$ for $j = 1, 2, \cdots, n$, define $\rho_j = \lambda_j / \mu_j$. ρ_j identifies the fraction of the time the transmitting buffer of node j is not empty, i.e., node j has a packet to transmit.

The mean queue size and delay for the jth queue are given by,

$$E[L_j] = \frac{\lambda_j}{\mu_j - \lambda_j} = \frac{\rho_j}{1 - \rho_j}, \quad E[D_j] = \frac{1}{\mu_j - \lambda_j},$$
$$j = 1, 2 \cdots, n. \quad (18)$$

Consider a path $x = x_\ell \to x_{\ell-1} \to \cdots \to x_1$ from source node x_ℓ to a destination node x_1, then the end-to-end delay for traffic originated at node x_ℓ is:

$$E[D_x] = \sum_{j=1}^{\ell} \frac{1}{\mu_{x_j} - \lambda_{x_j}} \qquad (19)$$

where, we can compute the arrival rate λ_j and the expected queuing delay $E[D_j]$ from Equations (16) and (18), respectively.

5. SIMULATION AND NUMERICAL RESULTS

Simulation of large-scale interconnection networks in data centers could become an intractable problem in terms of

scalability and cross-layer interactions. However, modularity, regularity, and hierarchical structure of the backplane interconnection network make it more feasible to partition the network into clusters and conduct simulation within and between clusters. The tandem queuing structure in Figure 7 is an example of a building block in fat-tree construction. A discrete-event continuous-time simulation model has been developed to verify the theoretical results. The simulation model has been structured as a set of stages of parallel $M/M/1$ queues interconnected according to the model described in Sections 2. While we implemented the model in both QualNet [3] and OPNET [2], due to the scalability issue, a C++ simulator has been developed using standard queuing libraries. Arrival to each queue was is governed by a Poisson process with rate (γ) and the packet service time is considered to be exponential with rate ($1/1500$) that corresponds to the average length of Ethernet packets (1500 bytes). $\rho = N\gamma/\mu < 1$ is enforced to satisfy the stability condition in Equation (17). The line speed (μ) is chosen to be 100 Mbps.

While various network configurations have been tested, here we consider the network in Figure 7 with the exogenous traffic $\vec{\gamma}$ and routing matrix $\mathbf{R}$.

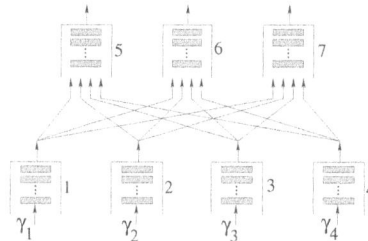

Figure 7: A 7-node switching center.

$$\vec{\gamma} = \begin{bmatrix} \gamma_1 \\ \gamma_2 \\ \gamma_3 \\ \gamma_4 \\ 0 \\ 0 \\ 0 \end{bmatrix} \mathbf{R} = \begin{bmatrix} 0 & 0 & 0 & 0 & 1/3 & 1/3 & 1/3 \\ 0 & 0 & 0 & 0 & 1/3 & 1/3 & 1/3 \\ 0 & 0 & 0 & 0 & 1/3 & 1/3 & 1/3 \\ 0 & 0 & 0 & 0 & 1/3 & 1/3 & 1/3 \\ 0 & 0 & 0 & 0 & 0 & 0 & 0 \\ 0 & 0 & 0 & 0 & 0 & 0 & 0 \\ 0 & 0 & 0 & 0 & 0 & 0 & 0 \end{bmatrix} \quad (20)$$

The endogenous arrival rates $\vec{\lambda}$ can be computed from Equation (16).

$$\vec{\lambda} = \begin{bmatrix} \gamma_1 \\ \gamma_2 \\ \gamma_3 \\ \gamma_4 \\ (\gamma_1 + \gamma_2 + \gamma_3 + \gamma_4)/3 \\ (\gamma_1 + \gamma_2 + \gamma_3 + \gamma_4)/3 \\ (\gamma_1 + \gamma_2 + \gamma_3 + \gamma_4)/3 \end{bmatrix} \quad (21)$$

The stability condition in Equation (17) must be held for each node ($\lambda_i < \mu_i$). The stability condition at each node does not necessarily guarantee the stability of the entire network because of traffic aggregation. Therefore, it is necessary to have $\max\{\lambda_i\} < \mu$, assuming $\mu_i = \mu$. Hence $\rho = \max\{\lambda_i\}/\mu < 1$. ρ basically is the probability that a packet arrives during a slot time. Assuming a uniform exogenous arrival process, $\gamma_i = \gamma$, for $i = 1, \cdots, n$, then the expected queuing length and delay including the service time for each packet can be computed from Equations (18) and (19), repectively.

$$E[L] = 3/4 \, \frac{1/3 - 1/3 \, (1 - \rho)^4}{\rho} \qquad (22)$$

$$E[D] = -\frac{\rho}{\gamma \, (-4 + 3\,\rho)} \qquad (23)$$

Figure 8 illustrates the delay performance of the tandem queues in Figure 7 obtained from the theoretical model and simulation.

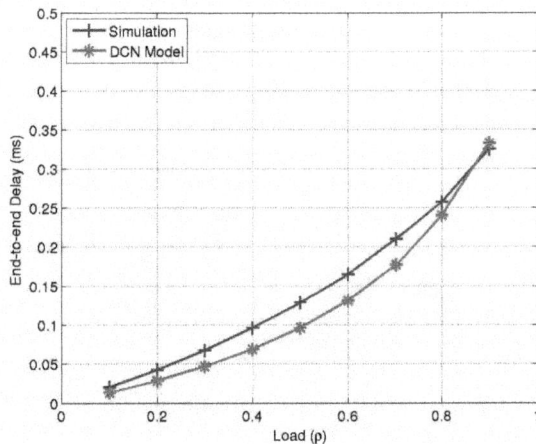

Figure 8: Delay performance of the tandem queues in Figure 7.

Similarly, the maximum throughput (bandwidth), for both cases are illustrated in Figure 9.

6. DESIGN ALTERNATIVES

The model is very useful to study various alternatives to design the network and cluster the servers. With various decompositions of I and O, one can compare the performance of various configurations in closed forms. The expected queuing delay including the service time for each packet can be computed from Equations (18) and (19). Assuming a uniform exogenous arrival process, $\gamma_i = \gamma$, for $i = 1, \cdots, n$, then the end-to-end delay and throughput performance for possible network configurations of $N = 12, M = 4$ are given in Table 2.

Figure 10 illustrates the normalized throughput for various 12×4 networks. Networks with contraction at higher stages give better throughput performance. Similarly, networks with contraction at higher stages give better delay performance, as shown in Figure 11. The throughput/delay performance for various decompositions of $N = 12, M = 4$ are shown in Figure 12.

The cost factor works on the opposite direction if it is formulated by the number of switches used. However, the

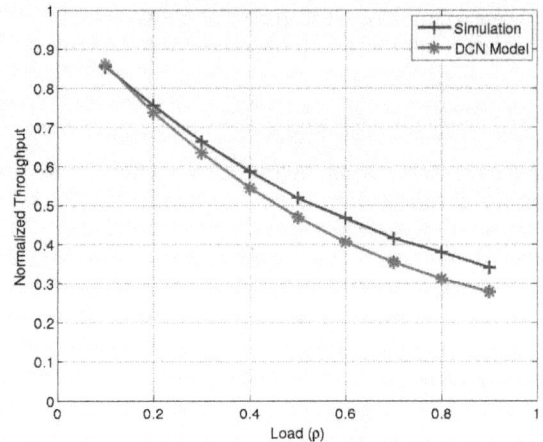

Figure 9: Normalized throughput performance of the tandem queues in Figure 7.

Table 2: Performance, $N = 12, M = 4$.

I	O	Throughput
$\langle 2,6 \rangle$	$\langle 2,2 \rangle$	$\frac{1}{3\rho} \left(1 - \left(1/2 + 1/2 \, (1 - 1/2\,\rho)^2 \right)^6 \right)$
$\langle 6,2 \rangle$	$\langle 2,2 \rangle$	$\frac{1}{3\rho} \left(1 - \left(1/2 + 1/2 \, (1 - 1/2\,\rho)^6 \right)^2 \right)$
$\langle 3,4 \rangle$	$\langle 2,2 \rangle$	$\frac{1}{3\rho} \left(1 - \left(1/2 + 1/2 \, (1 - 1/2\,\rho)^3 \right)^4 \right)$
$\langle 4,3 \rangle$	$\langle 2,2 \rangle$	$\frac{1}{3\rho} \left(1 - \left(1/2 + 1/2 \, (1 - 1/2\,\rho)^4 \right)^3 \right)$

I	O	End-to-end delay
$\langle 2,6 \rangle$	$\langle 2,2 \rangle$	$\rho / \left(2\gamma \, (3 - \rho) \right)$
$\langle 6,2 \rangle$	$\langle 2,2 \rangle$	$\rho \, (3 - 2\rho) / \left(6\gamma \, (3 - \rho) \, (1 - \rho) \right)$
$\langle 3,4 \rangle$	$\langle 2,2 \rangle$	$\rho \, (12 - 5\rho) / \left(12\gamma \, (3 - \rho) \, (2 - \rho) \right)$
$\langle 4,3 \rangle$	$\langle 2,2 \rangle$	$3\rho \, (\rho \, (2 - \rho)) / \left(4\gamma \, (3 - \rho) \, (3 - 2\rho) \right)$

switch size is a major factor in any cost calculation. We define the average switching cost as the ratio of total switching ports over the number of switches. In that case, similar to delay and throughput performance, networks with contraction at higher stages give better cost performance. This is shown in Figure 13.

A closer look at Equations (10) indicates that for a given $N \times M$ network, a monotonic increasing of the decomposition vector $I = \langle n_1, n_2, \cdots, n_L \rangle$, where $n_1 \geq n2 \geq \cdots, \geq n_L$, and monotonic increasing of the decomposition vector $O = \langle m_1, m_2, \cdots, m_L \rangle$, where $m_1 \geq m2 \geq \cdots, \geq m_L$ would give a better throughput performance.

7. CONCLUSIONS

Data centers are critical part of cloud computing and their performance, in terms of throughput and response time, is heavily affected by the underlying interconnection network. The interconnection network plays a significant role, in terms of scalability and communication cost, to form and interconnect clusters of servers. Simulating several thou-

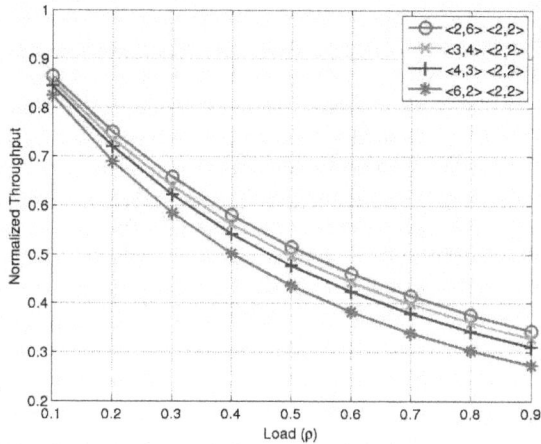

Figure 10: Load (ρ) vs. normalized throughput for various $N = 12, M = 4$ networks.

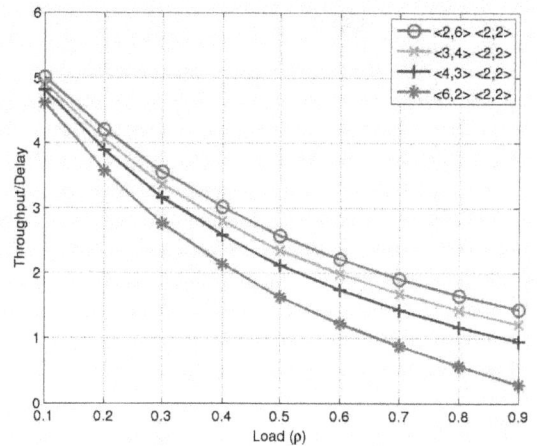

Figure 12: Throughput/Delay performance for various $N = 12, M = 4$ networks.

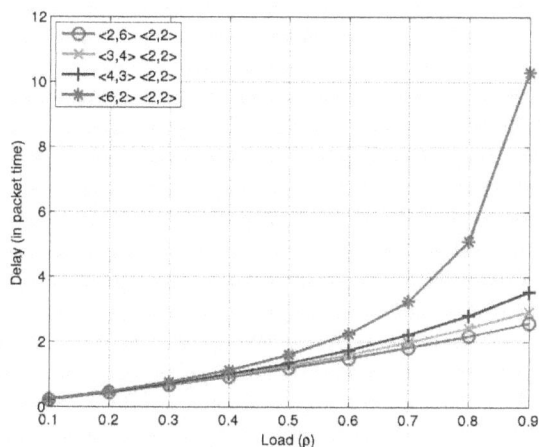

Figure 11: Load (ρ) vs. normalized delay for various $N = 12, M = 4$ networks.

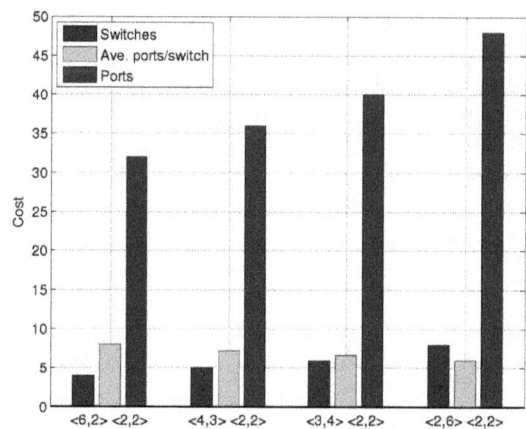

Figure 13: Cost performance for various $N = 12, M = 4$ networks.

sands of interconnected servers runs into a scalability problem, mainly due to the high memory consumption and the degradation in the computational speed. On the other hand, experiments are usually expensive and done on a very small scale comparing to the actual size of the data centers. Topological analysis along with distributed simulation can be employed to study various network configurations.

This paper introduced a new analytical model that can be used to efficiently design the underlying interconnection network in data centers. While the model is general, we employed the model to study the widely used fat-tree topology deployed in data centers. Two major performance criteria; delay and throughput have been used to study various fat-tree configurations. Among various fat-tree networks, we have shown that for a given $N \times M$ network, a monotonic increasing of the decomposition vector $I = \langle n_1, n_2, \cdots, n_L \rangle$, where $n_1 \geq n2 \geq \cdots, \geq n_L$, and monotonic increasing of the decomposition vector $O = \langle m_1, m_2, \cdots, m_L \rangle$, where $m_1 \geq m2 \geq \cdots, \geq m_L$ would give a better throughput and delay performance.

8. REFERENCES

[1] Cisco global cloud index 2011–2016, 2013.
[2] Opnet, 2014. http://www.riverbed.com.
[3] Qualnet, 2014. http://www.qualnet.com.
[4] M. Al-Fares, A. Loukissas, and A. Vahdat. A scalable, commodity data center network architecture. *SIGCOMM Comput. Commun. Rev.*, 38(4):63–74, Aug. 2008.
[5] T. Benson, A. Akella, and D. A. Maltz. Network traffic characteristics of data centers in the wild. In *Proceedings of the 10th ACM SIGCOMM conference on Internet measurement*, IMC '10, pages 267–280, New York, NY, USA, 2010. ACM.
[6] C. Clos. A study of non-blocking switching networks. *Bell System Technical Journal*, 32:406–424, Mar. 1953.
[7] D. Ersoz, M. S. Yousif, and C. R. Das. Characterizing network traffic in a cluster-based, multi-tier data center. In *Distributed Computing Systems, 2007. ICDCS'07. 27th International Conference on*, pages 59–59. IEEE, 2007.

[8] N. Farrington, G. Porter, S. Radhakrishnan, H. H. Bazzaz, V. Subramanya, Y. Fainman, G. Papen, and A. Vahdat. Helios: a hybrid electrical/optical switch architecture for modular data centers. In *Proceedings of the ACM SIGCOMM 2010 conference*, SIGCOMM '10, pages 339–350, New York, NY, USA, 2010. ACM.

[9] A. Greenberg, J. R. Hamilton, N. Jain, S. Kandula, C. Kim, P. Lahiri, D. A. Maltz, P. Patel, and S. Sengupta. VL2: a scalable and flexible data center network. *Communications of the ACM*, 54(3):95–104, Mar. 2011.

[10] C. Guo, G. Lu, D. Li, H. Wu, X. Zhang, Y. Shi, C. Tian, Y. Zhang, and S. Lu. BCube: a high performance, server-centric network architecture for modular data centers. In P. Rodriguez, E. W. Biersack, K. Papagiannaki, and L. Rizzo, editors, *SIGCOMM*, pages 63–74. ACM, 2009.

[11] C. Guo, H. Wu, K. Tan, L. Shi, Y. Zhang, and S. Lu. Dcell: a scalable and fault-tolerant network structure for data centers. In V. Bahl, D. Wetherall, S. Savage, and I. Stoica, editors, *SIGCOMM*, pages 75–86. ACM, 2008.

[12] B. Heller, S. Seetharaman, P. Mahadevan, Y. Yiakoumis, P. Sharma, S. Banerjee, and N. McKeown. Elastictree: saving energy in data center networks. In *Proceedings of the 7th USENIX conference on Networked systems design and implementation*, pages 17–17, Berkeley, CA, USA, 2010. USENIX Association.

[13] J. R. Jackson. Networks of waiting lines. *Operations Research*, 5, Aug. 1957.

[14] L. Kleinrock. *Queuing Systems, Volume I: Theory*. John Wiley, Inc., 1975.

[15] R. N. Mysore, A. Pamboris, N. Farrington, N. Huang, P. Miri, S. Radhakrishnan, V. Subramanya, and A. Vahdat. Portland: a scalable fault-tolerant layer 2 data center network fabric. In P. Rodriguez, E. W. Biersack, K. Papagiannaki, and L. Rizzo, editors, *SIGCOMM*, pages 39–50. ACM, Aug. 2009.

[16] J. H. Patel. Performance of processor–memory interconnections for multiprocessors. *IEEE Transactions on Computers*, C-30(10):771–780, Oct. 1981.

[17] G. Wang, D. G. Andersen, M. Kaminsky, K. Papagiannaki, T. E. Ng, M. Kozuch, and M. Ryan. c-through: part-time optics in data centers. *SIGCOMM Comput. Commun. Rev.*, 41(4):327–338, Aug. 2010.

A Stream-Based Architecture for the Management and On-Line Analysis of Unbounded Amounts of Simulation Data

Johannes Schützel
Modeling & Simulation Group
johannes.schuetzel@uni-rostock.de

Holger Meyer
Database Group
holger.meyer@uni-rostock.de

Adelinde M. Uhrmacher
Modeling & Simulation Group
adelinde.uhrmacher@uni-rostock.de

Institute of Computer Science
University of Rostock
Albert-Einstein-Str. 22
18059 Rostock, Germany

ABSTRACT

Conducting simulation studies can mean to execute a multitude of parameter configurations, for each of these we may need to execute a vast number of replications, and each single replication may mean the need to process a significant amount of data. Here, we propose a stream-based architecture that aligns data processing and buffering with the actual data usage during simulation to make the most of available memory. This turns away from the first-write-then-read approach, often utilizing databases or plain files as temporary storage. Instead, data are processed on the fly. By introducing a processing graph, which distinguishes between buffering and processing nodes, a flexible analysis of simulation data is achieved. As the data are processed close to their generation, the developed architecture fits well to a distributed execution of simulation studies. We illustrate how the stream-based architecture integrates into simulation workflows.

Categories and Subject Descriptors

I.6.6 [**Simulation And Modeling**]: Simulation Output Analysis

Keywords

Analysis, data storage, data streams, processing graph, simulation data management, simulation workflow.

1. INTRODUCTION

While development in computer simulation has started with providing bare simulation engines, now research aims towards providing thorough support for entire simulation

SIGSIM-PADS'14, May 18–21, 2014, Denver, CO, USA.
Copyright is held by the owner/author(s). Publication rights licensed to ACM.
ACM 978-1-4503-2794-7/14/05 ...$15.00.
http://dx.doi.org/10.1145/2601381.2601399.

processes [26, 28, 29]. The simulation process can vary significantly according to the purpose of the study and embraces diverse tasks, e.g., evaluating stop-policies and replication criteria for experiment steering, calculating averages and standard deviations, or analyzing spatial distributions of key players. Data collection and analysis, and partly storage are required by all of those tasks. Therefore, the approach pursued for data analysis and storage has an impact on the performance of the entire simulation study. This impact is rarely discussed and, if so, mostly in the context of parallel/distributed simulation, e.g., [18]. With increasing complexity of models, the amount of data that are produced by simulation is increasing and the question how to collect, analyze, and store the data efficiently becomes more urgent.

Since traditional database systems store data first or modify the underlying database and then evaluate queries specified over the stored data, they are often unable to perform in-depth analysis of massive data volumes on the fly [3, 23].

For processing data in real-time, data stream management systems (DSMS) have been introduced [5, 7, 12, 21, 24]. Data stream processing works on continuously flowing, potentially infinite streams (cf. [15]) of often very simple structured data, of which only a small portion is relevant and will be stored permanently. Multiple streams of data are filtered, aggregated, combined, summarized, and monitored using operators whose induced calculation effort can be predicted to enable meeting of real-time constraints. In general, on-the-fly analysis requires special algorithmic approaches [13].

Other approaches for query processing involving complex analysis tasks, e.g., [11], have started decomposing these tasks and annotating data with the corresponding analysis methods. Thereby, analysis tasks and sub-tasks move closer to the data into the database. Also, a closer intertwining of data and analysis is identified as essential for supporting decision processes [16]. Thus, recent developments in databases suggest to integrate simulation techniques into databases. We agree that state of the art data management and simulation techniques should move closer together. However, our starting point and focus is different.

Our approach is to exploit and integrate streaming techniques deeply into simulation experiments. In contrast to typical stream-based processing applications, in simulation we are in control of the data generation process, which releases us from considering real-time aspects. In simulation, where most of the data is of an inherently transient nature, we expect the simulation studies' performance to benefit significantly from on-the-fly processing and early data reduction. Even in cases where an early reduction is not possible, the intrinsic parallelism of the stream-based approach will be of advantage.

With our approach we move away from the strict processing pipeline of data collection, storage, and analysis. Instead, we aim at an architecture for data collecting, processing and storing that is interwoven with the workflow of "in-silico" experiments, and is sufficiently flexible during simulation and across simulation studies.

2. REQUIREMENTS

As stated above, our approach to data management and analysis focuses on features and characteristics that differ from those of existing approaches in modeling and simulation. In this section, we will discuss requirements for designing an integrated data management system for simulation in more detail.

2.1 Workflow of Simulation Experiments

To deeply integrate data management, analysis and storage into the simulation workflow, the latter deserves a closer inspection. As already stated, an experiment typically comprises multiple configurations with individual simulation runs or multiple replications in case of a stochastic model. These sources of simulation data can be arranged in a three layered structure (Figure 1). This structure is also reflected

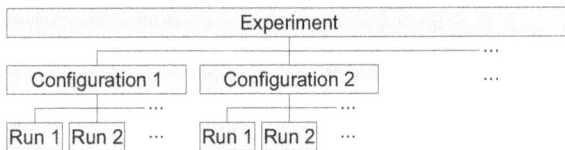

Figure 1: Hierarchical structure of a simulation experiment.

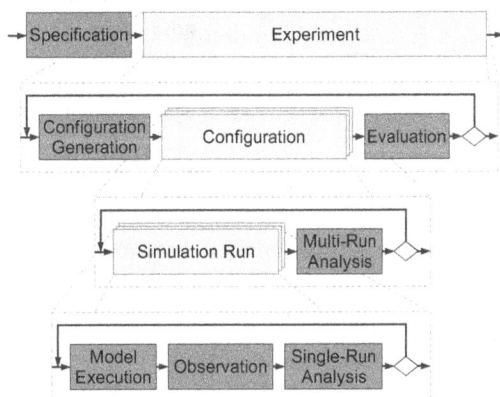

Figure 2: Layered view of the experiment workflow (adapted from [29]).

in the layers of the generalized experiment workflow, which

is shown in Figure 2. Therein, depending on the experiment design, repetition can be involved at different layers (represented by arrows from the right to the left). Furthermore, multiple configurations and simulation runs may be processed concurrently (indicated by stacked boxes). Simulation data are gained by observation only, situated at the bottom layer in Figure 2. However, the analysis and evaluation tasks at higher workflow layers involve accessing and processing data, mostly in a bottom-up manner, producing data as well. Consequently, the data management system must provide higher layer tasks access to data gained and processed at lower layers. Furthermore, tasks at all layers must be able to emit data.

2.2 General Objectives in Managing Simulation Data

In the following, *simulation data* or just *data* refer to units of information (data items) that are collected during simulation. Data items can be integers, floating point values, strings, structured types such as lists and maps, or objects. They may be timestamped with the simulation time at observation. Metadata annotated to individual simulation runs, configurations, or entire experiments are not subject of processing as they are used to document the experiment setup and thus rather static. Keeping metadata aside, data management involves

- to manage inputs, processing, and outputs of data,
- to process (i.e., to transform and analyze) data, and
- to provide the results for experiment steering, external use, or result reporting.

As stated, data can be collected and processed for controlling the experiment and data can be collected, processed, and exported for analyzing the model under study. Data are collected from the simulation by instrumentation and observation, for which there are sophisticated approaches that allow extracting and aggregating data from the model at certain time points during a simulation run [17, 30]. To decouple the data management from the specifics of modeling formalisms, the extraction and model structure spanning aggregation of data are considered a pre-step of the data management as understood in the following. With data management we will focus on analyzing time series.

2.3 Transformation & Analysis Capabilities

An example for data processing are replication criteria, on whose basis it is dynamically decided whether to execute additional replications (simulation runs) for a configuration (multi-run analysis in Figure 2). While a replication criterion is set up per configuration, its calculations base on data obtained from individual simulation runs. Consequently, data from multiple sources have to be merged. In case of replication criteria, variances or confidence intervals might be required to be calculated on merged data sets. Another example for data processing that has to be accomplished on-line are policies for stopping simulation runs. Such stop policies can include calculations that estimate whether the model reached a steady state, which is due to a simulation run's increasingly long trajectory often realized by analyzing the trajectory segment by segment. Consequently, required capabilities include time series processing that resembles the window-based processing on data streams [6]. Aside from analysis for experiment steering, simulation studies typically involve user defined analysis to understand the system under study. Such analysis can include processing and merging of data at all layers of the experiment workflow. Arbitrary functions can be required, operating on a per-item basis or on time series data. Further examples for analysis are checking a model against specifications based on temporal logic [10], the computation of predictive information on time series data [16], or the identification of re-occurring patterns over sliding time windows [3].

Generally speaking, required transformation capabilities include merging of data from multiple sources as well as filtering, projection, and windowing on time series. Furthermore, processing capabilities include, e.g., arithmetical operations, boolean operations, and statistical calculations.

2.4 Data Provision & Storage Capabilities

As stated, simulation data or processed data have to be provided or stored for different purposes. Data provision means to make processing results available

- within the simulation system (e.g., for steering tasks or user defined analyses), as well as
- outside of the simulation system (e.g., for on-line usage or external processing).

Data storage means exporting data from the simulation system, too, but aims at *persistent* storage using database systems or files, e.g., for experiment documentation, result reporting, or further off-line analysis.

With the data management system as provider and internal or external sinks as consumers, the consumers may require certain modes of data provision (cf. [2]). For instance, experiment steering decisions can be made at predefined points or can be triggered dynamically. In the former case, results of processing need to be buffered up to the predefined decision point where the results are fetched. In the other case, in which steering decisions need to be triggered, processing needs to actively forward resulting data on completion of calculations.

In a typical simulation study, certain data have to be stored persistently, at least for documenting the simulation experiment [33]. Depending on user- or application requirements, storing can be realized using database management systems, scientific data files (e.g., HDF, CDF, SDXF), comma separated value (CSV) files, user defined text or binary files, or other formats. Within these formats, the experimenter or the application following the experiment can demand specific schemes for organizing the data. This requires the possibility to integrate different storage formats and schemes. However, the data management system is supposed to relieve the experimenter from technical details of the storage solution he or she wants to put in. Since different portions of data can be required to be stored using distinct storage locations/formats/schemes, the data management should support appropriate flexibility while simplifying the employment of storage solutions for simulation studies.

2.5 Dynamicity of Processing

In the experiment workflow shown in Figure 2, evaluation, multi-run analysis, and single-run analysis tasks can appear, change, and disappear dynamically due to decision-based repetition and changing configurations. Not only due to

this, the data generation in simulation is highly dynamic, e.g.,

- sources of data can appear/disappear due to variable model structures or flexible observation,
- processing steps can become necessary/unnecessary,
- the number of inputs of a processing step can change,
- the amount of data to be buffered can change,
- sinks to which data may be provided/stored can change,
- sources and processing of data may migrate due to distributed simulation.

As the data management system is responsible for managing data flows and processing, it has to deal with these cases. The above also indicates, that processing steps, their order, and relation highly depend on the design of the experimental study. Therefore, appropriate adaptability is required.

3. A STREAM-BASED ARCHITECTURE

In the following, we present an architecture for simulation data management, which provides data related functionality as required by a simulation system. Figure 3 illustrates how the new data management system integrates into a simulation system.

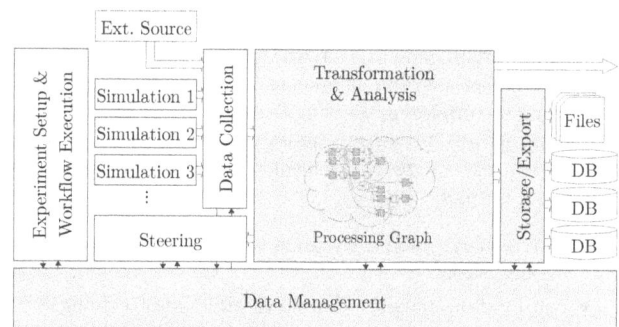

Figure 3: Overview of the data management and processing subsystem (gray) and its integration into the simulation system. Data processing takes place in Transformation & Analysis. Horizontal arrows: data flow. Vertical arrows: control/communication.

The Experiment Setup & Workflow Execution shown in Figure 3, belongs to the simulation system and executes the workflow described in Section 2.1. This includes to set up simulation runs (Simulation 1,2,3,...) as well as single-run analysis, multi-run analysis, and evaluation components (cf. Figure 2) that serve steering decisions in the experiment workflow (Steering). The Experiment Setup & Workflow Execution also sets up the Data Collection, according to requirements of Steering components and according to user specifications for instrumentation. The Data Management functions as a mediator for establishing the data flow (white block arrows) and the data processing, which takes place in Transformation & Analysis. The Experiment Setup & Workflow Execution also configures the Storage/Export that is responsible for managing database connections, output files and other external, possibly stream-based, data sinks (at the right in Figure 3).

The Transformation & Analysis is responsible for the actual processing of data in the architecture. It basically consists of a processing graph (cf. Figure 3). With the processing graph, our architecture adopts the stream-based processing paradigm. We believe that applying this paradigm to data processing within a simulation system provides a clean and flexible way to serve the requirements discussed above. This bases on the perception that simulation trajectories, which consist of successively generated data items, can be seen as item streams. Within a stream, items are related to each other in terms of their chronology and their source [6]. The same applies to time series extracted from simulation runs, where the course of the simulation determines the chronology and the data collector forms the source. Consequently, it seems natural to deal with such data as distinct streams and to transform and analyze the streams by routing their items through a processing graph such as that shown in Figure 4. Using graphs for stream processing is known from

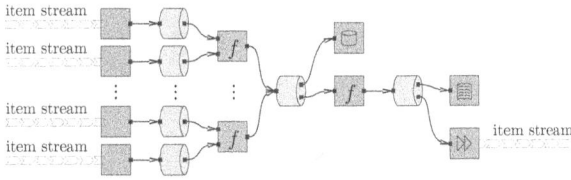

Figure 4: Example of a processing graph.

data stream management systems, where continuous queries are modeled as a graph of queues and operators [6]. Decomposing a complex processing task into simpler tasks and combining simple processing units into a processing graph has several advantages that meet our requirements, since processing graphs

- provide high flexibility for arbitrarily structured processing tasks,
- can be dynamically adapted at run time to changes of inputs, processing tasks, and outputs,
- allow to share computations and memory, and
- ease the reuse of processing units implemented for frequently encountered subtasks.

While designing the architecture of processing graphs, we identified two general tasks that can be distinguished: the transportation/transformation and the buffering of data (cf. separation of concerns principle [8]). Consequently, our processing graph is built of two kinds of nodes: Transporters and Queues. Why this separation ensures a clean architecture, becomes evident through the following example. We assume that a function $f(x_1, x_2)$ has to be calculated that takes its arguments x_1, x_2 from two streams, denoted by S_1 and S_2. As data items typically arrive at different times via S_1 and S_2, but f needs an item for x_1 and x_2 to be available at the same time, items have to be buffered, as illustrated by Figure 5a. Let us assume, that two functions g and h, both basing on f, have to be calculated:

$$g(x_1, x_2) = g_1(f(x_1, x_2))$$
$$h(x_1, x_2) = h_1(f(x_1, x_2))$$

Consequently, g and h could be calculated as shown in Figure 5b. If the inputs of g_1 and h_1 would be buffered directly at the functions, i.e., g_1 and h_1, both would get a copy of the result of f, which implies to buffer the same data twice. This

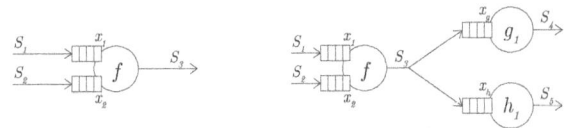

(a) Arguments need to be buffered if arguments can arrive asynchronously.

(b) Buffering directly at the functions might lead to a duplication of data.

Figure 5: Discussion of the buffering of input data for functions.

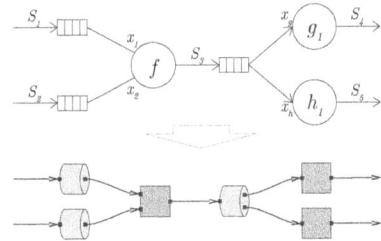

Figure 6: The same processing task as in Figure 5b but with buffers and functions separated. At the bottom, its realization in our architecture with Queues (pipe-shaped) and Transporters (box-shaped; here: FunctionStreams).

is avoided by distinguishing between two types of nodes, i.e., Queues that buffer data and Transporters that realize data transportation and transformation (Figure 6). Because n-ary functions are supplied by streams with possibly different characteristics (e.g., rate, timing), we defined that Transporters are served by Queues, except for Transporters that simply introduce streams of data to the processing structure (cf. leftmost boxes in Figure 4). This leads to a bipartite processing graph, or more specific, to a directed graph with alternating layers of Queues and Transporters.

Queues are not only introduced for sharing memory or for synchronizing inputs of n-ary functions, but also for allowing Transporters to operate on data windows. A data window is a bounded view on a sequence of data items. The boundaries of a data window move and/or adapt in size as the sequence evolves [6]. As Transporters may require specific window lengths and specific moving/adaption behavior, this seems to be contradictory to the idea of shared Queues. To this end, Queues maintain window information for each of their downstream Transporters, which will become clear in the next sections.

In the following sections, we describe the different node types, mostly in the order in which they occur in a processing graph.

3.1 InputStreams

InputStreams are Transporters that serve as entry points for item streams in the processing graph, as illustrated by Figure 7. InputStreams represent data sources, which are created by model instrumentation/observation or have its origin outside of the simulation system. Having distinguishable InputStreams for distinct data sources allows to link data sources to the processing graph and to establish further linkings in the processing graph. An InputStream can

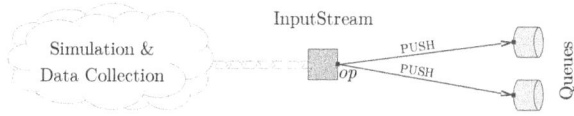

Figure 7: An InputStream serves as an entry point for data in a processing graph.

be followed by an arbitrary number of Queues to which incoming data items are pushed immediately (Pseudocode 1).

```
function INPUT(item)
    for all q ∈ op.queues do
        q.PUSH(item)
    end for
end function
```

Pseudocode 1: Immediate forwarding of a data item on its arrival via an InputStream's input interface.

3.2 Queues

Queues differ from Transporters as they are the only node type in the processing graph architecture that are designed for buffering data. Albeit implementing a fixed mechanism, they serve different buffering-related purposes, which are achieved through their interplay with downstream Transporters. Queues can be used for

- synchronizing the arguments for functions,
- realizing windowed views,
- supporting time-decoupled reading, and
- supporting bulk transfers to persistent storage.

Having a bipartite processing graph, Queues are always located between Transporters, as depicted in Figure 8. Queues

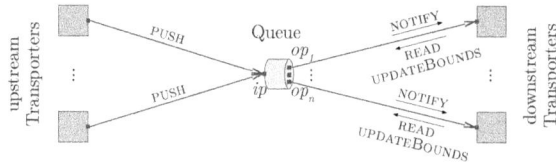

Figure 8: A Queue has one merging input port ip and any number of separate output ports $op_1, \ldots, op_n$.

have one input port (labeled ip in Figure 8) to which multiple data delivering Transporters can be connected. Incoming data items—no matter from which upstream Transporter they stem—are enqueued in the order of their arrival, thus conforming to the general semantics of a queue. By this, Queues add the possibility to serialize multiple streams into one stream.

A Queue buffers data items consecutively in the order they were received. The internal buffer structure has a flexible size, i.e., it increases without being limited when data items are enqueued and decreases when data items are dropped. In order to buffer data in behalf of Transporters with *different* buffering requirements, a Queue maintains boundary information for all Transporters that are connected via an output port, as exemplified by Figure 9. The algorithm

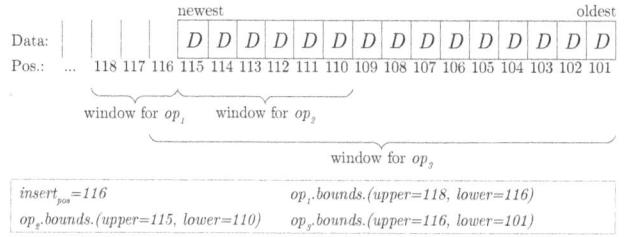

Figure 9: A Queue's internal buffer, in this example holding 15 data items (D). State information of the Queue in the lower box.

```
function PUSH(item)
    ENQUEUE(item)
    for all op ∈ OP do
        if insert_pos > op.bounds.upper then
            op.transp.NOTIFY
        end if
    end for
end function
```

```
function READ(op, r_l, r_u)
    assert op.bounds.lower ≤ (op.bounds.lower + r_l) ↩
            ≤ (op.bounds.upper + r_u) ≤ op.bounds.upper
    range ← (op.bounds.lower + r_l, op.bounds.upper + r_u)
    return COPYQUEUERANGE(range)
end function
```

```
function UPDATEBOUNDS(op, Δup, Δlo)
    assert Δup ≥ 0 ∧ Δlo ≥ 0 ∧ ↩
    (op.bounds.upper + Δup) ≥ (op.bounds.lower + Δlo)
    op.bounds ← op.bounds + (Δup, Δlo)
    DROPBELOW(min_{op_i ∈ OP}(op_i.bounds.lower))
end function
```

Pseudocode 2: Algorithm executed by a Queue when receiving a data item via PUSH. Functions READ and UPDATEBOUNDS can be called by downstream Transporters.

that is executed when a data item is received at the input port is defined by PUSH in Pseudocode 2. As soon as the upper boundary associated with an output port op lies in the buffer range, the corresponding Transporter $op.transp$ is notified. Via READ and UPDATEBOUNDS, a downstream Transporter is allowed to read a range (r_l, r_u) of data items from its window and to update its boundary information (Pseudocode 2). Please notice that with updating the bounds for an output port, also the minimum of all output ports' lower bounds is calculated and all items below that boundary are dequeued (dropped). This way, the life span of data items is determined by the requirements of downstream Transporters and by dropping items that are no longer needed, the amount of required memory is reduced.

3.3 FunctionStreams

FunctionStreams are the main data transforming/analyzing units in our architecture. They allow realizing n-ary functions while having a separate input port for each argument. Results, of which a FunctionStream may produce different ones, are released via output ports to downstream Queues, as shown in Figure 10.

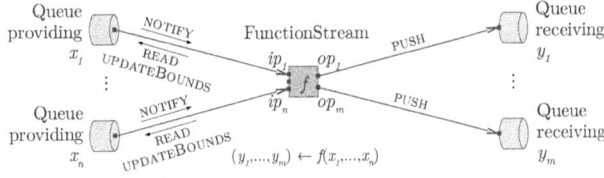

Figure 10: A FunctionStream can have n input ports for n arguments and m output ports for m result streams.

```
function NOTIFY(ip)
    ip.sufficientData ← true
    if (∀p ∈ IP : p.sufficientData = true) then
        for all ipᵢ ∈ IP do
            for all (rₗ, rᵤ) ∈ USERDEFREADS(ipᵢ) do
                ipᵢ.rd.partᵣₗ,ᵣᵤ ← ipᵢ.queue.READ(rₗ, rᵤ)
            end for
        end for
        (y₁, ..., yₘ) ← USERDEFFUNC(ip₁.rd, ..., ipₙ.rd)
        for all ipᵢ ∈ IP do
            (Δup, Δlo) ← USERDEFWINDOWSHIFT(ipᵢ)
            ipᵢ.queue.UPDATEBOUNDS(Δup, Δlo)
            ipᵢ.rd ← {}
            ipᵢ.sufficientData ← false
        end for
        for all i ∈ 1...m do
            if yᵢ is defined then
                for all q ∈ opᵢ.queues do
                    q.PUSH(yᵢ)
                end for
            end if
        end for
    end if
end function
```

Pseudocode 3: Exemplary algorithm executed by a FunctionStream when notified by an upstream Queue on input port ip. The $ip_i.sufficientData$-flags could also be handled by an user defined function instead of resetting all flags. More specific state handling (e.g., skip and/or count notifications, consider timestamps) could also be implemented.

As a Transporter node, a FunctionStream does not buffer data, but may use its upstream Queues to buffer inputs for argument synchronization, for realizing a window-based function, or for a combination of both, i.e., multiple arguments, each with an individual window. While Queues undertake the buffering task, determining *which portions* of data to transfer and *how much* data to buffer is a FunctionStream's individual concern (USERDEFREADS and USERDEFWINDOWSHIFT in Pseudocode 3). The function USERDEFFUNC implements the actual transformation and/or analysis, for which an internal state might be maintained (not shown). Input data that might be involved in multiple analysis cycles should remain in the upstream Queues and be read as often as demanded to avoid duplicative buffering.

As stated, the boundary-based buffering in the upstream Queues allows to implement windowed functions. An overview of window types is given, e.g., in [6], where window types are characterized by the particular movement of start and end boundaries, in compliance with our concept. For example, a FunctionStream that implements the *moving mean* with window size s, USERDEFWINDOWSHIFT will initialize the window in the first s by returning $(\Delta up, \Delta lo) = (1, 0)$ to shift the upper bound and afterwards returning $(1, 1)$ to shift the whole window whenever notified. The *moving mean* can be implemented by reading the whole window, calculating the sum and dividing by s. A more efficient implementation would maintain a window of size $s + 1$, read the most recent and the oldest value from the window, and compute with sum as internal state: $sum' = sum - v_{oldest} + v_{recent}$ and $mean = sum'/s$. A FunctionStream that implements the batch-based the MSER-m method for estimating the optimal truncation point in steady-state simulation [34] will use a disjunct window of size s that is shifted by (s, s). However, for window-less functions, USERDEFWINDOWSHIFT initially returns $(1, 0)$ and afterwards $(1, 1)$, resulting in notification on arrival of every individual data item.

3.4 OutputStreams

OutputStreams are introduced for streaming data from the processing graph back into the simulation system or to external stream sinks, as depicted in Figure 4. Maintaining a data window in its upstream Queue, an OutputStream can create packages of data items, which are pushed to the sink (Pseudocode 4). OutputStreams are supposed to be used

Figure 11: An OutputStream streams data arriving at its upstream Queue to a streaming sink inside or outside the simulation system.

```
function NOTIFY
    data ← ip.queue.READ(0, 0)   ▷ read complete window
    (Δup, Δlo) ← USERDEFWINDOWSHIFT(data.length)
    ip.queue.UPDATEBOUNDS(Δup, Δlo)
    PUSHOUT(data)
end function
```

Pseudocode 4: An OutputStream being notified by its upstream Queue simply reads and forwards windowed data.

for applications that are driven by the availability of processing results. However, it is crucial that the call of PUSHOUT returns fast rather than after time intensive processing at the sink side, because the OutputStream is blocked until this call returns and this blocks the algorithm of the upstream Queue. To achieve an item-wise forwarding from the upstream Queue to the sink, USERDEFWINDOWSHIFT just needs to return $(\Delta up, \Delta lo) = (1, 1)$. Applications for OutputStreams are sending analysis results back to the simulation system as well as streaming data to another simulation system, a physical system, a visualization, or a data logger.

3.5 ReadingPoints

While OutputStreams are designed for push communication, ReadingPoints are designed for applications where the flow of control requires pull communication, i.e., reading on demand. Here, extensive use is made of the upstream Queue, shown in Figure 12. The Queue buffers data until it leaves the window of interest, which can move automatically (on notification) or through external control. The semantics of a ReadingPoint is described by Pseudocode 5. For an automatically moving data window, USERDEFWINDOWSHIFT can be implemented accordingly, otherwise it returns $(0,0)$ and the window boundaries are moved by external control using EXTSHIFT.

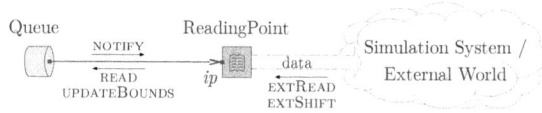

Figure 12: A ReadingPoint providing access to data for readers outside of the processing graph.

function NOTIFY
  $(\Delta up, \Delta lo) \leftarrow$ USERDEFWINDOWSHIFT
  $ip.queue.$UPDATEBOUNDS$(\Delta up, \Delta lo)$
end function

function EXTREAD(r_l, r_u)
  return $ip.queue.$READ(r_l, r_u)
end function

function EXTSHIFT$(\Delta up, \Delta lo)$
  $ip.queue.$UPDATEBOUNDS$(\Delta up, \Delta lo)$
end function

Pseudocode 5: A ReadingPoint does not forward any data on notification. Instead, EXTREAD and EXTSHIFT are exposed to the outside of the processing graph.

3.6 StoragePoints

There may be points in the processing graph at which data shall be automatically externalized to mass storage. StoragePoints serve the task of persistently storing data arriving at their upstream Queue (Figure 13). In contrast to OutputStreams, which also externalize data from the processing graph, StoragePoints send data to the Storage/Export unit that is responsible for handling databases and output files in the data management architecture (also cf. Figure 3).

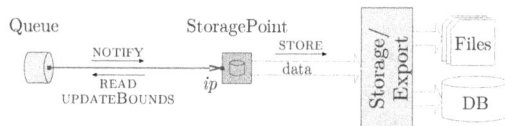

Figure 13: A StoragePoint storing data that accumulates at the upstream Queue to files or databases.

The operation of a StoragePoint is described by Pseudocode 6. Here, the function USERDEFWINDOWSHIFT controls the amount of data that is buffered at the upstream

Queue to be eventually transfered (in packets) to the Storage/Export unit. This is designed to increase performance, e.g., if a database is assigned to a StoragePoint. Within USERDEFWINDOWSHIFT, further communication with the Storage/Export unit could take place, as optimal transfer package sizes can depend on the actual storage sink or its current load.

function NOTIFY
  $data \leftarrow ip.queue.$READ$(0,0)$ ▷ read complete window
  $(\Delta up, \Delta lo) \leftarrow$ USERDEFWINDOWSHIFT$(data.length)$
  $ip.queue.$UPDATEBOUNDS$(\Delta up, \Delta lo)$
  STORE$(data)$
end function

Pseudocode 6: A StoragePoint being notified by its upstream Queue reads and stores windowed data.

3.7 The Storage/Export Unit

The Storage/Export unit is not part of the processing graph, but an important part in the data management architecture (cf. Figure 3). It is designed to mediate between the StoragePoints of the processing graph and storage sinks that are employed for persistent storage (e.g., DBMS, files). The Storage/Export unit not only unifies communication, but also handles the assignment of StoragePoints to storage sinks, since the existence of multiple StoragePoints does not necessarily mean, that each embodies another storage sink. Thus, it is possible to use a single database instance for the whole experiment, or certain database tables or files for particular data streams, or any other mapping.

In our concept, concrete storage sinks, such as DBMS or file writing libraries, are supposed to be encapsulated by individual plugins. A storage plugin is intended

- to handle the communication via the storage sink's interface,
- to establish a data scheme,
- to fit data sent by StoragePoints into the scheme, and
- if applicable, to determine and communicate performance related properties, to which assigned StoragePoints can adapt.

This concept allows to realize and easily employ arbitrary schemes, such as

- key-value relations,
- multi-column relations,
- individual relations per stream,
- one or separate relations per simulation run, configuration, or experiment,
- linear logs,

or any other scheme that suits the demands of the experimental study.

4. INTEGRATION INTO EXPERIMENTATION SYSTEMS

In this work, we consider experiment designs as described in Section 2.1. Such designs can include optimization algorithms or sensitivity analyzers, by which simulation configurations may be generated dynamically. Within configurations, replication criteria and run stop policies may decide about the number and duration of simulation runs, also dynamically. All these higher layer tasks as well as data analysis for system understanding depend on data from the simulation runs, which are at the lowest workflow layer (cf. Figure 2).

In the following, we use a small example to illustrate how the cross-cutting concern *data processing* can be realized in experimentation systems that follow the separation of concerns principle. Let us assume, a biologist has a population dynamics model with multiple species of which the two species x and y are of special interest. The biologist wants to examine the system's behavior under different initial configurations, e.g., different numerical ratios between the species [14]. A basic but relevant question, the biologist wants to answer first, is, "Given a model configuration, will neither x nor y die out?" Using linear temporal logic, where $G\psi$ connotes that ψ holds globally, the above question is transformable to the postulate $G(x_{count} > 0 \wedge y_{count} > 0)$. This postulate shall be checked by simulation. The biologist defines to stop the simulation when the x_{count} and y_{count} trajectories both reach a steady state, when in the simulation 3 years elapsed, or when one of the species x or y died out. Since the system under study is modeled as a stochastic process, one simulation run is not enough to get confidence that the species will never die out. Repeated simulation runs might lead to different results. Hence, our biologist applies a kind of statistical model checking (cf. [32]). Assume, he wants to confirm whether in at least 80 percent of the cases the species x and y do not die out:

$$Pr_{\geq 0.8}\big(G(x_{count} > 0 \wedge y_{count} > 0)\big) \qquad (1)$$

As for each simulation run the postulate $G(x_{count} > 0 \wedge y_{count} > 0)$ is either fulfilled or not, a set of stochastic runs can be seen as a Bernoulli experiment generating a mean fulfillment rate. For checking Hypothesis 1 (see formula above), enough simulation runs are intended be executed to reach the confidence $c = 0.95$ and the error tolerance $\varepsilon = 0.1$ for the generated mean fulfillment rate. For this, a confidence interval estimation method [4] is used.

The data management for this small example already spans two workflow layers: the simulation layer and the configuration layer (cf. Figure 2). At the simulation layer, the count of species x and y as well as the current simulation time has to be determined at each simulation step. Also at the simulation layer, it has to be determined when one of the following conditions is met:

- the simulation time exceeds 3.0,
- the time series x_{count} and y_{count} reach a steady state,
- the time series x_{count} or y_{count} contains the value 0.

The above single-run analyses belong to the so called *simulation run stop policy*, which determines when to stop a simulation run. Since the fulfillment of $(x_{count} = 0 \vee y_{count} = 0)$ corresponds to a violation of $G(x_{count} > 0 \wedge y_{count} > 0)$, the outcomes of the former formula are further processed to become inputs of a confidence interval calculation at the multi-run layer. Pre-processing at the single-run layer includes:

1. to negate the results of $(x_{count} = 0 \vee y_{count} = 0)$,
2. to check whether this returns *true* for the full length of the simulation run, and

3. to transform this result to 1 or 0 as final result of the simulation run.

As stated, the results of the above, which are one value per simulation run, are suspected to a confidence interval calculation for stopping the generation of further replications as soon as the desired confidence and error tolerance are met. The confidence interval calculations are part of the so called *replication criterion*, which operates at the multi-run layer. Also at the multi-run layer, but for user output, the mean fulfillment rate of $G(x_{count} > 0 \wedge y_{count} > 0)$ has to be calculated for a configuration. Since the mean value is a by-product of the confidence interval calculation, the confidence interval algorithm is intended to output the mean value as well.

4.1 Pre- and Post-work for Workflow Tasks

The calculations in our example refer to the simulation run stop policy, the replication criterion, and the user output. Other tasks that may be relevant in different simulation experiments are, e.g., optimization or sensitivity analysis over multiple configurations. Since these tasks probably require calculations at multiple workflow layers, the calculations are not only attributed to a task, but additionally to a workflow layer. Having in mind the processing nodes, which were introduced in the foregoing section, the calculations can be simply realized by constructing an appropriate processing graph. In order to be economical with main memory, our concept includes to assemble and disassemble parts of the processing graph as tasks and their calculations begin and end during workflow execution. This is a significant advantage of the graph-based processing architecture, since this avoids the accumulation of waste data and facilitates fast releasing of buffer space, which enables the simulation system to handle much more extensive studies or yet unbound execution of simulations (e.g., for on-line simulation applications). For this, we propose pre- and post-work routines for all workflow tasks as shown by Table 1. Figure 14 indicates, where pre- and post-work routines associated to certain layers are executed in the workflow.

Tasks	Pre-/post-work at layer:		
	Exp.	Conf.	Sim. run
Simulation run stop policies			x
Replication criteria		x	x
Optimizers, Sensit. analyzers	x	x	x
User defined analysis/output	x	x	x

Table 1: **Tasks and possible pre-/post-work at different workflow layers (marked with x).**

4.2 The Data Management Unit

The successive assembling and disassembling is made possible by the Data Management unit shown in Figure 3. This unit provides a common interface for setting up, tearing down and retrieving processing nodes. For that, the Data Management maintains a registry, which reflects the tree structure shown in Figure 1. Processing nodes are registered corresponding to the context of the pre-work routine by which they were set up. The context is defined by identifiers for the experiment, configuration, and simulation run,

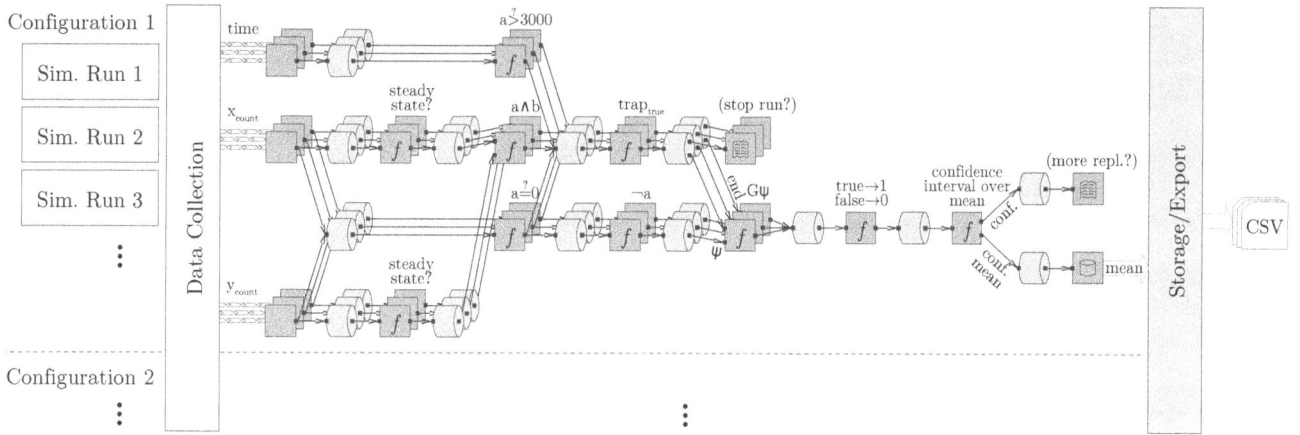

Figure 15: A processing graph for our example. Stacked nodes and links realize processing in behalf of parallel simulation runs. Configurations may also be executed in parallel.

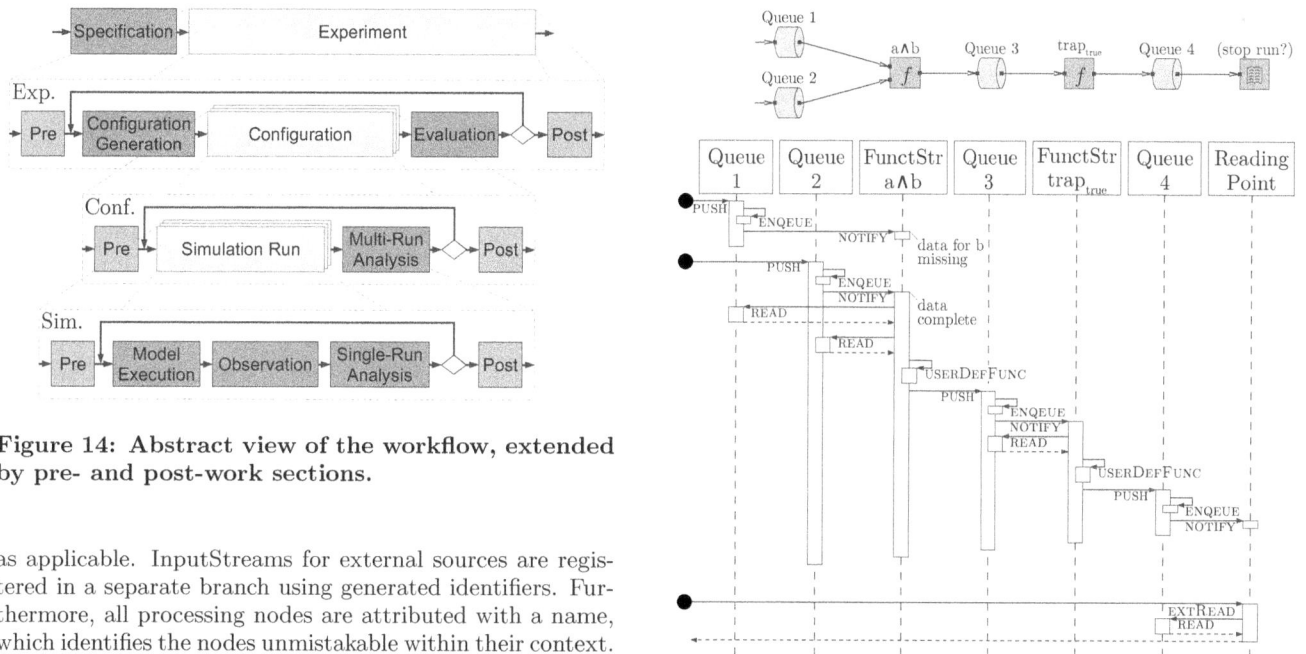

Figure 14: Abstract view of the workflow, extended by pre- and post-work sections.

Figure 16: Part of our example processing graph (top) and a sequence diagram showing calls that propagate data through the graph (for brevity, calls of updateBounds and most self-calls and checks are not shown).

as applicable. InputStreams for external sources are registered in a separate branch using generated identifiers. Furthermore, all processing nodes are attributed with a name, which identifies the nodes unmistakable within their context.

The tasks' pre- and post-work routines introduced above are intended to make use of the Data Management interface for assembling and disassembling the corresponding parts of the processing graph. Figure 15 illustrates how a processing graph for our example can look like.

5. DISCUSSION

Due to the semantics of the Queues and Transporters (cf. Pseudocodes 1–6), data items are propagated in a depth-first manner through the processing graph. Figure 16 shows an excerpt from our example processing graph and illustrates how the arrival of data at Queue 1 and Queue 2 triggers a nested call sequence that leads to the depth-first propagation. This way, FunctionStreams can evaluate data as soon as all inputs have sufficient data. This instantly produces results which may be read immediately after input data has been handed over for processing (cf. Figure 16, call of EXTREAD). Here, we take advantage of the fact that a simulation system is a *controllable* data source, since data

originating from simulation can be processed in line while blocking the source. This is in contrast to classical data stream sources [6]. However, the direct analysis and output scheme realized by OutputStreams fits to classical data streaming applications.

In our example, the FunctionStream labeled "trap$_{\text{true}}$" realizes a function that returns true once (and only once) it receives an item with the value **true**. This FunctionStream has a input window size of 1, telling the upstream Queue 3 to forward each single data item arriving from the FunctionStream labeled "a ∧ b". The existence of Queue 3 is dictated by the bipartiteness of the processing graph, but here, a direct forwarding/processing of results from "a ∧ b" to/by "trap$_{true}$" seems to be more intuitive and to induce less overhead. We motivated the placement of Queues in front of Transporters by cases such as of the FunctionStream "a ∧ b" (synchronization of arguments) or the ReadingPoint "stop run?" (asynchronous reads), as well as for window-based functions. Making exceptions from the bipartiteness directive would annihilate the simplicity achieved by the separation of Queues and Transporters, which are the basic building blocks for buffering and analysis&transport, respectively.

As indicated by our example in Section 4, the processing graph can consist of identical sub-graphs ascribed to parallel simulation runs or configurations. Such sub-graphs are mainly independent from each other, apart from possible merging points downstream. This is beneficial for exploiting parallelism on different layers [18]. Please notice that for an optimistic fine grained parallel execution of a model, the approach has to be extended, e.g. by specific queues that restrict the inflow of data items into the processing graph to those whose time stamps are larger than the global virtual time. As configurations, simulation runs, and model partitions may be computed distributedly, the processing graph can be partitioned as well and sub-graphs can be distributed to those machines where corresponding data is generated. Furthermore, the sub-graphs can be easily migrated along with the configurations, simulation runs, and model partitions. Data transfer between machines becomes necessary only at points, where data from different contexts are analyzed in behalf of the next higher layer processing tasks. In addition to support for parallel/distributed processing, load balancing is supported by the possibility to derive measures from the boundary information of shared Queues. This is because the accumulation of dissimilar amounts of data in front of n-ary FunctionStreams may correlate with different data rates and, thus, indicate imbalanced load on machines that generate the input data for the mentioned Function-Streams.

6. RELATED WORK

Each simulation system has to provide some means to collect, (analyze), and store data. Next to individually tailored simulation data output solutions, there are a few more general approaches for simulation data management.

In the simulation framework JAMES II, observation, analysis for experiment steering, and data storage are separate tasks which are fulfilled by exchangeable plugins [19, 22]. While the experimenter can choose, for instance, a replication criterion that implements confidence interval calculation, observers that deliver input data are set up independently. Data connections from observation to analysis are either realized manually by direct connections or automatically via data storages, implying that data is first stored and then read for analysis. Storing data to files or databases is also realized independently of observation This allows to use generic storage plugins together with model formalism-dependent or specifically tailored observation plugins. While JAMES II mediates data storages to be accessible by observation plugins, time series analysis as discussed herein is not actively supported nor is a streaming of data.

In the Data Collection Framework (DCF) developed for the network simulator ns-3, data is collected, processed and exported using a dataflow graph resembling our processing graph [25]. Therein, controllable Probes are placed into model code to expose values or events for data collection. Since Probes are clearly addressable in ns-3 models by "context strings", the DCF includes data collection functionality, which we excluded from data management for the sake of model-independence (also cf. [17, 30]). Through so-called Collectors, Adapters, and Aggregators, of which different variants are provided, data can be processed, transformed, and merged into different output formats, respectively, in a stream-based manner. Although it might be required to buffer data for Collectors that realize n-ary functions or batch-wise processing or for efficient output, there are no dedicated buffers and sharing of buffer space is not supported.

The Open Simulation Instrumentation Framework (OSIF) also includes simulation data collection and processing [27]. Therein, instrumentation code that is mixed into the model by aspect-oriented programming, provides data to Collectors (resembling our InputStreams) which forward them to a graph of Processors that filter, aggregate, or numerically process the data. As in our approach, the motivation for Processors, which accept data from multiple Collectors or Processors, are reuse, model-independent data processing, and composition of processing functions. While live analysis (for assessing confidence in the number and/or length of simulation runs), output, and post-mortem analysis are supported for a broader workflow covering whole simulation projects, there is no support to integrate processing deeply into the experiment workflow as understood in our work.

Simulation data management is also used as a base to integrate different simulators. By this, different aspects of a specialist discipline are covered through *one* integrated simulation system, e.g., for large-scale studies for oil production optimization [20]. In the latter, a data-driven architecture is presented to realize an automatic optimization workflow with two simulators whose configuration depends on outputs from the respective other simulator. In contrast to our approach, data are first stored near the simulations (supposed to be conducted on distributed machines) and then merged, converted, analyzed, and transported through a graph of buffers and "filters". Processed data is stored again, but at the destination, so that processing can be seen as modifying a data corpus that includes measurement data, simulation data, model parameters, and metadata.

Based on insights about the abundance, characteristics and usage of (multi-dimensional) scientific simulation data, such data were compared to streaming data [1]. Albeit in both domains vast amounts of data have to be pre-processed, summarized, compressed, and partly stored, experiments are found to be executed more efficiently when steered by the experimenter on the basis of ad-hoc queries, which are contradictory to the classical stream-based approach. As a consequence, an ad-hoc query system for simulation data (AQSim) is described, that generates indexes and synopses to prepare for queries [1]. While data are dissected and processed bottom-up in alignment with their multi-resolution structure, the methods found in AQSim focus on multi-dimensional data. Furthermore, queries are processed offline instead of on-the-fly.

7. CONCLUSION AND FUTURE WORK

We have developed a concept to realize a stream-based data management system and its integration into simulation systems. The developed architecture adopts a stream-based approach which allows an on-the-fly processing of time series data. With this we move away from a strict pipeline of generating data, collecting data, storing data, and analyzing data. Transient and persistent data are handled by the same concepts in a seamless manner. The introduced processing graph comprising Queues and a variety of Transporter nodes (InputStreams, FunctionStreams, OutputStreams, Reading-Points, and StoragePoints) supports asynchronously arriving inputs and flexible windowing approaches required for diverse types of time series analysis, e.g., statistical model checking.

By processing data close to their generation, often a lot of data can be thrown away early in the experiment which reduces the amount of data to be handled. Due to this "small big data" approach we expect an efficiency gain in comparison to more conventional approaches in many cases. This was also shown in experiments with a first prototype [31]. However, a more thorough evaluation is needed, as assembling and disassembling the processing graph requires additional efforts. Particularly large numbers of short runs will possibly imply an overhead that has to be taken into account. As a stream-based non-monolithic concept, distributed simulation studies are supported naturally and we expect the approach to scale well. However, this is subject to current studies.

The developed concept represents the inner workings of a data management system as part of a simulation system. However, for setting up the data processing in a convenient manner it has to be related to recent approaches for specifying an experiment, e.g., SESSL [9]. Referring to the latter, the data management becomes part of the semantics of the experiment specification language. So, the setup of the data processing that suits to the experiment design (i.e., the workflow) has to be generated automatically based on the experiment specification. Also more complex time series analyses, e.g., in the context of statistical model checking, need to be translated automatically into a processing graph. Therefore, future work will be dedicated to bringing the simulation experiment specification language SESSL and the developed stream-based data management together.

8. ACKNOWLEDGMENTS

This work is supported in part by the DFG via RTG 1424. Furthermore, we thank Jan Himmelspach who was involved at the beginning of this work and Stefan Leye who gave support in the field of stochastic simulation.

9. REFERENCES

[1] G. Abdulla, T. Critchlow, and W. Arrighi. Simulation data as data streams. *SIGMOD Record*, 33(1):89–94, 2004.

[2] L. Aldred, W. M. P. van der Aalst, M. Dumas, and A. H. M. ter Hofstede. Dimensions of coupling in middleware. *Concurrency and Computation: Practice and Experience*, 21(18):2233–2269, 2009.

[3] F. Ao, J. Meng, J. Du, F. Qin, and J. Yu. Application of data stream technique in simulation system. In *Proceedings of 4th IEEE International Conference on Software Engineering and Service Science*, pages 1059–1062, 2013.

[4] S. Asmusen and P. W. Glynn. *Stochastic simulation: Algorithms and analysis.* Stochastic Modelling and Applied Probability. Springer, New York, NY, 2007.

[5] D. Carney, U. Çetintemel, M. Cherniack, C. Convey, S. Lee, G. Seidman, M. Stonebraker, N. Tatbul, and S. B. Zdonik. Monitoring streams: A new class of data management applications. In *Proceedings of 28th International Conference on Very Large Data Bases*, pages 215–226, 2002.

[6] S. Chakravarthy and Q. Jiang. *Stream data processing: a quality of service perspective ; modeling, scheduling, load shedding, and complex event processing.* Number 36 in Advances in Database Systems. Springer, New York, NY, 2009.

[7] C. Cortes, K. Fisher, D. Pregibon, and A. Rogers. Hancock: a language for extracting signatures from data streams. In *Proceedings of the Sixth ACM SIGKDD International Conference on Knowledge Discovery and Data Mining*, pages 9–17, 2000.

[8] E. W. Dijkstra. On the role of scientific thought. In *Selected Writings on Computing: A personal Perspective*, Texts and Monographs in Computer Science, pages 60–66. Springer, New York, NY, 1982.

[9] R. Ewald and A. M. Uhrmacher. Setting up simulation experiments with SESSL. In *Proceedings of the 2012 Winter Simulation Conference*, page 379, 2012.

[10] F. Fages and A. Rizk. On the analysis of numerical data time series in temporal logic. In M. Calder and S. Gilmore, editors, *Computational Methods in Systems Biology*, volume 4695 of *Lecture Notes in Computer Science*, pages 48–63. Springer, Berlin Heidelberg, 2007.

[11] U. Fischer, L. Dannecker, L. Siksnys, F. Rosenthal, M. Böhm, and W. Lehner. Towards integrated data analytics: Time series forecasting in DBMS. *Datenbank-Spektrum*, 13(1):45–53, 2013.

[12] D. Florescu, C. Hillery, D. Kossmann, P. Lucas, F. Riccardi, T. Westmann, M. J. Carey, A. Sundararajan, and G. Agrawal. The BEA/XQRL streaming XQuery processor. In *Proceedings of the 29th International Conference on Very Large Data Bases*, pages 997–1008, 2003.

[13] J. Gehrke. Technical perspective — data stream processing: when you only get one look. *Communications of the ACM*, 52(10):96–97, 2009.

[14] L. R. Ginzburg and A. H. Resit. Consequences of ratio-dependent predation for steady-state properties of ecosystems. *Ecology (Durham)*, 73(5):1536–1543, 1992.

[15] L. Golab and M. T. Özsu. Issues in data stream management. *SIGMOD Record*, 32(2):5–14, 2003.

[16] P. J. Haas, P. P. Maglio, P. G. Selinger, and W. C. Tan. Data is dead... without what-if models. *Proceedings of the VLDB Endowment*, 4(12):1486–1489, 2011.

[17] T. Helms, J. Himmelspach, C. Maus, O. Röwer, J. Schützel, and A. M. Uhrmacher. Toward a language for the flexible observation of simulations. In *Proceedings of the 2012 Winter Simulation Conference*, pages 418:1–418:12, 2012.

[18] J. Himmelspach, R. Ewald, S. Leye, and A. M. Uhrmacher. Enhancing the scalability of simulations

by embracing multiple levels of parallelization. In *Proceedings of the Second International Workshop on High Performance Computational Systems Biology*, pages 57–66, 2010.

[19] J. Himmelspach and A. M. Uhrmacher. Plug'n simulate. In *Proceedings of the 40th Annual Simulation Symposium*, pages 137–143, 2007.

[20] T. M. Kurç, Ü. V. Çatalyürek, X. Zhang, J. H. Saltz, R. Martino, M. F. Wheeler, M. Peszynska, A. Sussman, C. Hansen, M. K. Sen, R. Seifoullaev, P. L. Stoffa, C. Torres-Verdín, and M. Parashar. A simulation and data analysis system for large-scale, data-driven oil reservoir simulation studies. *Concurrency — Practice and Experience*, 17(11):1441–1467, 2005.

[21] R. Motwani, J. Widom, A. Arasu, B. Babcock, S. Babu, M. Datar, G. S. Manku, C. Olston, J. Rosenstein, and R. Varma. Query processing, approximation, and resource management in a data stream management system. In *Proceedings of the 2003 Conference on Innovative Data Systems Research*, 2003.

[22] M&S Research Group, Institute of Computer Science, Rostock. JAMES II — Java Framework for Modeling & Simulation, 2014. http://jamesii.org, Accessed February 18, 2014.

[23] S. Muthukrishnan. *Data streams: algorithms and applications*. Now Publishers, Hanover, MA, 2005.

[24] F. Peng and S. S. Chawathe. XPath queries on streaming data. In *Proceedings of the 2003 ACM SIGMOD International Conference on Management of Data*, pages 431–442, 2003.

[25] L. F. Perrone, T. R. Henderson, M. J. Watrous, and V. D. Felizardo. The design of an output data collection framework for ns-3. In *Proceedings of the 2013 Winter Simulation Conference*, pages 2984–2995, 2013.

[26] L. F. Perrone, C. S. Main, and B. C. Ward. SAFE: simulation automation framework for experiments. In *Proceedings of the 2012 Winter Simulation Conference*, pages 249:1–249:12, 2012.

[27] J. Ribault, O. Dalle, D. Conan, and S. Leriche. OSIF: a framework to instrument, validate, and analyze simulations. In *Proceedings of the 3rd International ICST Conference on Simulation Tools and Techniques*, pages 56:1–56:9, 2010.

[28] S. Rybacki, F. Haack, K. Wolf, and A. M. Uhrmacher. Developing simulation models — from conceptual to executable model and back — an artifact-based workflow approach. In *Proceedings of the Seventh International Conference on Simulation Tools and Techniques*, 2014. To appear.

[29] S. Rybacki, S. Leye, J. Himmelspach, and A. Uhrmacher. Template and frame based experiment workflows in modeling and simulation software with WORMS. In *2012 IEEE Eighth World Congress on Services*, pages 25–32, 2012.

[30] J. Schützel, R. Ewald, and A. M. Uhrmacher. Towards a general foundation for formalism-specific instrumentation languages. In *Proceedings of the 2013 Winter Simulation Conference*, 2013.

[31] J. Schützel, J. Himmelspach, H. Meyer, A. Heuer, and A. M. Uhrmacher. Streaming data management for the online processing of simulation data. In *Proceedings of the 2012 Winter Simulation Conference*, 2012.

[32] K. Sen, M. Viswanathan, and G. Agha. On statistical model checking of stochastic systems. In K. Etessami and S. K. Rajamani, editors, *Computer Aided Verification*, volume 3576 of *Lecture Notes in Computer Science*, pages 266–280. Springer, Berlin Heidelberg, 2005.

[33] D. Waltemath, R. Adams, F. T. Bergmann, M. Hucka, F. Kolpakov, A. K. Miller, I. I. Moraru, D. Nickerson, S. Sahle, and J. L. Snoep. Reproducible computational biology experiments with SED-ML-the simulation experiment description markup language. *BMC Systems Biology*, 5(198):1–10, 2011.

[34] J. White, K.P., M. Cobb, and S. Spratt. A comparison of five steady-state truncation heuristics for simulation. In *Proceedings of the 2000 Winter Simulation Conference*, pages 755–760, 2000.

Exploring Many-Core Architecture Design Space for Parallel Discrete Event Simulation

Yi Zhang, Jingjing Wang, Dmitry Ponomarev, and Nael Abu-Ghazaleh
Department of Computer Science, Binghamton University
Binghamton, NY, USA
yzhang25@binghamton.edu, jwang36@cs.binghamton.edu,
dima@cs.binghamton.edu, nael@cs.binghamton.edu

ABSTRACT

As multicore and manycore processor architectures are emerging and the core counts per chip continue to increase, it is important to evaluate and understand the performance and scalability of Parallel Discrete Event Simulation (PDES) on these platforms. Most existing architectures are still limited to a modest number of cores, feature simple designs and do not exhibit heterogeneity, making it impossible to perform comprehensive analysis and evaluations of PDES on these platforms. Instead, in this paper we evaluate PDES using a full-system cycle-accurate simulator of a multicore processor and memory subsystem. With this approach, it is possible to flexibly configure the simulator and perform exploration of the impact of architecture design choices on the performance of PDES. In particular, we answer the following four questions with respect to PDES performance and scalability: (1) For the same total chip area, what is the best design point in terms of the number of cores and the size of the on-chip cache? (2) What is the impact of using in-order vs. out-of-order cores? (3) What is the impact of a heterogeneous system with a mix of in-order and out-of-order cores? (4) What is the impact of object partitioning on PDES performance in heterogeneous systems? To answer these questions, we use MARSSx86 simulator for evaluating performance, and rely on Cacti and McPAT tools to derive the area and latency estimates for cores and caches.

Categories and Subject Descriptors

I.6.8 [**Simulation and Modeling**]: Types of Simulation—
Discrete event, Parallel

General Terms

Design

Keywords

PDES, Multi-cores, full-system simulation

1. INTRODUCTION

Parallel Discrete Event Simulation (PDES) is a fine-grained application with irregular communication patterns and frequent synchronization. For these reasons, its performance and scalability have been severely constrained in computing platforms with high communication delays. The continuing emergence of multi-core and many-core architectures offers a significant promise with respect to PDES performance. Several recent studies evaluated the performance impact of multi-core chips on PDES [2, 14, 15, 7, 31]. However, these studies are limited to the existing hardware platforms with modest number of cores per chip [2, 14], or to specialized chips with larger core counts, such as the Tilera Tile64 architecture [15]. Therefore, while these prior works are still useful and more such studies are likely to emerge as the new multi-core processors are developed and brought to market, they can only answer a limited set of questions, and it is unclear whether the conclusions of these studies can be easily generalized beyond specific platforms and organizations being investigated.

In this paper, we expand the scope of PDES investigations on multi-core and many-core systems by employing a simulation-based approach. Specifically, instead of executing PDES on real platforms, we study its behavior using a cycle-accurate full-system simulator of a multi-core system. Simulation-based studies are extensively used by the computer architecture community where standard and emerging applications are evaluated against future hypothetical designs of single-core, or multi-core, processors and memory hierarchies. A major advantage of such an approach is that a simulator can be flexibly configured and the impact of a wide range of design options (most of which are not currently available in real designs, but could appear in some form in future processors) can be evaluated. In this framework, PDES serves as a benchmark of interest which we evaluate using the MarSSx86 simulator [27]. Marss is a recently developed cycle-accurate simulator of x86-based multi-core processors and memory hierarchy.

To the best of our knowledge, this is the first study that evaluates PDES on emerging architectures (rather than on existing architectures). Such simulation-based approach allows us to evaluate a much wider range of systems and explore the issues related to the architecture impact on PDES performance and scalability that are otherwise impossible to evaluate using traditional measurements on existing systems. Furthermore, using circuit, timing and area analysis tools, we study and compare PDES performance for various chip designs with the equivalent area, taking into account the area used by the cores and the on-chip cache hierarchy. Alternatively, we can also express possible performance and scalability improvements in PDES as a function of the additional chip area needed to achieve these improvements.

Specifically, this paper focuses on the following explorations and addresses the following questions:

First, we evaluate the trade-off between increasing the core count on a chip and using larger on-chip last-level cache. The optimal breakdown between these two resources depends on the applications running on the system. While placing more cores on a chip would allow for a higher degree of parallelism without having to cross the chip boundary, larger caches reduce expensive off-chip memory accesses. To understand this tradeoff in the context of PDES, we study the performance of PHOLD executing under ROSS simulator [6] on simulated hardware systems with several core/cache configurations ranging from the design where most of the chip area is dedicated to processing cores to the design where most of the area is dedicated to the on-chip caches.

Second, we evaluate the impact of the individual core designs on the performance of PDES. Specifically, we consider the choice between large out-of-order superscalar cores, smaller out-of-order cores, and simple in-order cores. In scenarios where fast event processing is on the critical path, more complex cores can offer a significant performance boost. However, since PDES is often dominated by communication, synchronization and rollback overhead, it is also conceivable that in-order cores will not result in significant overall slowdown for many models. At the same time, the use of simpler and smaller cores allows to place more of them on the same chip for the same total chip area, thus increasing the low-latency parallelization opportunities; our study considers these trade-offs.

Third, we investigate PDES performance issues on a heterogeneous many-core system that is composed of a number of high performance out-of-order cores and a number of small in-order cores. A particular question that we investigate on these systems with respect to PDES is whether or not a reconsideration of PDES object-to-core partitioning algorithms is required to adjust to the system heterogeneity. While previous work only considered evenly-sized partitions, we evaluate scenarios where a larger number of objects (and therefore, more work) is assigned to more powerful cores.

All simulation-based studies presented in this paper have been conducted using MARSS [27], a cycle accurate full system x86-64 architecture simulator. To obtain area estimates for various core designs with private caches, we used McPAT tool [21], so that all our designs are compared for the same total area. We obtained the latencies for differently-sized last-level caches using CACTI 5.3 [29] tool. The PDES workloads are based on classical PHOLD [10] models.

The key results and conclusions of our experiments are the following:

- For an area-unconstrained chip where the Level 3 (L3) cache size and the number of cores is fixed, and only the core counts vary, the best core choice is the modestly aggressive 2-way superscalar out-of-order core. For the simple PHOLD models, these cores perform nearly identical to much more aggressive 4-way out-of-order superscalar cores, but at the same time they significantly outperform simple in-order cores.

- For an area-constrained chip, a larger number of simple cores results in higher performance compared to the design with smaller number of more powerful cores for PHOLD models. That is, the advantages of thread-level parallelism that can be extracted from multiple cores on the same chip outweigh the advantages of instruction-level parallelism available within each core. Specifically, we show that the best performance is obtained when the largest possible number of small in-order cores are used.

- The size of the shared L3 cache has a limited impact on simulation performance (for PHOLD models) and it is more advantageous for performance to increase the number of cores at the expense of smaller last-level cache. This is because a significant locality in private L1 and L2 caches make the L3 cache less critical for performance. This conclusion is true even for the variation of PHOLD that intentionally increases the memory pressure by introducing an array manipulation loop inside each event.

- Heterogeneous multi-cores are detrimental to PDES performance, as the synchrony of the simulation progress on multiple (heterogeneous) cores is naturally distorted, resulting in the loss of efficiency. However, the degree to which performance is impacted depends on the composition of the system (e.g. the nature and number of individual cores), and some designs have only modest performance degradation. In general, the performance is limited by the slowest cores in the system, thus wasting the extra processing capabilities of more powerful cores.

- A heterogeneity-aware PDES object partitioning may somewhat alleviate the performance challenges of heterogeneous designs, but our initial results show that naive partitioning modifications (such as doubling the number of objects placed on the more powerful cores) only lead to further performance problems. Future research is needed to determine the proper partitioning for such systems.

The rest of the paper is organized as follows. Section 2 provides PDES background of the key PDES features relevant to this study. Section 3 describes our evaluation methodology and tools used for evaluating performance, area and latency. Section 4 presents the results of our experiments and provides discussion of these results. Section 5 describes the related work and we conclude in Section 6.

2. PDES BACKGROUND

In Discrete Event Simulation (DES), a model consists of a set of simulation objects with associated state [8, 20, 34]. For example, in a logic simulation, the objects may be the different gates in the model. The simulation begins with a number of scheduled events. For example, the initial list of scheduled events may be a set of test vectors presented at specified times to the inputs of the circuit. Events (containing timestamps that denote when the event is to take effect) are ordered by simulation time in a pending event queue. Simulation proceeds by processing the event with the earliest timestamp, which can cause changes in the simulation state (e.g., by changing the state of a gate) and schedule

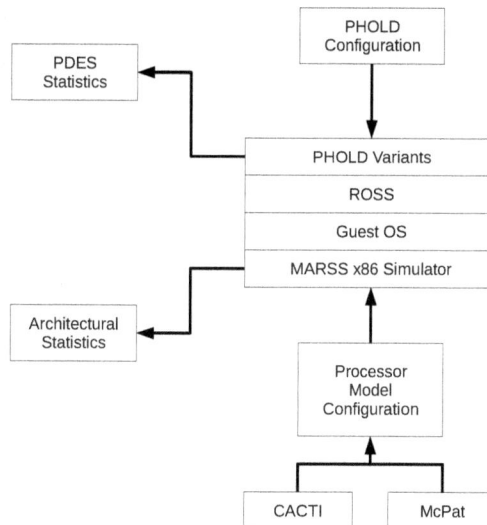

Figure 1: Evaluation and Simulation Methodology

one or more future events (*e.g.*, changing the value at the input of gates connected to the gates whose output logic level changed). Simulation time then advances to the timestamp of the next pending event. Simulation terminates when there are no more events or when a predetermined simulation state is reached.

Parallel Discrete Event Simulation (PDES) leverages parallel processing to accelerate the performance and capacity of DES [11]. The simulation model is partitioned across multiple simulation processes (called Logical Processes, or LPs). Each LP maintains a local pending event queue and carries out simulation as described above, repeatedly processing the earliest time stamp event. A locally processed event may generate events to remote LPs (that is, affecting state changes of an object managed by a remote LP). Thus, LPs communicate by exchanging time-stamped event messages [3, 9, 23, 28]. Correct simulation requires that all events be processed in their causal order such that parallel execution produces simulation results that are consistent with serial execution. Therefore, a synchronization model is needed to ensure that remote events are processed in their proper causal order.

Optimistically synchronized PDES simulators (that we consider in this study) do not enforce causality during event processing. When an event is received with an earlier processing time than the current simulation time, a causality error is detected [18]. The error is recovered from by rolling back the simulation to an earlier state and canceling event messages that were sent prematurely. Optimistic synchronization potentially hides the latency of communication by allowing LPs to process speculatively instead of waiting for events. However, optimism can lead to a number of problems as the speculative computation can generate premature events that later prove to be erroneous, leading to cascading (propagating) rollbacks [11].

PDES is historically difficult to parallelize: it is a fine grained application with frequent communication and complex dynamic dependency patterns. These characteristics can limit the ability of a parallel simulator to exploit the naturally available parallelism in models. Event process-

ing is typically of low computational complexity, as each event updates the state of an object and possibly schedules future events. Thus, significant communication occurs as events are generated to other objects. The amount of communication across cores depends on the locality of event messages. If event messages are frequently exchanged with remote LPs, significant communication occurs, placing substantial pressure on the memory subsystem of a multi-core processor. In the PHOLD benchmark that we use for this study, the amount of remote communication can be explicitly controlled. Additionally, as the degree of parallelism increases, contention for the use of the shared queues starts to play an important role.

3. EVALUATION METHODOLOGY

A number of tools and simulators were used in this study. Our modelling framework is summarized in Figure 1.

In order to perform cycle-accurate simulation of PDES, we used MARSSx86 [27] - a full-system simulator for x86 multi-core architectures. MARSS models different types of processing cores, including both in-order and out-of-order designs, and also provides flexible configurations for the on-chip cache hierarchy.

In order to estimate the area requirements of the individual cores, we used McPAT tool [21]. The three types of cores that we considered in this study include: a) large out-of-order core (Large OoO); b) small out-of-order core (Small OoO), and c) small in-order core. The configurations of each of these cores are listed in Table 1.

For the cache area, we used a cache byte equivalent area (CBE) model to estimate the size of the shared cache from available area [13]. Under this model, the cache size S can be calculated from A_{avail}, the available area and A_{unit}, the area of a fixed unit size of cache, as shown in Equation 1.

$$S = \frac{A_{avail}}{A_{unit}} \qquad (1)$$

We used 4.75 sq. mm per MB as the unit area for the shared L3 cache. For different cache sizes, we derived cache

Table 1: Core Model Configurations

	Large OoO	Small OoO	Small In-order
Issue Width	6	3	2
Commit Width	4	3	N/A
RoB Size	168	64	N/A
Instruction Queue Size	32	32	16
ALU	6	3	1
FPU	6	3	1
Load Queue Size	48	24	N/A
Store Queue Size	96	24	N/A
Private L1-I Cache Size	32KB	32KB	32KB
Private L1-D Cache Size	32KB	32KB	32KB
Private L2 Cache Size	256KB	256KB	256KB
Core Size (sqmm)	19.6154	13.0023	5.2573

access time estimates from Cacti 5.3 tool [29]. We used 32nm technology node for both CACTI and McPAT.

As a PDES simulation engine, we used ROSS-MT [14], a multi-threaded optimistic simulator specifically designed for multi-core environments. ROSS-MT is based on ROSS (Rensselaer's Optimistic Simulation System) [6], a PDES simulation engine with support for both conservative and optimistic time warp simulations.

Typically, PDES performance studies on the real systems are performed using PHOLD benchmark [10]. PHOLD is simple but effective synthetic model for testing the performance of the simulation system. In basic PHOLD, the simulation model is a collection of Logical Processes (LPs). Each Processing Element (PE) is allocated an equal number of LPs. Each LP is initialized with the same number of initial events. The simulation progresses by each LP randomly selecting a target and scheduling an event to that target. When the target receives an event, it randomly selects another LP and schedules an event. At any time during the simulation, the total event population is kept the same. For this study, we utilized PHOLD, but extended it with two additional parameters. The first parameter controls percentage of events that are generated remotely (i.e. to a simulation object running on a different core). The second parameter controls the event processing computational granularity (EPC), which reflects the amount of time that the CPU spends processing each event.

Using the modelling components described above, we performed evaluations in the following directions:

- A study of area-unconstrained homogeneous systems with fixed size of shared cache and variable number of cores.

- A study of area-constrained homogeneous systems, with a trade-off between the size of the on-chip cache and the number of cores. This includes the evaluation of PHOLD models with high memory pressure.

- A study of area-constrained heterogeneous systems composed of multiple types of cores.

For all area-constrained experiments, we assumed 220 square mm chip area for cores and caches, similar to Intel's Ivy-Bridge design [17]. The clock rate is modeled at 3.2 GHz for all of the experiments. Within that constraint, we vary the number and type of processing cores and the amount of shared on-chip L3 cache, to determine the design point that provides the best performance for PDES applications.

Our area-unconstrained model assumes an L3 shared cache of 16 MB, with the cache hit time of 17 cycles. Such a cache

occupies 76 sq. mm of area under the CBE model. The configuration of ROSS that we used for most of our experiments is shown in Table 2. All alterations of this configuration are explicitly described whenever they are used.

Table 2: ROSS Configuration for Evaluating Area-Unconstrained Homogeneous Systems

Model	PHOLD
Synchronization Method	Optimistic
Total LPs	24000
Simulation End Time	16
EPC	100
Remote Event Percentage	10%
Memory Pressure	None

3.1 Cache/Core Area Tradeoff

For evaluating the area tradeoffs, we conduct the experiments with increasing core count. Each core has a private L1 and L2 cache, which are kept fixed and included in the core area. The shared L3 cache size is calculated based on the available area remaining for it, using the CBE model mentioned above. CACTI 5.3 is used to derive the latency estimates for the considered L3 cache sizes. Tables 3 and Table 4 provide details of the cache sizes used in our experiments, their corresponding latencies (in cycles) were derived from CACTI.

3.2 Modelling High Memory Pressure

In an attempt to stress-test the core-cache trade-offs, we designed a modified PHOLD model that increases the memory pressure. This was achieved by adding several memory operations during each event processing. Specifically, we used event-private circular buffers, such that every circular buffer contains an array of pointers to a number of discrete blocks in memory. In the event handler, the contents of each block are copied to another block (not contiguous with the source block) within the same circular buffer. This involves a series of memory operations which affects a memory area of $BlockSize \times BlocksPerCircularBuffer$ in size for each event. The configuration of ROSS used for this experiment is shown in Table 5.

Table 5: Configuration of ROSS for Area-Constrained Homogeneous System with Memory Pressure

Model	PHOLD
Synchronization Method	Optimistic
Total LPs	24000
Simulation End Time	16
EPC	100
Remote Event Percentage	10%
Memory Pressure ($BlockSize \times BlocksPerBuffer$)	$256B \times 32, 128B \times 16$

3.3 Evaluating Heterogeneous Processors

For this evaluation, we only consider systems with two different types of cores. Using the three types of core models described above, we formed three possible combinations of cores:

- Large Out-of-order + Small Out-of-order

Table 3: Core Counts and Cache Size (Out-of-order cores)

Core#	Large OoO		Small OoO	
	L3 Cache Size (Byte)	L3 Cache Latency (Cycle)	L3 Cache Size (Byte)	L3 Cache Latency (Cycle)
2	39905280	23	42826048	24
3	35575104	22	39956224	23
4	31244992	19	37086464	23
5	26914816	18	34216640	22
6	22584640	17	31346880	19
7	18254528	16	28477056	19
8	13924352	13	25607296	18
9	9594176	11	22737536	17
10	5264064	7	19867712	17
11	933888	5	16997952	16
12	N/A	N/A	14128128	13
13	N/A	N/A	11258368	12
14	N/A	N/A	8388608	11
15	N/A	N/A	5518784	7
16	N/A	N/A	2649024	6

Table 4: Core Counts and Cache Size (Inorder cores)

Core#	L3 Cache Size (Byte)	L3 Cache Latency (Cycle)	Core#	L3 Cache Size (Byte)	L3 Cache Latency (Cycle)
3	45088768	24	23	21909696	17
5	42770816	24	25	19591808	17
7	40452928	23	27	17273856	16
9	38135040	23	29	14955968	13
11	35817088	22	31	12638080	12
13	33499200	20	33	10320192	11
15	31181312	19	35	8002240	8
17	28863424	19	37	5684352	7
19	26545472	18	39	3366464	7
21	24227584	18	41	1048576	6

- Large Out-of-order + Inorder

- Small Out-of-order + Inorder

As these experiments focus on the tradeoff between different types of cores, we fixed the shared L3 cache size to the 16 Megabytes cache with a latency of 17 cycles. This results in the remaining area of 144 sq.cm on the processor chip usable for the cores. The core combinations (with the number of cores of each type) used in our experiments are shown in the Table 6.

Table 6: Combinations of Cores Used in Evaluations of Heterogeneous Chips

Large OoO + Small OoO		Large OoO + Inorder		Small OoO + Inorder	
Large OoO	Small OoO	Large OoO	Inorder	Small OoO	Inorder
1	9	1	23	1	24
2	8	2	19	2	22
3	6	3	16	3	20
4	5	4	12	4	17
5	3	5	8	5	15
6	2	6	5	6	12
				7	10
				10	2

As the cores in a heterogeneous processor would have different capability, we also implemented workload partitioning for heterogeneous systems in an attempt to bridge the gap between the core processing capability and its actual load. The partitioning is performed by mapping different number of Logical Processors(LPs) to different cores using a specific ratio. With such partitioning strategy, cores with more computing power will receive more LPs, while the overall number of LPs would stay the same.

For example, for a heterogeneous processor with two small out-of-order cores and one in-order core, if the overall number of LPs is 2500 and the partitioning ratio is 2:1, then the two out-of-order cores will receive 1000 LPs each, and the in-order core will receive 500 LPs.

In this experiment, we tested 3 different partitioning ratios, as shown in Table 7.

Table 7: ROSS Configuration for Evaluating Area-Constrained Heterogeneous Systems

Model	PHOLD
Synchronization Method	Optimistic
Total LPs	24000
Simulation End Time	16
EPC	100
Remote Event Percentage	10%
Memory Pressure	NONE
Partitioning Ratio	1:1, 2:1, 4:1

4. PERFORMANCE EVALUATION

In this section we present performance evaluation of ROSS-MT using MARSSx86 simulator. In particular, we first evaluate the tradeoff between the L3 cache size and the core counts, and its impact on the performance of ROSS-MT. We follow this by evaluating the performance of ROSS-MT in the system with heterogeneous cores and examining the impact of object partitioning among the cores on the performance.

4.1 The Impact of L3 Cache Size and Core Counts

In our first experiment, we evaluated the performance of ROSS-MT using large out-of-order cores (large OoO), small out-of-order cores (small OoO), and small in-order cores (in-order) respectively, as shown in Figure 2. In this experiment, we fixed the size of the L3 cache at 16 MBytes. As shown in Figure 2, the performance of ROSS-MT scales when more cores are used. In addition, the performance of simulation when running on large out-of-order cores is close to the one running on small out-of-order cores, but is better than the performance obtained with in-order cores. This indicates that for the PHOLD model, a large out-of-order core has a similar processing speed with small out-of-order core, but is significantly faster than an in-order core. Thus, if the number of cores on the chip is fixed, the best performing design is the one that uses modestly aggressive out-of-order cores.

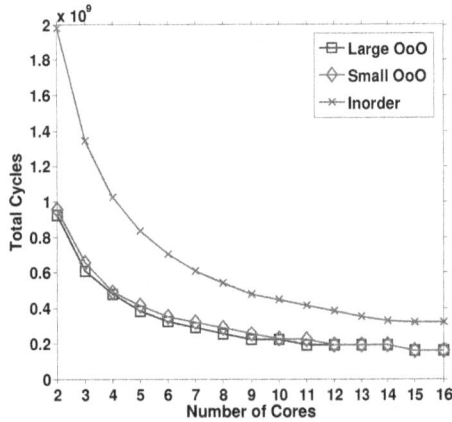

Figure 2: Experiments with Fixed L3 Cache Size

In the next experiment, we evaluate the performance of ROSS-MT when the L3 cache size varies. In this experiment, the chip area was fixed, meaning that the available size of the L3 cache becomes smaller, as more cores are placed on the chip. The size of the L3 cache and the core counts are calculated by Equation 1. Figure 3(a) and Figure 3(b) show the total cycles and the L3 hit rate respectively when the core count increases. At the point where 41 in-order cores are used (the maximum number of in-order cores that could fit on the chip according to our area model), PDES performance is better compared to using either 11 large out-of-order cores or 16 small out-of-order ones (the maximum number of out-of-order cores fitting in the same area).

In addition, the available size of the L3 cache decreases as the core count increases, thus reducing the L3 hit rate, as shown in Figure 3(b). As the penalty of a L3 cache miss cannot be ignored, we expect that the L3 cache misses can dominate the PDES performance at some point when the size of L3 cache is small. However, the experimental results in Figure 3 indicate that the performance of ROSS-MT is always better with more cores, even if the memory pressure exerted by each processing event is increased, as shown in Figure 4. The reason is that due to the high locality in the local L1 and L2 caches, the absolute number of accesses to L3 is fairly small, so the L3 performance has a limited impact in the simulation models that we consider for this study.

4.2 PDES on Heterogeneous Multi-Cores

In this subsection, we evaluate the impact of heterogeneous core combinations on the performance of ROSS-MT. In particular, we consider three different core compositions: large OoO + small OoO (Figure 5), large OoO + Inorder (Figure 6), and small OoO + inorder (Figure 7). In Figure 5, Figure 6, and Figure 7, the x-axis N x T indicates that the combination consists of N larger cores and T smaller ones. For example, the case marked "3x6" in Figure 5, refers to the design with 3 large out-of-order cores and 6 small out-of-order cores.

To study the performance of ROSS-MT on heterogeneous cores, a partitioning ratio was introduced in the previous section, with the purpose of distributing objects between larger cores and smaller ones. The motivation is to partially hide the impact of heterogeneity by assigning a larger fraction of objects to the more powerful cores. For example, when the partitioning ratio is set to four, the number of objects assigned to a larger core is four times more than those assigned to a smaller core.

We used the simulation efficiency to evaluate the quality of partitioning. In PDES, efficiency is calculated by dividing committed events to the total processed events. If objects are not properly partitioned among the cores, the progress of simulation on an overloaded core will lag behind, thus causing a large number of rollbacks (assuming an optimistic simulation). Figure 5(b), Figure 6(b) and Figure 7(b) show the simulation efficiency in each group of heterogeneous cores respectively. We selected three values of partitioning ratio: 1, 2, and 4. We observed that the power of the in-order cores (in terms of instruction throughput) is roughly half that of the out-of-order cores, and therefore the partitioning ratio of 2 represents an attempt to directly compensate for this disparity in order to achieve a more synchronous execution. Partitioning ratio of 4 overloads the fast cores even more.

When the partitioning ratio is set as either 2 or 4, the efficiency increases with the number of larger cores. This indicates that larger cores become overloaded , and are more likely to cause the simulation on the smaller ones to be rolled back. When the number of larger cores increases, the likelihood of communication occurring between larger cores and smaller ones reduces, thus increasing the efficiency. However, of these three partitioning ratios, the best efficiency is achieved for the ratio of 1, indicating that objects in the PHOLD model should be equally distributed among cores even though cores are heterogeneous. Therefore, a naive partitioning that matches the number of objects to the core's throughput capabilities does not work. It is likely that some fractional partitioning (the ratio being between 1 and 2) would lead to a better performance than that of equal partitioning, but additional experiments are needed to validate that claim.

We also evaluated the number of cycles for the PDES simulation in each group of heterogeneous cores, as shown in Figure 5(a), Figure 6(a), and Figure 7(a) respectively. In the case of partitioning ratio of 4, the performance of simulation in each experiment becomes better when more larger cores are used. Such performance improvement is obtained by improving the simulation efficiency. On the other hand, the trends are different when the partitioning ratio is set as either 1 or 2. For example, Figure 5(a) shows the number of cycles for simulation when both large out-of-order and small out-of-order cores are used. As both types

(a) Total Cycles

(b) L3 Cache Hit Rate

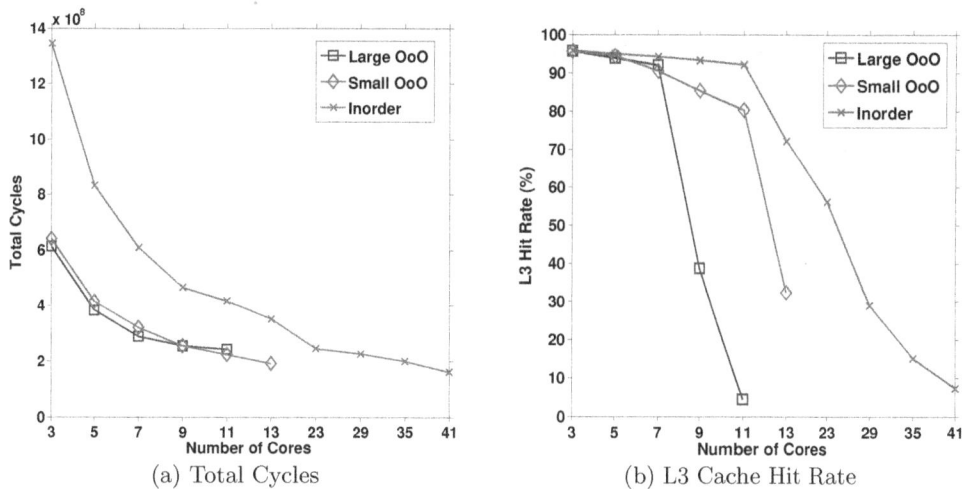

Figure 3: Tradeoff between L3 Cache Size and Core Counts

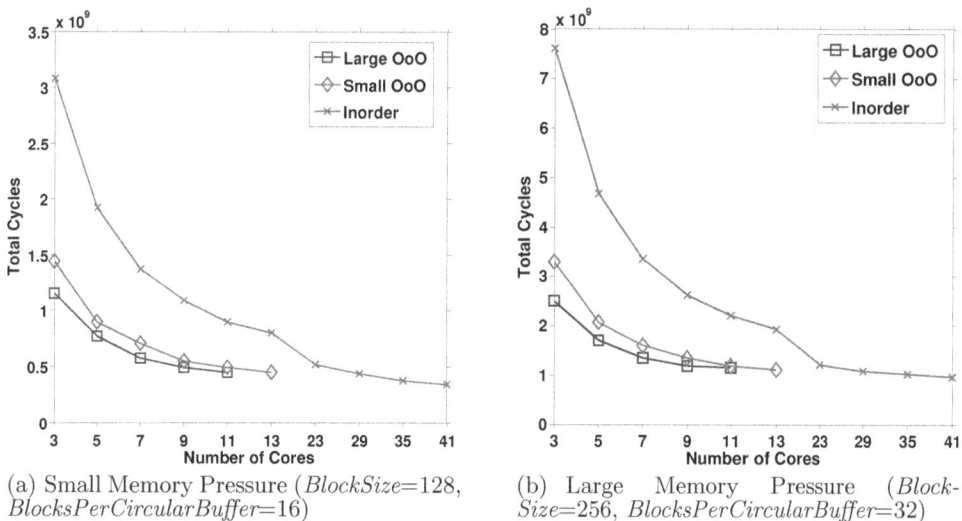

(a) Small Memory Pressure (*BlockSize*=128, *BlocksPerCircularBuffer*=16)

(b) Large Memory Pressure (*Block-Size*=256, *BlocksPerCircularBuffer*=32)

Figure 4: The Impact of Memory Pressure

of cores have a similar processing speed, the performance of simulation is mainly dependent on the total number of cores being used when the partitioning ratio is set as 1. In other words, the more cores are used, the better performance can be achieved. In the case of partitioning ratio of 2, the performance of simulation is dominated by the rollbacks.

Finally, Figure 6(a) and Figure 7(a) shows the number of cycles for ROSS-MT when the system is composed of large out-of-order cores and in-order cores, and small out-of-order cores and in-order cores respectively. In both experiments, when the partitioning ratio is set as either 1 or 2, the performance of simulation becomes worse when the number of in-order cores in the composition reduces. As we described in the previous subsection, it is advantageous to use more in-order cores when the size of chip area is limited. Again, notice that partitioning ratio of 1 provides the best performance out of these three points, and additional experiments are needed to determine the best-performing partitioning ratio.

5. RELATED WORK

The multi-core and many-core processor architectures can substantially reduce the communication cost of PDES. Several prior works analyzed PDES performance on these emerging systems and also explored performance optimization opportunities. Jagtap et al. [14, 15] designed a multi-threaded version of ROSS simulator, called *ROSS-MT*, to explicitly exploit shared memory hierarchy available on multi-core systems. This is in contrast to the process-based communication model used in baseline ROSS simulator, and in many other PDES engines. The performance of ROSS-MT was evaluated on two emerging many-core platforms: 48-core AMD Opteron Magny-Cours [14] and Tilera Tile64 [15]. The experimental results showed that ROSS-MT can scale well on both platforms, especially when a number of performance optimizations (specific to each platform) are applied.

Vitali et al. [32, 31] developed a different multi-threaded PDES simulator on multi-core platforms. A load-sharing scheme was implemented, allowing each simulation kernel instance to be executed by multiple threads. Wilsey et al. [7]

(a) Total Cycles

(b) ROSS Efficiency

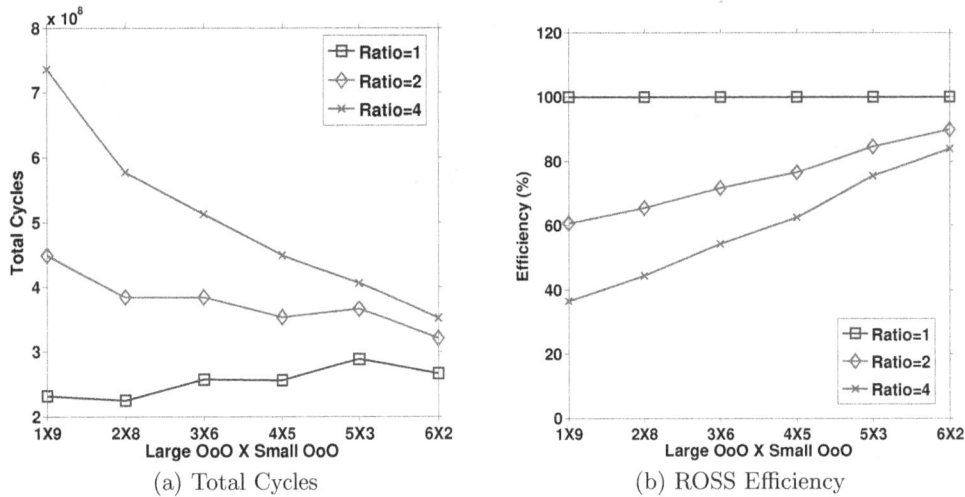

Figure 5: Core Composition between Large OoO and Small OoO

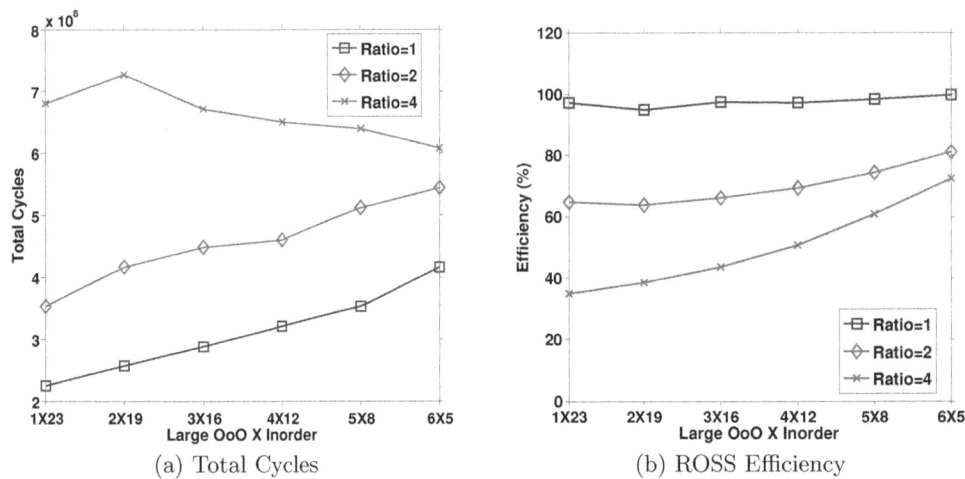

(a) Total Cycles

(b) ROSS Efficiency

Figure 6: Core Composition between Large OoO and Inorder

improved the performance of Time Warp simulation, by dynamically changing the frequency of each core during the simulation. In this approach, the cores having LPs with fewer rollbacks are overclocked, while the cores containing LPs with more rollbacks are underlocked.

Several studies focused on investigating the design trade-offs in multi-core architectures in order to improve the area efficiency of these systems. A study of [13] is an example of CMP design space exploration in terms of selecting different core designs (in-order and out-of-order) and also investigating the trade-offs between the core count and the cache capacity. In this paper, we perform a similar study in the context of multi-threaded PDES. Several studies focused on developing analytical models for the core, cache and on-chip interconnect area [1, 26, 33, 19]. The cache subsystem design has also been studied in great detail. For example, last level cache designs for data mining applications were explored in [16]. The work of [35] evaluated the impact of CMP cache sharing on multi-threaded applications and demonstrated benefits of cache-sharing aware program transformations. Oh et al. [26] and Wentzlaff [33] proposed

simple analytical models to study trade-offs between the core count and the cache capacity under finite die area. Analytical models for thermal implications of CMP designs [24] and its impact on network scalability [4] have also been developed.

The performance of parallel systems, however, depends not just on the CMP design but also on the characteristics of the workload [5]. Some studies have explored such interplay. Configuration workload characterization [25] demonstrated that architectural configuration alone or workload characterization alone were not sufficient to predict the performance of the system. The work of [12] developed analytical models for both architecture and workloads and studied the applications performance and power implications on a range of architectures. Lotfi et al. proposed Scale-out processor design [22] to address the inefficiency of current architectures (which are designed for high single thread performance) to achieve high server throughput. They proposed a chip architecture based on pods - an optimal performance-density building block specifically for scale-out workloads. The work by Vitali et al. [30] considered the memory access patterns

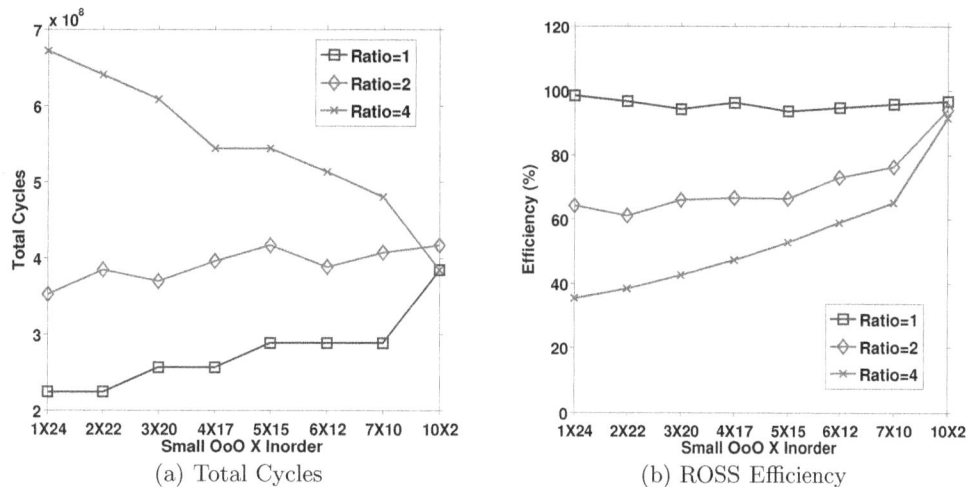

(a) Total Cycles	(b) ROSS Efficiency

Figure 7: Core Composition between Small OoO and Inorder

for various operations within optimistic simulation. They demonstrated a cache-aware memory manager that maps the simulation data structures in a way that maximizes the cache performance.

6. CONCLUSIONS

We presented a simulation methodology for evaluating performance of PDES applications on emerging hardware many-core architectures. Our approach allows for the exploration of the design space, including the evaluation of the designs with large number of cores as well as the designs with heterogeneous cores. To the best of our knowledge, ours is the first work that uses PDES as an application for such simulation-based studies.

The conclusions of our initial experiments with this simulation framework are that the shared L3 cache has a minimal performance impact for PHOLD-style PDES applications, and it is more advantageous for performance to utilize the available chip area for additional cores rather than caches. While modestly aggressive out-of-order cores provide noticeable performance benefits compared to the in-order cores for area-unconstrained designs, a better performance is achieved with a larger number of simple in-order cores when the chip area is constrained. We also demonstrated that core heterogeneity negatively impacts PDES performance as it naturally distorts the synchrony, increases the number of rollbacks and degrades simulation efficiency. We also showed that specific performance impact depends on the composition of cores.

The simulation framework described in this paper can also be applied to a number of more detailed studies, such as examining and understanding the causes and the impact of rollbacks in PDES in a repeatable and controlled fashion. The low-level details of other PDES subsystems can also be studied using this methodology - this is left for our future work. Future work will also examine further modifications to PDES object partitioning algorithms to tailor them to heterogeneous platforms and mitigate the negative impact of core heterogeneity on PDES performance.

7. ACKNOWLEDGEMENTS

This material is based on research sponsored by Air Force Research Laboratory under agreement number FA8750-11-2-0004 and by National Science Foundation grants CNS-0916323 and CNS-0958501. The U.S. Government is authorized to reproduce and distribute reprints for Governmental purposes notwithstanding any copyright notation thereon. The views and conclusions contained herein are those of the authors and should not be interpreted as necessarily representing the official policies and endorsements, either expressed or implied, of Air Force Research Laboratory, National Science Foundation, or the U.S. Government.

8. REFERENCES

[1] O. Azizi, A. Mahesri, S. Patel, and M. Horowitz. Area-efficiency in cmp core design: co-optimization of microarchitecture and physical design. *ACM SIGARCH Computer Architecture News*, 37(2):56–65, 2009.

[2] K. Bahulkar, N. Hofmann, D. Jagtap, N. B. Abu-Ghazaleh, and D. Ponomarev. Performance evaluation of PDES on multi-core clusters. In *Proceedings of the 2010 IEEE/ACM 14th International Symposium on Distributed Simulation and Real Time Applications, (DS-RT 10)*, pages 131–140, 2010.

[3] M. L. Bailey, J. V. Briner, Jr., and R. D. Chamberlain. Parallel logic simulation of VLSI systems. *ACM Computing Surveys*, 26(3):255–294, Sept. 1994.

[4] J. Balfour and W. Dally. Design tradeoffs for tiled cmp on-chip networks. In *Proceedings of the 20th annual international conference on Supercomputing*, pages 187–198. ACM, 2006.

[5] M. Bhadauria, V. Weaver, and S. McKee. Parsec: hardware profiling of emerging workloads for cmp design. In *Proceedings of the 23rd international conference on Supercomputing*, pages 509–510. ACM, 2009.

[6] C. D. Carothers, D. Bauer, and S. Pearce. Ross: A high-performance, low-memory, modular time warp system. *Journal of Parallel and Distributed Computing*, 62(11):1648 – 1669, 2002.

[7] R. Child and P. Wilsey. Dynamically adjusting core frequencies to accelerate time warp simulations in many-core processors. In *Principles of Advanced and Distributed Simulation (PADS)*, pages 35–43. IEEE, 2012.

[8] P. A. Fishwick. *Simulation Model Design and Execution: Building Digital Worlds*. Prentice Hall, Englewood Cliffs, NJ, 1995.

[9] R. Fujimoto. Parallel discrete event simulation. *Communications of the ACM*, 33(10):30–53, Oct. 1990.

[10] R. Fujimoto. Performance of time warp under synthetic workloads. 1990.

[11] R. M. Fujimoto. *Parallel and Distributed Simulation Systems*. Wiley Interscience, Jan. 2000.

[12] Z. Guz, O. Itzhak, I. Keidar, A. Kolodny, A. Mendelson, and U. Weiser. Threads vs. caches: modeling the behavior of parallel workloads. In *Computer Design (ICCD), 2010 IEEE International Conference on*, pages 274–281. IEEE, 2010.

[13] J. Huh, D. Burger, and S. Keckler. Exploring the design space of future cmps. In *Parallel Architectures and Compilation Techniques, 2001. Proceedings. 2001 International Conference on*, pages 199–210. IEEE, 2001.

[14] D. Jagtap, N. Abu-Ghazaleh, and D. Ponomarev. Optimization of parallel discrete event simulator for multi-core systems. In *Parallel & Distributed Processing Symposium (IPDPS), 2012 IEEE 26th International*, pages 520–531. IEEE, 2012.

[15] D. Jagtap, K. Bahulkar, D. Ponomarev, and N. Abu-Ghazaleh. Characterizing and understanding pdes behavior on tilera architecture. In *Workshop on Principles of Advanced and Distributed Simulation (PADS 12)*, July 2012.

[16] A. Jaleel, M. Mattina, and B. Jacob. Last level cache (llc) performance of data mining workloads on a cmp-a case study of parallel bioinformatics workloads. In *High-Performance Computer Architecture, 2006. The Twelfth International Symposium on*, pages 88–98. IEEE, 2006.

[17] D. James. Intel ivy bridge unveiled – the first commercial tri-gate, high-k, metal-gate cpu. In *Custom Integrated Circuits Conference (CICC)*, pages 1–4, 2012.

[18] D. Jefferson. Virtual time. *ACM Transactions on Programming Languages and Systems*, 7(3):405–425, July 1985.

[19] R. Kumar, V. Zyuban, and D. Tullsen. Interconnections in multi-core architectures: Understanding mechanisms, overheads and scaling. In *Computer Architecture, 2005. ISCA'05. Proceedings. 32nd International Symposium on*, pages 408–419. IEEE, 2005.

[20] A. M. Law and W. D. Kelton. *Simulation Modeling and Analysis*. McGraw-Hill, 3rd edition, 2000.

[21] S. Li, J. H. Ahn, R. D. Strong, J. B. Brockman, D. M. Tullsen, and N. P. Jouppi. Mcpat: An integrated power, area, and timing modeling framework for multicore and manycore architectures. In *Proceedings of the 42Nd Annual IEEE/ACM International Symposium on Microarchitecture*, MICRO 42, pages 469–480, New York, NY, USA, 2009. ACM.

[22] P. Lotfi-Kamran, B. Grot, M. Ferdman, S. Volos, O. Kocberber, J. Picorel, A. Adileh, D. Jevdjic, S. Idgunji, E. Ozer, et al. Scale-out processors. In *Proceedings of the 39th International Symposium on Computer Architecture*, pages 500–511. IEEE Press, 2012.

[23] J. Misra. Distributed discrete-event simulation. *Computing Surveys*, 18(1):39–65, Mar. 1986.

[24] M. Monchiero, R. Canal, and A. González. Design space exploration for multicore architectures: a power/performance/thermal view. In *Proceedings of the 20th annual international conference on Supercomputing*, pages 177–186. ACM, 2006.

[25] H. Najaf-Abadi and E. Rotenberg. Configurational workload characterization. In *Performance Analysis of Systems and software, 2008. ISPASS 2008. IEEE International Symposium on*, pages 147–156. IEEE, 2008.

[26] T. Oh, H. Lee, K. Lee, and S. Cho. An analytical model to study optimal area breakdown between cores and caches in a chip multiprocessor. In *VLSI, 2009. ISVLSI'09. IEEE Computer Society Annual Symposium on*, pages 181–186. IEEE, 2009.

[27] A. Patel, F. Afram, S. Chen, and K. Ghose. MARSSx86: A Full System Simulator for x86 CPUs. In *Design Automation Conference 2011 (DAC'11)*, 2011.

[28] P. F. Reynolds Jr. A spectrum of options for parallel simulation. In *Winter Simulation Conference*, pages 325–332. Society for Computer Simulation, 1988.

[29] S. Thoziyoor, N. Muralimanohar, J. Ahn, and N. Jouppi. Cacti 5.3. *HP Laboratories, Palo Alto, CA*, 2008.

[30] R. Vitali, A. Pellegrini, and G. Cerasuolo. Cache-aware memory manager for optimistic simulations. In *Proceedings of the 5th International ICST Conference on Simulation Tools and Techniques*, pages 129–138. ICST (Institute for Computer Sciences, Social-Informatics and Telecommunications Engineering), 2012.

[31] R. Vitali, A. Pellegrini, and F. Quaglia. Assessing load-sharing within optimistic simulation platforms. In *Proceedings of the 2012 Winter Simulation Conference*. IEEE, 2012.

[32] R. Vitali, A. Pellegrini, and F. Quaglia. Towards symmetric multi-threaded optimistic simulation kernels. In *Principles of Advanced and Distributed Simulation (PADS)*, pages 211–220. IEEE, 2012.

[33] D. Wentzlaff, N. Beckmann, J. Miller, and A. Agarwal. Core count vs cache size for manycore architectures in the cloud. 2010.

[34] B. P. Zeigler. *Multifacetted Modelling and Discrete Event Simulation*. Academic Press Inc. (London) Ltd., 24/28 Oval Road, London NW1, 1984.

[35] E. Zhang, Y. Jiang, and X. Shen. Does cache sharing on modern cmp matter to the performance of contemporary multithreaded programs? In *ACM Sigplan Notices*, volume 45, pages 203–212. ACM, 2010.

Transparent Multi-Core Speculative Parallelization of DES Models with Event and Cross-State Dependencies

Alessandro Pellegrini
pellegrini@dis.uniroma1.it

Francesco Quaglia
quaglia@dis.uniroma1.it

DIAG – Sapienza, University of Rome
Via Ariosto 25, 00185 Rome, Italy

ABSTRACT

In this article we tackle transparent parallelization of Discrete Event Simulation (DES) models to be run on top of multi-core machines according to speculative schemes. The innovation in our proposal lies in that we consider a more general programming and execution model, compared to the one targeted by state of the art PDES platforms, where the boundaries of the state portion accessible while processing an event at a specific simulation object do not limit access to the actual object state, or to shared global variables. Rather, the simulation object is allowed to access (and alter) the state of any other object, thus causing what we term *cross-state* dependency. We note that this model exactly complies with typical (easy to manage) sequential-style DES programming, where a (dynamically-allocated) state portion of object A can be accessed by object B in either read or write mode (or both) by, e.g., passing a pointer to B as the payload of a scheduled simulation event. However, while read/write memory accesses performed in the sequential run are always guaranteed to observe (and to give rise to) a consistent snapshot of the state of the simulation model, consistency is not automatically guaranteed in case of parallelization and concurrent execution of simulation objects with cross-state dependencies. We cope with such a consistency issue, and its application-transparent support, in the context of parallel and optimistic executions. This is achieved by introducing an advanced memory management architecture, able to efficiently detect read/write accesses by concurrent objects to whichever object state in an application transparent manner, together with advanced synchronization mechanisms providing the advantage of exploiting parallelism in the underlying multi-core architecture while transparently handling both cross-state and traditional event-based dependencies. Our proposal targets Linux and has been integrated with the ROOT-Sim open source optimistic simulation platform, although its design principles, and most parts of the developed software, are of general relevance.

Categories and Subject Descriptors

I.6.8 [**Simulation and Modeling**]: Types of Simulation—*Discrete Event, Parallel*

Keywords

PDES; Parallelism Transparency; Speculative Processing

1. INTRODUCTION

Traditionally, Parallel Discrete Event Simulation (PDES) has been based on explicitly partitioning the entire simulation model into distinct simulation objects (also referred to as Logical Processes) [7] to be dispatched concurrently, whose states are disjoint and whose memory access operations (upon event processing) are confined within the state of the simulation object executing the event. This approach implicitly requires the application programmers to shift from a sequential programming model where the application is designed and coded to run serially (namely to process one event at a time) and to have the possibility to access any valid memory location upon the execution of whichever event. In other words, parallelism is achieved by a-priori, namely at code design/development time, forcing separation of the accesses to slices of the simulation model state, each one representing an individual object.

Undoubtedly, such a classical PDES approach has been the only way to parallelism at the time when (massively) parallel architectures were mostly based on clusters of (single-core) machines. On the other hand, the advent (and the large diffusion) of shared-memory parallel machines, such as multi-core and SMP machines, offered the technical possibility to directly share state information across different objects, e.g., by relying on a unique address space and/or operating system supported shared memory. However, the synchronization approaches provided by the PDES literature, and the actual simulation platforms relying on them, definitely need to be adapted in order to support correct concurrent execution of simulation objects while jointly allowing the possibility to directly share data and masking synchronization (and hence actual parallelization) to the application programmer. We note that the final target along the path of supporting shared data across different simulation objects actually translated into enabling a sequential-style programming approach (augmented with the concept of "object", which allows for improving expressiveness while coding complex simulation models), characterized by full access capabilities to any valid memory location (logically belonging to the state of any involved object) upon executing whichever event, in either read or write mode.

One proposal along this direction has been recently provided in [19] for the case of simulation code based on the C programming language, where direct sharing of information across the simulation objects has been supported for the case of global variables included within the simulation program. This approach has been based on multi-versioning plus code instrumentation (for accessing multi-version chains) as the means to achieve programmer transparent concurrent accesses to global variables jointly to optimistic synchronization [12]. However, sharing based exclusively on global variables limits the actual possibility to share data in size, given that the storage for global variables is statically defined at compile time. Also, it still constraints the programmer, who is not allowed to directly access arbitrary slices of (dynamically-allocated) memory destined to keep portions of the simulation model (e.g. by having them logically representing the state of a generic simulation object).

In this article we exactly tackle the above problem, namely how to support direct access by concurrent simulation objects to memory areas that are dynamically allocated by any simulation object, and logically included within its local state via, e.g., pointer based referencing. The same pointers can be used as payloads of events so that the recipient simulation object can use them to directly access the local state of a different object, in either read or write mode. This breaks disjointness in memory access at the programming level, hence enabling the support for sequential-style DES programming (where any valid memory location keeping a portion of the state of whichever object, is accessible while processing any simulation event), and creates a new kind of dependency that we term *cross-state* dependency, which stands as complementary with respect to the classical event dependency proper of PDES. On the other hand, guaranteeing correct (e.g. causally consistent) execution of simulation events in the presence of cross-state dependency across concurrent simulation objects requires proper application-transparent synchronization mechanisms to be put in place, which we provide in this article.

Overall, the contributions by this article can be summarized as follows:

1) We present the design and implementation of an innovative memory management architecture, oriented to Linux systems, which allows to detect the materialization of cross-state dependencies across simulation objects that are run concurrently, in an application-transparent manner.

2) We present a synchronization scheme, entailing speculative processing, which takes into account both event and cross-state dependencies and allows the parallel run to mimic a classical sequential one where the simulation events are processed in non-decreasing timestamp order, while jointly being allowed to access any valid memory location belonging to the state of the simulation model (namely any memory location logically belonging to the state of some object). On the other hand, our scheme, which we name ECS (Event and Cross-State synchronization), allows running simulation events destined to different simulation objects concurrently (again transparently to the programmer).

All the presented software modules and algorithms have been integrated within the ROOT-Sim open source simulation package [10] and are available for download[1]. Further, experimental data for an assessment of the whole ECS architecture are provided.

The remainder of this article is organized as follows. In Section 2, we discuss literature results related to our proposal. The innovative memory management architecture transparently tracking cross-state dependencies and the actual ECS synchronization protocol are presented in Section 3. The results of the experimental study are provided in Section 4.

2. RELATED WORK

The issue of bypassing state disjointness for concurrent objects in PDES systems has been dealt with by several studies. The work in [2] discusses how state sharing can be emulated by using a separate simulation object hosting the shared data and acting as a centralized server. This proposal also introduces the notion of *version records*, where multi-versioning is used for shared data in order to cope with read/write operations occurring at different logical times, and to avoid unneeded rollbacks of the centralized server in case of optimistic synchronization. This is an approach similar to the one proposed in [17], where a theoretical presentation of algorithms to implement a Distributed Shared Memory mechanism is provided in terms of protocols to keep replicated instances of a variable coherent. In particular, one of the provided algorithms proposes to implement variables as multi-version lists where write operations install new version nodes and read operations find the most suitable version. The above approaches are different from what we propose given that read/write access to shared variables is mapped to message-passing (namely, event schedule operations), while we support a truly sequential-style access to any (by default sharable) buffer within the simulation object states, e.g., via pointers. Also, in our proposal sharing is not limited to a particular memory slice (such as the state image of the centralized server), while we allow access, and hence sharing, of any memory buffer representing a portion of the whole simulation model state. Also, by design the above approaches are strongly oriented to distributed simulation environments, while we target the trend of shared-memory/multi-core machines.

In another proposal [6] the notion of *state query* is introduced. A simulation object needing a portion of the state which belongs to a different object can issue a query message to it, and wait for a reply containing the suitable value. In case this value is later detected to be no longer valid, an anti-message is sent so as to invalidate the query. Again, this approach relies on message passing, and is not transparent to the application programmer.

The work in [9] proposes to integrate the support for shared state in terms of global variables, by basing the architecture on [3]. Although this proposal supports in-place read/write operations as we do (i.e., simulation objects directly access the only copy of the data, avoiding a commit phase at the end of the execution of an event), it provides no transparency, as the application-level code must explicitly register a simulation object as a reader/writer on shared variables. Our proposal avoids this limitation by also allowing the sharing of dynamically-allocated buffers, for which pre-declaration of the potential need to access cannot be raised at startup (hence intrinsically leading actual access

---

[1] http://svn.dis.uniroma1.it/svn/hpdcs/root_sim/trunk

to be determined as a function of the specific execution trajectory while running the application).

The issue of transparency has been tackled in [19], where shared data are allowed to be accessed by concurrent objects without the need for pre-declaring the intention to access. This has been achieved via user transparent software instrumentation, in combination with a multi-version scheme, either allowing the redirection of read operations to the correct version of the data (on the basis of the timestamp) or forcing rollbacks of causally inconsistent reads. However, this solutions is limited to the management of global variables, while our proposal is suited for allowing data sharing across dynamically allocated memory chunks logically incorporated within the state of each individual simulation object, while providing parallelism and synchronization transparency.

In the context of the High-Level-Architecture (HLA), proposals for supporting shared-state can be found in [8, 15]. They are again targeted at distributed environments, since they are based on a middleware component which relies on a timestamp-ordering approach for implementing a request/reply protocol. Additionally, these approaches are targeted at the conservative synchronization protocol, where there is no need to detect and handle causality violations, while we target optimistic synchronization.

The work in [4] proposes a framework targeted at multi-core machines and based on Time Warp, where so called Extended Logical Processes (Ex-LP), defined as a collection of LPs, have public attributes that are associated with variables which can be accessed by LPs in other Ex-LPs. The work proposes to handle shared attributes accesses by relying on a specifically targeted Transactional Memory (TM) implementation, where events are mapped to transactions and the actual implementation of the TM is based on [9]. One core difference between our proposal and the one in [4] is that the latter requires a-priori knowledge of the attributes to be shared, which need therefore to be a-priori mapped to TM managed memory locations. Rather, our proposal allows for sharing any memory area, without the need for a-priori knowledge of whether some sharing on a specific area can occur. This increases the level of transparency, again allowing a truly sequential-style programming model to be exposed to the programmer. In fact, she is allowed to let any simulation object that takes control touch any valid memory location within the global simulation state without the need for any particular care, just like it occurs in sequential-style programming and related sequential execution scenarios. Overall, we "transactify" the access to memory chunks across different concurrent objects without the need for marking data portions subject to transactional management by the programmer.

3. EVENT AND CROSS-STATE SYNCHRO-NIZATION

3.1 Cross-State Dependency Tracking

In this section we present the memory management architecture we have designed and developed in order to support cross-state dependency, and to actually track the materialization of such type of dependency across simulation objects that are run concurrently. Let us stress again that our architecture supports cross-state dependency in a fully transparent manner to the application level software. As an additional preliminary note, in our design we targeted PDES

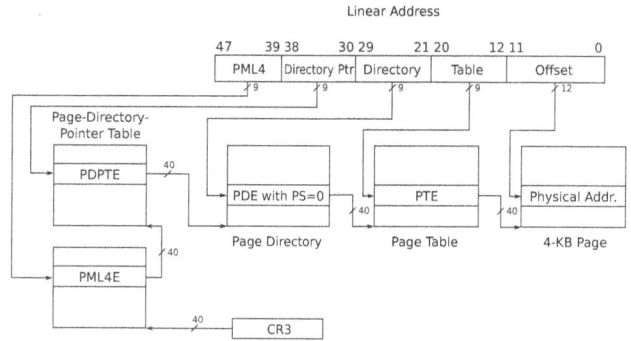

Figure 1: The paging scheme in x86_64 processors.

platforms relying on the multi-threading paradigm. These have been shown to provide a set of benefits and to support optimized resource usage policies (see, e.g., [4, 11, 27, 26]) when compared to the traditional counterpart where parallelization is achieved by running a set of single-threaded processes within the simulation platform. Overall, we designed a memory management architecture allowing not to loose the benefits from multi-threading.

On the basis of the above considerations, we target the scenario where multiple threads can take care of dispatching whichever simulation object for execution (although we will still rely on temporary-binding schemes between objects and worker threads in order to cope with, e.g., locality and other performance-related aspects), which takes place by simply calling an event-handler function, with proper input parameters, along that thread. Also, we target the C programming language, so that the event-handler function taking control at the application level is an ANSI-C function. As typical for DES-style coding rules, this function has a set of input parameters which includes the state base pointer, namely the memory address of the data structure starting from which the object is allowed to access any other dynamically allocated buffer belonging to its state via pointers.

In our architecture, virtual memory is destined for usage to any simulation object according to *stocks*. More in detail, when the object requests new memory buffers (which we support via the traditional malloc service, redirected to a proper memory allocator), the memory management architecture reserves an interval of page-aligned virtual memory addresses, namely the stock, which is achieved via the standard mmap POSIX API. We note that any page in the stock is an empty-zero page, thus being not really allocated in memory until the first read/write access to it is performed. This is the standard management performed by POSIX (e.g Linux) systems.

To understand how we use the stock for supporting cross-state dependency tracking, let us consider the actual paging scheme offered by x86_64 architectures. As shown in Figure 1, any 64-bit logical address has only 48 valid bits, which are used as access keys for a 4-level paging scheme, ultimately supporting pages of 4KB in size. The top level page table is called PML4 (or also PGD—Page General Directory) and keeps 512 entries. All the other page tables, operating at lower levels, also have 512 entries each. In our design, the stock of virtual memory pages destined for allocation of memory buffers for a given simulation object corresponds to the set of contiguous virtual-pages whose virtual-to-physical memory translation is associated with a single entry of the

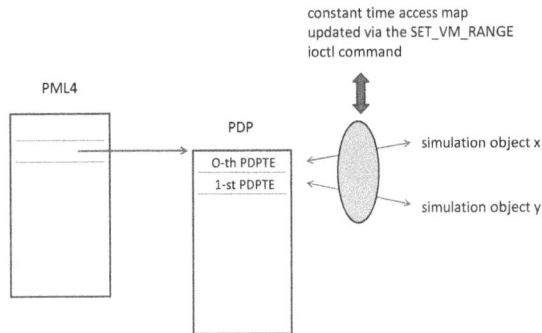

Figure 2: Example of association between stocks of virtual memory pages and simulation objects.

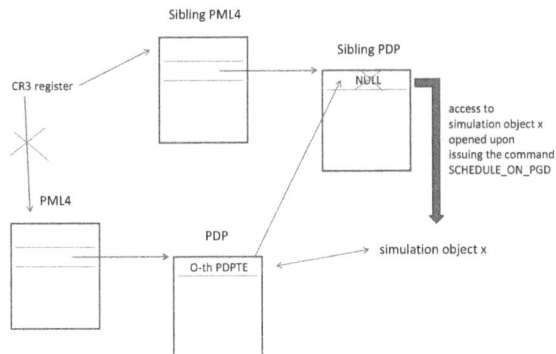

Figure 3: Example scenario where the memory stock associated with simulation object x is opened for access onto a sibling PDP page table.

second-level page table, which is called PDP—Page Directory Pointer (its entries are therefore referred to as PDPTE). Note that a single stock corresponds to 512^2 pages, for a total of 1GB of virtual memory. Hence, a single stock allows managing an object-state requesting up to 1GB of (dynamic) memory. On the other hand, reserving multiple stocks for a same simulation object will lead to manage object states reaching multiple gigabytes in size.

We have created a special device file (whose driver is loaded into the Linux kernel via an external module) which can be handled via proper `ioctl` commands, whose logic we have implemented within the driver. The `SET_VM_RANGE` command allows the special device to register the stocks to be reserved, and their association to the simulation objects (which are distinguished via classical unique numerical identifiers, as in typical PDES-platform implementations). When this command is issued, the state of the device file changes so that the driver sets up a kernel-level map (accessible in constant time) where for each reserved stock, which is logically related to one entry of a PDP page-table, the identifier of the simulation object destined to use that stock is recorded. In Figure 2 we show an example where a given PDP table has its 0-th entry, and hence the corresponding stock of virtual memory pages, reserved for object x, and its 1-st entry reserved for object y.

By this kind of organization, if simulation object x accesses any virtual address included in the stock reserved for object y, we know that such a memory access (which can be either in read or write mode in our execution model) is occurring outside the boundaries of its local state, and is actually involving the state of another object. Therefore, we are experiencing a cross-state dependency. We recall again that this may occur, e.g, if object y scheduled a simulation event destined to object x, carrying as payload the pointer to some memory buffer belonging to the state of y, just to indicate to x where to take (and possibly update) the information requested for processing the event.

The core problem to cope with in order to exploit the stocks as the means to capture whether the generic simulation object x (currently dispatched for execution along any worker tread WT_i within the PDES platform) is materializing a cross-state dependency is related to how to determine that event processing gives rise to a memory reference falling outside the boundaries of the stocks currently reserved for object x. We note that classical memory protection mechanisms supported by the operating system (and

related segmentation-fault handling schemes) are not suited for our purposes. Particularly, given that we are targeting multi-threaded PDES platforms, we cannot simply a-priori protect the access to stocks that are reserved for simulation objects other than x upon dispatching x along any worker thread WT_i. This is because these simulation objects might be requested to run concurrently with respect to x along other worker threads, which all share the same page table and experience the same protection rule as WT_i. Overall, closing to WT_i the access to the stocks not reserved for simulation object x upon dispatching it (e.g. via the `mprotect` POSIX API) would lead to a change of the state of the page table where any other thread would not be allowed to access those stocks. This would clearly hamper concurrency, also leading to unneeded memory faults (by threads running objects other than x) in contexts where the object x does not require any access to "remote" stocks while processing the event. On the other hand, addressing the above problem via (user transparent) code instrumentation would require to instrument not only memory write instructions (as typically done when supporting transparent incremental checkpointing in optimistic PDES platforms [28, 20]), but also all the memory reads, which would lead to overhead to be paid even in case no cross-state dependency, although admissible, will ever materialize (a scenario leading the tracking of memory read operations un-useful on the side of synchronization tasks related to cross-sate dependencies).

In order to cope with the above depicted core issue, we have devised a memory management architecture where any worker thread WT_i is associated with a sibling PML4 page table, whose entries point to sibling PDP page tables. The sibling page tables (both PML4 and PDP) destined for usage by a worker thread can be instantiated by relying on the `GET_PGD` command included in the special device file driver, which returns a descriptor for subsequent operations. By default, the entries of the sibling PDP page tables, which are associated with the stocks that have been destined for usage by the simulation objects, are all set to NULL. This means that they do not allow to reach the lower level page tables, hence not allowing access to any already allocated stock (therefore, any attempt to access the stocks will lead to a memory fault). On the other hand, when WT_i dispatches simulation object x for event execution, the entries of the PDP sibling tables that correspond to the virtual memory stocks destined for usage by x are "opened" to correctly allow the retrieval of the lower level page tables that contain the actual mapping of virtual-to-physical memory (or indications about whether the pages are not present, e.g., they are swapped-out pages). This is done by copying the corresponding entries of the original PDP tables into the destination entries within the sibling PDP page tables (see Figure 3 for an example scenario where the stock associated with simulation object x is again related to the 0-th entry of a given PDP page table). In our architecture, this operation can be executed via the additional SCHEDULE_ON_PGD command we have included within the special device file driver, which can be issued via the ioctl interface. In other words, via this command, the worker thread is allowed to switch to what we refer to as *simulation-object mode*, where the only accessible stock is the one associated with the dispatched object (say x in the example discussion), while the other stocks are no way accessible (given that their corresponding entries into the sibling PDP page tables are still set to NULL). As schematized in Figure 3, in our implementation this operation also leads to a change of the CR3 register (namely, the page table pointer register in x86_64 processors), thus allowing to switch to the sibling PML4 for virtual-to-physical address resolution purposes.

Having different sibling PML4 tables, associated with the different concurrent worker threads, leads to the possibility to concurrently dispatch and execute different simulation objets (this is done by having each worker thread opening the access to the stocks associated with the object it is currently dispatching) while still having the possibility to determine whether any of the dispatched objects is confining its memory references within its own stocks. The assumption underlying this type of organization is that, when there is the need for opening access to a given stock, the corresponding memory management information is already present in the corresponding PDP entry of the original page tables. This is not guaranteed by simply validating virtual memory addresses via mmap, which leaves memory into the empty-zero state. To overcome this problem, our architecture entails a stock allocation policy that beyond calling mmap, also explicitly writes a null byte into one single virtual page of the stock (the initial one). In this way, the Linux kernel traps the access to empty-zero memory and allocates the whole chain of page tables for managing the pages within the stock (although a single one of these pages is really allocated), which guarantees the existence of the PDP entry associated with the stock, to be filled into the corresponding sibling PDP entry upon dispatching the object owning the stock.

Two additional points need to be discussed. First, having all the stocks closed for access by the worker thread, except the one(s) related to the dispatched object, leads (as noted before) to memory faults in case of a memory access to stocks other than open one(s), namely in case of materialization of a cross-state dependency across concurrent simulation objects. However, these faults cannot be tracked (and handled) via classical segmentation-fault handling given that the "remote" stocks have already been validated via mmap, and the Linux kernel would simply lead the fault to reallocate the whole chain of page table entries for mapping the accessed virtual page in memory. This would lead the whole system to a state where for the same virtual page we would have multiple chains of page table entries representing its state (e.g. the frame used for mapping the page, which might be different along the multiple chains of page table entries) which is a

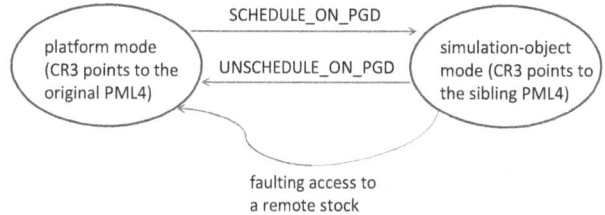

Figure 4: The state diagram for switch operations between original and sibling PML4 page tables.

discrepancy not directly hand-able by the Linux kernel (except if using invasive patches). To avoid this scenario, upon installing the driver for the special device file, via loading the external module, we change the IDT table (directly accessible via the IDT register) in order to make the pointer to the page-fault handler point to an ECS-proper handler (rather than the original do_page_fault kernel function). In case the fault is not related to accesses to remote stocks within the sibling paging scheme, then the original handler is invoked. Otherwise, the ECS-handler pushes control back to user mode in order to let the PDES platform to actuate ECS synchronization policies, exactly aimed at coping with cross-state dependencies.

Upon a memory-fault occurring on sibling PDP entries, due to cross-state dependency materialization, the faulting thread is put back into what we call *platform mode*, which implies that it is switched back onto the original PML4. This is done in order for this thread to operate any memory access required to reconcile the execution of the concurrent objects according to ECS synchronization. This aspect will be treated in detail in the next section. On the other hand, in case event processing at the currently dispatched object ends, the worker thread can switch back to platform mode on demand (hence gaining access to any memory location or data structure supporting the parallel execution) by using the UNSCHEDULE_ON_PGD command that we have implemented within the driver, which can be triggered by again exploiting the ioctl POSIX API. In Figure 4 we show the state diagram where the events causing the switch between simulation-object and platform modes are depicted.

Second, our architecture needs anyway to co-exist with the kernel scheduler, which poses issues on the side of managing the sibling PML4. Particularly, all the threads within a same Linux process share the same memory management information (the so called memory context), including the pointer to the original page table. This pointer is used by the kernel scheduler upon re-dispatching the thread after it has been context-switched off the CPU. Particularly, this pointer is reloaded into the page-table pointer register CR3 upon the occurrence of a context switch that gives control to the thread. However, if the thread was executing in simulation-object mode, CR3 would need to be filled with the address of the sibling PML4 (rather than the original page table). To achieve this, a minimal patch to Linux has been adopted, which has been located right at the end of the kernel schedule function. The patch simply checks whether the value of a special function-pointer we inserted into the kernel is not null, in which case the function-pointer is invoked, which gives control to a proper CR3 manager implemented within our external module. This manager checks whether the thread is running into simulation-object mode (which can be done by checking per thread meta-data that were setup via the SCHEDULE_ON_PGD command) and, in the positive case, it loads the sibling PML4 pointer into the CR3 register (thus maintaining the simulation-object mode when running the thread). Note that the aforementioned special pointer is exported as a kernel symbol, and can be set to a value different from NULL upon inserting the external module. If this pointer is not set the Linux kernel behaves as usual, by simply restoring the CR3 register according to the standard rules when the thread is rescheduled after a context switch.

Before ending the presentation of the memory management architecture, let us discuss two aspects related to the actual memory allocation support for the application code and to safety of dual-mode execution (platform vs simulation-object) in the presence of third party libraries. As for the first aspect, we integrated the memory management architecture with the DyMeLoR open source allocator [25, 20], explicitly targeting memory allocation needs in optimistic PDES platforms. It intercepts dynamic memory calls by the simulation object (e.g. malloc calls) and handles them by managing (and delivering to the simulation object) memory chunks located into a pre-reserved memory segment. DyMeLoR also keeps bitmaps to determine the currently in use chunks and the dirty ones, which allows for taking (incremental) snapshots and restoring past states of the simulation object (while allowing dynamic memory to be used by the object). Integration of DyMeLoR with the currently presented architecture has been straightforward given that, rather than relying on actual malloc implementations for pre-reserving the segment destined to allocate the chunks for a given simulation object, in the integrated architecture we let DyMeLoR rely on the stock allocator. Hence, the virtual memory segment managed by DyMeLoR boils down to the stock of virtual memory pages supported in the presented architecture. We note that identifying dirty chunks in DyMeLoR relies on compile/link time instrumentation of memory write instructions within the application level code. The outcoming memory access-tracking scheme is completely different from the support we are offering for cross-state dependency tracking, which is able to intercept read access (not only write access) to whichever application destined memory area without the need for instrumenting all the read operations.

As for the second aspect raised above, DyMeLoR is shipped with wrappers for ANSI-C stateless libraries, so that any memory allocation by these libraries (such as strdup) is still handled by DyMeLoR according to the above depicted scheme. Also, the third-party library interfaces are redirected to an actual logic which is statically linked to the application code, hence not requiring intervention by the dynamic linker. This automatically avoids page table updates while running in simulation-object mode which would otherwise be caused on sibling page tables by memory mapping actions by the dynamic linker (in case the shared libraries were invoked by the application code while running in simulation-object mode). The only limitation in terms of library usage by the application code is that the whole architecture does not yet support stateful libraries (e.g. strtok)[2],

whose data structures could be involved in read/write operations caused by library invocations by whichever concurrent simulation object, thus possibly creating indirect cross-state dependencies not catchable via the above described stock management policies. Coping with the employment of stateful libraries will be the target of future work.

As an additional note, our approach requires reloading the CR3 register anytime we switch between platform and simulation-object mode. The penalty incurred consists in flushing the TLB right upon loading a new value into CR3, which is done automatically by the firmware logic of x86_64 processors (this is anyhow required in order to make the access-rule of the target page table – original vs sibling – visible after the switch, which cannot be achieved without refilling the TLB). However, the data cache does not require to be invalidated, hence we expect that the cost for TLB renewal would look affordable as soon as a certain level of locality is exhibited while running either in platform or in simulation-object mode. As for this aspect, the reliance on DyMeLoR would favor locality in simulation-object mode, given that DyMeLoR implements policies aimed at maximizing virtual-memory contiguousness of the memory chunks delivered for usage by the simulation object.

Finally, we note that the on-demand switch to simulation-object mode or (back) to platform mode requires invoking the ioctl system call. While the cost of system calls has been traditionally considered an issue in high performance computing, especially when dealing with fine grain tasks, such costs are nowadays definitely reduced thanks to sysenter and sysexit machine instructions, which are explicitly designed for low-latency system calls, by relying on operating systems with a flat memory model and no segmentation. These instructions have been optimized by reducing the number of checks and memory references that are normally made so that a call or return has been shown to take less than one-fourth the number of internal clock cycles when compared to the traditional approach based on the int instruction, which was explicitly based on segment-gate retrieval and segmented-to-linear memory addressing translation.

3.2 The Enhanced Synchronization Scheme

In this section we provide the core mechanisms underlying ECS synchronization. The main difference between classical event-based synchronization and ECS lies in that ECS-synchronization tasks not only aim at letting each simulation object process its events in non-decreasing timestamp order (in accordance with the reference correctness criterion for PDES platforms only entailing event dependencies). Rather, ECS synchronization also aims at allowing any cross-state dependency materialized at simulation time t to let the involved object (namely the one accessing remote stocks reserved for other objects) to observe the state snapshot that would have been observed at simulation time t in a sequential-run, where simulation events were processed in globally non-decreasing timestamp order across all the objects.

We base ECS synchronization on the following two innovations:

---

[2]One exception is clearly the malloc library, for which the above described ad-hoc architecture has been put in place. On the other hand, for stdio one can rely on, e.g., the I/O

management subsystem presented in [1], explicitly targeting consistency of I/O operations in optimistic synchronization transparently to the application code.

A) the introduction of temporary object blocking phases, which may even lead to temporary block the execution of an already dispatched object (namely of an already dispatched simulation event at that object);

B) the introduction of so called *rendez-vous* events, which are kinds of system level simulation events not causing updates on the destination object state, but only driving block and unblock actions for processing activities at the objects. These will be exploited to temporarily disable a simulation object to perform updates of its state along the simulation-time axis, given that its state snapshot is currently being involved in a cross-state dependency.

Point A leads to an event processing model where control (along any worker thread) can return to the platform layer before an already started event-processing phase actually ends. This takes place according to an interrupt-driven scheme, different in nature from event-preemption ones that have been put in place in optimistic PDES systems to squash the execution of events that are detected to be causally inconsistent while still being processed, for either performance or infinite-loop avoidance reasons [24, 18]. In fact, these proposals have been typically based on polling (see, e.g., [24]) to be explicitly actuated by the event processing code, which is used to periodically query the platform layer to check whether no straggler event/antievent was delivered. On the other hand, point B leads to bridge PDES execution models with Transactional Memory models, particularly by having read/write operations across different stocks serialized according to the logical time for their occurrence.

In our proposal, each simulation object x is associated with a cross-state dependency set we refer to as CSD_x, which records the identifiers of all the simulation objects towards which x has materialized a cross-state dependency during the processing of an event. CSD_x is initialized as empty upon dispatching object x for the execution of any new event, and gets possibly updated while processing the event. ECS synchronization exploits the ad-hoc memory-fault management architecture presented in the previous section in order to detect that simulation object x is accessing a remote memory stock, say the stock associated with object y, in either read or write mode, while processing its next event, say e_x. The identity of the object towards which the cross-state dependency is being materialized (say y in our example discussion) is also known, given that the ECS memory-fault handler, which pushes the thread back in platform mode, notifies such an identifier into the thread user-mode stack. The memory fault occurrence gives rise to the following algorithmic steps:

1. Execution of e_x is temporarily blocked, hence object x transits into a block state;

2. A rendez-vous unique identifier is generated and assigned to the event e_x, which we refer to as $rvid(e_x)$.

3. A special rendez-vous event e_y^{rv} is scheduled for object y, marked with timestamp equal to the timestamp of event e_x, and with its rendez-vous identifier (formally $ts(e_y^{rv}) = ts(e_x)$ and $rvid(e_y^{rv}) = rvid(e_x)$). We note that rendez-vous events are not generated by the application layer, rather they are platform-generated events. Hence they do not have any associated processing rule at the application level.

Rendez-vous events are incorporated into the event list of the destination object as if they were traditional events. Given that we are targeting optimistic synchronization, this means that a rendez-vous event may be a straggler event (in case its timestamp is lower than the timestamp of some already processed event at the destination). They need therefore to be processed along the sequence of events of the destination, and the processing actions are platform-level actions proper of ECS (given that, as hinted above, no application level processing rule is – and needs to be – specified for rendez-vous events).

When a simulation object y is dispatched for processing a rendez-vous event e_y^{rv}, ECS performs the following algorithmic steps:

1. Object y is put into a block state;

2. A special rendez-vous acknowledgment event e_x^{rva} is scheduled for object x, marked with no-timestamp but with the same rendez-vous identifier of e_y^{rv} (formally $rvid(e_x^{rva}) = rvid(e_y^{rv})$).

On the other hand, when the rendez-vous acknowledgement event e_x^{rva} is delivered to the recipient simulation object x, ECS performs the following steps:

1. It inserts the identifier of the sender object, namely y, into CSD_x.

2. It puts the simulation object x back in the ready state (so that it can be eventually re-dispatched along some worker thread, thus resuming the execution of the originally interrupted event e_x).

At this point we know that simulation object y is blocked (thus not being currently allowed to process its events), hence the snapshot of its state is available to simulation object x for read/write operations, such as the operation that originally gave rise to the ECS memory fault and to the cross-state dependency being handled via the rendez-vous. However, upon re-dispatching object x (which leads to resuming the processing of e_x), the involved worker thread cannot transit into simulation-object mode by only opening the stock(s) associated with x into the sibling page tables. Rather, we also need to open access to the stock(s) associated with object y. In our architectural support, this can be still achieved via the SCHEDULE_ON_PGD command, given that this command has been augmented with capabilities to acquire a set of identifiers whose stocks need to be opened within the sibling page tables when the worker thread transits into simulation-object mode. Particularly, upon re-dispatching object x, the SCHEDULE_ON_PGD command is issued with in input the set $x \cup CSD_x$, which for our example discussion, contains the identifiers of both the objects x and y.

The above algorithmic steps can be iterated in case cross-state dependencies are materialized towards multiple simulation objects while processing the event e_x, which will lead to the scenario where simulation object x can be rescheduled multiple times (while being in the processing phase of e_x) with incrementally enlarged sets of open stocks. On the other hand, once a remote memory stock (associated with a distinct object) becomes open for access by object x during the processing phase of event e_x, any access to this stock by x while processing this event will not cause any additional ECS memory fault.

We only need to discuss how the finalization of the processing phase of e_x is handled. Essentially, we need to generate notifications that the stocks associated with simulation objects towards which cross-state dependencies have been materialized are no longer locked for access by object x. Hence, the owner simulation objects can resume their normal processing activities (thus they can resume from the block state). This is achieved via the following steps executed right after the processing of event e_x at object x:

1. An unblock-event e_k^{ub} is sent towards any object k whose identifier is logged within CSD_x. These events are marked again with no timestamp value, but with the rendez-vous identifier of the event e_x originating the cross-state dependency. Then CSD_x is reset as empty.

2. Upon the delivery of e_k^{ub}, the recipient simulation object is simply put back as ready for being dispatched (hence exiting the block state).

However, some additional mechanisms are required in order for ECS to provide correctness and to also ensure progress of the parallel run. These two aspects will be dealt with in the following subsections.

3.2.1 Correctness

Given that ECS targets speculative processing, where object blocking is never caused by native event dependencies, rather by the need for executing memory read/write operations on multiple stocks as in-memory transactions, some care must be taken when handling rollback phases. Particularly, when we process an event e_x that gives rise to a rendez-vous event e_y^{rv}, we need to define rules for handling the rollback phase of either object x or object y at a simulation time $t' < ts(e_x)$ (or equivalently $t' < ts(e_y^{rv})$). The peculiarity of this scenario is related to that e_x and e_y^{rv} are both causally related to each other. Particularly, if e_x is rolled back, then we need to rollback e_y^{rv} given that object x may have performed updates on the memory stocks destined to keep the state of simulation object y while processing e_x. On the other hand, the processing outcome of e_x is affected by values possibly read by object x from the stocks destined to y at time $ts(e_x)$. In case these values change due to a rollback of object y at a simulation time preceding $ts(e_y^{rv})$, the updated values should have been observed while processing e_x by object x.

In order to handle such mutual dependency, we devise the following scheme. When the event e_x is rolled back, we simply send an anti-event for the rendez-vous event e_y^{rv} that was scheduled while processing e_x. Given that e_y^{rv} was actually incorporated into the event list of the destination object y, the arrival of the anti-event gives rise to a classical annihilation that possibly rolls back y to the latest processed event with timestamp less than $ts(e_y^{rv})$. This solves the problem of rolling back object y due to the rollback of a rendez-vous generating event e_x on simulation object x.

On the other hand, in case the rollback is originated on object y, and pushes this object to a simulation time less than $ts(e_y^{rv})$ (which leads to undo the execution of e_y^{rv}), the following actions are taken by ECS. A special rendez-vous-restart event e_x^{rvr}, marked with the original rendez-vous identifier (namely $rvid(e_x)$) is sent out towards object x. This special event has the aim of annihilating the processing of the original instance (while not removing it from

the input queue), which will lead to ultimately undo e_y^{rv} via an anti-event. Given that when processed after the rollback, the event e_x will give rise to a rendez-vous marked with a different identifier (with respect to the rolled-back rendez-vous instance), no mismatch will occur in any annihilation phase for rendez-vous events associated with different incarnations of their generating event (which also avoids cycles in the annihilation process).

Also, all the other types of events used in ECS, such as acknowledgment and unblock events, are not actually incorporated into the event lists of the simulation objects, thus being inherently ephemeral, and not requiring particular care in the rollback scheme. Assuming FIFO communication across the objects, these events can be simply discarded at the recipient side if the rendez-vous associated with their corresponding identifier (e.g. $rvid(e_x)$ in case of the acknowledgement event sent to x upon the rendez-vous) is no more in place.

3.2.2 Progress

A bit more complex to deal with in ECS is the guarantee of progress. Specifically, care must be taken to avoid deadlocks and live-locks, and the domino-effect in the rollback scheme. Let us first consider the dealock/live-lock issue. A deadlock may arise in case of rendez-vous events cyclically involving a set of simulation objects, where the rendez-vous associated with the minimal timestamp along the cycle leads the simulation object raising this rendez-vous to wait for the rollback of a different object that is, in its turn, in the block state due to a different rendez-vous it issued, which needs to be completed. An example situation of this type is shown in Figure 5, where object x issues at time t_1 a rendez-vous towards object z, which is waiting for object y to reach time t_3 for a rendez-vous between z and y. On the other hand, object y is waiting for x to reach time t_2 for a rendez-vous with it. To avoid deadlock scenarios, we can simply adopt the rule that, in case a rollback needs to be executed by a simulation object x which is currently blocked due to a rendez-vous it generated while processing an event e_x, this object is simply resumed from the block state by also squashing the finalization of the rendez-vous (this will lead to manage the rollback of the rendez-vous as explained above, e.g., by issuing the anti-event for the already sent out rendez-vous event). We note that this implies that the current stack seen by the object also needs to be refilled with correct information (since, upon resuming, its context will no more be the processing context for the rendez-vous generating event). Details on how we handled this issue in our implementation, where the cross-state dependency tracking architecture and ECS have been integrated into the ROOT-Sim open source optimistic simulation platform, will be discussed in Section 4. We also note that annihilating the rendez-vous event via the corresponding anti-event is safe even in case the destination object is currently blocked waiting for the finalization of the rendez-vous. In fact, it can be simply resumed from the block state (again with proper stack image manipulation) and can be rolled back, thus possibly altering its state image safely given that the image does no more need to be locked for the access by a different object in a rendez-vous.

We note however that unblocking the object generating a rendez-vous so as to prevent deadlock in case a rollback is required may, in its turn lead to live-lock. Specifically, live-lock may in principle arise in case of simultaneous events materializing circular cross-state dependencies across mul-

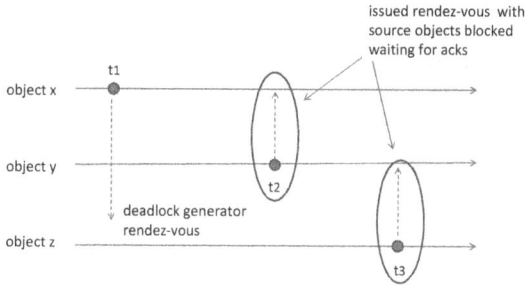

Figure 5: Example scenario with deadlock originated by a rendez-vous generating event at time t_1 processed by simulation object x.

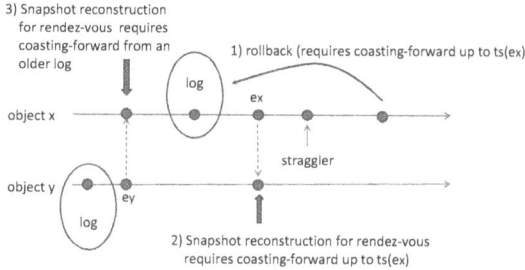

Figure 6: Example scenario with domino-effect due to a rollback originated on simulation object x.

tiple simulation objects. Each object x along the circle, executing an event e_x at simulation time $ts(e_x)$, is hit by another object due to a cross-state memory faulting access at the same simulation time, which may lead to request the rollback of the events generating the rendez-vous circularly. This is known to possibly lead the rollback circle to reappear indefinitely [14]. To overcome this problem, we need a priority management scheme for simultaneous events, that needs to be reflected also on the management of rendez-vous events. Particularly, if we have two events e_x and e_y such that $ts(e_x) = ts(e_y)$, and we have a priority scheme telling that $e_x \rightarrow e_y$ (namely, e_y is identified as causally dependent on e_x), then we need to enforce that any rendez-vous event e_y^{rv} generated by e_x is also causally related to e_y according to $e_y^{rv} \rightarrow e_y$. This way, the rendez-vous occurrences that are caused by events having the same timestmap are anyway sequentialized according to the priority scheme. We note however that the guarantee of progress in (optimistic) PDES systems in presence of simultaneous events is a more general problem, with respect to what we might experience in ECS, and has been extensively studied in literature [13]. Hence different literature solutions for tie-breaking simultaneous events (see, e.g., [16]) can be exploited for integration with ECS according to the scheme suggested above.

The final issue to cope with is the domino-effect in the rollback scheme. Particularly, by the ample literature on log/restore in optimistic PDES systems (see, e.g., [21, 22, 23]), we know that sparse state saving, which avoids logging the simulation object state after the processing of each event, allows for optimizing the performance tradeoff between logging cost and restore cost. However, state restore at time t requires the simulation object to be rolled back to the latest state log with time less than or equal to t, and to fictitiously reprocess intermediate events up to t

in a silent mode (namely with no interactions with other objects), which is also known to as coasting-forward. In ECS this is no longer possible since a coasting-forward event might be a rendez-vous generating event. Hence, in order for this to be re-processed, the simulation object originally hit by the rendez-vous also needs to rollback at the time of the rendez-vous, so as to provide its state snapshot for correct access by the object performing coasting-forward. It is easy to show that this may lead the originally rolling-back object to rollback further back along simulation time, according to the domino-effect. An example is shown in Figure 6, where in order to execute the coasting-forward involving event e_x at object x, we need to reconstruct the snapshot of object y at time $ts(e_x)$, But this leads to the need for processing e_y in a coasting-forward, which in turn leads x to restore its state to a time less than $ts(e_y)$. To avoid the need for executing coasting-forwards leading to rollback interactions with other objects (thus avoiding the domino-effect), our approach is based on complementing the selected sparse state saving algorithm by forcing the log of the state of a simulation object right after the processing of a rendez-vous generating event. This will lead to the scenario where no rendez-vous generating event will be ever included in the sequence of events between two subsequent logs of the same simulation object. Hence no rendez-vous generating event will need to be reprocessed in any coasting-forward phase. On the other hand, a rendez-vous generated event also needs to be excluded by any coasting-forward, since for these events the rendez-vous source object may have performed updates into the state of the target object. To avoid a rendez-vous generated event to be included in any coasting-forward phase, we can again force a state log of the involved object right after the event is processed.

4. EXPERIMENTAL STUDY

4.1 Test-bed Platform

We integrated ECS within the open source ROOT-Sim package [10], particularly the symmetric multi-threaded version presented in [27]. A few relevant modifications to this simulation platform have anyhow been made for integration purposes. Most relevantly, we have created stack-separation across the different simulation objects, by locating the stack of each object in the initial part of a stock of memory destined for object usage. Further, execution resume in the different stacks, by also providing the correct processor and stack image, has been supported via `setjump` and `longjump` POSIX APIs. These have also been used as the support for, e.g. squashing the stack image in case a rollback occurs while the simulation object is in the block state (which eventually leads the object to resume execution with a different context). As for the (temporary) binding of simulation objects to threads, we still relied on the already supported policies. Also, the simulation objects currently bound to a given worker thread are still dispatched according to the Lowest-Timestamp-First policy. However, simulation objects that are in the block state are not considered in the dispatching process (thus being again eligible for dispatching only after exiting the block state). We have run experiments on a 32-core HP ProLiant server equipped with 64GB of RAM and running Debian 6 on top of the 2.6.32-5-amd64 Linux kernel (augmented with our patch to the `schedule` function). A ROOT-Sim configuration with 32 symmetric worker threads

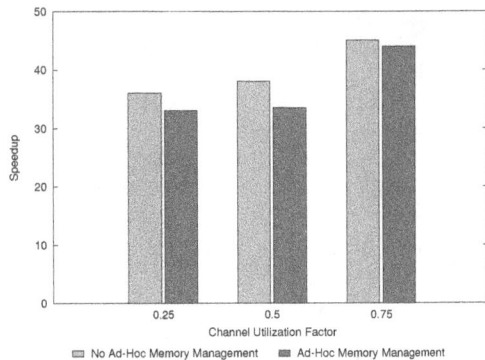

Figure 7: Relative speed-up by the parallel run without and with ad-hoc memory management vs the sequential run.

has been used in all the experiments, with GVT and fossil collection taking place each one second.

4.2 Experimental Data

This section is divided in two parts. Initially we provide data for an evaluation of the overhead by the core memory management support underlying ECS. To this aim we use a simulation model of a Personal Communication System (PCS) natively entailing disjointness of memory accesses by the different simulation objects. After, we present data related to the assessment of the whole ECS architecture, by also comparing the run-time behavior of models coded in such a way to be run on top of ECS (hence coded in sequential-style with no disjointness of memory accesses across different objects) with respect to the counterpart exclusively based on traditional PDES programming (only relying on event-dependencies via message passing). In this part of the study we rely on a model of NoSQL data-grid systems developed within the framework presented in [5].

4.2.1 Overhead Assessment

We evaluated the overhead by the presented memory management architecture by relying on a PCS model with 1024 wireless cells covering a square region, each one managing up to 1000 wireless channels. It models interference across different channels within a same cell, and power management upon call setup/handoff in a high fidelity fashion. This same model has been already used to assess the multi-threaded version of ROOT-Sim where we have integrated ECS, and its detailed description can be found in [26]. Two specific aspects are relevant for this study: 1) each simulation object models an individual cell, and the interactions between objects exclusively take place via handoff events of mobile devices across different cells (hence memory accesses by the different simulation objects are intrinsically disjoint); 2) the average granularity (CPU requirement) of the events is directly proportional to the wireless channel utilization factor, since the more channels are busy, the more complex is the calculation of interference and Signal-to-Interference Ratio (SIR) while simulating power regulation.

We have run this model with three different settings for the channel utilization factor, namely 25%, 50% and 75% (that gave rise to average granularity of the simulation events ranging from the order of 30 to 100 microseconds). Also, we considered three different execution modes: a classical sequential execution (relying on a calendar queue scheduler),

a parallel execution where no ad-hoc memory management facility is activated, and a parallel execution where we rely on the innovative memory management architecture. Note that the latter execution mode entails switching between object-mode and platform-mode (with refill of the CR3 register and implicit squash of the TLB) when changing the actual mode. Hence, such a mode allows us to assess the overhead for mode-switch operated by the support for ECS. In Figure 7 we show the variation of the speedup (vs the sequential run) we observed for simulating on the order of 1 million (committed) events in the different parallel execution modes (each sample is the average over 10 runs based on different random-generation seeds). By the data we see how the maximal loss in performance by the ad-hoc memory management architecture entailing switch between platform and object modes is on the order of 9% and is observed for the case of finer grain simulation events (namely for the case of 25% utilization factor). Such a performance penalty almost disappears for coarser grain configurations.

Successively we modified the PCS model in order to generate fictitious rendez-vous events periodically. When one fictitious rendez-vous event occurs, the executing object simply performs a dummy read operation into the state of an adjacent cell. However, we do not really enable ECS synchronization (in fact, no matter whether the dummy read access is not processed in timestamp order on the hit object), rather we only trap the access and open the stock associated with the object hit by the read operation. This way we are able to assess the overhead by ECS support when also including the management of memory faults and the activation of the ECS handler. For this experiment, we considered the PCS configuration with wireless-channel utilization factor set to 50%, and we varied the frequency of occurrence of the fictitious rendez-vous events between 1% and 10% of the total number of events processed. In Figure 8 we show the relative speedup achieved by the configuration with ad-hoc memory management and fault handling upon the occurrence of fictitious rendez-vous events vs the configuration with no ad-hoc memory management. By the data, we see how the ah-hoc architecture induces a speed-down that increases vs the frequency of fictitious rendez-vous events. Note that the speed-down is not only caused by the overhead for handling the memory faults. It is also due to the switch between platform and object modes, which is mandatory in order to create the per-thread memory view needed to trap the access to the state of other simulation objects. However, the speed-down is quite limited for relatively infrequent fictitious rendez-vous events, and becomes non-negligible only when moving towards scenarios with relatively frequent rendez-vous occurrences (say 10%).

On the other hand, the whole ad-hoc memory management architecture has been thought and realized to provide, transparently to the application code, a unique innovative support for handling cross-state dependencies in presence of concurrent objects. Hence the loss in performance in contexts where the model to be executed exhibits intrinsically disjoint accesses across different object-states (such as for the configurations in Figure 7) is the unavoidable price to be paid for the achievement of a run-time environment offering the above mentioned level of transparency.

4.2.2 Effectiveness Assessment

In this section we rely on NoSQL data-grid simulation models provided in [5], based on distributed/replicated cache

114

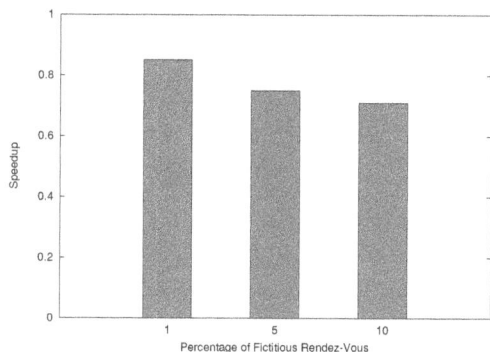

Figure 8: Relative speed-up by the ad-hoc memory management architecture vs the classical parallel run.

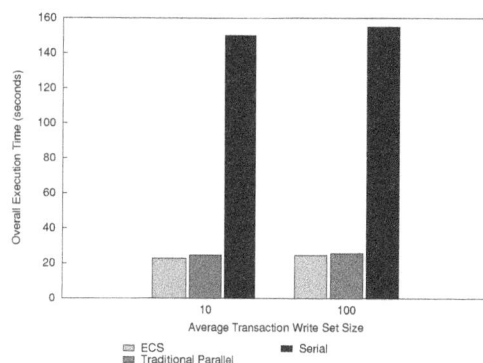

Figure 9: Execution times for the data-grid models.

serves, each keeping a subset of the whole set of keys in the entire data-set. Particularly, we consider a model where atomicity of the distributed transactions is ensured by running the 2-Phase-Commit (2PC) protocol across the nodes keeping keys that belong to the write set of the committing transaction. In these models, the simulated coordinator needs to schedule the arrival of a *prepare request* event to the involved sites, which needs to carry information about the write set. These sets may entail hundreds of data-item keys, and are populated at the coordinator while simulating the execution of the transaction. These sets are therefore instantiated by the transaction-coordinator simulation object within its local state. For this model we consider two different implementations, one not relying on ECS, which transmits the write set as the payload of the *prepare request* event[3], and another one based on ECS, where the write sets are directly accessed via pointers by the involved simulated nodes (hence the *prepare request* event only needs to carry the pointer indicating where to find the information related to the simulated 2PC phase). This model also entails a special simulation object which is a global statistics collector. For the case of non-reliance on ECS, the updates of the state of this object take place by explicitly scheduling *update statistics* events towards it. On the other hand, for the case of ECS synchronization, we have that each simulated node can directly access the state of the statistics collector simulation object in order to perform updates.

We simulated a NoSQL data-grid system with 64 nodes (with degree of replication 2 of each $\langle key, value \rangle$ pair in the data-grid), with closed-system configuration in terms of number of clients (and hence number of transactions) running within the system. Particularly, we set the number of active concurrent clients continuously issuing transactions to 64. This configuration resembles scenarios where the 64 clients operate as front end servers (co-located with the data-platform nodes) with respect to end-client applications. Also, we varied the amount of keys touched in write mode by transactions between 10 and 100, which gives rise to different dynamics/cost in terms of pack/unpack operations, message buffering and transmission for the case of non-ECS based synchronization, thus allowing us to study configurations with different performance tradeoffs.

In Figure 9 we report the execution time for simulating a predetermined simulation time interval for the operativity

of the NoSQL data-grid system. By the data we see how both ECS and the traditional message passing based parallel approach provide performance improvements over the sequential run. More important, the performance delivered by ECS is even slightly better that the one by the traditional parallel approach with disjoint accesses to the local state of the simulation objects. Overall, transparency of speculative parallelization with cross-state dependencies is achieved by also delivering performance comparable to the traditional parallel approach, which however does not mask message passing to the programmer, at least in relation to packing/unpacking of data to/from event payloads. Also, the traditional approach does not support direct memory writes into, e.g., the statistic collector object, thus requiring more complex coding schemes, aimed at realizing the updates via simulation events. On the contrary, with ECS we support such a direct memory update operation, hence offering to the programmer the possibility to code the model more simply, according to sequential programming style.

5. CONCLUSIONS

In this article we have presented ECS (Event and Cross-State), a new protocol for synchronizing the execution of concurrent simulation objects forming a DES model. The protocol allows breaking the classical limit of DES models, to be run concurrently on top of PDES platforms, where any object can access memory, and hence can touch the current state of the simulation model, limited to its local state. Rather, with ECS it is allowed to touch (in either read or write mode) any valid memory location. This capability has been achieved thanks to the design and implementation of an innovative memory management architecture, suited for Linux systems, which creates per-thread views of memory protection (within a same process) and tracks memory accesses in an efficient manner. The whole proposal supports cross-state access, joint to concurrency and speculative processing, in an application transparent manner. Hence, the programmer is allowed to rely on a sequential-style coding approach, where any memory location is implicitly accessible while processing any simulation event.

6. REFERENCES

[1] F. Antonacci, A. Pellegrini, and F. Quaglia. Consistent and efficient output-streams management in optimistic simulation platforms. In *Proceedings of the ACM SIGSIM Conference on Principles of Advanced Discrete Simulation*, pages 315–326. ACM, 2013.

---

[3]For this configuration the programmer is in charge of explicitly coding the pack/unpack of the write set.

[2] D. Bruce. The treatment of state in optimistic systems. *SIGSIM Simul. Dig.*, 25(1):40–49, July 1995.

[3] K. M. Chandy and R. Sherman. Space-time and simulation. *Proceedings of the SCS Multiconference on Distributed Simulation*, pages 53–57, 1989.

[4] L.-l. Chen, Y.-s. Lu, Y.-P. Yao, S.-l. Peng, and L.-d. Wu. A well-balanced Time Warp system on multi-core environments. In *Proceedings of the IEEE Workshop on Principles of Advanced and Distributed Simulation*, pages 1–9. IEEE Computer Society, 2011.

[5] P. Di Sanzo, F. Antonacci, B. Ciciani, R. Palmieri, A. Pellegrini, S. Peluso, F. Quaglia, D. Rughetti, and R. Vitali. A framework for high performance simulation of transactional data grid platforms. In *Proceedings of the 6th ICST Conference of Simulation Tools and Techniques*, SIMUTools, pages 63–72. ICST, Mar. 2013.

[6] A. Fabbri and L. Donatiello. SQTW: a mechanism for state-dependent parallel simulation. description and experimental study. In *Proceedings of the Workshop on Parallel and Distributed Simulation*, pages 82–89, jun 1997.

[7] R. M. Fujimoto. Parallel discrete event simulation. *Communications of the ACM*, 33(10):30–53, Oct. 1990.

[8] B. P. Gan, M. Low, J. Wei, X. Wang, S. Turner, and W. Cai. Synchronization and management of shared state in HLA-based distributed simulation. In *Proceedings of the Winter Simulation Conference*, pages 847–854, Dec. 2003.

[9] K. Ghosh and R. M. Fujimoto. Parallel discrete event simulation using space-time memory. In *Proceedings of the International Conference on Parallel Processing*, pages 201–208. CRC Press, 1991.

[10] HPDCS Research Group. ROOT-Sim: The ROme OpTimistic Simulator - v 1.0. http://www.dis.uniroma1.it/~hpdcs/ROOT-Sim/, Oct. 2012.

[11] D. Jagtap, N. Abu-Ghazaleh, and D. Ponomarev. Optimization of parallel discrete event simulator for multi-core systems. In *Proceedings of the International Parallel and Distributed Processing Symposium*, pages 520–531. IEEE Computer Society, 2012.

[12] D. R. Jefferson. Virtual Time. *ACM Transactions on Programming Languages and System*, 7(3):404–425, July 1985.

[13] V. Jha and R. Bagrodia. Simultaneous events and lookahead in simulation protocols. *ACM Transactions on Modeling and Computer Simulation*, 10(3):241–267, July 2000.

[14] J. I. Leivent and R. J. Watro. Mathematical foundations of Time Warp systems. *ACM Transactions on Programming Languages and Systems*, 15(5):771–794, 1993.

[15] M. Y. H. Low, B. P. Gan, J. Wei, X. Wang, S. J. Turner, and W. Cai. Shared state synchronization for HLA-based distributed simulation. *Simulation*, 82(8):511–521, Aug. 2006.

[16] H. Mehl. A deterministic tie-breaking scheme for sequential and distributed simulation. In *Proceedings of the Workshop on Parallel and Distributed Simulation*. ACM, 1992.

[17] H. Mehl and S. Hammes. How to integrate shared variables in distributed simulation. *SIGSIM Simulation Digest*, 25(2):14–41, Sept. 1995.

[18] D. M. Nicol and X. Liu. The dark side of risk (what your mother never told you about time warp). In *Proceedings of the Workshop on Parallel and Distributed Simulation*, pages 188–195. IEEE Computer Society, 1997.

[19] A. Pellegrini, R. Vitali, S. Peluso, and F. Quaglia. Transparent and efficient shared-state management for optimistic simulations on multi-core machines. In *Proceedings of the International Symposium on Modeling, Analysis and Simulation of Computer and Telecommunication Systems*, pages 134–141. IEEE Computer Society, 2012.

[20] A. Pellegrini, R. Vitali, and F. Quaglia. Di-DyMeLoR: Logging only dirty chunks for efficient management of dynamic memory based optimistic simulation objects. In *Proceedings of the Workshop on Principles of Advanced and Distributed Simulation*, pages 45–53. IEEE Computer Society, 2009.

[21] B. R. Preiss, W. M. Loucks, and D. MacIntyre. Effects of the checkpoint interval on time and space in Time Warp. *ACM Transactions on Modeling and Computer Simulation*, 4(3):223–253, July 1994.

[22] F. Quaglia. A cost model for selecting checkpoint positions in Time Warp parallel simulation. *IEEE Transactions on Parallel and Distributed Systems*, 12(4):346–362, Feb. 2001.

[23] R. Rönngren and R. Ayani. Adaptive checkpointing in Time Warp. In *Proceedings of the Workshop on Parallel and Distributed Simulation*, pages 110–117. Society for Computer Simulation, July 1994.

[24] A. Santoro and F. Quaglia. Software supports for event preemptive rollback in optimistic parallel simulation on myrinet clusters. *Journal of Interconnection Networks*, 6(4):435–457, 2005.

[25] R. Toccaceli and F. Quaglia. DyMeLoR: Dynamic Memory Logger and Restorer library for optimistic simulation objects with generic memory layout. In *Proceedings of the Workshop on Principles of Advanced and Distributed Simulation*, pages 163–172. IEEE Computer Society, 2008.

[26] R. Vitali, A. Pellegrini, and F. Quaglia. A load sharing architecture for optimistic simulations on multi-core machines. In *Proceedings of the 19th International Conference on High Performance Computing*, pages 1–10. IEEE Computer Society, Dec. 2012.

[27] R. Vitali, A. Pellegrini, and F. Quaglia. Towards symmetric multi-threaded optimistic simulation kernels. In *Proceedings of the Workshop on Principles of Advanced and Distributed Simulation*, pages 211–220. IEEE Computer Society, Aug. 2012.

[28] D. West and K. Panesar. Automatic incremental state saving. In *Proceedings of the Workshop on Parallel and Distributed Simulation*, pages 78–85. IEEE Computer Society, May 1996.

Synchronisation for Dynamic Load Balancing of Decentralised Conservative Distributed Simulation

Quentin Bragard, Anthony Ventresque, and Liam Murphy
Lero@UCD, School of Computer Science and Informatics,
University College Dublin, Ireland
quentin.bragard@ucdconnect.ie, anthony.ventresque@ucd.ie, liam.murphy@ucd.ie

ABSTRACT

Synchronisation mechanisms are essential in distributed simulation. Some systems rely on central units to control the simulation but central units are known to be bottlenecks [10]. If we want to avoid using a central unit to optimise the simulation speed, we lose the capacity to act on the simulation at a global scale. Being able to act on the entire simulation is an important feature which allows to dynamically load-balance a distributed simulation. While some local partitioning algorithms exist [12], their lack of global view reduces their efficiency. Running a global partitioning algorithm without central unit requires a synchronisation of all logical processes (LPs) at the same step.We introduce in this paper two algorithms allowing to synchronise logical processes in a distributed simulation without any central unit. The first algorithm requires the knowledge of some topological properties of the network while the second algorithm works without any requirement. The algorithms are detailed and compared against each other. An evaluation shows the benefits of using a global dynamic load-balancing for distributed simulations.

Keywords

Dynamic load-balancing; Synchronisation; Distributed simulation

1. INTRODUCTION

Distributed simulation is an important tool in many scientific fields. It has been designed to answer to problems such as processing power requirement, volatility or stability. However, using distributed systems instead of a single processor (running a non distributed simulation) leads to issues such as dividing and balancing efficiently the load, minimising the communication cost and synchronising LPs. A lot of work has been done in this area. For instance, [16, 32, 34] present algorithms - respectively called METIS, QuadTree and SParTSim - used to partition a simulated environment. QuadTree partitions the environment into smaller regions

SIGSIM-PADS'14, May 18–21, 2014, Denver, CO, USA.
Copyright 2014 ACM 978-1-4503-2794-7/14/05:.$15.00.
http://dx.doi.org/10.1145/2601381.2601386 .

according to spatial information. METIS tries to simplify a weighted graph before dividing it, then it projcts the partitions back on the original graph. SParTSim uses traffic characteristics, such as the importance of the roads, the number of vehicles, the number of neighbours per region, to partition road networks. Various work have tackled the problem of maximising the efficiency of the communication in general distributed systems. Message Passing Interface [31] is one of the most known communication system while some work try to develop their own library [22], especially in graph processing [7, 24, 21]. Synchronisation between the different parts of a distributed system is critical and synchronisation mechanisms can be classified in two categories [11, 20, 3, 19]: conservative or optimistic. The former does not allow any causality violations, i.e., any two events have to be processed in the same order in any LP where they are present, while the latter allows LPs to process events even if they may raise contradictions and need to be roll-backed. There is no strict consensus on which synchronisation mechanism is the best.

Once these three characteristics (workload partitioning among the LPs, communication, synchronisation) are set for a distributed simulation, there is still one element that can hamper the efficiency of the system: the system evolves and the load apply to each LP may vary. In that case, some LPs will have more work to compute while the others will be waiting, and the overall simulation will be slower. It is generally accepted that dynamic load-balancing is necessary for distributed simulations [12, 9, 37]. However, those work focus on local dynamic load-balancing as none of them uses a central unit to monitor the distributed simulation. While they offer fair results, they cannot compete with global load-balancing due to their lack of global information. The problem now is that centralised distributed simulations are not always a good solution - as they generate single points of failure for instance.

In this paper we address the question of the feasibility of overall synchronisation for dynamic load balancing of decentralised conservative distributed simulations. In short, (i) LPs can process a step at a time, and wait for their neighbours to finish their steps before processing the next one (*conservative*); (ii) there is *no central entity* to orchestrate/monitor the simulation; and (iii) the load in the system tend to be *imbalanced* after some time. This scenario is common in distributed simulations [37] and to the best of our knowledge there is no adequate solution that addresses it. We propose two novel algorithms that allow to provide an *overall synchronisation*[1] of the system at a particular step, i.e., stop all the LPs at the same step, so that some global process can happen (repartitioning to dynamically load balance the system in our case): TaSyn and GenSyn. TaSyn requires some topological information on the distributed simulation, such as eccentricity of each node, while GenSyn does not require any additional information and only floods the graph of LPs to figure out the best step to stop the simulation at. We show also in this paper that dynamic load-balancing mechanisms (either using TaSyn of GenSyn) can improve the processing time of a distributed simulation. In particular we find that the time saved using dynamic load-balancing, depending on the sensitivity of the algorithms to load imbalance in the system, is comprised between 7.4% and 15.1% (over 200 steps of simulation).

In the remainder of the paper we explain with more details the requirements of a global synchronisation mechanism (Section 2 and in general what distributed simulation are (Section 3). Section 4 details the two algorithms and compares them while Section 5 shows the impact of a dynamic global load-balancing on a distributed simulation. Finally, Section 6 concludes this paper and presents some future work.

2. MOTIVATION

Several approaches to synchronise distributed systems exist depending on the scale (LANs, WANs) or the kind of system (peer-to-peer, data-centre, clouds computing) [30, 25, 1]. However, those mechanisms are complex and deal with issues such as time-shift or fault-tolerance. While those issues are real at a physical level, they are not relevant in time-discrete distributed simulation, where time is measured logically by the number of steps executed by a LP. We can classify distributed simulations in two categories: distributed simulations with a central unit and distributed simulations where LPs share information locally. At the end of each step, LPs will report their activities to the central unit which will take decisions for the next step for the whole simulation. In this case, synchronising and stopping every LPs at the same step seems straightforward as the central unit knows the state of every LPs and can easily find the first step to stop at. However, distributed simulations with central unit are not always a good solution as the central unit can be a bottleneck. When information are shared locally, each LP communicates directly with its neighbours and LPs do not have a full knowledge of the network.

As workload is transferred through the distributed simulation, some LPs might receive more load than others and, therefore, take more time to complete their work. Each LP depending on the outputs of those slow ones will in turn be slowed down and eventually the whole simulation slows down. In order to prevent this issue, the simulation must find a way to globally balance the load over the LPs. However, without a central entity, this operation can be complex. First of all, a LP has to understand that the distributed simulation could have faster results. Different solutions can be imagined to evaluate a slowdown. The first way can be through synchronisation messages: each time the LPs synchronised, they send a message with their actual load and

compare the value with their neighbours or with the average load. It would be possible for a LP to periodically broadcast a message in order to share information about its load. However, if we want this solution to be more efficient than local dynamic load-balancing, we have to broadcast the message far away from its origin which will considerably increase the communication on the network. An ideal solution would be for a LP to be able to evaluate itself without sharing information with the rest of the simulation. While a LP alone cannot evaluate how much slower it is compared to its neighbour, it is possible for a faster LP to evaluate how much faster it is. After a step - or few steps with optimistic synchronisation mechanism - a LP requires to synchronise with its neighbours. Measuring the time between the end of its step and the last neighbour synchronising would give an idea about how faster the LP is. An evaluation can be conducted during the simulation without perturbing the processing just by measuring the slowest response time and compare it with a threshold. If during a couple of consecutive synchronisations, the latency is higher than usual, the problem might come from an unbalanced state of the simulation. Thus, the LP detecting the unusual latency is able to trigger an overall synchronisation.

3. RELATED WORK

Distributed simulation is the representation of the evolution of a system using multiple LPs working together. They can be used to simulate work such as adaptive mesh refinement [18], car crashes [29], behaviour simulation [5, 8], graph functions [6] and others. To respond to those requirements, distributed simulations can take a lot of forms: continuous or discrete time/space, time-step or event-driven, local or global communication (through a central unit). However, they all share the same basic requirements: a partitioning algorithm to distribute as evenly as possible the load among the LPs, a communication mechanism to allow LPs to exchange information and a synchronisation mechanism to allow LPs to organise themselves when needed.

3.1 Partitioning Algorithms

For the distributed simulation to be efficient, it is important to distribute the load as fairly as possible between each LP. As shown section 5, disparity among the load can have important consequences on the overall simulation time. A lot of research has been conducted to address this problem, leading to numerous algorithms including uniform and nonuniform space partitioning [33, 23, 2, 32], graph partitioning [16, 17] (some designed for specific tasks including road traffic partitioning [34, 36]), car crashes analysis [29] and others.

3.2 Communication Mechanism

The aim of the communication mechanism is to ensure that LPs share information throughout the simulation. It is a critical element as the very idea of LPs working together is based on their capacity to communicate. If the communication library is not efficient enough, it can lead to an important slow-down of the overall simulation. The most used communication library is MPI [31] as it is well-known to be efficient, simple to use and portable. Extensions of MPI have been developed to improve its efficiency. For instance, MPICH-G2 [15] has been designed to handle heterogeneous communication environments where commu-

---

[1]In this paper we use 'overall synchronisation' or 'synchronisation' for the same process of stopping all LPs at the same step.

nication latencies are nonuniform. To minimise the impact of the communication, some work try to load-balance the communication while partitioning the environment [34, 27].

3.3 Synchronisation Mechanism

Synchronisation mechanism is also required for an efficient distributed simulation. It ensures that messages are handled in the correct order of their timestamps. This law is called local causality constraint. Fujimoto [11] categorises synchronisation mechanisms in two classes: conservative synchronisation and optimistic synchronisation, dependant on the distributed simulation and no consensus seems to have emerged on wether to use one or the other.

3.3.1 Conservative Synchronisation

Conservative synchronisation is designed so that the local causality constraint cannot be violated. For instance, conservative time-stepped distributed simulations have to synchronise all LPs after each simulation step. When, and only when, a LP is sure that no message will arrive with a smaller timestamp, it proceeds the next step. In order to improve the communication, work such as [37] have their LPs synchronising only with their neighbours, allowing some time flexibility without violating the local causality constraint.

3.3.2 Optimistic Synchronisation

On the other side, optimistic synchronisation allows LPs to break the local causality constraint. In order to optimise the distributed simulation, LPs limit their synchronisation to every few steps instead of every step. Therefore, it is possible to receive a message which should have been handled at the step t while being already at the step $t + 1$. Rollback mechanisms are present to be able to go back to step t and handle the message. However, rollbacks have a heavy cost as the simulation has to reload its previous state and re-start the steps.

4. SYNCHRONISATION

Synchronising a simulation can be a critical task if a LP, or the user, wants to perform an action which can impact the whole distributed simulation. For instance, in distributed simulations, maintaining a good load-balance between LPs is important to get optimal results which force the simulation to balance itself during the simulation. While it is, in some cases, possible to foresee a change and therefore plan a modification of the partitioning before running the simulation, unpredictable load changes require dynamic partitioning. Load-balance can be done locally by exchanging, for instance, vertices or agents with its neighbours [12]. However, the risks are that it takes a while to correct the load-balance and that you increase the number of messages exchanged. Synchronising all LPs would offer the possibility to globally partition the simulation in one shot, saving time and network resources. In order to globally synchronise a time-stepped distributed simulation without using a central entity, two options are possible. Either moving forward in time until a chosen step or rollback until the latest checkpoint. Performing rollback - by state saving, or reverse computation - is a common operation in distributed simulations [28, 35]. However, this operation requires to periodically save the state of the LPs - or the operations executed in case of rollback by reverse computation - which is time-consuming. Moreover, when the simulation has performed

a rollback and is load-balanced again, it has to recompute steps which have already been done before. In addition, if rollbacks are indeed useful in distributed simulation using an optimistic synchronisation mechanism, it is not necessary with conservative synchronisation. On the other solution is, for some or all LPs, to go few steps forward. The first algorithm presented in this paper has been designed to quickly propagate the first safe step to stop at, without any global information, based on graph theory properties. The second algorithm presented propagates requests to all LPs in order to gather graph information and find the first possible step to stop at.

4.1 Graph Theory and Distributed Simulation

It is generally accepted that, as distributed simulations - and more generally a distributed systems - are composition of LPs linked together by communication channels, their structure can be compared to a graph with logical processes equivalent to vertices and communication channels equivalent to edges. The similarities can be extended to graph theory concepts such as:

- **Eccentricity** of a vertex is the maximum distance between a vertex and any other vertex. By extension, the eccentricity of a LP will be the maximum distance between a LP and any other LP. For instance, on 1, the eccentricity of F is 3 because it is at a maximum distance of 3 from every LP.

- **Diameter** and **Radius** are respectively the maximum and the minimum eccentricity. On 1, the maximum eccentricity is hold by A, E and H with a value of 4, therefore, the diameter of the graph is 4. In the same way, the minimum eccentricity is hold by C with a value of 2, thus, the radio of the graph is 2.

- **Peripheral vertices** are the vertices with an eccentricity equal to the diameter. In the same way, **central vertices** are the vertices with an eccentricity equal to the radius. The vertices left are called **pseudo-peripheral**. In this paper, we will use the vocabulary **peripheral LPs**, **central LPs** and **pseudo-peripheral LPs** to talk about the vertex equivalents in distributed system.

4.2 TaSyn: Topologically-aware Synchronisation

TaSyn, which stands for Topologically-aware Synchronisation, works using the eccentricity of a graph to find a step at which LPs can synchronise. Time-stepped distributed simulations using local conservative synchronisation allow a small time-flexibility between a LP and its neighbours. For instance, if the LP n_j has just completed the step $t - 1$, its neighbour n_i will receive the information required to compute the step t even if n_j is stuck at the end of $t - 1$. At the end of n_i's step, its neighbour, n_k will have enough information to compute the step $t + 1$ even if n_j has not moved from the end of the step $t - 1$. By transition, the difference of steps between two LPs in the simulation is logically smaller or equal to the distance which separate those two LPs. Therefore, the maximum difference of steps between any two LPs is smaller or equal to the eccentricity of those LPs. When computing the eccentricity of a LP, we know the maximum difference of steps between itself and any other LP in the distributed system. If the eccentricity is known before running the distributed simulation, a LP can safely request a general stop at the following step:

$$synchroStep = e(n_t) + s(n_t) \qquad (1)$$

with n_t the LP triggering TaSyn, $e(n_t)$ the eccentricity of n_t and $s(n_t)$ the current step of n_t. If we know the topology of the distributed simulation, algorithms such as Johnson's algorithm [14] offer the possibility to process the eccentricity of each node in the graph.

Algorithm 1: TriggerLP for TaSyn

---

1 **if** *triggered is false & synchronising is false* **then**
2   synchronising ← true;
3   synchroStep ← eccentricity + currentStep;
4   sendToAll("SYN "+synchroStep);

    // The LP can continue until reaching synchroStep

Algorithm 2: Regular LP for TaSyn

---

1 $\overrightarrow{parents}$ ← new array;
2 **foreach** *msg in msgBox* **do**
3   **if** *msg.startWith("SYN") is true & synchronising is false* **then**
4   synchronising ← true;
5   tempStep ← msg.split(" ")[1];
6 **if** *tempStep < synchroStep* **then**
7   synchroStep ← tempStep;
8    $\overrightarrow{parents}$.add(msg.sender);
9 **foreach** *n ∈ neighbours* **do**
10   **if** *n is not ∈ $\overrightarrow{parents}$* **then**
11   n.send("SYN "+synchroStep);

    // The LP can continue until reaching synchroStep

An important question to ask at this stage is: what happens if two LPs trigger the algorithm? If two LPs are at the same step and have the same eccentricity, they will send the same message. If a LP receives two messages at the same time, it will just assume that the two LPs are its parents. If one message comes later, it will just be discarded. When the value carried by the messages is not the same, the LP will select the lowest value as by definition, both values correspond to a safe step to stop at. Figure 1 presents a case of collision between LP F which has an eccentricity of 3 and is at the step 9 and LP H which has an eccentricity of 4 and is at step 10.

TaSyn is simple and straightforward but does not compute the first step where it is possible to stop because the triggering LP does not know at which step the other LPs are. It only knows that they are within the boundary of the constraint.

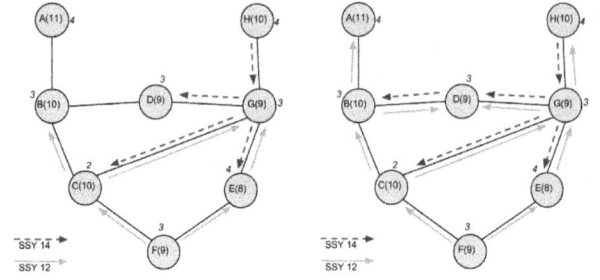

Figure 1: Collision in case of simultaneous trigger by *F* and *H*.

4.3 GenSyn: General Synchronisation

When it becomes important to stop the distributed simulation as soon as possible, GenSyn, which stands for General Synchronisation, can find the most ahead LP, and thus the first step to which it is safe to synchronise everyone. The algorithm works in three phases:

- **Propagation (PRP)**. The first phase consists in propagating a message through the distributed simulation to find the LP with the highest step. Each LP receiving one or more messages from its neighbours will compare its step with the step contained in each message. The LP will place the highest step in a message and forward it to all its remaining neighbours while the sender(s) id(s) will be stored. If the LP receives a message after it has propagated to its neighbours, the message is discarded. Figure 2(a) presents the propagation of the message if the LP F triggers GenSyn.

- **Answer (ANS)**. If after removing its parents, a LP has no other neighbour to propagate the message to, the second phase starts and the LP sends back to its parents an answering message containing the highest step stored. Each LP waits for an answer from all its children before forwarding back its own answer. Figure 2(b) shows how the answer will be sent back to the root LP F.

- **Confirmation (CNF)**. Once the triggering LP has received answers from all its neighbours, it sends a confirmation message with the highest step of the distributed simulation. Each neighbour stores the step contained in the confirmation message and continues its work until it reaches this step. Figure 2(c) presents the propagation of the confirmation message.

Algorithm 3: Leader LP for GenSyn

---

1 **if** *triggered is true & synchronising is false* **then**
2   synchronising ← true;
3   leader ← true;
4   sendToAll("PRP "+currentStep+" "+id);

In case of collisions, the LP arbitrary selects the smaller id between the LPs triggering the algorithm.

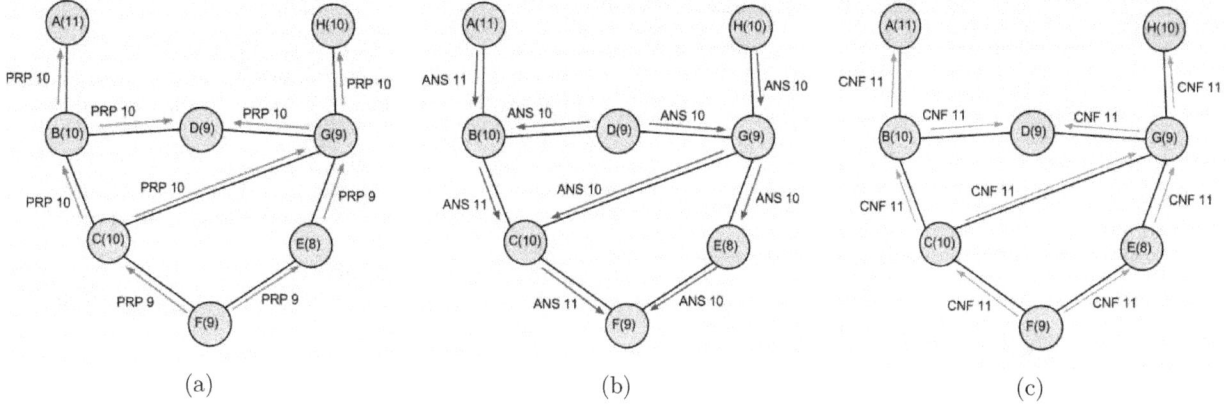

Figure 2: Evolution of the three steps of GenSyn. Each circle represents a LP and is labelled with LP id and latest processed step (in parenthesis).

4.4 Efficiency of GenSyn and TaSyn

Information about the eccentricity of each LP used by TaSyn makes it far less complex than GenSyn. However, despite the fact that this information is not always available, TaSyn's simplicity does not make it more efficient in every case. To compare the , we consider that each LP has to wait until the global synchronisation is finished to process the remaining steps. In other words, the communication phase and the processing phase will be executed sequentially - in practice, intermediate LPs can start processing steps if they know they are at a lower step compared to the potential maximum (i.e., they received propagation messages with a higher step than their actual one).

To reach the furthest neighbours, TaSyn requires a number of steps equal to the eccentricity of the triggering LP. The remaining step(s) to process for a LP will be the difference between the triggering LP current step added to its eccentricity and the current step of the LP. Therefore, Ta-Syn communication time ($CommTime_{TaS}$) and processing time ($StepTime_{TaS}$) requirements are:

$$CommTime_{TaS} = t_u \times e(n_t) \qquad (2)$$

$$t_s \times e(n_t) \leq StepTime_{TaS} \leq t_s \times (e(n_t) + s(n_t) - min(s(n))) \qquad (3)$$

As the communication phase of GenSyn consists in crossing the network 3 times, its communication phase is 3 times longer than TaSyn. The maximal number of steps required before reaching the synchronisation step is given by the difference between the highest step and the lowest step present on the simulation. From that point, GenSyn communication time ($CommTime_{GenS}$) and processing time ($StepTime_{GenS}$) requirements are defined as:

$$CommTime_{GenS} = t_u \times 3 \times e(n_t) \qquad (4)$$

$$0 \leq StepTime_{GenS} \leq t_s \times (max(s(n)) - min(s(n))) \qquad (5)$$

with $CommTime_{TaS}$ and $CommTime_{GenS}$ respectively TaSyn and GenSyn's communication times, $StepTime_{TaS}$ and $StepTime_{GenS}$ respectively TaSyn and GenSyn's processing times, t_u the time required to send a message to a neighbours, n_t the LP triggering the algorithm, $e(n)$ the

eccentricity of the LP n, t_s the time required to process a step and $s(n)$ the step of LP n. The minimum value for the processing time happens when the LPs are all close to be at the same step which means $max(s(n)) - min(s(n)) = 0$, while the maximum processing time occurs when the LPs are at completely different steps and then $max(s(n)) - min(s(n)) = max(e(n))$. For the comparison, we will assume that we are in the worst case, $max(s(n)) - min(s(n)) \rightarrow max(e(n))$ but the process is identical for the case 1 and for the intermediate values. By adding equations 2 to 3 and equations 4 to 5, we obtain the total time required respectively by TaSyn and GenSyn. As we want to compare them according to the topology of the graph, the communication time and the processing time, we can write:

$$TotalTime_{GenS} = TotalTime_{TaS}$$

$$t_u \times 3 \times e(n_t) + t_s \times max(e(n)) = t_u \times e(n_t) + t_s \times 2 \times e(n_t)$$

$$t_u \times (2 \times e(n_t)) = t_s \times (2 \times e(n_t) - max(e(n))) \qquad (6)$$

In graph theory, it is proven than $radius \leq diameter \leq 2 \times radius$ [4]. As explained before, the diameter is the maximum eccentricity so $dia = max(e(n))$ and the radius the minimum eccentricity $rad = min(e(n))$. In the case of $dia = 2rad$, if n_t is a pseudo-peripheral LP - $rad \leq e(n_t) \leq dia$ - from equation 6, the relation between the communication time and the processing time is given by:

$$t_u = \frac{t_s \times (2 \times e(n_t) - dia)}{2 \times e(n_t)} \qquad (7)$$

If n_t is a central LP - $rad = e(n_t)$ -, as $dia = 2 \times radius$, the equation 7 can be reduced to:

$$t_u = \frac{t_s \times (dia - dia)}{2 \times e(n_t)}$$

$$t_u = 0 \qquad (8)$$

Finally, if n_t is a peripheral LP - $dia = e(n_t)$ -, for the same reason, we can reduce equation 7 to:

$$t_u = \frac{t_s \times (2dia - dia)}{2 \times dia}$$

Algorithm 4: GenSyn LP for TaSyn

```
1  parents ← new array;
2  foreach msg in msgBox do
3  |   tempRootId ← msg.split(" ")[2];
4  |   if rootId == null then
5  |   └   rootId ← tempRootId;
6  |   else if tempRootId < rootId then
7  |   └   rootId ← tempRootId;nbPrp ← 0;nbAns ← 0;
8  foreach msg in msgBox do
9  |   if msg.startWith("PRP") is true then
10 |   |   nbPrp ← nbPrp + 1;
11 |   |   tempStep ← msg.split(" ")[1];
12 |   |   triggered ← true;
13 |   |   parents.add(msg.sender);
14 |   |   if synchronising is true then
15 |   |   |   synchronising ← true;
16 |   |   └   currentMaxStep ← step;
17 |   |   if tempStep > currentMaxStep then
18 |   |   └   currentMaxStep ← tempStep;
19 |   |   if nbPrp == neighbours.size() then
20 |   |   |   foreach p ∈ parents do
21 |   |   |   |   if n is ∈ parents then
22 |   |   |   |   └   n.send("ANS "+currentMaxStep);
23 |   |   |   parents.clear();
24 |   |   else
25 |   |   └   prpToSend ← true;
26 |   else if msg.startWith("ANS") is true then
27 |   |   nbAns ← nbAns + 1;
28 |   |   currentStepMax ← msg.split(" ")[1];
29 |   |   if leader is true & nbAns == neighbours.size()
        |   |   then
30 |   |   |   stoppingStep = currentStepMax;
31 |   |   └   sendToAll("CNF "+stoppingStep);
32 |   |   else if nbPrp+nbAns == neighbours.size()
        |   |   then
33 |   |   |   foreach p ∈ parents do
34 |   |   |   └   p.send("ANS "+currentMaxStep);
35 |   |   └   parents.clear();
36 |   else if msg.startWith("CNF") is true &
        |   confirmation is false then
37 |   |   confirmed ← true;
38 |   |   stoppingStep ← msg.split(" ")[1];
39 |   |   parents.add(msg.sender);
40 |   |   foreach n ∈ neighbours do
41 |   |   |   if n is not ∈ parents then
42 |   |   |   └   n.send("CNF "+stoppingStep);
43 if prpToSend is true then
44 |   foreach n ∈ neighbours do
45 |   |   if n is not ∈ parents then
46 |   |   └   n.send("PRP "+currentMaxStep);
```

$$t_u = \frac{1}{2} \times t_s \qquad (9)$$

Equation 8 proves that, if the LP triggering the algorithm is a central node, TaSyn will always be faster than GenSyn. However, if the triggering LP is a peripheral node, GenSyn will be faster than TaSyn if the communication time is less than twice the processing time. Identically, if the LP trigger is a pseudo-peripheral node, the relation between the communication time and the processing time is given by the equation 7.

Using the same way, if we are in the case of $dia = rad$, all LPs have the same status and the equation resulting is:

$$t_u = t_s \qquad (10)$$

Which means that no matter which LP triggers the algorithm, GenSyn will outperform TaSyn if the communication time is smaller than the processing time.

If we are in the case where $rad < dia < 2rad$, by declaring $dia = 2rad - x$ with $0 < x < rad$, we obtain the following equations:

$$t_u = t_s \times \frac{x}{2rad} \qquad (11)$$

$$t_u = \frac{t_s}{dia} \qquad (12)$$

$$t_u = t_s \times \frac{dia}{2 \times e(n_t)} \qquad (13)$$

for a triggering LP respectively a central node 11, a peripheral node 12 and a pseudo-peripheral node 13.

This comparison shows that neither TaSyn nor GenSyn outperforms the other. Therefore, the user can select which algorithm is more suitable for its distributed simulation depending on the following features: communication time, processing time, network topology and the position of the node if known.

5. EXPERIMENTATION

To test their efficiency, we implement our algorithms into the simulator of distributed system Peersim [26] and simulate the behaviour of the distributed simulation.

5.1 PeerSim

PeerSim has been developed to simulate and test distributed (peer-to-peer) systems. Its main features are its scalability, which allows it to run algorithms on hundreds of thousands of nodes quickly, its modularity as all the components are configurable and its graph abstraction, useful to import networks as graphs and use topological information. PeerSim also implements two types of simulations, event-based and cycle-based. We choose to implement our algorithm with the cycle-based simulation as we are studying time-stepped simulations. For each PeerSim cycle, LPs are randomly selected and executed one after another.

5.2 Scenario

We measure the impact of dynamic load-balancing by using a distributed simulation implementing our algorithms against a reference distributed simulation. Our distributed simulation will be able to perform a global dynamic load-balancing but not the reference. We simulate a 200 steps-long stepped-based distributed simulation using Peersim.

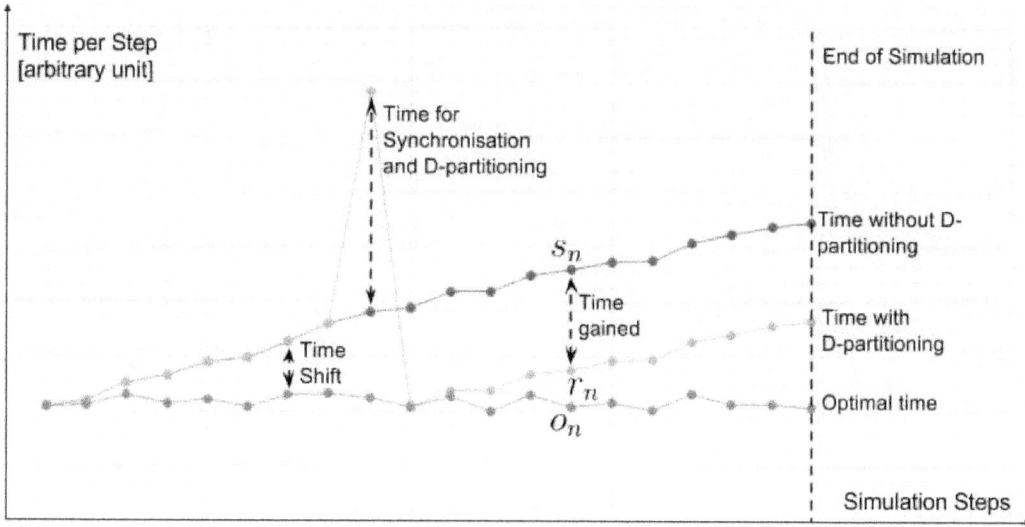

Figure 3: Expected synchronisation impact over the simulation.

Each Peersim cycle, the LPs increase a value until they reach their maximum load. It is a simple task representing the LPs doing their part of the simulation. When a LP reaches it maximum load, it sends to its neighbours an end-of-step message and waits until all its neighbours send back the same message. Once the end-of-step messages are gathered, the LP calls a method to increase or decrease its maximum load of 1%, depending of a random value. This phase represents the fact that a distributed simulation seldom stays at the optimal state of a perfect load-balance. Then, the LPs will proceed to the next step with more load, or less load, than its neighbours. It is very likely that, after a while, some LPs will have a lot more, or a lot less, work than others and will slow down the simulation, or have to wait a long time. From this point, the simulations using GenSyn and TaSyn will try to synchronise the distributed simulation in order to perform a dynamic partitioning which will bring-back the load-balanced state. On the other side, the reference simulation will have to continue with its unbalanced state. It will allow us to compare the effect of the dynamic-load balancing against its absence and measure its impact in term of simulation time.

In order to trigger the global synchronisation algorithms, and therefore the dynamic partitioning, a LP will compare the time it requires to simulate a step against the time it has to wait its neighbours. We will set 4 different thresholds in order to compare their impact. We have chosen as thresholds: $StepTime = \{1/2, 1/4, 1/8, 1/16\}$ $WaitingTime$. For the scenario of our algorithm, we did not implement any specific partitioning algorithm to run when the LPs are synchronised which could, in some cases, take a certain time. Following the same idea, our LPs communicate by shared memories which cannot be compared, in term of time, with messages sent in the network. However, we will present our results being aware of those two missing constraints.

5.3 Metrics

The first observation we expect is a global impact such as represented by the Figure 3. Optimal time means the time to process the simulation if the system is perfectly load-balanced. As the simulation is losing its load-balanced state, the time want measure the average time required by all the LPs to move to the next step, which means both the processing-time and the waiting-time. This measure will show us the impact of the load-balancing on each step of the simulation and on the overall simulation. The time gained over the whole simulation will be obtained from:

$$TotalTimeGained = \sum_{i=0}^{n}(\frac{\sum_{j=0}^{m}(s_j)}{m} - \frac{\sum_{j=0}^{m}(r_j)}{m}) \quad (14)$$

where n is the number of steps, m the number of LPs, $s_i \in S$ the values of the simulation without the synchronisation and $r_i \in R$ the values of the simulation including a synchronisation. The different measurements according to each threshold will allow us to evaluate the efficiency of a load-balancing methods regarding the unbalanced state. In order to obtain the efficiency per synchronisation, we will divide the percentage of time gained by the number of synchronisations. The efficiency of the synchronisation will allow us to discuss over the time we can spend running a real partitioning algorithm. Lastly, we will measure and compare the reduction of waiting time obtained thanks to the load-balancing. We will trigger our algorithms using the four different thresholds introduced above.

5.4 Results

Our first concern was to observe the behaviour expected from Figure 3 and all the measurements confirm our expectations. Figure 4(a) presents this behaviour around step 80 while figure 4(b) presents it three times around steps 50, 115 and 165. Both figure 4(c) and (d) show this behaviour several times along the simulation. These are a series a great figures that show exactly what we expected: the system diverge to a imbalanced state and both GenSyn and TaSyn allows it to come back to a balanced state, more or less

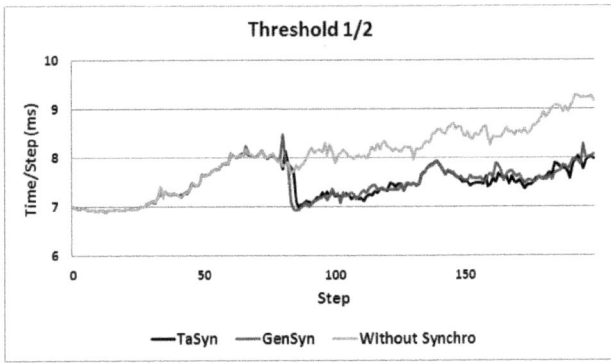

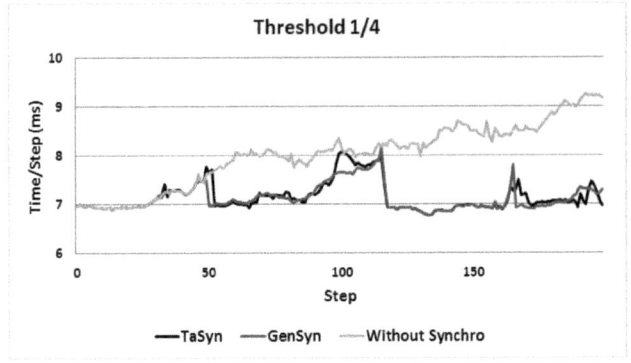

(a)   (b)

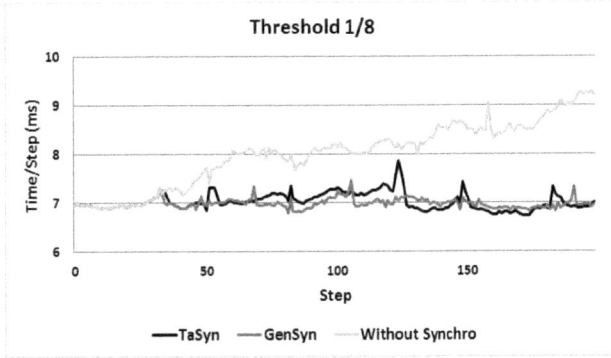

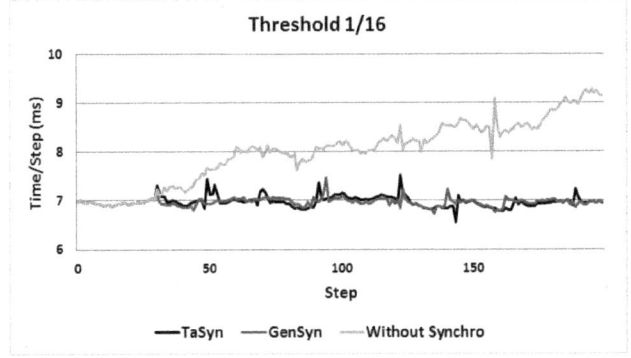

(c)   (d)

Figure 4: Evolution of the time required per step over the simulation. The lower the better.

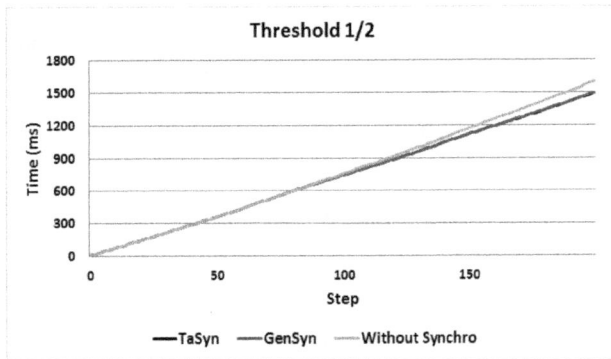

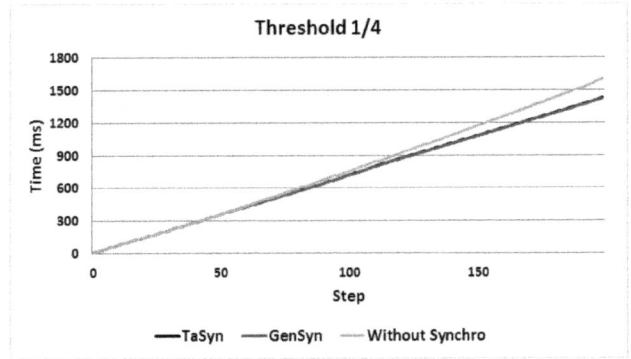

(a)   (b)

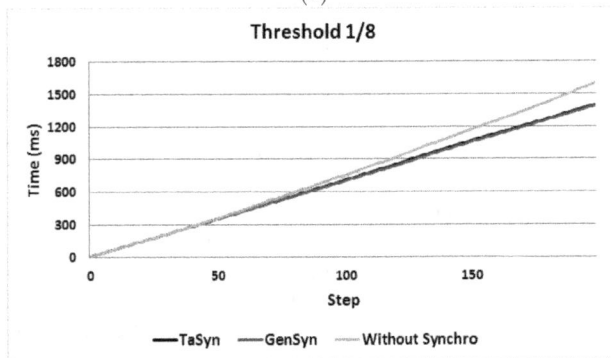

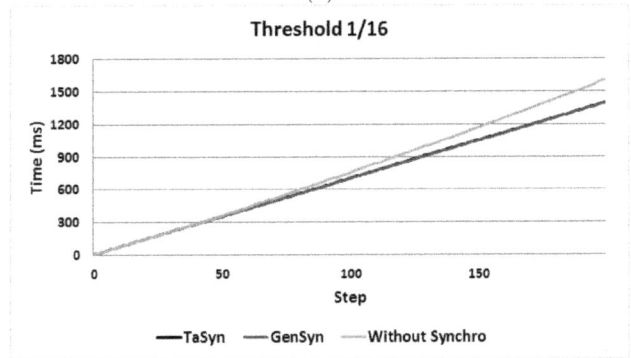

(c)   (d)

Figure 5: Simulation time for the whole simulation. The lower the better.

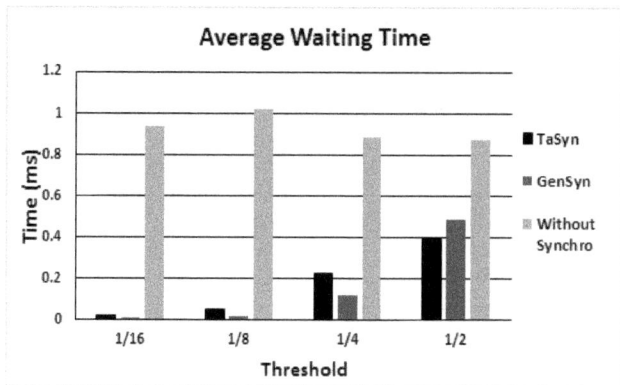

Figure 6: Average waiting time of each case over the four thresholds.

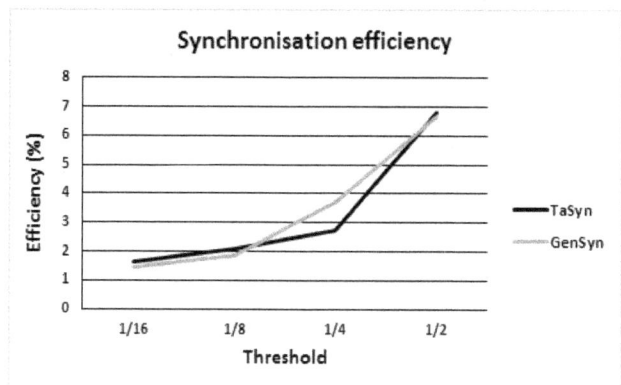

Figure 7: Efficiency of a dynamic partitioning according to the threshold of the trigger.

quickly depending on the sensitivity of the algorithms (i.e., threshold).

Figures 5(a-d) present the overall time required to execute the 200 steps of the simulation. As expected, a divergence is observed on all figures. Moreover, while the sensitivity of the synchronisation trigger increases, the gap between the reference simulation and the two other keeps increasing. It results from the number of synchronisations as the more the simulation synchronises, the more the load-balance will be brought back closer to it optimal state. We can note as well that the curves are linear which leads to think that the longer the simulation will be, the more time will be gained. We find that the gain is very similar for TaSyn and GenSyn: from 7.4% for a TaSyn and threshold of 1/2 (7.6% for GenSyn), to 15.1% for GenSyn and a threshold of 1/16 (14.9% for TaSyn) - 13.5% for GenSyn and a threshold of 1/4 (13.2% for TaSyn), 14.9% for GenSyn and a threshold of 1/8 (14.5% for TaSyn). This is a very good results as processing time is often the critical metric for distributed simulations.

Figure 6 presents the time lost in average by each LP at each step (we compare to the average time for a simulation without imbalance). At the optimal state, each LP will finish its step at the same time and the waiting time will be limited to the time required to exchange end-of-step messages. While the reference simulation misuses between 0.9ms and 1ms per step, the average waiting-time decreases as we increase the sensitivity of the trigger. If the synchronisation is triggered more often, the simulation will be brought closer to the optimal load-balance state more often.

Efficiency of the synchronisation is an important measure. As we did not implement any time-consuming load-balancing algorithm - what they usually are [13] - we need a way to evaluate how many times we have at our disposition to add the time required for the load balancing and the exchange of synchronisation messages. Figure 7 presents the efficiency of a synchronisation in our different test-cases. On a simulation of 200 steps, the efficiency of a synchronisation would be close to 7% for both TaSyn and GenSyn with a trigger set at 1/2. However, the efficiency decreases rapidly at 3.5% for GenSyn and 2.8% for TaSyn with a trigger set at 1/4. It seems to stabilise around 2% and 1.8% for a trigger respectively at 1/8 and 1/16. In a real situation, we would also have to take care of the efficiency of the load-balancing algorithm used to determine how much time we can allow to it and how many times we can run it during the distributed

simulation. However, those results are the proof that there is certainly room for improvement.

6. CONCLUSION

This paper introduces two algorithms TaSyn and GenSyn which are able to synchronise globally a time-stepped conservative distributed simulation. This global synchronisation makes global actions possible, such as a global-scale load-balancing in an environment where information are only shared locally or unpredictable requirement to dump the memory because of imminent failure. GenSyn and TaSyn complexities have been compared and we have proven that their efficiency depends on the structure of the distributed simulation as well as the communication latency and the time required to perform a step. We have also compared, by simulation through PeerSim, a distributed simulation able to perform a global dynamic load-balancing against a distributed simulation which cannot load-balance itself. The results show that dynamically load-balancing a distributed simulation is an important operation which offers great improvements on the simulation time.

As future work we would like to compare our fully decentralised approach and high level architectures (HLA) and investigate whether TaSyn/GenSyn can still be applied (e.g., replace the synchronisation management offered by RTI). We are also interested in implementing our algorithms in distributed simulations (e.g., [5]) to evaluate the overhead of synchronisation and load-balancing on a real system. Eventually, our main target now is to compare global and local load-balancing on the system.

7. ACKNOWLEDGEMENT

This work was supported, in part, by Science Foundation Ireland grant 10/CE/I1855 to Lero - the Irish Software Engineering Research Centre (www.lero.ie)

8. REFERENCES

[1] K. Arvind. Probabilistic clock synchronization in distributed systems. *Parallel and Distributed Systems, IEEE Transactions on*, 5(5):474–487, May 1994.

[2] J. W. Barrus, R. C. Waters, and D. B. Anderson. Locales and Beacons: Efficient and Precise Support For Large Multi-User Virtual Environments. In *VRAIS*, pages 204–213, 1996.

[3] D. W. Bauer Jr., C. D. Carothers, and A. Holder. Scalable time warp on blue gene supercomputers. In *PADS*, pages 35–44, 2009.

[4] B. Bollobás. *Modern Graph Theory*. Springer, Heidelberg, corrected edition, 1998.

[5] Q. Bragard, A. Ventresque, and L. Murphy. dsumo: Towards a distributed sumo. In *First SUMO conference*, Berlin, Germany, 2013.

[6] S. Brin and L. Page. The anatomy of a large-scale hypertextual web search engine. *Comput. Netw. ISDN Syst.*, 30(1-7):107–117, Apr. 1998.

[7] R. Chen, X. Weng, B. He, and M. Yang. Large graph processing in the cloud. In *SIGMOD*, pages 1123–1126, 2010.

[8] I. D. Couzin, J. Krause, N. R. Franks, and S. A. Levin. Effective leadership and decision-making in animal groups on the move. *Nature*, 433(7025):513–516, 2005.

[9] K. D. Devine, E. G. Boman, R. T. Heaphy, B. A. Hendrickson, J. D. Teresco, J. Faik, J. E. Flaherty, and L. G. Gervasio. New challenges in dynamic load balancing. *Applied Numerical Mathematics*, 52(2–3):133 – 152, 2005.

[10] A. Ferscha and S. K. Tripathi. Parallel and distributed simulation of discrete event systems. 1998.

[11] R. M. Fujimoto. Parallel and distributed simulation. In *WSC*, pages 122–131, 1999.

[12] B. Hendrickson and K. Devine. Dynamic load balancing in computational mechanics. *Computer Methods in Applied Mechanics and Engineering*, 184(2-4):485 – 500, 2000.

[13] S. Iqbal and G. F. Carey. Performance analysis of dynamic load balancing algorithms with variable number of processors. *Journal of Parallel and Distributed Computing*, 65(8):934 – 948, 2005.

[14] D. B. Johnson. Efficient algorithms for shortest paths in sparse networks. *J. ACM*, 24(1):1–13, Jan. 1977.

[15] N. T. Karonis, B. Toonen, and I. Foster. Mpich-g2: A grid-enabled implementation of the message passing interface. *Journal of Parallel and Distributed Computing*, 63(5):551–563, 2003.

[16] G. Karypis and V. Kumar. Metis - unstructured graph partitioning and sparse matrix ordering system, version 2.0. Technical report, 1995.

[17] G. Karypis and V. Kumar. Multilevel k-way partitioning scheme for irregular graphs. *Journal of Parallel and Distributed Computing*, 48(1):96 – 129, 1998.

[18] B. Kirk, J. Peterson, R. Stogner, and G. Carey. libmesh: a c++ library for parallel adaptive mesh refinement/coarsening simulations. *Engineering with Computers*, 22(3-4):237-254, 2006.

[19] S. Lin, X. Cheng, and J. Lv. Micro-synchronization in conservative parallel network simulation. In *PADS*, pages 195–202, 2008.

[20] J. Liu and R. Rong. Hierarchical composite synchronization. In *PADS*, pages 3–12, July 2012.

[21] Y. Low, J. Gonzalez, A. Kyrola, D. Bickson, C. Guestrin, and J. M. Hellerstein. Graphlab: A new parallel framework for machine learning. In *Conference on Uncertainty in Artificial Intelligence (UAI)*, 2010.

[22] E. Lusk and K. Yelick. Languages for high-productivity computing: the darpa hpcs language project. *Parallel Processing Letters*, 17(01), 2007.

[23] M. R. Macedonia, M. J. Zyda, D. R. Pratt, D. P. Brutzman, and P. T. Barham. Exploiting Reality with Multicast Groups: A Network Architecture for Large-scale Virtual Environments. In *IEEE Virtual Reality Annual International Symposium*, 1995.

[24] G. Malewicz, M. H. Austern, A. J. Bik, J. C. Dehnert, I. Horn, N. Leiser, and G. Czajkowski. Pregel: A system for large-scale graph processing. In *SIGMOD*, pages 135–146, 2010.

[25] D. L. Mills. Internet time synchronization: the network time protocol. *Communications, IEEE Transactions on*, 39(10):1482–1493, 1991.

[26] A. Montresor and M. Jelasity. Peersim: A scalable p2p simulator. In *Peer-to-Peer Computing, 2009. P2P '09. IEEE Ninth International Conference on*, pages 99–100, 2009.

[27] L. Nyland, J. Prins, R. Yun, J. Hermans, H.-C. Kum, and L. Wang. Modeling dynamic load balancing in molecular dynamics to achieve scalable parallel execution. In *Solving Irregularly Structured Problems in Parallel*, volume 1457, pages 356–365. 1998.

[28] K. Perumalla. Parallel and distributed simulation: Traditional techniques and recent advances. In *WSC*, pages 84–95, 2006.

[29] S. Plimpton, SteveAttaway, S. Attaway, B. Hendrickson, J. Swegle, C. Vaughan, and D. Gardner. Parallel transient dynamics simulations: Algorithms for contact detection and smoothed particle hydrodynamics. *J. Par. Distrib. Computing*, 50:50–1, 1998.

[30] P. Ramanathan, K. Shin, and R. Butler. Fault-tolerant clock synchronization in distributed systems. *Computer*, 23(10):33–42, Oct 1990.

[31] M. Snir, S. W. Otto, D. W. Walker, J. Dongarra, and S. Huss-Lederman. *MPI: The Complete Reference*. MIT Press, Cambridge, MA, USA, 1995.

[32] A. Steed and R. Abou-Haidar. Partitioning Crowded Virtual Environments. In *VRST*, pages 7–14, 2003.

[33] D. J. Van Hook, S. J. Rak, and J. O. Calvin. Approaches to Relevance Filtering. In *Workshop on Standards for the Interoperability of Distributed Simulations*, pages 26–30, 1994.

[34] A. Ventresque, Q. Bragard, E. S. Liu, D. Nowak, L. Murphy, G. Theodoropoulos, and J. Q. Liu. Spartsim: A space partitioning guided by road network for distributed traffic simulations. In *IEEE/ACM DS-RT*, 2012.

[35] X. Wang, S. Turner, M. Low, and B.-P. Gan. Optimistic synchronization in hla based distributed simulation. In *PADS*, pages 123–130, May 2004.

[36] Y. Xu and G. Tan. An offline road network partitioning solution in distributed transportation simulation. In *IEEE/ACM DR-ST*, pages 210–217, Oct 2012.

[37] T. Zou, G. Wang, M. V. Salles, D. Bindel, A. Demers, J. Gehrke, and W. White. Making time-stepped applications tick in the cloud. In *2Nd ACM Symposium on Cloud Computing*, pages 20:1–20:14, 2011.

Accelerating Parallel Agent-based Epidemiological Simulations

Dhananjai M. Rao
CSE Department
Miami University, Oxford, OHIO, USA
raodm@miamiOH.edu

ABSTRACT

Background: Simulations play a central role in epidemiological analysis and design of prophylactic measures. Spatially explicit, agent-based models provide temporo-geospatial information that cannot be obtained from traditional equation-based and individual-based epidemic models. Since, simulation of large agent-based models is time consuming, optimistically synchronized parallel simulation holds considerable promise to significantly decrease simulation execution times.

Problem: Realizing efficient and scalable optimistic parallel simulations on modern distributed memory supercomputers is a challenge due to the spatially-explicit nature of agent-based models. Specifically, conceptual movement of agents results in large number of inter-process messages which significantly increase synchronization overheads and degrades overall performance.

Proposed solution: To reduce inter-process messages, this paper proposes and experimentally evaluates two approaches involving single and multiple active-proxy agents. The Single Active Proxy (SAP) approach essentially accomplishes logical process migration (without any support from underlying simulation kernel) reflecting conceptual movement of the agents. The Multiple Active Proxy (MAP) approach improves upon SAP by utilizing multiple agents at boundaries between processes to further reduce inter-process messages thereby improving scalability and performance. The experiments conducted using a range of models indicate that SAP provides 200% improvement over the base case and MAP provides 15% to 25% improvement over SAP depending on the model.

Categories and Subject Descriptors

I.6.8 [**Simulation and Modeling**]: Types of Simulation—
Discrete event, Parallel

General Terms

Algorithms; Performance

Keywords

Time Warp; Logical Process Migration; Ghosting; Performance Improvement

1. INTRODUCTION

Humanity continues to face a multitude of global socioeconomic challenges due to annual epidemics and punctuated pandemics of highly virulent zoonoses such as avian influenza (H5N1, H7N9) and the 2009 swine flu (H1N1) pandemic. Moreover, diseases such as seasonal Influenza are of global importance because they annually affect about 90 million people globally, causing about 250,000 to 500,000 human fatalities [32] and billions of dollars of annual losses due to recurrent epidemics both in humans and livestock.

Importance of Modeling and Simulation (M&S) in epidemiology: Epidemiological Modeling and Simulation (M&S) plays a pivotal role in study and analysis of diseases, phylodynamics, and design of prophylactic measures to contain epidemics [27, 21, 30]. Encouraged by advancement in computing technology and catalyzed by the need for detailed epidemiological analysis of emergent diseases, Agent-based Modeling (ABM) is gaining importance over traditional epidemiological modeling [27, 21, 30]. Figure 1 illustrates an ABM viewed in SEARUMS, the M&S environment used in this study, and Section 3 provides additional details on ABM.

Need for Parallel Simulation: Unfortunately, the advantages of ABMs are realized at the cost of significantly higher simulation execution time because ABMs are computationally demanding. For example, a single threaded (not counting garbage collector and other background Java threads) simulation of 3,088 (namely model M4 discussed in Section 9) mobile agents in SEARUMS requires about 25 hours on a 3.5 GHz Intel i7-3770K CPU. The issue of long simulation execution times is magnified by the need to conduct a large number of simulation replications (~200,000 replications are not uncommon [9]) with different parameters to analyze various scenarios.

A PDES Environment (prior research): Parallel simulation holds considerable promise to significantly decrease simulation execution times and thereby enabling effective use of ABMs. Accordingly, our earlier investigations focused on developing a modeling, simulation, and analysis environment called SEARUMS for study and analysis of the role

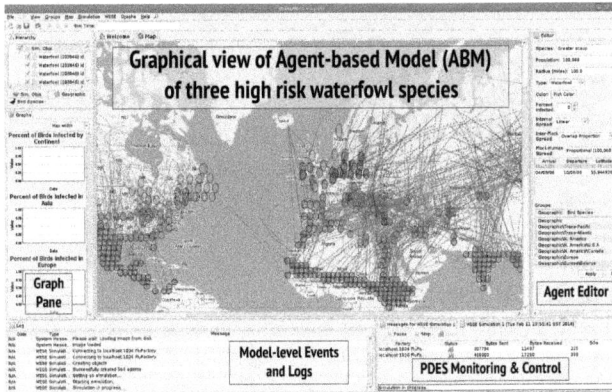

Figure 1: Screenshot of an Agent-based Model (ABM) viewed in SEARUMS, the M&S environment used in this study (see Section 2 for details.)

of migratory waterfowl in intercontinental spread of Avian Influenza [26, 25]. The graphical frontend is in Java while the simulation infrastructure operates as an optimistically synchronized Parallel Discrete Event Simulation (PDES) in C++. Figure 1 shows a screenshot of SEARUMS [26] while Section 2 presents an overview of the environment.

1.1 Motivation: Scalability Problems

The Time Warp synchronized PDES infrastructure of SE-ARUMS provided good performance improvement over the initial conservatively synchronized, Java-based multithread-ed kernel as reported in our earlier publication [24]. However, the PDES did not efficiently scale as the number of mobile agents in the model was increased even when optimism was throttled. The root cause of the issue was experimentally identified to be large number of Inter-Process Messages (IPMs) that increased synchronization overheads and degraded performance. IPMs arise because agents are initially partitioned to different compute nodes (on the compute cluster used for PDES) and they do not *physically* move (the C++ objects for an agent is fixed on a compute node), but only move *logically* by changing state. However, as illustrated in Figure 2, as agents logically move they have to interact with agents on a different compute node giving raise to IPMs. Consequently, as simulation time advances from t_0 to t_2 ($t_0 < t_1 < t_2$), the communication patterns change increasing IMPs.

IPMs negatively impact synchronization resulting in degraded scalability and performance as illustrated by the charts in Figure 3. The graphs in Figure 3 also illustrate the strong correlation (Pearson correlation coefficient $r = 0.98$, p-value < 0.0001) between IPMs (Figure 3(a)) and rollbacks (in Figure 3(b)) as well as a strong correlation ($r = 0.96$, p-value < 0.0001) between inter-process messages and simulation execution time (Figure 3(c)).

1.2 Solution Overview & Paper Outline

In continuation with the foregoing discussions, the volume of Inter-Process Messages (IPMs) arising due to movements of agents had to be reduced to improve scalability and performance. Reducing IPMs requires that interacting agents must be predominantly on the same compute node – implying that as agents *logically* migrate they must be corre-

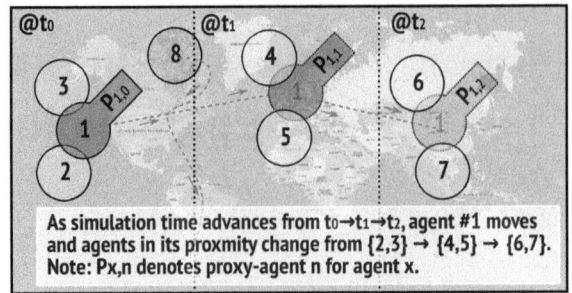

(a) Conceptual view of changes in commucation patterns due to movements of an agent

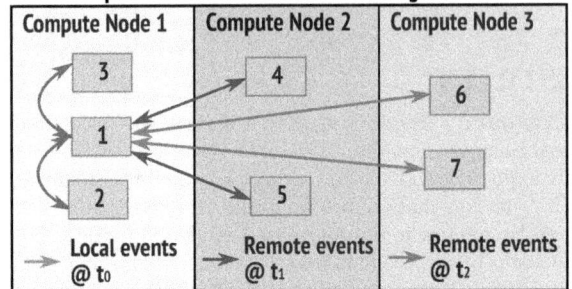

(b) Corresponding change from local to remote events as C++ objects for agents are on the same compute node.

Figure 2: Overview of Problem: Increase in Inter-Process Messages (IPMs) due to conceptual movement of agents

spondingly repartitioned or relocated to a different compute node.

Accordingly, the notion of *proxy* agents for each mobile agents was introduced on each compute node used for PDES. As an agent logically migrates across process boundaries, it logically deactivates itself after activating an appropriate proxy on a different compute node. Therefore, only one proxy-agent is active at any given time. This strategy, called Single Active Proxy (SAP) approach, is discussed in further detail in Section 5. SAP essentially accomplishes logical (rather than physical [18]) process migration, events thereby reducing IPMs.

However, as detailed in Section 6, the SAP approach still experienced performance issues at boundary cases when an agent's neighborhood spans two more partitions. Consequently, a Multiple Active Proxy (MAP) approach is proposed to address three different boundary cases that arose in SAP approach. The MAP approach extends the SAP approach by permitting multiple proxies to be active at the boundary cases when an agent spans two or more partitions to minimize IPMs. Section 7 presents the MAP approach followed by Section 8 that contrasts SAP and MAP with related research investigations. Section 9 discusses results from various experiments conducted to assess SAP and MAP approaches. Section 10 concludes the paper by summarizing the outcomes and inferences drawn from this paper.

2. SEARUMS: M&S ENVIRONMENT

SEARUMS is the epidemiological modeling, parallel simulation, and analysis software system used in this study. An architectural overview of SEARUMS is shown in Figure 4 and a screenshot of its Graphical User Interface (GUI) is

Number of inter-process messages (exchanged over network)

The following data point deviates from nominal curve (dotted line) due to Boundary Cases (BCs) BC #2 and BC #3 discussed further in the paper arising due to partitioning. As the number of cores increases, the effects occur consistently, as per expectations.

(a) Inter-Process Messages (IPMs)

Optimistic Synchronization overheads

The chart shows strong correlation between inter-process messages and rollbacks, which impact PDES efficiency and performance.

(b) Rollbacks

Scalability issues observed in a model

Data for model model M3 that has 10,076 agents out of which 44 agents are mobile.

In all charts, the shaded area tracks the 95% confidence interval indicated by the vertical bars at each data point

(c) PDES execution time

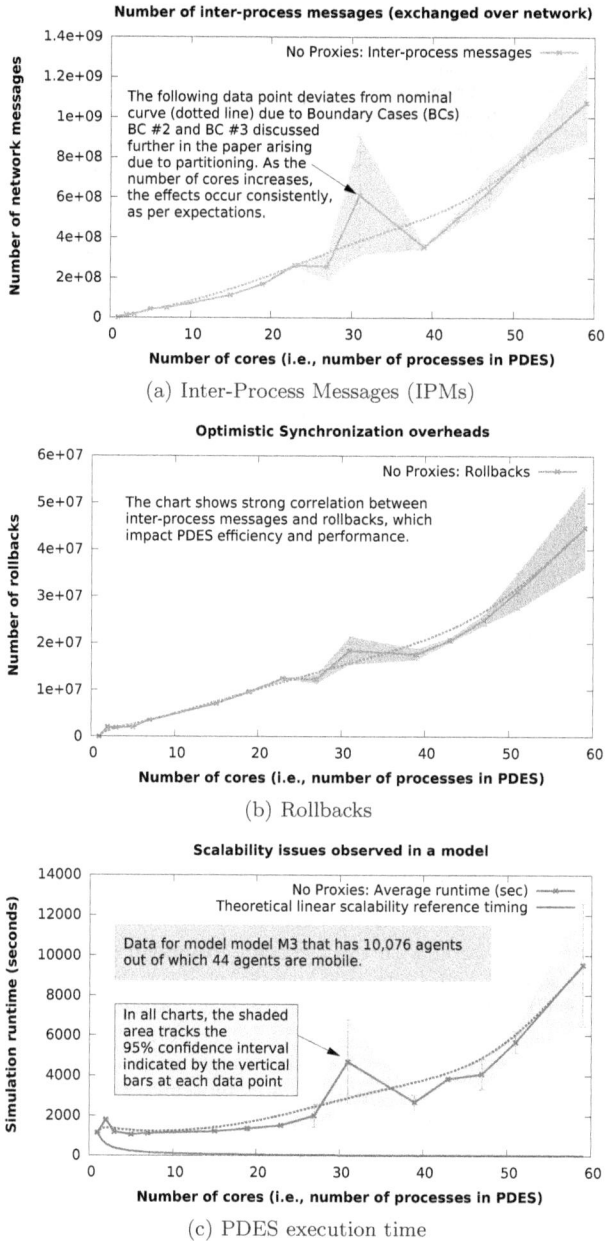

Figure 3: Experimental data (*without proposed solution* from model M3 discussed in Section 9) illustrating lack of scalability in PDES execution

shown in Figure 1. The GUI and associated frontend components have been developed in Java. The frontend modules enable execution of simulations in an offline, non-GUI mode to ease experimental analysis. These modules also handle partitioning of model using several different strategies.

The backend parallel simulation infrastructure of SEARUMS has been developed in C++ using WESE. WESE is a general purpose, web-enabled, Time Warp synchronized framework that eases development of parallel and distributed simulations [22]. It has been developed by suitably extending the WARPED simulation kernel [6] which provides the core Time Warp infrastructure. WESE further customizes

WARPED to provide web-based features for modeling, parallel simulation, I/O stream centralization, monitoring, and control.

In WESE a `Factory` is deployed on a compute node and acts as an agent repository as well as a simulation server that is part of a PDES. The `communication subsystem` can be configured to operate using different network protocols and handles the tasks of interacting with other WESE factories used for PDES. A `session manager` (on each `Factory` used for PDES) is used to coordinate, monitor, and control a PDES. The `session manager` also handles the task of creating local agents partitioned to execute on the `Factory`.

Life cycle activates of agents along with inter-agent interactions are accomplished by suitably scheduling various virtual timestamped events. In order to facilitate discovery of neighbors, agents report change in their position to one or more `EcoArea` agents and interrogate the `EcoArea` agents to identify neighboring agents. Neighbor discovery and other event-driven interactions occur only when needed and do not follow an High Level Architecture (HLA) type publish-subscribe approach.

Agents executing on a compute node share a scheduling system for management of virtual timestamped events generated during simulation. Therefore, events exchanged between agents on the same WESE compute node never cause rollbacks. However, the agents are not coerced into synchronizing with each other. Conversely, inter-node events, that are exchanged over the network give raise to straggler events resulting in rollbacks. The Time Warp infrastructure of WESE uses traditional state saving and rollback-based mechanism to recover from causal violations. A Global Virtual Time (GVT) based approach is used for garbage collection and management of optimistic I/O streams. Further details on the various software modules constituting the frontend and backed of SEARUMS is available in the literature [24, 26].

3. BACKGROUND: EPIDEMIC MODELS

Modeling and Simulation (M&S) plays a pivotal role in epidemiological analysis, phylodynamics, bionomics, and design of prophylactic measures to contain epidemics [27, 21, 30]. Epidemiological models are classified into Equation-based models (EBMs) (also called compartmental models), Individual-based Models (IBMs), and Agent-based Models (ABMs) [27, 21, 30]. EBMs use Ordinary Differential Equations (ODEs) to model transition of population between disease states or compartments such as: Susceptible $\rightarrow$ Infected $\rightarrow$ Recovered (SIR) [3]. Unlike EBMs that model the population as homogeneous aggregate compartments, IBMs model individuals in the population to explore heterogeneity, phylodynamics, antigenic drift, and other important epidemiological phenomena. However, IBMs are stochastic models and typically do not embody geospatial characteristics of diseases [21, 30].

Agent-based Models (ABMs) further extend IBMs to provide additional details in interactions between individuals, including geospatial characteristics, enabling in depth analysis of various phenomena and prophylactic measures [21, 27]. In contrast to EBMs, ABMs are descriptive rather than prescriptive models. Consequently, ABMs are most effective in epidemiological analysis of emergent diseases whose characteristics are not well understood [21, 27]. Furthermore, unlike EBMs and IBMs, ABMs can be readily extended to embody other aspects of the system. Moreover, ABMs enable more vivid and intuitive temporo-geospatial visualization for various analysis. However, the advantages of ABMs are realized at the cost of increased simulation execution times because ABMs are computationally demanding. Nevertheless, ABMs are gaining importance because PDES methodologies coupled with proliferation of affordable supercomputing provide an effective solution to meet computational demands making ABM an attractive approach. The investigations reported in this paper focus on improving scalability and performance of parallel simulation of spatially explicit, epidemiological ABMs.

4. MODELS IN SEARUMS

The SEARUMS models used in this study are agent-based, spatially-explicit models of global epidemiology of avian influenza. The Agents embody the classical SIR (Susceptible → Infected → Removed) mathematical models [3] and are used to describe the epidemiological behaviors of the the three salient entities, namely: waterfowl, poultry, and humans. The agents are specifically designed to ease effective use of real world statistical data. The conceptual design of each agent is based on discrete time Markov processes [26] that implement the SIR mathematical model. Figure 5 presents an overview of the Markov processes along with the SIR mathematical model constituting the three main agents in the models used in this study. Various discrete state transitions and inter-agent interactions are accomplished via virtual timestamped events.

The spatial interactions between agents are modeled using one or more `EcoArea` agents that represents Earth's surface. Typically, in a PDES the number of `EcoArea` agents correspond to the number of compute nodes used for simulation. The Earth's surface is evenly subdivided into non-overlapping regions and assigned to each `EcoArea`. `EcoAreas` receive updates from agents overlapping its area whenever an agent changes selected attributes, such as: current coordinate, infection percentages, and population changes. The `EcoArea` components tracks agents in its purview and uses the information to detect and trigger interactions between overlapping agents by scheduling events.

4.1 Model Generation and Validation

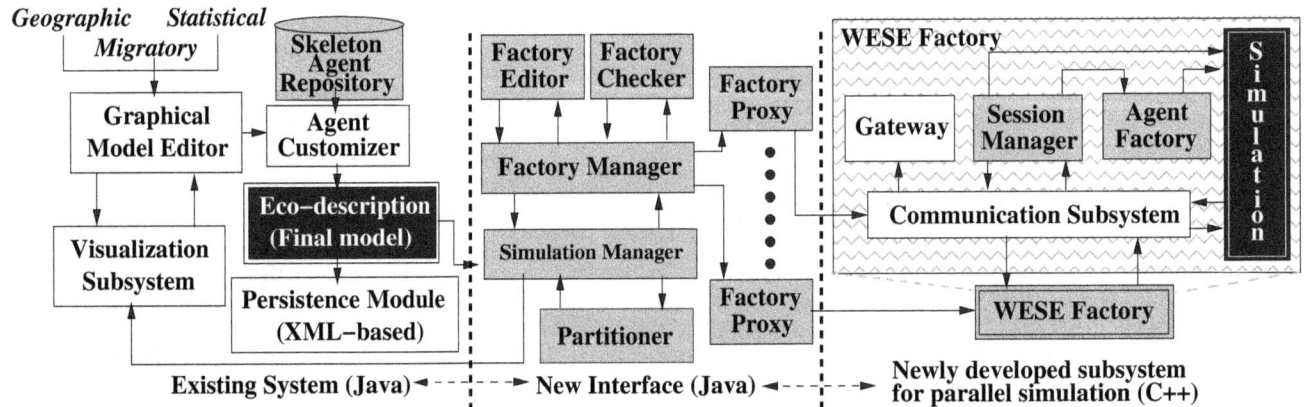

$$ds/dt = \lambda - [\mu + \lambda(t)]s(t)$$
$$d\lambda/dt = [\nu + \mu]\lambda(t)[R_0 s(t) - 1]$$

where $s(t)$ is the proportion of population remaining susceptible at time t, and R_0 is the basic reproductive rate, μ is death rate, ν is recovery rate, and $\lambda(t)$ is infection rate.

Figure 5: Overview of Susceptible → Infected → Recovered (SIR) state transitions in various agents.

The models used in this study have been developed using real-world statistical data on: waterfowl migration [12], high risk waterfowl species [10], global poultry population and distribution [11], and global human population distribution information [28]. We have already published approaches for verification of the models using bioinformatics and viral isolates [23] as well as statistical analysis against temporo-geospatial data on epidemic outbreaks reported by the World Health Organization (WHO) [25]. Readers are referred to our earlier publications [26, 25, 23] for details on model generation, verification, and various analysis. However, pertinent sections of our prior publications are included in the appendix.

5. SINGLE ACTIVE PROXY (SAP)

In continuation with the foregoing discussions in Section 1.1 about the problem, the volume of Inter-Process Messages (IPMs) arising due to movements of agents had to be reduced to improve scalability and performance. Reducing IPMs requires that interacting agents must be predominantly on the same compute node – implying that as agents *logically* migrate they must be correspondingly repartitioned or relocated to a different compute node. Accordingly, the notion of *proxy* agents was introduced in the simulation. Proxy agents are agents that are automatically created for each mobile agent on each compute node used for PDES as

Figure 4: Architectural overview of SEARUMS showing core software subsystems.

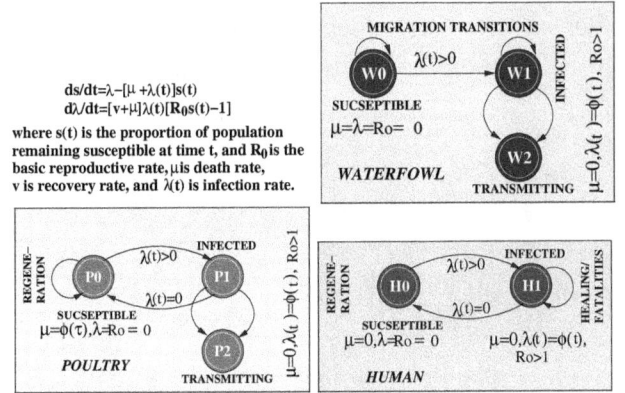

130

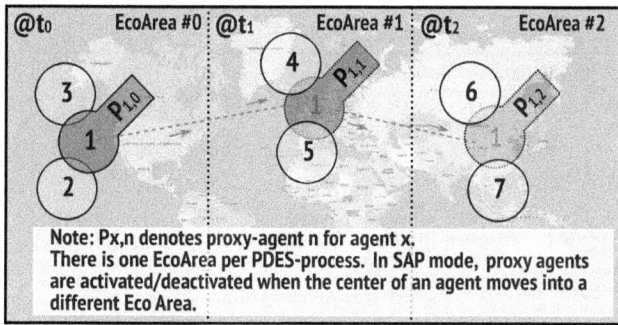

Figure 6: Overview of Single Active Proxy (SAP) approach (with 3 EcoArea agents on 3 PDES-processes)

Algorithm 1: Single Active Proxy (SAP) Approach

```
 1  begin initialization(state)
 2    if inLocalEcoArea(state->latitude,
          state->longitude) then
 3        state->isActive = true;
 4        registerWithEcoArea();
 5        scheduleLifeCycleEvents();
 6    else
 7        state->isActive = false;
 8    end if
 9  end initialization
10  begin processEvent(state, event)
11    if state->isActive then
12        proessEvent(event);
13        if ! inLocalEcoArea(state->latitude,
              state->longitude) then
14            state->activeProxy =
                  unregisterFromEcoArea();
15            activateProxy(state, state->activeProxy);
16            state->isActive = false;
17        end if
18    else
19        if isProxyEvent(event) then
20            activate();
21            state->isActive = true;
22        else
23            rescheduleEvent(state->activeProxy,
                  event->recvTime + DELTA);
24        end if
25    end if
26  end processEvent
```

shown in Figure 6. As the center of an agent logically moves across `EcoArea` boundaries, it logically deactivates itself after activating an appropriate proxy on a different compute node. Therefore, only one proxy-agent is active at any given time and consequently this strategy is called Single Active Proxy (SAP) approach.

An simplified pseudo code for the SAP approach is shown in Algorithm 1. Initially, one deactivated proxy agent is automatically created on each PDES-process for every mobile agent in a given model. Deactivated agents do not perform any operations and remain dormant in the simulation. However, based on the initial geographical location of an agent, the appropriate proxy activates itself and performs the normal operations of the agent. When the agent migrates across its local `EcoArea`, the active proxy first deactivates itself *logically* removing itself from the simulation. The proxy then schedules an activation event (which includes the current state) to the appropriate proxy object on a different `EcoArea`. For example when agent #1 in Figure 6 moves from `EcoArea` #0 to `EcoArea` #1 proxy agent $P_{1,0}$ deactivates itself while activating proxy agent $P_{1,1}$. The activated proxy then resumes life cycle activities for the agent and as a consequence, the SAP approach essentially accomplishes logical (rather than physical [18]) process migration.

The dormant proxies have an extra role of forwarding events (as they may already be scheduled) to the active proxy. Activation, deactivation, and forwarding of events are performed using sub-simulation cycles. Specifically, simulation time is defined as a double precision value and fractional times are used to represent subcycles. Consequently, the overall resulting state of various agents is identical with the base case (without SAP). Moreover, tools for post-simulation analysis of simulation logs ignore the subcycles. Consequently, the filtered simulation logs used for various analysis are identical in all cases.

6. BOUNDARY CASES IN SAP

The Single Active Proxy (SAP) approach provided significant improvement in scalability and performance over the base case as discussed in Section 9. However, the simulations continued to experience some performance degradation as the number of mobile agents in the model increased. Experimental analysis indicated that the SAP approach still experienced increased inter-process messages and rollbacks

when an agent spans two or more partitions, as enumerated in the following three different Boundary Cases (BCs):

1. **BC #1**: The first case occurs when agents transitioning from one `EcoArea` to another across PDES-process boundaries as illustrated for agent #1 in Figure 7. In this transitional period only one proxy is active in SAP and has to interact with agents in two different PDES-processes resulting in increased Inter-Process Messages (IPMs) and degrades performance in models with many mobile agents.

2. **BC #2**: The second case occurs when a mobile agent is resting but happens to spans across two `EcoAreas` as illustrated by the set of agents {#6, #7, #8} in Figure 7. Since agents span two or more `EcoAreas`, it gives raise to copious amounts of Inter-Process Messages (IPMs) which results in degraded performance. The frequency of this scenario steadily increases as the number of `EcoAreas` or partitions increases. This issue conspicuously manifests itself even without SAP (as expected) as highlighted by the chart in Figure 3(a).

3. **BC #3**: The third BC occurs when an agent's movement oscillates between two or more partitions, similar to the pathway of agent #9 shown in Figure 7. In this scenario, proxy agents often experience cascading rollbacks which degrades performance.

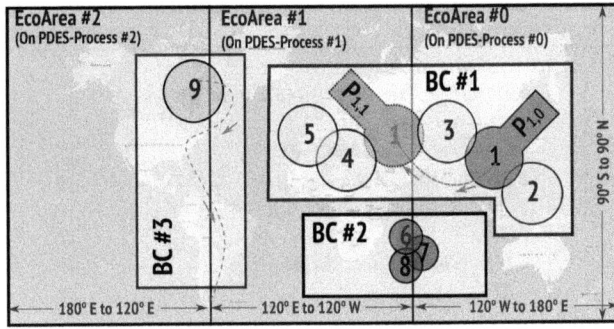

Figure 7: Illustration of three Boundary Cases (BCs) that impact SAP approach

7. MULTIPLE ACTIVE PROXY (MAP)

The Multiple Active Proxy (MAP) approach is proposed to extend SAP approach and address the three boundary cases (BCs) discussed in Section 6 to provide a more comprehensive solution. The MAP approach extends the SAP approach by permitting multiple proxies to be active at the boundary cases when an agent spans two or more partitions. Recollect that an agent has one proxy preallocated on each EcoArea (*i.e.*, PDES-process). Consequently, in MAP approach two or more proxies can be active when boundary cases arise. The pseudo code in Algorithm 2 provides additional details about the MAP implementation.

In MAP approach, each active proxy "ghosts" operations of related proxies and handles interactions with other agents on its local partition, thereby eliminating Inter-Process Messages (SAP) that occur at boundary cases in SAP mode. Moreover, each proxy agent also performs various life cycle tasks by scheduling events to itself. Ghosting of life cycle tasks by active proxies does increase the net number of events in the simulation. However, these events are local events that do not significantly degrade performance.

At the end of handling local interactions, the active proxies exchange messages (which are inter-process messages) to consistently update the states of all active proxies using a straightforward protocol. Each proxy maintains a summary of location interactions which includes list of neighbors infected and amount of infection received from neighbors. The summary information is sent via timestamped events to other active proxies, if any. Upon receiving summary information from another active proxy, each proxy appropriately updates its local state. At the end of the phase of event exchanges all proxies have the same, consistent state. The straightforward protocol involves $O(n_a^2)$ events, where n_a is number of active proxies per agent. However, n_a is typically a small value (in the range 2 to 4) and therefore is not a significant overhead.

Once an agent no longer spans multiple partitions, relevant proxies deactivate themselves eliminating "ghosting" and the simulation continues to proceed in SAP mode. MAP minimizes the number of Inter-Process Messages (IPMs) at boundary cases thereby improving upon the efficiency gained by utilizing SAP. In this context, it must be noted that the final resulting state in both MAP and SAP approaches is the same as that of the original agent's state. Consequently, the results from the simulations used for various analysis are identical in all cases.

Algorithm 2: Multiple Active Proxy (MAP) Approach

```
 1  begin initialization(state)
 2      ecoAreas=ecoAreas(state->latitude,
        state->longitude);
 3      if localEcoArea ∈ ecoAreas then
 4          state->isActive = true;
 5          registerWithEcoArea();
 6          scheduleLifeCycleEvents();
 7      else
 8          state->isActive = false;
 9      end if
10  end initialization
11  begin processEvent(state, event)
12      if state->isActive then
13          prevEcoAreas=ecoAreas(state->latitude,
            state->longitude);
14          proessEvent(event);
15          if ! inLocalEcoArea(state->latitude,
            state->longitude) then
16              state->activeProxy =
                unregisterFromEcoArea();
17              state->isActive = false;
18          else
19              newEcoAreas=ecoAreas(state->latitude,
                state->longitude) - prevEcoAreas;
20              if newEcoAreas != φ then
21                  activeProxies(newEcoAreas);
22              end if
23          end if
            // Synchronize active proxy states
24          activeProxyStateCoherence();
25      else
26          if isProxyEvent(event) then
27              activate();
28              state->isactive = true;
29          else
30              rescheduleEvent(state->activeProxy,
                event->recvTime + DELTA);
31          end if
32      end if
33  end processEvent
```

---

8. RELATED RESEARCH

The proposed research is a novel integration several major topics in of Modeling and Simulation (M&S), including: agent-based epidemic modeling, spatially-explicit models, and optimistic PDES. Several investigations have been reported on these topics and this section compares the proposed research with some of the closely related investigations. Readers are referred to the references and literature for a more comprehensive survey of related works [26, 25].

Agent-based models (ABMs) have been employed for large scale epidemiological analyses for various diseases [7, 17]. Parker and Epstien [17] discusses the issues involved in design and development of a Java-based, Global-Scale Agent Model (GSAM) distributed platform for epidemiological modeling using over 6 billion interacting agents. Similar to GSAM, the proposed research avoids "physical" process migration but unlike GSAM the proposed research involves "logical" process migration using proxy agents. However, in contrast to agents in GSAM, the mobile agents in our model explicitly embody migration and inter-agent interactions without relying on contact matrices or contact networks [17]. Moreover, the agents in our research are different in that they do not represent a single entity but a collection of collocated entities, striking a better balance between model resolution and execution costs. Our modeling approach is useful for M&S of 21 billion migrating waterfowl using surveillance and satellite telemetry data for that is available only in aggregate forms [12].

The use of ABMs with explicit agent mobility distinguishes the proposed research from work from those reported by Barrett *et al* [1], Bisset *et al* [2], and Perumalla *et al* [19]. These three investigations use a reaction-diffusion approach involving contact graphs for epidemic modeling. The use of contact graphs or social networks for epidemic modeling has been discussed by other researchers as well [9, 15, 13]. Although, the migratory flyways for waterfowl are specified in our models, the contacts between agents are not preordained but discovered based on probabilistic movements of agents. However, similar to these three investigations we aim to utilize PDES to accelerate performance of epidemic simulations.

The proposed Single Active Proxy (SAP) and Multiple Active Proxies (MAP) approach discussed in Section 5 and Section 7 essentially accomplishes logical process migrations in contrast to physical process migration that has been extensively investigated in conservative as well as optimistic PDES [14, 18]. Unlike SAP that involves logical process migration, strategies involving physical movement of logical processes have been proposed for dynamic partitioning [20]. However, unlike the application-specific, logical migration accomplished by SAP, almost all of the efforts reported in the literature focus on providing a generic infrastructure for physical process migration. Consequently, the earlier investigations involve extensions to the underlying simulation kernel. On the other hand, the proposed investigations focus on model-level extensions that can be applied to both conservative and optimistic PDES.

The SAP and MAP approaches are distantly related to "ghosting" in multi-resolution simulations in which multiple representations of entities are maintained [29]. However, MAP approach is different than the concept of "ghosting" in that the agents are not at different resolutions and in fact strive to be identical copies of each other. Migration of portions of shared states for adaptive load management of multi-agent systems have been explored [16]. Similarly, distribution and maintenance of consistent states and sub-states is an integral aspect of the Data Distribution Management (DDM) service in the High Level Achitecture (HLA) [31]. In contrast, the MAP approach does not subdivide states of agents but aims to replicate complete, consistent state resulting multiple, identical proxy agents in the simulation. Furthermore, interactions between agents uses an on-demand request-response approach rather than the publish-subscribe approach used in HLA. Maintaining, identical coherent states for proxy agents also distinguishes MAP approach from the *passive* agent sharing approch used in RepastHPC [4]. In RepastHPC copies of agents are passive in that changes to the copies are not transmitted to the actual agent [4]. Conversely, in MAP changes to proxy agents are used to obtain a globally consistent state for the actual and proxy agents.

Table 1: Characteristics of models used for conducting the experiments

ID	Number of Agents			Total
	Waterfowl (mobile)	Poultry (stationary)	Humans (stationary)	
M1	44	1314	1314	2672
M2	44	4251	2160	6455
M3	44	4763	5269	10076
M4	3088	0	0	3088

9. EXPERIMENTS

The experiments conducted to evaluate the effectiveness of the Single Active Proxy (SAP) and Multiple Active Proxies (MAP) mode were performed using four different models. Table 1 shows the number of agents constituting each models. `Waterfowl` agents indicate the number of mobile entities while `Poultry` and `Human` agents are stationary. The migratory flyways of the waterfowl and their population has been generated from GROMS database [12] [25, 12] and validated using statistical and bioinformatics analysis [25, 23].

The models M1, M2, and M3 have a varying number of humans and poultry agents at different scales of detail. Agent data at were generated from poultry and human Geographic Information Systems (GIS) data obtained from NASA's SEDAC database [28]. Unlike the first three models in Table 1, model M4 serves as a stress-test case in which all agents are mobile.

All the experiments were conducted on a distributed memory super computing cluster running Red Hat Enterprise Linux (RHEL 6.5). Each compute node had two hex-core Intel Xeon X5650 CPUs @ 2.67 GHz (with 12 MB L2 cache) yielding 5333 bogomips on each of the 12 cores. Each compute node had 48 GB of RAM averaging to 4 GB per core. The nodes were interconnected using QDR infiniband interconnect. Note that the experiments were performed using the non-GUI mode supported by SEARUMS to avoid GUI overheads. Furthermore, the Java frontend was executed on a separate compute node and model-logs were turned off to eliminate any resource contentions or I/O overheads for all performance tests reported in this section.

9.1 Calibration

The objective of the first phase of experimentation was to identify the optimal simulation configuration for the base case with did not utilize the SAP or MAP optimization. The objective was to identify suitable settings to obtain the best possible performance for base case comparisons. The medium sized model M2 was used for these experiments. For all of the tests the surface of Earth was vertically partitioned because most migratory flyways are in North-South direction. Consequently, vertical partitioning minimizes interprocess messages even in the base case. Effects of different strategies for partitioning this model have been reported in our earlier publication [24]. The number of `EcoAreas` correspond to the number of processes used for PDES with one `EcoArea` assigned to each PDES-process. Furthermore, each `EcoArea` handles agents in an evenly divided, nonoverlapping vertical region of Earth's surface.

The charts in Figure 8 illustrate the effect of three Time Warp parameters that influence overall performance of the simulations [24]. The calibration experiments enable iden-

(a) Calibration of Polling delay

(b) Calibration of Time Window

(c) Calibration of GVT duration

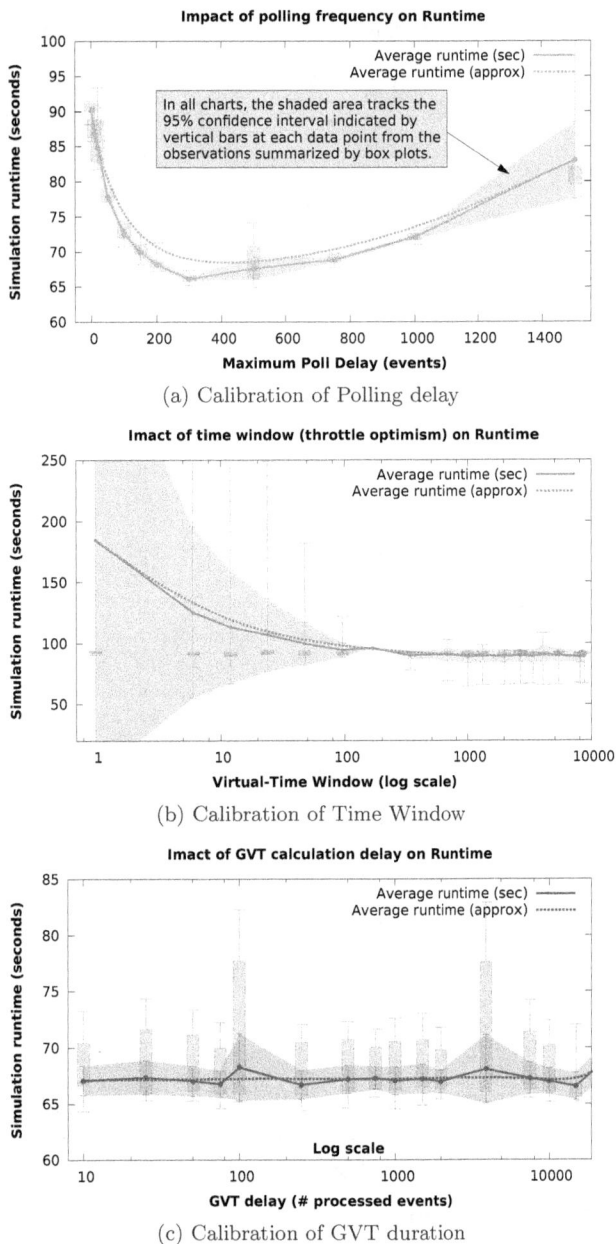

Figure 8: Experimental calibration (*without proposed solution*) of influential parameters to identify optimal settings for base case measurements. The tests were conducted using 12 PDES-processes (on 4 compute nodes, 3 processes per node)

tification of suitable settings for these three parameters for a given computational platform and minimize noise in the experimental data. The graph in Figure 8(a) illustrates the effect of changing the maximum delay between successive checks for Inter-process Messages (IPM) arriving over the network. Consistent with expectations, neither small nor large settings are effective with ideal value lying at the inflection point of the characteristic curve.

The need for controlling optimism is pervasive to spatially-explicit, optimistic simulations running on both shared and distributed memory architectures [5, 8, 24]. The chart in Figure 8(b) illustrates the effect of varying the time window used for throttling. Small time windows curtail optimism too aggressively and consequently the PDES cannot use available optimism effectively. Consequently, a significant variation in runtimes is observed because the simulation becomes network-bound, waiting for messages to arrive. On the other hand, when the time window is large the simulation experiences more overheads due to rollbacks and runtimes signficiantly vary hindering effective comparisons. Accordingly, an intermediate value of 144 hours (in simulation-time units) corresponding to the minimum variance point has been used.

The Global Virtual Time (GVT) computation delay parameter had the least impact on the simulation as shown in Figure 8(c). The impact of GVT period is not pronounced because the compute nodes have large caches and RAM. However, as expected, the variance in timings increases for small and large GVT values. Therefore a intermediate value of 4000 events has been used for experimentation. The charts in Figure 8 indicate that the PDES is most sensitive to polling delay and least sensitive to GVT delay.

9.2 Experimental Evaluation of SAP & MAP

The influential parameter settings identified via the calibration discussed in Section 9.1 were used to conduct all the experiments for evaluating the proposed Single Active Proxy (SAP) and Multiple Active Proxy (MAP) modes. The observations collated from experiments conducted using a range of configurations with for different models (see Table 1) are shown by the charts in Figure 9 and Figure 10. The x-axis of all the charts corresponds to the number of parallel PDES-processes (*i.e.*, Linux processes), with each process running on an independent core. The solid lines on each one of the charts tracks average values obtained from 10 runs. The corresponding dotted lines show the approximate curve fitting for the observations to emphasize general trends in the data due to the occurrence of Boundary Cases (BCs) as discussed in Section 6. The error bar at each of the data points indicates the 95% confidence interval computed from the 10 runs and the lightly shaded region tracks the confidence interval to highlight statistical significance of the observations.

In all the charts in Figure 9 and Figure 10, the `base case` configuration corresponds to simulations conducted without the use of proxies. However, the base case curves are not included in the charts for model `M4` because the configuration without proxies was practically unusable due to long simulation execution times (over 24 hours with over 32 cores) and the experiments had to be abandoned. The long simulation execution times arise because of the large number of mobile agents in the model. Note that, although model `M4` has fewer total number of agents than even `M2` model, all of its agents are mobile waterfowl agents. Consequently, model `M4` is a "worst case" model for simulating with the base case configuration (*i.e.*, without proxies) resulting in long execution times.

The charts for model `M1` in Figure 9 already highlight the effectiveness of the Single Active Proxy (SAP) and Multiple Active Proxies (MAP) approaches. However, for `M1` both the SAP and MAP approaches are pretty close in runtime for most configurations, with the MAP approach performing about 10% to 15% better. The small difference is expected because the MAP approach operates as SAP ex-

134

cept for boundary cases. Furthermore, the M1 model is the smallest and lacks sufficient workload to effectively utilize the available compute power. Consequently, even with SAP and MAP the number of rollbacks offset advantages of PDES and the time for simulation actually increases.

The graphs for model M2 in Figure 9 and model M3 in Figure 10 illustrate the advantages of SAP and MAP approach. Furthermore, the advantages of MAP is a bit more prominent in these two models. The SAP approach consistently outperforms the the base case by about 2x while the MAP approach provides another 15% to 25% performance boost on top of SAP. In these two models the overall effect of MAP is still muted because the models do not have many mobile agents in them. Nevertheless, the advantages of MAP are a bit more prominent as the number of PDES-processes (synonymous to number of cores used for PDES) are increased. The MAP approach provides much better scalability that SAP for both M2 and M3 models. On the other hand, the SAP approach starts experiencing degradation in scalability around 20 cores and 40 cores for models M2 and M4 respectively. The degradation in scalability occurs sooner for M2 than for M3 because M2 is a smaller model with less workload and with increased availability of compute power the model optimistically advances only to suffer from increased rollbacks, as evidenced by the charts in Figure 9.

The advantages of MAP approach is more pronounced in the case of model M4 that has a large number of mobile agents. The abundance of mobile agents increases the chances of Boundary Cases (BCs) discussed in Section 6 in SAP as the number of PDES-processes are increased. The approximated runtime curve for M4 shown in Figure 10 shows that initially the runtime decreases with increase in PDES-processes demonstrating good scalability. However, the scalability tappers off around 40 cores and further increase in PDES-processes worsens the runtime. However, the MAP approach continues to provide much better scalability and about 20% to 25% performance improvement in the configurations with more than 25 PDES processes. Reprising the discussion from earlier paragraph, the base case data for model M4 are not shown in in Figure 10 as the experiments were abandoned due to extremely long simulation times that exceeded 24 hours in several configurations.

The experimental results shown in Figure 9 and Figure 10 also illustrate the strong correlation between Inter-Process Messages (IPMs), the number of rollbacks, and simulation execution time. Note that the count of IPMs includes anti-messages used by the Time Warp protocol for optimistic synchronization and increase in rollbacks degrades scalability and performance of the PDES. However, the SAP approach is effective in eliminating a large fraction of IMPs by essentially accomplishing logical process migration using a set of proxies. Furthermore, the MAP approach improves upon SAP by further reducing IPMs and consequently providing more reliable scalability.

10. CONCLUSIONS

The application of simulation-based analysis using spatially explicit, agent-based models is gaining momentum for epidemiological analysis of emergent diseases such as avian influenza [27, 21, 30]. We have developed a modeling, parallel simulation, and analysis environment called SEARUMS to meet the computational demands of agent-based models. In SEARUMS, Parallel Discrete Event Simulation (PDES) is

accomplished by partitioning various agents and the geospatial components used to coordinate various interactions. The PDES uses Time Warp algorithm for optimistic synchronization to effectively utilize inherent parallelism in the model [24] and operated well for models with many stationary agents but few mobile agents.

However, the optimistically synchronized PDES backend of SEARUMS experienced performance degradation when the number of mobile agents in the model were increased. The investigation reported in this paper focused on identifying and addressing the scalability and ensuing performance degradation. Exploratory investigations (presented in Section 1.1) identified that the large volume of Inter-Process Messages (IPMs) exchanged over the network was magnifying synchronization issues resulting in degraded scalability. The IPMs arise because as the mobile agents *logically* move they have to interact with agents on a different compute node causing increase in volume of IPMs.

The investigations proposed and assessed the effectiveness of using *proxy* agents on each PDES-process for each agent. Specifically, as an agent migrates across process boundaries, a proxy deactivates while activating another proxy on a different process. Initially, only one proxy was permitted to be active at any given time resulting in a Single Active Proxy (SAP) approach. The SAP approach provided significant performance improvements as indicated by the experimental results discussed in Section 9. However, the SAP approach did not address bottlenecks arising due to three different Boundary Cases (BCs) as discussed in Section 6. Consequently, a Multiple Active Proxy (MAP) approach was proposed and assessed.

The Multiple Active Proxy (MAP) approach extends SAP approach and permits multiple proxy agents to be active only in boundary case scenarios while operating in SAP mode otherwise. The MAP mode essentially permits "ghosting" of an agent where multiple active proxies handle local interactions occurring on the same PDES-process and using Inter-Process Messages (IPMS) to maintain consistent states. Experimental evaluation of the MAP approach discussed in Section 9 indicates that the MAP approach provides more reliable scalability along with a modest performance boost of 15% to 25% on top of SAP.

The SAP and MAP approaches are implemented at the model-level using the default infrastructure provided by the PDES kernel. Since the proposed solutions do not depend on any special support from the underlying PDES kernel, they can be readily implemented in any infrastructure, including conservatively synchronized parallel simulations. Nevertheless, the MAP approach involving "ghosting" can be incorporated as general-purpose infrastructure in PDES kernels. The optimized PDES significantly reduces simulation execution times, easing exploratory analyses, and highlights the current and future importance of parallel simulations in epidemiology, bionomics, and related fields.

11. REFERENCES

[1] C. L. Barrett, K. R. Bisset, S. G. Eubank, X. Feng, and M. V. Marathe. Episimdemics: An efficient algorithm for simulating the spread of infectious disease over large realistic social networks. In *Proceedings of the 2008 ACM/IEEE Conference on Supercomputing*, SC '08, pages 37:1–37:12, Piscataway, NJ, USA, 2008. IEEE Press.

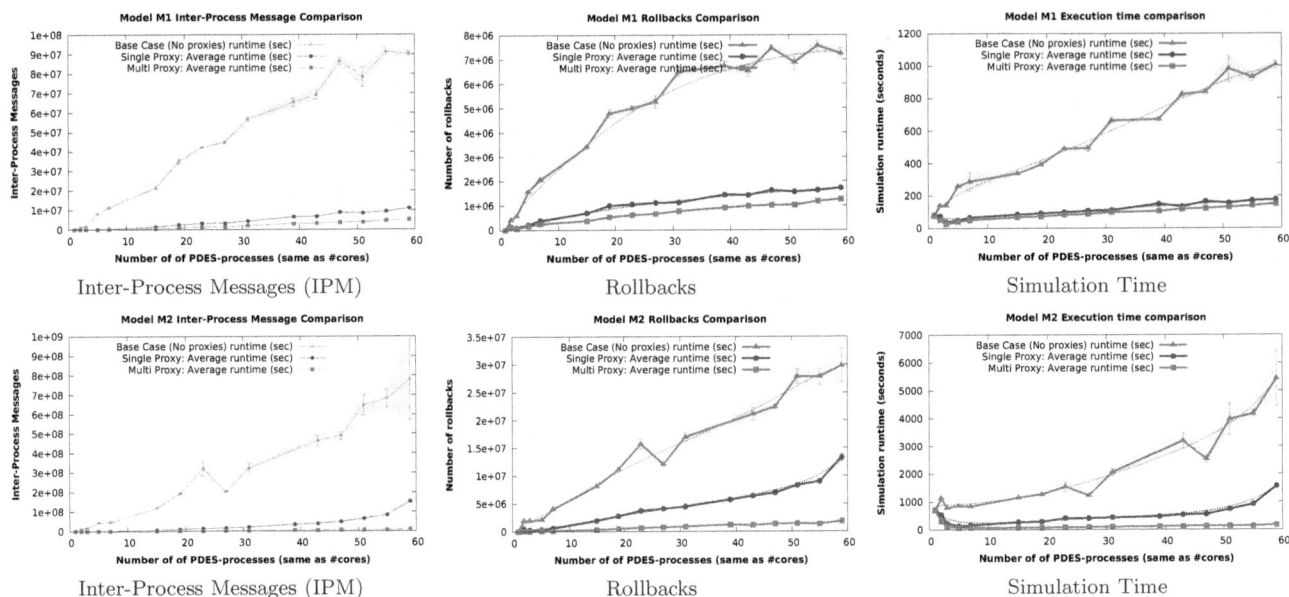

Inter-Process Messages (IPM)	Rollbacks	Simulation Time

Figure 9: Comparison of Inter-Process Messages (IPM), rollbacks, and simulation execution time for the models M1 and M2 shown in Table 1 in the following three configurations: no proxies (base case), Single Active Proxy (SAP) approach, and Multiple Active Proxies (MAP) approach. Note that number of PDES-processes is the same as the number of CPU-cores used for simulation (one PDES-process per CPU-core).

[2] K. R. Bisset, J. Chen, X. Feng, V. A. Kumar, and M. V. Marathe. Epifast: A fast algorithm for large scale realistic epidemic simulations on distributed memory systems. In *Proceedings of the 23rd International Conference on Supercomputing*, ICS '09, pages 430–439, New York, NY, USA, 2009. ACM.

[3] F. Brauer and C. Castillo-Chavez. *Mathematical Models for Communicable Diseases*. SIAM, 3600 Market Street, Philadelphia, PA 19104-2688, USA, 2013.

[4] N. Collier and M. North. Parallel agent-based simulation with repast for high performance computing. *SIMULATION*, 2012.

[5] E. Deelman and B. K. Szymanski. Simulating spatially explicit problems on high performance architectures. *Journal of Parallel and Distributed Computing*, 62(3):446–467, Mar. 2002.

[6] T. Dickman, S. Gupta, and P. A. Wilsey. Event pool structures for pdes on many-core beowulf clusters. In *Proceedings of the 2013 ACM SIGSIM Conference on Principles of Advanced Discrete Simulation*, SIGSIM-PADS '13, pages 103–114, New York, NY, USA, 2013. ACM.

[7] J. M. Epstein. Modelling to contain pandemics. *Nature*, 460:687–687, 2009.

[8] S. Eubank. Scalable, efficient epidemiological simulation. In *Proceedings of the 2002 ACM symposium on Applied computing*, pages 139–145, Mar. 2002.

[9] N. M. Ferguson, D. A. T. Cummings, C. Fraser1, J. C. Cajka, P. C. Cooley, and D. S. Burke. Strategies for mitigating an influenza pandemic. *Nature*, 442:448–452, 2006.

[10] M. Gilbert, X. Xiao, J. Domenech, J. Lubroth, V. Martin, and J. Slingenbergh. Anatidae migration in the western palearctic and spread of highly pathogenic avian influenza H5N1 virus. *Emerging Infectious Diseases*, 12(11), 2006.

[11] GLiPHA. Global Livestock Production and Health Atlas (GLiPHA): Animal Production and Health Division of Food and Agriculture Organization of the United Nations, 2014.

[12] GROMS. Global Register of Migratory Species (GROMS): Summarising Knowledge about Migratory Species for Conservation, Jul 2013.

[13] M. E. Halloran, N. M. Ferguson, S. Eubank, J. Ira M. Longini, D. A. T. Cummings, B. Lewis, S. Xu, C. FraserÂğ, A. Vullikanti, T. C. Germann, D. Wagener, R. Beckman, K. Kadau, C. Barrett, C. A. Macken, D. S. Burke, and P. Cooley. Modeling targeted layered containment of an influenza pandemic in the united states. *Proceedings of the National Academy of Sciences of the United States of America*, 105(12):4639–4644, Mar. 2008.

[14] S. Jafer, Q. Liu, and G. Wainer. Synchronization methods in parallel and distributed discrete-event simulation. *Simulation Modelling Practice and Theory*, 30(0):54 – 73, 2013.

[15] I. M. Longini, A. Nizam, S. Xu, K. Ungchusak, W. Hanshaoworakul, D. A. T. Cummunings, and M. E. Halloran. Containing pandemic influenza at the source. *Sience*, 309(5737):1083–1087, 2005.

[16] T. Oguara, D. Chen, G. Theodoropoulos, B. Logan, and M. Lees. An adaptive load management mechanism for distributed simulation of multi-agent systems. In *Distributed Simulation and Real-Time Applications, 2005. DS-RT 2005 Proceedings. Ninth*

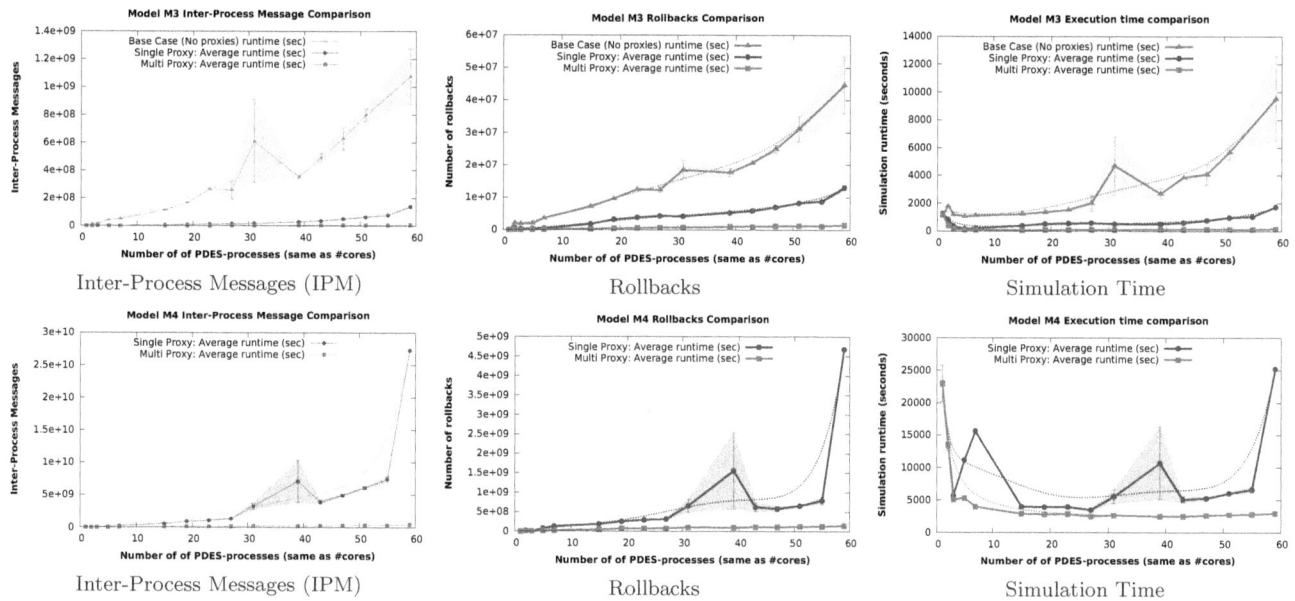

Figure 10: Comparison of Inter-Process Messages (IPM), rollbacks, and simulation execution time for the models M3 and M4 shown in Table 1 in the following three configurations: no proxies (base case), Single Active Proxy (SAP) approach, and Multiple Active Proxies (MAP) approach. Note that number of PDES-processes is the same as the number of CPU-cores used for simulation (one PDES-process per CPU-core).

IEEE International Symposium on, pages 179–186, Oct 2005.

[17] J. Parker and J. M. Epstein. A distributed platform for global-scale agent-based models of disease transmission. *ACM Trans. Model. Comput. Simul.*, 22(1):2:1–2:25, Dec. 2011.

[18] S. Peluso, D. Didona, and F. Quaglia. Supports for transparent object-migration in pdes systems. *Journal of Simulation*, 6:279–293, 2012.

[19] K. S. Perumalla and S. K. Seal. Discrete event modeling and massively parallel execution of epidemic outbreak phenomena. *SIMULATION*, 2012.

[20] P. Peschlow, T. Honecker, and P. Martini. A flexible dynamic partitioning algorithm for optimistic distributed simulation. In *Principles of Advanced and Distributed Simulation, 2007. PADS '07. 21st International Workshop on*, pages 219–228, June 2007.

[21] L. L. Pullum and O. Ozmen. Early results from metamorphic testing of epidemiological models. In *BioMedical Computing (BioMedCom), 2012 ASE/IEEE International Conference on*, pages 62–67, 2012.

[22] D. M. Rao. *Study of Dynamic Component Substitution*. PhD thesis, University of Cincinnati, 2003.

[23] D. M. Rao. Enhancing temporo-geospatial epidemiological analysis of h5n1 influenza using phylogeography. In *Proceedings of the Great Lakes Bioinformatics Conference 2014 (GLBIO'14)*, University of Cincinnati, Ohio, USA, May 2014. International Society for Computational Biology (ISCB). (submitted).

[24] D. M. Rao and A. Chernyakhovsky. Parallel simulation of the global epidemiology of avian

influenza. In *Proceedings of the 2008 Winter Simulation Conference*, pages 1583–1591, Dec. 2008.

[25] D. M. Rao and A. Chernyakhovsky. Automatic generation of global agent-based model of migratory waterfowl for epidemiological analysis. In *Proceedings of the 27th European Simulation and Modelling Conference (ESM'2013)*, Lancaster University, Lancaster, UK, oct 2013. EuroSis. Best paper award.

[26] D. M. Rao, A. Chernyakhovsky, and V. Rao. Modeling and analysis of global epidemiology of avian influenza. *Environmental Modelling & Software*, 24(1):124–134, jan 2009.

[27] B. Roche, J. Drake, and P. Rohani. An agent-based model to study the epidemiological and evolutionary dynamics of influenza viruses. *BMC Bioinformatics*, 12(1):87, 2011.

[28] SEDAC. SocioEconomic Data and Applications Center (SEDAC): Gridded Population of the World, Oct 2014.

[29] A. Tolk. *Engineering Principles of Combat Modeling and Distributed Simulation*. Wiley, 2012.

[30] E. M. Volz, K. Koelle, and T. Bedford. Viral phylodynamics. *PLoS Computational Biology*, 9(3):e1002947, 2013.

[31] J. Wang and T. Zheng. A hybrid multicast-unicast assignment approach for data distribution management in {HLA}. *Simulation Modelling Practice and Theory*, 40(0):39 – 63, 2014.

[32] WHO. Influenza (seasonal) fact sheet, Feb. 2014. Citations for 90 million annual infections and 500,000 annual deaths.

Multi-fidelity Modeling & Simulation Methodology for Simulation Speed Up

Seon Han Choi, Sun Ju Lee, Tag Gon Kim
Department of Electrical Engineering
Korea Advanced Institute of Science and Technology (KAIST)
Daejeon, Republic of Korea
[shchoi, sjlee]@smslab.kaist.ac.kr, tkim@ee.kaist.ac.kr

ABSTRACT

M&S-based analysis has been performed for simulation experiments of all possible input combinations as a 'what-if' analysis causing the simulation to be extremely time-consuming. To resolve this problem, this paper proposes a multi-fidelity M&S methodology for enhancing simulation speed while minimizing accuracy loss and maximizing model reusability, in the M&S-based analysis. Target systems of this methodology are continuous and discrete event system. The proposed multi-fidelity M&S methodology consists of 4 steps: 1) target model selection and Interest Region definition, 2) low-fidelity model development, 3) multi-fidelity model composition, 4) selected target model substitution. Also this methodology proposes structure of multi-fidelity model and its mathematical specifications for the third step. This methodology is applied without any modification of existing models and simulation engine for maximizing model reusability. Case study applies this methodology to Torpedo Tactics Simulation model and the Vehicle Allocation Simulation model. The result shows that simulation speed increases at least 1.21 times with 5% accuracy loss. We expect that this methodology will be applicable in various M&S-based analysis for enhancing simulation speed.

Categories and Subject Descriptors

I.6.5 [**SIMULATION AND MODELING**]: Model Development
– *Modeling methodologies*;
I.6.8 [**SIMULATION AND MODELING**]: Types of Simulation
– *Continuous, Discrete event*

General Terms

Algorithms, Design, Performance, Theory

Keywords

Multi-fidelity M&S; Simulation speed up; Interest Region; Model reusability

1. INTRODUCTION

The Modeling and Simulation (M&S) method has been widely used for solving problems in real world that cannot be solved with numerical and analytical methods [1]. Problem solving by M&S provides new insights that other methods cannot in design/analysis/acquisition of system. For example, in defense

field, analysis of future operational capability through battle experiments [2], performance acquisition of the next generation weapons system, and analysis of tactics [3] are achieved with the M&S method. Problem solving processes using M&S on general, especially the M&S-based analysis, have been performed in simulation experiments of full-factorial design as a "what-if" analysis causing the simulation to be extremely time-consuming (see Table 1). To reduce the simulation time (i.e. to enhance simulation speed), many researches are conducted in various aspects, such as Event-based DEVS Execution Environment [4] and Simulation-based optimization [5].

Table 1. Example of M&S-based analysis: Anti-Torpedo Sim [3]

Combat Entity	Experimental Case (Factor)		
	Experimental Factor	Description	Level of factor
Submarine	F1	Wire-guided tactic	2
Warship	F2	Detection range	4
	F3	Avoidance angle	2
	F4	Delivery angle	3
Torpedo	F5	Torpedo speed	3
Decoy	F6	Source level	2
	F7	Operating time	4
	F8	Decoy speed	3
Total Case	$2^3 \times 3^3 \times 4^2 \times 50 = 3456 \times 50 = 172800$		
Execution Time	$172800 \times 20(\text{sec}) = 3456000(\text{sec}) = \textbf{40(day)}$		

This paper centers on the multi-fidelity M&S concepts to enhance the simulation speed in the M&S-based analyses. The fidelity is defined as the degree of similarity between a model and the system properties being modeled [6]. A high-fidelity model has high accuracy in model output and simulation speed is slow; a low-fidelity model has low accuracy in model output and simulation speed is relatively high. Accordingly, multi-fidelity M&S means bring the models with various fidelity levels under certain conditions during simulation. Due to the use of appropriate low-fidelity models, simulation speed increases with minimization of accuracy loss.

In recent years, the multi-fidelity M&S has been applied in many application fields such as aerospace engineering [7][8], submarine system [9], computational fluid dynamics [10][11], and supply chain system [12]. However, all of the researches focused on practical issues and on ad hoc approaches. In other words, there has been no formal representation for the multi-fidelity model and no model reusability of existing simulation models. Therefore, this paper proposes a multi-fidelity M&S methodology for enhancing simulation speed while minimizing accuracy loss and maximizing model reusability.

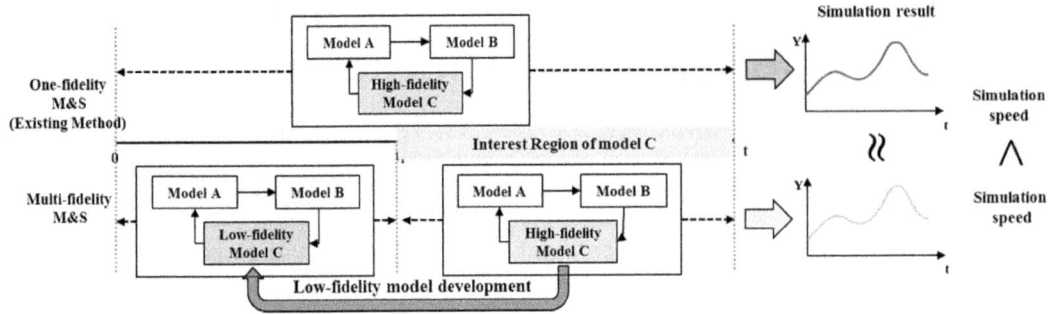

Figure 1. Interest Region concept of multi-fidelity M&S

The target model for applying this methodology is an existing model which consumes too much time due to many requisite experiments. In order to enhance simulation speed without significant loss in accuracy, it is important to know when to use low-fidelity model during simulation. For this, we firstly define an important concept called Interest Region. Interest Region is a region where the model output has a serious effect on the overall simulation result. For example (see Figure 1), when Interest Region of the sub-model C is determined, multi-fidelity M&S uses high-fidelity model C in Interest Region and low-fidelity model C in the outside of Interest Region. However, overall simulation result of multi-fidelity M&S is almost same as one-fidelity M&S (Existing method), which uses high-fidelity model C in overall simulation region. The reason is that output of the low-fidelity model has a little influence on the overall simulation result in the outside of Interest Region. Furthermore, because using low-fidelity model whose simulation speed is relatively faster than high-fidelity model's, multi-fidelity M&S can enhance simulation speed.

To maximize the model reusability, the target model (existing model) is considered as a high-fidelity model, which is not modified when applying this methodology. Also low-fidelity model is developed from the high-fidelity model. Its simulation speed is faster than the high-fidelity model's while accuracy of output is lower than the high-fidelity model's. Also this methodology includes the formal representation of multi-fidelity model with high/low-fidelity models and is applied to the existing model without any modification of simulation engine.

This paper is organized as follows. Section 2 provides a background and Section 3 introduces the proposed multi-fidelity methodology. The case study is described in Section 4 and a conclusion is given in Section 5.

2. BACKGROUND

2.1 Target System

2.1.1 Continuous system

Continuous system is described by a differential equation, and variables in the model are changing continuously as time increases (e.g. Analog circuit). Below is the formal representation of continuous system [13]. Continuous model consists of 3 sets (input, output, and state) and 2 functions (state transition function, and output function). Input, output, and state variable have continuous values according to the time. The state transition function is represented by a differential equation and the output function is described with state and input variables. The execution of continuous model solves the state transition function and calculates the output function, as time increases in simulation engine.

$$CM = \, < X, S, Y, f, g >$$

- X, Y are the set of inputs and outputs.
- S is the set of states.
- $f : \frac{d}{dt} S(t) = f(\, S(t), X(t), t\,)$ is the state transition function.
- $g : Y(t) = g(\, S(t), X(t), t\,)$ is the output function.

2.1.2 Discrete event system

Discrete event system is described by the DEVS (Discrete EVent system Specification) formalism [14] and state variables of model have discrete value while time increases continuously (e.g. War game). Below is the formal representation of discrete event system.

$$DEM = \, < X, S, Y, \delta_{ext}, \delta_{int}, \lambda, ta >$$

- X, Y are the set of inputs and outputs.
- S is the set of states.
- $Q = \{(s, e) | \, s \in S, 0 \le e \le ta(s)\}$
- $\delta_{int} : Q \longrightarrow Q$ is the internal transition function.
- $\delta_{ext} : Q \times X \longrightarrow S$ is the external transition function.
- $\lambda : Q \longrightarrow Y$ is the output function.
- $ta : S \longrightarrow \mathbb{R}$ is the time advance function.

Discrete event model consists of 3 sets (input, output, and state) and 4 functions (internal/external state transition function, output function, and time advance function). Input and output are events consisting the occurrence time and value. For example, the event called 'package arriving' consists of the arriving time (occurrence time) and contents of the package (value). State has discrete values and it is changed by two cases. When input comes, state variables are changed, and if none of the input comes until certain time, output occurs and state variables are changed. The former is called external transition and conducted by the external transition function. The latter is called internal transition and conducted by the internal transition function with the output function. The amount of time (state time) that state can remain for is decided by time advance function.

2.2 Fidelity of Model

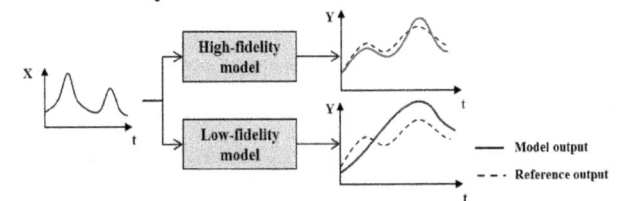

Figure 2. Fidelity of model

For the models that represent the same target system component, fidelity is compared by their output for the same input. High-fidelity model has lower output error than low-fidelity model, when it is compared by reference output (see Figure 2).

Table 2. Measurement method of output error

Error	Continuous system	Discrete event system
Value Error		
	Value Error(t_i) $$= \left| \frac{(V_R(t_i) - V_M(t_i))}{V_R(t_i)} \right|$$	Value Error(E_i) $$= \left| \frac{(V_R(E_i) - V_M(E_i))}{V_R(E_i)} \right|$$
Time Error		
	Time Error(v_i) $$= |t_i - t_i'|$$	Time Error(E_i) $$= \left| \frac{(ET_R(E_i) - ET_M(E_i))}{ET_R(E_i)} \right|$$

To compare the fidelity between two models quantitatively, this paper suggests ϵ which means the difference between two outputs (i.e. output error). It is measured in two aspects, because the output of continuous model and discrete event model consists of time and value. In continuous model, Time Error (i.e. delay) is defined to be the time difference between two same values of output, and Value Error is defined as the value ratio between two output values in same time. In discrete event model, Time Error means the difference between two ET (time interval from input event to output event) of same output events and Value Error is defined to be the value ratio between two same events in the same time (see Table 2). For each aspect, ϵ is calculated by RMSE (Root Mean Square Error).

$$\epsilon = \sqrt{\frac{\sum_{i=1}^{N} Error^2}{N-1}}$$

In the formula, the *Error* can be the Value Error or Time Error, and it is decided according to simulation objective. N is the number of samples. For example, when the *Error* is the Value Error in continuous model, N is the number of time samples. When the *Error* is Time Error in discrete event model, N is the number of events. The range of ϵ is $[0, +\infty)$. 0 means the output of two models are exactly same in condition of same input. The larger ϵ is, the more difference is. In other words, large ϵ means low-fidelity model about the reference model possessing reference output. The reference model can be real system or validated model. We assume that the target model is valid, and it is reference model.

In continuous system, value of output is determined by the value of state variables, and these state variables are determined in state transition function. Time of output is decided in output function. Therefore, state transition function and output function are related to determine the fidelity of continuous model. However, in

discrete event model, value of output is decided in output function and time of output is decided in time advance function. Therefore, these two functions are related to determine the fidelity of discrete event model. Also input, output, and state variables of high-fidelity model and low-fidelity model are same; because the fidelity is compared in output for the same input (changing of variables in model is related to resolution of model [14][15]).

3. MULTI-FIDELITY M&S METHODOLOGY

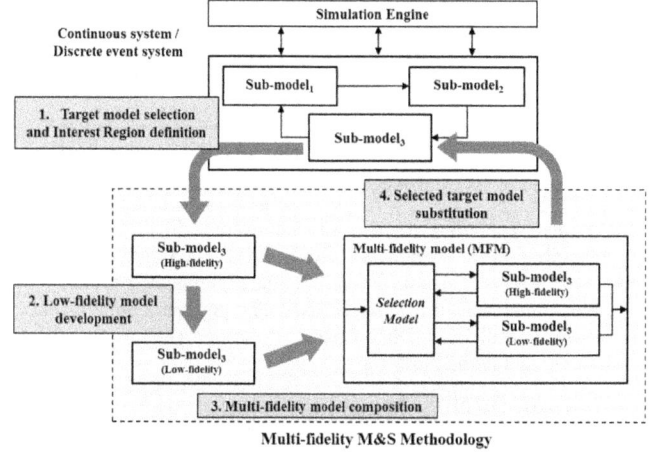

Figure 3. Proposed multi-fidelity M&S methodology

Proposed multi-fidelity M&S methodology consists of 4 steps: 1) target model selection and Interest Region definition, 2) low-fidelity model development, 3) multi-fidelity model composition, 4) selected target model substitution (see Figure 3). The target systems of this methodology are continuous and discrete event system. To maximize model reusability, this methodology is applied without any modification of existing models and simulation engine. The following sections will explain each step in detail.

3.1 Target Model Selection and Interest Region Definition

The first step consists of selecting a target model from the entire model and defining Interest Region of the selected target model. The selection criteria for the target model are below.

- A model based on continuous model formalism or discrete event model formalism

- A model executed frequently during simulation and needed a high computation power (The model which has high ETR)

- A model with Interest Region smaller than overall simulation region

The first criterion is needed to maximize the model reusability. When the model does not meet the second criterion, we cannot get meaningful simulation speed up even if the methodology is applied to that model. Section 3.4 will explain it in detail. If Interest Region is the same as overall simulation region, we cannot use the low-fidelity model. To find the target model efficiently, the criteria are applied step by step. First, make the list of candidate models fulfilling the first criterion and sort the list in ascending order of ETR (Execution Time Ratio: The ratio of the model execution time to overall execution time). From the top of the list, define Interest Region of the model and apply the methodology if it meets the third criterion.

In order to define Interest Region of model, first, describe the overall simulation region with several variables that the model can access. The several variables are the set of Interest Region Variable (IRV) which can be time variable (logical simulation time), input variables, state variables, or new variables representing a combination of input variable and state variable.

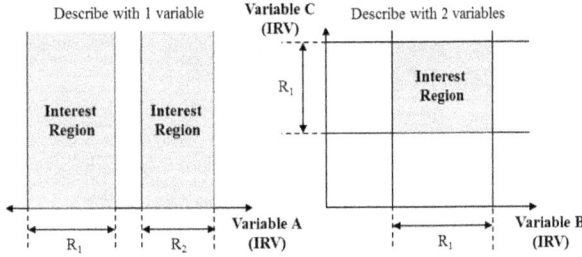

Figure 4. Interest Region definition with IRV and R

After that, according to the simulation objective, define the Interest Region (R in Figure 4) of IRV. R must be smaller than the range of IRV. IRV can have many R and experiment is needed to decide optimal size of R in some cases. The important point is that IRV and R will be Fidelity Change Condition (FCC) of multi-fidelity model in the third step.

3.2 Low-fidelity Model Development
The second step is to develop the low-fidelity models from the target model selected in the first step. The low-fidelity models should have lower accuracy of output and lower execution time than the target model. The following sub-sections will explain this in detail for continuous model and discrete event model.

3.2.1 Continuous model
As mentioned in background, the fidelity of continuous model is determined by the state transition function and the output function. Therefore, low-fidelity model development is to simplify these two functions. Because this is the modeling issues, there are various methods. This paper suggests two methods: Elimination and Projection. Elimination means deleting the terms, which have little effect to the accuracy of output in the state transition function. On the other hand, Projection means fixing the value of variables in the state transition function. Following example will explain low-fidelity model development.

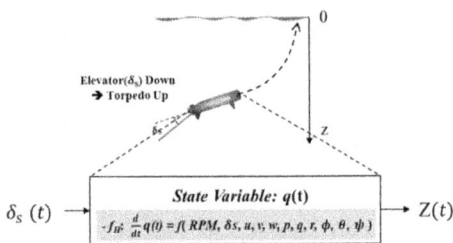

Figure 5. Example model: Torpedo maneuver

The example model is the Torpedo maneuver model [16] (see Figure 5). Input and output variables of this model are Elevator ($\delta_S(t)$) and Depth ($Z(t)$) of torpedo and the state variable is Pitch ($q(t)$). The state transition function of the model is differential equation which consists of many terms. In this model, value of output is important, according to simulation objective. Therefore, developing low-fidelity model is to make state transition function simple. Depending on the level of eliminating terms, mid-fidelity model and low-fidelity model can be developed by using Elimination method (see Figure 6).

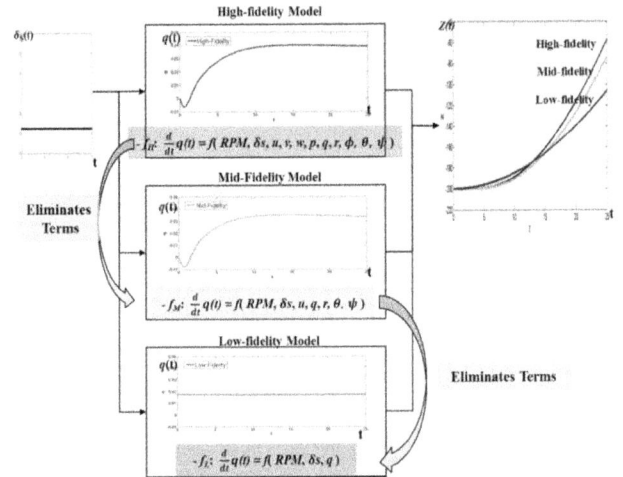

Figure 6. Example of low-fidelity model development: Torpedo maneuver model [16]

The state transition function of low-fidelity has fewer terms than that of high-fidelity model. As the more terms are eliminated, the accuracy of function decreases (see Figure 6), while the calculation speed increases. Therefore, the low-fidelity model has Value Error in comparison with the high-fidelity model (see Figure 6). Table 3 shows the execution time and ϵ for the same input. As the fidelity decreases, execution time of model decreases and ϵ increases.

Table 3. Comparison of models: Torpedo maneuver model

	High-fidelity	Mid-fidelity	Low-fidelity
Execution Time (Sec)	8.01	7.50	4.08
ϵ	0	0.08	0.22

3.2.2 Discrete event model
The fidelity of discrete event model is determined by the output function and time advance function. Therefore, low-fidelity model development is to make these two functions simple. Specifically, that is to simplify the algorithms in these two functions. These algorithms decide the time of each state in the time advance function and the output value in the output function. As is the case of continuous model, there are various methods. Following example will explain low-fidelity model development.

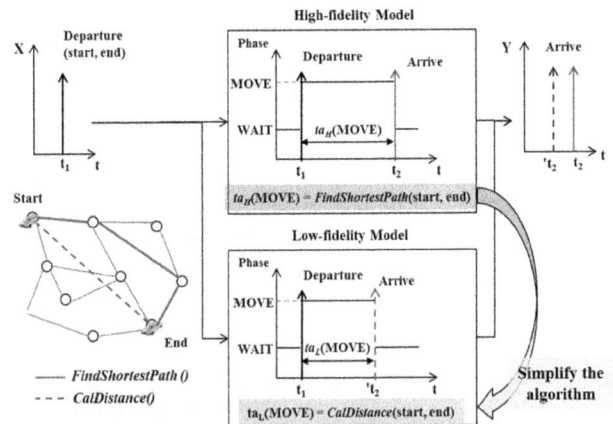

Figure 7. Example of low-fidelity model development: Vehicle model

The example model is the Vehicle model (see Figure 7). In this model, time of ouptut is important, according to simulation objective. Therefore, developing low-fidelity model is to make time advance function simple. When input (Departure) comes, the state of vehicle model change to MOVE from WAIT. Then the vehicle model makes the output after the state time of MOVE. High-fidelity model calculates the state time of MOVE by using Dijkstra algorithm [17], which finds the shortest path with given the Start and the End, in graph. However, the Dijkstra algorithm needs too much time to calculate. Low-fidelity model is developed by making this algorithm simple. The low-fidelity model uses the simple algorithm which just calculates distance between the Start and the End. The accuracy of simple algorithm is lower than Dijkstra algorithm's, while its calculation speed is much faster than Dijkstra algorithm's. Therefore, the low-fidelity model has Time Error in comparison with the high-fidelity model (see Figure 7). For the same input (2000 Departure event), Table 4 shows the execution time and ϵ. The low-fidelity model has 0.21 output error, while the execution time of it is lower than high-fidelity model's.

Table 4. Comparison of models: Vehicle model

	High-fidelity	Low-fidelity
Execution Time (Sec)	2.79	0.41
ϵ	0	0.21

In summary, the low-fidelity model that we developed should have lower accuracy of output and lower execution time than the high-fidelity model. In continuous model, development of low-fidelity model is to make transition function and output function simple. In discrete event model, that is to make time advance function and output function simple. Someone who knows well about the high-fidelity model or target system can develop low-fidelity models efficiently.

3.3 Multi-fidelity Model Composition

After selecting the target model in the first step and developing low-fidelity models based on target model in the second step, the next step is to composite a Multi-fidelity model (MFM) automatically. For automatic composition, the formal structure and specification are needed (see Figure 8).

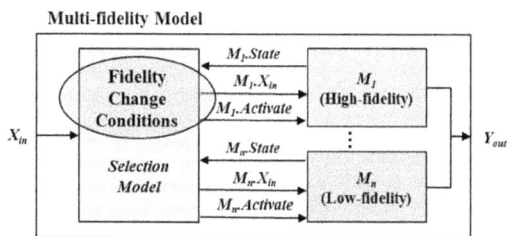

Figure 8. Structure of multi-fidelity model

$$MFM = <X, Y, SM, \{M_i\}, MCS>$$
- $X = \{X_{in}\}$ is the set of inputs
- $Y = \{Y_{out}\}$ is the set of outputs
- $\{M_i\} = \{M_1, \ldots, M_n\}$ is the set of models with various fidelity
- SM is the Selection Model
- $MCS \subseteq EIC \cup EOC \cup IC$ is the model coupling scheme
  $EIC \subseteq X \times SM.X$ is the external input coupling
  $EOC \subseteq \cup_{i=1}^{n} M_i.Y \times Y$ is the external output coupling
  $IC \subseteq (SM.Y \times \cup_{i=1}^{n} M_i.X) \cup (\cup_{i=1}^{n} M_i.Y \times SM.X)$
       is the internal coupling

MFM consists of the internal models (the target model and low-fidelity models) and SM. Since MFM is the substitution of the target model, input and output are the same as the target model. The SM changes internal models according to Fidelity Change Conditions (FCC) during simulation. FCC is composed of IRV and R which were decided in the second step. SM has two important roles. First, when input comes, SM decides whether the current internal model changes with FCC, and if the model is not changed, SM sends the coming input to the model (i.e. Input Bypass). Otherwise, SM changes the model, copies the state from the current internal model to the next internal model for continuing simulation, and sends the coming input to the next internal model (i.e. Model Change with State Copy). For this, state transfer message ($M_i.State$) from the current internal model and state copy message ($M_i.Activate$) to the next internal model are added. In continuous model, SM is expressed as algorithm model; in discrete event model, SM is expressed as atomic model. The following sub-sections will explain this in detail.

3.3.1 Continuous model

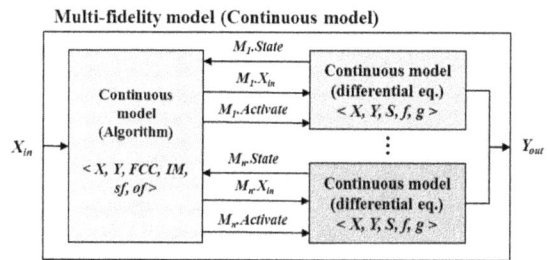

Figure 9. Structure of multi-fidelity model: Continuous model

Figure 9 shows the structure of multi-fidelity model of continuous model. The internal models are expressed as existing continuous model specifications mentioned in the background, and SM is expressed as algorithm model which existing continuous simulation engine can simulate (see Figure 10).

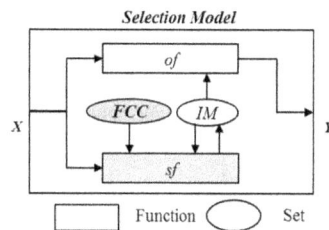

Figure 10. Structure of selection model: Continuous model

The set of inputs of SM consists of external input sent to the current internal model, and state input transferred from the current internal model. The set of outputs of SM consists of the external output for Input Bypass, and activate output for Model Change with State Copy. SM has two sets of states, FCC and IM. IM represents the current internal model, and consists of the current internal model, the state value of the model, and the Boolean variable representing a change of the model. The two important roles of SM are conducted by a Selection Function (sf) mapped to state transition function and an Output Function (of). The sf decides whether the current internal model is changed with FCC, when external input comes. If the current internal model is not changed, the of sends the external input to the model. Otherwise, the of sends the state of the current internal model and the external input, to next internal model (see Figure 11).

$$CSM = <X, Y, IM, FCC, sf, of>$$

- $X = \{X_{in}\} \cup \{M_1.State, ..., M_n.State\}$ is the set of inputs.
  ($M_i.State$ is the state input of internal model(M_i))

- $Y = \{M_1.X_{in}, ..., M_n.X_{in}\} \cup \{M_1.Activate, ..., M_n.Activate\}$
  is the set of outputs. ($M_i.X_{in}$ is the bypass output of M_i,
  $M_i.Activate$ is the activate output of M_i)

- $IM = \{(M_i, State, bChange)|\ M_i \in \{M_i\},$
  $State$ is the state value of M_i,
  $bChange \in \{True, False\}\}$
  is the set of internal model states

- $FCC = \{(v,r)|\ v \in IRV, r \in R\}$
  is the set of fidelity change conditions.

- $sf: X \times S \times FCC \longrightarrow S$ is the selection function.

- $of: X \times S \longrightarrow Y$ is the output function

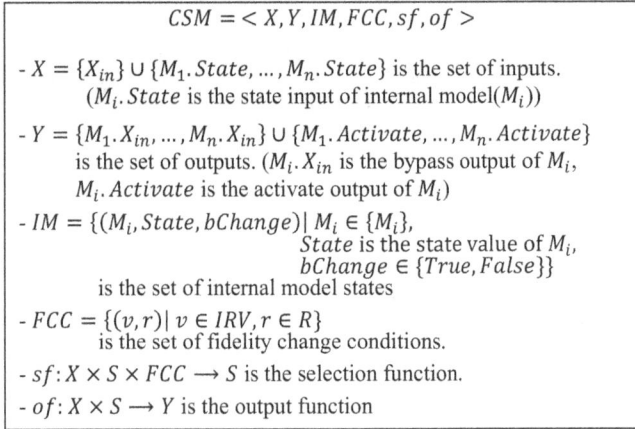

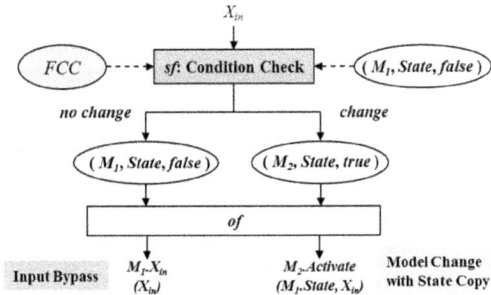

Figure 11. Two important roles of selection model: Continuous model

3.3.2 Discrete event model

Figure 12 shows the structure of multi-fidelity model of discrete event system. The internal models are expressed as DEVS mentioned in background, and *SM* is expressed as DEVS Atomic model (see Figure 13). Unlike the continuous model, discrete event model can be executed when it has no input or internal transition. Therefore, MFM of discrete event model have additional message, ($M_i.Stop$) which stops execution of current internal model when it is changed. Furthermore, to stop the internal transition, a state (Stop state) whose state time is infinite, is added to the internal model. When the internal model get a stop message, its state changes to the Stop state and it waits until getting an activate message. When it receives the activate message, its state shifts to some state included in the message.

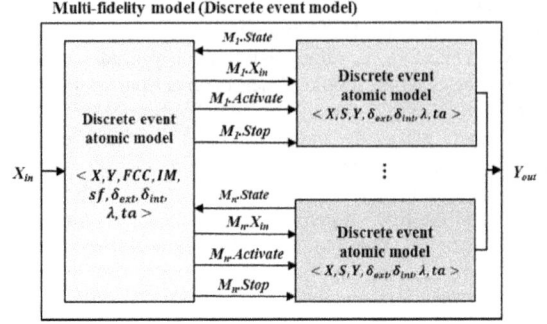

Figure 12. Structure of multi-fidelity model: Discrete event model

Except for the stop message, the set of inputs and outputs are the same as *SM* of continuous model. *SM* has two sets of state, FCC and IM. FCC is the same as *SM* in continuous model, while IM is slightly different. IM consists of the input (X_{in}), current internal model, the state value of the internal model, and four steps for message delivery. In discrete event model, these IM are mapped to 4 phases which are $M_i.\textbf{Wait}$, $M_i.\textbf{Check}$, $M_i.\textbf{Active}$, and $M_i.\textbf{Change}$. Unlike the continuous model, the two important roles of *SM* are conducted by series of phase transition. The basic phase is $M_i.\textbf{Wait}$, according to the current internal model M_i. When input X_{in} comes, the phase moves to $M_i.\textbf{Check}$ and *SM* checks the whether the M_i changes with *sf* and FCC. Also if the model is not changed, the phase changes to $M_i.\textbf{Wait}$ and *SM* sends the X_{in} to the model. Otherwise, the phase shifts to $M_j\textbf{Activate}$, according to next internal model M_j, and *SM* sends the stop message to the M_i. Then, the phase moves to $M_j.\textbf{Change}$, and *SM* sends the activate message to the M_j. Finally, the phase changes to $M_j.\textbf{Wait}$, and *SM* sends the X_{in} to the current internal model M_j. After that, SM is waiting until the X_{in} comes. The series of phase transition of Input Bypass is below. (brackets mean the output message, $\Rightarrow$ means the external transition, and $\longrightarrow$ means the internal transition)

$$M_i.\textbf{Wait} \Rightarrow M_i.\textbf{Check} \longrightarrow (M_i.X_{in}) \longrightarrow M_i.\textbf{Wait}$$

The series of phase transition of Model Change with State Copy is below.

$$M_i.\textbf{Wait} \Rightarrow M_i.\textbf{Check} \longrightarrow (M_i.Stop) \longrightarrow M_j.\textbf{Activate}$$
$$\longrightarrow (M_j.Activate) \longrightarrow M_j.\textbf{Change} \longrightarrow (M_j.X_{in}) \longrightarrow M_j.\textbf{Wait}$$

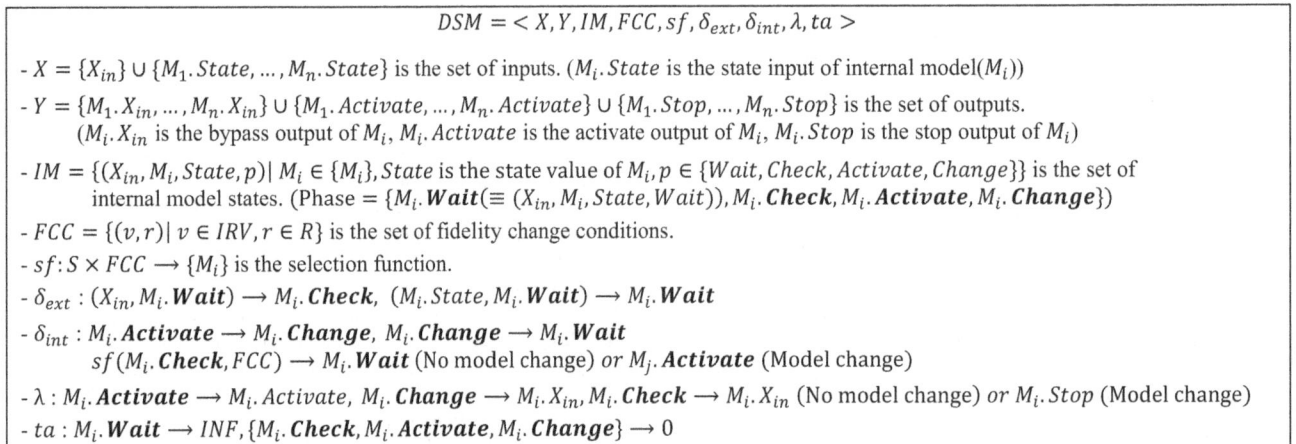

$$DSM = <X, Y, IM, FCC, sf, \delta_{ext}, \delta_{int}, \lambda, ta>$$

- $X = \{X_{in}\} \cup \{M_1.State, ..., M_n.State\}$ is the set of inputs. ($M_i.State$ is the state input of internal model(M_i))

- $Y = \{M_1.X_{in}, ..., M_n.X_{in}\} \cup \{M_1.Activate, ..., M_n.Activate\} \cup \{M_1.Stop, ..., M_n.Stop\}$ is the set of outputs.
  ($M_i.X_{in}$ is the bypass output of M_i, $M_i.Activate$ is the activate output of M_i, $M_i.Stop$ is the stop output of M_i)

- $IM = \{(X_{in}, M_i, State, p)|\ M_i \in \{M_i\}, State$ is the state value of $M_i, p \in \{Wait, Check, Activate, Change\}\}$ is the set of
  internal model states. (Phase $= \{M_i.\textbf{Wait}(\equiv (X_{in}, M_i, State, Wait)), M_i.\textbf{Check}, M_i.\textbf{Activate}, M_i.\textbf{Change}\}$)

- $FCC = \{(v,r)|\ v \in IRV, r \in R\}$ is the set of fidelity change conditions.

- $sf: S \times FCC \longrightarrow \{M_i\}$ is the selection function.

- $\delta_{ext} : (X_{in}, M_i.\textbf{Wait}) \longrightarrow M_i.\textbf{Check}, (M_i.State, M_i.\textbf{Wait}) \longrightarrow M_i.\textbf{Wait}$

- $\delta_{int} : M_i.\textbf{Activate} \longrightarrow M_i.\textbf{Change}, M_i.\textbf{Change} \longrightarrow M_i.\textbf{Wait}$
  $sf(M_i.\textbf{Check}, FCC) \longrightarrow M_i.\textbf{Wait}$ (No model change) *or* $M_j.\textbf{Activate}$ (Model change)

- $\lambda : M_i.\textbf{Activate} \longrightarrow M_i.Activate, M_i.\textbf{Change} \longrightarrow M_i.X_{in}, M_i.\textbf{Check} \longrightarrow M_i.X_{in}$ (No model change) *or* $M_i.Stop$ (Model change)

- $ta : M_i.\textbf{Wait} \longrightarrow INF, \{M_i.\textbf{Check}, M_i.\textbf{Activate}, M_i.\textbf{Change}\} \longrightarrow 0$

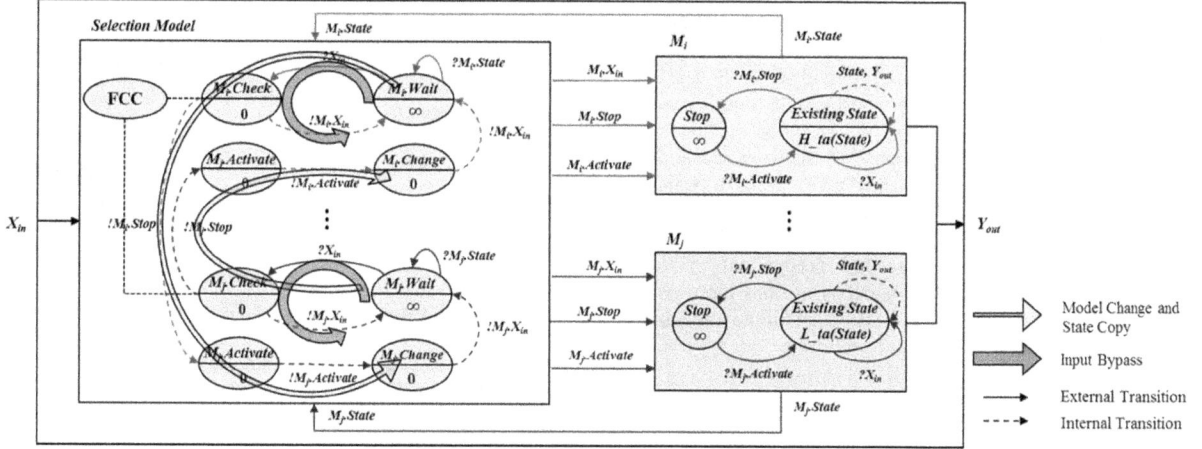

Figure 13. Structure of selection model: Discrete event model

The MFM substitutes the target model without any modification of existing simulation engine, and other models. This increases the model reusability. Small modifications used to add more messages and the Stop state in case of discrete event model are unrelated to model logic, since they are just subsidiary functions. If IRV with R and internal models are given, the MFM is composited automatically and it leads to reducing time for applying this methodology.

3.4 Simulation Speed Evaluation

This section suggests the formula of speed up when applying the proposed methodology, and tells that which parts should be modified to get the maximum speed up.

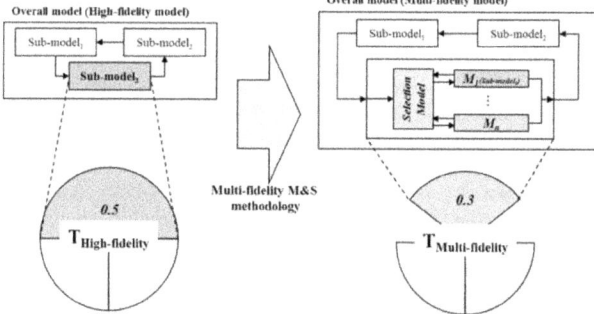

Figure 14. Execution time reduction of multi-fidelity methodology

Figure 14 illustrates that how to reduce the execution time when applying the multi-fidelity methodology. The time reduction means that reducing the execution time of target sub-model. Therefore, if the ETR of target sub-model is low, we can't get meaningful simulation speed up when the methodology is applied to that model. $T_{High-fidelity}$ and $T_{Multi-fidelity}$ are defined as the overall execution time of high-fidelity model and multi-fidelity model, respectively. Speed up is defined as below.

$$Speed\ Up = \frac{T_{High-fidelity}}{T_{Multi-fidelity}} = \frac{1}{1 - ETR(1 - A\sum_{i=1}^{n} a_i r_i - E)}$$

ETR: The ratio of the target model execution time to overall execution time. ($0 < ETR \leq 1$)

A: The coefficient of structure overhead (Input Bypass) in the

MFM. ($1 < A$)

a_i: The ratio of M_i execution time to target model execution time. ($0 < a_i < 1$)

r_i: The ratio of M_i simulation region to overall simulation region. ($0 < r_i < 1, \sum_{i=1}^{n} r_i = 1$)

E: The overhead rate of model exchange in the MFM. ($E \propto$ # of model exchange, $0 < E < 1$)

The maximum speed up is using only the fastest low-fidelity model during overall simulation.

$$Speed\ Up_{Max} = \frac{1}{1 - ETR(1 - A \times \min(a_i))}$$

The efficiency means the ratio of actual speed up to maximum speed up when applying the proposed methodology.

$$Efficiency = \frac{Speed\ Up}{Speed\ Up_{Max}} = \frac{1 - ETR(1 - A \times \min(a_i))}{1 - ETR(1 - A\sum_{i=1}^{n} a_i r_i - E)}$$

Based on these formulae of speed up, to maximize the speed up, first, select the target model with large ETR. Second, simplify the C and sf in SM and that leads to reducing A. Third, reduce the Interest Region (i.e. increase the simulation region where low-fidelity is used) and that is related to increasing r_i and reducing a_i. The last is to minimize the frequency of model exchange and it is related to reduce E. The third and fourth are related to maximization of the efficiency.

4. CASE STUDY

4.1 Torpedo Tactics Simulation

4.1.1 Overview of torpedo tactics simulation model

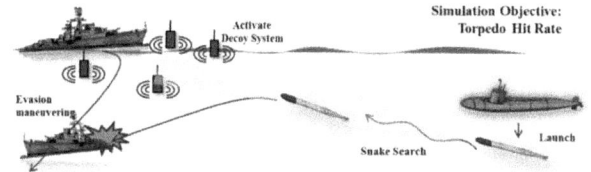

Figure 15. Scenario of TTS

The example of continuous model is Torpedo Tactics Simulation (TTS) whose objective is to get the torpedo hit rate according various parameters such as firing range, type of torpedo, speed of torpedo, type of decoy, number of decoy, and so on. Because of various parameters with large range, considerable time is needed to get the result. Therefore, we apply the proposed methodology to TTS for simulation speed up. Figure 15 shows a scenario of TTS. A submarine placed a distance away from a warship launches a torpedo and it finds the warship by using snake search tactic. If it finds the warship, it chases and hits the warship. When detecting it, the warship drops several decoys with evasive maneuvers. If hit target by torpedo is decoy, it finds the warship again by using circle search tactic. If it does not hit the target until the limit moving distance, it explodes itself.

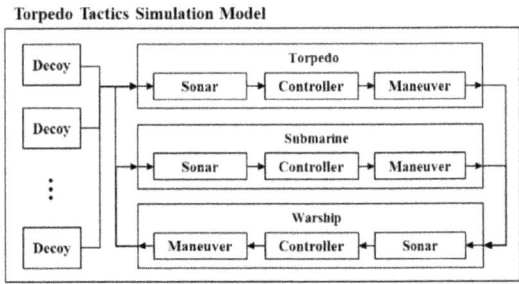

Figure 16. Overall model structure of TTS model

The TTS model consists of many sub models (see Figure 16). All of the models are based on continuous model specification and implemented with C++ language.

4.1.2 Apply the multi-fidelity M&S methodology

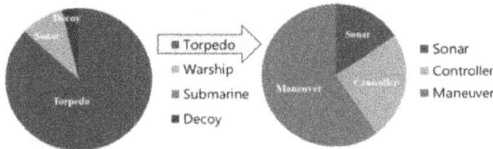

Figure 17. ETR of sub models in TTS

The first step is to select the target model and define Interest Region. TTS is based on the continuous model specification, so all of the sub models satisfy the first criterion. To find the sub

models which meet the second criterion, we got ETR of sub models (see Figure 17).

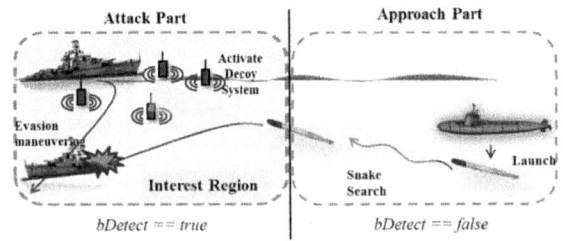

Figure 18. Interest Region of Torpedo maneuver model

Because the torpedo maneuver model has the highest ETR, we defined Interest Region of the maneuver model, to identify whether it meets the third criterion. To define Interest Region, we described overall simulation with 'bDetect' which is a Boolean variable and represents whether the torpedo detects the target. When the 'bDetect' is true, output of the maneuver model has a serious effect on the overall simulation result (torpedo hit rate). Therefore, Interest Region of the maneuver model is when the 'bDetect' is true, and the R is 'true'. In this case, the experiment to decide optimal size of R is not needed because the IRV has only two values. The torpedo maneuver model meets the three criteria. Therefore, it is the target model for applying this methodology. The second step is to develop the low-fidelity models from the torpedo maneuver model. The maneuver model has 6 state variables (u, v, w, p, q, r) which represent velocity and angular velocity of each axis (X, Y, Z). The state transition function of the maneuver model is very complex differential equation which is based on the Newton Equation, and calculates the change amount of state variables with various parameters such as thrust force, gravity force, drag force and so on [16]. Developing the low-fidelity models means to simplify the state transition function. For this, Elimination and Projection method mentioned in 3.2.1 are used. The third step is to composite a MFM automatically. The internal models are the existing torpedo maneuver model and low-fidelity model developed in the second step. Also FCC is composed with IVA and R decided in the first step. The last step is to substitute the maneuver MFM composed in previous step for the maneuver model. Figure 19 shows the overall process of applying of proposed methodology to TTS.

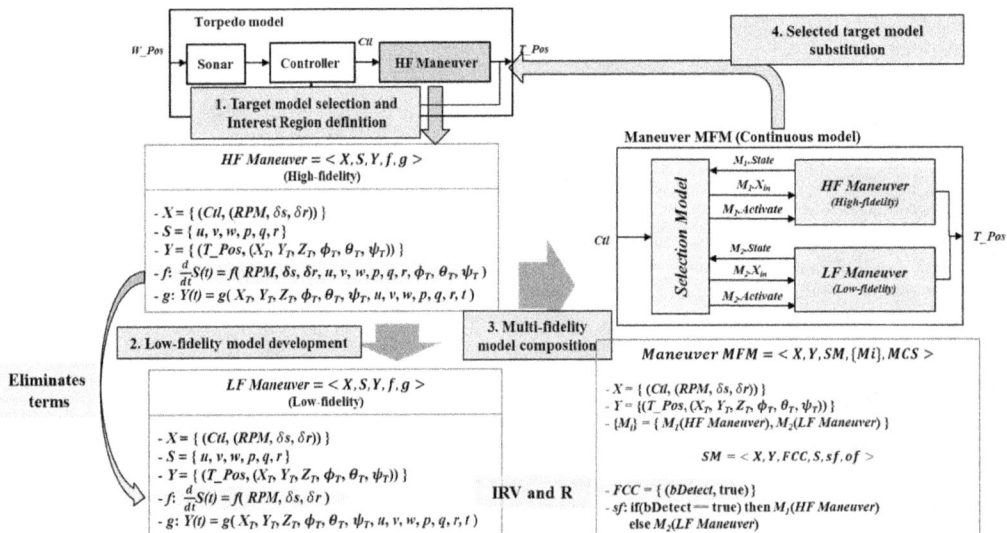

Figure 19. Overall process of multi-fidelity M&S methodology: Torpedo Tactics Simulation

4.1.3 Simulation result

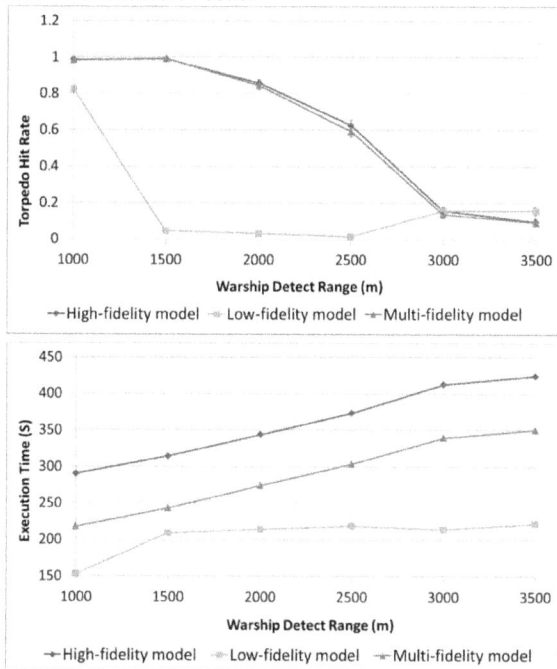

Figure 20. Simulation result of TTS

Torpedo hit rate can be measured with various parameters, but in this case study, it is measured according to the warship detect range. Figure 20 shows the torpedo hit rate and execution time according to the warship detect range. To accomplish the standard error is within 0.031 with confidence level 95%, torpedo hit rate and execution time are calculated in 1000 times launching. In the graph, High-fidelity model means simulation with existing TTS model, Low-fidelity model means simulation with TTS model whose maneuver model is substituted with low-fidelity model, and multi-fidelity model means simulation with TTS model whose maneuver model is substituted with the maneuver MFM. The torpedo hit rate of High-fidelity model and Multi-fidelity model are almost same, but Low-fidelity model has much accuracy loss. However, execution time of Multi-fidelity model is lower than the one of High-fidelity model, i.e., simulation speed increases about 1.25 times with 70% efficiency (see the section 3.4). Therefore, the result shows that proposed methodology can increase the simulation speed without significant loss in accuracy. Furthermore, without modification of simulation engine, and other existing models, the proposed methodology is applied and that means maximizing model reusability.

4.2 Vehicle Allocation Simulation

4.2.1 Overview of vehicle allocation simulation model

The example of discrete event time model is Vehicle Allocation Simulation (VAS) which has the objective to decide the optimal number of vehicle by measuring the average waiting time of customer and average utilization rate of vehicle according various parameters such as organization of map, distribution of customer, speed of vehicle, and so on. As is the case of the TTS, it takes lots of time to get the simulation result. Therefore we apply the proposed methodology to VAS for simulation speed up.

Figure 21 shows a scenario of VAS. The map is described as graph. A vertex represents a crossing and an edge represents a road. Customers and vehicles can be on a vertex, and stations are

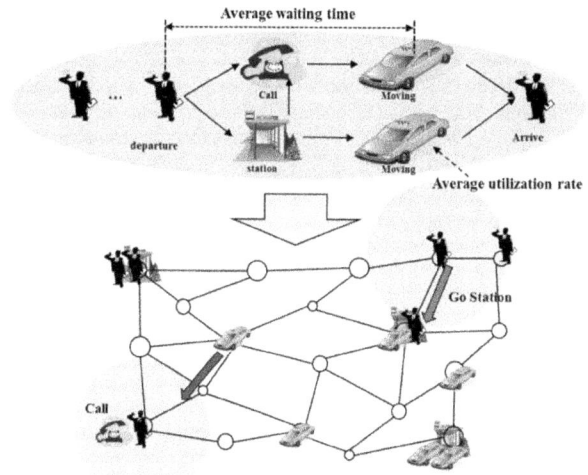

Figure 21. Scenario of VAS

on several vertexes. Customers who have the own destination, are generated in each vertex with some weight. If station is within some distance of the vertex where the customer is generated, the customer goes to the station and takes a vehicle. Otherwise, the customer calls a vehicle and the closest vehicle from the customer is allocated. If there is no vehicle in the station, the customer waits for a vehicle. After some time later, the customer calls a vehicle. If a vehicle picks up a customer who waits in a station or calls the vehicle, it goes to destination of the customer. After arriving, it goes to the nearest station and waits for a customer. It goes to the popular station, after some time has passed. A vehicle can take a call from customers in moving and waiting without picking up a customer.

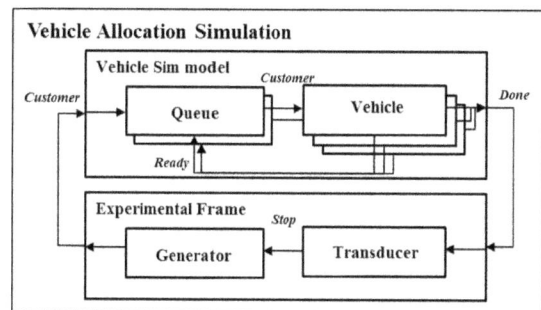

Figure 22. Overall model structure of VAS model

The VAS model consists of many sub models (see Figure 22). All of the models are based on DEVS formalism and implemented with DEVSim++ [18].

4.2.2 Apply the multi-fidelity M&S methodology

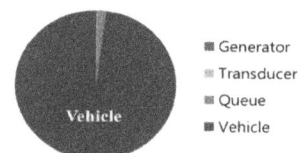

Figure 23. ETR of sub models in VAS

The first step is to select the target model and define Interest Region. VAS is based on the DEVS formalism, so all of the sub models satisfy the first criterion. To find the sub models which meet the second criterion, we got the ETR of sub models (see Figure 23). Because the vehicle model has the highest ETR, we defined Interest Region of the vehicle model to know whether it meets the third criterion. To define Interest Region, we described overall simulation with 'Distance' which is positive number and means expected distance between departure and destination of a customer. The simulation results (average waiting time and average utilization rate) are more affected when 'Distance' has high value. Therefore the Interest Region of the vehicle model is when the 'Distance' has high value. In this case, the experiment to decide optimal size of R is needed because the size of R has various values. Large Interest Region, which means high-fidelity model is used in simulation for much time, makes the simulation result more accurate and the execution time longer. While, smaller Interest Region makes the simulation result inaccurate and the execution time shorter. Therefore, by using the experiment, the optimal size of R is decided according to an optimal condition that is set by user.

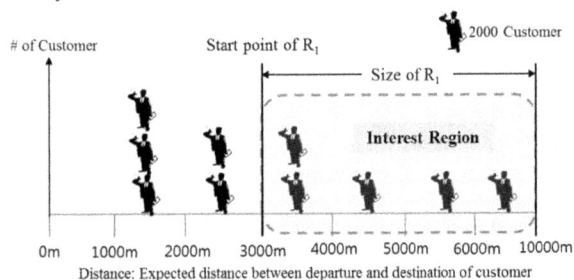

Figure 24. Interest Region of Vehicle model

The second step is to develop the low-fidelity model from the vehicle model. The developed low-fidelity model is the same as one mentioned at 3.2.2. To calculate the state time of MOVE in time advance function, the high-fidelity model use the Dijkstra algorithm, while the low-fidelity model use the simple algorithm which calculates distance between the Start and the End. The third step is to composite a MFM automatically. The internal models are the existing vehicle model and the low-fidelity model developed in the second step. Also in this step, the experiment deciding optimal size of R is conducted. Table 5 shows the experimental design. This experiment checks the measurement values according to the various Start points of R from 1000 to 3500. The experiment group is multi-fidelity model whose vehicle model is substituted with the vehicle MFM, and the control group is high-fidelity model (existing VAS) and low-fidelity model whose vehicle model is substituted with the low-fidelity model.

Table 5. Experiment design for deciding optimal size of R

Group	Model	IRV	Start point	Measurement value
Experiment Group	Multi-fidelity model		1000, 1500, 2000, 2500, 3000, 3500	Accuracy of simulation result (average waiting time), Execution time (sec)
Control Group	High-fidelity model, Low-fidelity model	Distance		

Figure 25 shows the trade-off relation between execution time and accuracy of simulation result, according to the Start point of R. As is mentioned, if the Start point of R increases (i.e. the size of R or

Interest Region decrease), execution time is short, while accuracy of simulation result is high.

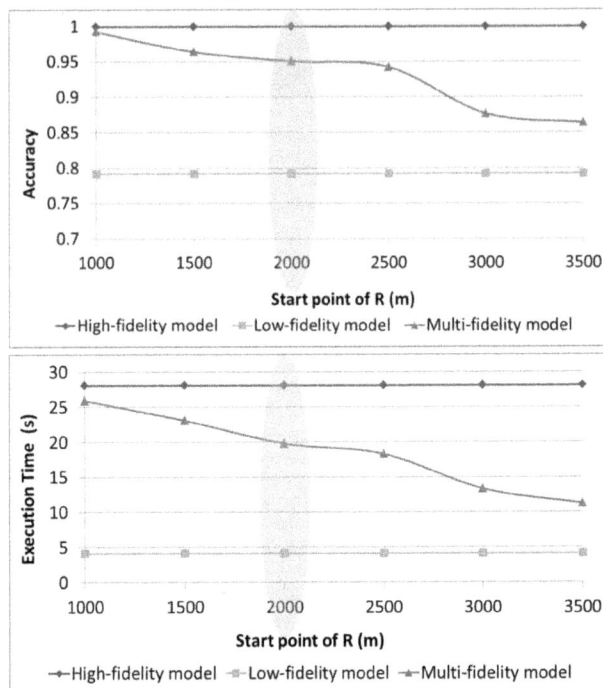

Figure 25. Experiment result for deciding optimal size of R

Based on the experiment result, we should decide the optimal size of R. The optimal condition is as follows.

> The optimal size of R has minimum execution time among the candidates whose accuracy of simulation result is within a permissible error.

If the permissible error is 0.05, the set of candidates are 1000, 1500, and 2000. Among the candidates, 2000 has the minimum execution time. Therefore, the optimal size of R is (2000, 10000) in the condition of this permissible error. The optimal size of R will be changed with the permissible error. However in this case study, we decide that the optimal size of R is (2000, 10000). The last step is to substitute the vehicle MFM composed in previous step for the vehicle model. Figure 26 shows the overall process of applying proposed methodology to VAS.

4.2.3 Simulation result

To increase the reliability of simulation result, real data is used to decide the value of several parameters. First, the map is constructed based on real map data [19] in scale of 400m. Major crossings correspond to vertex, and roads and its real distance between each crossing correspond to edge and its weight. The number of customer, destination of customer, and speed of vehicle are decided based on the government report [20]. Based on these parameters, Figure 27 shows the average waiting time, average utilization rate, and execution time according to the number of vehicle. The meanings of High-fidelity model, Low-fidelity model, and Multi-fidelity model are the same as TTS. The simulation result of High-fidelity model and Multi-fidelity model are same, but Low-fidelity model has much accuracy loss. However, execution time of Multi-fidelity model is lower than the one of High-fidelity model, i.e., simulation speed increases about 1.21 times with 65% efficiency (see the section 3.4). The efficiency of VAS is lower than the one of TTS because of the high frequency

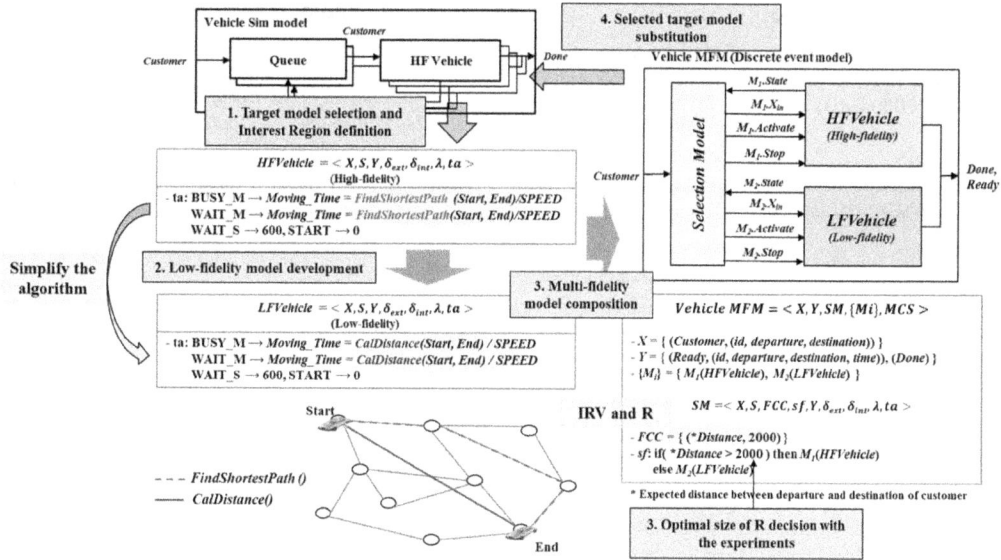

Figure 26. Overall process of multi-fidelity M&S methodology: Vehicle Allocation Simulation.

of model exchange in the vehicle model (see Figure 28). The high frequency of model exchange decreases the efficiency of this methodology, as mentioned. Nevertheless, the result shows that proposed methodology can increase the simulation speed without significant loss in accuracy. Furthermore, without modification of simulation engine, and other existing models, the proposed methodology is applied and that means maximizing model reusability.

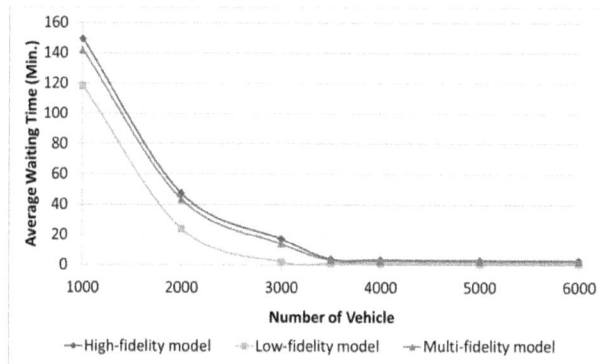

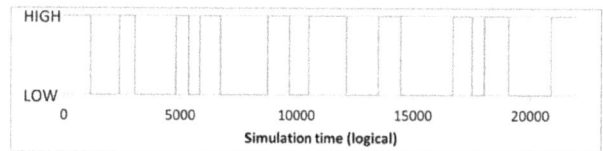

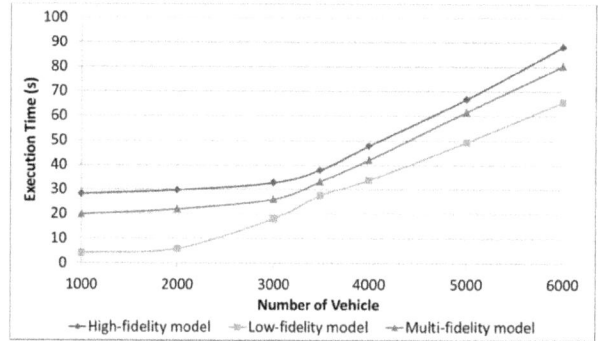

Figure 27. Simulation result of VAS

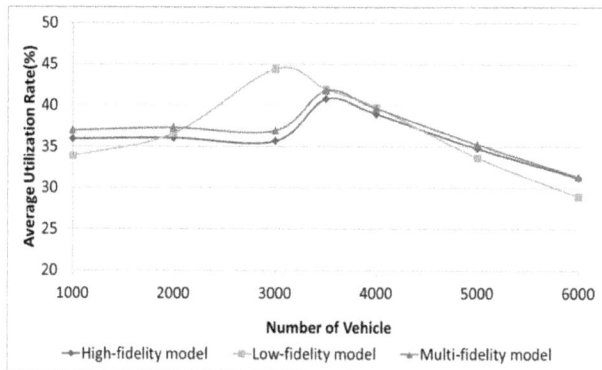

Figure 28. Frequency of model exchange in a vehicle model

5. CONCLUSION

This paper proposes the multi-fidelity M&S methodology for enhancing simulation speed while minimizing accuracy loss and maximizing model reusability, in M&S-based analysis. The target systems of this methodology are continuous and discrete event systems. The proposed methodology consists of 4 steps: 1) target model selection and Interest Region definition, 2) low-fidelity model development, 3) multi-fidelity model composition, 4) selected target model substitution. To maximize model reusability, this methodology is applied without any modification of existing models and simulation engine.

The case studies show effectiveness of the proposed methodology in simulation speed up and model reusability. Examples of continuous system and discrete event system are the Torpedo Tactics Simulation model and the Vehicle Allocation Simulation model. The proposed methodology enhances the simulation speed about 1.25 times and 1.21 times in each example, without any modification of existing models and simulation engine.

6. ACKNOWLEDGMENTS

This work was partially supported by Defense Acquisition Program Administration and Agency for Defense Development under the contract. (UD110006MD)

7. REFERENCES

[1] Kim, T.G. 2007. Modeling and Simulation Engineering. *Communication of the Korea Information Science Society.* 14(6), 3-17.

[2] Kim, J.H., Moon, I.C., and Kim, T.G. 2012. New insight into doctrine via simulation interoperation of heterogeneous levels of models in battle experimentation. *Simulation: Transactions of The Society for Modeling and Simulation International.* 88(6), 649-667.

[3] Seo, K.M., Song, H.S., Kwon S.J., and Kim, T.G. 2011. Measurement of Effectiveness for an Anti-torpedo Combat System Using a Discrete Event Systems Specification-based Underwater Warfare Simulator. *The Journal of Defense Modeling and Simulation: Applications, Methodology, Technology,* 8(3), 157-171.

[4] Kwon, S. J., and Kim, T.G. 2012. Design and Implementation of Event-based DEVS Execution Environment for Faster Execution of Iterative Simulation. In *Proceedings of the Spring Simulation Multiconference* (Orlando, USA, March 26-29, 2012). p. 14.

[5] Hong, J.H., Seo, K.M., and Kim, T.G. 2013. Simulation-based optimization for design parameter exploration in hybrid system: a defense system example. *Simulation: Transactions of The Society for Modeling and Simulation International.* 89(3), 362-380.

[6] IEEE. 2011. IEEE Recommended Practice for Validation of Computational Electromagnetics Computer Modeling and Simulation. *IEEE Std 1597.2^{TM}-2010,* p. 113.

[7] Vitali, R., Haftka, R.T., and Sankar, B.B. 2002. Multi-fidelity design of stiffened composite panel with a crack. *Structural and Multidisciplinary Optimization,* 23(5), 347-356.

[8] Gano. S.E. 2005. *Simulation-based design using variable fidelity optimization.* Doctoral Thesis, University of Notre Dame, 14-30.

[9] Molina-Cristobal, Arturo, Patrick R. Palmer, and Geoffrey T. Parks. 2011. Multi-fidelity Simulation modeling in optimization of a hybrid submarine propulsion system. In *Proceedings of the European Conference on Power Electronics and Applications* (Birmingham, UK, Aug. 30-Sept. 1, 2011). 1-10.

[10] Peng, W., Yun, Z., Zhengping, Z., Lei, Q., and Zhixiang, Z. 2013. A Novel Multi-fidelity Coupled Simulation Method for Flow Systems. *Chines Journal of Aeronautics,* 26(4), 868-875.

[11] Zhou, Z., Ong, Y. S., Nair, P.B. Keane, A. J., and Lum, K. Y. 2007. Combining global and local surrogate models to accelerate evolutionary optimization. *System, Man, and Cybernetics, Part C: Applications and Review, IEEE Transactions on,* 37(1), 66-76.

[12] Celik, N., Lee, S., Vasudevan, K., and Son, Y.J. 2010. DDDAS-based multi-fidelity simulation framework for supply chain systems. *IIE Transactions,* 42(5), 325-341.

[13] Lim, S.Y., Kim, T.G. 2001. Hybrid Modeling and Simulation Methodology based on DEVS Formalism. In *proceedings of Summer Computer Simulation Conference* (Vancouver, Canada, July 16-20, 2001). 188-193.

[14] Zeigler, Bernard P., Herbert Praehofer, and Tag Gon Kim. 1976. *Theory of modeling and simulation.* John Wiley, New York, 510 pages.

[15] Hong, S.Y., and Kim, T.G. 2012. Specification of multi-resolution modeling space for multi-resolution system simulation. *Simulation: Transactions of The Society for Modeling and Simulation International.* 89(1), 28-40.

[16] Fossen, T.I. 1994. *Guidance and control of ocean vehicles.* Wiley, England.

[17] Dijkstra, Edsger W. 1959. A note on two problems in connexion with graph. *Numerische mathematic,* 1(1), 269-271.

[18] Tag Gon Kim. 2006. DEVSIM++ v3.0 Developer's Manual, http://smslab.kaist.ac.kr, accessed at Jan. 2014.

[19] Naver Map. http://maps.naver.com, accessed at Jan. 2014.

[20] Gyeonggi Research Institute. 2011. Analysis of O/D passenger traffic in capital area. http://www.gri.re.kr, accessed at Jan. 2014.

Towards Semantic Model Composition via Experiments

Danhua Peng
Albert-Einstein-Str. 22
University of Rostock
18059 Rostock, Germany
danhua.peng2@uni-
rostock.de

Roland Ewald
Albert-Einstein-Str. 22
University of Rostock
18059 Rostock, Germany
roland.ewald@acm.org

Adelinde M. Uhrmacher
Albert-Einstein-Str. 22
University of Rostock
18059 Rostock, Germany
adelinde.uhrmacher@uni-
rostock.de

ABSTRACT

Unambiguous experiment descriptions are increasingly required for model publication, as they contain information important for reproducing simulation results. In the context of model composition, this information can be used to generate experiments for the composed model. If the original experiment descriptions specify which model property they refer to, we can then execute the generated experiments and assess the validity of the composed model by evaluating their results. Thereby, we move the attention to describing properties of a model's behavior and the conditions under which these hold, i.e., its semantics. We illuminate the potential of this concept by considering the composition of Lotka-Volterra models. In a first prototype realized for JAMES II, we use ML-Rules to describe and execute the Lotka-Volterra models and SESSL for specifying the original experiments. Model properties are described in continuous stochastic logic, and we use statistical model checking for their evaluation. Based on this, experiments to check whether these properties hold for the composed model are automatically generated and executed.

Categories and Subject Descriptors

I.6.4 [**Simulation and Modeling**]: Model Validation and Analysis—*Semantic Composability*; I.6.7 [**Simulation and Modeling**]: Simulation Support Systems—*Model Composition, Simulation Experiments*

Keywords

Reuse of models; Simulation Experiments; Validation; Semantic Composition

1. INTRODUCTION

Model composition holds the promise of easily assembling complex models from predefined building blocks. Generally, a component is developed as a replaceable part of a system, to be used in unforeseen contexts and for different

purposes [39]. Appropriate interface definitions are crucial for this, as they shall provide just the information necessary to (re-)use the component [4]. For many technical areas, libraries of model components have been proven highly effective [8]. Traditionally, model components are viewed as portable building blocks [39] and model composition refers to combining the inputs and outputs of the model components [1]. In non-technical areas like computational biology, however, no libraries of model components could be established yet. Nevertheless, there are public libraries for complete models [18], which are frequently reused as a starting point for model extension or composition [29]. Different approaches towards composing models are distinguished in this context [36]. For example, *Fusion* merges existing models into one model, whereas *Aggregation* creates models by composing models via interfaces.

Unlike model components, which are designed to work in an "unforeseen" context, it is clear that a model designed to answer a specific question of interest—and thus being validated with this question in mind—is not simply reusable in an any context, i.e., cannot simply be composed with another model [3, 25]. Various levels of composability can be distinguished [40], often summarized as syntactic and semantic composability [27]. Semantic composability, which also refers to a model's underlying abstractions and assumptions (this is called conceptual composability in [40]), is particularly challenging to ensure, as these assumptions are rarely stated explicitly and exhaustively. In the following, we try to circumvent this problem by looking at how those assumptions are reflected by simulation experiments and their outcome.

Experiments and their results play a key role in refining and successively enriching models, which is also reflected in workflows that intertwine phases of experimenting and modeling, e.g., [32]. These experiments shall serve as a starting point to tackle the issue of conceptual interoperability and, more generally, the support of modeling by automatic experimentation. Thus, our study does *not* focus on the automatic composition of models and the different manners in which composition can be done, but rather on how to automatically provide important feedback to the user during a modeling process that includes the reuse of different models, i.e., to check whether properties that hold for the reused models also hold for the composed one.

Throughout the paper, we will use Lotka-Volterra models as a running example to illuminate our approach.

2. EXAMPLE: COMPOSITION OF LOTKA-VOLTERRA MODELS

The Lotka-Volterra model, one of the classic predator-prey models, is a well-known example of a mathematical model of population biology (as described in [30], it was first presented in [19, 41]). It describes the interaction between populations, i.e., predators and prey, in a rather abstract manner. Here, we focus on a specific variant of the Lotka-Volterra model, where one predator species hunts one prey species and the prey depends on an unlimited supply of food. To avoid an exponential growth of the prey population in the absence of predators, competition among prey is also considered. Let N_1 denote the prey population size and N_2 denote the predator population size, so that the deterministic equations are (cf. [30, p. 176]):

$$\mathrm{d}N_1/\mathrm{d}t = N_1 * (b - k * N_1 - a * N_2) \qquad (prey)$$
$$\mathrm{d}N_2/\mathrm{d}t = N_2 * (-d + c * N_1) \qquad (predator)$$

where b is the birth rate of the prey, d is the mortality rate of the predator, a and c are the interaction coefficients, and k is the competition coefficient.

Different questions can drive the modeling and simulation of prey and predator systems. For example, one may be interested in the stationary states of the system, e.g., the "coexisting state", where both prey and predator populations exist, the "prey state", where the predators die out and only prey survive, or the "empty state", where predators first extinguish the prey population and afterward die out [6]. Similarly, it may also be interesting to compare the size of the predator and prey populations. These questions are reflected in different *hypotheses*, i.e., under which circumstance, e.g., parameter values and initial state, does a certain *statement* or *property* hold.

Assuming we develop a set of Lotka-Volterra models, each characterized by some hypotheses and experiments: what properties of the composed model can be deduced? For example, if we have two Lotka-Volterra models and for each of those the hypothesis "coexisting state" has been shown to hold, can we assume that the hypothesis still holds in a composed model where two predator species hunt the same prey, or two prey species are hunted by the same predator? What does a violation, i.e., a falsified hypothesis, tell us about the conceptual validity of our composition?

In the following, we approach these questions based on concrete simulation studies that focus on three properties. Two properties, "coexisting state" and "empty state", are commonly checked in Lotka-Volterra models [6]. The third, "recovery comparison", states that the prey population will recover faster than the predator population if both populations has been disturbed significantly, i.e., both populations are quite small.

2.1 Ingredients

To test our approach, we need a modeling formalism, an execution algorithm, a way to describe simulation experiments, and a way to describe the model properties that shall be satisfied.

2.1.1 Model Description and Execution

We use ML-Rules [21] to describe the Lotka-Volterra models, which is a rule-based, multi-level modeling language for (cell) biological systems that has been realized for JAMES II [16]. ML-Rules can describe a dynamic hierarchy of nested species, and also supports downward and upward causation across different levels of the hierarchy. For each rule, arbitrary reaction rate kinetics using any kind of mathematical expression and constraints are allowed to specify state transitions in a flexible manner. Several other modeling formalisms supported by JAMES II would also allow to define these comparatively simple models. However, as we aim at applying our technique to concrete cell biological modeling and simulation studies, e.g., to extend the Wnt-pathway model from [22] to include membrane dynamics, we use ML-Rules here as well. We use the reference stochastic simulation algorithm from [21], which is based on Gillespie's approach [11], to simulate the models (instead of the faster but approximative tau-leaping variant [15]).

2.1.2 Experiment Description

SESSL (*Simulation Experiment Specification via a Scala Layer*) is an embedded domain-specific language for simulation experiments [9]. It serves as an additional software layer between users and simulation systems, facilitates the reuse and execution of simulation experiments, and offers various features, e.g., for experiment design and simulation-based optimization. As already mentioned, a variety of experiments are executed during the development of a simulation model, e.g., sensitivity analysis or parameter estimation [32]. The user might wish to store experiments and results together with the model. Models can be annotated with SESSL specifications, which can also be generated. So far, SESSL was focused on the execution of experiments, similar to other approaches for simulation experimentation (e.g., NEDL [14]). It did not allow to specify which model properties shall hold, i.e., what the experiment results should look like. However, an explicit and formal description of the expected outcome is required for our approach.

In general, the motivation of simulation experiments is rarely stated in a formal manner. This is in contrast to verification and model checking approaches, where the property of the system to be checked needs to be formally defined [24]. Consequently, experiments that combine techniques from simulation and verification, e.g., in statistical model checking, include explicit formal statements about the properties of the trajectories that are checked. Nevertheless, SESSL is easy to extend, so we choose to use it for experiments description.

2.1.3 Property Description

Linear Temporal Logic (LTL) is widely used to check the properties of individual trajectories [10, 47], and thus allows to express a broad range of dynamic model properties. To check an output trajectory π, we rely on a JAMES II-based reimplementation of the model-checking algorithm introduced by Fages et al. [10]. The original algorithm captures the following operators of LTL: X (next), G (global), F (finally), and U (until). We extended the algorithm to include the R operator (release) as well (see [2]). However, LTL might not suffice to describe all properties of interest. Thus, we allow to express custom properties via predefined predicates, which must also provide the corresponding algorithms to check them on a trajectory.

ML-Rules is based on Continuous-Time Markov Chain (CTMC) semantics, so that the results are stochastic and multiple replications are required for analysis. For some replications a property may hold, for others it may not hold. Thus, we need to express our expectation regarding replications with probabilities. In analogy to Continuous Stochastic Logic (CSL) [46, 35], which has been proposed as a formalism for expressing properties of CTMC, we define $Pr_{\bowtie p}(\phi)$ with $\bowtie \in \{<, \leq, >, \geq\}$ and an initial state s so that

$$s \vDash Pr_{\bowtie p}(\phi) \iff Prob(\pi \in Path(s) | \pi \vDash \phi) \bowtie p \quad (1)$$

We extended SESSL to support the definition of such probabilistic statements, where ϕ could be an LTL formula or a predefined predicate. In contrast to [46, 35], however, we currently do not support nested probabilities.

Statistical model checking relies on executing stochastic models, and on hypotheses testing. Consider the null hypothesis H_0 that some property does *not* hold in s, and the alternative hypothesis H_1 that the property does hold in s: the probability to accept H_1 although H_0 is true (false positive) should be at most $\alpha \in (0, 1]$, and the probability to accept H_0 although H_1 is true (false negative) should be at most $\beta \in (0, 1]$. α and β are error bounds for statistical model checking, and as it is quite difficult to ensure a low probability for both types of errors, typically an indifference region of size 2δ is defined. Different approaches exist to minimize the amount of needed replications (e.g., see [45]). For our proof of concept, we follow the approach outlined in [35, p. 5–6] and find the smallest number of replications, n, so that the probability of false positives (false negatives) is smaller than α (β) when assuming a binomially distributed number of successful checks for ϕ, with parameters n and $p - \delta$ (n and $p + \delta$). Again, p denotes the assumed probability (see Equation 1).

2.2 The basic Lotka-Volterra Model

Figure 1 shows the parameters, the species, the initial state, and the reaction rules of a Lotka-Volterra model defined in ML-Rules. Please note that predators and prey are modeled as populations whose individuals encounter the events of death or reproduction stochastically. In the original Lotka-Volterra model equations, five parameters (i.e., a, b, c, d and k, see Section 2) as well as the initial predator and prey population sizes can be set by the modeler. To simplify the example, we reduced the parameter space and thus our ML-Rules models do not distinguish between the interaction coefficients, so both have the same value ($a = c$), and we keep the competition coefficient $k = 0.002$ constant.

A model with the fox being the predator and the rabbit being the prey shall illuminate the experiments. As a first property, we tested the "coexisting state", i.e.,

$$G(\#Rabbit > 0 \wedge \#Fox > 0).$$

We assume that both predators and prey will survive, with a probability of 0.8, i.e.,

$$s \vDash Pr_{\geq 0.8}(G(\#Rabbit > 0 \wedge \#Fox > 0)).$$

The experiment is specified in SESSL (see Figure 2) and executed with JAMES II. The parameter value ranges for which the simulation output fulfills this statement are:

```
1   a: 0.014;
2   b: 0.6;
3   d: 0.7;
4   k: 0.002;
5   nFood:100;
6   nPredator:10;
7   nPrey:100;
8   Food();
9   Predator();
10  Prey();
11
12  >>INIT[(nFood) Food + (nPredator) Predator + (nPrey) Prey];
13
14  // Prey reproduces
15  Food:f + Prey:x -> Food + 2 Prey @b*#x;
16  // Prey dies by competition
17  Prey:x + Prey:z -> Prey @k*#z*#x;
18  // Predator reproduces based on successful hunting
19  Predator:y + Prey:x -> 2 Predator @a*#y*#x;
20  // Predator dies
21  Predator:y -> @d*#y;
```

Figure 1: A Lotka-Volterra model described in ML-Rules

```
1   val exp = new Experiment with Observation with Hypotheses {
2     model = "file-mlrj:/./LotkaVolteraFoxRabbit.mlrj"
3     scan(
4       "a" <~ range(0.010, 0.001, 0.015),
5       "b" <~ range(0.6, 0.1, 1.0),
6       "d" <~ range(0.1, 0.1, 1.0),
7       "nPrey" <~ range(100,100),
8       "nPredator" <~ range(10,10))
9     stopCondition = AfterWallClockTime(minutes=2) or
          AfterSimTime(10)
10    observe("Rabbit","Fox")
11    observeAt(range(0.0, 0.1, 10))
12    assume(
13    Pr(G(variable("Rabbit") > 0 and variable("Fox") > 0)) >= 0.8)
14  }
```

Figure 2: SESSL experiment specification to test the "coexisting state" hypothesis in a basic Lotka-Volterra model.

$$a : 0.010 - 0.015, b : 0.6 - 1.0, d : 0.5 - 1.0$$
$$nPrey = 100, nPredator = 10$$

These parameter ranges define the initial states s (see Equation 1) for which the property has been shown to hold with the given probability, by statistical model checking. Please note the parameters for the initial values of prey ($nPrey$) and predators ($nPredator$) have been fixed. For simplicity, we set the probability p in all our experiments to 0.8.

Similarly, for the properties "empty state" and "recovery comparison", experiments using the same model are executed. For the "empty state" (i.e., the prey dies out first, then the predators die out), the property ϕ can be expressed in LTL as

$$((\#Prey = 0) \; R \; (\#Predator > 0)) \wedge F \; (\#Predator = 0).$$

Taking the probability (and multiple replications) into account, the property which needs to be tested is denoted as $Pr_{\geq 0.8}(\phi)$. In SESSL, this can be expressed as

```
assume(
  Pr(((Negation(variable("Rabbit") > 0)) R (variable("Fox") > 0)
    ) and (Negation(G(variable("Fox") > 0))))) >= 0.8)
```

From the experiments, we learn that this property holds for the initial states s where

$$a : 0.050 - 0.070, b : 0.1 - 0.4, d : 0.7 - 1.0$$
$$nPrey = 100, nPredator = 30$$

Both, property and parameter assignments, together form our hypothesis regarding the model behavior.

The "recovery comparison" property — if both populations are disturbed at the beginning to have the same small size, the prey population will recover faster — is difficult to be expressed in LTL. Therefore, this property is currently implemented as a predefined predicate (see Section 2.1.3). The initial sizes of both predator and prey population are set to a common low value. In principle, the predicate is evaluated by comparing the time points where the first peak occurs in each population. The earlier the first peak occurs, the faster the population has recovered. However, the population trajectories contain random fluctuations, and many sophisticated methods have been developed to find optima in time series with noise (e.g., [34, 7]). We use a more simple approach, which may not be as rigorous but appears to be sufficient for our purpose. In our method, a certain time point is selected and only the time points between the initial and the selected time point are considered. From those, the time point with the maximum value is identified, and the recovery rate is calculated as the slope between the initial value and this maximum. If the maximum equals the initial value, then the recovery rate is calculated as the slope between initial and selected time point. Although such a manual implementation of predicates is not too difficult in JAMES II, it is not acceptable for all users. Therefore, future work will be aimed at extending the language constructs currently used for describing properties of trajectories.

Again, experiments are executed to check the above property. The hypothesis that the probability of The property "recovery comparison" is satisfied with a probability larger than 0.8 for the following initial states:

$$a : 0.010 - 0.028, b : 0.6 - 1.0, d : 0.5 - 1.0$$
$$nPrey : 10, nPredator : 10$$

2.3 Composing Lotka-Volterra Models

Given two Lotka-Volterra models as shown in Figure 1, i.e., each having two species, these can be composed in three ways: the *same prey* composition, the *same predator* composition and the *food chain* composition.

In the *same predator* composition, one predator species and two prey species constitute the composed model. The predator hunts on both prey species. This type of composition requires that the predators in the two model components are the same. Similarly, in the *same prey* composition, there are two predator species and one prey species in the composed model, and both predator species hunt on the same prey. In the *food chain* composition, the prey in one reused model has the role of the predator in the other model component. Thus, in the composed model, it is a food chain where one species functions as both, prey and predator.

```
1  Food:f + Rabbit:x -> Food + 2 Rabbit @b*#x;
2  Rabbit:x + Rabbit:z -> Rabbit @k*#z*#x;
3  Wolf:y + Rabbit:x -> 2 Wolf @a*#y*#x;
4  Wolf:y -> @d*#y;
5
6  Fox:y + Rabbit:x -> 2 Fox @a*#y*#x;
7  Fox:y -> @d*#y;
```

Figure 3: An example of the same prey composition.

```
1  Food:f + Rabbit:x -> Food + 2 Rabbit @b*#x;
2  Rabbit:x + Rabbit:z -> Rabbit @k*#z*#x;
3  Fox:y + Rabbit:x -> 2 Fox @a*#y*#x;
4  Fox:f -> @d*#f;
5
6  Wolf:w + Fox:y -> 2 Wolf @a*#y*#w;
7  Wolf:w -> @d*#w;
```

Figure 4: An example of the food chain composition.

Similar to the model in Figure 1, we developed and experimented with Lotka-Volterra models for foxes and rabbits, wolves and rabbits, wolves and foxes, and wolves and sheep. Now we wish to compose those. As outlined in [26], the modeler needs to decide during the composition whether a species with the same name refers to the same species in the composed model. If not, renaming is required. For example, if the wolves were hunting another kind of rabbit, its name needs to be changed. Besides renaming species, the modeler could also change the configuration of parameters during composition. In the food chain composition, for example, the species that is now both prey and predator may need a readjusted initial population size in the composed model.

We create three composed models to evaluate our approach, one for each type of composition. An example of the same prey composition, in which both wolves and foxes hunt rabbits, is shown in Figure 3. An example of the food chain composition, in which wolves hunt foxes and foxes hunt rabbits, is shown in Figure 4. Additionally, we created a same predator composition, where the composed model contains one predator that feeds on two prey, i.e., wolves hunt both sheep and rabbits.

2.4 Generating Experiments for Hypotheses

As mentioned before, we consider three properties to be checked (see Section 2.2) and three types of composition (see Section 2.3). Two basic two-species Lotka-Volterra models (see Section 2.2) are reused for each composition. For both models, all three hypotheses are checked, each by its corresponding experiment. All of these hypotheses shall be checked again for composed model. To do so, experiments for the composed model will be generated, based on the experiments that were used to check the hypotheses for the reused models.

Each hypothesis consists of two parts, i.e., parameter value ranges and the property that shall hold (see Section 2.2). The parameter value ranges are reflected by the parameter configuration of the corresponding experiment, whereas the property is a formal statement that depends on the names of model variables (e.g., species names, species population and so on). As described before, these names may be changed by

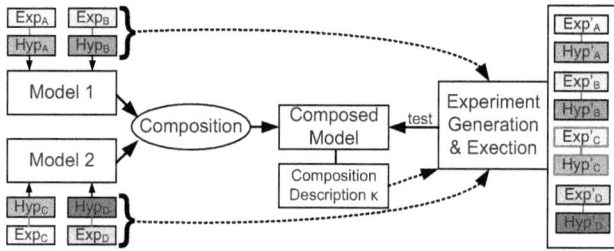

Figure 5: Our overall approach considers the hypotheses of the individual models (colored boxes), as well as the simulation experiments to check them, and supports semantic model composition by first adapting them to the composed model (Hyp'_A etc., right-hand side) and then testing them. The user is notified whenever a hypothesis does not hold for the composed model (e.g., Hyp'_C, see red outline).

the modeler during composition. Therefore, the hypotheses to be checked need to be refined according to those changes.

No species need to be renamed in our example, but the parameter value ranges need reconsideration when generating experiments for the composed model (see Section 3). For the food chain composition, we also adjusted the initial population size of the fox, which is both the prey and the predator in this case. Other details of the experiment setup, such as the simulation stopping criterion, will be copied from the experiments that were defined on the reused models. The hypotheses we consider refer to probabilities, so we follow the approach outlined in Section 2.1.3 to determine the number of necessary replications.

With all this information, we can now execute the newly generated simulation experiments, to check the hypotheses from the reused models on the composed model. We describe our concept and algorithms for this task in the following.

3. THE CONCEPT

The main idea we put forward in this paper is to support semantic composition by automatically adapting and checking hypotheses that are defined on the reused models. To do so, our approach relies on additional information in form of a composition description (see Section 3.2.1). It is then able to identify hypotheses that do not hold in the composed model (or, in case of probabilistic statements, are very unlikely to hold). Figure 5 gives an overview of the general approach.

3.1 Basic Notation

We assume that each model m has an interface, comprising a set of parameters and a set of interaction points [31]. Both are defined by their names and their domain, e.g., the set of parameters $P(m) = \{p_i | i = 1, \ldots, n\}$ with p_i being a tuple $(name, \mathcal{D}_i)$, where $\mathcal{D}_i$ is the domain of the parameter's possible values. Similarly, the set of interaction points of a model is defined, i.e., $IP(m) = \{ip_i | i = 1, \ldots, v\}$ with IP_i being a tuple $(name, \mathcal{D}_i)$. Interaction points are used for aggregating models [29] and for collecting data from the model. Please note that all variables of a model become interaction points when using exchange formats like SBML [17].

Let $\mathbb{A} = \mathcal{D}_1 \times \ldots \times \mathcal{D}_n$ be the set of all permissible parameterizations of the model m. We call an element $a \in \mathbb{A}$

an *assignment*, and the finite subset $A \subseteq \mathbb{A}$ of assignments for which the model has been simulated the *experiment assignments*.

We consider the simulation of a model to be a black box. Given a certain assignment $a \in \mathbb{A}$, and an experiment $exp(a)$, it will generate output in the form of $Y(a)$.

Because simulation can be stochastic, there may be multiple sets of finite trajectories T_i per observation: $Y(a) = \{T_i, i = 1, \ldots, k\}$. Each trajectory set T_i consists of all observed data from a single run, in the form of trajectories tr_i, i.e., $T_i = \{tr_i, i = 1, \ldots, l\}$. We further assume each trajectory tr_i consists of a unique name, e.g., a biological species to be observed, and a sequence of time-stamped data d_i:

$$tr_i = (name, (t_1, d_1), \ldots, (t_z, d_z)).$$

Each trajectory set T_i should also contain corresponding data for each interaction point, i.e.,

$$\forall (name_{ip}, D_{ip}) \in IP(m) : \exists tr_i \in T_i,$$
$$name = name_{ip} \text{ and } d_j \in D_{ip} \ j \in 1 \ldots z.$$

So far, we have discussed parameter assignments and the output of the experiments in terms of trajectories, which depends on these assignments. Now, we define the properties of a model's behavior. We use a variant of the continuous stochastic logic (CSL) [46, 35] for the stochastic case, which works on multiple replications and where a property expressed in LTL is checked for each replication (see Section 2.1.3). For a certain statement or property $Pr_{\bowtie p}(\phi)_i$, a given assignment set $A_i \subseteq \mathbb{A}$ defines for which parameter assignments $Pr_{\bowtie p}(\phi)_i$ is true. Together, this yields a hypothesis $h_i = \langle A_i, Pr_{\bowtie p}(\phi)_i \rangle$, i.e.,:

$$\forall a \in A_i : \langle a, exp_i(a) \rangle \vDash Pr_{\bowtie p}(\phi)_i. \quad (2)$$

This can be evaluated with statistical model checking, i.e.,

$$\langle a, exp(a) \rangle \vDash Pr_{\bowtie p}(\phi) \iff Prob(\pi \in Path(s) | \pi \vDash \phi) \bowtie p$$

where π represents the T_i, s is the initial state of the model (determined by a and $exp(a)$), and $Y(a) \subseteq Path(s)$. Please note that each hypothesis h_i has a corresponding experiment description exp_i. In the following, we therefore simplify Equation 2 to the shorthand notation $A_i \vDash Pr_{\bowtie p}(\phi)_i$.

The above definition of a hypothesis makes the goal of its corresponding experiment explicit. Statements about the behavior of the model and information about configurations (in terms of parameter assignments) become the focus of interest. The above argumentation neglects information that is essential for reproducing simulation results (like stop criteria, the simulator to use, etc.) which are part of specifying an experiment, $exp(a)$. However, we build on this information when executing the experiments to test the generated hypothesis for the composed model (see Section 2.4). Finally, we assume that each reused model m is annotated with a set of hypotheses $H_m = \{h_i, i = 1, \ldots, q\}$.

3.2 Experiment Generation

3.2.1 Basic Algorithm

We assume that a composed model m_c is created by reusing two models, m_1 and m_2, and that the type of composition is

Algorithm 1 Basic algorithm.

m_c: composed model
H_{m_1}: Hypotheses defined for model m_1
H_{m_2}: Hypotheses defined for model m_2
κ: composition description
u: user preferences

```
1   // Generate possible hypotheses
2   H_mc ← createHypotheses(H_m1, H_m2, κ, u)
3   // Return set for successful hypotheses
4   H+ ← ∅
5   // Return set for failure hypotheses
6   H- ← ∅
7   // Check hypotheses in composed model m_c
8   for each hypothesis h = A_h ⊨ Pr⋈p(φ)_h ∈ H_mc
9     A ← sampleAssignments(h, κ, u)
10    A+ ← ∅
11    A- ← ∅
12    for each assignment a ∈ A
13      exp_a ← generateExperiment(m_c,a,exp_h,Pr⋈p(φ)_h)
14      Y(a) ← run(exp_a)
15      result ← check(Pr⋈p(φ)_h, Y(a))
16      if result is invalid
17        switch(u.returnPreference(h))
18          case strict: return error
19          case record: A- ← A- ∪ a
20                       continue
21        end
22      else
23        A+ ← A+ ∪ a
24      end
25    end for
26    //Add successful hypothesis:
27    H+ ← H+ ∪ {A+ ⊨ Pr⋈p(φ)_h}
28    //Add failure hypothesis:
29    H- ← H- ∪ {A- ⊭ Pr⋈p(φ)_h}
30  end for
31  return H+,H-
```

defined by some $c \in C = \{c_i, i = 1, \ldots, r\}$. In our example, we distinguish the *same prey*, the *same predator*, and the *food chain* composition types (see Section 2.3). Besides the composition type, the modeler may also change the names of some model entities, or change the value ranges of some model parameters. For example, in the food chain composition the initial value of the species population is adjusted during composition (see Section 2.3). These changes, along with the composition type c, are stored in a composition description κ, which describes the overall model composition.

An additional structure for user preferences, u, allows users to influence how hypothesis testing and hypothesis creation are executed. This improves the flexibility of our approach. For instance, some hypotheses must never be violated, e.g., in our example the hypothesis referring to the "empty state" property (prey should always becomes extinct first, followed by the predators, see Section 2.2). A violation of this hypothesis could thus be defined as an error. On the other hand, a violation of the hypothesis referring to the "coexisting state" property (no species becomes extinct, see Section 2.2) may even be *expected* in a composed Lotka-Volterra model, and could thus be tolerated.

Algorithm 1 depicts the procedure of generating experiments for the composed model, based on information about experiments done with the reused models. The input of the algorithm are the composed model m_c, the hypothesis sets H_{m_1}, H_{m_2}, which are defined for the two reused models m_1 and m_2, respectively, the composition description κ, and the user preferences u. First of all, a hypothesis set

H_{m_c} of the composed model m_c is created by a function **createHypotheses** (line 2), which will be described in algorithm 2. Additionally, two hypothesis sets to record the result of hypothesis testing, H_+ and H_-, are created (line 4, 6). H_+ stores all hypotheses that hold for the composed model. Similarly, if there are some assignments $a \in A_-$ for which the statement $Pr_{\bowtie p}(\phi)_h$ is not true, this will be stored in H_- as $A_- \nvDash Pr_{\bowtie p}(\phi)_i$.

For each hypothesis $h \in H_{m_c}$, experiment assignments A are generated through sampling. This is implemented in a function **sampleAssignments** (line 9), which takes the given hypothesis h, the composition description κ, and the user preferences u as input. While we currently sample uniformly from the assignment set A_h of the given hypothesis, other sampling methods may yield much better results. For example, one could draw samples from nearly orthogonal latin hypercubes (e.g., [33]), or focus on the boundaries of A_h in the parameter space. Since larger sample sizes are computationally more expensive, we expect that the quality of the sampling method will have a large impact on the overall performance. Therefore, users should also be able to adjust the sampling procedure to their requirements, e.g., to generate more samples if the available hardware is sufficiently powerful. This can be expressed via the user preferences u. Similarly, more sophisticated sampling methods may require additional information on the actual model composition, e.g., to generate more samples for parameters shared by both model components.

The sampling results in a set A of experiment assignments. For each assignment a, the algorithm now generates a suitable experiment exp_a. For this, it relies on the composed model m_c, the assignment a, the experiment exp_h that is associated with the hypothesis h, and the statement $Pr_{\bowtie p}(\phi)_h$ of the hypothesis h (line 8), all of which are passed to the function **generateExperiment** (line 13). Currently, this function takes an experiment specification defined in SESSL and adapts it to the composed model and the new assignment. Internally, this function retrieves the experiment definition that corresponds to $Pr_{\bowtie p}(\phi)_h$, which we assume to be preserved from experiments with the reused models m_1 and m_2 (see Section 3.2.2 for details). For example, these definitions can be specified with SESSL, as shown in Figure 2. Apart from the model to be simulated, which is now m_c, the parameters to be used, which are now defined by a, and the number of required replications, which now depends on α, β, and δ (see Section 2.1.3), every aspect of the experiment can stay the same. Thus, this function simply reconfigures the corresponding experiment to work with m_c and a.

With all the details configured, the simulation experiment exp_a can now be executed by invoking **run** (line 14). The output of the simulation execution is a trajectories set $Y(a)$. Then, the statement $Pr_{\bowtie p}(\phi)_h$ will be checked against $Y(a)$. If the check is successful, the assignment a will be stored in the set A_+, which contains all assignments where the current hypothesis h has been corroborated. If the check is unsuccessful, i.e., the result is invalid (lines 16–22), what happens next depends on the user preferences u. If the statement $Pr_{\bowtie p}(\phi)_h$ does not hold for the assignment a, a user may want to let the whole procedure fail as early as possible, because this indicates problems in the model composition or the reused models. On the other hand, it may also be reasonable to check all hypotheses first, and to record which

Algorithm 2 Creation of hypotheses.
H_{m_1}: Hypotheses defined for model m_1
H_{m_2}: Hypotheses defined for model m_2
κ: composition description
u: user preferences

```
1   function createHypotheses(H_m1, H_m2, κ, u)
2       H_mc ← ∅
3       // Create new hypotheses on composed model m_c
4       for each hypothesis h = A_h ⊨ Pr⋈p(φ)_h ∈ (H_m1 ∪ H_m2)
5           Pr⋈p(φ)'_h ← renameVariables(Pr⋈p(φ)_h, κ_names)
6           A_h' ← updateBounds(A_h, κ_A, u)
7           if (A_h' = ∅)
8               switch(u.strictness)
9                   case strict: return error
10                  case tolerant: continue
11                  case retry: A_h' ← κ_A
12              end
13          end
14          H_mc ← H_mc ∪ {A_h' ⊨ Pr⋈p(φ)'_h} //Add new hypothesis
15      end
16  return H_mc
```

hold and which do not hold, because this could simplify the later analysis of potential causes. Both approaches are supported by defining $u.returnPreference(h)$ either as **strict** (line 18), which fails early, or as **record** (line 19), which continues the experiments.

3.2.2 Creation of Hypotheses

The creation of hypotheses is described in Algorithm 2. This function works on the hypotheses sets of the two reused models, H_{m_1} and H_{m_2}, and also needs the composition description κ and the user preferences u as input. It iterates over all hypotheses in the two hypothesis sets H_{m_1} and H_{m_2} (line 4). For each hypothesis $h = A_h \models Pr_{\bowtie p}(\phi)_h$, the for-loop generates a new statement $Pr_{\bowtie p}(\phi)'_h$ and new experiment assignments $A_{h'}$. The new statement $Pr_{\bowtie p}(\phi)'_h$ is generated by renaming variables, i.e., it depends on the composition description κ (line 5, see Section 2.4). If a variable name has been changed, e.g., substituted with another name in the composed model, this is recorded in κ_{names}. Therefore, we apply all name changes given in κ_{names} to the corresponding variables in statement $Pr_{\bowtie p}(\phi)_h$, which then forms the new statement $Pr_{\bowtie p}(\phi)_h$. This is handled by the function **renameVariables** in Algorithm 2 (line 5).

After model composition, the experiment assignments of the reused models and the experiment assignments of the composed model will usually have different dimensions. One reason for this is that parameters of *both* reused models are included in the composed model. Thus, the experiment assignments of each original hypothesis, A_h, need to be refined to suit the experiment assignment dimensions of the composed model. This is done in a function called **updateBounds**, which takes the assignments A_h, the experiment assignments of the composed model, κ_A, and the user preferences u as input (line 6).

The dimensions of the composed model's experiment assignments, κ_A, are part of the composition description and assumed to be defined by the modeler during composition. This can also be done implicitly. For example, our prototype currently calculates the minimum and maximum value for each parameter of the reused models, by iterating over the experiment assignments of all their hypotheses. To construct

κ_A, we use these minimal and maximal parameter values as boundaries, and then join these parameter intervals of the reused models together. If a parameter is defined in both reused models, we use the overall minimum and maximum value. In this way, we can define valid parameter ranges for the composed model without user intervention. Still, if the modeler explicitly sets one parameter to a constant value during the composition, κ_A will be reduced accordingly.

Our prototype currently implements **updateBounds** in a simple way. For each dimension of κ_A, the intersection of the corresponding intervals in A_h and κ_A is calculated. If there is no such dimension in A_h, e.g., because the corresponding parameter is defined in the composed model but not the reused model, the interval from κ_A is used. There are other ways to generate the new experiment assignments $A_{h'}$, e.g., in some situations it may be preferable to compute a union of the parameter intervals (and not an intersection). To let the user have control over this aspect, the function also takes user preferences as input.

Even with these precautions regarding an update of the parameter bounds, it is still possible that A'_h is empty. In our prototype implementation of **updateBounds**, this means there is at least one parameter with non-overlapping bounds in A_h and κ_A. In this case, the user preference regarding the *strictness* of hypothesis generation determines how to proceed. This is shown in lines 8–12 of Algorithm 2. As κ_A describes for which parameter bounds the composed model shall be used, a lack of assignments that fall within these bounds could mean that the composition itself is problematic. Thus, the hypothesis creation function should stop and return an error message (**strict** mode, line 9). However, it could also mean that over-constrained hypotheses are the problem, i.e., they are of less importance for the composed model and should be discarded (**tolerant** mode, line 10). Besides these options, a user might also be more interested in exploring the validity of model properties for the new parameter bounds of the composed model, and would thus like to check them with the experiment assignments in κ_A (**retry** mode, line 11). Anyhow, the newly defined experiment assignments $A_{h'}$ will then be used to define a new hypothesis (line 14).

We assume that for each hypothesis $h = A_h \models Pr_{\bowtie p}(\phi)_h$, defined for either m_1 or m_2, there is also a corresponding experiment definition exp_h that allows to check whether $Pr_{\bowtie p}(\phi)_h$ is true for a certain assignment $a \in A_h$ and the reused model. As described in Section 3.2.1, this experiment definition can be reused with minimal adaptations. Thus, it allows us to check whether $Pr_{\bowtie p}(\phi)'_h$ is true for a certain assignment $a' \in A'_h$ and m_c. The advantage of this approach is that the actual experiment definition can be arbitrarily complex, e.g., in terms of output analysis, experiment design, or stopping conditions. Anyhow, we omit the explicit handling of experiments from the pseudo-code for simplicity.

3.2.3 Interpretation of Generated Output

If Algorithm 1 finds a problem, it will return a (set of) counterexamples H_-. It is easy to re-check these counterexamples on the model for which they have been defined originally. This is important, because the hypotheses that characterize the reused models may have been checked insufficiently, i.e., they may not even be valid for the original models. Depending on the outcome of testing the corresponding model component (m_1 or m_2), the user knows whether there

Hypothesis & Experiment Definition (SESSL)

- Experiment specifications   - Composition results
- Hypotheses   - Errors

Hypothesis Creation & Experiment Execution

- Output data   - Statement evaluation (true ∨ false)
- Statement

Statement Evaluation on Output (e.g. LTL Model Checking)

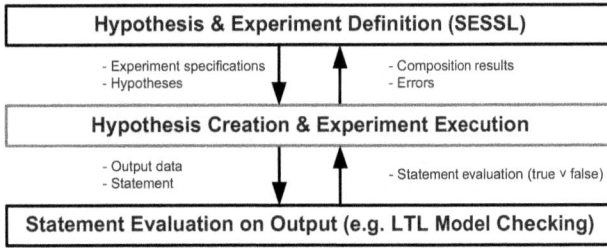

Figure 6: The three layers of our prototype implementation: a SESSL extension is used to specify experiments and hypotheses on model components (upper layer) and the middle layer generates the new hypotheses and executes all experiments (red box). The lower layer evaluates each statement against the generated output.

	Same Prey	Same Predator	Food Chain
Coexisting state	√ / √	⊘ / ⊘	√ / ⊘
Empty state	√ / √	√ / √	⊘ / √
Recovery comparison	√ / √	⊘ / √	√ / ⊘

Table 1: Results overview. For each composition type, the hypotheses of the two reused models are checked. Each cell contains the results of checking both hypotheses that refer to the same property (one hypothesis from each of the reused models). The symbol √ represents hypotheses that hold, whereas the symbol ⊘ represents those that do not hold.

is a problem with the composition (i.e., the counterexample is true for m_1, but not for m_c) or a problem with the hypothesis set of the original model component (i.e., the counterexample is true for neither m_1 nor m_c). Such checks can be easily triggered automatically, so that a user can quickly see what kind of problem has been encountered. Extending our prototype in that regard will be subject to future work.

4. IMPLEMENTATION & RESULTS

4.1 Implementation

Our implementation of the concepts described in Section 3 consists of three distinct layers, as summarized in Figure 6.

The first layer provides the user interface, i.e., it allows to define hypotheses and their corresponding simulation experiments for individual models. Currently, this user interface is realized as an extension of SESSL [9] that provides the functionality to define hypotheses regarding the simulation output. It can be used to augment SESSL experiments by mixing in the **Hypotheses** trait, as shown in line 1 of Figure 2. Besides defining simulation experiments, the main task of this layer is the creation of an object hierarchy that represents a hypothesis. Both the experiment specification and the hypothesis representation are handed over to the second layer. Many other kinds of user interfaces could be developed on top of this layer, e.g., to specify hypotheses via a graphical user interface.

The second layer implements our overall concept (see Algorithms 1 and 2) and defines the type hierarchy for the hypotheses that are currently supported, i.e., so far LTL-Expressions, probabilistic statements ($Pr_{\bowtie p}(\phi)$), and custom predefined predicates (see Section 2.1.3). This layer is integrated into JAMES II, so that it can leverage its plug'n simulate approach [16] to ensure its flexibility regarding future extensions, as well as its applicability to the various modeling formalisms already supported by JAMES II.

The third layer is triggered by the second layer to check the generated hypotheses against the simulation output of the composed model. It is implemented on top of JAMES II as well. So far, this layer provides a re-implementation of the model checking approach followed in [10], as well as support for custom predicates. We consider the integration of additional model checking approaches to be future work.

Finally, note that our prototypical implementation is still mostly independent of concrete simulation systems, i.e., it can be integrated into other simulation systems with relatively little effort. This is because the plug-in system of JAMES II is used as a foundation, but our prototype requires none of its simulation-specific abstractions.

4.2 Result Analysis

Table 1 gives an overview about the results of our example (see Section 2), where √ means that the property also hold in the composed model, and ⊘ that it does not hold (at least not with the expected probability $p \geq 0.8$). For each type of composition (see Section 2.3), the hypotheses referring to the two reused models are checked for the composed model.

If we look at the results, we see that two predators feeding on the same prey is unproblematic (i.e., the *same prey* composition). This is to be expected, as the prey still controls the behavior of the predator(s). The situation is different if a predator feeds on two prey species (i.e., the *same predator* composition). Here, the weaker prey is likely to become extinct, which is not uncommon. In case of the *food chain* composition, only the hypothesis of one reused model holds in the composed model, while the hypothesis of the other reused model does not hold. This indicates that this composition type might not be valid. Actually, in the given example we would expect the wolves to also feed on rabbits as soon as rabbits are around, and not only on foxes (cf. Figure 4).

Table 2 shows the results in more detail. Here, another interesting observation is that one hypothesis regarding "Recovery comparison" for the *same predator* composition holds for 9 out of 10 tested assignments in the composed model. Thus, the likelihood to find a counterexample is low, i.e., this would be difficult to find out if the hypotheses were checked manually. This illustrates the potential of our approach in preventing users from coming to incorrect conclusions regarding the hypotheses that hold in a composed model.

5. DISCUSSION

5.1 Related work

Other approaches that address semantic composition of models depend on the existence of a perfect model, based on which the composed models can be validated [44, 38]. The validity of the composed model is measured by comparing its simulation executions with that of the perfect model, which are represented by Labeled Transition Systems [37].

Original statement	Composition Type	Composition Description	$|A_+|$	$|A_-|$	Counterexample
Coexisting State(Rabbit, Fox)	The Same Prey	–	10	0	–
Coexisting State(Rabbit, Wolf)	The Same Prey	–	10	0	–
Coexisting State(Rabbit, Wolf)	The Same Predator	–	3	7	a:0.015;b:0.7;d:0.5; nRabbit:100;nWolf:10;nSheep:100
Coexisting State(Sheep, Wolf)	The Same Predator	–	1	9	a:0.012;b:0.9;d:0.5; nRabbit:100;nWolf:10;nSheep:100
Coexisting State(Rabbit, Fox)	The Food Chain	nFox:30	10	0	–
Coexisting State(Fox, Wolf)	The Food Chain	nFox:30	5	5	a:0.014;b:0.7;d:0.9; nRabbit:100;nWolf:10;nFox:30
Recovery Comparison(Rabbit, Fox)	The Same Prey	–	10	0	–
Recovery Comparison(Rabbit, Wolf)	The Same Prey	–	10	0	–
Recovery Comparison(Rabbit, Wolf)	The Same Predator	–	9	1	a:0.024;b:0.9;d:0.5; nRabbit:10;nWolf:10;nSheep:10
Recovery Comparison(Sheep, Wolf)	The Same Predator	–	10	0	–
Recovery Comparison(Rabbit, Fox)	The Food Chain	–	10	0	–
Recovery Comparison(Fox, Wolf)	The Food Chain	–	10	0	–
Empty State(Rabbit, Fox)	The Same Prey	–	10	0	–
Empty State(Rabbit, Wolf)	The Same Prey	–	10	0	–
Empty State(Rabbit, Wolf)	The Same Predator	–	10	0	–
Empty State(Sheep, Wolf)	The Same Predator	–	10	0	–
Empty State(Rabbit, Fox)	The Food Chain	nFox:30	0	10	a:0.055;b:0.3;d:0.8; nRabbit:100;nWolf:30;nFox:30
Empty State(Fox, Wolf)	The Food Chain	nFox:30	10	0	–

Table 2: Detailed results. The column "Original statement" shows the properties and the related species. All properties are checked regarding their probability ($p \geq 0.8$), which is omitted for simplicity. In "Composition Description", additional information regarding the composition are given (if necessary). $|A_+|$ and $|A_-|$ are the number of assignments for which the property holds and does not hold, respectively. In our example, we set the sampling number to 10, thus $|A_+| + |A_-| = 10$. A counterexample is given for invalidated hypotheses (see rows with gray background).

However, it may not be easy to find a perfect model. In contrast, our approach makes use of models being annotated with experiments and hypotheses about a model's behavior. Through checking the hypotheses of the reused models in the composed model, some information about the validity of the composed model are provided. Hence, in our approach, the semantic model composition is studied from a different view.

With the initiative MIASE (Minimum Information About a Simulation Experiment) [42], and associated methods like SED-ML (a description language for experiments) [43], the systems biology community set out to define standards to annotate models with experiment descriptions. While these annotations are typically aimed at reproducing simulation results, we use this information about experiments to derive hypotheses that ensure semantically more reasonable composition, and for testing hypotheses by adapting the original experiment specifications. Thereby, we move the attention from describing the details needed to reproduce or execute an experiment to the goal that drives an experiment, i.e., the definition of the hypothesis to be tested.

Increasingly, trajectories produced by simulation are checked regarding specific properties, often defined in temporal logic. Some approaches work with deterministic models [10], while others work with stochastic models [35]. This is reflected in the language that is used to express the properties that shall hold. Whereas linear temporal logic (LTL) is focused on one trajectory, continuous stochastic logic (CSL) has been developed to check Continuous Time Markov models. In our approach we rely on a hybrid approach, i.e., we use LTL to check individual traces and adopt a CSL construct as an external wrapper to express the expected probability. However, currently the nesting of probabilistic operators is not

supported. To evaluate the LTL formulas, we use the algorithm presented in [10], and to account for the stochasticity we adopt the approach from [35] (see Section 2.1.3).

As properties defined in temporal logic can be interpreted as a discrete target function, this approach can easily be applied for optimizing the model, e.g., to fit the parameter values of a model, including the parameters of rules that link two or more models [20]. Those approaches depend on users specifying explicitly the entire experiment from scratch, including the goal of the individual experiment in terms of the parameter value ranges to be searched and the property to be checked. In our approach, we extract this information by reusing "old" experiment descriptions, i.e., we interpret an experiment description as a hypothesis that holds for a reused model (and experiment, e.g., regarding parameter assignments), and can thus be used to automatically generate and check this hypothesis for the composed model. Thus, our approach takes a next step to generate hypotheses and experiments automatically, by reusing hypotheses and experiment descriptions of the models that shall be reused.

Techniques similar to ours have also been developed in the field of software testing. For example, program analysis via symbolic execution can be combined with model-checking and observations from actual program executions to automatically generate software tests [28]. These tests can be considered as experiments to test developer hypotheses regarding a program, e.g., that it should not crash for valid input. Test generation may even exploit the composition of a program, which in this context means to construct the overall set of execution paths by considering the execution paths of each procedure individually [13]. Like the sampling of experiment assignments (see Section 3.2.1), the generation of test data is crucial to find bugs, i.e., to invalidate a hypothesis. Metaheuristics have been successfully applied to this task [23], and we plan to integrate similar techniques to our prototype.

5.2 Limitations and future work

A limitation of our approach is that the falsification or corroboration of hypotheses referring to the composed model and certain assignments still have to be interpreted by the user. There does not seem to be an easy way to automate this step. However, the approach provides additional valuable information to the user for evaluating the composed model. A suitable presentation of this information still has to be developed.

The current language to describe properties (see Section 2.1.3) is not able to easily express all interesting aspects even in our comparatively simple experiments with the Lotka-Volterra models. Therefore, future work will be dedicated to enhance the expressiveness of these LTL terms, e.g., integrating regular expressions to describe repeating patterns [5] (e.g., oscillations), or integrating user-defined functions. Both will be facilitated by the design of SESSL as a domain-specific language embedded in Scala.

Our current approach only considers individual trajectories and replications of those. However, some properties refer to differences between the trajectories sets of multiple assignments. For example, the ratio-dependent theory states that if an ecosystem has richer resources, there should be higher equilibrium abundances on all trophic levels, in comparison to an ecosystem with less resources [12]. So, if we have more food for rabbits available, we would expect a higher number of both, rabbits and foxes. To also allow for these kind of properties to be checked, the current design of Algorithm 1 has to be adapted, as it requires to compare the relation between the results of different assignments.

Compared to the original hypotheses, the hypotheses that are currently checked on the composed model are only different referring to possibly renamed species and the sampling of parameter values for which the statements shall hold. Depending on the number of hypotheses to be checked, some preprocessing could allow a more efficient evaluation of LTL formulas, e.g., by joining some formulas together or by reordering their operators, and should thus be considered in the future. In addition, as already mentioned in Section 3.2, sampling methods may have a strong impact on overall performance and need to be investigated further.

6. CONCLUSION

An explicit, unambiguous specification of experiments is increasingly required to support the reproduction of simulation results in many application domains. This information can also be very valuable to support a semantically meaningful reuse of models. The underlying idea of our approach is that, if models are annotated with experiments and their corresponding hypotheses, then it becomes possible to automatically generate new experiments and hypotheses for composed models, and to automatically execute the new experiments to check the hypotheses, independently of what kind of composition, e.g., aggregation or fusion, is used.

Obviously, the results of these experiments help assessing the validity of the newly composed model, referring to the questions the reused models have been designed for.

Our approach has been realized in the context of the modeling and simulation framework JAMES II. For experiment specification and execution, we use the embedded domain-specific language SESSL, which we extended to allow the definition of experiment hypotheses. The hypotheses comprise statements about the behavior of the system and parameter ranges within which this behavior has been observed. As we are working with stochastic models, the statements shall hold with a specific probability. To do so, statements of the form $Pr_{\bowtie p}(\phi)$ are defined by adopting concepts from continuous stochastic logic and linear temporal logic (see Section 5.1), where ϕ describes a property of an individual trajectory (and thus is tested on individual trajectories), whereas assessing the probability p with which ϕ can be observed depends on statistical model checking methods, i.e., it is based on simulation replication.

After our promising results with the Lotka-Volterra model, we plan to apply our approach to current modeling and simulation studies in the area of cell biology, where a Wnt-pathway model [22] is successively extended by other models that describe membrane-related dynamics or diffusion processes in more detail, and which come with their own experiments and hypotheses. The results will shed new light on the validity of the newly developed models, or, in some cases, also on the validity of hypotheses assumed to hold for the reused models. We expect our approach to significantly improve the development process of these new models, as it helps to ensure a semantically meaningful reuse of the existing models.

Acknowledgments

This research is partly supported by the CSC (China Scholarship Council), the German research foundation, (Grant No. EW 127/1-1), and the National Natural Science Foundation of China (Grant No. 61374185). We thank Tom Warnke for providing his implementation of the algorithm presented in [10].

7. REFERENCES

[1] J. Bézivin, S. Bouzitouna, M. D. Del Fabro, et al. A canonical scheme for model composition. In *Model Driven Architecture–Foundations and Applications*, pages 346–360. Springer, 2006.

[2] E. Clarke, O. Grumberg, and D. Peled. *Model Checking*. MIT Press, 1999.

[3] P. K. Davis and R. H. Anderson. Improving the composability of DoD models and simulations. *JDMS*, 1(1):5–17, Apr. 2004.

[4] L. De Alfaro and T. A. Henzinger. Interface-based design. In *Engineering Theories of Software-intensive Systems*, volume 195 of *NATO Science Series: Mathematics, Physics, and Chemistry*, pages 83–104. Springer, M. Broy, J. Gruenbauer, D. Harel, and C.A.R. Hoare, 2005.

[5] G. De Giacomo and M. Y. Vardi. Linear temporal logic and linear dynamic logic on finite traces. In *Proceedings of the Twenty-Third International Joint Conference on Artificial Intelligence*, IJCAI'13, pages 854–860. AAAI Press, 2013.

[6] M. Droz and A. Pękalski. Different strategies of evolution in a predator-prey system. *Physica A: Statistical Mechanics and its Applications*, 298:545–552, 2001.

[7] P. Du, W. A. Kibbe, and S. M. Lin. Improved peak detection in mass spectrum by incorporating continuous wavelet transform-based pattern matching. *Bioinformatics*, 22(17):2059–2065, 2006.

[8] H. Elmqvist, S. E. Mattsson, and M. Otter. Object-oriented and hybrid modeling in modelica. *Journal Européen des systèmes automatisés*, 35(1):1–10, 2001.

[9] R. Ewald and A. M. Uhrmacher. SESSL: A Domain-Specific Language for Simulation Experiments. *ACM Transactions on Modeling and Computer Simulation*, 2014 (to appear). See `http://sessl.org`.

[10] F. Fages and A. Rizk. On the analysis of numerical data time series in temporal logic. In *Computational Methods in Systems Biology*, 2007.

[11] D. T. Gillespie. Exact Stochastic Simulation of Coupled Chemical Reactions. *Journal of Physical Chemistry*, 81(25), 1977.

[12] L. Ginzburg and H. Akçakaya. Consequences of ratio-dependent predation for steady-state properties of ecosystems. *Ecology*, 73(5):1536–1543, 1992.

[13] P. Godefroid. Compositional dynamic test generation. In *Proceedings of the 34th Annual ACM SIGPLAN-SIGACT Symposium on Principles of Programming Languages*, pages 47–54, New York, NY, USA, 2007. ACM.

[14] A. Hallagan, B. Ward, and L. F. Perrone. An experiment automation framework for ns-3. In *Proceedings of the 3rd Int'l ICST Conference on Simulation Tools and Techniques*. ICST, 2010.

[15] T. Helms, M. Luboschik, H. Schumann, and A. M. Uhrmacher. An approximate execution of rule-based multi-level models. In *Proceedings of the 11th International Conference on Computational Methods in Systems Biology*, 2013.

[16] J. Himmelspach and A. M. Uhrmacher. Plug'n simulate. In *Proceedings of the 40th Annual Simulation Symposium*, ANSS '07, pages 137–143, Washington, DC, USA, 2007. IEEE Computer Society.

[17] M. Hucka, L. Smith, D. Wilkinson, M. Hucka, et al. The systems biology markup language (SBML): language specification for level 3 version 1 core. *Nature Precedings*, Oct. 2010.

[18] C. Li, M. Donizelli, N. Rodriguez, et al. BioModels Database: An enhanced, curated and annotated resource for published quantitative kinetic models. *BMC Systems Biology*, 4:92, Jun 2010.

[19] A. Lotka. *Elements of Physical Biology*. Williams & Wilkins Company, 1925.

[20] E. D. Maria, F. Fages, and S. Soliman. On coupling models using model-checking: Effects of irinotecan injections on the mammalian cell cycle. In *Proceedings of Computational Methods in Systems Biology*, pages 142–157. Springer, 2009.

[21] C. Maus, S. Rybacki, and A. M. Uhrmacher. Rule-based multi-level modeling of cell biological systems. *BMC Systems Biology*, 5(166), 2011.

[22] O. Mazemondet, M. John, S. Leye, A. Rolfs, and A. M. Uhrmacher. Elucidating the sources of beta-catenin dynamics in human neural progenitor cells. *Plos One*, 7(8):e42792–e42792, 2012.

[23] P. McMinn. Search-based software test data generation: a survey. *Software Testing, Verification and Reliability*, 14(2):105–156, June 2004.

[24] D. Nicol, C. Priami, H. Nielson, and A. Uhrmacher, editors. *Simulation and Verification of Dynamic Systems*. Dagstuhl Seminar Proceedings 0161, 2006. ISSN 1862-4405.

[25] C. M. Overstreet, R. Nance, and O. Balci. Issues in Enhancing Model Reuse. In *First International Conference on Grand Challenges for Modeling and Simulation*, 2002.

[26] D. Peng, A. Steiniger, T. Helms, and A. Uhrmacher. Towards Composing ML-Rules Models. In *Proceedings of the 2013 Winter Simulation Conference*, 2013.

[27] M. D. Petty and E. W. Weisel. A composability lexicon. In *Spring Simulation Interoperability Workshop (SISO)*, pages 181–187, 2003.

[28] C. Păsăreanu and W. Visser. A survey of new trends in symbolic execution for software testing and analysis. *International Journal on Software Tools for Technology Transfer*, 11(4):339–353, Oct. 2009.

[29] R. Randhawa, C. a. Shaffer, and J. J. Tyson. Model aggregation: a building-block approach to creating large macromolecular regulatory networks. *Bioinformatics (Oxford, England)*, 25(24):3289–95, Dec. 2009.

[30] E. Renshaw. *Modelling Biological Populations in Space and Time*. Cambridge Studies in Mathematical Biology. Cambridge University Press, 1991.

[31] M. Röhl and A. M. Uhrmacher. Definition and analysis of composition structures for discrete-event models. In *Proceedings of the 2008 Winter Simulation Conference*, pages 942–950, 2008.

[32] S. Rybacki, F. Haack, K. Wolf, and A. Uhrmacher. Developing simulation models - from conceptual to executable model and back - an artifact-based workflow approach. In *SimuTools*, 2014.

[33] S. Sanchez and H. Wan. Work smarter, not harder: A tutorial on designing and conducting simulation experiments. In *Proceedings of the 2012 Winter Simulation Conference (WSC)*, pages 1–15, Dec 2012.

[34] F. Scholkmann, J. Boss, and M. Wolf. An efficient algorithm for automatic peak detection in noisy periodic and quasi-periodic signals. *Algorithms*, 5(4):588–603, 2012.

[35] K. Sen, M. Viswanathan, and G. Agha. On statistical model checking of stochastic systems. In K. Etessami and S. Rajamani, editors, *Computer Aided Verification*, volume 3576 of *Lecture Notes in Computer Science*, pages 266–280. Springer Berlin Heidelberg, 2005.

[36] C. A. Shaffer, R. Randhawa, and J. J. Tyson. The role of composition and aggregation in modeling macromolecular regulatory networks. In *Proceedings of the 38th conference on Winter simulation*, pages 1628–1636. Winter Simulation Conference, 2006.

[37] J. Srba. On the power of labels in transition systems. In *Proceedings of the 12th International Conference on Concurrency Theory*, pages 277–291, 2001.

[38] C. Szabo and Y. Teo. An approach for validation of semantic composability in simulation models. *. . . on*

161

Principles of Advanced and Distributed Simulation, pages 3–10, June 2009.

[39] C. Szyperski, D. Gruntz, and S. Murer. *Component Software: Beyond Object-oriented Programming.* ACM Press Series. ACM Press, 2002.

[40] A. Tolk. What comes after the semantic web - pads implications for the dynamic web. In *Workshop on Principles of Advanced and Distributed Simulation (PADS),* page 55. IEEE Computer Society, 2006.

[41] V. Vito. Variazioni e fluttuazioni del numero d'individui in specie animali conviventi. *Mem. R. Accad. Naz. dei Lincei,* 2:31–113, 1926.

[42] D. Waltemath, R. Adams, D. A. Beard, F. T. Bergmann, et al. Minimum Information About a Simulation Experiment (MIASE). *PLoS Computational Biology,* 7(4):e1001122, 2011.

[43] D. Waltemath, R. Adams, F. Bergmann, M. Hucka, et al. Reproducible computational biology experiments with SED-ML - the simulation experiment description markup language. *BMC Systems Biology,* 5:198, 2011.

[44] E. Weisel, M. Petty, and R. Mielke. Validity of models and classes of models in semantic composability. *Proceedings of the Fall 2003 SIW,* 2003.

[45] H. L. Younes and R. G. Simmons. Statistical probabilistic model checking with a focus on time-bounded properties. *Information and Computation,* 204(9):1368 – 1409, 2006.

[46] H. L. S. Younes and R. G. Simmons. Probabilistic verification of discrete event systems using acceptance sampling. In *Proceedings 14th International Conference on Computer Aided Verification, volume 2404 of LNCS,* pages 223–235. Springer, 2002.

[47] P. Zuliani, A. Platzer, and E. M. Clarke. Bayesian statistical model checking with application to simulink/stateflow verification. In *Proceedings of the 13th ACM International Conference on Hybrid Systems: Computation and Control,* HSCC '10, pages 243–252, New York, NY, USA, 2010. ACM.

Phold Performance for Distributed Network Simulation under Conservative Synchronization Methods in ns-3

Jared Ivey
School of Electrical and
Computer Engineering
Georgia Institute of
Technology
Atlanta, GA 30332-0250
j.ivey@gatech.edu

George Riley
School of Electrical and
Computer Engineering
Georgia Institute of
Technology
Atlanta, GA 30332-0250
riley@ece.gatech.edu

Brian Swenson
School of Electrical and
Computer Engineering
Georgia Institute of
Technology
Atlanta, GA 30332-0250
bswenson3@gatech.edu

Categories and Subject Descriptors

I.6.8 [**Computing Methodologies**]: Simulation and Modeling—*Discrete Event, Parallel*

General Terms

Experimentation, Performance

Keywords

Parallel Discrete-Event Simulation; ns-3

1. INTRODUCTION

Parallel and distributed discrete event simulation allocates the processing requirements of simulation executions across multiple logical processors (LP) with the intent of leveraging increased processing power to decrease execution time. With multiple simulated events occurring simultaneously across multiple LPs, the simulation must appropriately synchronize the execution of these events to either prevent or repair out-of-order events. This synchronization may be implemented either conservatively, communicating in some way across LPs to confirm that events are executed in order and blocking events set to execute at a specified time in the future, or optimistically, allowing the various processes to execute freely to a certain extent and synchronizing using rollback and anti-messages when errors are detected in event ordering.

Conservative synchronization algorithms simply avoid processing events out of order. LP A may communicate to a different LP B the time at which it may receive remote events by sending null messages holding the timestamp of A denoting the smallest time stamp that B can expect to receive from A. In this way, LP B will only process events up to the time specified by A. An alternative conservative synchronization method requests a global consensus among LPs (through calls to collecting methods such as MPI_Allgather)

SIGSIM-PADS'14, May 18–21, 2014, Denver, CO, USA.
ACM 978-1-4503-2794-7/14/05.
http://dx.doi.org/10.1145/2601381.2601410.

to agree upon a time value lookahead, and any remote event received with a timestamp greater than the current time plus lookahead will be held unscheduled until the event timestamp falls within the granted time.

Selection of a specific synchronization algorithm within parallel discrete event simulators depends as much on design requirements as it does personal preference. Opinions and results vary on whether optimistic or conservative synchronization algorithms provide better real-time performance based on a variety of parameters and situations. More specifically, within both optimistic and conservative synchronization methods, the choice of rollback with anti-messages, null messages, or global consensus of granted time among other tactics provide additional sources of research and debate.

The discrete event network simulator, ns-3, currently provides two conservative synchronization options for performing distributed simulations. The GrantedTimeWindowMpiInterface provides a simulation implementation that determines the granted time before which an LP may safely process its events using calls to MPI_Allgather to retrieve the lowest bound timestamps (LBTS) from all LPs. The lookahead value derived from the propagation delays between remote point-to-point channels is added to this LBTS to produce a granted time window within which an LP may process pending events. This interface also incorporates a check that the total transmitted and received packets for the entire simulation at a particular time are equal to ensure that transmitted packets from an LP have been received by another LP such that no transient messages exist. The NullMessageMpiInterface constructs a bundle of remote channel neighbors connected via point-to-point links that hold the channel delays from a node on one LP to a node on another LP. These delay values are used within both packet and null messages to update the guaranteed time before which a node may safely process the events in its event list.

The work in progress discussed in this paper examines modified versions of both synchronization options supported by ns-3. In choosing to analyze the performance of the simulation implementations under a Phold simulation model, the interfaces in ns-3 have been modified to allow all LPs to transmit packet messages to each other as individual nodes without any simulated network routing nor any simulated IP overhead. In this way, only the event scheduler and synchronization algorithms of ns-3 are used to send MPI messages directly between applications. As expected, initial experiments for the GrantedTimeWindowMpiInterface demonstrated an increase in performance as the lookahead value is increased. Further research will be performed with the GrantedTimeWindowMpiInterface and the NullMessageMpiInterface to gather insights concerning their performance in order to provide a framework for predicting appropriate circumstances for selecting one synchronization method over the other with confidence.

2. EXPERIMENTAL SETUP

The Phold simulation model provides a performance benchmark for parallel and distributed simulations. Under this model, each LP initially transmits a packet to another randomly selected LP at a randomly selected time in the future. When an LP processes receipt of a packet, it randomly selects an LP to which it transmits another packet at another random time. This process may continue across all LPs until each LP has transmitted a specified maximum number of packets. Selection of LPs is based on a uniform random variable, providing equal likelihood of selection across all 128 LPs. Selection of transmit times is based on an exponential random variable value with mean 0.9 seconds which is added to the current simulation time. In addition, the specified lookahead value is added to cross-LP transmit times to ensure that events would not be processed out of order.

Additional parameters included in the simulations are percentage of remote packet transmissions, number of initial packets injected into the system, and run value provided to the random number generator. Percentages of remotely transmitted packets serve as a sanity check since lower percentages will provide fewer packets travelling across LPs and more packets being accepted and processed within LPs over less time, resulting in increased performance. Introducing a set of local packets into each LP at the beginning of the simulation favorably augments performance results to better view any visible data trends. The research conducted in this work in progress employed an initial packet injection of 100 packets per LP. The run value provides a way to assess the repeatability of results. If all other parameters remain the same, using the same run value (as well as the same seed) for multiple simulation executions will produce identical simulation results (but not necessarily equivalent performance results), and using a different run value across simulation executions will result in different simulation results.

3. RESULTS & DISCUSSION

Experimental simulations using the Phold simulation model and modified versions of the GrantedTimeWindowMpiInterface have been performed across the following parameters:

- lookahead values: 1 - 10, 15, 20 and 25 ms

- remote percentages: 10, 50, and 90%

- maximum number of transmitted packets: 16,777,216 and 67,108,864 packets (131,072 and 524,288 packets per 128 LPs, respectively)

As shown in Figure 1, under the described setup and parameters, transmit rate increases as lookahead increases. These results can be explained by the idea that a higher lookahead value results in increased granted time windows leading to fewer calls to MPI_Allgather. Fewer calls to MPI_Allgather decrease the number of chances that the simulation may enter a "blocking" mode. For 16,777,216 transmitted packets,

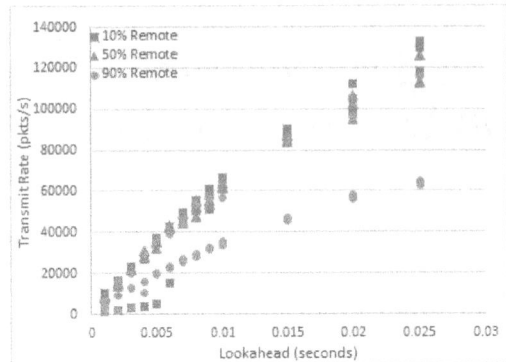

Figure 1: Transmit rate as a function of lookahead for distributed simulations using GrantedTimeWindowMpiInterface with 16,777,216 total packets transmitted across 128 LPs. The transmit rate is derived from the total transmitted packets divided by wall clock time.

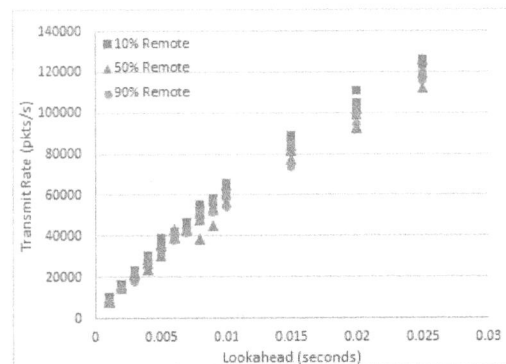

Figure 2: Transmit rate as a function of lookahead for distributed simulations using GrantedTimeWindowMpiInterface with 67,108,864 total packets transmitted across 128 LPs. The transmit rate is derived from the total transmitted packets divided by wall clock time.

differences in performance can also be seen between the 90% and 10/50% cases, another reasonable result since fewer locally transmitted and received packets would result in more processing effort through MPI send and receive calls.

Further research will be done for the modified versions of both the GrantedTimeWindowMpiInterface and the NullMessageMpiInterface. Under the GrantedTimeWindowMpiInterface, additional simulations with more and fewer packets than currently presented will be performed to determine trends based simply on processing effort. Increasing the tested lookahead range will shed some insight on whether the results presented in Figure 1 map to a particular regression (linear, logarithmic, etc.). These increased ranges in transmitted packets and lookahead values must also be considered for simulations using the modified NullMessageMpiInterface; however, additional work and testing still remains to confirm proper functionality based on these modifications.

Securing Industrial Control Systems with a Simulation-based Verification System

Dong Jin
Department of Computer Science
Illinois Institute of Technology
dong.jin@iit.edu

Ying Ni
Department of Computer Science
Illinois Institute of Technology
yni6@hawk.iit.edu

ABSTRACT

Today's quality of life is highly dependent on the successful operation of many large-scale industrial control systems. To enhance their protection against cyber-attacks and operational errors, we develop a simulation-based verification framework with cross-layer verification techniques that allow comprehensive analysis of the entire ICS-specific stack, including application, protocol, and network layers.

1. INTRODUCTION

Protection of industrial control systems (ICSes) is a critical component of protecting against a potential "cyber Pearl Harbor" [2] — an attack that devastates the critical infrastructure and paralyzes the nation. ICSes represent a wide variety of networked information technology systems connected to the physical world to monitor and control physical processes. ICSes perform vital functions in national critical infrastructures, such as electricity, oil, gas, and water distribution; transportation systems; and even weapons systems. The disruption of these control systems could have a significant impact on public safety and health, and lead to large financial losses. Modern ICSes are increasingly adopting Internet technology to boost control efficiency, which also increases the risk of attacks and failures inherited from the commodity network infrastructure. In practice, a common way to implement security policy in ICSes is direct deployment of commercial off-the-shelf products, such as firewalls and antivirus software, which only provide fine-grained protection at single devices. Without a way to check system-wide requirements, serious security vulnerabilities can and do exist in real implementations of critical systems. To ensure that the entire system functions correctly, we need to verify not only the network layer, such as reachability among end-hosts as being verified by tools like VeriFlow [3], but also application behaviors. That would seem to be impossible in traditional networks, since many applications are outside the network operator's control. How can the operator know what applications are running and what defines "correct op-

eration" for them? Fortunately, most ICSes have a small set of applications whose run is restricted and controlled by the operator. That unique property of ICSes allows us to investigate modeling and verification techniques to check applications with the key idea of *cross-layer verification* for detection of malicious activities and system errors. We address two key research issues: (1) the network should be giving applications an environment with required performance properties (Section 2.1), and (2) the applications should be behaving correctly on the network (Section 2.2). To answer those questions, we are developing a simulation-based framework to perform system-wide properties verification in large-scale ICSes.

2. VERIFYING ICS APPLICATIONS WITH CROSS-LAYER VERIFICATION

Figure 1 overviews the system design. The core component is the verification framework, which uses a model-checking approach to verify models against the constraints, such as security and performance requirements. Violations indicate cyber-attacks or misconfigurations. The verification framework takes inputs of network states, such as forwarding tables and topologies, from the network model, and inputs of correct application behaviors from the state-machine-based application models. The network and application models are simulated, and the verification framework is emulated (with a modified version of VeriFlow [3]) in a parallel discrete event network simulation/emulation testbed, S3FNet [4]. Our ongoing work of verifying network performance properties and the approach to extend the verification framework from the network layer to the application layer is described in the remainder of the section.

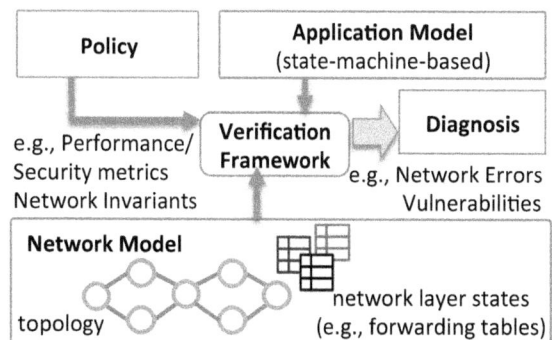

Figure 1: Simulation-based Verification System

2.1 Verifying Network Performance Metrics

Meeting specification-based performance requirements is crucial for ICS to function correctly. For example, a generic object-oriented substation event message must be delivered within 4 ms, according to IEC 61850. Typical network model-checking tools formalize packet header and location changes as state transitions. Continuous states are needed to model metrics like latency, which is not practical for large-scale systems because of the exponentially increasing state space. One approach is to leverage VeriFlow's forwarding graph model, and model the network forwarding behaviors as *weighted forwarding graphs*, e.g., we can assign delays to the links (graph edges) as weights, and compute the sum of delays when traversing the graph to check the end-to-end delay requirements). Verification of such invariants requires more storage space for link attributes and more operations during traversals than the reachability test in VeriFlow. Both storage and time increases is bounded by a constant factor times the size of the network.

We implemented the weighted forwarding graph in VeriFlow, and performed a case study in our testbed. We simulated a network consisting of 172 routers following a Rocketfuel [5] topology (AS 1755), and simulated the BGP activities by replaying traces collected from the Route Views Project [1]. We initialized the network with a BGP trace containing 90,000 updates. We then fed 1 million updates, and measured the end-to-end delay verification cost of the updates. The experiments were performed on a Dell PowerEdge R720 server with two 8-core processors (2.00GHz) and 64 GB RAM, and installed with 64-bit Linux OS. The results are shown in Figure 2. Our system is able to verify the end-to-end requirement on 86% updates within 10 ms, with mean verification time of 6.08 ms. However, the system exhibit long tail properties because a small fraction of updates result in the generation of large number of forwarding graphs.

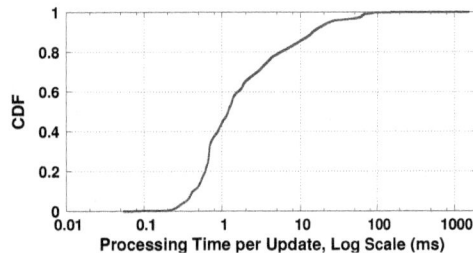

Figure 2: CDF of Update Verification Time

There are many questions we want to explore. Can we leverage knowledge from upper layers to verify performance metrics in ICSes, (e.g., the transport layer will naturally provide flow-based delay and throughput)? Can we leverage the network traffic and application domain knowledge to verify performance metrics of the physical infrastructure of an ICS, such as transmission system effectiveness, power quality and distribution reliability?

2.2 Verifying Application Semantics

Verification of applications can efficiently capture attacks that are not seen by lower layers, or some attacks may be detected much earlier in the application layer, because of the richer semantic information available. Therefore, we are exploring

(i) How to express application layer behavior. Given the fact that an ICS runs a small set of *managed applications*, it is effective to take a specification-based modeling approach for characterizing the correct behaviors. We conduct semantics analysis based on the application protocol specifications, and create models based on correct packet payloads and communication patterns. (1) Modeling packet payloads is based on the analysis of packet content to define what an application should do and reveal what an application intends to do. For example, the DNP3 protocol uses an 8-bit integer to represent the function code, in which 37 out of 256 combinations are predefined, and only a subset of the 37 function codes are supported in a real SCADA. A specification-based policy is therefore generated; any DNP3 requests with a function code out of the range may indicate that a reconnaissance scan from an adversary, exploitation of an unknown backdoor, or a denial-of-service attempt. Generation of such rules will require extensive vulnerability assessments of the particular protocols; (2) Modeling packet sequences is based on the analysis of the communication patterns among network components. For instance, in the DNP3 protocol, an "OPERATE" packet, is almost always issued right after a "SELECT" packet to control remote field devices chosen by the "SELECT" packet. The unmatched requests and responses are signs of denial-of-service attacks or replay attacks. We investigate protocol-specific analyzers that maintain flow-based states from the observed traffic, and useful info can be extracted from correlated packets of the same flow. It was recently proposed that state estimation and contingency analysis in power systems can be performed based on measurements from a specific set of substations [6]. We will leverage that algorithm to reduce the state space and further analyze the strongly correlated states to verify appropriate communication patterns.

(ii) How to check the model against what is actually happening. Verification of application and network models against a set of constraints (e.g., security requirements and network invariants) can expose malicious activities and system faults. To achieve that goal, we are developing a formal cross-layer verification framework to mathematically prove to validate different types of critical operations. The framework will be built hierarchically in several layers including a model of the network, a set of pre-defined operations and policies, protocol specifications, and a verification theorem. The layers will be implemented in ACL2, which is a software tool combining a programming language, a logic, and a theorem prover based on Common Lisp. ACL2 can automate most of the proof effort using techniques such as rewriting and mathematical induction, but we will investigate means to guide the proof by adding lemmas that the mechanical prover cannot deduct by itself.

3. REFERENCES

[1] University of Oregon Route Views Project.
[2] E. Bumiller and T. Shanker. Panetta Warns of Dire Threat of Cyberattack on U.S., New York Times, October 2012.
[3] A. Khurshid, X. Zou, W. Zhou, M. Caesar, and P. B. Godfrey. Veriflow: Verifying network-wide invariants in real time. In *Proc of NSDI*, 2013.
[4] D. M. Nicol, D. Jin, and Y. Zheng. S3F: The Scalable Simulation Framework revisited. In *Proc of WSC*, 2011.
[5] N. Spring, R. Mahajan, and D. Wetherall. Measuring ISP topologies with Rocketfuel. Aug. 2002.
[6] T. Yang, H. Sun, and A. Bose. Transition to a two-level linear state estimator – part 1: architecture. *IEEE Transactions on Power Systems*, 26(1):46–53, 2011.

Integrated Simulation and Emulation Using Adaptive Time Dilation

Hee Won Lee, David Thuente, and Mihail L. Sichitiu
North Carolina State University
Raleigh, NC 27695
{hlee17, djthuent, mlsichit}@ncsu.edu

ABSTRACT

Simulation and emulation techniques are commonly used to evaluate the performance of complex networked systems. Simulation conveniently predicts the behavior of a complex networked system while usually requiring fewer simplifying model assumptions often necessary for theoretical analysis. In contrast, emulation does not need to re-implement the target real systems, so it may improve on the implementation efficiency of simulation while maintaining much of the realism of testbeds. A hybrid approach in which simulation nodes connect to emulation hosts can be used to combine the advantages of both approaches. In this paper, we propose integrating simulation with emulation using adaptive time dilation to evaluate system performance. If a simulator schedules its events in real time and the simulation time keeps up with the real time, then the hybrid system works very well and meets its deadlines. However, a heavily-loaded simulator can introduce significant simulation delays and thereby create situations where these delays impact the accuracy of the system. Our approach uses time dilation to reduce simulation delays and thus increasing the accuracy of the integrated simulation and emulation system. Our adaptive time dilation dynamically controls the time dilation factor to avoid system overloads for both the simulation and the emulation components and to improve the execution correctness of the hybrid system.

Categories and Subject Descriptors

C.2.4 [**Computer-Communication Networks**]: Distributed Systems—*Distributed applications*; C.4 [**Computer Systems Organization**]: Performance of Systems—*Modeling techniques*; D.4.8 [**Operating Systems**]: Performance—*Modeling and prediction*

Keywords

Simulation; Emulation; Virtualization; Time Dilation; ns-3; KVM

1. INTRODUCTION

Modern networks have evolved into highly complex systems that are difficult to debug and to evaluate their performance. Moreover, the network protocols and distributed applications currently in use are sometimes too complex to accurately model their behavior.

Simulation is a primary technique for evaluating the performance of networked systems. Simulation generally uses event-driven models to predict the behavior of complex networked systems while requiring fewer simplifying model assumptions than usually necessary for theoretical analysis. However, unless a simulation model accurately captures the behavior of the real system, the simulation results may be significantly different from those of real systems.

Emulation testbeds [9, 2] can directly use actual implementation code and thus avoid the verification and validation issues required for simulators. While emulation offers much of the realism of testbeds, it is often expensive to scale to a large number of emulated elements.

A hybrid approach using both simulation and emulation can take advantage of both approaches. While simulation is a powerful tool for evaluating large networks, emulation makes it possible to use real protocol implementations, real application code, and even real operating systems (OSs). For instance, the work in [30] integrates S3F [36], a scalable simulation framework, with network emulation OpenVZ [8].

Time dilation allows the passage of virtual time (i.e., time passage from the perspective of a virtual node) to proceed at a slower rate than real time by a specified factor, which is referred to as *time dilation factor* (TDF) [28]. When TDF > 1, time dilation creates, to the virtual machines, the illusion of increased performance [28].

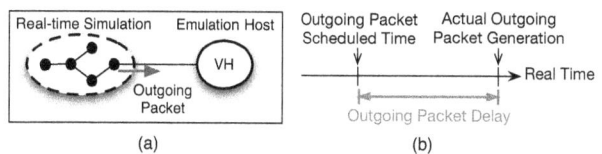

Figure 1: (a) Example topology with an integrated emulation and simulation system with the simulator sending one packet to the emulator. (b) If the simulator is overloaded, outgoing packets can be delayed with respect to their original scheduled times.

In this paper, we propose an approach integrating simulation with emulation using adaptive time dilation in order to keep the simulation and emulation appropriately synchronized and thereby improve accuracy. Usually, when a simulation node exchanges packets with an emulation host, the simulator schedules its events in real time under the assumption that simulation time passes faster than real time. However, when using real-time scheduling, the events' simulation time may fall behind the real time. Therefore, if an outgoing packet is generated from a simulation node with an emulation host as its destination, *outgoing packet delay* can be introduced, as shown in Fig. 1. When the simulator is heavily loaded with a large-scale network topology, outgoing packet delay can be significant and thereby reducing the accuracy of a hybrid simulation and emulation system. Time dilation can reduce the outgoing packet delay, since the simulator can process more events as the virtual time passage rate slows down.

For the emulation, time dilation can prevent CPU overload of the physical hosts (PHs), as time dilation allows virtual hosts (VHs) to perceive higher processing power and network capacity than in real time [27].

Many emulation approaches have used lightweight virtualization to increase scalability [44, 43, 14, 20]. These systems emulate part of the real code (e.g., the network protocol stack), but not an entire application or the OSs. In contrast, our approach uses full virtualization to create fully self-contained VHs and allows our system to emulate unmodified OSs.

Our adaptive time dilation mechanism dynamically changes the time passage rate of the simulator(s) and fully-virtualized hosts, while controlling physical system loads.

The remainder of the paper is organized as follows. In Section 2, we describe our adaptive time dilation approach that can reduce simulation delay in a hybrid simulation and emulation environment. Section 3 presents our system implementation. In Section 4, we discuss our TDF controller tuning and evaluate our integrated simulation and emulation system. Finally, related work in Section 5 is followed by our conclusion in Section 6.

2. PROPOSED APPROACH

Our system emulates applications on unmodified OSs with each running as a *virtual host* (VH). Simulators are used to simulate networks that can exchange packets with the VHs.

For scalability, multiple PHs can be used for mapping the VHs and simulators to host machines. Once all elements (i.e. VHs and simulators) are ready to start, our integrated simulation and emulation system proceeds at a variable time rate with precise synchronization between all VHs and the simulator.

Figure 2(a) depicts a sample network with Windows/Linux/FreeBSD clients connected to a server through several routers. Figure 2(b) shows a possible mapping of the elements in the real-world topology into virtual elements on five physical machines. The server and the clients can be emulated via a virtualizing technology (in our system we use KVM [10, 5]). The four routers and their links are modeled using a simulator (in our work ns-3 [7]).

Previous emulation systems [17, 20, 30, 14] avoid using full virtualization in order to use available resources efficiently because scalability of the emulated systems was considered more important than full isolation among VMs. In contrast, our approach uses full virtualization to emulate unmodified OSs and unmodified applications.

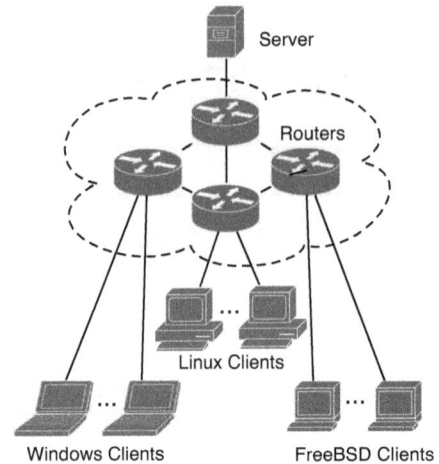

(a) An example of a real-world topology

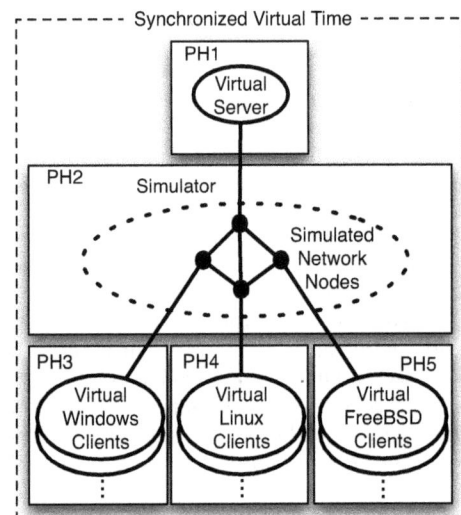

(b) Corresponding integrated simulation and emulation topology

Figure 2: Overview of the proposed approach with (a) an example of a real world topology and (b) a possible mapping of the virtual elements to physical hosts

2.1 The Effects of Time Dilation on Simulation

When the simulator schedules its events in real time, delays can be introduced due to excessive execution time. Time dilation can reduce these delays.

Consider the topology shown in Fig. 3(a). VH1 running on PH1 generates and sends a packet to VH2 running on PH3, and the packet passes through a simulator running on PH2. A packet that arrives at the simulator is transformed into a simulation event, which in turn triggers the generation of follow-up events. When the simulator completes the processing of all the events generated by the live packet injection, it then creates an outgoing live packet as appropriate.

As the simulator uses real-time scheduling with a best-effort policy, an outgoing packet delay may occur due to

(a) Network topology

(b) No time dilation (TDF = 1)

(c) Time dilation (TDF = 2)

(d) Time dilation (TDF = 4)

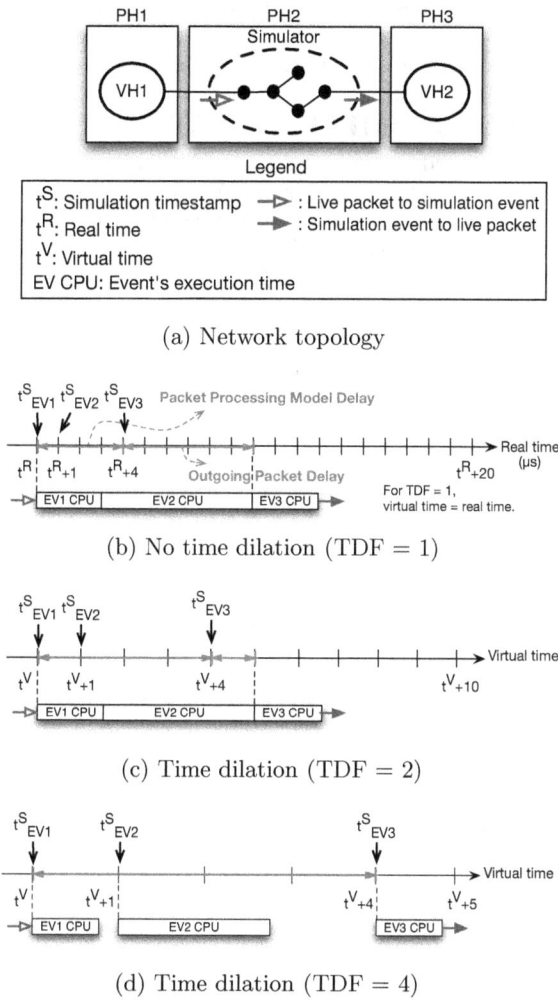

Figure 3: The effect of reduction in outgoing packet delay by time dilation. (a) The simulator transforms a live packet into simulation events, processes the events, and creates an outgoing packet. (b) Real-time scheduler running in real time (TDF=1) introduces outgoing packet delay. (c) Time dilation, where virtual time passes at half the rate of real time (TDF=2), can reduce outgoing packet delay. (d) An even larger TDF=4 can completely eliminate outgoing packet delay.

the simulation events' execution time. Under a best-effort policy, if the timestamp of an event to be processed falls behind real time, the event is processed immediately provided processing resources are available.

For an illustrative explanation, assume that the simulator generates three events to handle an incoming live packet, as shown in Fig. 3(b) (in reality, in ns-3, about 13 events are generated for forwarding a packet through a simulated network node). When a live packet arrives at the simulator at t^R in real time, the simulator creates event 1 with timestamp t^S_{EV1}. Event 2 handles a propagation delay on a communication channel, and event 3 generates an outgoing live packet for VH2.

We refer to the time that it takes for the simulator to process a packet in the time unit of the simulator (i.e., the

timestamp of ns-3) as *packet process model delay*. Hence, packet process model delay is t^S_{EV3} - t^S_{EV1} in Fig. 3. *Outgoing packet delay* is the time difference between event 3's scheduled timestamp (t^S_{EV3}) and the actual time at which the simulator starts to process event 3. Outgoing packet delay is a key metric for accuracy and we will explore adaptive time dilation to reduce it.

Assume that event 1 is scheduled by the simulator to finish after 1 μs. In the example in Fig. 3(b), however, the simulator takes 3 μs to process event 1. Event 1 triggers the follow-up events: events 2 and 3. Assume the execution of events 2 and 3 takes 7 μs and 3 μs respectively. Since event 3 is scheduled at time t^S_{EV3} (4 μs after t^S_{EV1}) in simulation time but is sent out after 10 μs from the start of t_{EV1}, an outgoing packet delay of 6 μs occurs in this case.

As shown in Fig. 3(c), when using a time dilation factor of two (TDF = 2), virtual time passes at half of the real-time rate. While the execution time of the events does not change, the simulator now runs in virtual time whose passage rate is $\frac{1}{TDF}$ $(= \frac{1}{2})$ with respect to real time. Event 1, 2, and 3 are then executed along the axis of virtual time (not real time as in Fig. 3(b)) at the scheduled timestamps t^S_{EV1}, t^S_{EV2}, and t^S_{EV3} respectively. Therefore, the outgoing packet delay is reduced to 2 μs in real time (= 1 μs in virtual time).

In Fig. 3(d), when TDF = 4, events 1 and 2 finish their computation before the next event's scheduled time. In this case the simulator has a chance to catch up with the real time events. Hence, outgoing packet delay is completely eliminated.

Therefore, outgoing packet delay can be reduced or completely eliminated by increasing the TDF. When the simulator is heavily loaded with many incoming packets or simulation events, the simulator may not be able to process all events in real time, thus increasing outgoing packet delay and degrading throughput.

2.2 The Effects of Time Dilation on Emulation

If virtual time passes at a slower rate, physical resources appear faster to virtual nodes [27], as the CPU can execute more instructions per unit of virtual time. Hence, a PH can support more VHs, or heavier traffic generators can be executed in a VH without a degradation of the emulated performance.

In addition, when virtual time slows down and a VH generates traffic, the virtual nodes (e.g., simulators and the other VHs) receive the traffic at a slower rate in real time. Consequently, time dilation reduces the workload of physical systems running virtual nodes at the cost of an increase in emulation time.

2.3 Virtual Time

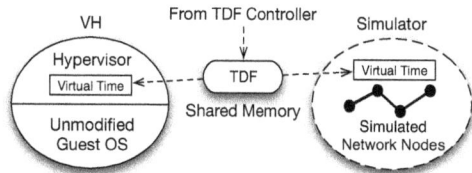

Figure 4: Synchronization of virtual elements

Virtual elements, including VHs and simulators, have their own time generators usually using the real time clock of their PH as a reference. All virtual elements running on our system are instead synchronized to a virtual clock with a common time passage rate by sharing a TDF value as shown in Fig. 4.

The ratio between the virtual time passage rate and real time is $\frac{1}{TDF}$. Hence, given the real time t^R, virtual time t^V can be obtained by:

$$t^V = t^V_{start}(n) + \frac{t^R - t^R_{start}(n)}{TDF(n)}, \qquad (1)$$

where $t^V_{start}(n)$ is the value of starting point of nth TDF change (epoch) in virtual time and $t^R_{start}(n)$ is the value of starting point of nth TDF change in real time.

In our approach, the simulators use virtual time t^V instead of real time t^R for their real-time scheduler, while VHs use virtual time t^V generated by the modified hypervisors such that unmodified guest OSs can be used in the VHs.

Since each simulator keeps track of virtual time based on the TDF stored in shared memory, the simulator readjusts the virtual time rate whenever the TDF is changed. For VHs' virtual time, we control the hypervisor time by changing the interrupt frequency of the hypervisor according to the value of TDF. Since the guest OS of the hypervisor creates its own time based on the interrupt frequency, the guest's time passage rate changes according to TDF. Since all virtual elements use a common TDF (i.e., the system TDF), their virtual times are all synchronized.

2.4 Adaptive Time Dilation

Our approach is to control the time passage rate such that outgoing packet delay is reduced or maintained at a low level. Time passage rate control is also used to prevent VHs from overloading their PHs.

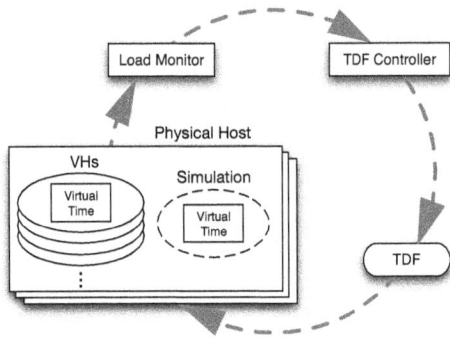

Figure 5: Virtual time control mechanism using TDF to control the system load

Our virtual time control mechanism is shown in Fig. 5. For each PH, a load monitor is periodically checking the CPU loads. The TDF controller then computes a new TDF based on its PH's CPU loads and broadcasts the TDF to all the controllers running on the other PHs. The computed TDF from each controller is the minimum TDF value that is required in a PH to prevent simulators and VHs from introducing outgoing packet delay created by PH overloads.

When a TDF controller receives the other PHs' TDF messages, it updates the current running TDF with the *maxi-*

mum of all values received from all PHs. Using the maximum of the TDF values guarantees that no virtual elements are overloaded (even if some of the PHs may be underloaded).

3. SYSTEM IMPLEMENTATION

Our proposed system uses ns-3, which is a widely used discrete-event network simulator. We chose ns-3 because its real-time scheduler uses CPU resources efficiently by using sleep-waiting and busy-waiting; however, our system works independent of the simulator choice.

For VHs, there are several hypervisors that support full virtualization (e.g. KVM [10, 5], Xen [13], and Virtual-Box [12]). Our system uses the KVM hypervisor, which was recommended [42] as the optimal choice for high performance computing environments; however, our approach is equally applicable to other hypervisors.

In this section, we first present our system architecture and then our virtual time implementation. Lastly, we define TDF_{load}, the TDF used for system load control.

3.1 System Architecture

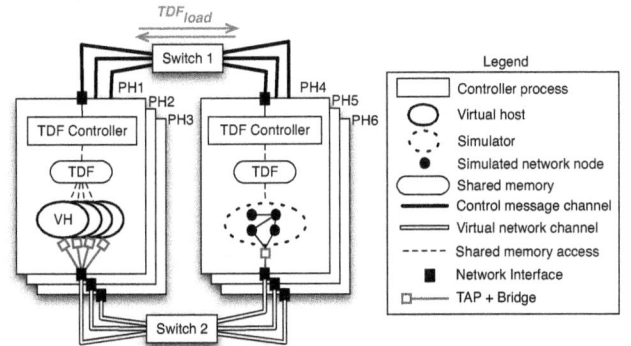

Figure 6: System architecture

Fig. 6 depicts our system architecture that synchronizes VHs and simulators distributed over PHs with a dynamic TDF. The TDF controller on each PH monitors system loads, computes TDF_{load}, and periodically broadcasts the TDF_{load} to all the controllers running on the other PHs. The system TDF is defined as the maximum of the TDF_{load} of all the PHs:

$$TDF_{system} = max(TDF_{load,PH1}, TDF_{load,PH2}, ...), \quad (2)$$

where TDF_{load,PH_i} is the minimum TDF required to maintain the system loads below a target level in PH_i.

The TDF controller stores the system TDF value in the shared memory of each PH, and the VHs use this TDF value to control the progress of their virtual clocks. Since VHs distributed over multiple PHs use a common TDF value, they are all synchronized.

Virtual elements such as VHs and simulators are connected through TAP [11] interfaces and bridges; TAP is a virtual network kernel device that simulates a link layer handling Ethernet frames. For example, as illustrated in Fig. 6, a simulator creates one or more TAP interfaces, which can be bridged to a real network interface to communicate with VHs running in other PHs.

The TDF control messages use a physically-isolated control channel through switch 1, while virtual elements (i.e., VHs and simulators) use a virtual network channel through switch 2 to communicate with each other. The isolated control channel assures robust TDF control operations and eliminates control traffic from affecting the virtual network traffic.

3.2 Virtual Time Implementation

We modify the real time scheduler of ns-3 to use virtual time instead of real time. For VHs, the hypervisors also use virtual time.

The ns-3 real-time scheduler obtains real time by calling `GetRealtime()`, a method of the `WallClockSynchronizer` class [7]. We replace `gettimeofday()`, a POSIX system call to retrieve the PH's real time in `GetRealTime()`, with our function `get_virtualtime()`. Our function that computes virtual time, `get_virtualtime()`, is an implementation of (1), where t^R is obtained by `gettimeofday()` and TDF is retrieved from shared memory. The KVM hypervisor also uses our function `get_virtualtime()` to obtain its virtual time.

In short, the ns-3 simulator and the KVM hypervisor both replace `gettimeofday()` with our function `get_virtualtime()` to obtain the time and hence all virtual elements' time passes at a rate of $\frac{1}{TDF}$ with respect to real time.

3.3 TDF for System Load Control

When the load monitor obtains a new CPU load, the TDF controller computes a new TDF, TDF_{load}. A desirable TDF control property is that the computed TDF adapts rapidly to current loads, while the frequency of TDF changes is minimized for system stability. To meet these conflicting requirements, the TDF controller uses three parameters: α for the exponential moving average (EMA), *Gain*, and *Insensitivity* that balance the TDF responsiveness with system stability as seen below.

EMA can be used to prevent rapid changes in the current load ($Load_{current}$) from changing TDF_{load} too rapidly. The EMA value of a system load for a monitoring interval, denoted by $Load_{EMA}(n)$, is computed as:

$$Load_{EMA}(n) = (1 - \alpha) \cdot Load_{EMA}(n - 1)$$
$$+ \alpha \cdot Load_{current}. \qquad (3)$$

Gain determines how rapidly TDF_{load} will adapt to system loads. If $Load_{EMA}(n)$ is greater than a target CPU load ($Load_{target}$), TDF_{load} increases, and vice versa as well. The magnitude of the increase or decrease is directly proportional to the value of the *Gain*.

Insensitivity is used to minimize the number of TDF changes until there are significant deviations of $Load_{EMA}$ from a target CPU load $Load_{target}$.

In summary, $TDF_{load}(n)$ is given by:

$$TDF_{load}(n) = TDF_{load}(n - 1)$$
$$+ Gain \cdot sgn(Load_{EMA}(n) - Load_{target})$$
$$\cdot \left| 2 \cdot \frac{Load_{EMA}(n) - Load_{target}}{Load_{target}} \right|^{Insensitivity}, \qquad (4)$$

where $sgn(x)$ is the sign of x, and $|x|$ is the absolute value of x.

When the load monitor obtains a new current load, $Load_{current}$, the TDF controller computes a new TDF, TDF_{load} using (3) and (4). The TDF controller computes the new TDF_{load} depending on the configuration of the control parameters α,

Gain, and *Insensitivity* that reflect different priorities of the system such as responsiveness versus stability.

4. PERFORMANCE EVALUATION

In this section, we evaluate the performance of the integrated simulation and emulation system.

4.1 Experimental Setup

For the evaluation we used three identical physical hosts (PHs): each PH is a Dell PowerEdge R210 with two 1 Gigabit Ethernet interfaces, which are connected to two separate 1 Gbps switches. The first interface is used for exchanging TDF control messages, and the second interface is used for emulating links between virtual nodes, i.e., virtual elements on different PHs communicate through the second interface.

We use KVM (qemu-kvm-0.13.0) for full virtualization and ns-3 (ns-3.12.1) for simulation. Ubuntu Linux (ubuntu-10.04-server-amd64) is used for both PHs and VH guest OSs.

4.2 TDF Controller Tuning

The goal of the TDF controller is to adapt the system TDF to CPU loads in the PHs, while minimizing the number of TDF changes. We determine the parameters α in (3) and *Gain*, and *Insensitivity* in (4) for a responsive, yet stable TDF_{load} control.

The current TDF is controlled to maintain the current PH CPU load $Load(i)$ close to a target CPU load TDF_{load}. The tracking error between the current load $Load(i)$ and the target load $Load_{target}$ can be quantified as:

$$C_1 = \frac{\sum_{i=1}^{N} (Load_{target} - Load(i))^2}{N}, \qquad (5)$$

where the summation is taken over a measurement period with N samples. Similarly, the change in TDF_{load} can be measured by:

$$C_2 = \sum_{i=1}^{N-1} \left(\frac{TDF_{load}(i+1) - TDF_{load}(i)}{t(i+1) - t(i)} \right)^2, \qquad (6)$$

where the summation is taken over the same measurement period of N.

The normalized value of C_1, denoted by $\overline{C}_1$, is obtained by dividing C_1 by the average of C_1 values over a measurement period (60 seconds in our experiments). Similarly, $\overline{C}_2$ is the normalized value of C_2.

While we consider two objectives (low tracking error corresponding to a low value of C_1 and infrequent TDF_{load} changes corresponding to a low value of C_2), we favor infrequent TDF_{load} changes over better tracking and thus we define the total cost as:

$$C = \overline{C}_1 + w\overline{C}_2, \qquad (7)$$

where w, the relative weight assigned to $\overline{C}_2$, is greater than one. Experimentally we find that the values of w between 5 and 20 results in relatively infrequent TDF_{load} changes; therefore, we choose $w = 10$. Our TDF controller operates as designed (i.e., the rapid adaptation of TDF to system loads and the minimization of the number of TDF changes) when $\alpha \leq \frac{1}{8}$, *Gain* of $1 \sim 3$, and *Insensitivity* of $4 \sim 10$. Under these ranges of α, *Gain*, and *Insensitivity*, the total cost C is minimized in our experiments. For all the experiments we use $\alpha = \frac{1}{64}$, *Gain* $= 1$ and *Insensitivity* $= 10$, as the PH running the simulator changes the CPU load rapidly. We also use the target CPU load $Load_{target} = 60\%$, at which VHs are able to generate traffic without packet losses.

Finally, we use a TDF control interval of 10 ms (which is also a CPU load checking interval), as a smaller TDF control interval starts to affect system loads.

4.3 Evaluation Topology

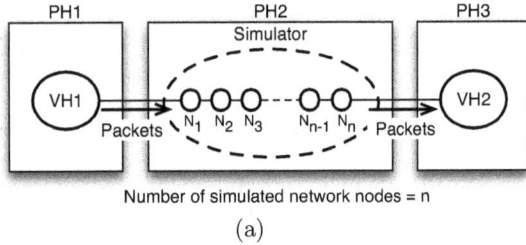

Number of simulated network nodes = n

(a)

Figure 7: Evaluation Topology

When the simulator schedules its events in real time, outgoing packet delay can be introduced due to the simulator execution time. In order to measure outgoing packet delay, we construct an evaluation topology, as shown in Fig. 7. This topology is used for the performance evaluation of our approach.

The simulator running in PH2 creates n simulated network nodes, each of which simulates a network node (i.e., a host or router) with the Internet protocol stack and two CSMA network devices. We use the network devices to connect simulated network nodes through CSMA channel models in ns-3. The CSMA channel model has two configurable parameters: data rate and delay for modeling transmission and propagation delay respectively. The number of simulated network nodes, n, does not include the ghost nodes for VHs.

VH1 running on PH1 generates packets and sends them toward VH2 running on PH3. The packets passes through simulated network nodes on PH2.

4.4 Outgoing Packet Delay

We discuss the effect of time dilation on outgoing packet delay, and then investigate how network nodes' processing delays can affect outgoing packet delay.

4.4.1 The Effect of Time Dilation

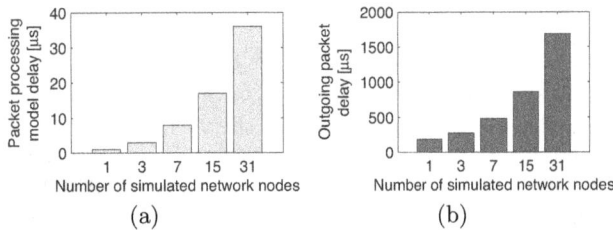

Figure 8: The simulator measures (a) packet processing model delay and (b) outgoing packet delay, while processing a UDP packet in the topology of Fig. 7, where the CSMA channel model delay is 0 μs.

In the topology of Fig. 7, a CSMA channel model connects VH1 to the first simulated network node (N_1), and another CSMA channel model connects the last simulated network node (N_n) to VH2. The data rate and delay of the CSMA channel model are 1 Gbps and 0 μs respectively. VH1 generates 200 146-byte UDP packets (the UDP payload size = 100 bytes) at a constant bit rate of one packet per second. Figures 8 (a) and (b) show the average packet processing model delay and the average outgoing packet delay respectively, both measured in the simulator.

When a packet arrives at the simulator, the packet is transformed into a series of events. The real-time scheduler processes all the events. The ns-3 simulator computes packet processing model delay. The packet process model delay is the time that it takes for the simulator to process a packet in the time units of the simulator and is shown in Fig. 8(a). As the number of simulated network nodes increases, the packet processing model delay increases proportionally because a packet passes through more simulated network nodes and CSMA channels.

Outgoing packet delay is the delay between the instant when the simulator generates a packet towards VH2 and the scheduled time of that packet. As the number of simulated network nodes increases, outgoing packet delay also increases, as shown in Fig. 8(b). As the real-time scheduler in ns-3 simulates the behavior of a physical layer (i.e., the CSMA channel in our experiments), unless we use a hardware-based simulator such as a FPGA-based channel simulator [18], it is difficult or impossible for the simulation to keep pace with real time, because the execution time that it takes to process events for the physical layer behaviors (e.g., transmission delay, propagation delay, inter-frame gaps, etc.) is much larger than the scheduled time. As each network node in the simulation introduces additional delays, the simulator falls further and further behind real time as a packet progresses through the simulated network nodes. Hence, as the number of simulated network nodes and CSMA channels increase, outgoing packet delay also increases almost proportionally.

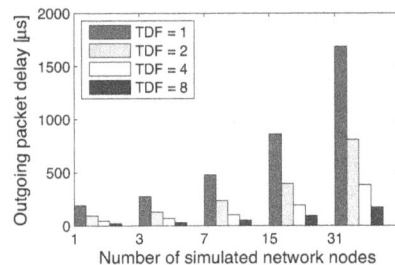

Figure 9: Increasing TDF decreases outgoing packet delay.

We can decrease the outgoing packet delay from the ns-3 simulator by slowing the virtual time. As time proceeds at a slower rate (i.e., TDF increases), the outgoing packet delay is reduced almost linearly. For instance, as shown in Fig. 9, when the simulator runs 31 nodes in real time, there is an outgoing packet delay of 1685 μs. When TDF increases to 2, 4, and 8, the outgoing packet delay decreases to 808, 384, and 171 μs respectively.

4.4.2 Consideration of Network Node's Processing Delay

The ns-3 network simulator does not include a model for the network node's processing delay. The work in [32] proposes a methodology to capture processing delay models from communication software running on real devices.

A network node's processing delay can significantly affect the total packet delay. Hence, for our evaluation we measure a physical node's processing delay.

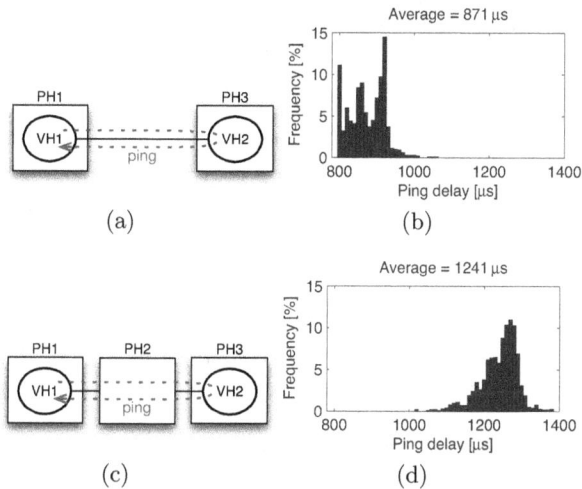

Figure 10: **Experiments for measuring the processing delay of a PH: ping delay distribution without (a), (b) and with (c), (d) a PH in the path**

In order to measure a node's processing delay, we conduct delay measurements on two different network topologies illustrated in Fig. 10. We first measure a ping delay between two VHs without a PH between VHs, as shown in Fig. 10(a). We send a 64-byte ICMP packet every second. Figure 10(b) shows a delay distribution for a total of 1000 ICMP packets. The average ping delay of 1000 ICMP packets is 871 μs.

We then measure another ping delay on the configuration shown in Fig. 10(c). In this configuration, VH1 sends the same ICMP packets to VH2 through a real physical machine (PH2). The average delay of 1000 ICMP packets on this configuration is 1241 μs, and the distribution is shown in Fig. 10(d).

Hence, the average processing delay of a real node (PH2) is $\frac{1241-871}{2} = 185\mu s$. In our performance evaluation, we use $185\mu s$ for simulating the nodes' processing delay.

In order to model a node's processing delay in simulation, we use an additional 185 μs of CSMA channel model delay. Since a packet is transmitted from simulated network node 1 (N_1) to simulated network node n (N_n) in the topology of Fig. 7, we add the CSMA channel delay on each node's outgoing link; i.e., for simulated network node N_1, the delay addition is placed on N_1's right-side CSMA channel. Hence, packet processing model delay linearly increases by ~ 185 μs per simulated network node. For instance, for 31 simulated network nodes, the packet processing model delay is 185 $\mu s \times$ 31 nodes = 5735 μs while the other delays such as inter-frame gaps and transmission delays are negligible by comparison.

While packet processing model delay increases approximately linearly with the number of simulated network nodes

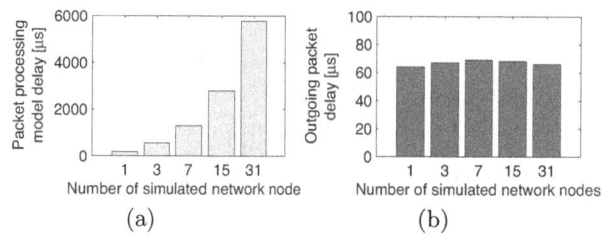

Figure 11: **The simulator measures (a) packet processing model delay and (b) outgoing packet delay, while processing a 146-byte UDP packet in the topology of Fig. 7, where the CSMA channel model delay is 185 μs.**

in Fig. 11(a), outgoing packet delays are almost constant, as shown in Fig. 11(b). When CSMA channel delay is sufficiently large (185 μs) for the simulation to keep pace with real time, the outgoing packet delay is expected to be completely removed, but a delay of approximately 60 μs is still present: after the ns-3 real-time scheduler performs a sleep and spin wait for a CSMA channel model delay of 185 μs, the `CsmaNetDevice` of the ns-3 simulator receives a packet and then sends it to `TapBridge` for a real packet generation. This process takes approximately 60 μs. Since outgoing packet delay occurs only at the last node (i.e., N_n), it remains almost constant, independent of the number of simulated network nodes.

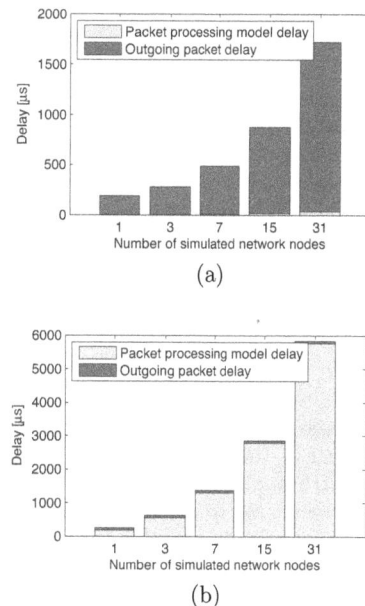

Figure 12: **Comparison of the packet processing model delay and the outgoing packet delay when CSMA channel model delay is (a) 0 μs and (b) 185 μs**

For comparison, Fig. 12 juxtaposes the packet processing model delay and the outgoing packet delay shown in Fig. 8 (for CSMA channel delay = 0 μs) and Fig. 11 (for CSMA channel delay = 185 μs). Recall that outgoing packet delay is our key metric for accuracy. When comparing Fig. 12 (a) and (b), as CSMA channel delay of 185 μs is included for nodes' processing delay, the outgoing packet delay is signif-

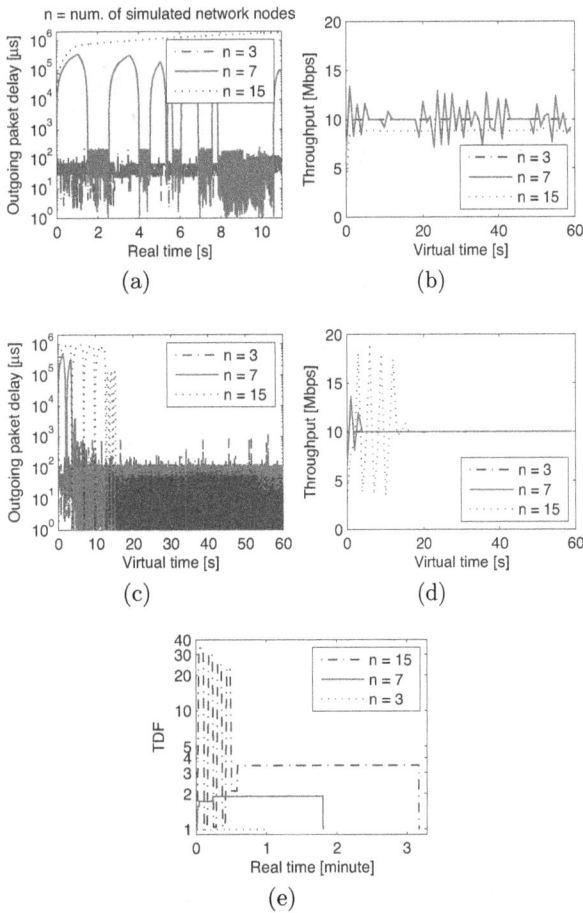

Figure 13: Without time dilation, as the number of simulated network nodes increases, outgoing packet delay significantly increases in (a), and throughput is degraded in (b). When using adaptive time dilation, outgoing packet delay is reduced to ∼ 100 μs in (c), and throughout reaches the packet generation rate (10 Mbps) in (d). Our TDF controller increases TDF for a larger number of simulated network nodes in (e).

icantly reduced. Even though the real-time scheduler simulates a physical layer, if the nodes' processing delay is captured in the model (through the CSMA channel delay in our setup), the simulator is able to catch up with real time, resulting in a significant reduction in the delay introduced by the simulator.

4.5 Evaluation of Adaptive Time Dilation

When the simulator is heavily loaded due to network traffic, outgoing packet delay can increase. In this section, we show how adaptive time dilation can reduce outgoing packet delay under several traffic scenarios. For all the scenarios, we use a data rate 10 Mbps and we model the 185 μs of node processing delay by using the CSMA channel model.

4.5.1 UDP Traffic Scenario

In this section we test UDP traffic on our evaluation topology (Fig. 7). VH1 sends towards VH2 1046-byte UDP packets (the UDP payload size = 1000 bytes) at 10 Mbps.

The simulator can be overloaded by a large number of simulated network nodes or a large traffic load. Under the influx of 10-Mbps UDP packets, with a single simulated network node (n = 1), the simulator can almost process all the events in time, i.e., the outgoing packet delay is approximately 60 μs in our experiments. We do not show this result to avoid cluttering Fig. 13(a). However, as the number of simulated network nodes increases, the outgoing packet delay significantly increases as shown in Fig. 13(a). When n = 7, peaks and troughs occur, as the simulator is repeatedly overloaded and underloaded by the traffic loads. When n = 15, the outgoing packet delay continues to increase since the simulator is not able to process all the events in time. As the number of simulated network nodes increases, throughput is also degraded, as shown in Fig. 13(b).

As the TDF controller dynamically changes TDF according to CPU loads, outgoing packet delay is maintained at approximately 100 μs regardless of the number of simulated network nodes. When the number of simulated network nodes is 15, outgoing packet delay is even lower due to the effect of time dilation, as shown in Fig. 13(c). Figure 13(c) also shows that as the number of simulated network nodes increases, it takes more time for the simulation to reach a steady state. With adaptive time dilation, throughput is approximately the same as the offered load (i.e., 10 Mbps), as shown in Fig. 13(d).

As the number of simulated network nodes increases, our TDF controller increases the TDF to reduce simulation loads and, consequently, simulation run time increases, as shown in Fig. 13(e).

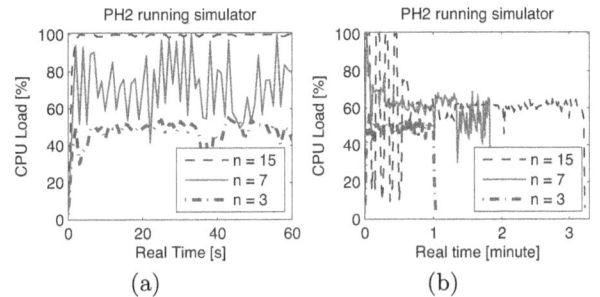

Figure 14: CPU loads (a) without and (b) with adaptive time dilation.

Our TDF controller controls CPU loads at $Load_{target} = 60\%$, as shown in Fig. 14. As the number of simulated network nodes increases, the PH2's CPU load also increases, as shown in Fig. 14(a). However, when using adaptive time dilation, even if the number of simulated network nodes increases, the CPU loads are controlled near the target load 60%. The CPU loads of PH1 and PH3 are much lower than 60%, meaning that in our system at an equal traffic load, the simulator has a much higher CPU load than the VHs.

4.5.2 TCP Traffic Scenario

We generate TCP traffic on our evaluation topology (Fig. 7). We run an iperf [4] client on VH1 and an iperf server on VH2, while changing the number of simulated network nodes on PH2.

Without time dilation (TDF = 1), as the number of simulated network nodes increases, outgoing packet delay significantly fluctuates, as shown in Fig. 15(a) . However, when

(a)

(b)

(c)

(d)

(e)

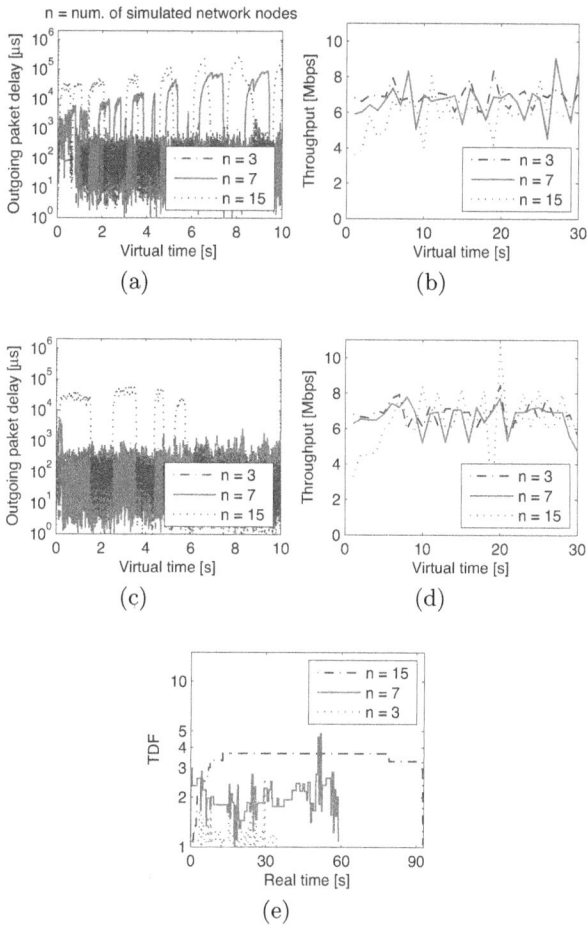

Figure 15: Without time dilation, as the number of simulated network nodes increases, outgoing packet delay significantly fluctuates in (a), and the corresponding throughput is shown in (b). When using adaptive time dilation, outgoing packet delay is reduced to approximately 200 μs in (c), and the corresponding throughput is shown in (d). Our TDF controller increases TDF for larger number of simulated network nodes in (e).

(a)

(b)

(c)

(d)

Figure 16: Each VH on PH1 sends 1.25-Mbps UDP packets to the corresponding VH on PH3 through the simulator in (a). With adaptive time dilation, outgoing packet delay, throughput and TDF are shown in (b), (c), and (d) respectively.

using adaptive time dilation, the outgoing packet delay is controlled to about 200 μs when the number of simulated network nodes is $n = 3$, 7 and 15. Throughput variance in Fig. 15(d) is slightly reduced by adaptive time dilation, as compared with Fig. 15(b).

As shown in Fig. 13(e), for seven simulated network nodes, TDF is stably maintained at $TDF \approx 2$ for UDP traffic. However, as shown in Fig. 15(e), TDF changes are frequent for TCP traffic, since TCP produces bursty traffic. On the other hand, since TCP gradually increases traffic over time, for 15 simulated network nodes, there are no TDF oscillations as seen for UDP traffic (compare Fig. 13(e) with Fig. 15(e)).

4.5.3 Multiple VHs Scenario

In this section, we create a scenario where multiple VHs run on a PH, as shown in Fig. 16(a). We run 8 VHs in PH1 and 8 VHs in PH3. VH1 running on PH1 sends UDP packets

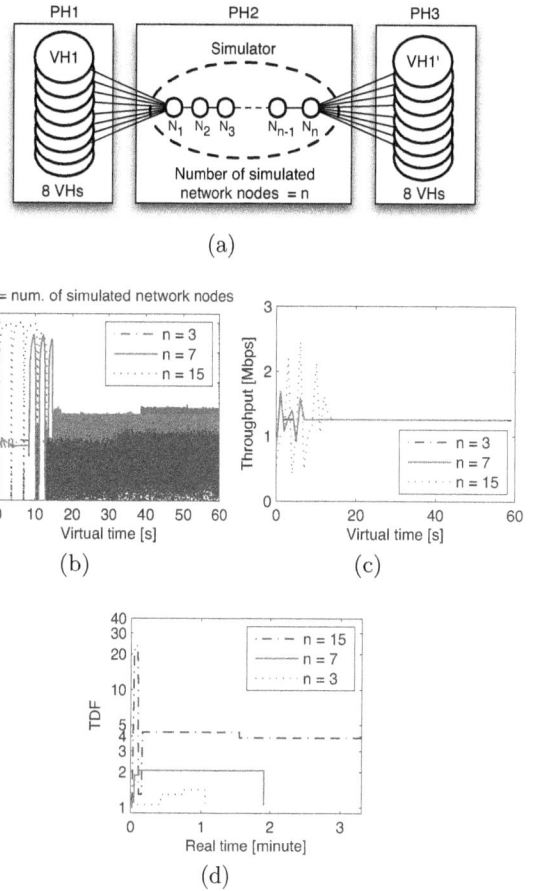

at 1.25 Mbps (constant bit rate) towards VH1' running on PH3. The size of each UDP packet is 1046 bytes. VH2 on PH1 sends UDP packets at the same rate towards VH2' on PH3, and so on. Since the 8 VHs on PH1 generate a total of 10 Mbps ($= 1.25$ Mbps $\times$ 8 VHs), the simulator processes the same amount of traffic as in the previous UDP scenario discussed in Section 4.5.1, where a single VH on PH1 generated 10-Mbps UDP packets.

As shown in Fig. 16(b), the outgoing packet delay has slightly increased compared to Fig. 13(c). While the same amount of traffic (i.e., 10 Mbps) passes through the simulator in total, multiple VHs can create more variance in traffic patterns. Hence, the simulator may sometimes process a closely bunched series of packets such that the simulator can often be busier, thus slightly increasing outgoing packet delay. As the number of simulated network nodes increases, time dilation decreases outgoing packet delay. As shown in Fig. 16(c), despite a slight increase in the outgoing packet delay, throughput remains the same as in Fig. 13(d). On the other hand, the TDF changes for the multiple VHs scenario in Fig. 16(d) are similar to those for the UDP traffic scenario in Fig. 13(e).

5. RELATED WORK

The work in this paper builds on a large body of related work from many different areas, including time dilation, hybrid simulation and emulation systems, real time emulation systems and large-scale emulation systems.

Time control: The approach in SliceTime [41] is to alternately suspend and resume the entire system in order to connect VMs to discrete event simulations [33] that may lag behind in time under heavy system loads [40]. DieCast [27] uses time dilation, which allows virtual time to pass slower than real time such that physical resources appear to virtual nodes to be faster [28]. The Open Network Emulator uses a temporal model referred to as *relativistic time* and employs a lightweight virtualization framework called *Weaves* to enhance scalability [17, 20]. *Weaves* emulates multiple instances of an application or protocol stack inside a single OS process [35]. The approach in [43, 14] uses a timeslice-based scheduler; as the scheduler gives a timeslice to a VE (Virtual Environment), the VE consumes the timeslice and stops its operation.

The approaches in [40, 41, 28, 27] are static in that the relative ratio between real and virtual time is fixed for the life of the VMs. NETplace [23] and NETbalance [24] use epoch-based virtual time [22] for implementing a dynamic time dilation. While the dynamic time dilation in [22] uses a threshold-based load control mechanism, our TDF controller maintains system loads at a target level. Our TDF control mechanism towards a target system load can perform more accurately for a hybrid simulation and emulation environment in that real-time simulation is sensitive to system loads.

In parallel discrete event simulation, conservative algorithms use lookahead for time synchronization [37]. While these algorithms send null messages to compute lookahead, our approach does not exchange null messages. Instead, our adaptive time dilation approach sends TDF messages, which may change the time passage rate of virtual elements. In the algorithm of [37], time proceeds for an amount of lookahead and stops, but in our approach, once TDF changes, virtual time continues to proceed at the rate of $\frac{1}{TDF}$.

Hybrid simulation and emulation: As mentioned in Introduction, the work in [30] integrates S3F [36], a scalable simulation framework, with the OpenVZ [8]-based network emulation. Each VE is synchronized with the simulation clock in S3F. The S3F simulation engine controls VEs' execution to preserve the causal relationship of the whole network scenario [30].

ROSENET [26, 25] is a network emulation approach that uses a remote high-fidelity simulation along with a low-fidelity emulator serving a locally executing real-time application to improve scalability and accuracy.

WHYNET [45] consists of a wireless network emulator (TWINE [44]), simulated radio devices, and physical testbeds. Physical elements includes 801.11-based networks, sensor networks, and SDR/MIMO radio platforms. TWINE [44] embeds the simulated physical and MAC layers into the operating system for scalability.

The approach in [38] incorporates a physical layer emulator for OFDM-based IEEE 802.11 communications into the ns-3 simulator. The work in [21] simulates heterogeneous systems by using a discrete-event simulator, TOSSIM, that implements the lowest layer of components in the TinyOS API, and EmSIM that provides a real code simulation capability.

Real-time emulation: CORE (Common Open Research Emulator) is a real-time network emulator that emulates the network stack of routers or hosts through virtualization, and that simulates the links which connect them together [15]. CORE employs the lightweight virtualization to allow over a hundred virtual machines to run on a single emulation server. Wireless channel emulators use hardware to simulate wireless channel propagation in real time [39, 31, 18]. RAMON (Rapid-Mobility Network emulator) is a software/hardware emulator that allows the ns-2 simulator to interact with hardware components including access points (APs), attenuators, laptops, and smart phones, while emulating mobility in wireless networks [29]. MNE (Mobile Network Emulator) simulates the mobility of wireless nodes [34]. Since MNE operates in real time, it uses simplistic propagation models that do not require significant amounts of processing.

Large-scale emulation: Several large testbeds partially employ or significantly depend on emulation techniques. PlanetLab [9] is a distributed overlay network designed to evaluate planetary-scale network services, allowing multiple services to run concurrently, each in its own *slice* [16, 19]. Emulab [2] offers integrated access to emulated PC nodes, an 802.11 a/b/g testbed, and universal software defined radios (USRP devices). Emulab can also be expanded into PlanetLab testbeds, allowing for live Internet experimentation. GENI [3] provides researchers across the country with collaborative environments on which new network architectures and their implementations can be tested, while supporting scalable experimentation on shared and heterogeneous infrastructure. DETERlab [1] supports experimentation on next-generation cyber security technologies, and uses the Emulab cluster testbed software to control and manage a pool of PCs. ModelNet [6] emulates the delays, losses, and throughput of packets traveling between different application instances.

6. CONCLUSION

In this paper, we proposed an approach integrating simulation with emulation by using adaptive time dilation. VHs and simulators are synchronized to a common virtual time passage rate. When the simulator schedules its events in real time, event processing can easily overload the simulator, as the simulation load increases. Our TDF controller dynamically changes a virtual time rate such that outgoing packet delay is minimized in the simulator. Without using virtual time in our evaluation, the simulator becomes heavily loaded as TCP and UDP traffic passes through it, and thus increases outgoing packet delay. Our adaptive time dilation approach dynamically changes TDF such that outgoing packet delay is minimized. Since our integrated simulation and emulation approach uses full virtualization, unmodified OSs and applications can be used in the system.

7. REFERENCES

[1] DeterLab. http://www.isi.deterlab.net.
[2] Emulab. http://www.emulab.net.
[3] GENI Project. http://www.geni.net.
[4] Iperf. http://iperf.sourceforge.net.
[5] KVM. http://www.linux-kvm.org.

[6] ModelNet. http://modelnet.ucsd.edu.

[7] ns-3. http://www.nsnam.org.

[8] OpenVZ. http://wiki.openvz.org.

[9] PlanetLab. http://www.planet-lab.org.

[10] QEMU. http://wiki.qemu.org.

[11] Universal TUN/TAP Device Driver. http://vtun.sourceforge.net/tun.

[12] VirtualBox. http://www.virtualbox.org.

[13] Xen. http://www.xenproject.org.

[14] Y Zheng, D M Nicol, D Jin1 and N Tanaka, A virtual time system for virtualization-based network emulations and simulations, Journal of Simulation, 1 June 2012.

[15] AHRENHOLZ, J., DANILOV, C., HENDERSON, T., AND KIM, J. CORE: A real-time network emulator. In *Military Communications Conference, 2008. MILCOM 2008. IEEE* (Nov. 2008), pp. 1–7.

[16] BAVIER, A., BOWMAN, M., CHUN, B., CULLER, D., KARLIN, S., MUIR, S., PETERSON, L., ROSCOE, T., SPALINK, T., AND WAWRZONIAK, M. Operating system support for planetary-scale network services. In *Proceedings of the 1st conference on Symposium on Networked Systems Design and Implementation - Volume 1* (Berkeley, CA, USA, 2004), USENIX Association, pp. 19–19.

[17] BERGSTROM, C., VARADARAJAN, S., AND BACK, G. The distributed open network emulator: Using relativistic time for distributed scalable simulation. In *Principles of Advanced and Distributed Simulation, 2006. PADS 2006. 20th Workshop on* (2006), pp. 19–28.

[18] BORRIES, K., JUDD, G., STANCIL, D., AND STEENKISTE, P. FPGA-based channel simulator for a wireless network emulator. In *Vehicular Technology Conference, 2009. VTC Spring 2009. IEEE 69th* (April 2009), pp. 1–5.

[19] CHUN, B., CULLER, D., ROSCOE, T., BAVIER, A., PETERSON, L., WAWRZONIAK, M., AND BOWMAN, M. PlanetLab: an overlay testbed for broad-coverage services. *SIGCOMM Comput. Commun. Rev. 33* (July 2003), 3–12.

[20] DUGGIRALA, V., AND VARADARAJAN, S. Open network emulator: A parallel direct code execution network simulator. In *Proceedings of the 2012 ACM/IEEE/SCS 26th Workshop on Principles of Advanced and Distributed Simulation* (Washington, DC, USA, 2012), PADS '12, IEEE Computer Society, pp. 101–110.

[21] GIROD, L., STATHOPOULOS, T., RAMANATHAN, N., ELSON, J., ESTRIN, D., OSTERWEIL, E., AND SCHOELLHAMMER, T. A system for simulation, emulation, and deployment of heterogeneous sensor networks. In *Proceedings of the 2Nd International Conference on Embedded Networked Sensor Systems* (New York, NY, USA, 2004), SenSys '04, ACM, pp. 201–213.

[22] GRAU, A., HERRMANN, K., AND ROTHERMEL, K. Efficient and scalable network emulation using adaptive virtual time. In *Computer Communications and Networks, 2009. ICCCN 2009. Proceedings of 18th Internatonal Conference on* (Aug. 2009), pp. 1–6.

[23] GRAU, A., HERRMANN, K., AND ROTHERMEL, K. NETplace: Efficient runtime minimization of network emulation experiments. In *Performance Evaluation of Computer and Telecommunication Systems (SPECTS), 2010 International Symposium on* (July 2010), pp. 265–272.

[24] GRAU, A., HERRMANN, K., AND ROTHERMEL, K. NETbalance: Reducing the runtime of network emulation using live migration. In *Computer Communications and Networks (ICCCN), 2011 Proceedings of 20th International Conference on* (Aug. 2011), pp. 1–6.

[25] GU, Y., AND FUJIMOTO, R. Applying parallel and distributed simulation to remote network emulation. In *Simulation Conference, 2007 Winter* (Dec 2007), pp. 1328–1336.

[26] GU, Y., AND FUJIMOTO, R. Performance evaluation of the rosenet network emulation system. In *Distributed Simulation and Real-Time Applications, 2007. DS-RT 2007. 11th IEEE International Symposium* (Oct 2007), pp. 276–283.

[27] GUPTA, D., VISHWANATH, K. V., AND VAHDAT, A. DieCast: Testing distributed systems with an accurate scale model. In *Proc. of NSDI* (2008), pp. 407–421.

[28] GUPTA, D., YOCUM, K., MCNETT, M., SNOEREN, A. C., VAHDAT, A., AND VOELKER, G. M. To infinity and beyond: time warped network emulation. In *In ACM Symposium on Operating Systems Principles* (2005).

[29] HERNANDEZ, E., AND HELAL, A. RAMON: rapid-mobility network emulator. In *Local Computer Networks, 2002. Proceedings. LCN 2002. 27th Annual IEEE Conference on* (Nov. 2002), pp. 809–817.

[30] JIN, D., ZHENG, Y., ZHU, H., NICOL, D. M., AND WINTERROWD, L. Virtual time integration of emulation and parallel simulation. In *Proceedings of the 2012 ACM/IEEE/SCS 26th Workshop on Principles of Advanced and Distributed Simulation* (Washington, DC, USA, 2012), PADS '12, IEEE Computer Society, pp. 201–210.

[31] KAHRS, M., AND ZIMMER, C. Digital signal processing in a real-time propagation simulator. *Instrumentation and Measurement, IEEE Transactions on 55, 1* (Feb. 2006), 197–205.

[32] KRISTIANSEN, S., PLAGEMANN, T., AND GOEBEL, V. Modeling communication software execution for accurate simulation of distributed systems. In *Proceedings of the 2013 ACM SIGSIM Conference on Principles of Advanced Discrete Simulation* (New York, NY, USA, 2013), SIGSIM-PADS '13, ACM, pp. 67–78.

[33] LAW, A. M., AND KELTON, D. M. *Simulation Modeling and Analysis*, 3rd ed. McGraw-Hill Higher Education, 1999.

[34] MACKER, J., CHAO, W., AND WESTON, J. A low-cost, ip-based mobile network emulator (MNE). In *Military Communications Conference, 2003. MILCOM 2003. IEEE* (Oct. 2003), vol. 1, pp. 481–486.

[35] MUKHERJEE, J., AND VARADARAJAN, S. Weaves: A framework for reconfigurable programming. *International Journal of Parallel Programming 33* (2005), 279–305. 10.1007/s10766-005-3591-5.

[36] NICOL, D., JIN, D., AND ZHENG, Y. S3f: The scalable simulation framework revisited. In *Simulation Conference (WSC), Proceedings of the 2011 Winter* (2011), pp. 3283–3294.

[37] NICOL, D. M. The cost of conservative synchronization in parallel discrete event simulations. *J. ACM 40*, 2 (Apr. 1993), 304–333.

[38] PAPANASTASIOU, S., MITTAG, J., STROM, E., AND HARTENSTEIN, H. Bridging the gap between physical layer emulation and network simulation. In *Wireless Communications and Networking Conference (WCNC), 2010 IEEE* (2010), pp. 1–6.

[39] PICOL, S., ZAHARIA, G., HOUZET, D., AND EL ZEIN, G. Hardware simulator for MIMO radio channels: Design and features of the digital block. In *Vehicular Technology Conference, 2008. VTC 2008-Fall. IEEE 68th* (Sept. 2008), pp. 1–5.

[40] WEINGÄRTNER, E., SCHMIDT, F., HEER, T., AND WEHRLE, K. Synchronized network emulation: matching prototypes with complex simulations. *SIGMETRICS Perform. Eval. Rev. 36* (August 2008), 58–63.

[41] WEINGÄRTNER, E., SCHMIDT, F., LEHN, H. V., HEER, T., AND WEHRLE, K. SliceTime: a platform for scalable and accurate network emulation. In *Proceedings of the 8th USENIX conference on Networked systems design and implementation* (Berkeley, CA, USA, 2011), NSDI'11, USENIX Association, pp. 19–19.

[42] YOUNGE, A., HENSCHEL, R., BROWN, J., VON LASZEWSKI, G., QIU, J., AND FOX, G. Analysis of virtualization technologies for high performance computing environments. In *Cloud Computing (CLOUD), 2011 IEEE International Conference on* (July 2011), pp. 9–16.

[43] ZHENG, Y., AND NICOL, D. A virtual time system for openvz-based network emulations. In *Principles of Advanced and Distributed Simulation (PADS), 2011 IEEE Workshop on* (2011), pp. 1–10.

[44] ZHOU, J., JI, Z., AND BAGRODIA, R. Twine: A hybrid emulation testbed for wireless networks and applications. In *INFOCOM 2006. 25th IEEE International Conference on Computer Communications. Proceedings* (2006), pp. 1–13.

[45] ZHOU, J., JI, Z., VARSHNEY, M., XU, Z., YANG, Y., MARINA, M., AND BAGRODIA, R. Whynet: A hybrid testbed for large-scale, heterogeneous and adaptive wireless networks. In *Proceedings of the 1st International Workshop on Wireless Network Testbeds, Experimental Evaluation & Characterization* (New York, NY, USA, 2006), WiNTECH '06, ACM, pp. 111–112.

TimeKeeper: A Lightweight Virtual Time System for Linux

Jereme Lamps, David M. Nicol, Matthew Caesar
University of Illinois at Urbana-Champaign
{lamps1, dmnicol, caesar}@illinois.edu

ABSTRACT

We present TimeKeeper: a simple lightweight approach to embedding Linux containers (LXC) in virtual time. Each container can be directed to progress in virtual time either more rapidly or more slowly than the physical wall clock time. As a result, interactions between an LXC and physical devices can be artificially scaled, e.g., to make a network appear to be ten times faster with respect to the software within the LXC than it actually is. Our approach also supports synchronized (in virtual time) emulation, by grouping LXCs together into an *experiment* where the virtual times of containers are kept synchronized, even when they advance at different speeds. This has direct application to the integration of emulation and simulation within a common framework.

Categories and Subject Descriptors

C.2.4 [**Computer-Communication Networks**]: Distributed Systems—*distributed applications*; D.4.4 [**Operating Systems**]: Communications Management—*message sending, communication management*; D.4.8 [**Operating Systems**]: Performance—*measurements, simulation*; I.6.3 [**Simulation and Modeling**]: Applications—*Miscellaneous*

Keywords

Simulation, Emulation, LXCs, Virtualization, Time Dilation, CORE, Linux Kernel

1. INTRODUCTION

Virtual machine managers (VMM) multiplex the execution of virtual machines (VM), i.e., software stacks, in such a way that the VMs behave as though they are running on individual pieces of hardware. A question of great interest to us is how the advancement of time in a VM is perceived. For example, suppose that an application in one VM sends a message to another, and includes in that message the time at which the message was sent. What is the value of that time variable? In most systems the system clock will give the time, but the system clock in a VMM *typically* reflects time advancement of the VMM, not its VMs. A Xen VM has an associated *domain time*, which reflects the amount of wall-clock time that the VM has received. The domain time advances with the system clock while the VM is served, and stops advancing when it no longer has CPU service. However, domain time is used in Xen for scheduling, and not as a measure of virtual time.

The idea for embedding Xen in virtual time was originally expressed in the context of testing distributed applications [7]. The basic idea is to make virtual time in a VM advance more slowly than real time, in order to make the (real) network connected to the VM appear to be performing faster. The approach associates with each VM an integer-valued *time dialation factor*, or TDF. A TDF of n reduces the advancement rate of a VM in time by a factor of n; for example, a TDF of 2 makes virtual time in the VM advance at half the rate of wall-clock time. This approach (and subsequent ones [6]) rescale a VM's notion of time with reference to a *physical* network, in order to emulate a seemingly accelerated rate of interaction between the VM and the network.

We are motivated by a different objective, to virtualize time in a VM in order integrate its behavior with a network *simulator* such as S3F [11] or ns-3 [13]. This goal raises new considerations. A network simulator can represent a much larger infrastructure than a real network in a typical lab, which creates the need to emulate in virtual time many VMs; this in turn raises the importance of minimizing overhead. In particular, we want to have VMs "jump" over epochs in virtual time where nothing of interest occurs, rather than rescale time and have the VM crawl through the epoch just to advance its clock to its next interaction with the network simulator. An example is a web-server, whose behavior is to wait for a request, formulate and issue a database query, wait for the IO system's response, report the response and then wait for another request. Depending on what the experiment is measuring, the VM might be directed to reset its virtual time to the time of a request or IO completion and completely bypass epochs where the process is suspended. Another new consideration is the need to advance a group of VMs through virtual time so that their virtual clocks are closely synchronized, even if they advance those clocks at different rates by virtue of different TDFs.

A final goal is to bring virtual time to the Linux kernel in a minimally invasive way, that exposes an API to support our motivating problem of integrating emulation and simulation, and is general enough to support other uses of virtual time. These considerations have led us to develop *Time-Keeper*, a small set of modifications to the Linux kernel that allows for the creation of LXCs, each with their own virtual clock. There are two main distinctions separating this project from previous ones. First, our approach becomes an integral (and very small) part of the Linux kernel, giving it the potential to become mainstream. Second, our approach is much lighter weight than Xen [2] or OpenVZ [16] (admittedly at the cost of less generality than Xen). Finally, our approach to virtual time synchronization is more sophisticated than that which has been applied to Xen's to date, and has greater flexibility of interaction between emulation and simulation than previous solutions based on OpenVZ.

2. RELATED WORK

Related work exists in the area of simulation/emulation, and in the area of virtual time. We discuss these separately.

2.1 Simulation/Emulation

In simulation computer systems are modeled entirely in software. Simulation has the attractive property of being scalable and repeatable. There are various simulation tools available today, such as J-Sim [9], ns-2 [12], OMNeT++ [14], and ns-3 [13]. J-Sim is a component-based simulation environment, where each link, node, and protocol is a component. Components have ports associated with them, and a component contract describes how data should be handled if it arrives at a specific port. Event executions are in real-time, thus improving the fidelity of the simulation. OMNet++ and ns-2 are both popular discrete event simulators. Both simulators are written in C++, while ns-2 provides the interface through OTcl. In ns-2, models are flat, meaning that creating subnetworks is not possible. On the other hand, OMNeT++ supports a hierarchical module structure which makes it easier to develop complex models in a methodical manner. Many papers have compared the performance of ns-2 and OMNeT++, concluding that ns-2 is not nearly as scalable or easy to use as OMNeT++ [10, 15, 20]. Also, there is ns-3, a discrete event simulator that is aimed to overcome ns-2's shortcomings. It is developed in C++, and it is designed to be modular, scalabale, and extensible. Papers have conducted studies testing the performance of ns-3 and other simulators, concluding ns-3 to be the most efficient [20]. In addition, ns-3 is a hybrid approach, allowing for emulation as well.

In contrast to simulation, emulation involves a testbed or a physical network to provide more realistic results. Two common testbeds that provide emulation are Emulab [21] and PlanetLab [17]. Emulab provides the experimenter with the ability to create arbitrary networks, and allocates specific nodes from the testbed for a specific amount of time. The experimenter can run specific operating systems on the hardware, and is granted *root* access. This allows for controllable and predictable experiments; however, it is limited by the size of the testbed, and may not be suitable for all types of tests. On the other hand, PlanetLab is a global research network consisting of nodes throughout the globe. At the time of writing, PlanetLab consists of 1181 nodes at 572 sites. A distinction between PlanetLab and Emulab is that PlanetLab gives you an LXC on various nodes, while Emulab will give you sole access to the machine. Therefore, experiments on PlanetLab will not be reproducible, because

other users may be running experiments on the same nodes simultaneously.

There also exist hybrid solutions, supporting both simulation and emulation, such as the Common Open Research Emulator (CORE) [1] and ns-3 [13]. This allows the simulator to be interfaced with real-world communication systems for more realistic measurements.

2.2 Virtual Time Systems

There have been many recent papers dealing with giving systems a sense of virtual time, e.g., [3, 5, 6, 19, 22]. DieCast [6] makes modifications to the Xen hypervisor to give VM's a concept of virtual time. DieCast also scales the performance of physical hardware components. This is a useful option if you want to create an experiment where the number of nodes in the experiment is greater than the number of nodes in your testbed. SVEET! [3] is a performance evaluation testbed running on Xen-based VMs that implements time virtualization techniques if the simulation is overloaded. It sets a static TDF to slow down both the simulator and the VMs. Our work differs from both DieCast and Sveet, as we use lightweight LXCs with Linux kernel modifications instead of Xen-based VMs. We can also dynamically change TDFs, as well as support the synchronization of LXCs virtual times, even if they have different TDFs. In some ways our approach resembles that of Zheng et al., [22] who developed a virtual time system for simulation and emulation using OpenVZ. Like our solution, they modified time-related system calls to return virtual time as opposed to the system time. However, our work is different, as it uses LXCs, and brings the notion of a time dialation factor to the forefront. The OpenVZ system scales measured elapsed time as we do, but that scaling factor is fixed.

3. DESIGN

We designed TimeKeeper with three objectives. First, we wanted to develop a lightweight solution. This minimizes overhead for time-dilated processes. Next, we wanted a simple solution which would allow researchers to create and test their own time-dilated processes. Finally, we wanted TimeKeeper to easily integrate with existing emulators/simulators. We next expand on these objectives.

3.1 Lightweight

We want to spin up many time-dilated processes simultaneously, with minimal overhead. An attractive option is to use Linux Containers (LXCs) [8], a virtualization method which allows multiple individual Linux instances to be running on a single host while sharing the kernel. LXC produces less overhead than traditional virtual machine monitors, such as Xen [2] or VMWare [18], as they require separate kernels for each VM. We also attempted to minimize the number of changes made to the Linux kernel. For example, to support basic time-dilation within a process, we need only add 36 bytes to the process' *task_struct* (the *task_struct* is a data structure in Linux that stores information about a particular process). These changes required modifying only 7 files in the kernel and adding fewer than than 100 lines of code. To support advanced time-dilation features, such as running processes with different TDFs within the same *experiment*, we developed a linux kernel module which may be dynamically loaded into the kernel at runtime.

3.2 User Interface

In order to make TimeKeeper easy to use, we developed a simple and intuitive application programming interface (API) to create and manage time-dilated processes. The presented API is simply a subset of functions which Time-Keeper provides. The API exports the following functions:

- **clone_time(unsigned long flags, float dilation, int should_start):** causes a new process to be cloned from the calling process. You can set specific flags just as you would in the *clone()* system call. The *dilation* argument is the dilation factor of the new process, and the *should_start* argument will start the new process immediately with a value of 0, and not start the new process with a value of 1. This is useful if you wish to clone numerous processes, and then start them all at the same time (as in an *experiment*).

- **start_experiment(int count, ...):** causes a series of cloned processes all to be started at the same time. *Count* represents the number of processes in the experiment, followed by a variable number of pid integers.

- **dilate(int pid, float dilation):** changes the dilation factor of a process. *Pid* represents the unique ID of the process, and *dilation* is the new dilation factor of the process. This can be called on both processes that were created through the *clone_time()* function, as well as general processes.

- **freeze(int pid):** stops the process from executing. The time at which it stopped executing is remembered.

- **unfreeze(int pid):** allows a previously frozen process to continue executing. In between the time in which the process was frozen and unfrozen, the process does not perceive the passage of time. For example, if a process was frozen at time $t=10$ *seconds*, and unfrozen at time $t=20$ *seconds*, the process will resume at time $t=10$ *seconds*.

- **leap(int pid):** changes the container's virtual time to be identical to that of the container with id *pid*. Applied to a frozen process, it causes that container to leap over an epoch of virtual time, without modification to its TDF.

3.3 Ease of Integration

Finally, we wanted to be sure TimeKeeper could be integrated with other simulation or emulation systems. As proof of concept, we integrated TimeKeeper with CORE [1]. We chose to initially integrate with CORE as it already uses LXCs. Therefore, changes needed to the framework would be minimal. In addition, the framework itself is highly customizable. With only a few modifications to the graphical user interface (GUI) to allow setting dilation factors, plus minor changes to the backend we were able to run simple time dilated experiments. The results can be found in section 5.

4. IMPLEMENTATION

We sought a solution that can run different LXCs at different TDF's. We wanted to be able to run LXCs individually with no synchronization, or grouped together in an experiment where processes with different TDF's must progress

---

Algorithm 1: Finding current time of a time dilated task

```
def gettimeofday(tv):
    Data: struct timeval which gets returned to the user
    if task→v_s_t > 0:
        new_p_p_t = now() - task→v_s_t
        new_p_v_t = (new_p_p_t - task→p_p_t)/d_f +
        task→p_v_t
        time = new_p_v_t + task→v_s_t
        task→p_p_t = new_p_p_t
        task→p_v_t = new_p_v_t
        tv = ns_to_timeval(time)
    else:
        Do normal gettimeofday(tv)
```

Figure 1: Pseudocode For Gettimeofday Algorithm

uniformly together in virtual time. The following subsections describe modifications to the linux kernel and the development of a linux kernel module respectively that will provide needed functionality.

4.1 Kernel Modifications

We added only 36 bytes (5 variables) to the linux *task_struct* in order to give each dilated process its own perception of time. The variables added are:

- 4 bytes *dilation_factor (d_f)* represents the time dilation factor of the process.

- 8 bytes *virtual_start_time (v_s_t)* represents the point in virtual time (in ns) at which a process starts progressing by its TDF.

- 8 bytes *past_virtual_time (p_v_t)* represents how much virtual time has passed since the last time the process inquired about the current time.

- 8 bytes *past_physical_time (p_p_t)* represents how much physical time has passed since the last time the process inquired about the current time.

- 8 bytes *freeze_time (f_t)* is used to determine if a process is currently frozen or not. A value of 0 means it is not frozen, where a value greater than 0 represents the point in time (in ns) in which a process was frozen. This is a variable internal to TimeKeeper.

The *gettimeofday()* system call was modified to return the virtual time for a process if it has a *virtual_start_time* set; if the *virtual_start_time* is not set, then *gettimeofday()* performs normally. The pseudocode for the gettimeofday modifications can be found in Figure 4.1.

Consider a quick example for clarification, using a process with a TDF of 2. Note this means for every 2 seconds of clock time, the process will perceive only 1 second of virtual time. We assume the process is started at the system time of 20 seconds. At this point in time, $d\_f=2$, $v\_s\_t=20$, $p\_v\_t=0$, and $p\_p\_t=0$. Suppose this process performs a computation for 10 seconds, and then calls *gettimeofday()*. Following the pseudocode, a new_p_p_t will be calculated by subtracting the current system time from the v_s_t. So the new_p_p_t = 30s - 20s = 10s. A new_p_v_t is then calculated by finding the time which has elapsed since the last past_physical_time, scaling it appropriately based on the TDF, and finally adding it to the last past_virtual_time.

Thus, new_p_v_t = (new_p_p_t - p_p_t)/d_f + p_v_t = (10s - 0s)/2 + 0 = 5s. So the virtual_time = v_s_t + new_p_v_t = 25 seconds, which is the correct virtual time for the described scenario. Note, before *gettimeofday()* returns, new_p_p_t and new_p_v_t are stored into p_p_t and p_v_t respectively. At the end of this function, the state of the process is: *d_f=2, v_s_t=20s, p_p_t=10s, and p_v_t=5s* and the global time is 30s. Now assume the process runs for an additional 20 seconds, and checks its time once again. new_p_p_t = 50s - 20s = 30s and new_p_v_t = (new_p_p_t - p_p_t)/d_f + p_v_t = (30s - 10s)/2 + 5 = 15s. So the virtual_time returned is 20s+15s = 35s. As you can see, this is consistent with what is expected, as the process was started at 20 seconds, and has been running with a TDF of 2 for 30 seconds of physical time.

In order to accurately maintain the process' perception of time, we can not simply alter the *gettimeofday()* system call, we must modify system calls such as *sleep()* and *poll()* as well. The *sleep()* system call takes an integer as an argument, which represents the number of seconds the program should sleep before it continues its execution. We modified the *sleep()* system call such that it is scaled with the calling process' TDF. For example, if a process with a TDF of 2 calls *sleep(10)*, it will sleep for 20 seconds of wall clock time. However, due to its TDF, it will believe it slept for 10 seconds. The *poll()* system call waits for a set of file descriptors to become ready so it may perform I/O. *Poll()* takes a *timeout* value as an argument, which corresponds to the minimum number of milliseconds the system call will block. Similarly to *sleep()*, *poll()* was modified so a process with a specified TDF will run as anticipated.

4.2 Kernel Module

Some of the more complicated time dilation functionality was developed in the form of a loadable linux kernel module, e.g., the ability to *freeze* and *unfreeze* a process' advancement in virtual time. In addition, TimeKeeper is able to synchronize containers, so we are able to group processes together with different TDF's and still manage to insure their virtual times are synchronized.

To *freeze* or *unfreeze* a process, TimeKeeper makes use of a variable that was added to each process' *task_struct*: *freeze_time (f_t)*. If the user wishes to *freeze* a process, its *f_t* is set to the current, non-dilated system time, and a SIGSTOP signal is sent to the process, removing it from the CPU and putting it in a stopped state. When the user wishes to *unfreeze* a frozen process, the process' *p_p_t* is updated to reflect the amount of physical time the process was frozen *(p_p_t = p_p_t + (current_system_time - f_t))*. A SIGCONT signal is then sent to the process, allowing it to run on the CPU once again. Finally, *f_t* is reset to 0. To continue the example in the previous section. Assume the process was frozen immediately after it last checked its time (virtual_time=35s, system_time=50s). The current state of the process is: *d_f=2, v_s_t=20s, p_p_t=30s, p_v_t=15s, f_t=50s*. The process is first frozen for 10 seconds, then unfrozen and immediately checks the time. When it is unfrozen, the *p_p_t* is changed to *(p_p_t + (current_system_time - f_t)) = (30s + (60s-50s)) = 40s*. When it checks the time with the updated *p_p_t* value, it returns 35s, therefore not recognizing any time has passed since it was frozen.

In addition to freezing and unfreezing a process' perception of time, TimeKeeper is also responsible for grouping processes with different TDF's into a single *experiment*, where all of the processes virtual times progress uniformly.

TimeKeeper maintains a linked list of all processes in the experiment, a tunable knob called a *timeslice* which specifies the amount of phyiscal time the *leader* LXC should be allowed to run in each interval, and another tunable knob that specifies how many processors can be used for LXCs in the experiment (DED_CPU). We would set DED_CPU to be two CPUs less than the total number of CPUs in the system. This would allow standard background tasks to still run successfully, even when performing a CPU-intensive experiment. When an *experiment* is initialized, TimeKeeper determines the process with the highest TDF, known as the *leader*. Knowing the *leader* is a necessity, as the *leader's* virtual time will be progressing slower than any other process in the experiment. Therefore, we need to scale down the running time of other processes in the experiment accordingly. For example, if the *leader* has a TDF of 2 and there is another process with TDF of 1, the process with a TDF of 1 will need to run for one half the time the *leader* runs.

Once the *leader* has been determined, each process is dedicated to a specific CPU, where multiple processes may be dedicated to the same CPU, and set to have a scheduling policy of SCHED_FIFO (first-in first-out). We set each process' scheduling policy as SCHED_FIFO so it will have priority over other tasks not in the experiment, as well as not get pre-empted until we say so. Each process will receive a fraction of the *timeslice* in which it will be allowed to run on its dedicated CPU, this fraction is based on the process' TDF in respect to the *leader's* TDF, and maintained by a high-resolution timer (*hrtimer*) [4]. To run a process, it is unfrozen with TimeKeeper's previously mentioned *unfreeze* capability, and its *hrtimer* is set to expire when its fraction of the *timeslice* is up. When the *hrtimer* for a process expires, that process is frozen, and the next process whose turn it is to run on the CPU gets unfrozen and has its *hrtimer* set. When all processes in the experiment have been allowed to run for their fraction of the *timeslice*, the round is up. At the end of each round, the *leader* will be recalculated if new processes were added to the experiment, or if the past *leader* finished executing. Each process' virtual time is compared to the expected virtual time. If a process' virtual time exceeds the expected virtual time, that process will be forced to run for less time in the following round (by setting the *hrtimer* to expire earlier). If a process' virtual time is below the expected virtual time, that process will be allowed to run for additional time in the following round. The next round begins when all processes know how long they should be allowed to run for in the next round. See Figure 4.2 for the basic psuedocode.

5. EVALUATION

In this section, we will discuss our preliminary results regarding the accuracy of *hrtimers*, and our virtual time systems ability to keep the LXCs synchronized. In addition, we look into scalability of the system, the overhead TimeKeeper may create, as well as how efficiently TimeKeeper can keep LXCs running in real-time. Unless otherwise specified, experiments were conducted on a Dell Studio XPS Desktop, with 24 GB of RAM, and 8 Intel Core i-7 CPU X 980's @ 3.33GHz. The machine is running 32-bit Ubuntu with a modified 3.10.9 Linux kernel.

Algorithm 2: Simplified Process Synchronization and Hrtimer Interrupt

```
def synchronize(timeslice):
    expected_time = calcExpectedVirtualTime()
    foreach task in experiment do
        dilated_time = calcDilatedTime(task)
        difference = expected_time - dilated_time
        task→offset = calcOffsetNeeded(task, difference)
    foreach CPU in DED_CPU do
        task = getNextTask(CPU)
        unfreeze(task)
        task→setHrTimer(timeslice - task→offset)
    return
def hrtimerInterrupt(task):
    freeze(task)
    nextTask = getNextTask(task→CPU)
    if nextTask == NULL:
        synchronize(timeslice)
    else:
        unfreeze(nextTask)
        nextTask→setHrTimer(timeslice - nextTask→offset)
    return
```

Figure 2: Pseudocode for LXC Synchronization Algorithm

timeslice	μ	σ
$300ms$	862ns	1130ns
$30ms$	401ns	680ns
$3ms$	341ns	592ns
$300\mu s$	523ns	2306ns
$30\mu s$	351ns	2128 ns
$3\mu s$	481ns	3312ns
$1\mu s$	2404ns	4213ns
$300ns$	2925ns	6012ns

Table 1: Mean and Standard Deviation of Timer Error for Different Timeslice Lengths

5.1 hrtimer accuracy

The effectiveness of TimeKeeper's ability to keep virtual clocks synchronized is highly dependent on the *hrtimers* ability to fire interrupts at precise moments in time. If we want a particular LXC to run for $3\mu s$ at a time, then we would want the *hrtimer* associated with that particular LXC to trigger an interrupt as close to $3\mu s$ as possible. For the initial test, we set different *hrtimers* to periodically fire at different time intervals (*timeslice*), and measured what time the *hrtimer* interrupt actually fired. We collected 200 data points for every different time interval. From there, we calculated the mean (μ) and standard deviation (σ) of the error. Table 1 presents the results.

Taking the first row as an example, when the timer was scheduled to fire an interrupt every $300ms$, on average the interrupt occurred 862ns from what was expected. This is excellent accuracy, there are five orders of magnitude between the error and the *timeslice*. The magnitude of the variation in error is roughly constant; the error size relative to *timeslice* is still an order of magnitude smaller with a 30 micro-second *timeslice*, and is roughly equal with a 3 micro-second *timeslice*. These comparisons tell us something very important about the level of granularity we can effectively use in combined emulation/simulation scenarios. If 10% error in timing is acceptable and a simulated message takes on the order of 100 micro-seconds to pass on the network from

# of LXCs	timeslice	μ	σ
10	.3ms	596ns	1084ns
10	3ms	685ns	1129ns
10	30ms	1028ns	1766ns
10	300ms	812ns	1447ns
80	.3ms	196ns	375ns
80	3ms	193ns	374ns
80	30ms	258ns	535ns
80	300ms	333ns	628ns

Table 2: Mean and Standard Deviation of Error as a Function of Timeslice and #LXCs

one device to another, we can expect to get a little over three *timeslices* in during the message's passage through the network simulator. *This* means that if a container is sensitive to IO from the simulator only at *timeslice* boundaries (as is the case with the virtual-time OpenVZ system), there may be as much as a 33% error in the virtual time at which the container "sees" the message. The take-away message here is that Linux timers are very accurate, but if we are to be able to take advantage of that accuracy when interfacing emulated LXC containers and a network simulator we will have to find a way to integrate simulator time and container time at a finer granularity than the *timeslice*. This constitutes one of our areas of future work.

5.2 Synchronization

To integrate our emulation with network simulation we will need to keep LXCs closely synchronized. We performed a set of experiments to evaluate how tightly we are able to do so. In these experiments, TimeKeeper aimed to have each LXC achieve a target virtual time by the end of each *timeslice*. For each LXC and each *timeslice* we measure the deviation of the virtual time the LXC actually achieved at that *timeslice* from the target goal. For each set of experiments we compute the mean error μ and the the standard deviation of the error σ, taken over all LXCs and synchronizations, and observe the behavior of these errors as a function of the number of LXCs and the size of the *timeslice*. Our first round of experiments used the same TDF for all containers; each container was engaged in the compute-intensive task of computing the factorial of a large number.

For the first experiment, we used a TDF of 10 for each container, and recorded measurements for 150 *timeslice* intervals. The results are summarized in Table 2, and reveal some interesting information. First, it demonstrates that TimeKeeper is effective at keeping virtual times synchronized on the *timeslice* sizes used. TimeKeeper is seemingly more effective at keeping the experiment synchronized when the *timeslice* length is $3ms$ rather than $300ms$. At the time of this writing we are unsure of the underlying cause for this difference, and are working at additional instrumentation in an effort to uncover an understandable explanation.

To give better insight into the distribution of error, we also plotted two cumulative distribution functions (CDFs). Figure 3 shows us a CDF when the number of LXCs in the experiment range from 10-80, and the *timeslice* interval is constant at $3ms$. Regardless of whether the experiment had 10 LXCs or 80 LXCs, TimeKeeper was able to keep every LXCs virtual time within $4\mu s$ of the expected virtual time for more than 90% of each *timeslice* interval. However, this comes at a cost. The more LXCs you add to the experi-

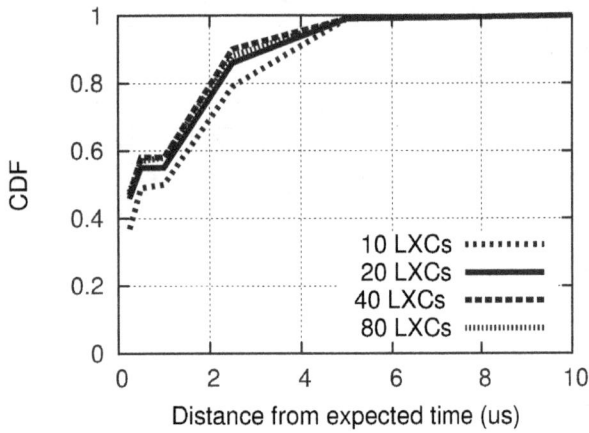

Figure 3: CDF with timeslice=3ms as a function of #LXCs

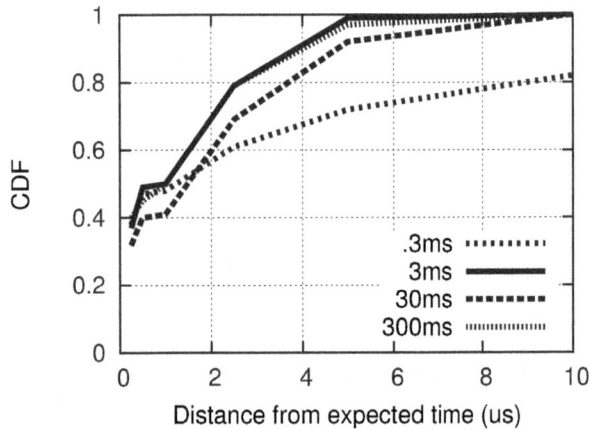

Figure 4: CDF with 10 LXCs as a function of timeslice length

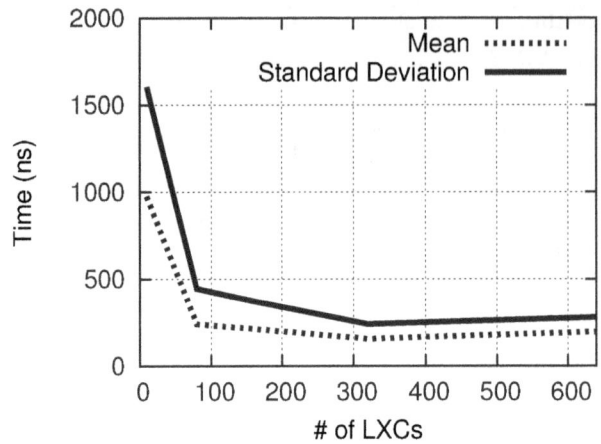

Figure 5: Testing Scalability with a Timeslice of 3ms and a TDF of 1/10

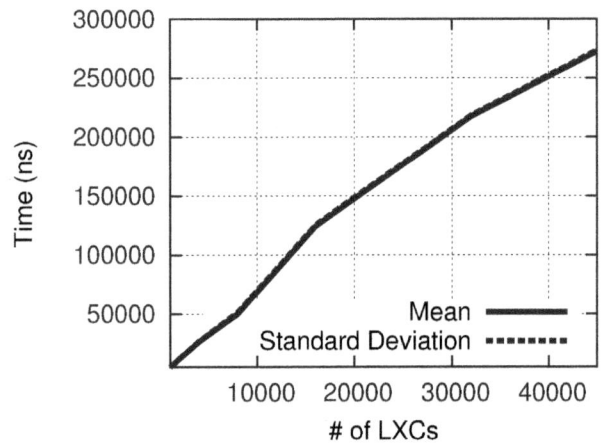

Figure 6: Testing Scalability with the Product of #LXCs and TDF Constant

ment, the longer it takes for the experiment virtual time to progress. This will be explored more fully in Section 5.3. Figure 4 shows us a CDF when we have an experiment size of 10 LXCs (where 5 LXCs have a TDF of 10, and 5 LXCs have a TDF of 1), and we vary the *timeslice* interval lengths. In general, TimeKeeper is able to keep the experiment virtual time in sync, but we noticed when the *timeslice* interval is .3ms that it did not perform as well. These results correspond with what we found in Table 1 (where the *hrtimers* were not as accurate at a granularity of .3ms as opposed to higher granularities).

5.2.1 Scalability

Figure 5 demonstrates scalability, plotting how the mean and standard deviation of the error behaves as the number of containers grows. Again we see the interesting phenomena that the error decreases with increasing numbers of containers; the error is also contained almost always to be less than half a micro-second.

We obtained access to a larger machine, with 32 cores and 64Gb of memory. This allowed us to bring TimeKeeper up and observe how many containers we can sustain. We successfully did one experiment using 45,000 containers, which

represents two orders magnitude increase of what could be done on that same machine with openVZ containers.

We performed an experiment aimed at measuring the mean and standard deviation of the time error found when TimeKeeper tries to keep all LXC containers in an experiment synchronized. For this we keep the product of number of containers with the TDF constant, at approximately 20. The intuition is we are trying to keep the rate (in wall-clock time) at which virtual time advances in the system as a whole constant—increasing the number of containers means the number of times a container is given service per unit wallclock time decreases, so each time it gets service it has to advance simulation time farther. Now in these experiments the *timeslice* length is kept constant.

Figure 6 displays the results, and reveals an interesting consequence of the scaling we employ. As the number of LXCs increases, the TDF decreases, which means that the advance in virtual time per unit wall-clock tick increases. The error of timers *in wall-clock time* is unaffected by the number of containers, however this fixed error is *amplified* by the amplification of virtual time advancement. This explains the linear increase in error. We'd get essentially the same curve—but with different y-axis values—by using a different

184

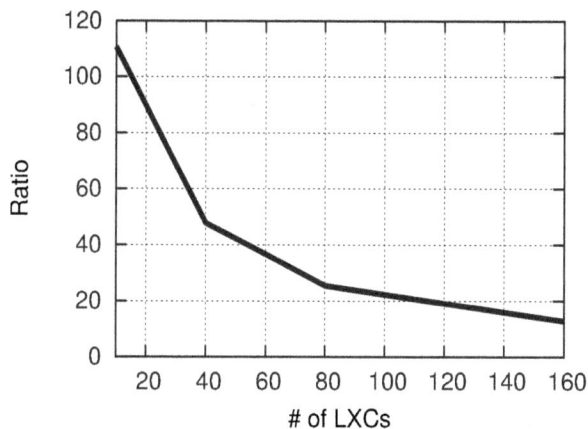

(a) 6 Dedicated CPUs and 24 GB RAM

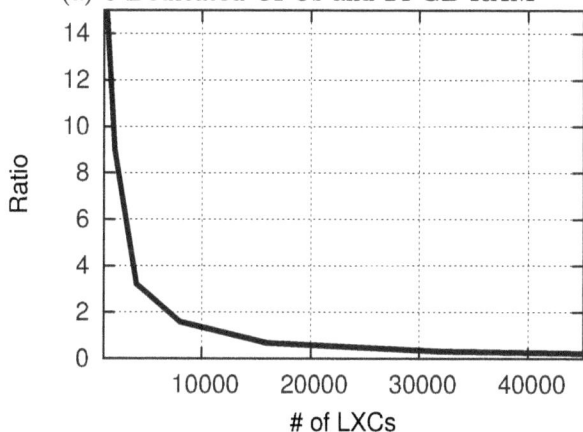

(b) 28 Dedicated CPUs and 64 GB RAM

Figure 7: Overhead Ratio with Timeslice=3ms as a Function of #LXCs

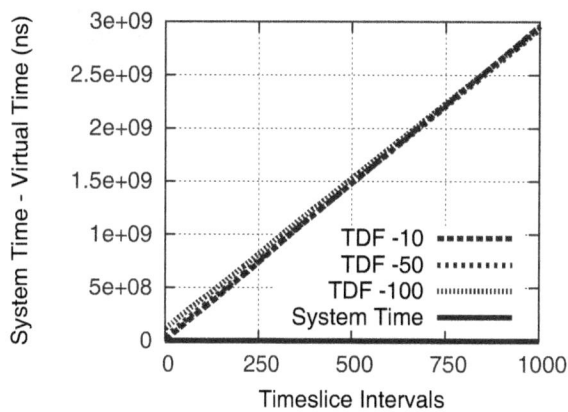

(a) 6/(TDF+1) #LXCs

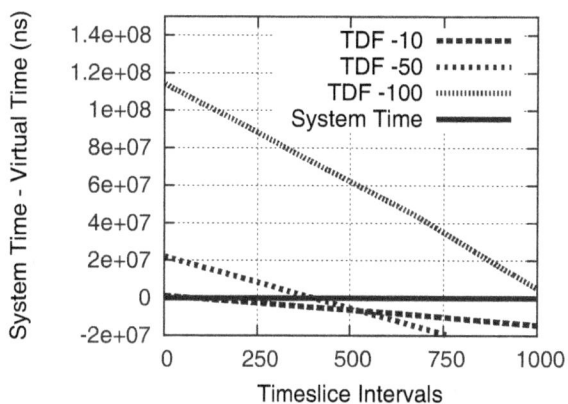

(b) 6/(TDF+1) +1 #LXCs

Figure 8: Determining Maximum #LXCs Where Real-Time is Maintained

constant product of TDF and #LXCs. A product that is larger by a factor of 10 will yield errors that are a factor of 10 smaller. Two main points should be appreciated from this data. One, that TimeKeeper has managed as many as 45,000 synchronized containers on a commodity server, and second, that the error of timers in real-time has more impact on the errors in virtual time the faster the containers are accelerated through virtual time.

5.3 Overhead

We measured the scheduling overhead of TimeKeeper, by dividing the amount of physical time progression of the leader LXC by the amount of time spent in the synchronization method of TimeKeeper. We call this the *overhead ratio* (OR). The larger the OR value, the more efficient the emulation. We ran multiple experiments with different TDFs and *timeslice* lengths. We learned that as *timeslice* length increases, so does the OR. This is intuitive, as a larger *timeslice* will call TimeKeeper's synchronization function less frequently.

Figure 7(a) shows how the OR changes as the number of LXCs in an *experiment* increases. For this particular experiment, the *timeslice* was set to 3ms, and we scaled the number of LXCs from 10-160. As the number of LXCs grew, the OR decreased. This is because TimeKeeper must manage more LXCs, and managing these additional LXCs results in more

overhead. This overhead can be reduced by dedicating more CPUs to the LXCs in the experiment.

The overhead ratio calculated on a machine with 32 cores (28 dedicated cores) and 45,000 LXCs was **.23** and is shown in Figure 7(b). This is to be expected, and reducing that overhead is a topic of future study. For example, the task of setting the timers for all LXCs to initiate the *timeslice* can be accomplished with a tree structure, rather than the serial structure our current implementation employs.

5.4 Maintaining Real-Time

We also wanted to determine how efficient TimeKeeper is at keeping LXCs running in real-time. When we say real-time, we mean that for every instant in time, all LXCs in the experiment will have a virtual time that is greater than or equal to the system time. Obviously, we will only be able to keep an experiment in real-time if all of its TDFs are all less than or equal to 1. For the experiment, we assumed all LXCs have the same TDF. Therefore, the maximum number of LXCs in an experiment we can keep in real-time is: N/TDF, where N is the number of dedicated CPUs on the machine, and we are assuming no overhead. However, our system does have overhead, so our experiment will determine just how close we can get to this upper bound. We ran experiments with 6 dedicated CPUs, a *timeslice* of 3ms, and TDFs of 1/10, 1/50, and 1/100 with increasing numbers

185

of LXCs per experiment, until we found the tipping point (the point where we could no longer keep the experiment as a whole in real-time). We calculated the virtual time of each LXC and compared it to the system time at the end of each *timeslice* interval. Our results are in Figure 8. We found the maximum number of LXCs to be: $6/(TDF+1)$, any more LXCs cause a tipping point and the experiment can no longer be kept in real-time. Figure 8(a) displays the virtual time of the experiment with respect to the system time using this tipping point. As you can see, all experiments virtual time is *increasing* linearly in respect with the system time. Figure 8(b) displays the same thing, but this time, adding just 1 more LXC to each experiment, ie: $6/(TDF+1)+1$. This is obviously the tipping point, as all three experiments virtual time is now *decreasing* with respect to the system time.

6. CONCLUSION

We introduced TimeKeeper: a lightweight, simplistic, and easily integrated solution to provide LXCs with their own view of virtual time. TimeKeeper was integrated into the CORE framework, and collected promising results. We demonstrated TimeKeeper's ability to keep the LXCs virtual time synchronized to within half a micro-second of error. In addition, scalability was also tested, with experiments pushing upwards of 45,000 LXCs, each with their own virtual time, all on a single commodity server.

7. ACKNOWLEDGMENTS

This work was supported in part by the Boeing Corporation, and in part by by the Department of Energy under Award Number DE-OE0000097. [1]

8. REFERENCES

[1] J. Ahrenholz, C. Danilov, R. Henderson, and H. Kim. Core: a real-time network emulator. In *Proceedings of the 2008 International conference for military communications (MILCOM'08)*, 2002.

[2] P. Barham, B. Dragovic, K. Fraser, S. Hand, T. Harris, A. Ho, R. Neugebauer, I. Pratt, and A. Warfield. Xen and the art of virtualization. In *Proceedings of the 19th ACM Symposium on Operating System Principles*, 2003.

[3] M. Erazo, Y. Li, and J. Liu. Sveet! a scalable virtualized evaluation environment for tcp. In *Testbeds and Research Infrastructures for the Development of Networks & Communities and Workshops*, 2009.

[4] T. Gleixner and D. NieHaus. Hrtimers and beyond: Transforming the linux time subsystems. In *Proceedings of the Linux Symposium (Ottawa, Ontario, June 2006)*, 2002.

[5] A. Grau, S. Maier, K. Herrmann, and K. Rothermel. Time jails: A hybrid approach to scalable network emulation. In *Proceedings of PADS'08*, 2008.

[6] D. Gupta, K. Vishwanath, and A. Vahdat. Diecast: Testing distributed systems with an accurate scale model. *NSDI'08*, 2008.

[7] D. Gupta, K. Yocum, M. McNett, A. Snoeren, A. Vahdat, and G. Voelker. To infinity and beyond: Time-warped network emulation. In *Proceedings of the twentieth ACM symposium on Operating systems principles*, 2005.

[8] M. Helsley. Lxc: Linux container tools. *IBM developerWorks Technical Library*, 2009.

[9] J-sim official. https://sites.google.com/site/jsimofficial/, 2014.

[10] M. Koksal. A survey of network simulators supporting wireless networks, 2008.

[11] D. Nicol, D. Jin, and Y. Zheng. S3f: The scalable simulation framework revisited. In *Proceedings of the 2011 Winter Simulation Conference*, 2011.

[12] The network simulator - ns-2. http://www.isi.edu/nsnam/ns/, 2014.

[13] The ns-3 project. https://www.nsnam.org/, 2014.

[14] Omnet++ community site. http://www.omnetpp.org/, 2014.

[15] Omnet++ vs ns-2: A comparison. http://ctieware.eng.monash.edu.au/OMNeTppComparison, 2014.

[16] Openvz: a container-based virtualization for linux. http://openvz.org/MainPage, 2014.

[17] A. Vahdat, K. Yocum, K. Walsh, P. Mahadevan, D. Kostic, J. Chase, and D. Becker. Scalability and accuracy in a large-scale network emulator. In *Proceedings of the 5th Symposium on Operating Systems Design and Implementation*, 2002.

[18] Vmware virtualization software. http://www.vmware.com/, 2014.

[19] E. Weingartner, F. Schmidt, H. Vom Lehn, T. Heer, and K. Wehrle. Slicetime: a platform for scalable and accurate network emulation. In *Proceedings of the 8th USENIX conference on Networked systems design and implementation*, 2011.

[20] E. Weingartner, H. vom Lehn, and K. Wehrle. A performance comparison of recent network simulators. In *Proceedings of the IEEE International Conference on Communications*, 2009.

[21] B. White, J. Lepreau, L. Stoller, R. Ricci, S. Guruprasad, M. Newbold, M. Hibler, C. Barb, and A. Joglekar. An integrated experimental environment for distributed systems and networks. In *Proceedings of the 5th Symposium on Operating Systems Design and Implementation*, 2002.

[22] Y. Zheng, D. Nicol, D. Jin, and N. Tanaka. A virtual time system for virtualization-based network emulation and simulation. In *Journal of Simulation*, 2011.

[1] Disclaimer: This report was prepared as an account of work sponsored by an agency of the United States Government. Neither the United States Government nor any agency thereof, nor any of their employees, makes any warranty, express or implied, or assumes any legal liability or responsibility for the accuracy, completeness, or usefulness of any information, apparatus, product, or process disclosed, or represents that its use would not infringe privately owned rights. Reference herein to any specific commercial product, process, or service by trade name, trademark, manufacturer, or otherwise does not necessarily constitute or imply its endorsement, recommendation, or favoring by the United States Government or any agency thereof. The views and opinions of authors expressed herein do not necessarily state or reflect those of the United States Government or any agency thereof.

Hierarchical Resource Management for Enhancing Performance of Large-scale Simulations on Data Centers

ZengXiang Li, Xiaorong Li, Long Wang
Institute of High Performance Computing
Agency for Science, Technology and Research
(A*STAR) Singapore
{liz,lixr,wangl}@ihpc.a-star.edu.sg

Wentong Cai
School of Computer Engineering
Nanyang Technological University Singapore
{aswtcai}@ntu.edu.sg

ABSTRACT

More and more interests have been shown to move large-scale simulations on modern data centers composed of a large number of virtualized multi-core computers. However, the simulation components (Federates) consolidated in the same computer may have imbalanced simulation workloads. Similarly, the computers involved in the same simulation execution (Federation) may also have imbalanced simulation workloads. Hence, federates may waste a lot of computer resources on time synchronization with each other. In this paper, a hierarchical resource management system is proposed to enhance simulation execution performance. Federates in the federation are enraptured in their individual Virtual Machines (VMs), which are consolidated on a group of virtualized multi-core computers. On the computer level, multiple VMs share the resource of the computer according to the simulation workloads of their corresponding federates. On the federation level, some VMs are migrated for workload balance purpose. Therefore, computer resources are fully utilized to conduct useful simulation workloads, avoiding the synchronization overheads. Experiments using synthetic and real simulation workloads have verified that the hierarchical resource management system enhances simulation performance significantly.

Keywords

Large-scale simulation, Data Center, Virtualization, Time Synchronization, Resource Provisioning, Migration, Workload Balance

1. INTRODUCTION

A large-scale simulation is usually built to study a complex real or artificial system. It divides the target system into a collection of subsystems, each simulated by a simulation component, and executes the simulation components on parallel and/or distributed computers. In *High Level Architecture* (HLA) (IEEE 1516 standard) terminology [14], the

simulation components are referred to as federates, while the entire simulation is referred to as a federation. In order to simulate a complex system in desired fidelity, the simulation execution is usually time and resource consuming. For this reason, we have witnessed recently increasing interests in moving large-scale simulations to data centers for the purpose of obtaining large amount of resources at low prices.

The system model of a large-scale simulation executed on a modern data center is shown in Figure 1. The typical building blocks of the data center are multi-core computers. For instance, a computer may be installed with 4 Intel Xeon processors each of which may have 10 CPU cores. Thanks to the increasing resources, a number of federates are able to run on the same computer. In addition, virtualization technology [1] has been deployed widely in data centers. Federates are encapsulated and executed on the resident virtual machines (VMs) with their own guest operating systems. Therefore, federates developed by different participants can be consolidated in the same computer without leaking confidential information. In addition, most modern data centers provide a shared storage, which is uniformly and fast accessible from individual computers. Hence, the VM disk file can be saved in the shared storage.

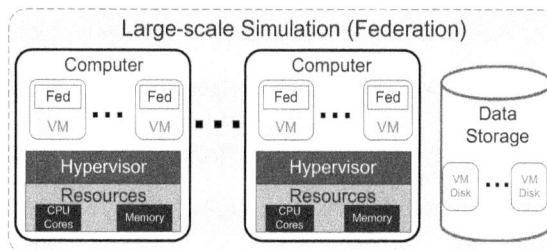

Figure 1: Overview of a large-scale simulation on a modern data center

Generally, federates modeling different sub-system may have different simulation workloads. For instance, federates might have different number of simulated objects (e.g., vehicles in a traffic simulation). Moreover, the workload of each federate might change dynamically during the simulation execution. Hence, the federates consolidated in the same computer may have imbalanced simulation workloads. Similarly, the computers involved in the same simulation execution (Federation) may also have imbalanced simulation workloads. As a result, federates in the same federation might advance their simulation time with different speeds.

However, to guarantee the correct simulation results, federates should process events, either generated by the federate itself (internal events) or received from other federates (external events), in time stamp (TS) order. To achieve this, federates must synchronize with each other in their simulation time advancement. For this reason, the simulation execution speed is determined by the slowest federate (i.e., the federate with highest workload). The time synchronization can be conducted in either conservative [4, 6] or optimistic [16] manners. In this paper, we focus on optimistic synchronization which allows a federate to process events and to advance simulation time freely. However, the faster federate (in terms of simulation time) may conduct over-optimistic executions and rollback its execution on receiving straggler messages (i.e., messages with TS smaller than federate's simulation time) from the slower federate. In other words, besides the useful simulation workload, the federate may spend considerable computer resources on synchronization overheads (i.e., over-optimistic executions and execution rollbacks).

To enhance the simulation performance, we have previously proposed an adaptive resource provisioning mechanism on VM platforms [19], However, it only supports small-scale simulation executions on a single computer. In this paper, we extend our work for large-scale simulations executed on multiple computers, by proposing a hierarchical resource management system. On the computer level, the computer resources are shared by the VMs according to the simulation workload of their corresponding federates. Hence, federates consolidated in the same computers are able to advance their simulation time with comparable speeds, avoiding synchronization overheads. On the federation level, a centralized coordinator composed of speed alignment and workload balance modules is deployed. The speed alignment module align simulation execution speeds of all computers to the slowest one. Consequently, the computers with light simulation workloads will not occupy all available resources. In order to use more computer resources for the simulation execution, the workload balance module migrate VMs from heavily-loaded computers to lightly-loaded computers. In theory, the centralized coordinator with these modules is able to make computers balanced and thus fully utilized, while keeping comparable execution speeds. Therefore, all available computer resources are used for conducting useful simulation workloads rather than the synchronization overheads. From this point of view, our proposed hierarchical resource management system is able to obtain the maximum simulation execution speed.

The rest of the paper is organized as follows: Section 2 discusses the related work. Section 3 illustrates the details of our proposed hierarchical resource management. Section 4 describes the experiment design and discusses the experimental results. Finally, Section 5 concludes the paper and outlines the future work.

2. RELATED WORK

A number of workload balance mechanisms have been proposed for accelerating large-scale simulations. Workload balance among federates can be achieved by migrating simulated objects [3]. However, it was assumed that the simulated objects must be movable and that they can be processed by all federates in the federation. Workload balance among computers can be achieved by migrating federates (i.e., OS processes) from heavily-loaded computers to lightly-loaded computers. However, the existing federate migration protocols are too complex [5, 18, 28], as they must guarantee the state consistent in the entire federation and rebuild the connections among federates. Both of the above object and federate migration mechanisms require cooperation of simulation model developers and introduce considerable overhead on data transfer. What is worse, other federates in the federation might be interrupted, e.g., they are informed to redirect communications to the migrated federates, and required to resend messages for the purpose of avoiding message loss. To solve above problems, Peluso et al. [24] have proposed a global memory management architecture supporting application-transparent migration of simulated objects among federates. However, its implementation is nontrivial and requires OS support.

In our hierarchical resource management system, federates in the same computer are allowed to have different simulation workloads. They are able to advance simulation time in comparable speeds, by adjusting VM capabilities according to their simulation workloads. Furthermore, our method does not introduce much additional overhead and takes effect (i.e., speedup or slowdown the corresponding federates) immediately. To achieve workload balance among computers, the entire VM (i.e., the federate and guest OS) is migrated in a transparent manner. VM migration has been widely used to accommodate the increasing application workloads [27] and to achieve workload balance on computers [30]. However, the existing load balance mechanisms usually assume that the VMs are executed independently. In contrast, the VMs used for a large-scale simulation are highly coupled. Migrating one VM might affect the execution speeds of the VMs on both source and destination computers, and finally, affect the execution speed of the entire federation. Therefore, a new load balancing mechanism is proposed in this paper, for the purpose of obtaining maximum simulation speed.

Recently, more and more interests are shown to execute large-scale simulations on Cloud and data centers [9, 13]. In order to explore the increasing capacities of multi-core computers, researchers have proposed to design simulations in multi-threaded manner [10, 15]. In addition, approaches were proposed to solve the problem of workload imbalance by globally scheduling events with least simulation time [7] or by re-allocating different numbers of CPU cores to federates according to their simulation workloads [31]. In this paper, federates, as sequential simulation components [12] are developed and executed as single-threaded processes [21]. We will investigate how to extend our work to multi-threaded simulations in the future.

To the best of our knowledge, limited work has been conducted on accelerating simulations by harnessing virtualization technologies. Yoginath and Perumalla [33] have evaluated the performance of large-scale simulations using either conservative or optimistic synchronization approaches on Cloud and VM platforms. To solve workload imbalance problem, they have also proposed a global VM scheduler [32] which collects the simulation time of all federates and schedules their resident VMs in least-simulation-time-first order. However, its implementation is non-trivial, as the simulation application, the guest operating system and the VM scheduler in hypervisor must be modified. Moreover, it is difficult to extend the global VM scheduler in the environment with multiple computers. In contrast, our proposed hierarchical resource management system is implemented in a transparent manner for large-scale simulations on multiple computers.

3. HIERARCHICAL RESOURCE MANAGEMENT SYSTEM

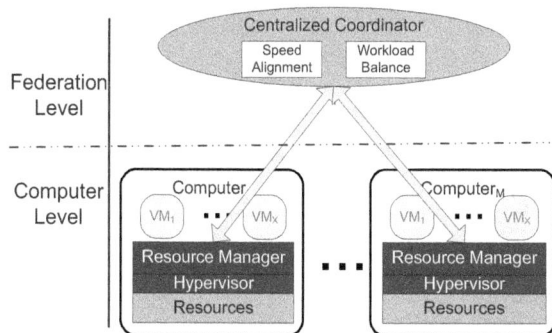

Figure 2: Architecture of hierarchical resource management system

The architecture of the proposed hierarchical resource management system is illustrated in Figure 2. On the computer level, a resource manager is deployed in each computer based on the VM Hypervisor. It dynamically reallocates resources to VMs according to the simulation workload of their corresponding federates. Hence, federates in the same computer will advance their simulation time with comparable speed. On the federation level, a centralized coordinator composed of *speed alignment* and *workload balance* modules is deployed. Due to the workload imbalance among computers, federates in different computers may have different execution speeds. To solve the problem, the speed alignment module reduces the resource provisioning of all federate on lightly-loaded computers. Consequently, federates in different computers can also advance their simulation time with comparable speeds. In the meantime, the workload balance module migrates VMs (or federates) from heavily-loaded computers to lightly-loaded computers. This will increase the execution speed of the heavily-loaded computers, and thus, increase the execution speed of the entire federation. In the meantime, more computer resources are used for the simulation execution. During the simulation execution, a number of federates are migrated iteratively for the purpose of achieving workload balance among all computers. Consequently, the computers can be fully utilized, while keeping comparable execution speeds. Therefore, all available computer resources are used for conducting useful simulation workloads without being wasted on the synchronization overheads. From this point of view, our proposed hierarchical resource management system is able to obtain the maximum simulation execution speed, using the same number of computers.

In the hierarchical resource management system, we assume that there are N federates in the federation, and that M computers are involved in the federation execution. The involved computers may have different number of VMs (or, Federates) and different number of CPU cores. For simpli-

fication, we use X and Y to denote the number of VMs and CPU cores of a computer respectively.

3.1 Computer Level

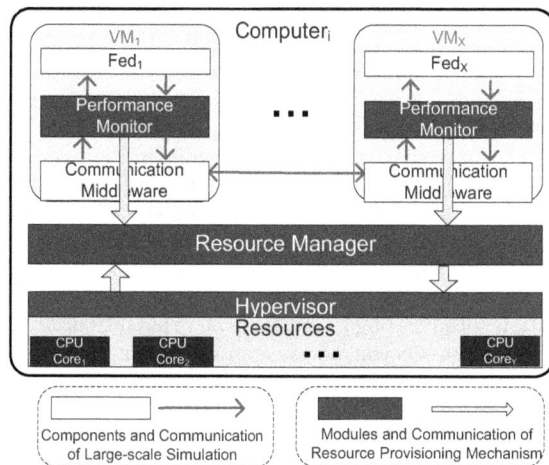

Figure 3: Resource provisioning mechanism for VMs consolidated in the same computer

In each computer, a resource provisioning mechanism, which was previously proposed by us in [19], is reused to ensure that federates on the computer have comparable execution speed. It is composed of performance monitor and resource manager modules as illustrated in Figure 3. It periodically reallocates computer resource to VMs according to the dynamic simulation workloads of their corresponding federates. In other words, the simulation execution is divided into a number of successive control intervals. At the end of each interval, the performance monitor is responsible for measuring the execution speed of its corresponding federate; while the resource manager is responsible for adjusting resource shares of the VMs, making the federates have the same predicted execution speeds in the next control interval.

The performance monitor is inserted between the federate and the simulation middleware [1]. Similar to the approaches in [25], the performance monitor is transparent to both the federates and the simulation middleware. It intercepts the simulation service requests invoked by the federate, and then, stands for the federate to invoke corresponding service requests to the simulation middlware. Intuitively, the execution speed of a federate can be measured as the advanced simulation time in a control interval divided by the control interval length. However, execution rollbacks might happen during a control interval. If so, the federate decreases its simulation time and wastes processing time on over-optimistic executions and execution rollbacks. Hence, the execution speed measured in this manner may not accurately characterize the useful simulation workload of the federate. In some extreme cases, the measured execution speed might even be a negative value. To solve this problem, the control interval are further partitioned into a number of small epochs. For instance, an epoch can be bounded by two subsequent time advancement requests initiated by the

---

[1] The simulation middleware, e.g., HLA RunTime Infrastructure [23], is responsible for connecting federates to build a federation.

federate. By intercepting the time advancement requests, the performance monitor can calculate the advanced simulation time and the elapsed execution time in each epoch. It can also detect the straggler messages, by intercepting the callbacks delivered to the federate. Finally, the execution speed can be measured correctly by excluding those epochs with over-optimistic executions and execution rollbacks.

The resource manager is developed as a bridge between performance monitors and Hypervisor. According to the studies [2, 26], the cap value of VMs precisely specifies their allocated computing capabilities. It can be any integer value (denoted as c) between 1 and 100, indicating that $c\%$ time slots of one CPU core are scheduled for the VM. In addition, changing cap value does not introduce additional overhead, and the new cap value can take effect immediately [26]. Therefore, the resource manager is able to control federate execution speed through adjusting the capability of its resident VM in an efficient and fine-grained manner. Take the ith federate as an example, at the end of kth control interval, the resource manager retrieves the *measured execution speed* denoted as $MES_i(k)$ from the performance monitor. Suppose that the caps of its resident VM at k^{th} and $(k+1)^{th}$ control intervals are set to $Cap_i(k)$ and $Cap_i(k+1)$ respectively, we can get the *predicted execution speed* (*PES*) at the $(k+1)^{th}$ control interval as:

$$PES_i(k+1) = \frac{MES_i(k)}{Cap_i(k)} \times Cap_i(k+1) \qquad (1)$$

An algorithm is developed in the resource manager to maximize $PES(k+1)$ of all federates while satisfying the following conditions.

- Federates can only consume the available resource on the computer i.e., $\sum_{i=1}^{X} Cap_i(k+1) \leq Y \times 100$

- Each federate, which is usually single-threaded [21], consumes at most one CPU core, i.e., $Cap_i(k+1) \leq 100$

- Federates should have the same *PES*, i.e., $PES_i(k+1) = PES_j(k+1)$ where i and $j \in \{1, 2, ..., X\}$

In summary, the resource provisioning mechanism periodically reallocates computer resource to VMs, making federates have comparable execution speeds and thus avoiding time synchronization overhead.

3.2 Federation Level

As mentioned above, the resource provisioning mechanism ensures federates consolidated in the same computer have the same *PES*. Therefore, we can set the *Computer Predicted Execution Speed* (denoted as *CPES*) as the *PES* of the federates. By default, all computer resources are distributed to VMs. That is, the sum of cap values of the VMs on the computer (denoted as *CCap*) is equal to $100 \times Y$, i.e., $CCap = \sum_{1}^{X} Cap_i = 100 \times Y$. If so, each computer achieves the maximum *CPES*, which is denoted as *MaxCPES*. However, a group of computers are usually involved to execute a large-scale simulation. These computers might have different numbers of federates and the federates might have different simulation workloads. Consequently, different computers might have different *MaxCPES*. However, due to the time synchronization, the execution speed of the entire federation is determined by the slowest computer. Federates located on lightly-loaded computers waste

resources on time synchronization overheads. To solve the problem, a centralized coordinator composed of speed alignment and workload balance modules is deployed as shown in Figure 2.

Algorithm 1 Speed alignment and workload balance modules in centralized coordinator

1: $\mathbf{P} = \{P_1, P_2, \cdots, P_M\}$;
2: **for** Each $P_j \in \mathbf{P}$ **do**
3:     Fetch $MaxCPES_j$ and $\overrightarrow{Cap_j}$
4: **end for**
   //Speed Alignment Module
5: $FPES = \min_{j=1}^{M} MaxCPES_j$;
6: **for** Each $P_j \in \mathbf{P}$ **do**
7:     $\omega_j = \frac{FPES}{MaxCPES_j}$;
8:     $CPES_j = \omega_j \times MaxCPES_j$
9:     $CCap_j = \omega_j \times 100 \times Y$
10:     $\overrightarrow{Cap_j} = \omega_j \times \overrightarrow{Cap_j}$
11:     $\overrightarrow{PES_j} = \omega_j \times \overrightarrow{PES_j}$
12: **end for**
   //Workload Balance Module
13: Choose $P_u \in \mathbf{P}$ where $CCap_u = \max_{P_j \in \mathbf{P}} CCap_j$;
14: Choose $P_v \in \mathbf{P}$ where $CCap_v = \min_{P_j \in \mathbf{P}} CCap_j$;
15: $\Psi = CCap_u$
16: $\kappa = -1$
17: **for** each Cap_i in $\overrightarrow{Cap_u}$ **do**
18:     **if** $Cap_i < CCap_u - CCap_v$ **then**
19:         **if** $\Psi > \max(CCap_u - Cap_i, CCap_v + Cap_i)$ **then**
20:             $\kappa = i$
21:             $\Psi = \max(CCap_u - Cap_i, CCap_v + Cap_i)$
22:         **end if**
23:     **end if**
24: **end for**
25: **if** $\kappa \neq -1$ **then**
26:     Migrate the κth federate from P_u to P_v
27:     $CCap_u = CCap_u - Cap_\kappa$
28:     $CCap_v = CCap_v + Cap_\kappa$
29:     $\lambda = \frac{100 \times Y}{\Psi}$
30:     $FPES = \lambda \times FPES$
31:     **for** Each $P_j \in \mathbf{P}$ **do**
32:         $CPES_j = \lambda \times CPES_j$
33:         $CCap_j = \lambda \times CCap_j$
34:         $\overrightarrow{Cap_j} = \lambda \times \overrightarrow{Cap_j}$
35:         $\overrightarrow{PES_j} = \lambda \times \overrightarrow{PES_j}$
36:     **end for**
37: **end if**
38: **for** Each $P_j \in \mathbf{P}$ **do**
39:     Send $CPES_j$, $CCap_j$ and $\overrightarrow{Cap_j}$
40: **end for**

The implementation details of the centralized coordinator is shown in Algorithm 1. $\mathbf{P}$ denotes the set of all computers involved in the simulation execution. Firstly, the centralized coordinator fetches $MaxCPES$ and the vector of VM cap values from all computers (Lines 2 to 4). Because of time synchronization, the *Federation Predicted Execution Speed* (denoted as $FPES$) is equal to $\min_{j=0}^{M} MaxCPES_j$ (Line 5). Then, the speed alignment module calculates a factor ω, i.e., the ratio of $FPES$ to $MaxCPES$ which is always smaller than one, for each computer. Based on the factor, each computer is decelerated from $MaxCPES$ to $FPES$, by decreasing the VM cap values. Consequently, federates, either on the same computer or on the different computers, have the same PES. Due to the prediction error and VM scheduling, the real federate execution speed might be slightly different from the predicted execution speed, i.e., $MES_i(k+1) \approx PES_i(k+1)$. Therefore, federates in the federation have comparable execution speeds, avoiding most of time synchronization overheads. (Refer to our experiments in Section 4.3)

Generally, the lower the simulation workload on the computer, the greater $MaxCPES$, and thus, the smaller ω, which indicates that the less resources are utilized on the computer. In order to use more computer resources for the simulation execution, a workload balance module is developed in the centralized coordinator. It migrates VMs from heavily-loaded computers to lightly-loaded computers for the purpose of achieving workload balance among all computers. If so, all computer have the same $MaxCPES$, which is equal to $FPES$. Consequently, all computers have $\omega = 1$, i.e., all computer resources are used for the simulation execution. In the meantime, computer resources are not wasted on the synchronization overheads, as all federates have the same PES. Therefore, our proposed hierarchical resource management system is able to obtain the maximum simulation execution speed, using the same number of computers.

In current stage, we assume that only one federate is migrated in each control interval [2]. Hence, the workload balance module should make the migration decision (i.e., which federate should be migrated to which computer) for the purpose of achieving maximum $FPES$. For simplification, we assume that computers are homogeneous with the same number (Y) of CPU cores available. After the speed alignment, only the slowest computer (P_u) with greatest $\omega = 1$, uses all resources (i.e., $CCap_u = \max_{P_j \in \mathbf{P}} CCap_j = 100 \times Y$). The fastest computer (P_v) with smallest ω has most idle resource (i.e., $CCap_v = \min_{P_j \in \mathbf{P}} CCap_j$). In order to increase $FPES$, one of the federates located in P_u should be migrated to P_v (Line 17). The VM is selected if migrating it to P_v can minimize Ψ (i.e., the maximum $CCap$ value of all computers). It is worthwhile to point out that, the VMs with cap values greater than $CCap_u - CCap_v$ are never migrated (Line 18), as migrating it will make $CCap_v$ greater than $100 \times Y$.

After the selected VM is migrated from P_u to P_v, the $CCap_u$ and $CCap_v$ should be updated accordingly (Line 27 and 28). In the meantime, we can get $\Psi < 100 \times Y$, i.e., no computer has fully utilized its resources. In order to use more computer resources for the simulation execution, the cap values of all VMs are increased by a factor of $\lambda = \frac{100 \times Y}{\Psi} > 1$. After that, the new $CPES$ and the vector of VM cap values are sent to corresponding computers. Finally, the resource manager in each computer set the VM cap values accordingly by calling a hypercall of the Hypervisor. According Equation 1, PES of the federate increases linearly with the Cap value of its resident VM. Therefore, the PES of federates increase by a factor of λ, according to the increased Cap values of their resident VMs. Since federates in the federation have the same PES, the federation execution speed $FPES$ also increases by a factor of λ.

In virtualized data centers, VMs are migrated using the live VM migration method [8], which can migrate VMs, while running their overlying applications with liveness constraints [3]. Since the entire VM state has been transferred, the federate state is consistent in the source and destination computers. Similarly, the OS state (e.g., TCP control block for active connections) are transferred consistently. In addition, the IP address of the migrated VM is moved to a new physical location and the routers are configured to send packets to the new physical address. In this way, the migrated VM is able to maintain all open network connections. Therefore, the live VM migration procedure is transparent to the simulation developer. They do not have to recode simulation program for state saving and restoration; and do not have to rebuild connections with other federates or conduct network redirection. Moreover, the federation execution is not interrupted during the migration procedure.

However, it is still a challenge to transfer entire VM states in an efficient fashion. The VM states may be kept in both disk storage and memory. Since most modern data centers have a shared data storage (as shown in Figure 1) to save VM disk files, the disk storage transfer can be avoided. As for the VM states kept in memory, a pre-copy protocol [29] is adopted by the live VM migration method [8] to copy memory pages iteratively from the source computer to the destination computer, without stopping the execution of the VM being migrated. It can significantly reduce the downtime, i.e., the period during which the federate is inactive due to there being no executing VM. However, the total migration time, i.e., the duration between when migration is initiated and when the original VM may be finally discarded, is still considerable due the large amount of data transfer on the network [17]. To reduce the data transfer overhead, we propose to reduce the memory size before starting VM migration. For instance, the memory cache can be simply dropped as there is another copy in the shared data storage. In addition, the memory size can be further reduced by writing dirty pages to the shared data storage manually.

4. EXPERIMENTS

4.1 Experimental Design

Nae et al. [22] have introduced the concepts of *Massively Multiplayer Online Games* (MMOGs) ecosystem and proposed a dynamic resource provisioning method. In the MMOGs ecosystem, game operators rent resources (CPU, Network and Memory) from data centers for running the MMOG servers. They are able to dynamically adjust the amount of renting resources according to the workload of MMOGs (e.g., the number of players and their interactions). We develop an HLA-based simulation to simulate the MMOGs ecosystem. It can be used to study the effect of dynamic resource provisioning schemes using different workload prediction algorithms and different resource hosting policies. The HLA-based simulation is used to evaluate our proposed hierarchical resource management system.

In the HLA-based simulation, each federate simulates the game servers in a data center. It generates a local event to

---

[2] In order to achieve workload balance quickly, we will also investigate in the future migrating a group of VMs concurrently, while keeping the migration overhead marginal.

[3] This method has been supported in the latest hypervisors (e.g., Xen 4.2)

(a) Migration Overhead

(b) Total Migration Time

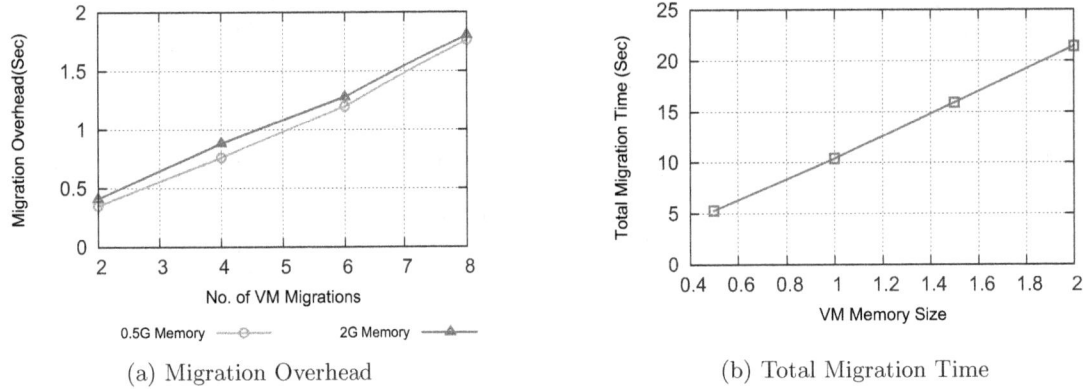

Figure 4: Performance evaluation for live VM migrations during simulation execution

simulate the performance of game servers in each time step (i.e., 10 seconds). Each local event calculates the response time of each interaction initialized by players connected to the data center and measures the quality of game experience from the perspective of those players, using the resources rented from the data center. Therefore, the computer resources required for processing a local event increases proportionally with the increasing number of players connected to the data center. In addition, federates might send external events to each other to simulate the communication between different data centers. The probability of generating external events is denoted as $P_{ExternEvent}$. The TS of an external event equals to TS of the processing internal event plus a *lookahead* (LA) [12], indicating that the external event will affect the receiving federate after LA simulation time. Different values of $P_{ExternEvent}$ and LA parameters has been investigated in [19]. In this paper, we simply set the $P_{ExternEvent}$ and LA as 1 and 105 respectively.

The simulation model employs optimistic synchronization using infrequent state saving [11]. The simulation length is 2 days, including the first day as the warm up period. It is executed on an *Service Oriented HLA RunTime Infrastructure* (SOHR) [23]. For efficiency consideration, the communication among federates use JAVA socket instead of the heavy Grid service invocation. Experiments are carried out on a small cluster with 4 computers, each of which is installed with 16 Intel Xeon 2.67 GHz CPU cores, 64 GB RAM, CentOS 6.4 and Xen 4.2. A group of VMs (one VCPU core, 0.5 2 GB RAM, 10 G disk and CentOS 6.4) are created for executing federates in the federation. One computer works as the NFS server to save VM disk files. Hence, VMs can be migrated without moving their disk files.

4.2 Performance of VM Migration

Experiments are designed to evaluate the performance of live VM migrations during simulation execution. For simplification, we use a federation execution with two federates only. Synthetic workload is introduced to the MMOGs simulation model. The number of players in each federate follows a normal distribution $N(\mu, \sigma^2)$. Federates are assumed to have balanced workload, more exactly, $\mu = 500$ and $\sigma = 15$. The first federate is executed on one computer, while the second federate might be migrated to and fro on another two computers. The VM migration overhead is defined as

the simulation execution time in the execution scenario with VM migrations minus that in the execution scenario without VM migrations. As shown in Figure 4(a), the VM migration overhead is marginal and increases with the number of migrations. In addition, the migration overhead increase slightly with the memory size of the migrated VMs. This is because, a pre-copy protocol is adopted by the live VM migration method (refer to section 3.2). The simulation execution is not interrupted during the most part of memory state transferring during the VM migration.

Besides VM migration overhead, the total migration time (i.e., the duration between when migration is initiated and when the original VM may be finally discarded) is also important to the simulation performance. Usually, a VM is migrated to another computer when the original computer is heavily-loaded. However, during the total migration time, the migrated VM still executes on the original computer. The longer is the total migration time, the slower the original computer is able to release corresponding computer resources. Thus, the benefit of VM migration on workload balance among computers is neutralized. As shown in Figure 4(b), the total migration time is considerable and increases linearly with the memory size. In order to reduce the total migration time, we have proposed methods to reduce the VM memory size before migration (refer to section 3.2).

4.3 Performance of Resource Management

Experiments using both synthetic and real workloads are conducted to evaluate the performance of the hierarchical resource management system. The federation is composed of 24 (or 16 for real workload) federates (with fedIndex=1, 2 ...) executed on 3 (or 2 for real workload) computers (with comIndex=1, 2 ...), each of which use four CPU cores. Initially, 8 federates are executed in each computer and the cap value of each VM is 50. Four execution scenarios are studied. In the *Fixed* scenario, the caps of all VMs are fixed at 50. In the *Adaptive* scenario, the resource provisioning mechanism is used to adjust cap values of those VMs consolidated on the computer. In the *Aligned* scenario, the speed alignment module in the centralized coordinator aligns the execution speeds of different computers. In the *Balanced* scenario, the workload balance module in the centralized coordinator migrates VMs among computers for workload balance purpose. In the *Adaptive*, *Aligned* and *Balanced* scenarios, the con-

Table 1: Simulation performance using synthetic simulation workload

	Imbalanced Computer				Imbalanced Federate			
	Fixed	Adaptive	Aligned	Balanced	Fixed	Adaptive	Aligned	Balanced
Speed	97.7	98.1	94.9	125.8	53.1	91.3	88.6	97.1
Rollbacks	70.2	67.8	31.2	30.4	206.4	73.7	30.9	30.8
Efficiency	0.662	0.669	0.927	0.926	0.399	0.645	0.901	0.905
Resource	1200	1200	896	1099	1200	1200	890	970

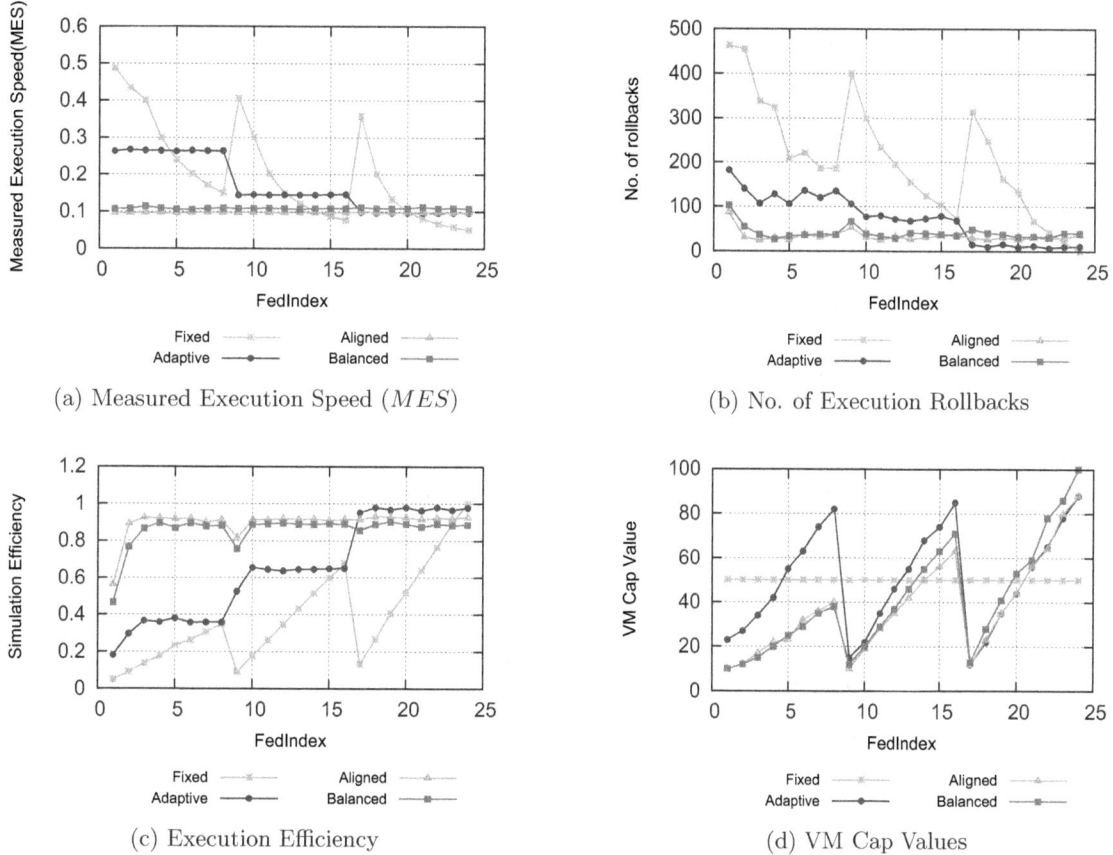

(a) Measured Execution Speed (*MES*)

(b) No. of Execution Rollbacks

(c) Execution Efficiency

(d) VM Cap Values

Figure 5: Performance of individual federates in *Imbalanced Federate* case for synthetic simulation workload

trol interval length is set to 30 seconds. In order to compare simulation performance in different scenarios, four measurements are considered. The simulation *speed* is defined as the ratio of advanced simulation time (i.e., one day or 86400 seconds) to the simulation execution time. The simulation *rollback* is the average number of rollbacks happened in all federates in the federation. Due to the simulation rollbacks, a federate may process extra events besides the useful events. The execution efficiency of the federate is defined as the ratio of useful events to total events processed [20]. Hence, the simulation *efficiency* is measured as the averaged execution efficiency of all federates. The simulation *resource* is the sum of cap values of all computers.

For the synthetic simulation workload, the number of players in each federate follows a normal distribution $N(\mu, \sigma^2)$. The experimental results are shown in Table 1. Two cases are studied: 1> *Imbalanced Computer* and 2> *Imbalanced Federate*. In the *Imbalanced Computer* case, the simulation

workload on computers is proportion to *ComIndex* (i.e., $\mu = 400 \times comIndex$ and $\sigma = 3 \times comIndex$). Since federates located in the same computer have the same simulation workload, the *Fixed* and *Adaptive* scenarios have similar simulation performance. In the *Aligned* scenario, the lightly-loaded computers do not allocate all resources to federates. Hence, we can observe the decreased resource usage, decreased number of rollbacks and increased simulation efficiency. In practice, the speed alignment cannot ensure that all federates in the federation have the exact same execution speed. Hence, it cannot avoid all simulation rollbacks and the execution efficiency is slightly smaller than one. As a result, the simulation speed is slightly lower than that in the *Adaptive* scenario. In the *Balanced* scenario, three federates are migrated from P_3 to P_1 for workload balance purpose during the simulation warm up period. Hence, almost all computer resources are utilized. As a result, the simulation speed has been increased by 28.2% and 32.6% compared to the *Adaptive* and *Aligned* scenarios respectively.

In the *Imbalanced Federate* case, the simulation workload of federates on the same computer is proportion to $fedIndex$, and the simulation workload on computers is proportion to $ComIndex$, i.e., $\mu = 100 \times (fedIndex \mod 8) \times comIndex$; and $\sigma = 3 \times (fedIndex \mod 8) \times comIndex$. In addition to Table 1, Figure 5 further illustrates the performance of individual federates in the federation. Figure 5(a) and 5(d) show the averaged measured execution speed (i.e., MES) and the averaged VM cap values of federates in all control intervals during simulation execution; Figure 5(b) and 5(c) show the number of rollbacks and the simulation efficiency of federates in the entire simulation execution.

In the *Fixed* scenario, the same amount of computer resources are allocated to all federates(Figure 5(d)). Due to the imbalance workload, federates have different simulation speeds (Figure 5(a)). The faster federate encounters more execution rollbacks (Figure 5(b)) and lower execution efficiency(Figure 5(c)). In the *Adaptive* scenario, each computer distributes its resources according to the simulation workload of the corresponding federates (Figure 5(d)). Hence, it can increase simulation speed of each computer, and thus increase the simulation speed on the entire federation. As we can see in Table 1, the simulation speed has been increased by 71.9% in the *Adaptive* scenario compared to the *Fixed* scenario. Due to workload imbalance, federates located on different computers have different simulation performance. The higher simulation workload on the computer, the slower its overlying federates, with less rollbacks and higher efficiency. In the *Aligned* scenario, smaller amount of computer resources are allocated to federates on lightly-loaded computers compared to the *Adaptive* scenario. As a result, all federates in the federation have comparable simulation speed, encounter small number of rollbacks and achieve high execution efficiency. Since the federation execution speed is determined the slowest federate, the *Aligned* scenario have similar simulation speed as the *Adaptive* scenario (as shown in Table 1). Similar to the *Aligned* scenario, federates in the *Balanced* scenario have comparable simulation speed, encounter small number of rollbacks and achieve high execution efficiency. To achieve workload balance, F_{24} and F_{20} are migrated from P_3 to P_1 during warm up period. Consequently, more resources are used for the simulation executions (refer to Figure 5(d) and Table 1). Consequently, MES of individual federates (Figure 5(a)) and the simulation speed (Table 1) increases accordingly. It is worthwhile to point-out that the federate with the highest simulation workload (i.e., F_{24}) has been accelerated as much as possible by allocating one entire CPU core (i.e., $cap = 100$). Due the speed alignment, all other federates in the federation have comparable speeds as F_{24}, without using all resources on the computers. As shown in Table 1, the sum of the VM Cap values is 970 only. For this reason, the simulation speed in the *Balanced* scenario is only increased by 6.4% and 9.6% compared to the *Adaptive* and *Aligned* scenarios.

For the real simulation workload, the number of players connected to the data centers are retrieved from the traces of RuneScape [22], which have strong diurnal pattern. In the case that the data centers locate at regions in different time zones, the corresponding federates may have different simulation workloads at the same simulation time. As shown

in Figure 6, the time difference between the data centers simulated by these two federates is around 12 hours.

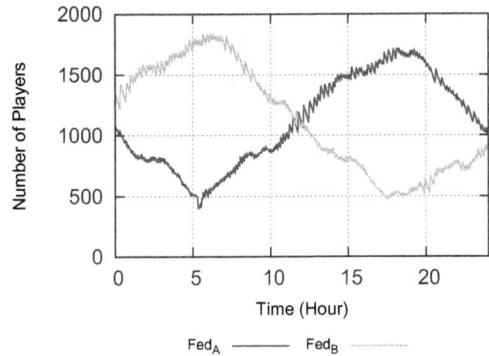

Figure 6: Simulation workload with diurnal pattern

Similar to the synthetic simulation workload, two cases are also studied for the real simulation workload. In the *Imbalanced Computer* case, the 8 federates located in each computer have the same simulation workload. However, federates on P_1 have workloads following Fed_A trace; while federates on P_2 have workload following Fed_B trace. The simulation performance of different scenarios is shown in Table 2. Since federates on each computer have the same simulation workload, computer resources are distributed evenly among the federates in both *Fixed* and *Adaptive* scenarios. Hence, they have similar simulation performance as shown in Table 2. Figure 7 shows the execution speed of the two computers (i.e., the minimum MES of all federates on the computer) in each control interval. In the *Adaptive* scenario, the computer speeds have strong diurnal pattern. The higher the simulation workload (Figure 6), the lower execution speed of the computer (Figure 7(a)). In the *Aligned* scenario, computers have similar execution speed, which are approximate to the minimum speed of the two computers in the *Adaptive* scenario. Since the federation execution speed is determined by the slowest federate, the *Aligned* scenario obtains comparable simulation speed as the *Adaptive* scenario, while reducing resource usage significantly (Table 2). In the *Balanced* scenario, four federates on P_2 are exchanged for the another four federates on P_1 during warm up period. Hence, computers can always have balanced workload during entire the simulation execution. For this reason, the simulation execution uses almost all resources in the computers; computers have comparable execution speeds which are much greater than the *Aligned* scenario (Figure 7(b) and 7(c)). As a result, the simulation speed has been increased by 23.3% and 32.2% in the *Balanced* scenario compared to the *Adaptive* and *Aligned* scenarios respectively.

In the *Imbalanced Federate* case, federates on P_1 (or P_2) still have simulation workload following the trace of Fed_A (or Fed_B) in Figure 6. However, federates located in the same computer have different simulation workloads which are proportion to their $fedIndex$. More exactly, the number of players is equal to the number of player in Fed_A (or Fed_B) $\times 0.5 \times (fedIndex \mod 8)$. Similar to the synthetic simulation workload, the *Adaptive* scenario accelerates simulation execution by 76.8% compared to the *Fixed* scenario; the *Aligned* scenario obtains comparable simulation speed as the *Adaptive* scenario, while reducing resource usage signif-

Table 2: Simulation performance using real simulation workload

	Imbalanced Computer				Imbalanced Federate			
	Fixed	Adaptive	Aligned	Balanced	Fixed	Adaptive	Aligned	Balanced
Speed	79.2	79.9	74.5	98.5	22.4	39.6	38.2	43.6
Rollbacks	54.8	53.8	34	30.5	156.8	57.1	25.3	31.1
Efficiency	0.65	0.643	0.895	0.911	0.372	0.629	0.955	0.949
Resource	800	800	652	792	800	800	656	715

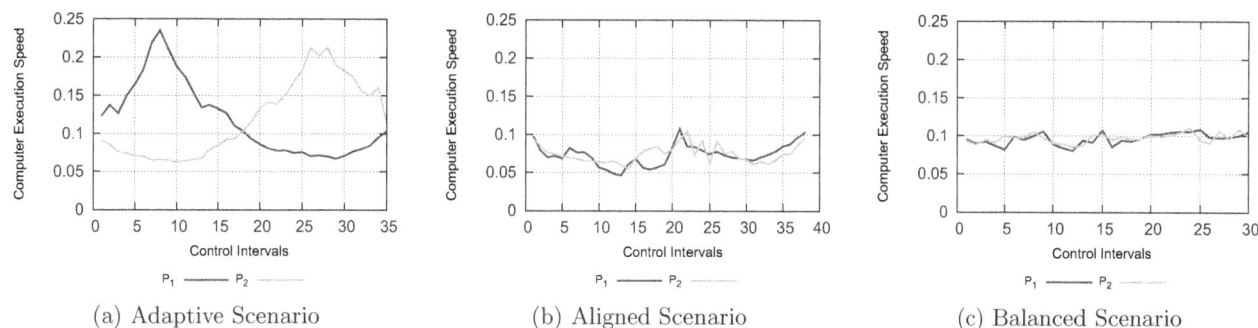

(a) Adaptive Scenario   (b) Aligned Scenario   (c) Balanced Scenario

Figure 7: Computer execution speeds in *Imbalanced Computer* case for real simulation workload

icantly; the *Balanced* scenario obtains maximum simulation speed. During some simulation execution periods, some federates with highest workload have been accelerated as much as possible by setting VM Cap value at 100. Due the the speed limit of these federates, not all computer resources are used for the simulation execution. As shown in Table 2, the sum of the VM Cap values is 715 only. For this reason, the simulation speed in the *Balanced* scenario is not increased very significantly, more exactly, 10.1% and 14.1% compared to the *Adaptive* and *Aligned* scenarios respectively.

5. CONCLUSIONS

In this paper, a hierarchical resource management system is proposed to enhance the performance of large scale simulations on modern data centers. Simulation components (Federates) are enraptured in individual Virtual Machines (VMs), which are consolidated on a group of multi-core computers. On the computer level, a resource provisioning mechanism is proposed. It ensures federates on the same computer have comparable execution speeds by reallocating computer resources to VMs according to simulation workloads. On the federation level, a centralized coordinator composed of speed alignment and workload balance modules is deployed. The speed alignment module ensures federates on different computers have comparable execution speeds; while the workload balance module achieves workload balance through live VM migrations. Experiments using synthetic and real simulation workloads have verified that the hierarchical resource management system increases resources utilized for useful simulation workload and decreases resources wasted on time synchronization. Therefore, it can speedup simulation executions significantly using the same computers.

Currently, a centralized coordinator is deployed for federation level resource management. However, it may turn to be a hot spot due to the increasing simulation scale. In the future, we will design the coordinator in a distributed manner.

In addition, migration decisions, as shown in Algorithm 1, are made without considering the migration penalty. For instance, moving VM state changes the network dynamics significantly which may increase the message delivery delay among federates. What is worse, simulation workloads of federates may change dramatically after the migration, which may decrease the benefit of the federate migration [27]. To solve the problem, we will take migration overhead and dynamic simulation workloads into account while making the migration decisions. More benchmarks and real-world workloads will be used to evaluate our improved resource management system. In the meantime, our resource provisioning and workload balance mechanisms will also be applied for high performance computing and big data processing applications on Cloud and VM platforms.

6. ACKNOWLEDGMENTS

This work is supported under future data center technology thematic strategic research programme by Singapore Agency for Science, Technology and Research (A*STAR) with grant number 112 172 0015.

7. REFERENCES

[1] P. Barham, B. Dragovic, K. Fraser, S. Hand, T. Harris, A. Ho, R. Neugebauer, I. Pratt, and A. Warfield. Xen and the art of virtualization. *SIGOPS Oper. Syst. Rev.*, 37(5):164–177, Oct. 2003.

[2] S. K. Barker and P. Shenoy. Empirical evaluation of latency-sensitive application performance in the Cloud. In *Procs of conf. on Multimedia systems (MMSys'10)*, pages 35–46, 2010.

[3] L. Bononi, M. Bracuto, G. D'Angelo, and L. Donatiello. An adaptive load balancing middleware for distributed simulation. *Frontiers of High Performance Computing and Networking*, 4331:873–883, 2006.

[4] R. E. Bryant. Simulation of packet communication architecture computer systems. Technical report, Massachusetts Institute of Technology, Massachusetts Institute of Technology. Cambridge, MA, USA, 1977.

[5] W. Cai, Z. Yuan, M. Y.-H. Low, and S. J. Turner. Federate migration in HLA-based simulation. *Future Generation Computer System*, 21(1):87–95, 2005.

[6] K. M. Chandy and J. Misra. Distributed simulation: A case study in design and verification of distributed programs. *IEEE Trans. on Software Engineering*, 5(5):440–452, 1979.

[7] L. Chen, Y. Lu, Y. Yao, S. Peng, and L. Wu. A well-balanced time warp system on multi-core environments. In *Procs of Workshop on Principles of Advanced and Distributed Simulation (PADS'11)*, pages 1–9, 2011.

[8] C. Clark, K. Fraser, S. Hand, J. G. Hansen, E. Jul, C. Limpach, I. Pratt, and A. Warfield. Live migration of virtual machines. In *Procs of Symposium on Networked Systems Design & Implementation (NSDI'05)*, pages 273–286, 2005.

[9] G. D'Angelo. Parallel and distributed simulation from many cores to the public Cloud. In *Procs of Conference on High Performance Computing and Simulation (HPCS'11)*, pages 14–23, 2011.

[10] G. D'Angelo, S. Ferretti, and M. Marzolla. Time warp on the go. In *Procs of Conf. on Simulation Tools and Techniques (SIMUTOOLS'12)*, pages 242–248, 2012.

[11] J. Fleischmann and P. A. Wilsey. Comparative analysis of periodic state saving techniques in time warp simulators. In *Procs of workshop on Parallel and distributed simulation (PADS'95)*, pages 50–58, 1995.

[12] R. M. Fujimoto. *Parallel and Distributed Simulation Systems*. Wiley Interscience, 2000.

[13] R. M. Fujimoto, A. W. Malik, and A. J. Park. Parallel and distributed simulation in the Cloud. *SCS Modeling and Simulation Magazine, Society for Modeling and Simulation, Intl.*, 1, July 2010.

[14] IEEE. *1516-2010 IEEE Standard for Modeling and Simulation (M&S) High Level Architecture (HLA)– Framework and Rules*, August 2010.

[15] D. Jagtap, N. Abu-Ghazaleh, and D. Ponomarev. Optimization of parallel discrete event simulator for multi-core systems. In *Procs of International Parallel and Distributed Processing Symposium (IPDPS'12)*, pages 520–531, 2012.

[16] D. R. Jefferson. Virtual time. *ACM Trans. Program. Lang. Syst*, 7(3):404–425, 1985.

[17] C. Jo, E. Gustafsson, J. Son, and B. Egger. Efficient live migration of virtual machines using shared storage. In *Procs of conf. on Virtual execution environments (VEE'13)*, pages 41–50, 2013.

[18] Z. Li, W. Cai, S. J. Turner, and K. Pan. Federate migration in a service oriented HLA RTI. In *Procs of Symposium on Distributed Simulation and Real-Time Applications (DS-RT '07)*, pages 113–121, 2007.

[19] Z. Li, X. Li, T. N. B. Duong, W. Cai, and S. J. Turner. Accelerating optimistic HLA-based simulations in virtual execution environments. In *Procs of Conf. on Principles of Advanced Discrete Simulation (PADS'13)*, 2013.

[20] A. Malik, A. Park, and R. Fujimoto. Optimistic synchronization of parallel simulations in Cloud computing environments. In *Procs of Conf. on Cloud Computing (CLOUD'09)*, pages 49–56, 2009.

[21] D. E. Martin, T. J. McBrayer, and P. A. Wilsey. Warped: A time warp simulation kernel for analysis and application development. In *Procs of Hawaii International Conf. on System Sciences Volume 1: Software Technology and Architecture (HICSS'96)*, pages 383–386, 1996.

[22] V. Nae, A. Iosup, S. Podlipnig, R. Prodan, D. Epema, and T. Fahringer. Efficient management of data center resources for massively multiplayer online games. In *Procs of conf. on Supercomputing (SC'08)*, pages 10:1–10:12, 2008.

[23] K. Pan, S. J. Turner, W. Cai, and Z. Li. A service oriented HLA RTI on the Grid. In *Procs of Int. Conf. on Web Services (ICWS 2007)*, pages 984–992, 2007.

[24] S. Peluso, D. Didona, and F. Quaglia. Supports for transparent object-migration in PDES systems. *Journal of Simulation*, 6(4):279–293, 2012.

[25] F. Quaglia. A middleware level active replication manager for high performance HLA-based simulations on SMP systems. In *Procs of Symposium on Distributed Simulation and Real-Time Applications (DS-RT'06)*, pages 219–226, 2006.

[26] D. Schanzenbach and H. Casanova. Accuracy and responsiveness of CPU sharing using Xen's cap values. Technical report, Computer and Information Sciences Dept., University of Hawai at manoa, 2008.

[27] Z. Shen, S. Subbiah, X. Gu, and J. Wilkes. Cloudscale: Elastic resource scaling for multi-tenant Cloud systems. In *Procs of Symposium on Cloud Computing (SOCC'11)*, pages 5:1–5:14, 2011.

[28] G. S. H. Tan, A. Persson, and R. Ayani. HLA federate migration. In *Procs of Annual Simulation Symposium*, pages 243–250, 2005.

[29] M. M. Theimer, K. A. Lantz, and D. R. Cheriton. Preemptable remote execution facilities for the V-system. In *Procs of symposium on Operating systems principles (SOSP '85)*, pages 2–12, 1985.

[30] H. F. van Rietschote, C. W. Hobbs, and M. P. Saptarshi. Migrating virtual machines among computer systems to balance load caused by virtual machines, May 2010.

[31] R. Vitali, A. Pellegrini, and F. Quaglia. Towards symmetric multi-threaded optimistic simulation kernels. In *Procs of Workshop on Principles of Advanced and Distributed Simulation (PADS'12)*, pages 211–220, 2012.

[32] S. Yoginath and K. Perumalla. Optimized hypervisor scheduler for parallel discrete event simulations on virtual machine platforms. In *Procs of Conf. on Simulation Tools and Techniques (SIMUTOOLS'13)*, 2013.

[33] S. B. Yoginath and K. S. Perumalla. Empirical evaluation of conservative and optimistic discrete event execution on Cloud and VM platforms. In *Pros of Conference on Principles of Advanced Discrete Simulation (SIGSIM-PADS '13)*, pages 201–210, 2013.

Power Consumption of Data Distribution Management for On-Line Simulations

SaBra Neal, Gaurav Kantikar, Richard Fujimoto

School of Computational Science and Engineering
Georgia Institute of Technology
Atlanta, GA 30332, USA
sneal6@gatech.edu, gaurav.kanitkar@gmail.com, fujimoto@cc.gatech.edu

ABSTRACT

With the growing use of mobile devices, power aware algorithms have become essential. Data distribution management (DDM) is an approach to disseminate information that was proposed in the High Level Architecture (HLA) for modeling and simulation. This paper explores the power consumption of mobile devices used by pedestrians in an urban environment communicating through HLA DDM services operating over a mobile ad-hoc network (MANET). The computation and communication power requirements of Grid-Based and Region-Based implementation approaches to DDM are contrasted and quantitatively evaluated through experimentation and simulation.

General Terms

Data Distribution Management, multicasting, crowdsourcing

Keywords

Data Distribution Management (DDM), multicasting, ns-3, crowdsourcing, fixed grid method, federates, regions.

1. INTRODUCTION

Dynamic Data Driven Application Systems (DDDAS) are applications that continuously monitor, analyze, and adapt operational systems in order to better assess and/or optimize their behavior. Applications arise in many areas such as transportation, medicine, disaster management, and manufacturing, among others [2]. Many DDDAS applications involve sensing and computation on mobile devices, utilizing communications through wireless networks. Power consumption in these applications is a major concern because battery life often limits the effectiveness of DDDAS applications utilizing mobile platforms.

Mobile computing is a research area that is receiving much interest with the rapidly growing use of mobile devices. A majority of the U.S. population uses smartphones. Popular operating systems such as android, iOS etc. have emerged and are constantly undergoing changes. Most of these operating systems support sensors such as GPS, photo and video camera, accelerometer and also provide location and map based services, providing a rich source of data for on-line applications.

SIGSIM-PADS'14, May 18–21, 2014, Denver, Colorado, USA.
Copyright © 2014 ACM 978-1-4503-2794-7/14/05...$15.00.
10.1145/2601381.2601409

Mobile ad-hoc networks (MANETS) provide communication services for mobile devices without relying on fixed infrastructure. They provide communication services among a set of mobile and fixed location devices and have received much attention by the research community.

Crowdsourcing has begun to emerge as a paradigm for collecting information. Crowdsourcing is the practice of obtaining needed services, ideas, or content by soliciting contributions from a large group of people and especially from the online community rather than from traditional employees or suppliers. A well-known example is the 2009 DARPA Balloon Challenge where teams were tasked with finding 10 red weather balloons placed across the U.S. using social media to gather information [12]. The winning team from the Massachusetts Institute of Technology correctly located the ten balloons in less than nine hours. Their winning strategy included a financial incentive for recruiting members and used a recursive pyramid money scheme to keep members interested and to continue to recruit other members until the balloons were found. The DARPA challenge demonstrated that certain surveillance tasks could be accomplished much more rapidly and at a much lower cost than traditional means for collecting information.

Mobile on-line simulations have also received much attention in recent years. For example, in mobile traffic simulations fed by online data sources were used to predict congestion in urban transportation systems [14]. Such simulations find use in many DDDAS applications, as discussed earlier.

Here, we are concerned with DDDAS applications that use techniques such as crowd sourcing, MANETS and predictive simulations operating on mobile platforms to analyze operational systems. Specifically, we are concerned with the amount of power consumed in such applications, e.g., as a pedestrian carries a mobile device throughout the system. We assume that MANETS are used to disseminate information throughout the system.

Data distribution management (DDM) is a set of services defined in the High Level Architecture [8] to distribute information in distributed simulation environments. DDM services are implemented by Run-Time Infrastructure (RTI) software. Several different approaches to implementing the DDM services have been proposed including grid-based implementations, region-based implementations, and hybrid approaches that utilize a combination of ideas from the grid and region-based approaches [11]. These approaches have certain computation and communication requirements, as will be discussed later. However, to our knowledge, DDM services have yet to be examined from the standpoint of power consumption requirements. This is the focus of the work described here. We examined the grid- and region-based approaches for this study because they represent two very different approaches to DDM that have been widely reported in the literature. Specifically, we focus on power consumption issues in using DDM services for DDDAS applications including crowd-sourced information that is used to drive mobile distributed simulations.

The rest of this paper is organized as follows. Section 2 reviews different approaches to implementing the HLA Data Distribution Management services, focusing on the Grid and Region-based methods that are studied here. Section 3 describes tradeoffs that arise between grid-based and region-based implementations with respect to power consumption for computation and communications. Factors of the implementation that impact power consumption include the grid cell and region size. Section 4 describes the application scenarios used in our experiments to compare power consumption for these two approaches. Section 5 presents the results of power consumption measurement of DDM computations on a representative mobile device. Section 6 presents the results of power consumption that takes place during communication when grid-based DDM method is implemented over a MANET using the NS3 simulator. Section 7 summarizes the results and presents conclusions and areas of future work.

2. APPROACHES TO DATA DISTRIBUTION MANAGEMENT

Data Distribution Management services are defined in the HLA to reduce traffic flow over the network. The DDM services define an N-dimensional coordinate system known as the routing space. Publication and subscription regions are defined within this routing space to characterize the information contained in messages and to specify what information federates are interested in receiving, respectively. Typically, the routing space represents a geographical area. Data producers specify which regions are relevant to a message by associating a publication region with each message. Data receivers specify the areas of the routing space in which they have interest by associating subscription regions with their data subscriptions. If the publication region associated with a message overlaps a federate's subscription region, the message is routed to that federate. The grid-based and region-based implementations are well known approaches to realizing the HLA DDM services.

2.1 Grid-Based Approach

The grid-based DDM approach divides the routing space into fixed sized grid cells. A s group is assigned to each grid cell. When a federate subscribes to a subscription region it joins each multicast group whose cell overlaps with the subscription region. When a message is sent, it is transmitted to each multicast group associated with a grid cell overlapping with the publication region associated with the message. A matching computation must take place to determine which grid cells overlap with each publication region to determine the multicast groups that are used to transmit the message.

Figure 1 shows an example of the grid-based DDM approach. In this example the publisher region P1 would publish messages to all federates whose subscription region include the grid cells that overlap with P1, i.e., cells 10, 11, 15, 16, 20, and 21. Similarly, S1 overlaps with grid cells 1, 2, 6, 7, 11, 12, 16 and 17. Note that in this case, federates subscribed to S1 will receive two identical copies of the message – messages sent to groups 11 and 16. Federates subscribed to region S2 will not receive the message because they are subscribed to groups 13, 14, 18, 19, 23 and 24. It

may be noted that federates may receive extra (irrelevant) messages, i.e., it is possible a message will be received even though the publication and subscription regions do not overlap. This occurs if the non-overlapping regions have a grid cell in common. If communications are reliable, the grid-based approach will result in all federates whose subscription region overlap with the publication region of the message receiving at least one copy, however as noted earlier, duplicate or additional (irrelevant) messages may be received, and must be filtered at the receiver.

The number of duplicate and irrelevant messages that are sent and received by federates is of particular concern here because these result in unnecessary power consumption. The size of the grid cells can have a large impact on the cost of sending data and receiving irrelevant data [8]. D.J. Van Hook and S.J. Rak explored the effect of grid cell space sizes and the effect it has on multicast group assignment and communication cost. They concluded that communication cost becomes increasingly greater the larger the size of the grid cell because it causes an increase in irrelevant and duplicated messages. This issue has been explored by Tan and Xu who ran several experiments on the sending of data using grid-based DDM. They proposed an alternate approach called Agent-based DDM to decrease the number of irrelevant messages sent across a network [10].

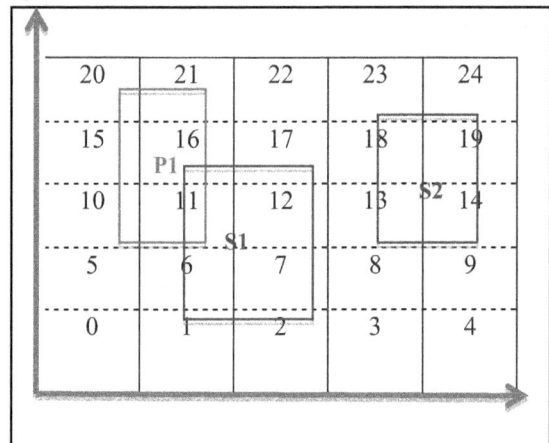

Figure 1: Grid-Based DDM

To implement this approach to DDM the space was divided into fixed size grid cells. Federates were created and added to the space. Each federate was assigned a single publication and a single subscription region. The grid-based matching computation executes the following:

```
For all grid cells:
    For all federates:
            Check if Publication/subscription regions overlap with
            the grid cell
            If regions overlap, add the respective grid_id to the
            pub/sub multicast group of the respective grid cell.
```

On a publication (or subscription) region update, the program first compares the coordinates of the updated publication (or subscription) region to the coordinates in its publication (or subscription) multicast group. All the grid cells from the multicast group for whom coordinates do not overlap are removed from the group. The next step is to compare the coordinates of the updated region with remaining grid cells and add all those grid cells to the multicast group for whom the coordinates overlap.

2.2 Region-Based Approach

The region-based approach does not use grid cells. Rather, a multicast group is defined for each publication region. Federates join the multicast groups associated with publication regions that overlap the subscription regions to which the federate is subscribed. This is a direct implementation of the DDM services, and is sometimes referred to as the "brute force" approach to DDM.

Region-based matching is clearly more efficient than the grid-based approach in terms of message communications in that there are no duplicate or irrelevant messages. Publication regions are checked against subscription regions to identify overlaps and information is then distributed when overlaps exist. Region-based DDM has been implemented on the MAK high performance RTI by Wood [13]. Implementation of region-based DDM does incur additional messages depending on the implementation. For example, if a centralized implementation is used, region changes must be communicated to the server in order to determine the new composition of the multicast groups.

The drawback of the region-based approach is a matching computation must be performed to determine which subscription regions overlap with which publication regions. This computation must be repeated each time a publication or subscription region changes.

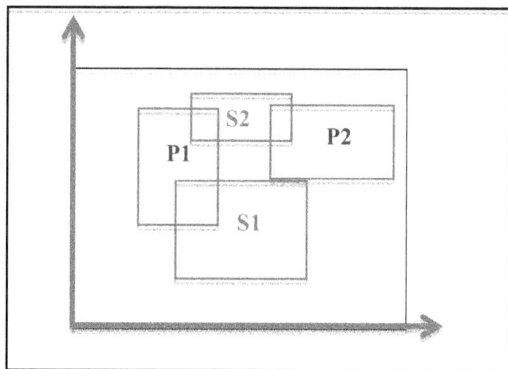

Figure 2: illustrates an example of Region-Based DDM. In this example P1 publishes information to federates who are subscribed to regions S1 and S2. P2 publishes information to federates who are subscribed to region S2.

In this implementation federates were added to the entire space. Each federate was assigned a publication as well as a subscription region. The matching algorithm executes the following:

```
For all federates (F1):
  For all federates (F2):
      Check if Publication region of F2 overlaps with the
      subscription region of F1.
      If regions overlap, add the respective federate_id to the
      publication multicast group of F2.
```

On a publication region update, the matching algorithm is executed only for the federate with the updated region.

On a subscription region update, the updated subscription region is compared against all publication regions. If the regions overlap, the program adds the federate to the multicast group associated with the federate's publication region. If the regions do not overlap, the federate (if present) leaves the corresponding multicast group.

3. POWER CONSUMPTION TRADEOFFS

Power consumption of the DDM services using the grid-based and region-based approaches is somewhat complex because it must consider several tradeoffs. The region-based approach must consume power to compute overlaps among publication and subscription regions. This computation is $O(N^2)$ where N is the total number of publication/subscription regions used in the entire federation. Whenever a publication (subscription) region changes the new region must be compared against all other subscription (publication) regions to determine overlaps with the new region. This computation could be reduced by overlaying a grid structure onto the routing space, however, this hybrid approach to the region-based scheme is not investigated here. In addition, if the DDM mechanism is implemented centrally at one device, communications with this device is necessary whenever regions change, necessitating additional power consumption. If the DDM implementation is distributed, e.g., across a set of devices, communications among these devices is similarly required whenever regions change to coordinate management of the groups.

The grid-based approach requires computation to determine overlaps between regions and grid cells when a region changes, however, this computation is $O(1)$. This will be significantly less than that for the region-based approach. Further, the grid-based approach allows a fully distributed implementation without the need for coordination messages that are necessary in the region-based approach when regions change. However, the grid-based approach incurs additional power consumption to transmit irrelevant and duplicate messages, something that is not required in the region-based approach. The amount of additional communication will depend on factors such as the grid cell size, the number of federates, the size and location of publication and subscription regions, and the number of hops between communicating nodes in the MANET.

The tradeoffs among these factors clearly depend on the specific scenario that is used and particulars of the DDM design. In the following we empirically evaluate these questions through a combination of measurement and simulation. The scenario used in this work is based on a college campus where individuals walk from one location to another. A two-dimensional routing space is used that corresponds to the college campus itself. Mobile units publishing data are assumed to send information concerning observations made by the mobile unit, i.e., their publication region corresponds to an area not far from their current location. Subscription regions represent areas of interest to a particular mobile device and are typically further removed from the location of the subscriber federate.

4. SCENARIO AND EXPERIMENTAL SETUP

Our scenario consists of federates (mobile devices) moving throughout the simulated college campus. The federates report observations concerning an object, e.g., a vehicle that the federates might be attempting to monitor. Federates report information or receive information, e.g., observations made by a particular mobile device as it moves throughout the environment. This simulated environment is approximately 1280 meters by 1280 meters. The simulation consists of two major components, the Data Distribution Management component that manages federate publication and subscription regions and determines the composition of multicast groups and the NS3 (network simulator) component that routes packets among federates over a MANET.

The Data Distribution Management component was created for three different sets of experiments. The experiments determine power consumption for three different grid cell sizes (10X10, 20X20, and 40X40). The DDM grid-based method consists of creating grid cells that are overlaid on top of the simulated area. This grid cells are then used to assign federates to multicast groups based on the publication and subscription regions. Each federate has a single publication and subscription region. Each federate's publication region covers an area that is a half of a mile away from their current location and their subscription region covers an area that is a mile away from its current location. Each grid cell has its own multicast group. A federate sends messages to, or joins a particular multicast group based on the location of their regions. The federate joins every multicast group of the respective grid cells that their regions cover. These assigned multicast groups are used to determine who receives packets when a publication is made. Changing federate region locations take place during the simulation when an update event occurs. The DDM grid-based method then determines the federate's new assigned multicast groups based on their new region locations. Federates first leave their current multicast group before joining a new multicast group. These new region locations are determined based on the current location of the federate at the time during the simulation when this event takes place, the regions are reassigned using the coordinates of the current location of the federate. The grid-based DDM mechanism handles assigning all of the multicast groups that NS3 uses in order to multicast packets to the federates.

The amount of power consumed for computation is determined through direct measurement of the associated algorithms on a mobile device. The amount of power consumed for communications over the MANET is determined through simulation using the NS3 network simulator.

NS3 is used to send packets to respective multicast groups. The NS3 component of the experiment consists of creating a wireless ad hoc network that uses the OLSR (Optimized Link State Routing) routing protocol to route packets to federates. Packets sizes of 1000 bytes were used for these experiments.

The federates follow a mobility pattern that reflects the movement of pedestrians moving through the campus. Mobility files were created using the mobility scenario generation tool Bonnmotion [1]. The SMOOTH model was used in order to reflect mobility patterns of pedestrians moving through the campus. SMOOTH is a simple way to model human movement. SMOOTH consider walking behavior to be self-similar. This principle is the grounding foundation for generating mobility models, since patterns of human walking behavior are considered self-similar the model can be used for any scale of larger models. SMOOTH is a simplified version of the original mobility model SLAW, which produces the same mobility patterns with the need of more parameters [4]. The model generates mobility patterns based on seven features: the distribution of the movement of nodes, the distribution of nodes, the pause time distribution, popular waypoints in the network, closest waypoints that mobile nodes tend to visit first, the distribution of mobile nodes in a non-uniform network, and mobile nodes with common interest form communities of interest [5]. The parameters of SMOOTH that reflect the dynamics of the university campus used in this study were used as inputs for our mobility trace files that include: the size of the area and clusters that represent common places on campus were people tend to linger for long periods of times. The clusters in the experiments represent a Commons area, the student center, recreational center, a commercial region, and an instructional center on the Georgia Tech campus.

The distance of the waypoints between the clusters were a part of the inputs used in order to generate accurate trace files that reflect the system under investigation. Once these trace files are created they are then stored in trace files and used as input to NS3. The files are then imported into NS3 to be used as the mobility model for the simulation. Once the mobility model was set for the simulation the closest federate to the vehicle being observed sends a packet. The nodes that receive the message are those that have been determined by the DDM component of our experiment that their subscription region overlaps with grid cells that are a part of the federate's publication region.

The NS3 Wi-Fi radio energy model was used to measure the amount of power consumed by devices attached to each federate. Every ten seconds during the simulation an update event occurs. During this update federates update their current location and create new publication and subscription regions. The federate that is now closest to the object being monitored then becomes the new source for publishing a message to those federates that are members of the multicast groups that contain the source federate publication regions and overlapping subscriber regions. The amount of energy consumed by these devices while federates are sending and receiving packets during the simulation are continuously added until communication between federates end. These measurements are then converted to watts to reflect the amount of power consumed during communication.

5. POWER CONSUMPTION: COMPUTATION

The associated DDM computations were implemented on a Google Nexus 4 smart phone, using PowerTutor to measure power consumption for the android device [3]. Power Tutor is a smartphone application that measures the power consumption of CPU, Wi-Fi, 3G, and applications running on Google based android devices. The focus of this experiment only considers power consumed by the CPU.

The routing space was assumed to be a 400 x 400 unit space. For the grid-based implementation, the routing space was divided into 400 grid cells of 20x20 units each. The number of federates were varied from 100 to 1000 incrementing by 100 for each experiment. The publication and subscription regions of every federate were chosen randomly within the routing space. The code for both implementations was written in Java using the Android Development Tool (ADT) plugin for the Eclipse IDE and was tested on the Nexus 4 smartphone while monitoring the CPU power consumption using PowerTutor application. The consumption results obtained from these measurements are shown in Figures 3 (energy) and 4 (power).

From Figure 3 it is clear that the region-based implementation consumes much more energy than the grid-based approach with the same parameters. This result is expected since the grid-based method reduces the computation cost involved by dividing the routing space into grid cells. We also observe that in the grid-based method, the incremental power consumption is proportional with the number of federates and this can be attributed to the fact that the number of computations involved is directly proportional to the number of federates.

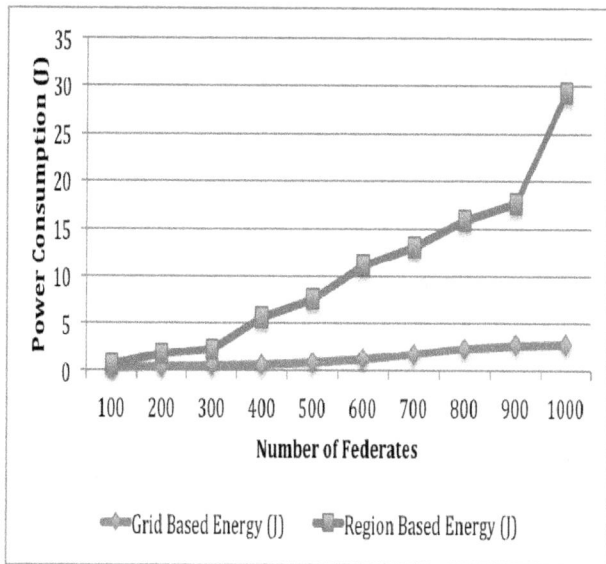

Figure 3: Energy Consumption results for computation in region-based and grid-based DDM.

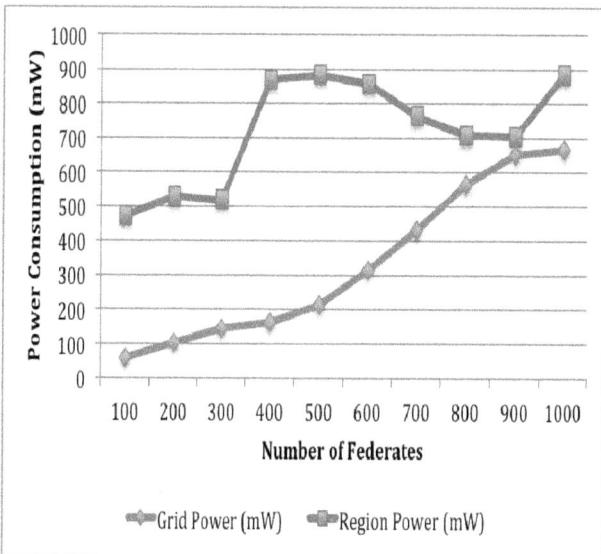

Figure 4: Power consumption results for computation in region-based and grid-based DDM.

On the other hand, in the region-based method, though the power consumed increases initially with the number of federates, it does not increase significantly beyond a few hundred federates. It should be kept in mind that the power is calculated in mW and thus even though the graph indicates that the power consumed in the region-based method does not significantly change, the total amount of energy consumed does increase as is shown in the Figure 3.

The computational cost in the region-based method is $O(N^2)$, where N is the number of federates. The above result is consistent with this observation.

6. POWER CONSUMPTION: COMMUNICATIONS
6.1 Grid Cell Size Experiment

The previous section compared the power consumption for computation using the grid-based and region-based implementations of DDM. Here, we examine the power consumed for communications, specifically for the grid-based approach as the size (and thus the number) of grid cells is varied. We also examine the power consumed for communications for the grid-based approach as the grid cell size is varied for different publication and subscription region size..

The number of multicast groups increases with the number of grid cells. This will affect the number of irrelevant messages (i.e., messages sent to a federate whose subscription region does not overlap with the publication region) and duplicate messages. Increasing the number of grid cells results in a finer grid cell structure that may reduce the number of non-overlapping publication and subscription regions that have a common grid cell, resulting in fewer irrelevant messages. On the other hand, if the publication and subscription regions are sufficiently close to cause irrelevant messages, having a larger number of grid cells (multicast groups) may result in magnifying the number of irrelevant messages. This is apparent when one considers the case of subscription and publication regions that do not overlap, but have a long edge in parallel with each other that are in close proximity.

Concerning duplicate messages, consider a publication and subscription region that do overlap. Smaller grid cells will result in more multicast groups in common with the overlapping portion of the subscription and publication regions, which would, in turn, increase the number of duplicate messages.

Another factor that impacts power consumption concerns the fact that the DDM mechanism is operating over a MANET. The number of hops for a single message will depend on the location of the communicating federates and mobile nodes forwarding the message. Some messages will consume more power than others because they must traverse several hops to reach their final destination.

We simulated the grid-based Data Distribution Management approach using NS3 with from 10 to 90 federates for different grid cell sizes in order to investigate these tradeoffs and estimate the amount of power that was consumed [6]. The grid cell sizes used were 10X10, 20X20, and 40X40. Our results, shown in Figure 5 indicate that increasing the number of grid cells causes an increase in power consumption. We believe this is due to an increase in duplicate messages, as described earlier. One would anticipate that as the number of federates increases the amount of power consumption would also increase, Figure 6 indicates that this case is true. The experiment that used the 10X10 grid cell size produces the least amount of power consumption.

Figure 7 shows the number of packets sent and received for differing number of federates at all three different grid cell sizes. It is seen that power consumption tracks the number of messages sent and received, confirming one's intuition that power consumption for these experiments largely depends on the amount of communication. For the 10X10 case fewer packets are sent and received resulting in reducing the amount of power consumption in comparison to the 20X20 and 40X40 experiment. This result is a reflection of the small amount of communication taking place. With the cost of less power consumption comes the loss of efficiency. It may be noted that this data does not take into account the power required to filter duplicate and irrelevant messages, which should also increase in proportion with the amount of communication.

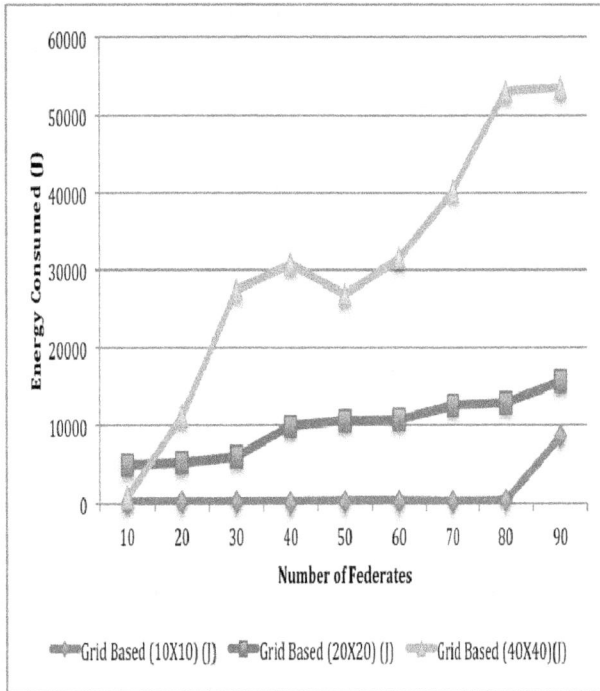

Figure 5: DDM Energy Consumption for communications

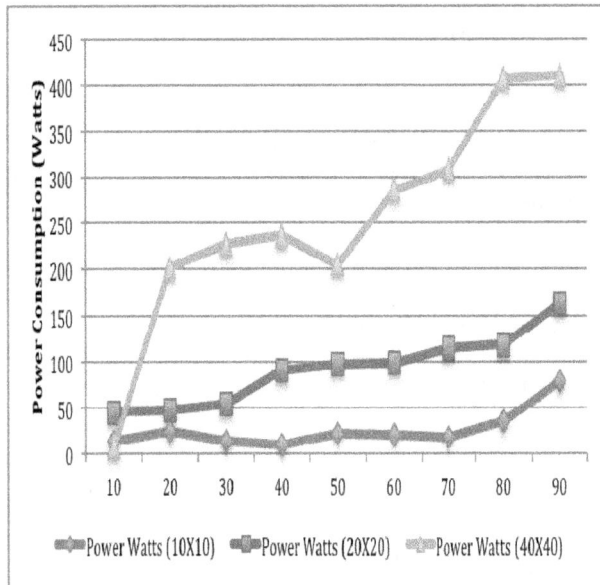

Figure 6: DDM-Grid Power Consumption for communications.

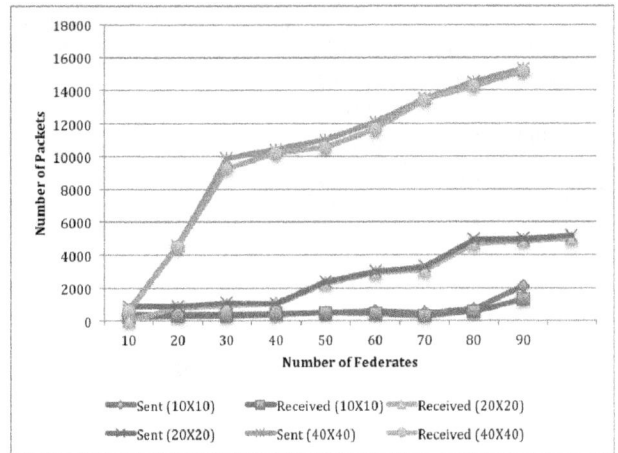

Figure 7: DDM Grid Packets Sent and Received.

The results from our experiments reflect that power consumption during communication for grid-based Data Distribution Management is greatly impacted by grid cell size. A larger number of grid cells increases the number of multicast groups which can increase the amount of communication and result in increased power consumption.

6.2 Publication and Subscription Region Size Experiment

This experiment was conducted using the same set up as the initial experiment described in Section 6.1 with a modification to the region sizes for each federate, the subscription region size was decreased to half of a mile and the publication region was decreased to a quarter of a mile. The purpose of this experiment is to see the impact that region sizes have on power consumption. One would anticipate that the size of a federates publication and subscription region has a significant affect on the amount of power consumed. Our results are consistent with this expectation as shown in Figure 8.

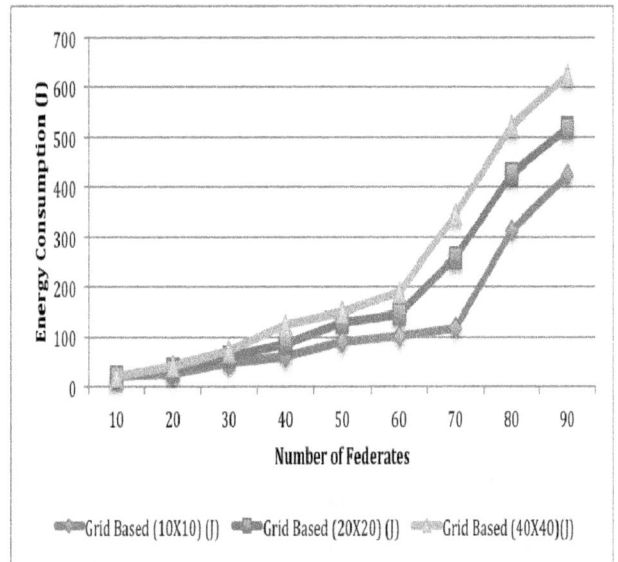

Figure 8: DDM-Grid Energy Consumption for communication from smaller region scenario

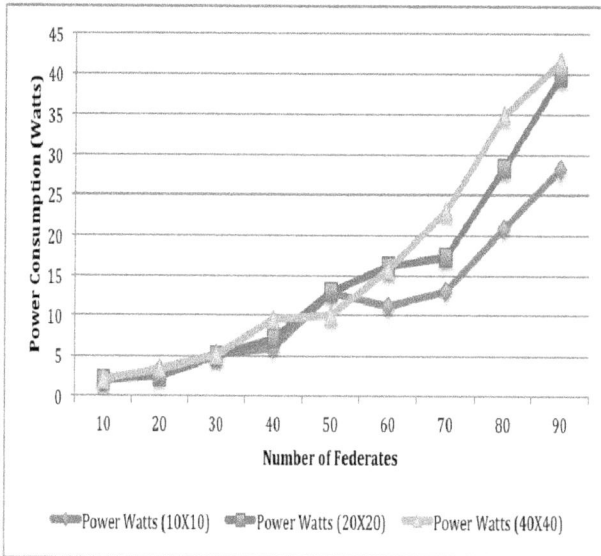

Figure 9: Power Consumption for DDM-Grid Based Communication for smaller region scenario

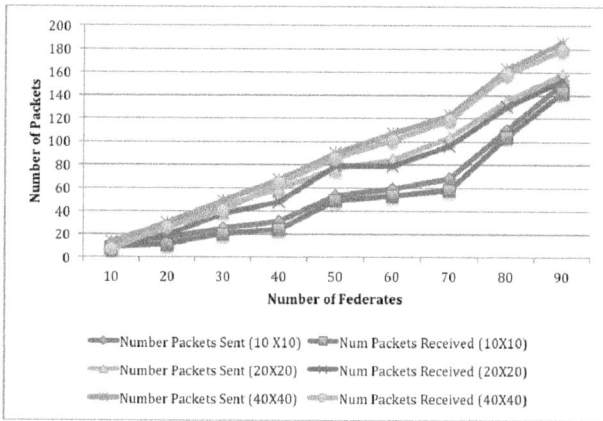

Figure 10: DDM Grid Packets Sent and Received with Smaller Region Sizes

Figure 8 shows the amount of energy that was consumed for different grid sizes using smaller regions. As before, Figure 8 shows that the amount of energy consumed increases as the grid cell sizes decreases. However, the difference in energy consumption among the three different grid cell sizes is much less than before. This result can be attributed to the fact that the number of multicast groups to which each federate is now subscribed and publishes has significantly decreased with a smaller region size. A federate now sends and receives fewer packets due to the smaller region sizes. Figure 9 shows the amount of power consumed presents a strong positive correlation between the amount of power and the change in grid cell size. Figure 10 shows that the number of packets sent and received decreases significantly compared to Figure 7 where publication and subscription region were twice as large. Comparing these two experiments we can draw the conclusion that the larger the publication and subscription region size the more power will be consumed during communication.

7. CONCLUSIONS AND FUTURE RESEARCH

Communication and computation cost are the key factors to choosing any algorithm when power consumption is an important issue. Our experiments evaluate the tradeoffs of choosing grid-based or region-based DDM when determining the effects that their methods cause on power consumption. Region-based DDM has a $O(N^2)$ computation cost. The results of our experiments reflect that when comparing overlaps of publication and subscription regions when using region-based DDM the power consumption increases at a significant rate because of the direct comparison of each region against all other regions. Grid-based DDM requires much less computation. Because all grid cells have their own designated multicast group minimal computation is needed to determine which federates will receive information when a publication is made. Communication has an inverse affect on grid-based DDM power consumption. As the size of the grid cell decreases the amount of power consumed increases. Although little computation is need for grid-based DDM much more communication takes place when a publication is made because of the large number of multicast groups. Choosing grid cell sizes has a direct impact on power consumption because a larger number of grid cells may result in more power consumed. Although more power is consumed with a larger number of cells the efficiency of communication may be reduced. Finding the optimal grid cell size in terms of power consumption is an area of future research. As the region size decreases there is less communication and correspondingly less power consumption. This highlights the need to restrict the size of publication and subscription regions to the minimum required size in order to keep power consumption low.

When choosing which Data Distribution Management method is more power efficient with respect to power consumption both computation and communication costs should be considered. Region-based DDM methods have many tradeoffs with respect to power consumption for computation and communications. Our experiments reveal the effects that DDM computation has on power consumption when comparing grid-based and region-based methods. Region-based DDM consumes significantly more power than grid-based DDM for computation as the number of federates is increased. Our experiments indicate that when evaluating the effects that grid cell size plays on power consumption, the communication cost is affected by several factors. The largest factor is the number of packets that were sent and received. The decrease in grid cell size results in an increase in the number of multicast groups causing an increase in the number of packets that must be sent and received during communication between federates. Our experiments also indicate that the decrease in federate publication and subscription region size results in fewer message communications and less power consumption. As before, the number of multicast groups affects the number of packets that must be sent and received during the execution, however, the impact on power consumption is less compared to the case using larger region sizes.

This work represents a preliminary investigation of the power consumed by DDM implementations. A more comprehensive study of the power consumed by grid-based and region-based DDM approaches is needed. A theoretical model that can predict the amount of power consumed by these approaches may be useful. Other future work includes evaluating the power consumed by other Data Distribution Management methods for computation and communication. For example, the hybrid method that combines grid cells with the region-based approach may reduce the power consumed for computation [11]. Evaluation of power consumption needs for specific application scenarios is another area of future research. As mobile computing, MANETs, crowdsourcing, and DDDAS approaches become more common, power consumption issues will become an increasingly important concern.

ACKNOWLEDGEMENT

Funding for this project was provided by AFOSR Grant FA9550-13-1-0100.

REFERENCES

[1] Aschenbruck, N., et al. (2010). Bonnmotion: a mobility scenario generation and analysis tool. Proceedings of the 3rd International ICST Conference on Simulation Tools and Techniques, ICST (Institute for Computer Sciences, Social-Informatics and Telecommunications Engineering).

[2] Darema, F. (2004). Dynamic data driven applications systems: A new paradigm for application simulations and measurements. Computational Science-ICCS 2004, Springer: 662-669.Fujimoto, R., et al. (2007). Ad hoc distributed simulations. Proceedings of the 21st International Workshop on Principles of Advanced and Distributed Simulation, IEEE Computer Society.

[3] Gordon, Mark, Lide Zhang, Birjodh Tiwana, Robert Dick, Zhuoqing Morley Mao, and Lei Yang. "PowerTutor." *PowerTutor*. N.p., 2009. Web. 20 Nov. 2013.

[4] Lee, K., et al. (2009). Slaw: A new mobility model for human walks. INFOCOM 2009, IEEE, IEEE.

[5] Munjal, A., et al. (2011). "SMOOTH: a simple way to model human walks." ACM SIGMOBILE Mobile Computing and Communications Review **14**(4): 34-36.

[6]NS-3, "The ns3 network simulator," http://www.nsnam.org/, 2011.

[7] Pan, K., et al. (2009). Implementation of data distribution management services in a service oriented HLA RTI. Winter Simulation Conference, Winter Simulation Conference.

[8] Rak, S. J. and D. J. Van Hook (1996). Evaluation of grid-based relevance filtering for multicast group assignment. Proc. of 14th DIS workshop, Citeseer.

[9] Riley, G. F. and T. R. Henderson (2010). The ns-3 network simulator. Modeling and Tools for Network Simulation, Springer: 15-34.

[10] Tan, G., et al. (2001). An agent-based DDM for high level architecture. Proceedings of the fifteenth workshop on Parallel and distributed simulation, IEEE Computer Society.

[11]Tan, G., et al. (2000). A hybrid approach to data distribution management. Distributed Simulation and Real-Time Applications, 2000.(DS-RT 2000). Proceedings. Fourth IEEE International Workshop on, IEEE.

[12] Tang, J. C., et al. (2011). "Reflecting on the DARPA red balloon challenge." Communications of the ACM **54**(4): 78-85. [13] Wood, D. D. (2002). Implementation of DDM in the MAK High Performance RTI. Proceedings of the Simulation Interoperability Workshop, Citeseer.

[14] R. M. Fujimoto, M. Hunter, J. Sirichoke, M. Palekar, H.-K. Kim, W. Suh, "Ad Hoc Distributed Simulations," *Principles of Advanced and Distributed Simulation*, June 2007

Computing as Model-Based Empirical Science

Paul Fishwick
University of Texas at Dallas
800 W. Campbell Rd., AT10
Richardson, TX 75080
1+972-883-4389
Paul.Fishwick@utdallas.edu

ABSTRACT

Is computer science a science? This question has been asked since the inception of the field in the 1940s. Computer Science is certainly a science in the sense of a mature body of knowledge, including systematic method and practice. Many in the field have argued that the *body of knowledge* argument is sufficient. To provide a more substantive argument in favor of a science interpretation, other researchers have suggested that computer science is an artificial, experimental science not unlike economics. To build from, and complement prior views, we claim that *computing is an empirical science*, similar to that of physics or biology. Demonstrating this claim requires broadening the foundations of computing to include analog systems, and *employing modeling and simulation as a fundamental approach* toward observing computing in natural and artificial contexts. An example model of mixed discrete-event/continuous information is presented in support of this claim.

Categories and Subject Descriptors

C.1.3 [**Other Architectural Styles**]: Analog computers; D.1 [**Programming Techniques**]: General, Visual programming; D.2.6 [**Programming Environments**]: Graphical environments, Interactive environments; H.1.1 [**Systems and Information Theory**]: General systems theory; I.6.1 [**Simulation Theory**]: Types of simulation (continuous and discrete); I.6.5 [**Model Development**]: Modeling methodologies; I.6.8 [**Types of Simulation**]: Combined, Visual.

General Terms

Design, Experimentation, Languages, Theory

Keywords

Virtual Analog, Creative Automata, Abstraction, Modeling

1. INTRODUCTION

Is Computer Science a science? Newell and Simon (1976), and then later (Simon 1996) answer this question in the affirmative. They structure their arguments on symbol manipulation and artificial intelligence as core elements that comprise the scientific enterprise of computing. Cerf recently challenged the Computer Science community with that same question (Cerf 2012a). He ends his essay with "I hope you…will encourage others in our

professional to join ACM in the question for the science in our discipline." He then made subsequent comments (Cerf 2012b) addressing editorial feedback that he had received, and noted "Modeling is a form of abstraction and is a powerful tool in the lexicon of computer science." He also noted "abstraction and modeling are key to making things analytic." Denning had earlier made a related inquiry (Denning 2007) and also wrote in the Editor's Introduction to (Cerf 2012b) "he [Cerf] called on all ACM members to commit to building a strong science base for computer science. Cerf cites numerous open questions, mostly in software development, that cry out for experimental studies."

Whereas Simon and Newell build upon symbol manipulation as being at the core, Denning (2013) summarizes conclusions from a symposium (Denning 2012) on the issue of the scientific attributes of Computer Science, including "We can now say 'computing is the study of information processes, artificial and natural.'"

In the opening statement of that symposium, Denning notes that the issue of computing as being a science has persisted since the beginnings of the field in the 1940s. Indeed, classic texts on foundations within computing, Turing's manuscript on computability (Turing 1936) serves as a central reference within computer science. Turing's highly mathematical essay on computable numbers is remarkable from the standpoint of *his description of a machine*, with a tape containing squares, and physical operations such as scanning (e.g., reading) and writing. Even though Turing did not construct a physical counterpart to his hypothetical machine, the simulated mechanical apparatus can be said to have informed his thought process. Turing's use of machines as a means to reason about mathematics will be mentioned later when referencing 19th century British scientific modeling practice.

In our quest for understanding computing, and in determining to what degree it may be considered a science, we must ask ourselves whether computer science can be viewed as more than a systematic study. Is it also an empirical science? Is it possible to take a walk in the forest, or on a busy city street, and see the dynamics of information flow? We contend that computer science is a fundamental science in the strong sense since it represents not only a body of knowledge, but also embodies a well-defined type of observation and analysis of information flow. This method is defined similarly to approaches used within the field of modeling and simulation. Thus, the essence of computer science as a science is defended through modeling and simulation theory and practice. Modeling is the key practice in defense of computing as an empirical science. Our position on modeling, and *computing as science,* is not to suggest that computing is only a science. Computing already has a strong presence as an engineering discipline; hence the phrase "Computing *as* Empirical Science" rather than "Computing *is* Empirical Science."

2. PRINCIPLES OF COMPUTING

To identify core principles in computer science, we review the history of computing (Ifrah 2001). We then look at early computers and study the concepts and elements of those devices. Since computing stresses information process according to Denning, counting devices provide the first evidence of computing. As Ifrah documents, the first stage in the development of counting was found in notched bones, frequently referred to as "tally sticks" from 35,000BCE to 20,000BCE. A tally stick contains external memory (i.e., a representation of number) and a non-automatic, human method for altering memory. The rich variety inherent within the history of computing involves advancing technology to automate tasks that were previously performed by hand. We should not want to limit our understanding of computing concepts to the use of a specific technology, or class of technology, such as digital. Technology allows computing to become more efficient, and yet the principles of computing are not guided by efficiency. Table 1 provides a partial list of principles based on computing history.

Table 1: Computing Principles

Category	Concepts
Information	Data, Memory
System	Time, Input, Output, State, Event
Control	Sequence, Iteration, Feedback, Branch
Model	Dynamic (logic, flow-based), Shape, Knowledge

The history of computing involves many mechanisms from early examples involving gear trains, as contained within clockwork or automata to machines constructed from electromechanical and fully electronic designs. Most of the machines, including very early mechanical varieties exemplify principles listed in Table 1. In the case of analog computing, information is distributed rather than localized into a central store. The last category labeled Model includes three varieties with the first being the primary center of activity within modeling and simulation.

If we witness fruit falling from a tree, or several streams of water cascading into a pool then we are witnessing computing with the aid of naïve physics (Hayes 1979, Forbus 1984, Baillargeon 1994, Smith 1994), a physical view of computing. Similarly, automobiles on the road allow us to see information processes such as merging, queuing, and the formation of stacks when a line of automobiles is slowed by a vehicle and the most recent arrival within that stack "pops out" to bypass the blockage; remaining cars "peel off" accordingly. The following assumptions are required for this perspective:

- *A1*: Computer science is the study of information dynamics within discrete and continuous space.

- *A2*: Computer science is defined without regard to a specific technology.

A1 is similar to Denning (2012), but we broaden the core of computer science to encompass both discrete and continuous space. *A1* captures the essence of scientific inquiry where computing is not limited to an intentional design (e.g., a computer) but is rather a phenomenon to be observed. Without analog computing—typically a form of computing grounded in continuous space—computer science as a science would be difficult to justify in an empirical sense. With the analog included, computing becomes ubiquitous because the field is then more closely linked to reality. *A2* also speaks to the analog inclusion, but also emphases that computing is not limited by technology. The notion of *A2* is well known to natural or unconventional computing communities (Ballard 1999). If technology does not provide constraints, then mechanisms from the Middle Ages may provide substantial material for a science of information dynamics due to the size and visibility of the mechanical components when seen in diagrams and in scale models. A side benefit is that the word "automata," whether of the 20th century mathematical category or the older "artificial life" mechanical variety, can be defined in terms of both discrete as well as continuous space information flow.

Programs are consequently models that may employ a variety of technologies for their definitions. The technology of print is economical and therefore common, and yet programs made out of virtual environment assets or custom materials are possible. Technologies such as 3d printing, sandbox physics-based game engines, and augmented reality can result in program structures that may have significant pedagogical value. It is in this value that our approach makes a strong claim—that through a model-based science, students come to learn basic concepts within computing and within practices of computing (e.g., computer programming).

3. MODEL-BASED EXAMPLE

3.1 Overview

As with sciences such as physics, biology, and chemistry, we turn our attention to a specific object or scenario where the goal is to apply a scientific method to yield knowledge. We seek knowledge in the form of information dynamics. Furthermore, we can experiment with the object and create models of the object's structure and behavior. The model can subsequently be employed to create predictions of more general situations. The prior examples of automobile stack formation represent one example. The cascading water flows in nature represent another. Information dynamics can be easily observed. However, there is a special class of object, which we call "information-rich" that deserves our attention. An information-rich object is simply that which contains an unusual density of models, each of which contains computer science concepts and methods. The general area of mechanism—machines of the past prior to the development of highly integrated electronic circuits—represents an information-rich object class. We will use an object designed by Leonardo da Vinci in 1497 to illustrate the empirical approach to computer science—his cam hammer design. We do not claim that the cam hammer is a computer, but rather that we can observe fundamental computing concepts through studying this mechanism.

3.2 Computing in Da Vinci's Cam Hammer

The cam hammer was designed to automate the machining of materials through hammering them with a force that would exceed that deliverable by a blacksmith. Figure 1 has a left and right figure. The left figure is Da Vinci's original hammer design, and the figure on the right is a wooden scale model built by the author.

Consider the original design. The crank handle is on the left (far side of mechanism), and the "snail cam" rotates clockwise. We consider that the start position is an angle of zero radians, and that the hammer is resting on the anvil. As the crank is turned, the hammer rises since it is attached to a lever arm connected to a cam follower. When there is a full 2π radian turn, the hammer falls and repeats its cyclic process. Even though the lever's fulcrum is located directly below the cam, there is a mechanical advantage created by the follower and what amounts to a variable length lever inherent within the cam geometry. Figure 2 shows that when the angle rotates to 2π, the follower is ready to slip back to its start position, allowing the hammer to drop.

Figure 1. Leonardo Da Vinci's original cam hammer design (left) and author's wooden model (right). Original from Madrid Codex I, Biblioteca Nacional de España

3.3 Modeling Strategies

An informal and cursory examination of the device yields many of the principles found within programming. For example, the hammer's rising and falling is a loop, and the discontinuity in the snail cam represents a conditional branching resulting from a discrete event. We see object-oriented principles since the device is a physical object with sub-components, each with behaviors that are encapsulated within those pieces. The models are not models of software as it is generally understood, but rather of the mechanism whose structure is isomorphic to software. Therefore a heuristic for finding computing in objects such as the cam hammer is to *make models of these objects and then simulate them.* The models that we design and make may involve numerous technologies. Many of the model designs can be found in educational texts (Fishwick 1995) and in model design handbooks (Fishwick 2008).

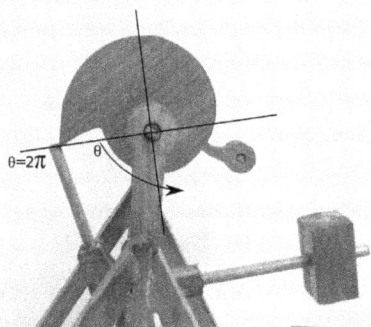

Figure 2. Cam behavior reaching its discrete event position at angle 2π.

3.4 Conceptual Models

A conceptual model is one where there is information about an artifact at a fairly high level of abstraction. This approach to modeling, which often precedes gradually more detailed iterations, is sometimes defined in terms of soft systems methodology's role in modeling. For example, consider the following:

> *The hammer rises and falls in response to the turning of the crank.*

This is a simulation model constructed from natural language. In terms of parts of speech, there are some abstract concepts of sub-objects and behavior. In the field of System Dynamics (Roberts et al. 1982), causal graphs are covered as an early phase as part of a incremental chain of model construction. An example graph can be formed from a linear event chain:

1. Human powers crank
2. Crank turns
3. Cam rotates
4. Cam follower rotates
5. Lever rotates
6. Hammer rises and falls

Robinson et al (2012) cover a range of conceptual modeling techniques and practices within this area.

3.5 Program and Control Flow

For the many who are familiar with text-based programming, it is often useful to create a model using text either in the syntax of a given language such as C++, Java, or pseudocode. Figure 3 provides a rudimentary text-based model of the cam hammer's function without any knowledge of physics.

This model, like the others we discuss, needs to be seen in the empirical light in which it is offered—a model that serves to illuminate the foundational computing concepts inherent in an object's structure and operation. These concepts are specified on the left and right sides of the program (Fig. 3). For example, the concept of iteration is seen in two places: a turning of the hand-crank ten times, and the rotation of the cam. As for all stable objects, the cam itself is a memory device with its stored memory value being equal to one of its changing degrees of freedom: current angular orientation.

Branching for physical objects undergoing motion is reached when there is a boundary, or discontinuity, in the motion path. The radius (r) of the cam is defined as equal to angle theta. Thus, the cam geometry defines the conditional branching function in wood. When the discontinuity is encountered (theta at or very near 2*PI), there is a phase transition and the hammer stops rising and falls. All such discontinuities can result in discrete events from a simulation perspective, and correspondingly in conditional branching from a programming perspective. Similar programming patterns involving branching occur when a moving ball being simulated strikes a wall or bounces on the floor. Seeing discontinuities in the cam, or when a ball strikes a wall, provides us with deep computing insight on branching.

The cam hammer becomes an evocative object (Turkle 2011) and "we think with" models—in Figure 3, a model based on the common technologies belonging to writing and print. This aspect of the technologies of modeling is covered in Care (2010) where extensive treatment is given to other types of technologies that yield other forms of models used in analog computing. Figure 4 shows a control flow model (e.g., flowchart) for the cam hammer function depicted in Figure 3.

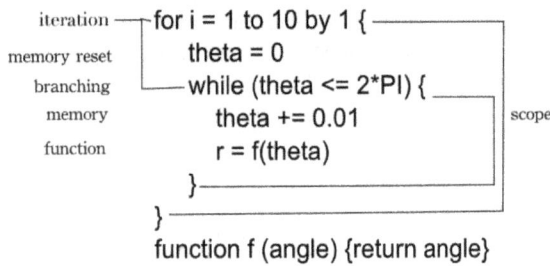

```
iteration ──┌─for i = 1 to 10 by 1 {─────────┐
memory reset │    theta = 0                   │
branching    └── while (theta <= 2*PI) {───┐  │
memory           theta += 0.01            │  │ scope
function         r = f(theta)              │  │
             }───────────────────────────┘  │
           }──────────────────────────────────┘
       function f (angle) {return angle}
```

Figure 3. Da Vinci's cam hammer in pseudocode.

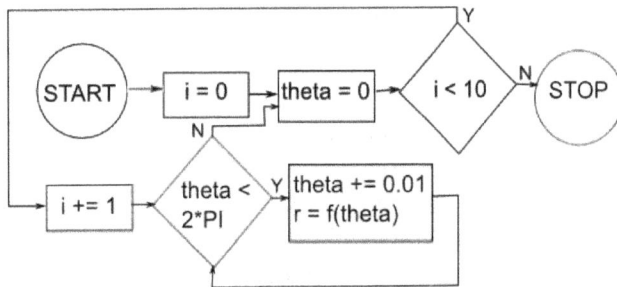

Figure 4. Flowchart model corresponding to Figure 3.

3.6 Data Flow

While control flow provides us with a way of modeling directives, as if we were giving commands to an agent, data flow modeling centers the perspective of the material that moves through the environment—a *systems* view. For the cam hammer, this flow is captured through variables that comprise work, power, and energy. Despite the physical nature of these concepts, the concepts can all be seen as information flows fundamentally, and so we note evidence for a scientific method based on information dynamics. A model sketch of data flow is illustrated in Figure 5.

The icon on the far left in Figure 5 is a clock, which outputs a time synchronous periodic clock signal. This feeds into the integrator as a time reference. The integrator component integrates the angular speed of the cam, and of the crankshaft, since the two are coupled through a rigid link. The output of the integrator is the angle and the cam geometry is defined as the identity function (r = theta). The block on the far right contains a finite state machine with two phases: R for rising hammer and F for falling hammer. The hammer falls when r reaches 2*PI. The hammer will take time to fall, so a differential equation (not shown) is located inside of state F. As this equation is solved over time, the hammer will, under the influence of gravity, fall to the anvil at which time the y=0 triggers an event that begins the R phase again. Even though this is not a fully developed model, it is similar in structure to models that can be designed in simulation environments such as Ptolemy (Lee and Seshia 2011) and Modelica (Fritzson 2011).

3.7 Role of Modeling in Computer Science

Denning makes a strong case for computer science as a discipline (Denning 1999) and yet as previously noted at the start of this

paper, there are still nagging questions regarding *computer science as a science* in the sense of classical areas of study such as physics. He makes the point that Computer Science is involved with information processes and then posits that the fundamental question underlying all of computing is "What can be (efficiently) automated?" Our claim is similar to Denning's with regard to information dynamics and processing, however, we suggest that the fundamental question is "Where is the information?" By changing the question to one that has an empirical tone rather than one based more strictly on automation or on machine efficiency, we achieve a better understanding of computing from the standpoint of *modeling practice*. Modeling plays a central role in computing since it is not only a means for designing and organizing software (Booch et al. 2005), but more importantly, a foundational means for studying information processes which already exist in nature and in the artificial.

Denning notes "The digital computer plays the central role in the field because it is a universal computing machine." There are two issues with this statement. The first is that whether or not information is grouped in discrete chunks is not as central to computer science as the information dynamics aspect: information is stored in memory, processed, and moved without respect to a specific technology; it can just as easily flow down the rotating rods in Vannevar Bush's analog differential analyzer as it can through wires via electric potentials. Discrete events in space and time will always be there and come with their own model types.

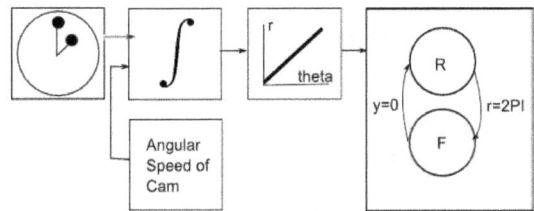

Figure 5. Data flow model

Figure 4 is a rudimentary example of this where the discontinuity in the cam's geometry causes a logical conditional branch within the control flow. The second note is with regard to universality. Universality in computing is not necessary for pedagogical purposes or for a wide range of real-world problems. If a computer solves a problem for which it is intended, then the computer and its computing are sufficient. Also, since analog computing is captured by the data flow paradigm, we observe that data flow machines can be designed to be universal in the Turing-complete sense with relative ease. So, universality is unnecessary in making the case for computer science as science.

Modeling and Simulation as a discipline, and as a core area within Computer Science, plays a major role in observing information flows. Models within the simulation field began as analog and then shifted to digital in underlying computer architectures. However, the analog has never disappeared—instead, it is in the user interface as a human-interactive front end to the visually less observational digital hardware. This interactive aspect of the analog points to "analog as analogy" (Gentner et al. 2001) rather than in the stricter definition of analog computing being limited to continuous-space measurement.

3.8 Philosophy and Education

A criticism that could be directed at this argument for Computer Science is "Aren't we really just arguing for the importance of modeling and simulation?" For example, with Da Vinci's cam hammer, others have made simulations of this artifact as animations driven by key-frame modeling. The response to this potential criticism is that, in the way that we in Computer Science organize our discipline and teach fundamentals, modeling and simulation is currently viewed as a set of tools, or an applied domain within science and engineering. This application-view is valid, and yet insufficiently narrow.

If students can be taught to see information flows around them, and then they study these flows with the same rigor allowed for physics and biology, then there are two consequences: 1) computer science becomes an empirical practice in how it is conveyed and taught, and 2) modeling and simulation plays a critical role in all of computer science, including learning how to think about programming. Thinking in analogies, and learning elements of analog computing and cybernetics (Ashby 1957) can be of assistance in connecting models to real-world entities. One of the earliest, sophisticated examples of analog computing was the Antikythera mechanism (Marchant 2010), capturing the mathematics of the solar system as known circa 100BCE.

Warren Weaver's comment (Owens 1986) about Bush's efforts in differential analyzers is as provocative today as it was when first issued:

> It seems rather a pity not to have around such a place as MIT a really impressive Analogue Computer, for there is vividness and directness of meaning of the electrical and mechanical processes involved...which can hardly fail, I would think, to have a very considerable educational value. A digital electronic computer is bound to be a somewhat abstract affair, in which the actual computational processes are fairly deeply submerged.

The analog has never really gone away since images of paper being organized into simulated manila folders are seen in most drag-and-drop computer interfaces. We prefer the term *virtual analog* to describe this approach where, much like a quartz movement watch with rotating hands, the digital is underneath for reasons of efficiency, but the analog remains to serve a natural aid to humans who tend to think and act mechanically. The term virtual analog can be found in the computer music literature from the mid 1990s, and was first coined as *hybrid simulation* (McLeod 1968). Current software supporting systems thinking in one form or another have analog interfaces where the models are highly interactive and visual—ghosts of an analog past.

On the central role of modeling and simulation as key to our cognition, significant research has centered on the central role of modeling as a mediating activity in science (Hesse 1963, Morgan and Morrison 1999, Bailer-Jones 2002). Models are language constructs that play analogical or metaphorical roles in our understanding of phenomena. The analog nature of models is not without controversy has been framed within the "Duhem vs. Campbell" debate (Mellor 1968). Throughout most of history, models were physical (de Chadarevian and Hopwood 2004). The central role that is played by model design, categories, and lifecycles is discussed by Balci (2012), Fishwick (1995), and Tolk et al. (2013). Zeigler et al. (2000) define a mathematical framework for modeling. Ören and Yilmaz (2013) define different ways in which simulation models can be characterized.

That the universe is computational is covered in several theories combined under the umbrella term *digital physics* (DP 2014).

Examples from reality as a computational phenomenon result from quantum computation (Lloyd 2007) and complex systems arising from cellular automata (Wolfram 2002). While the emphasis on information is similar to our claims, the limiting of information measurement and observation is not required to be only at the most microscopic levels of spacetime, nor is it required to be digital in character. Instead, information can be continuous, and evidence of the universe as a sort of giant computer exists at human scale in the form of observable information flows.

Computational thinking (Wing 2008) is a constructive movement and frequently employs modeling and simulation as method (Lee, Martin et al. 2011), and yet what is needed as we progress toward computer science as empirical science are educational approaches that begin with students taking photographs, measuring, and exploring the world around them. Investigating an old tractor by the side of the road or a grove of trees swaying in the wind are excellent ways in which to observe information structure and dynamics. This observational phase is a natural precursor to the use of modeling and simulation as a form of experiment (Radder 2003). Computer science is not limited to metallic boxes and enclosures. Modeling and simulation should ideally be situated at the core of computational thinking rather than as an application methodology.

4. Observations on Modeling

4.1 Modeling as Experience

A salient point about modeling is that it is a human experience, with agency, an embodied condition rather than a purely formal one. Bissell and Dillon (2012) collected a series of essays describing how modeling is experienced and historically how modeling has been perceived. In that same volume, Monk (2012) characterizes the practice of modeling as "creating reality." Beynon (2012) cautions us against treating software on the basis of "functional abstractions." He develops his Empirical Modeling (EM) thesis, which is based partially on William James' radical empiricism. Experiential approaches are also encouraged within mathematics (Bailey et al. 2007) although models here tend to be limited to traditional typographic notation and theorem proving.

The experiential aspect of modeling suggests that when we take modeling within a software engineering context, we take the view that the model is a model of information dynamics present within a physical system, and not only *a model of software*. This distinction is subtle but important if computer science is to be considered an empirical science.

4.2 Models of Mathematics

The concept that information is everywhere and that since information undergoing dynamical flow is at the core of computing, we observe information scientifically through the practice of modeling and simulation. We have claimed that these models are also *models of computing* rather than simply models of physical phenomena. However, this argument leads to a broader question regarding mathematics. If computing can be seen as the extension of mathematics covering information dynamics, then perhaps we can also see mathematics everywhere as well. The notion that "all is mathematics" at the core of existence is as old as the wisdom handed down to us from the Greeks, but has recently resurfaced within the physics community (Tegmark 2014).

Another way of seeing that mathematics and extensions in the form of computer science (e.g., the mathematics of information dynamics) are at the heart of reality is by researching scientists through history who have viewed modeling as a means to practice and think about mathematics. Care (2010) discusses this trend as embodied within analog computing. The 19th century scientists including Maxwell and Thompson (later, Lord Kelvin) regularly opined in writing on *the use of mechanical models to understand a mathematical reality underlying nature.* Uspenskii (1961). Szücs includes a diagram (1980, fig. 6.1) captioned "models of addition" in which mechanical model components are presented. These components, such as those involving gears and pulleys, are portrayed as models that help us to reason mathematically.

As a closing note on abstraction and its role in mathematics and computing, we refer briefly to Kelvin's tide machine, which contained a series of ball and disc integrators such as the one in Figure 6. We see that this mechanical device and the standard long S in type denoting integration serve the same purpose: they are both models of the concept of integration using different technologies. And, therefore, this concept as an abstraction is a function of collective relation of multiple representations rather than an objective characteristic of a singular representation. Kelvin's ball and disc integrator in action, the pouring the morning coffee into a cup, or marbles dropped into a tin can all map to the integration concept. Abstraction *is the process* (Fishwick 1988) by which these isomorphic behaviors become known as one in the mind.

Figure 6. A close-up view of a mechanical ball and disc integrator for Kelvin's harmonic tide machine. Image courtesy of WikiMedia Commons.

5. CONCLUSIONS

We observed early in the paper that, mainly through the writings of Denning and Cerf, that computer science is still searching for itself and yet no one doubts that the discipline is a well-developed science in the sense of "science" being a systematic body of knowledge. The issue arises when the claim toward empiricism is raised. Newell and Simon point out that even in this light, computing is an experimental science. Simon refers to this effect as the "science of the artificial." He also points out that computer science is in good company—scientifically speaking—with other areas of study, such as economics.

We are issuing the strong claim for computer science—that it is an empirical quest for knowledge in addition to its engineering role. We propose that modeling and simulation contains a set of methodologies that create a foundation for computer science as empirical science. While this claim may create philosophical tensions and a host of new questions, we also suggest that through a stronger emphasis on modeling, computer science education may be significantly improved especially where it can be linked to federal and state mathematics and science standards.

The argument within the paper narrows down to a specific, concrete recommendation: to sense computing as information processes, we must observe via the senses as with any empirical science. We should spend time seeing information, and journaling our efforts through the usual means including physical measurement as way to enhance perception. Methods such as photography, video, audio recording, field notes, and sketching are particularly useful.

The notion of computing as empirical science breaks the myth that computing should be construed as either programming or as technology. Computing wears two hats: science and engineering. Even as computing does provide the world with advanced technologies, its potential is deeper and more profound since it provides us with a unique way to see the world as information structure and process.

6. FUTURE DIRECTIONS

The author teaches a Creative Automata class, where students are encouraged to participate in three-phase studies. Phase 1 reflects the subject of this paper—for students to see computing in their surroundings. Students are introduced to an "object of the day." Each object is captured by a photograph or video of something occurring in the vicinity. Students are then encouraged at the start of each class to identify core computer science concepts (e.g., iteration, memory management, conditional branching) in what they observe. For information-rich objects, they can find mechanism in places such as open HVAC systems in buildings, bicycle racks, pool pumps, and by observing organizational behavior of employees and customers in the student hub.

Phase 2 involves the creation of Javascript-based prototypes representing a model of the computing found in Phase 1, as well as the scene or object being modeled. Phase 3, however, is a synthetic rather than analytic step where students create new representations based on what they observed in Phase 1. For example, seeing a mechanism inside of household furniture (e.g., two latches that must both be pulled to unlock a sliding behavior) yields the information flow of a Boolean logic gate, suggesting computing occurring inside of the furniture. A student can then represent models of entirely different phenomena using latches similar in look-and-feel to those in the furniture. Information carriers in the form of furniture latches can, therefore, be employed during synthesis of other models containing logic gates. This creative approach to representation of computing concepts is termed *Aesthetic Computing* (Fishwick 2006). The analytic-synthetic dualism is possible since computing can be uniquely characterized as both an empirical science and a form of engineering.

7. ACKNOWLEDGMENTS

I thank anonymous reviewers for their attention to detail, with many good suggestions for improvement. I also acknowledge the creative endeavors of all current and former students in the modeling and simulation, Aesthetic Computing, and Creative Automata classes. Discussions with Karen Doore, in particular, have revealed new ways of applying the "science approach" to Computer Science education. Colleagues in Arts & Technology (ATEC) and Computer Science at the University of Texas at Dallas have provided a rich environment for cross-disciplinary discussions necessary for development of this manuscript. Recently, I have benefited from in-depth interchange with several individuals. For details on analog computing practice, discussions with Alex Bochannek, former curator of the Analog Computing section of the Computer History Museum in Mountain View, California, were most useful. I have benefited also from conversations on the history of technology and engineering with David Channell, and on the philosophy of mathematics with Joselle Kehoe, both at the University of Texas at Dallas. Empirical and experimental investigations in modeling were discussed with Meurig Beynon at the University of Warwick.

8. REFERENCES

[1] Ashby, W. R. 1957. An introduction to cybernetics. Chapman & Hall, London.

[2] Bailey, D. H., Borwein, J. M., Calkin, N. J., Girgensohn, R., Luke, D. R., and Moll, V. H. 2007. Experimental mathematics in action. A. K. Peters, Wellesley, MA.

[3] Baillargeon, R., 1994. How do infants learn about the physical world? *Current Directions in Psychological Science*, 3(5): 133-140.

[4] Balci, O. 2012. A life cycle for modeling and simulation, Simulation: Transactions of the Society for Modeling and Simulation International, 88(7): 870-883.

[5] Ballard, D. H. 1999. An introduction to natural computation. Bradford Books.

[6] Bailer-Jones, D. M. 2002. Models, Metaphors, and Analogies, *The Blackwell Guide to the Philosophy of Science*, Wiley-Blackwell.

[7] Beynon, M. 2012. Modelling with Experience: Construal and Construction for Software. In Bissell, C. and Dillon, C. Eds, Ways of Thinking, Ways of Seeing: Mathematical and Other Modelling in Engineering and Technology, Springer-Verlag, Berlin. pp. 197-228.

[8] Bissell, C. and Dillon, C. Eds. 2012, Ways of Thinking, Ways of Seeing: Mathematical and Other Modelling in Engineering and Technology, Springer-Verlag, Berlin. pp. 1-28.

[9] Booch, G., Rumbaugh, J. and Jacobson, I. 2005. The unified modeling language user guide, 2nd Ed., Addison-Wesley Professional Publishing.

[10] Börstler, J., Kuzniarz, L., Alphonce, C., Sanders, W. B., and Smialek, M. 2012. Teaching software modeling in computing curricula, ITiCSE-WGR '12, Association for Computing Machinery, pp. 39-50.

[11] Care, C. 2010. Technology for modeling: electrical analogies, engineering practice, and the development of analog computing. Springer-Verlag, London.

[12] Cerf, V. G. 2012a. Where is the science in computer science? Communications of the ACM, 55(10): 5.

[13] Cerf, V. G. 2012b. The science in computer science: Computer Science Revisited, Ubiquity, December 2012, pp. 2-4.

[14] De Chadarevian, S. and Hopwood, N. 2004. Eds, Models: the third dimension of science, Stanford University Press.

[15] Denning, P. J. 1999. Computer science: the discipline, Ralston, A., Reilly, E. D., and Hemmendinger, D., Eds. Encyclopedia of Computer Science. Wiley Publishing.

[16] Denning, P. J. 2005. Is computer science science? Communications of the ACM, 48(4): 27-31.

[17] Denning, P. J. 2012. Ubiquity symposium: the science in computer science opening statement, Ubiquity, December 2012, pp. 2-5.

[18] Denning, P. J. 2013. The science in computer science, Viewpoint, Communications of the ACM, 56(5): 35-38.

[19] DP (Digital Physics). 2014. http://en.wikipedia.org/wiki/Digital_physics , Last accessed April 9, 2014.

[20] Fishwick, P. A. 1988. The role of process abstraction in simulation, *IEEE Transactions on Systems, Man, and Cybernetics*, 18(1): 18-39.

[21] Fishwick, P. A. 1995. Simulation model design: building digital worlds, Prentice Hall, Englewood Cliffs, NJ.

[22] Fishwick, P. A., Ed. 2006. Aesthetic Computing, MIT Press.

[23] Fishwick, P. A. Ed, 2008. Handbook of Dynamic System Modeling, Chapman & Hall/CRC Computer & Information Sciences Series.

[24] Forbus, K. 1984. Qualitative process theory, *Artificial Intelligence*, 24, 85-168.

[25] Fritzson, P. 2011. Introduction to modeling and simulation of technical and physical systems with Modelica. Wiley-IEEE Press.

[26] Gentner, D., Holyoak, K. J., and Kokinov, B. N., Eds. 2001. The analogical mind: perspectives from cognitive science. Bradford Books.

[27] Hayes, P. 1979. The Naïve physics manifesto, In Michie, D., Ed., Expert systems in the micro-electronic age, Edinburgh University Press, 242-270.

[28] Hesse, M. 1963. Models and analogies in science, Sheed and Ward, London, England.

[29] Ifrah, G. 2001. The universal history of computing: from the abacus to the quantum computer. John Wiley and Sons.

[30] Lee, E. A. and Seshia, S. A. 2011, Introduction to Embedded Systems, A Cyber-Physical Systems Approach, http://LeeSheshia.org, ISBN 978-0-557-70857-4, 2011.

[31] Lee, I., Martin, F., Denner, J., Coulter, B., Allan, W., Erickson, J., Malyn-Smith, J., and Werner, L. 2011. Computational thinking for youth in practice. In ACM Inroads, 2(1): 32-37.

[32] Levi, M. 2009. The mathematical mechanic: using physical reasoning to solve problems, Princeton University Press.

[33] Lloyd, S. 2007. Programming the cosmos: a quantum computer scientist takes on the cosmos. Vintage Publishing.

[34] Marchant, J. 2010. Ancient astronomy: mechanical inspiration, Nature 468 (7323): 496-498.

[35] McLeod, J. 1968. Simulation: the dynamic modeling of ideas and systems with computers, McGraw-Hill Book Company.

[36] Mellor, D. H. 1968. Models and analogies in science: Duhem versus Campbell? *History of Science Society*, The University of Chicago Press, 59(3): 282-290.

[37] Monk, J. 2012. Creating Reality. In Bissell, C. and Dillon, C. Eds, Ways of Thinking, Ways of Seeing: Mathematical and Other Modelling in Engineering and Technology, Springer-Verlag, Berlin. pp. 1-28.

[38] Morgan, M. S., and Morrison, M. 1999. Models as mediators: perspectives on natural and social science, Cambridge University Press.

[39] Newell, A., Simon, H. A., 1976. Computer Science and Empirical Inquiry: Symbols and Search. Communications of the ACM, 19(3): 113-126.

[40] Ören, T. and Yilmaz, L. 2013. Philosophical aspects of modeling and simulation. Tolk, A., Ed. *Ontology, Epistemology & Teleology for Modeling and Simulation*, Springer-Verlag, Berlin-Heidelberg, pp. 157-172.

[41] Owens, L. 1986. Vannevar Bush and the differential analyzer: the text and context of an early computer. *Technology and Culture*. 27(1): 63-95.

[42] Radder, H. 2003. The philosophy of scientific experimentation. University of Pittsburgh Press.

[43] Roberts, N. 1982. Introduction to computer simulation: the systems dynamics approach. Addison-Wesley.

[44] Robinson, S., Brooks, R., Kotiadis, K., and Van Der Zee, D-J. 2012. Conceptual modeling for discrete-event simulation, CRC Press.

[45] Simon, H. A. 1996. The sciences of the artificial, 3rd ed., MIT Press, Cambridge, MA

[46] Smith, B. and Casati, R. 1994, *Philosophical Psychology* 7/2, 225-244.

[47] Szücs, E. 1980. Similitude and modelling. Elsevier Scientific Publishing Company.

[48] Turing, A. M. 1936. On computable numbers, with an application to the entscheideungsproblem.

[49] Tegmark, M. 2014. Our mathematical universe: my quest for the ultimate nature of reality. Knoff Publishing.

[50] Tolk, A., Heath, B. L., Ihrig, M., Padilla, J. J., Page, E. H., Suarez, E. D., Szabo, C., Weirich, P., and Yilmaz, L. 2013. Epistemology of modeling and simulation. In *Proceedings of the 2013 Winter Simulation Conference*, Pasupathy, R., Kim, S.-H., Tolk, A., Hill, R., and Kuhl, M. E., Eds, Institute for Electrical and Electronics Engineers (IEEE), pp. 1152-1166.

[51] Turkle, S. 2011. Evocative objects: things we think with. MIT Press.

[52] Uspenskii, V. A. 1961. Some applications of mechanics to mathematics, Pergammon Press.

[53] Wing. J. 2008. Computational thinking and thinking about computing. Philosophical Transactions of the Royal Society A, 366, pp. 3717-3725.

[54] Wolfram, S. 2002. A new kind of science, Wolfram Media.

[55] Zeigler, B. P. Kim, T. G., Praehofer, H. 2000. Theory of modeling and simulation, Academic Press.

The Earth System Modeling Framework: Interoperability Infrastructure for High Performance Climate and Weather Models

Cecelia DeLuca

Cooperative Institute for Research in Environmental Sciences
NOAA Earth System Research Laboratory/University of Colorado
Boulder, CO
cecelia.deluca@noaa.gov

Abstract

Weather forecasting and climate modeling are grand challenge problems because of the complexity and diversity of the processes that must be simulated. The Earth system modeling community is driven to finer resolution grids and faster execution times by the need to provide accurate weather and seasonal forecasts, long term climate projections, and information about societal impacts such as droughts and floods. The models used in these simulations are generally written by teams of specialists, with each team focusing on a specific physical domain, such as the atmosphere, ocean, or sea ice. These specialized components are connected where their surfaces meet to form composite models that are largely self-consistent and allow for important cross-domain feedbacks. Since the components are often developed independently, there is a need for standard component interfaces and "coupling" software that transforms and transfers data so that outputs match expected inputs in the composite modeling system.

The Earth System Modeling Framework (ESMF) project began in 2002 as a multi-agency effort to define a standard component interface and architecture, and to pool resources to develop shareable utilities for common functions such as grid remapping, time management and I/O. The ESMF development team was charged with making the infrastructure sufficiently general to accommodate many different numerical approaches and legacy modeling systems, as well as making it reliable, portable, well-documented, accurate, and high performance. To satisfy this charge, the development team needed to develop innovative numerical and computational methods, a formal and rigorous approach to interoperability, and distributed development and testing processes that promote software quality.

ESMF has evolved to become the leading U.S. framework in the climate and weather communities, with users including the Navy, NASA, the National Weather Service, and community models supported by the National Science Foundation. In this talk, we will present ESMF's evolution, approach, and future plans.

Categories and Subject Descriptors
D.2.10 Design; D.2.11 Software Architecture

Keywords
Earth system modeling framework, high performance computing; component architecture; weather forecasting; climate modeling

Short Bio
CECELIA DeLUCA is the head of the NOAA Environmental Software Infrastructure and Interoperability group and the lead on national and international software infrastructure projects in the Earth system sciences. Her interests lie in the development of large, high-performance software systems and governance models that promote community and multi-agency ownership. She is an advocate for open source software and the development of shareable infrastructure for modeling and data services. Her education combines liberal arts (A.L.B. Harvard 1992), engineering (M.S. Boston University 1994), and atmospheric science (M.S. Massachusetts Institute of Technology 1996). Projects she has led include the premier U.S. weather and climate framework, the Earth System Modeling Framework (ESMF); the National Unified Operational Prediction Capability (NUOPC) Layer, a set of templates and conventions that increase the interoperability of ESMF-based modeling applications; and Earth System CoG, a collaboration environment and user interface for the Earth System Grid Federation (ESGF), an international network of data nodes that serves the model data on which the Intergovernmental Panel on Climate Change (IPCC) and other national and international climate assessments are based. She is also a co-lead on the international Earth System Documentation (ES-DOC) project, which originates and governs a metadata schema that comprehensively describing Earth system models and creates associated tools for collecting, displaying, and comparing that metadata.

SIGSIM-PADS'14, May 18–21, 2014, Denver, Colorado, USA.
ACM 978-1-4503-2794-7/14/05.
http://dx.doi.org/10.1145/2601381.2611130

Author Index

www.ingramcontent.com/pod-product-compliance
Lightning Source LLC
Chambersburg PA
CBHW061415210326
41598CB00035B/6228